Computing Concepts with C++ Essentials

Computing Concepts with C++ Essentials

Cay S. Horstmann
San Jose State University

John Wiley & Sons, Inc.
New York ◆ Chichester ◆ Brisbane ◆ Toronto ◆ Singapore ◆ Weinheim

ACQUISITIONS EDITOR	Regina Brooks
MARKETING MANAGER	Jay Kirsch
SENIOR PRODUCTION EDITOR	Tony VenGraitis
DESIGN DIRECTOR	Madelyn Lesure
MANUFACTURING MANAGER	Mark Cirillo
PHOTO EDITOR	Lisa Passmore
ILLUSTRATION COORDINATOR	Sandra Rigby

This book was set in Stempel Schneidler by Publication Services, Inc., and printed and bound by R. R. Donnelley/Crawfordsville. The cover was printed by Phoenix Color.

Recognizing the importance of preserving what has been written, it is a policy of John Wiley & Sons, Inc. to have books of enduring value published in the United States printed on acid-free paper, and we exert our best efforts to that end.

The paper in this book was manufactured by a mill whose forest managements programs include sustained yield harvesting of its timberlands. Sustained yield harvesting principles ensure that the number of trees cut each year does not exceed the amount of new growth.

Library of Congress Cataloging in Publication Data:

Horstmann, Cay S., 1959-
  Computing concepts with C++ essentials / Cay S. Horstmann.
    p. cm.
  Includes bibliographical references.
  ISBN 0-471-13770-7 (alk. paper)
  1. C++ (Computer program language) 2. Computers. I. Title.
QA76.73.C153H669 1996 96-39307
005. 13"3–dc21 CIP

Printed in the United States of America

10 9 8 7 6 5 4 3 2

Preface

This book gives a traditional introduction to computer science using modern tools. As computer scientists, we have the good fortune of being able to introduce students to an activity that is accessible, satisfying, and deep rather than broad: namely, the activity of *programming*. Like the majority of computer scientists, I believe that programming is the central theme of computer science. Thus, this course teaches students how to program.

While this book remains traditional in outlook, it uses modern techniques in three ways.

First, the programming language is a subset of C++. Although C++ is far from a perfect educational language, it makes pragmatic sense to use it. C++ is required for advanced computer science courses. Convenient and inexpensive programming environments are available on all major platforms. C++ is sufficiently expressive to teach programming concepts. This book avoids pointers through the use of modern features of the ANSI C++ standard—in particular, reference parameters, the stream library, the `string` class, and the `vector<T>` template. Pointers are used only for linked lists and polymorphism.

The second modern aspect is the early use of objects. Objects are introduced in two stages. From Chapter 2 on, students learn to *use* objects—in particular strings, streams, and graphical shapes. Students become comfortable with the concepts of creating objects and calling member functions. Then the book follows a traditional path, discussing branching and loops, functions, and procedures. Chapter 8 teaches how to *implement* classes and member functions.

The third modern aspect is the use of graphics. Students enjoy programming graphics. There are many programming examples in which the numbers and the visual information reinforce each other. This book uses a very simple graphics library that is available on a number of popular platforms. Unlike traditional graphics libraries, this library uses objects in a very straightforward and effective way.

The choice of programming language has a very visible impact on any book on programming. However, the purpose of the book is to teach computing concepts, not C++, which is just a tool toward that end. In 1997 there will be a Java version of this book that teaches the same concepts, in the same order, using Java instead of C++.

Sample Curricula

This book contains more material than could be covered in one semester, so you will need to make a choice of chapters to cover. The core material of the book is:

Chapter 2. Fundamental Data Types
Chapter 3. Objects
Chapter 4. Decisions
Chapter 5. Iteration
Chapter 6. Functions
Sections 9.1–9.4 Arrays

The following chapters are optional:

Chapter 1. Introduction
Chapter 7. Testing and Debugging
Chapter 8. Classes
Chapter 10. Files
Chapter 11. Modules
Chapter 12. Algorithms
Chapter 13. Data Structures
Chapter 14. Inheritance

The following graph shows the dependencies between the chapters.

Dependencies Between Sections

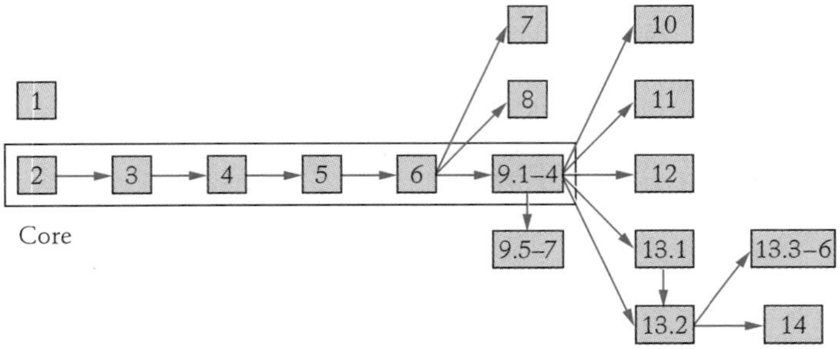

The material in Chapters 12 though 14 is meant as an introduction to these topics, not a definitive treatment.

A good choice for a semester-long course is to teach Chapters 2 though 11. This will comfortably lead students into a second-semester course on data structures. If you are not concerned about separate compilation, you can omit Chapter 11 and cover Chapter 12 instead.

If the second semester uses C instead of C++, you may want to omit Chapter 11 and instead cover Appendix 3 to get students up to speed in C.

If the second semester covers object-oriented design in detail, you can omit Chapter 8, Sections 9.5 though 9.7, and Chapters 13 and 14. Your students will then be using classes, but they will not implement them.

If you choose to cover inheritance but skip Chapter 13, you will need to cover Section 13.2 on pointers. That section is independent of the remainder of Chapter 13.

The book covers the following knowledge units from the ACM curriculum guidelines.

AL1: Basic Data Structures (6 of 13 hours)
AL2: Abstract Data Types (2 of 2 hours)
AL3: Recursion (2 of 3 hours)
AL6: Sorting and Searching (2 of 6 hours)
PL3: Representation of Data Types (2 of 2 hours)
PL4: Sequence Control (2 of 4 hours)
PL5: Data Control, Sharing and Type Checking (2 of 4 hours)
PL6: Run-Time Storage Management (2 of 4 hours)
PR: Introduction to a Programming Language (12 of 12 hours)
SE1: Fundamental Problem-Solving Concepts (16 of 16 hours)
SP1: Historical and Social Context of Computing (3 of 3 hours)

The Use of C++

It is impossible to teach all of C++ to beginning programmers in one semester. This book purposefully omits a number of useful but technically complex C++ topics, such as copy construction and destruction, run-time type identification, function pointers, parameterized types, exception handling, name spaces, and operator overloading.

This book does not teach programming "close to the metal". For example, strings are treated as fundamental types. Characters are simply strings of length 1. This approach may offend those who feel that students should understand the C implementation of strings, but it has been a great hit with students, who no longer have to deal with character array overruns and dangling character pointers. There is exactly one place in the book where I missed the `char` type. (Challenge: Find it.)

Since the focus of the book is on computing concepts, I try not to dwell on syntactical wrinkles of C++. Consider the `#include` directive. In my opinion, the distinction between `<...>` and `"..."` delimiters is just the kind of clutter that serves no useful purpose in an introductory course. The directive `#include "iostream.h"` will find the system header just fine (provided there is no file named iostream.h in the current directory). If you think it is not a great burden to learn about the distinction between system headers and private headers, there is an Advanced Topic note in the book to back you up.

C++ has two styles of comments: the C-style /**/ and the C++-style //. The // style is great if you want to dash off a one-line comment, but it is a true pain for comments extending over multiple lines. I don't want to use two comment styles in the book. Furthermore, I would like to encourage students to write comments *as long as they need to be* rather than cramming them into the remainer of the current line. Therefore, I chose to use the /* */ comments. Naturally, everyone has a strong personal preference in this regard. It is an exceedingly minor matter, and if your preference doesn't match mine, please feel free to use whatever style you like best.

Occasionally, a choice of programming style was prompted by anticipating widespread use of the ANSI standard C++ libraries. For example, iterators are pointerlike objects that describe locations in containers. For technical reasons, iterators do not support the -> operator. Therefore, I chose to use the more mundane `(*p).m` for pointers as well. Again, if you don't agree, feel free to use the other syntax.

About the Code Library

To use this book, you need a copy of the code library. You can obtain the library via the World Wide Web (http://www.horstmann.com/ccc). Simply uncompress the library and place all files into your working directory. Then include the header file ccc.h (which stands for Computing Concepts with C++) in your programs. There is no need to build a project or to link in a separate library.

This book uses the ANSI C++ Boolean type, string class, and vector template throughout. Since not all compilers currently support these features, the code library that accompanies this book contains an implementation that has been tested on most major C++ compilers. The header file ccc.h includes the compiler version or the book library version of the string and header file, as appropriate.

The ccc.h header defines a small number of the utility functions to make life simpler for the students. For example, a function `round (x)` does the same thing as `(int)(x + 0.5)`. A function `uppercase` returns a string with all lowercase characters turned into uppercase—a feature that is inexplicably missing in the standard library. Look at Appendix 2, Section A2.15 for a listing of these functions. There are also definitions for π and e.

The graphics library is purposefully kept simple. There are just four shapes: points, lines, circles, and text. To display a shape, make an object and send it to the graphics window: `cwin << circle`. Students can learn the entire library in an hour. The library has been ported to several major platforms.

There are two simple classes, `Time` and `Employee`, that are used for many programming examples. They add some realism and reinforce the concept that most real-life programs do not just manipulate numbers and strings. These two are automatically included with the ccc.h header.

How to Use This Book

The material in this book is divided into three parts: the essential, the useful, and the optional. To cover the essential material, simply skip over all side notes. It is perfectly reasonable to ignore all side notes completely during lectures and assign them for home reading.

Three of the side note sets are useful for the students, namely the Common Errors, Productivity Hints, and Quality Tips. Students quickly discover the Common Errors and read them on their own. You may need to encourage them to read the Quality Tips. The Productivity Hints may be challenging to some students, but those with some computer experience tend to find them very helpful.

The Random Facts and Advanced Topics are optional. The Random Facts provide historical and social information on computing, as required to fulfill the "historical and social context" requirements of the ACM curriculum guidelines. Most students will read the Random Facts on their own while pretending to follow the lecture. You will need to suggest those Advanced Topics that you think are important. By the way, not all of them are truly "advanced". Occasionally, alternative syntax (such as the // comment delimiter) is explained in an Advanced Topic.

Most examples are in the form of complete, ready-to-run programs. The programs are available electronically, and you can give them to your students.

Appendix 1 contains a style guide for use with this book. I have found it highly beneficial to require a consistent style for all assignments. I realize that my style may be different from yours. If you have strong feelings about a particular issue, or if this style guide conflicts with local customs, feel free to modify it. The style guide is available in electronic form for this purpose.

Appendix 2 contains a summary of all C++ constructs and library functions and classes used in this book.

To make it possible to smuggle this book into a curriculum that is otherwise based on C or low-level C++, Appendix 3 contains a crash course in C that shows how the higher-level C++ features map to C.

Acknowledgments

I would like to thank my acquisitions editor Steven Elliot for encouraging me to write this book, and my editor Regina Brooks at John Wiley & Sons for guiding the book through the development process. Her many constructive suggestions greatly improved this book, as did those of the reviewers: John Cordero, University of Southern California; Wanda Dann, Syracuse University; David G. Kay, University of California, Irvine; Ron McCarty, Pennsylvania State University; Don McKnight, Los Medanos College; Bruce Mielke, University of Wisconsin, Green Bay;

and Charles M. Williams, Georgia State University. Thanks to my student assistants, Michael Carney, Darrel Cherry, and Jiaoyang Zhou, with their help with the random facts and the code library, and to Lisa Passmore of John Wiley & Sons for her photo research. At Publication Services, Jerome Colburn did a splendid job with the copyediting; Jan Fisher adroitly handled the communications with John Wiley & Sons; Kathryn Wright kept the production process well coordinated; and the art was rendered expertly by Paul Edwards and his studio team. John Johnson of Teapot Graphics designed the stunning cover. My love and apologies go once again to my family, who had to suffer through yet another book project that never seemed to end.

Contents

Chapter 3 Objects 89

Chapter 4 Decisions 127

Chapter 5 Functions 173

Appendix A2 C++ Language Summary 599

Appendix A3 Moving from C++ to C 617

CHAPTER 1

Introduction

Objectives

- To understand the activity of programming
- To learn about the architecture of computers
- To learn about machine languages and higher-level programming languages
- To become familiar with your compiler
- To compile and run your first C++ program
- To recognize syntax and logic errors

1.1 What Is a Computer?

You have probably used a computer for work or fun. Many people use computers for everyday tasks such as balancing a checkbook or writing a term paper. Computers are good for such tasks. They can handle repetitive chores, such as totaling up numbers or placing words on a page, without getting bored or exhausted. More importantly, the computer presents you the checkbook or the term paper on the screen and lets you fix up mistakes easily. Computers make good game machines because they can play sequences of sounds and pictures, involving the human user in the process.

Actually, what makes all this possible is not just the computer. The computer must be programmed to perform these tasks. One program balances checkbooks; a different program, probably designed and constructed by a different company, processes words; and a third program plays a game. A computer itself is a machine that stores data (numbers, words, pictures), interacts with devices (the monitor screen, the sound system, the printer), and executes programs. Programs are sequences of instructions and decisions that the computer carries out to achieve a task.

Today's computer programs are so sophisticated that it is hard to believe that they are all composed of extremely primitive operations. A typical operation may be one of the following.

Put a red dot onto this screen position.

Send the letter A to the printer.

Get a number from this location in memory.

Add up these two numbers.

If this value is negative, continue the program at that instruction.

Only because a program contains a huge number of such operations, and because the computer can execute them at great speed, does the computer user have the illusion of smooth interaction.

The flexibility of a computer is quite an amazing phenomenon. The same machine can balance your checkbook, print your term paper, and play a game. In contrast, other machines carry out a much narrower range of tasks; a car drives, and a toaster toasts. Computers can carry out a wide range of tasks because they execute different programs, each of which directs the computer to work on a specific task.

1.2 What Is Programming?

A computer program tells a computer, in minute detail, the sequence of steps that are needed to fulfill a task. The act of designing and implementing these programs is called computer programming. In this course, you will learn how to program a computer—that is, how to direct the computer to execute tasks.

To use a computer you do not need to do any programming. When you write a term paper with a word processor, that program has been programmed by the manufacturer and is ready for you to use. That is only to be expected—you can drive a car without being a mechanic and toast bread without being an electrician. Many people who use computers every day in their careers never need to do any programming.

Quite a few computer users actually do some programming, even though they may not think of themselves as programmers. Many software packages allow a sophisticated user to automate certain repetitive tasks. A user can record *macros,* sequences of actions that can be replayed many times. For example, a word processor user might write a macro translating all quotes "like this" into *smart quotes* “like this”. Writing a macro involves three steps. First, you must have a clear understanding of the exact steps that need to be carried out. Then you must teach the application program how to carry out the steps. The mechanism for that teaching depends on the program. In a spreadsheet, you put macro instructions in special cells; in a word processor, you may need to record keystrokes and mouse clicks. Finally, you must come up with a mechanism to deliver the functionality of the macro for later use by yourself or by another user. Typically, you must attach the macro to a name, a keystroke, or a button with an icon.

Of course, a professional computer scientist or software engineer does a great deal of programming. Since you are taking this first course in computer science, it may well be your career goal to become such a professional. Programming is not the only skill required of a computer scientist or software engineer; indeed, programming is not the only skill required to create successful computer programs. Nevertheless, the activity of programming is central to computer science. It is also a fascinating and pleasurable activity that continues to attract and motivate bright students. The discipline of computer science is particularly fortunate that it can make such an interesting activity the foundation of the learning path.

To write a computer game with motion and sound effects or a word processor that supports fancy fonts and pictures is a complex task that requires a team of many highly skilled programmers. Your first programming efforts will be more mundane. The concepts and skills you learn in this course form an important foundation, and you should not be disappointed if your first programs do not rival the sophisticated software that is familiar to you. Actually, you will find that there is an immense thrill even in simple programming tasks. It is an amazing experience to see the computer carry out a task precisely and quickly that would take you hours of drudgery, to make small changes in a program that lead to immediate improvements, and to see the computer become an extension of your mental powers.

1.3 The Anatomy of a Computer

To understand the programming process, we need to have a rudimentary understanding of the building blocks that make up a computer. We will look at a personal

Figure 1

Central Processing Unit

computer. Larger computers have faster, larger, or more powerful components, but they have fundamentally the same design.

At the heart of the computer lies the *central processing unit* (CPU) (see Figure 1). It consists of a single *chip,* or a small number of chips. A computer chip (integrated circuit) is a component with a plastic or metal housing, metal connectors, and inside wiring made principally from silicon. For a CPU chip, the inside wiring is enormously complicated. For example, the Pentium chip (a popular CPU for personal computers at the time of this writing) is composed of over three million structural elements, called *transistors*. Figure 2 shows a magnified detail view of a CPU chip. The CPU performs program control, arithmetic, and data movement. That is, the CPU locates and executes the program instructions; it carries out arithmetic operations such as addition, subtraction, multiplication, and division; it fetches data from external memory or devices or stores data back. All data must travel through the CPU whenever it is moved from one location to another. (There are a few technical exceptions to this rule; some devices can interact directly with memory.)

The computer stores data and programs in *memory.* There are two kinds of memory. *Primary storage* is fast but expensive; it is made from memory chips (see Figure 3): so-called *random-access memory* (RAM) and *read-only memory* (ROM). Read-only memory contains certain programs that must always be present—for example, the code needed to start the computer. Random-access memory might have been better called "read-write memory", because the CPU can read data from it and write data

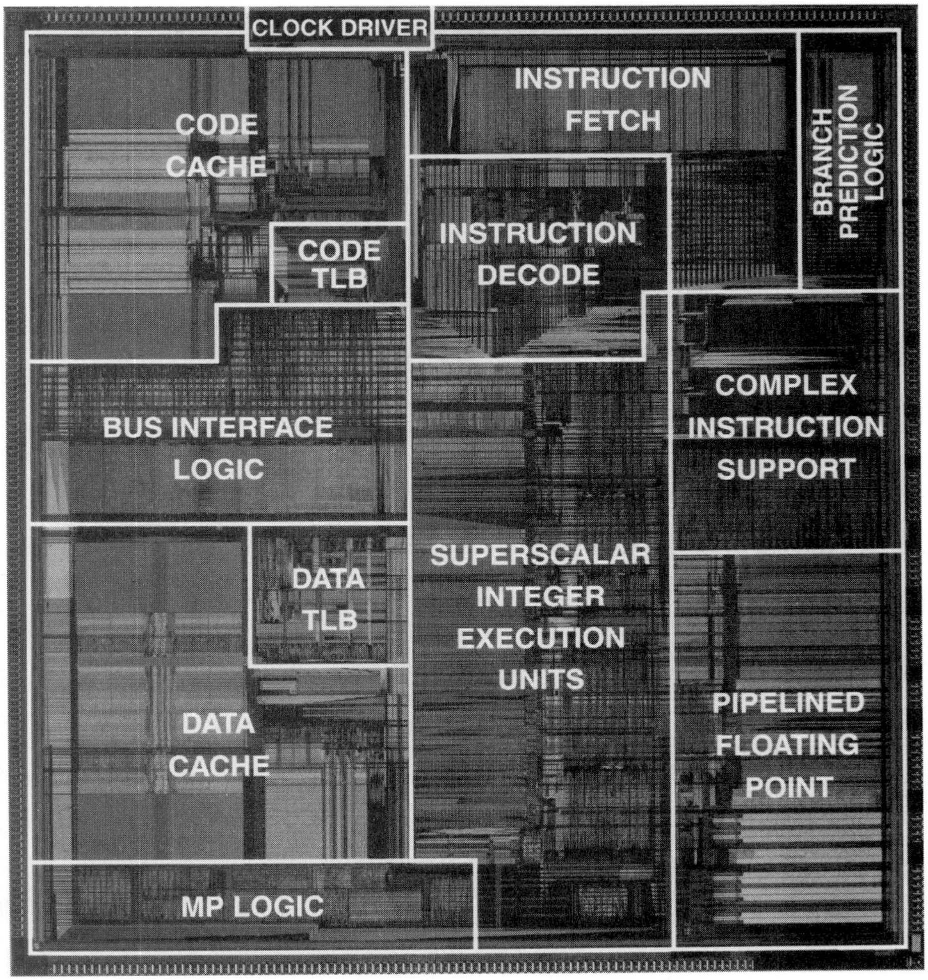

Figure 2

CPU Chip Detail

back to it. That makes RAM suitable to hold changing data and programs that do not have to be available permanently. RAM memory has two disadvantages. It is comparatively expensive, and it loses all its data when the power is turned off. *Secondary storage,* usually a *hard disk* (see Figure 4) provides less expensive storage that persists without electricity. A hard disk consists of rotating platters, which are coated with a magnetic material, and read/write heads, which can detect and change the magnetic flux on the platters. This is essentially the same storage process that is used in audio or video tapes. Programs and data are typically stored on the hard disk and loaded

Figure 3

RAM Chips

Figure 4

A Hard Disk

into RAM when the program starts. The program then updates the data in RAM and writes the modified data back to the hard disk.

You will often use another kind of magnetic storage device: a so-called *floppy disk* or *diskette* (see Figure 5). As the name suggests, a floppy disk consists of a flexible round base, covered with a magnetic material, inside a plastic cover. Like a hard

Figure 5

A Floppy Disk

disk, a floppy disk can also store data and programs, and the data is kept without electricity. The most common use for a floppy disk is to move data from one computer to another; you can copy data from your home computer and bring the disk to school to continue working with it, or you can put the disk in the mail. Because a floppy disk is not an integral part of the computer system, it is called an *external storage device.*

Floppy drives are inexpensive, comparatively rugged and convenient, but they suffer from one disadvantage: One floppy disk cannot hold nearly as much data as a hard disk. That is not so much a problem for your personal data; it is quite likely that all the homework you will produce in this class will easily fit on one floppy. However, audio and video information takes up much more space than a floppy disk provides. That kind of information is typically distributed on a CD-ROM (compact disc read-only memory; see Figure 6). A CD-ROM looks just like an audio CD and is read by a laser device (in fact, a CD-ROM reader on a personal computer can also play an audio CD). A CD-ROM can hold a large amount of information, and it can be manufactured inexpensively, but it is a read-only device: It can be used only to deliver programs and data from the manufacturer to the user, not by the user to store more data. To store large amounts of user data, *data tapes* (see Figure 7) are commonly

Figure 6

A CD-ROM Drive

used. Like audio and video tape cassettes, data tapes contain a long strip of magnetic tape for reading and writing data. Data tapes are inexpensive but slow. To locate data in the middle of the tape, the tape must be wound to the portion containing the data—a much slower task than moving a head across a rotating platter.

Some computers are self-contained units, whereas others are interconnected through *networks*. Home computers are usually not networked, but the computer in your computer lab is probably connected to a network. Through the network cabling, the computer can read programs from central storage locations or send data to other computers. For the user of a networked computer it may not even be obvious which data reside on the computer itself and which are transmitted through the network.

To interact with a human user, a computer requires other peripheral devices. The computer transmits information to the user through a display screen, loudspeakers, and printers. The user can enter information and directions to the computer by using a keyboard or a pointing device such as a mouse. Figure 8 shows a typical personal computer equipped with these devices.

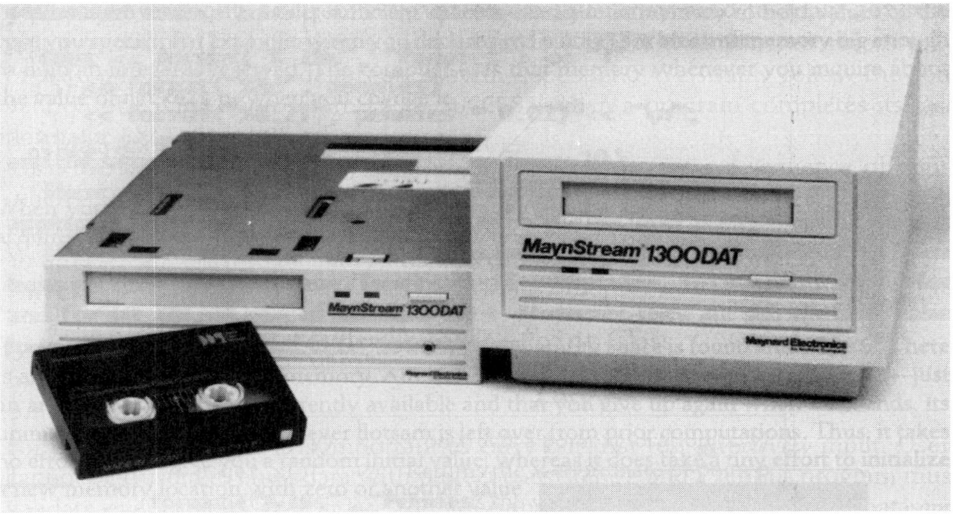

Figure 7

Tape Backup Drives and Data Tape

Figure 8

A Personal Computer

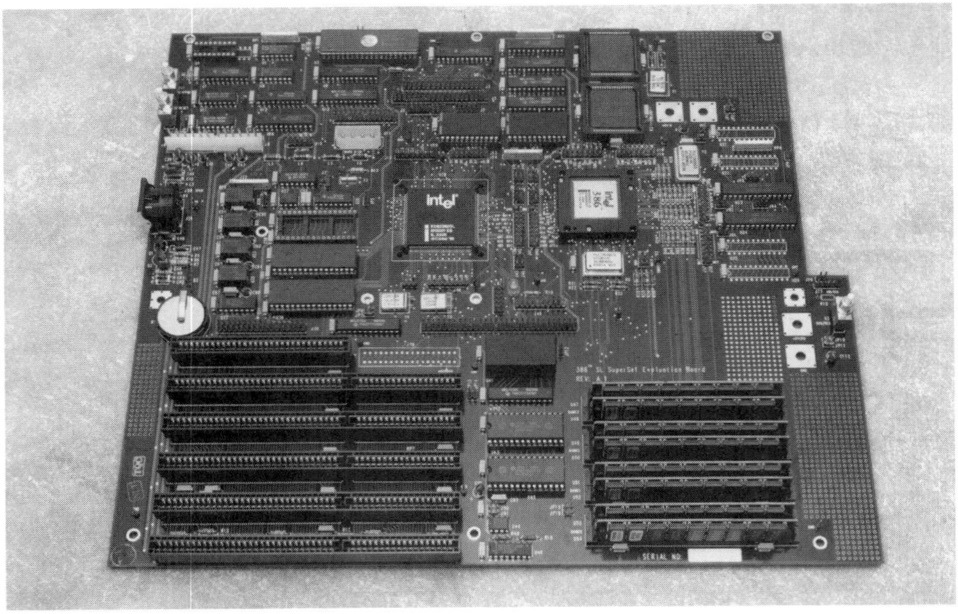

Figure 9

A Motherboard

The central processing unit, RAM memory, and the electronics controlling the hard disk and other devices are interconnected through a set of electrical lines called a *bus.* Data travels along the bus from the system memory and peripheral devices to the CPU and back. Figure 9 shows a *motherboard,* which contains the CPU, the RAM, and card slots, through which cards that control peripheral devices connect to the bus.

Figure 10 gives a schematic overview of the architecture of a computer. Program instructions and data (such as text, numbers, audio or video) are stored on the hard disk, on a CD-ROM, or elsewhere on the network. When a program is started, it is brought into RAM memory, from where the CPU can read it. The CPU reads the program an instruction at a time. As directed by these instructions, the CPU reads data, modifies it, and writes it back to RAM memory or the hard disk. Some program instructions will cause the CPU to place dots on the display screen or printer or to vibrate the speaker. As these actions happen many times over and at great speed, the human user will perceive images and sound. Some program instructions read user input from the keyboard or mouse. The program analyzes the nature of these inputs and then executes the next appropriate instructions.

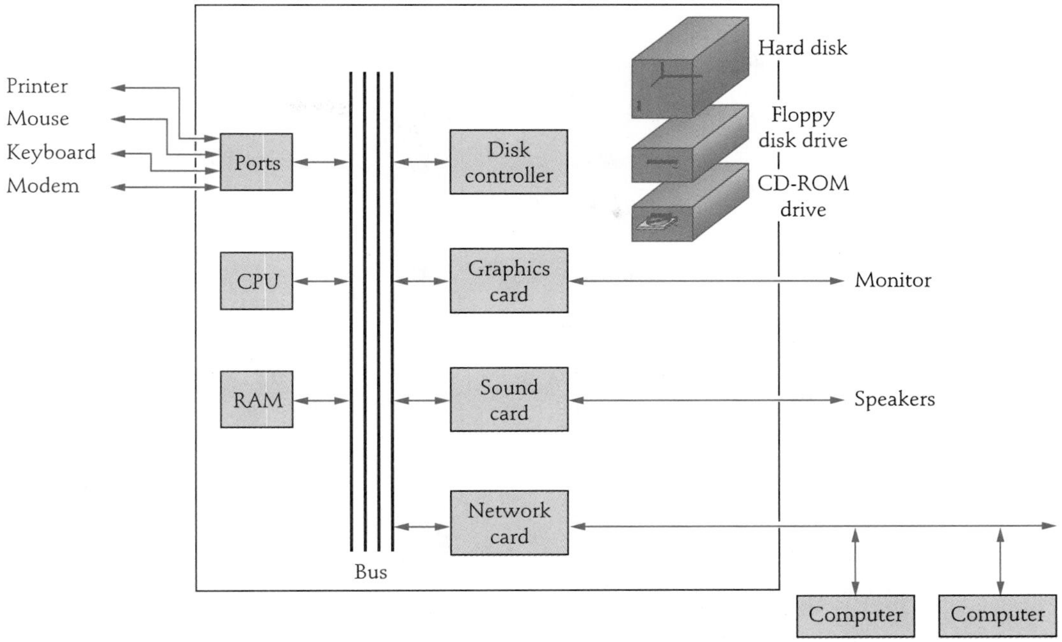

Figure 10

Schematic Diagram of a Personal Computer

Random Fact 1.1

The ENIAC and the Dawn of Computing

The ENIAC (*e*lectronic *n*umerical *i*ntegrator *a*nd *c*omputer) was the first usable electronic computer. It was designed by J. Presper Eckert and John Mauchly at the University of Pennsylvania and was completed in 1946—two years before transistors were invented. The computer was housed in a large room and consisted of many cabinets containing about 18,000 vacuum tubes (see Figure 11). Vacuum tubes burned out at the rate of several tubes per day. An attendant with a shopping cart full of tubes constantly made the rounds and replaced defective ones. The computer was programmed by connecting wires on panels. Each wiring configuration would set up the computer for a particular problem. To have the computer work on a different problem, the wires had to be replugged.

Work on the ENIAC was supported by the U.S. Navy, which was interested in computations of ballistic tables that would give the trajectory of a projectile, depending on the wind resistance, initial velocity, and atmospheric conditions. To compute the trajectories, one must

Figure 11

The ENIAC

find the numerical solutions of certain differential equations; hence the name "numerical integrator". Before machines like ENIAC were developed, humans did this kind of work, and until the 1950s the word "computer" referred to these people. The ENIAC was later used for peaceful purposes such as the tabulation of U.S. Census data.

1.4 Translating Human-Readable Programs to Machine Code

On the most basic level, computer instructions are extremely primitive. The processor executes *machine instructions.* A typical sequence of machine instructions is

1. Move the contents of memory location 40000 into register AX.
2. Subtract the value 100 from register AX.
3. If the result is positive, continue with the instruction that is stored in memory location 11280.

Actually, machine instructions are encoded as numbers so that they can be stored in memory. On an Intel 80386 processor, this sequence of instruction is encoded as the sequence of numbers

161 40000 45 100 127 11280

On a processor from a different manufacturer, the encoding would be quite different. When this kind of processor fetches this sequence of numbers, it decodes them and executes the associated sequence of commands.

How can we communicate the command sequence to the computer? The simplest method is to place the actual numbers into the computer memory. This is, in fact, how the very earliest computers worked. However, a long program is composed of thousands of individual commands, and it is a tedious and error-prone affair to look up the numeric codes for all commands and place the codes manually into memory. As we said before, computers are really good at automating tedious and error-prone activities, and it did not take long for computer programmers to realize that the computers themselves could be harnessed to help in the programming process.

The first step was to assign short names to the commands. For example, `MOV` denotes "move", `SUB` "subtract", and `JG` "jump if greater than 0". Using these commands, the instruction sequence becomes

```
MOV AX, [40000]
SUB AX, 100
JG  11280
```

That is a lot easier to read for humans. To get the instruction sequences accepted by the computer, though, the names must be translated into the machine codes. This is the task of another computer program: a so-called *assembler.* It takes the sequence of characters `M O V  A X` and translates it into the command code 161, and carries out similar operations on the other commands. Assemblers have another feature: they can give names to *memory locations* as well as to instructions. Our program sequence might have checked that some interest rate was greater than 100%, and the interest rate was stored in memory location 40000. It is usually not important where a value is stored; any available memory location will do. By using symbolic names instead of memory addresses, the program gets even easier to read:

```
MOV AX, [INT_RATE]
SUB AX, 100
JG  INT_ERROR
```

It is the job of the assembler program to find suitable numeric values for the symbolic names and to put those values into the generated code sequence.

Assembler instructions were a major advance over programming with raw machine codes, but they suffer from two problems. It still takes a great many instructions to achieve even the simplest goals, and the exact instruction sequence differs from one processor to another. For example, the above sequence of machine codes has a completely different meaning on the Sun SPARC processor. That is a real problem for people who invest a lot of time and money producing a software package. If a computer becomes obsolete, the program must be completely rewritten to run on the replacement system.

In the mid-1950s, higher-level programming languages began to appear. In these languages, the programmer expresses the idea behind the task that needs to be performed, and a special computer program, a so-called *compiler*, translates the higher-level description into machine instructions for a particular processor.

For example, in C++, the high-level programming language that we will use in this course, we might give the following instruction:

```
if (int_rate > 100) cout << "Interest rate error";
```

This means, "If the interest rate is over 100, display an error message." It is then the job of the compiler program to look at the sequence of characters `i f ( i n t _ r a t e > 1 0 0 )` and translate that into

161 40000 45 100 127 11280

Compilers are quite sophisticated programs. They have to translate logical statements, such as the `if`, into sequences of computations, tests, and jumps, and they must find memory locations for variables like `int_rate`. In this course, we will generally take the existence of a compiler for granted. If you become a professional computer scientist, you may well learn more about compiler-writing techniques later in your studies.

Higher-level languages are independent of the underlying hardware. For example, the instruction `if (int_rate > 100)` does not rely on particular machine instructions. In fact, it will compile to different code on an Intel 80386 and a Sun SPARC processor.

1.5 Programming Languages

Programming languages are independent of specific computer architecture, but they are human creations. As such, they follow certain conventions. To ease the translation process, those conventions are much stricter than they are for human languages. When you talk to another person, and you scramble or omit a word or two, your conversation partner will usually still understand what you have to say. Compilers are less forgiving. For example, if you omit the quotation mark close to the end of the instruction,

```
if (int_rate > 100) message_box("Interest rate error);
```

the C++ compiler will get quite confused and complain that it cannot translate an instruction containing this error. That is actually a good thing. If the compiler were to try to guess what you did wrong and tried to fix it, it might not guess your intentions correctly. In that case, the resulting program would do the wrong thing—quite possibly with disastrous effects, if that program controlled a device on whose functions someone's well-being depends. When a compiler reads programming instructions in a programming language, it will translate them into machine code only if the input follows the language conventions exactly.

Just as there are many human languages, there are many programming languages. Consider the instruction

```
if (int_rate > 100) message_box("Interest rate error");
```

This is how you must format the instruction in C++. C++ is a very popular programming language, and it is the one we use in this book. But in Pascal (another programming language in common use) the same instruction would be written as

```
if int_rate > 100 then message_box('Interest rate error');
```

In this case, the differences between the C++ and Pascal versions are slight: for other constructions, there will be far more substantial differences. Compilers are language-specific. The C++ compiler will translate only C++ code, whereas a Pascal compiler will reject anything but legal Pascal code. For example, if a C++ compiler reads the instruction `if int_rate > 100 then ...`, it will complain, because the condition of the `if` statement isn't surrounded by parentheses `( )`, and the compiler doesn't expect the word `then`. The choice of the layout for a language construct like the `if` statement is somewhat arbitrary, and the designers of different languages choose different tradeoffs among readability, easy translation, and consistency with other constructs.

1.6 Programming Language Design and Evolution

There are many hundreds of programming languages in existence today. That is actually quite surprising. The idea behind a high-level programming language is to provide a medium for programming that is independent from the instruction set of a particular processor, so that one can move programs from one computer to another without rewriting them. Moving a program from one programming language to another is a difficult process, however, and it is rarely done. Thus, it seems that there would be little use for so many programming languages.

Unlike human languages, programming languages are created with specific purposes. Some programming languages make it particularly easy to express tasks from a particular problem domain. Some languages specialize in database processing; others in "artificial intelligence" programs that try to infer new facts from a given base of knowledge; others in multimedia programming. The Pascal language was purposefully kept simple because it was designed as a teaching language. The C language was developed to be translated efficiently into fast machine code, with a minimum of housekeeping overhead. C++ builds on C by adding features for "object-oriented programming", a programming style that promises easier modeling of real-world objects.

Special-purpose programming languages occupy their own niches and are not used much beyond their area of specialization. It may be possible to write a multimedia program in a database language, but it is likely to be challenging. In contrast, languages like Pascal, C, and C++ are general-purpose languages. Any task that you would like to automate can be written in these languages.

The initial version of the C language was designed about 1972, but features were added to it over the years. Because different compiler writers added different features, the language actually sprouted various dialects. Some programming instructions were understood by one compiler but rejected by another. Such divergence is an immense pain to a programmer who wants to move code from one computer to another, and an effort got underway to iron out the differences and come up with a standard version of C. The design process ended in 1989 with the completion of the ANSI (American National Standards Institute) Standard. In the meantime, Bjarne Stroustrup of AT&T added features of the language Simula (an object-oriented language designed for carrying out simulations) to C. The resulting language was called C++. From 1985 until today, C++ has grown by the addition of many features, and a standardization process in currently underway.

C and C++ are good examples of languages that grow in an incremental fashion. As users of the language perceived shortcomings, they added features. In contrast, languages such as Pascal and Ada are designed in a more orderly process. One individual, or a small team, sets out to design the entire language, trying to anticipate the needs of its future users. Such planned languages have a great advantage: Because they are designed with one vision, their features tend to be logically related to each other, and separate features can be combined easily. In contrast, "grown" languages are typically a little messy; different features were designed by people with different tastes. Once a feature is a part of the language, it is difficult to remove it. Removing a feature breaks all existing programs that use it, and their authors would be very upset at the prospect of having to rewrite them. So grown languages tend to accumulate a patchwork of features that do not necessarily interact well with each other.

Furthermore, planned languages are generally designed with more thought. There is more attention to readability and consistency. In contrast, a new feature in a grown language is often added in a hurry to solve a specific need, without thinking through the ramifications. You can see one trace of that phenomenon in the Pascal and C++ `if` statements. The Pascal version

```
if int_rate > 100 then...
```

is easier to read than the C version

```
if (int_rate > 100)...
```

because the `then` keyword helps the human reader along. It is actually easier to compile too, because the `then` keyword tells the compiler where the condition ends and the action begins. In contrast, C++ needs the parentheses `( )` to separate the condition from the action. Why the difference? The trick with the `then` keyword was actually well known when Pascal and C were designed. It was used in Algol 60, a visionary language that has greatly influenced language design in the succeeding years. (Computer scientist Tony Hoare said of Algol 60: "Here is a language so far ahead of its time, that it was not only an improvement on its predecessors, but also on nearly all its successors." [1]) The designer of Pascal used `if... then` because it is a good solution. The designers of C were not as competent in language design. Either they did not know about the construction or they did not appreciate its benefits. Instead, they imitated the poorly designed `if` statement from FORTRAN, another early programming language. One of them later regretted their decision, but by then it was too late: The `if (...)` construction had been used millions of times, and nobody was willing to change existing, working code.

Languages that are designed by competent planners are generally easier to learn and use. Grown languages have the edge in the marketplace, however. Consider, for example, C++. Because C++ is simply C with some additions, any program written in C will continue to work under C++. Thus, programmers can reap the benefits of the new object-oriented features in C++ without having to throw away their existing C programs. That is a huge benefit. In contrast, the Modula 3 language was designed from the ground up to offer the benefits of object-oriented programming. There is no question that Modula 3 is easier to learn and use than C++, but for a programmer who already knows C the picture is different. That programmer can easily move C code to C++, whereas rewriting all the code in Modula 3 would be painful. This rewrite is difficult for two reasons. A serious program consists of many thousands or even millions of lines of code, and translating it line by line is obviously time-consuming. There is more to a programming language than just its syntax and conventions, though. The C language enjoys tremendous *tool support* from software packages that help programmers manage their C programs. These tools find errors, archive code, speed up programs, and help in combining useful parts of code from various sources. When a new language such as Modula 3 comes along, it has only rudimentary tool support, making it doubly hard to embrace for an ongoing project. In contrast, C tools can be easily modified to work with C++.

At this time, C++ is the premier language for general-purpose programming. For that reason, we use a subset of C++ in this book to teach you how to program. This allows you to benefit from the excellent C++ tools and to communicate easily with other programmers, many of whom use C++ every day. The drawback is that C++ is not all that easy to learn and has its share of traps and inconveniences. I don't want to give you the impression that C++ is a terrible language. It has been designed and refined by many very bright and hard-working people, and it has a tremendous application range, from very hardware-oriented programs to the highest levels of abstraction. By sticking to a small subset of the language, we will avoid most of the problems, and I will point out possible pitfalls and how you can avoid them. The purpose of this course is not to teach you all of C++ but to teach you the art and science of writing computer programs.

Random Fact 1.2

Standards Organizations

As this book is written, there is not yet a standard version of C++, but two organizations, the American National Standards Institute (ANSI) and the International Organization for Standardization (ISO), are jointly developing such a standard.

Why have standards? You encounter the benefits of standardization every day. When you buy a light bulb, you can be assured that it fits in the socket without having to measure the socket at home and the bulb in the store. In fact, you may have experienced how painful the lack of standards can be if you have ever purchased a flashlight with nonstandard bulbs. Replacement bulbs for such a flashlight can be difficult and expensive to obtain.

The ANSI and ISO standards organizations are associations of industry professionals who develop standards for everything from car tires and credit card shapes to programming languages. Having a standard for a programming language such as C++ means that you can take a program that you developed on one system with one manufacturer's compiler to a different system and be assured that it continues to work.

An ISO standard goes through three phases: technical analysis, consensus building, and formal approval. The technical analysis for the emerging C++ standard has just been completed at the time of this writing (1995), and the interested public is invited to submit comments to the committee. It is currently expected that final approval will occur about 1997.

To find out more about standards organizations, check out the following World Wide Web sites: `www.ansi.org` and `www.iso.ch`.

1.7 Becoming Familiar with Your Computer

For many readers this will be your first programming course, and you may well be doing your work on an unfamiliar computer system. You should spend some time making yourself familiar with the computer. Because computer systems vary widely, this book can only give an outline of the steps you need to follow. Using a new and unfamiliar computer system can be frustrating, especially if you are on your own. Look for training courses that your campus offers, or just ask a friend to give you a brief tour.

Step 1. Login

If you use your own home computer, you don't need to worry about this step. Computers in a lab, however, are usually not open to everyone. Access is usually restricted to those who paid the necessary fees and who can be trusted not to mess up the configuration. You will likely need an account number and a password to gain access to the system.

Figure 12

A Startup Screen with Icons

Step 2. Locate the C++ Compiler

Computer systems differ greatly in this regard. Some systems let you start the compiler by selecting an icon (see Figure 12) or menu. On other systems you must use the keyboard to type a command to launch the compiler. On most personal computers there is a so-called *integrated environment* in which you can write and test your programs. On other computers you must first launch one program that functions like a word processor, in which you can enter your C++ instructions; then launch another program to translate them to machine code; and then run the resulting machine code.

Step 3. Understand Files and Folders

As a programmer, you will write C++ programs, try them out, and improve them. You will be provided a place on the computer to store them, and you need to find out where that place is. You will store your programs in *files*. A C++ file is a container of C++ instructions. Files have names, and the rules for legal names differ from one system to another. On some systems, file names cannot be longer than eight characters. Some systems allow spaces in file names; others don't. Some distinguish between upper- and lowercase letters; others don't. Most C++ compilers require that C++ files end in an *extension* `.cpp` or `.C`; for example, `test.cpp`.

Figure 13

A Directory Hierarchy

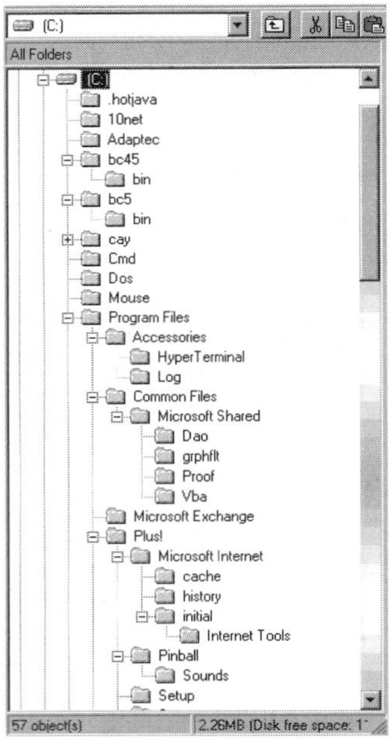

Files are stored in *folders* or *directories*. These file containers can be nested. A folder can contain files as well as other folders, which themselves can contain more files and folders (see Figure 13). This hierarchy can be quite large, especially on networked computers where some of the files may be on your local disk, others elsewhere on the network. While you need not be concerned with every branch of the hierarchy, you should familiarize yourself with your local environment. Different systems have different ways of showing files and directories. Some use a graphical display and let you move around by clicking the mouse on folder icons. In other systems, you must enter commands to visit or inspect different locations.

Step 4. Write a Simple Program

In the next section, we will introduce a very simple program. You will need to learn how to type it in, how to run it, and how to fix mistakes.

Step 5. Save Your Work

You will spend many hours typing C++ programs in and improving them. The resulting program files have some value, and you should treat them as you would other important property. A conscientious safety strategy is particularly important for computer files. They are more fragile than paper documents or other more tangible objects. It is easy to delete a file by accident, and occasionally files are lost because of a computer malfunction. Unless you kept another copy, you must then retype the contents. Because you are unlikely to remember the entire file, you will likely find yourself spending almost as much time again as you did to enter and improve it in the first place. This costs time, and it may cause you to miss deadlines. It is therefore crucially important that you learn how to safeguard files and get in the habit of doing so *before* disaster strikes. You can make safety or *backup* copies of files by saving copies on a floppy or by saving them onto another folder.

Productivity Hint 1.1

Backup Copies

Backing up on floppy disks is the easiest and most convenient method for most people. If you can't back up onto floppies, you can back up onto separate folders on your hard disk—but then you need to back up those folders, typically onto data tape, in case the hard disk dies. Here are a few pointers to keep in mind.

- *Back up often.* Backing up a file takes only a few seconds, and you will hate yourself if you have to spend many hours recreating work that you could have saved easily. I recommend that you back up your work once every thirty minutes, and every time before you run a program that you wrote.
- *Rotate backups.* Use more than one floppy disk for backups, and rotate them. That is, first back up onto the first floppy disk and put it aside. Then back up onto the second floppy disk. Then use the third, and then go back to the first. That way you always have three recent backups. Even if one of the floppy disks has a defect, you can use one of the others. The next day, switch to a new set of three. How many simultaneous backups should you keep? It is a tradeoff between convenience and paranoia. I suggest you keep seven sets of three, one set for each weekday.
- *Back up source files only.* The compiler translates the files that you write into files consisting of machine code. There is no need to back up the machine code files, since you can recreate them easily by running the compiler again. Focus your backup activity on those files that represent your effort. That way your backup disks won't fill up with files that you don't need.
- *Pay attention to the backup direction.* Backing up involves copying files from one place to another. It is important that you do this right—that is, copy from your work location to the backup location. If you do it the wrong way, you will overwrite a newer file with an older version.
- *Check your backups once in a while.* Double-check that your backups are where you think they are. There is nothing more frustrating than to find out that the backups are not there when you need them. This is particularly true if you use a backup program that stores files on an unfamiliar device (such as data tape) or in a compressed format.
- *Relax, then restore.* When you lose a file and need to restore it from backup, you are likely to be in an unhappy, nervous state. Take a deep breath and think through the recovery process before you start. It is not uncommon for an agitated computer user to wipe out the last backup when trying to restore a damaged file.

1.8 Compiling a Simple Program

We are now ready to write and run our first C++ program. The traditional choice for the very first program in a new programming language is a program that displays a simple greeting: "Hello, World!". We follow that tradition. Here is the "Hello, World!" program in C++.

Program hello.cpp

```
#include "iostream.h"
#include "stdlib.h"

int main()
{  cout << "Hello, World!\n";
   return EXIT_SUCCESS;
}
```

We will explain this program in a minute. For now, you should make a new program file and call it `hello`. Add the extension `.cpp` or `.C` that your compiler requires. Enter the program instructions and compile and run the program, following the procedure that is appropriate for your compiler.

By the way, C++ is *case-sensitive.* You must enter upper- and lowercase letters exactly as they appear in the program listing. You cannot type `MAIN` or `Return`. On the other hand, C++ has *free-form layout.* Spaces and line breaks are not important. You can write the entire program on a single line,

```
int main(){cout<<"Hello, World!\n";return EXIT_SUCCESS;}
```

or write every keyword on a separate line,

```
int
main()
{
cout
<<
"Hello, World!\n"
;
return
EXIT_SUCCESS;
}
```

However, good taste dictates that you lay out your programs in a readable fashion, so you should follow the layout in the program listing.

When you run the program, the message

```
Hello, World!
```

will appear on the screen. On some systems, you may need to switch to a different window to find the message.

Now that you saw the program working, it is time to understand its makeup. The first line,

```
#include "iostream.h"
```

tells the compiler to read the file iostream.h. That file contains definition for the *stream input/output* package. Our program performs output onto the screen and therefore requires the services provided in iostream.h. You must include this file into all programs that read or write text. Similarly, we include a file stdlib.h to make available a part of the *standard library* to our program.

By the way, you will see a slightly different syntax, #include <iostream.h>, in many C++ programs. See Advanced Topic 2.2 in Chapter 2 for more information on this issue.

The construction

```
int main()
{
   return EXIT_SUCCESS;
}
```

defines a *function* called main. A function is a collection of programming instructions that carry out a particular task. Every C++ program must have a main function. Most C++ programs contain other functions besides main, but it will take us until Chapter 5 to learn how to write other functions. The instructions or *statements* in the *body* of the main function—that is, the statements inside the curly braces {}—are executed one by one. Note that each statement ends in a semicolon ;

```
cout << "Hello, World!\n";
return EXIT_SUCCESS;
```

A sequence of characters enclosed in quotation marks

```
"Hello, World!\n"
```

is called a *string*. We must enclose the contents of the string inside quotation marks so that the compiler knows we literally mean "Hello, World!\n". In this short program, there is actually no possible confusion. Suppose, on the other hand, we wanted to display the word *main*. By enclosing it in quotation marks, "main", the compiler knows we mean the sequence of characters m a i n, not the function named main. The rule is simply that you must enclose all text strings in quotation marks, so that the compiler considers them plain text and not program instructions.

Actually, the text string "Hello, World!\n" should not be taken *completely* literally. We do not want the odd-looking \n to appear on the screen. The two-character sequence \n actually denotes a single, nonprinting character, a so-called *newline*. When the newline character is sent to the display, the cursor is moved to the first column in the next screen row. If you don't send a newline character, then the next displayed item will simply follow the current string on the same line. In this program we only printed one item, but in general we will want to print multiple items, and it is a good habit to end all lines of output with a newline character.

The backslash \ character is used as a so-called *escape* character. The backslash does not denote itself; instead, it is used to encode other characters that would otherwise be difficult or impossible to show in program statements. There are a few other backslash combinations that we will encounter later. Now, what do you do if you actually want to show a backslash on the display? You must enter two in a row. For example,

```
cout << "Hello\\World!\n";
```

would print

```
Hello\World!
```

Finally, how can you display a string containing quotation marks, such as

```
Hello, "World"!
```

You can't use

```
cout << "Hello, "World"!\n";
```

As soon as the compiler reads `"Hello, "`, it thinks the string is finished, and then it gets all confused about `World` followed by a second string `"!\n"`. Compilers have a one-track mind, and if a simple analysis of the input doesn't make sense to them, they just refuse to go on, and they report an error. In contrast, a human would probably realize that the second and third quotation marks were supposed to be part of the string. Well, how do we then display quotation marks on the screen? The backslash escape character again comes to the rescue. Inside a string the sequence \" denotes a literal quote, not the end of a string. The correct display statement is therefore

```
cout << "Hello, \"World\"!\n";
```

To display values on the screen, you must send them to an entity called `cout`. The << operator denotes the "send to" command. You can also print numerical values. For example, the statement

```
cout << 3 + 4;
```

displays the number 7.

Finally, the `return` statement denotes the end of the `main` function. When the `main` function ends, the program terminates. The EXIT_SUCCESS value is a signal that the program ran successfully. In this small program there was nothing that could have gone wrong during the program run. In other programs there might be problems with the input or with some devices, and you would then have `main` return the value EXIT_FAILURE to indicate an error. By the way, the `int` in `int main()` indicates that `main` returns an integer value, not a fractional number or string. The values EXIT_SUCCESS and EXIT_FAILURE are defined in the file stdlib.h.

Common Error 1.1

Omitting Semicolons

In C++ every statement must end in a semicolon. Forgetting to type a semicolon is a common error. It confuses the compiler because the compiler uses the semicolon to find where one statement ends and the next one starts. The compiler does not use line ends or closing braces to recognize the end of statements. For example, the compiler considers

```
cout << "Hello, World!\n"
return EXIT_SUCCESS;
```

a single statement, as if you had written

```
cout << "Hello, World!\n" return EXIT_SUCCESS;
```

and then it doesn't understand that statement, because it does not expect the keyword `return` in the middle of an output command. The remedy is simple. Just scan every statement for a terminating semicolon, just as you would check that every English sentence ends in a period.

1.9 Errors

Experiment a little with the hello program. What happens if you make a typing error such as

```
cot << "Hello, World\n";
cout << "Hello, World\";
cout << "Hell, World\n";
```

In the first case, the compiler will complain. It will say that it has no clue what you mean by `cot`. The exact wording of the error message is dependent on the compiler, but it might be something like "Undefined symbol cot". This is a *compile-time error* or *syntax error.* Something is wrong according to the language rules, and the compiler finds it. When the compiler finds one or more errors, it refuses to translate the program to machine code, and as a consequence you have no program that you can run. You must fix the error and compile again. In fact, the compiler is quite picky, and it is common to go through several rounds of fixing compile-time errors before compilation succeeds for the first time.

If the compiler finds an error, it will not simply stop and give up. It will try to report as many errors as it can find, so you can fix them all at once. Sometimes, however, one error throws it off track. This is likely to happen with the error in the second line. The compiler will miss the end of the string because it thinks that the \" is an embedded quote character. In such cases, it is common for the compiler to emit bogus error reports for neighboring lines. You should fix only those error messages that make sense to you and then recompile.

The error in the third line is of a different kind. The program will compile and run, but its output will be wrong. It will print

```
Hell, World!
```

This is a *run-time error* or *logic error.* The program is syntactically correct and does something, but it doesn't do what it is supposed to do. The compiler cannot find the error, and it must be flushed out when the program runs, by testing it and carefully looking at its output.

During program development, errors are unavoidable. Once a program is longer than a few lines, it requires superhuman concentration to enter it correctly without slipping up once. You will find yourself omitting semicolons or quotes more often than you would like, but the compiler will track down these problems for you.

Logic errors are more troublesome. The compiler will not find them—in fact, the compiler will cheerfully translate any program as long as its syntax is correct—but the resulting program will do something wrong. It is the responsibility of the program author to test the program and find any logic errors. Testing programs is an important topic that we will encounter many times in this course. Another important aspect of good craftsmanship is *defensive programming:* structuring programs and development processes in such a way that an error in one place of a program does not trigger a disastrous response.

The error examples that we saw so far were not difficult to diagnose or fix, but as you learn more sophisticated programming techniques, there will also be much more room for error. It is an uncomfortable fact that locating all errors in a program is very difficult. Even if you can observe that a program exhibits faulty behavior, it may not at all be obvious what part of the program caused it and how you can fix it. There are special software tools, so-called *debuggers,* that let you trace through a program to find *bugs*—that is, logic errors. In this course you will learn how to use a debugger effectively.

Note that all these errors are different from the kind of errors that you are likely to make in calculations. If you total up a column of numbers, you may miss a minus sign or accidentally drop a carry, perhaps because you are bored or tired. Computers do not make these kind of errors. When a computer adds up numbers, it will get the correct answer. Admittedly, computers can make overflow or roundoff errors, just as pocket calculators do, when you ask them to perform computations whose result falls outside their numeric range. An overflow error occurs if the result of a computation is very large or very small. For example, most computers and pocket calculators overflow when you try to compute 10^{1000}. A roundoff error occurs when a value cannot be represented precisely. For example, $\frac{1}{3}$ may be stored in the computer as 0.3333333, a value that is close to, but not exactly equal to $\frac{1}{3}$. If you compute $1 - 3 \times \frac{1}{3}$, you may obtain 0.0000001, not 0, as a result of the roundoff error. We will consider such errors logic errors, because the programmer should have chosen a more appropriate calculation scheme that handles overflow or roundoff correctly.

You will learn a three-part error management strategy in this course. First, you will learn about common errors and how to avoid them. Then you will learn defensive programming strategies to minimize the likelihood and impact of errors. Finally, you will learn debugging strategies to flush out those errors that remain.

Common Error 1.2

Misspelling Words

If you accidentally misspell a word, then strange things may happen, and it may not always be completely obvious from the error messages what went wrong. Here is a good example of how simple spelling errors can cause trouble:

```
#include "iostream.h"

int Main()
{  cout << "Hello, World!\n";
   return EXIT_SUCCESS;
}
```

This code defines a function called `Main`. The compiler will not consider this to be the same as the `main` function, because `Main` starts with an uppercase letter and the C++ language is *case-sensitive*. Upper- and lowercase letters are considered to be completely different from each other, and to the compiler `Main` is no better match for `main` than `rain`. The compiler will cheerfully compile your `Main` function, but when the linker is ready to build the executable file, it will complain about the missing `main` function and refuse to link the program. Of course, the message "missing `main` function" should give you a clue where to look for the error.

If you get an error message that seems to indicate that the compiler is on the wrong track, it is a good idea to check for spelling and capitalization. All C++ keywords, and the names of most functions, use only lowercase letters. If you misspell the name of a symbol (for example `out` instead of `cout`) the compiler will complain about an "undefined symbol". That error message is usually a good clue that you made a spelling error.

1.10 The Compilation Process

Some C++ development environments are very convenient to use. You just enter the code in one window, click on a button or menu to compile, and click on another button or menu to run your code. Error messages show up in a second window, and the program runs in a third window. Figure 14 shows the screen layout of a popular C++ compiler with these features. With such an environment you are completely shielded from the details of the compilation process. On other systems you must carry out every step manually.

Even if you use a convenient C++ environment, it is useful to know what goes on behind the scenes, mainly because knowing the process helps you solve problems when something goes wrong.

You first enter the program statements into a text editor. The editor stores the text and gives it a name such as **`hello.cpp`**. If the editor window shows a name like **`noname.cpp`**, you should change the name. You should *save* the file to disk frequently, because otherwise the editor only stores the text in the computer's RAM memory. If something goes wrong with the computer and you need to restart it, the contents of the RAM (including your program text) are lost, but anything stored on a hard disk or floppy disk is permanent even if you need to restart the computer.

When you compile your program, the compiler translates the C++ *source code* (that is, the statements that you wrote) into so-called *object code*. Object code consists of machine instructions and information on how to load the program into memory prior to execution. Object code is stored in a separate file, usually with extension

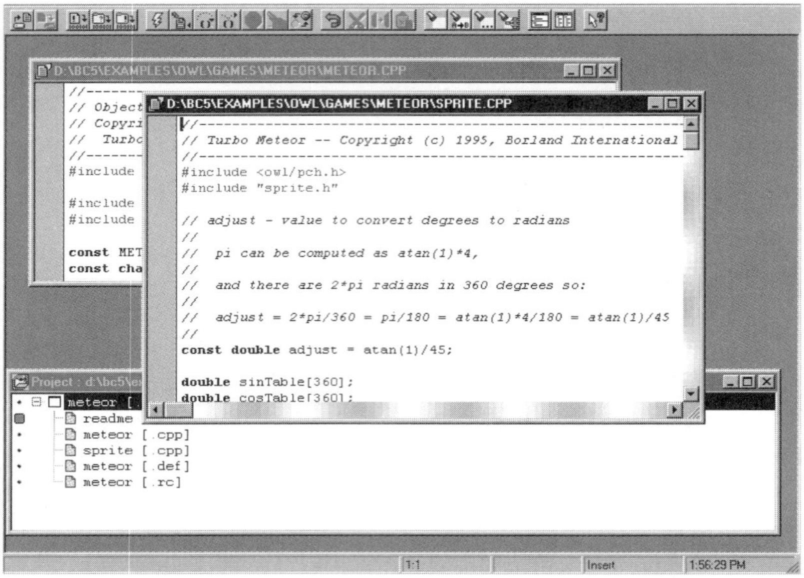

Figure 14

Screen Layout of an Integrated C++ Environment

`.obj` or `.o`. For example, the object code for the hello program might be stored in hello.obj.

The object file contains only the translation of the code that you wrote. That is not enough to actually run the program. To display a string on a window, quite a bit of low-level activity is necessary. The authors of the iostream package (which defines `cout` and its functionality) have implemented all necessary actions and placed the required machine code into a *library.* A library is a collection of code that has been programmed and translated by someone else, ready for you to use in your program. (More complicated programs are built from more than one object file and more than one library.) A special program called the *linker* takes your object file and the necessary parts from the iostream library and builds an *executable file.* (Figure 15 gives an overview of these steps.) The executable file is usually called hello.exe or just hello, depending on your computer system. It contains all machine code necessary to run the program. You can run the program by typing `hello` at a command prompt, or by clicking on the file icon, even after you exit the C++ environment. You can put that file on a floppy and give it to another user who doesn't have a C++ compiler or who may not know that there is such a thing as C++, and that person can run the program in the same way.

Figure 15

From Source Code to Executable Program

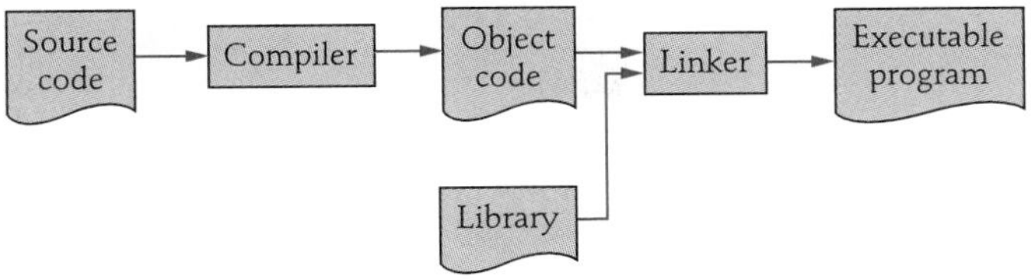

Figure 16

Edit–Compile–Debug Loop

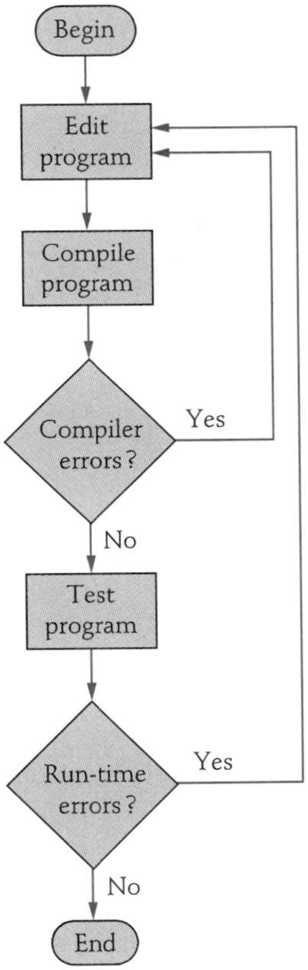

Your programming activity centers around these files. You start in the editor, writing the source file. You compile the program and look at the error messages. You go back to the editor and fix the syntax errors. When the compiler succeeds, the linker builds the executable file. You run the executable file. If you find an error, you can run the debugger to execute it a line at a time. Once you find the cause of the error, you go back to the editor and fix it. You compile, link, and run again to see whether the error has gone away. If not, you go back to the editor. This is called the *edit–compile–debug loop* (see Figure 16), and you will spend a substantial amount of time in this loop in the months and years to come.

1.11 Algorithms

We will soon learn how to program calculations and decision making in C++. But before we look at the mechanics of implementing computations in the next chapter, let us consider the planning process that precedes the implementation.

You may have run across advertisements that encourage you to pay for a computerized service that matches you up with a love partner. Let us think how this might work. You fill out a form and send it in. Others do the same. The data are processed by a computer program. Is it reasonable to assume that the computer can perform the task of finding the best match for you? Suppose your younger brother, not the computer, had all the forms on his desk. What instructions could you give him? You can't say, "Find the best-looking person of the opposite sex who likes inline skating and browsing the Internet". There is no objective standard for good looks, and your brother's opinion (or that of a computer program analyzing the digitized photo) will likely be different from yours. If you can't give instructions for someone to solve the problem by hand, there is no way the computer can magically solve the problem. The computer can only do what you can do by hand. It just does it faster, and it doesn't get bored or exhausted.

Now consider the following investment problem:

> You put $10,000 into a bank account that earns 6% interest per year. Interest is compounded monthly. How many years does it take for the account balance to be double the original?

Could you solve this problem by hand? Sure, you could. If the interest rate is 6% per year, it is 0.5% per month. So you figure out the balance as follows:

Month	Balance	
0	$10,000.00	
1	$10,050.00	$= \$10,000.00 * 1.005$
2	$10,100.25	$= \$10,050.00 * 1.005$
3	$10,150.75	$= \$10,100.25 * 1.005$
4	$10,201.51	$= \$10,150.75 * 1.005$

You keep going until the balance goes over $20,000. Then you convert the months to years, and you have the answer.

Of course, carrying out this computation is intensely boring. You could tell your younger brother to do it. Seriously, the fact that a computation is boring or tedious is irrelevant to the computer. Computers are very good at carrying out repetitive calculations quickly and flawlessly. What is important to the computer (and your younger brother) is the existence of a systematic approach for finding the solution. The answer can be found just by following a series of steps that involves no guesswork.

Here is such a series of steps:

Step 1. Start with the table

After month	Balance
0	$10,000.00

Step 2. Repeat steps 2a . . . 2c while the balance is less than $20,000.

Step 2a. Add a new row to the table.
Step 2b. In column 1 of the new row, put one more than the preceding month value.
Step 2c. In column 2 of the new row, place the value of the preceding balance value, multiplied by 1.005 (0.5%).

Step 3. Divide the last number in the month column by 12, and report it as the number of years required to double the investment.

Of course, these steps are not yet in a language that a computer can understand, but we will learn soon how to formulate them in C++. What is important is that the method that we described be

- Unambiguous
- Executable
- Terminating

The method is *unambiguous* because there are precise instructions what to do in every step and where to go next. There is no room for guesswork or creativity. The method is *executable* because each step can be carried out in practice. Had we asked to use the actual interest rate that will be charged in months to come, and not a fixed rate of 6% per year, our method would not have been executable, because there is no way for anyone to know what that interest will be. Finally, the computation will eventually come to an end. With every step, the balance goes up by at least $50, so eventually it must reach $20,000.

A solution technique that is unambiguous, executable, and terminating is called an *algorithm.* We have found an algorithm to solve our investment problem, and thus we can find the solution with the computer. The existence of an algorithm is an essential prerequisite for programming a task. Sometimes finding an algorithm is very simple. At other times it requires ingenuity or planning. If you cannot find an algorithm, you cannot use the computer to solve your problem. You need to satisfy yourself that an algorithm exists, and that you understand its steps, before you start programming.

Chapter Summary

1. Computers execute very basic operations in rapid succession. The sequence of operations is called a computer program. Different tasks (such as balancing a checkbook, printing a letter, or playing a game) require different programs. Programmers produce computer programs to make the computer solve new tasks.

2. The central processing unit (CPU) of the computer executes one operation at a time. Each operation specifies how data should be processed, how data should be brought into the CPU or out of the CPU, or what operation should be selected next.

3. Data values can be brought into the CPU for processing from storage or from input devices such as the keyboard, the mouse, or a communications link. Processed information is sent back from the CPU to storage or to output devices such as the display or a printer.

4. Storage devices include random-access memory (RAM) and secondary storage. RAM is fast, but it is expensive and loses its information when the power is turned off. Secondary storage devices use magnetic or optical technology to store information. Access time is slower, but the information is retained without the need for electrical power.

5. Computer programs are stored as machine instructions in a code that depends on the processor type. Writing instruction codes directly is difficult for human programmers. Computer scientists have found ways to make this task easier by using assembly language and higher-level programming languages. The programmer writes the programs in such a "language," and a special computer program translates it into the equivalent sequence of machine instructions. Assembly language instructions are tied to a particular processor type. Higher- level languages are independent of the processor. The same program can be translated to run on many different processor types from different manufacturers.

6. Programming languages are designed by computer scientists for a variety of purposes. Some languages are designed for specific purposes, such as database processing. In this course, we use C++, a general-purpose language that is suited for a wide range of programming tasks. C++ is popular because it is based on the C language, which is already in widespread use. To be efficient and compatible with C, the C++ language is less elegant than some newly designed languages, and C++ programmers have to live with a few unfortunate compromises. However, many excellent development tools support C++.

7. Set aside some time to become familiar with the computer system and the C++ compiler that you will use for your class work. Develop a strategy for keeping backup copies of your work before disaster strikes.

8. Every C++ program contains `#include` directives, to access necessary features such as input and output, and a function called `main`. In a simple program, `main` just displays a message on the screen and then returns with a success indicator.

9. Errors are a fact of life for the programmer. Syntax errors are faulty constructs that do not conform to the rules of the programming language. They are detected by the compiler, and no program is generated. Logic errors are constructs that can be translated into a running program, but the resulting program does not perform the action that the programmer intended. The programmer is responsible for inspecting and testing the program to guard against logic errors.

10. C++ programs are translated by a program called a compiler into machine code. In a separate step, a program called a linker combines that machine code with previously translated machine code for input/output and other services to build your program.

11. An algorithm is a description of steps to solve a problem that is unambiguous, executable, and terminating. That is, the description leaves no room for interpretation, the steps can be carried out in practice, and the result is guaranteed to be obtained after a finite amount of time. In order to solve a problem by computer, you must know an algorithm for finding the solution.

Further Reading

[1] C. A. R. Hoare, "Hints on Programming Language Design," *Sigact/Sigplan Symposium on Principles of Programming Languages, October 1973*. Reprinted in *Programming Languages, A Grand Tour,* ed. Ellis Horowitz, 3rd Ed., Computer Science Press, 1987.

Review Exercises

Exercise R1.1. Explain the difference between using a computer program and programming a computer.

Exercise R1.2. Name the various ways in which a computer can be programmed that were discussed in this chapter.

Exercise R1.3. Which parts of a computer can store program code? Which can store user data?

Exercise R1.4. Which parts of a computer serve to give information to the user? Which parts take user input?

Exercise R1.5. Rate the storage devices that can be part of a computer system by (*a*) speed and (*b*) cost.

Exercise R1.6. Describe the utility of the computer network in your department computer lab. To what other computers is a lab computer connected?

Exercise R1.7. Assume a computer has the following machine instructions, coded as numbers:

160 *n*:	Move the contents of register AX to memory location *n*.
161 *n*:	Move the contents of memory location *n* to register AX.
44 *n*:	Add the value *n* to register AX.
45 *n*:	Subtract the value *n* from register AX.
50 *n*:	Add the contents of memory location *n* to register AX.
51 *n*:	Subtract the contents of memory location *n* from register AX.
52 *n*:	Multiply register AX with the contents of memory location *n*.
53 *n*:	Divide register AX by the contents of memory location *n*.
127 *n*:	If the result of the last computation is positive, continue with the instruction that is stored in memory location *n*.
128 *n*:	If the result of the last computation is zero, continue with the instruction that is stored in memory location *n*.

Assume that each of these instructions and each value of *n* requires one memory location. Write a program in machine code to solve the investment doubling program.

Exercise R1.8. Design mnemonic instructions for the machine codes in the preceding exercise and write the investment-doubling program in assembler code, using your mnemonics and suitable symbolic names for variables and labels.

Exercise R1.9. Explain two benefits of higher programming languages over assembler code.

Exercise R1.10. List the programming languages mentioned in this chapter.

Exercise R1.11. Explain at least two advantages and two disadvantages of C++ over other programming languages.

Exercise R1.12. On your own computer or on your lab computer, find the exact location (folder or directory name) of

- The sample file hello.cpp, which you wrote with the editor
- The standard header file iostream.h
- The header file ccc.h, which you need for most programs in this book

Exercise R1.13. Explain the special role of the \ escape character in C++ character strings.

Exercise R1.14. Write three versions of the hello.cpp program that have different syntax errors. Write a version that has a logic error.

Exercise R1.15. How do you discover syntax errors? How do you discover logic errors?

Exercise R1.16. Write an algorithm to settle the following question: A bank account starts out with $10,000. Interest is compounded monthly at 6% per year (0.5% per month). Every month, $500 is withdrawn to meet college expenses. After how many years is the account depleted?

Exercise R1.17. Consider the question of the preceding exercise. Suppose the numbers ($10,000, 6%, $500) were user-selectable? Are there values for which the algorithm you developed would not terminate? If so, change the algorithm to make sure it always terminates.

Exercise R1.18. The value of π can be computed according to the following formula:

$$\frac{\pi}{4} = 1 - \frac{1}{3} + \frac{1}{5} - \frac{1}{7} + \frac{1}{9} - \cdots$$

Write an algorithm to compute π. Since the formula is an infinite series and an algorithm must stop after a finite number of steps, you should stop when you have the result determined up to six significant digits.

Exercise R1.19. Suppose you put your younger brother in charge of backing up your work. Write a set of detailed instructions how he should carry out his task. Explain how often he should do it, and what files he needs to copy from which folder to which floppy disk. Explain how he should verify that the backup was carried out correctly.

Programming Exercises

Exercise P1.1. Write a program that prints out a message "Hello, my name is Hal!". Then, on a new line, the program should print the message "What would you like me to do?". Then it is the user's turn to type in an input. We haven't yet learned how to do it—just use the following line of code:

```
string user_input = get_line(cin);
```

Finally, the program should ignore the user input and print the message "I am sorry, I cannot do that."

This program uses `string` data and the `get_line` function. To access these features, you must place the line

```
#include "ccc.h"
```

before the `main` function. The file ccc.h accompanies this book and needs to be properly installed on your system.

Here is a typical program run. The user input is printed in color.

```
Hello, my name is Hal!
What would you like me to do?
Clean up my room
I am sorry, I cannot do that.
```

When running the program, remember to hit the Enter key after typing the last word of the input line.

Exercise P1.2. Write a program that prints out a message "Hello, my name is Hal!" Then, on a new line, the program should print the message "What is your name?" As in Exercise P1.1, just use the following line of code:

```
string user_name = get_line(cin);
```

Finally, the program should print the message "Hello, *user name.* I am glad to meet you!" To print the user name, simply use

```
cout << user_name;
```

As in Exercise P1.1, you must place the line

```
#include "ccc.h"
```

before the `main` function.

Here is a typical program run. The user input is printed in color.

```
Hello, my name is Hal!
What is your name?
Dave
Hello, Dave. I am glad to meet you.
```

Exercise P1.3. Write a program that computes the sum of the first ten positive integers, $1 + 2 + \cdots + 10$. *Hint:* Write a program of the form

```
int main()
{  cout <<
   return EXIT_SUCCESS;
}
```

Exercise P1.4. Write a program that computes the *product* of the first ten positive integers, $1 \times 2 \times \cdots \times 10$, and the sum of the reciprocals $1/1 + 1/2 + \cdots + 1/10$. This is harder than it sounds. First, you need to know that the * symbol, not a $\times$, is used for multiplication in C++. Try out writing the program, and check the results against a pocket calculator. The program's results aren't likely to be correct. Then write the numbers as *floating-point* numbers, `1.0`, `2.0`, ..., `10.0`, and run the program again. Can you explain the difference in the results? We will explain this phenomenon in Chapter 2.

Exercise P1.5. Write a program that displays your name inside a box on the terminal screen, like this:

```
Dave
```

Do your best to approximate lines with characters like `| - +`.

CHAPTER 2

Fundamental Data Types

Objectives

- To understand integer and floating-point numbers
- To write arithmetic expressions in C++
- To appreciate the importance of comments and good code layout
- To be able to define and initialize variables and constants
- To recognize the limitations of the `int` and `float` types and the overflow and roundoff errors that can result
- To learn how to read user input and display program output
- To be able to change the values of variables through assignment
- To use the ANSI C++ standard `string` type to define and manipulate character strings
- To be able to write simple programs that read numbers and text, process the input, and display the results

In this and the four following chapters you will learn the basic skills needed to write programs in C++. Only in Chapter 6 will we have all necessary tools for actually coding the investment problem at the end of Chapter 1.

This chapter teaches how to manipulate numbers and character strings in C++. The goal of this chapter is to write simple programs using these basic data types.

2.1 Number Types

Consider the following simple problem. I have 8 pennies, 4 dimes, and 3 quarters in my purse. What is the total value of the coins?

Here is a C++ program that solves this problem:

Program coins1.cpp

```
#include "iostream.h"
#include "stdlib.h"

int main()
{  int pennies = 8;
   int dimes = 4;
   int quarters = 3;

   float total = pennies * 0.01 + dimes * 0.10
      + quarters * 0.25; /* total value of the coins */

   cout << "Total value = " << total << "\n";

   return EXIT_SUCCESS;
}
```

In this program we manipulate two kinds of numbers. The coin counts (`8`, `4`, `3`) are *integers*. Integers are whole numbers without a fractional part (including zero and negative whole numbers). The numerical values of the coins (`0.01`, `0.10`, and `0.25`) are called *floating-point numbers.* Floating-point numbers can have decimal points. They are called "floating-point" because of their internal representation in the computer. The numbers 250, 2.5, 0.25, and 0.025 are all represented in a very similar way: namely, as a sequence of the significant digits—2500000—and an indication of the position of the decimal point. When the values are multiplied or divided by 10, only the position of the decimal point changes; it "floats". (Actually, internally the numbers are represented in base 2, but the principle is the same.) As you probably guessed, `int` and `float` are the C++ names for integers and floating point-numbers.

Why have two number types? We could just use

```
float pennies = 8;
```

There are two reasons for having separate types, one philosophical and one pragmatic. By indicating that the number of pennies is an integer, we make explicit an assumption: There can be only a whole number of pennies in the purse. The program would have worked just as well with floating-point numbers to count the coins, but it is generally a good idea to choose programming solutions that document one's intentions. Pragmatically speaking, integers are more efficient than floating-point numbers. They take less storage space and are processed faster.

In C++, multiplication is denoted by an asterisk `*`, not a raised dot $\cdot$ or a cross $\times$. (There is no key for these symbols on most keyboards.) For example, $d \cdot 10$ is written as `d * 10`. Do not write commas or spaces in numbers in C++. For example, 10,150.75 must be entered as `10150.75`. To write numbers in exponential notation in C++, use E*n* instead of "$\times 10^n$". For example, 5.0×10^{-3} becomes `5.0E-3`.

The output statement

```
cout << "Total value = " << total << "\n";
```

shows a useful feature: *stream* output. You can display as many items as you like (in this case, the string `"Total value = "`) followed by the value of `total` and a string containing a newline character, to move the cursor to the next line. Just separate the items that you want to print by `<<`. Alternatively, you could write three separate output statements

```
cout << "Total value = ";
cout << total;
cout << "\n";
```

This has exactly the same effect as displaying the three items in one statement.

Note the *comment*

```
/* total value of the coins */
```

next to the definition of `total`. This comment is purely for the benefit of the human reader, to explain in more detail the meaning of `total`. Anything enclosed between `/*` and `*/` is completely ignored by the compiler. Comments are used to explain the program to other programmers or to yourself. There is a second comment style, using the `//` symbol, that is very popular. See Advanced Topic 2.3 for details.

The most important feature of our sample program is the introduction of *symbolic names*. We could have just programmed

Program coins2.cpp

```
#include "iostream.h"
#include "stdlib.h"

int main()

{  cout << "Total value = "
      << 8 * 0.01 + 4 * 0.10 + 3 * 0.25 << "\n";

   return EXIT_SUCCESS;
}
```

This program computes the same answer. Compare it with our first program, though. Which one is easier to read? Which one is easier to update if we need to change the coin counts, such as by adding some nickels? By giving the symbolic names `pennies`, `dimes`, and `quarters` to the counts, we made the program more readable and maintainable. This is an important consideration. You introduce symbolic names to explain what a program does, just as you use variable names such as p, d, and q in algebra.

In C++, each variable has a *type*. By defining `int pennies`, we proclaim that `pennies` can hold only integer values. If you try to put a floating-point value into the `pennies` variable, the fractional part will be lost.

You define a variable by first giving its type and then its name, such as `int pennies`. You may also add an *initialization value*, such as `= 8`. Then you end the definition with a semicolon. Even though the initialization is optional, it is a good idea always to initialize variables with a specific value. See Quality Tip 2.1 for the reason.

Variable names in algebra are usually just one letter long, such as p or A, maybe with a subscript such as p_1. In C++, it is common to choose longer and more descriptive names, such as `price` or `area`. You cannot type subscripts; just tag an index behind the name: `price1`. You can choose any variable names you like, provided you follow a few simple rules. Names must start with a letter, and the remaining characters must be letters, numbers, or the underscore (_) character. You cannot use other symbols such as `$` or `%`. Spaces are not permitted inside names either. Furthermore, you cannot use *reserved words* such as `float` or `return` as names; these words are reserved exclusively for their special C++ meanings. Variable names are also *case-sensitive*, that is, `Area` and `area` are *different* names. It would not be a good idea to mix the two in the same program, because it would make that program very confusing to read. To avoid any possible confusion, we will never use any uppercase letters in variable names in this book. You will find that many programmers use names like `listPrice`; however, we will always choose `list_price` instead. (Because we cannot have spaces inside names, `list price` is not permissible.)

Quality Tip 2.1

Initialize Variables When You Define Them

You should always initialize a variable at the same time you define it. Let us see what happens if you define a variable but leave it uninitialized.

If you just define

```
int nickels;
```

the variable `nickels` comes into existence and memory space is found for it. However, it contains some random value, since you did not initialize the variable. If you mean to initialize the variable to zero, you must do so explicitly:

```
int nickels = 0;
```

Why does an uninitialized variable contain a random value? It would seem less trouble to just put a 0 into a variable than to come up with a random value. Anyway, where does the random value come from? Does the computer roll electronic dice?

When you define a variable, sufficient space is set aside in memory to hold values of the type you specify. For example, when you declare `int nickels`, a block of memory big enough to hold an integer is reserved. The compiler uses that memory whenever you inquire about the value of `nickels` or when you change it.

`nickels` 

When you initialize the variable, `int nickels = 0`, then a zero is placed into the newly acquired memory location:

`nickels` 

If you don't specify the initialization, however, the memory space is found and left as is. There is already *some* value in the memory. After all, you don't get freshly minted transistors—just an area of memory that is currently available and that you give up again when `main` ends. Its uninitialized value is just whatever flotsam is left over from prior computations. Thus, it takes no effort at all to give you a random initial value, whereas it does take a tiny effort to initialize a new memory location with zero or another value.

If you don't specify an initialization, the compiler assumes that you are not quite ready to come up with the value that you want to store in the variable. Maybe the value needs to be computed from other variables, like the `total` in our example, and you haven't defined all components yet. It is quite reasonable not to waste time initializing a variable if that initial value is never used before it is overwritten with the truly intended value.

However, suppose you have the following sequence of events:

```
int nickels; /* I'll get around to setting it presently */
int dimes = 3;
float total = nickels * 0.05 + dimes * 0.10; /* Error */
nickels = 2 * dimes;
/* Now I remember—I have twice as many nickels as dimes */
```

This is a problem. The value of `nickels` has been used before it has been set. The value for `total` is computed as follows: Take a random number and multiply it by 0.05, then add the value of the dimes. Of course, what you get is a totally unpredictable value. This is no use at all.

There is an additional danger here. Because the value of `nickels` is random, it may be different every time you run the program. Of course, you would get tipped off pretty soon if you ran the program twice and you got two different answers. However, suppose you ran the program ten times at home or in the lab, and it always came up with one value that looked reasonable. Then you turned the program in to be graded, and it came up with a different and unreasonable answer when the grader ran it. How can this happen? Aren't computer programs supposed to be predictable and deterministic? They are—as long as you initialize all your variables. On the grader's computer the uninitialized value for `nickels` might have been −15,054, when on your machine on that particular day it happened to have been 6.

What is the remedy? *Reorder the definitions* so that all of the variables are initialized. This is usually simple to do:

```
int dimes = 3;
int nickels = 2 * dimes;
/* I have twice as many nickels as dimes */
float total = nickels * 0.05 + dimes * 0.10; /* OK */
```

Quality Tip 2.2

Choose Descriptive Variable Names

We could have saved ourselves a lot of typing by using shorter variable names, as in

```
#include "iostream.h"
#include "stdlib.h"

int main()
{  int p = 8;
   int d = 4;
   int q = 3;

   float t = p * 0.01 + d * 0.10 + q * 0.25;
      /* total value of the coins */

   cout << "Total value = " << t << "\n";

   return EXIT_SUCCESS;
}
```

Compare this program with the previous one, though. Which one is easier to read? There is no comparison. Just reading `pennies` is a lot less trouble than reading `p` and then *figuring out* that it must mean "pennies".

In practical programming, descriptive variable names are particularly important when programs are written by more than one person. It may be obvious to *you* that `p` must stand for pennies and not percentage (or maybe pressure), but is it obvious to the person who needs to update your code years later, long after you were promoted (or laid off)? For that matter, will you remember yourself what `p` means when you look at the code six months from now?

Of course, you could use comments:

```
#include "iostream.h"
#include "stdlib.h"

int main()

{  int p = 8; /* pennies */
   int d = 4; /* dimes */
   int q = 3; /* quarters */

   float t = p + d * 0.10 + q * 0.25;
      /* total value of the coins */

   cout << "Total value = " << t << "\n";

   return EXIT_SUCCESS;
}
```

That makes the definitions pretty clear, but the computation `p + d * 0.10 + q * 0.25` is still cryptic.

If you have the choice between comments and self-commenting code, choose the latter. It is better to have clear code with no comments than cryptic code with comments. There is a good reason for this. In actual practice, code is not written once, handed to a grader, and subsequently forgotten. Programs are modified and enhanced all the time. If the code explains itself, you just have to update it to new code that explains itself. If the code requires explanation, you have to update both the code and the explanation. If you forget to update the explanation, you end up with a comment that is worse than useless because it no longer reflects what is actually going on. The next person reading it must waste time to understand whether the code is wrong or the comment.

Advanced Topic 2.1

Numeric Ranges and Precisions

Unfortunately, `int` and `float` values do suffer from one problem. They cannot represent arbitrarily large integer or floating-point numbers. On many microprocessors, integers range only between about −30,000 and about +30,000. On other, newer processors they usually have a range of about −2 billion to +2 billion. If you want to represent the world population, you can't use an `int`. Floating-point numbers are somewhat less limited; they can go up to 10^{37} (for comparison, the earth weighs about 6×10^{27} grams). However, floating-point numbers suffer from a different problem: *precision*. They store only six to seven significant digits. For example, if you compute `539999.0 * 1.0525`, the result should be `568348.9475`. Try it out with a calculator; then run the following program:

```
#include "iostream.h"
#include "stdlib.h"

int main()
{  float price = 539999.0;
   float amount_due = price * 1.0525;

   cout << amount_due << "\n";

   return EXIT_SUCCESS;
}
```

The program prints `568348.9375`. It is off by a penny!

For our programming projects, the limited range and precision of `int` and `float` are usually acceptable. If they are not, there is a whole zoo of extended types that can help you out—see Advanced Topic 2.2 for more information.

Advanced Topic 2.2

Other Numeric Types

If `int` and `float` are not sufficient for your computational needs, there are other data types you can turn to. On many compilers for personal computers, `int` data have a fairly restricted range (from −32768 to 32767, to be exact). (This is because integers are represented using

16 bits, allowing for 2^{16}, or 65536, different values. Half of the values (from -1 to -32768) are negative. There is one less positive value, because 0 also needs to be represented.) This is insufficient for most applications. The simplest remedy is to use the `long` type. Long integers typically have a range from $-2{,}147{,}483{,}648$ to 2,147,483,647.

Some C++ compilers have an integer type `short` with shorter-than-normal integers, which are useful to conserve space. There are `unsigned` variations of the integer data types: `unsigned int`, `unsigned short`, `unsigned long`. Data of this type can never be negative, and the positive range is twice as large as that for the signed varieties. For example, if `int` has a range of -32768 to 32767, then `unsigned int` has a range of 0 to 65535. We will not use short or unsigned integers in this course.

The precision of `float` values, commonly 23 binary digits or 6 to 7 decimal digits, is insufficient for many programs. For example, you need more than seven digits to compute the cost of a home mortgage in dollars and cents. The `double` data type implements *double-precision* floating-point numbers, with about 13 decimal digits of precision and exponents ranging from about 10^{-300} to about 10^{300}. Another type, `long double`, yields even more precision.

Advanced Topic 2.3

Alternative Comment Syntax

In C++ there are two methods for writing comments. You already learned that the compiler ignores anything that you type between /* and */. The compiler also ignores any text between a // and the end of the current line:

```
float t = p * 0.01 + d * 0.10 + q * 0.25;
    // total value of the coins
```

This is easier to type if the comment is only a single line long. But if you have a comment that is longer than a line, then the /* . . . */ comment is simpler:

```
/*
In this program, we compute the value of a set of coins. The
user enters the count of pennies, nickels, dimes, and quarters.
The program then displays the total value.
*/
```

It would be somewhat tedious to add the // at the beginning of each line and to move them around whenever the text of the comment changes.

In this book we keep it simple and always use the /* */–style comments. If you like the // style better, by all means go ahead and use it. Or you can use // for comments that will never grow beyond a single line, and /* . . . */ for longer comments. The readers of your code will be grateful for *any* comments, no matter which style you use.

Random Fact 2.1.

The Pentium Floating-Point Bug

In 1994, Intel Corporation released what was then its most powerful processor, the Pentium. Unlike previous generations of Intel's processors, the Pentium had a very fast floating-point unit. Intel's goal was to compete aggressively with the makers of higher-end processors for engineering workstations. The Pentium was an immediate huge success.

In the summer of 1994, Dr. Thomas Nicely of Lynchburg College in Virginia ran an extensive set of computations to analyze the sums of reciprocals of certain sequences of prime numbers. The results were not always what his theory predicted, even after he took into account the inevitable roundoff errors. Then Dr. Nicely noted that the same program did produce the correct results when run on the slower 486 processor, which preceded the Pentium in Intel's lineup. This should not have happened. The optimal roundoff behavior of floating-point calculations has been standardized by the Institute of Electrical and Electronics Engineers (IEEE), and Intel claimed to adhere to the IEEE standard in both the 486 and the Pentium processors. Upon further checking, Dr. Nicely discovered that indeed there was a very small set of numbers for which the product of two numbers was computed differently on the two processors. For example,

$$4,195,835 - ((4,195,835/3,145,727) \times 3,145,727)$$

should of course evaluate to 0, and it did compute as 0 on a 486 processor. On a Pentium processor, however, the result was 256.

As it turned out, Intel had independently discovered the bug in its testing and had started to produce chips that fixed it. The bug was caused by an error in a table that was used to speed up the floating-point multiplication algorithm of the processor. Intel determined that the problem was exceedingly rare. They claimed that under normal use a typical consumer would only notice the problem once every 27,000 years. Unfortunately for Intel, Dr. Nicely had not been a normal user.

Now Intel had a real problem on its hands. It figured that replacing all Pentium processors that it had already sold would cost it a great deal of money. Intel already had more orders for the chip than it could produce, and it would be particularly galling to have to give out the scarce chips as free replacements instead of selling them. Intel's management decided to punt on the issue and initially offered to replace the processors only for those customers who could prove that their work required absolute precision in mathematical calculations. Naturally, that did not go over well with the hundreds of thousands of customers who had paid retail prices of $700 and more for a Pentium chip and did not want to live with the nagging feeling that perhaps, one day, their income tax program would produce a faulty return.

Ultimately, Intel had to cave in to public demand and replaced all defective chips, at a cost of about 475 million dollars.

What do you think? Intel claims that the probability of the bug occurring in any calculation is extremely small—smaller than many chances we take every day, such as driving to work in an automobile. Indeed, many users had used their Pentium computers for many months without reporting any ill effects, and the computations that Professor Nicely was doing are hardly examples of typical user needs. As a result of its public relations blunder, Intel ended up paying a large amount of money. Undoubtedly, some of that money was added to chip prices and thus actually paid by Intel's customers. Also, a large number of processors, whose manufacture consumed energy and caused some environmental impact, were destroyed without benefiting anyone. Could Intel have been justified in wanting to replace only the processors of those users who could reasonably be expected to suffer an impact from the problem?

Suppose that, instead of stonewalling, Intel had offered you the choice of a free replacement processor or a $200 rebate. What would you have done? Would you have replaced your faulty chip, or would you have taken your chance and pocketed the money?

2.2 Input and Output

The program of the preceding section was not very useful. If I have a different collection of coins in my purse, I must change the variable initializations, recompile the program, and run it again. In particular, I must always have a C++ compiler available to adapt the program to new values. It would be more practical if the program could ask how many coins I have of each kind, and then compute the total. Here is such a program.

Program coins3.cpp

```
#include "iostream.h."
#include "stdlib.h"

int main()
{  cout << "How many pennies do you have? ";
   int pennies;
   cin >> pennies;

   cout << "How many nickels do you have? ";
   int nickels;
   cin >> nickels;

   cout << "How many dimes do you have? ";
   int dimes;
   cin >> dimes;

   cout << "How many quarters do you have? ";
   int quarters;
   cin >> quarters;

   float total = pennies * 0.01 + nickels * 0.05
      + dimes * 0.10 + quarters * 0.25;
      /* total value of the coins */

   cout << "Total value = " << total << "\n";

   return EXIT_SUCCESS;
}
```

When this program runs, it will ask, or *prompt,* you:

```
How many pennies do you have?
```

The cursor will stay on the same line as the prompt, and you should enter a number and then press the Enter key. Then there will be three more prompts, and finally the answer is printed and the program terminates.

Figure 1

Processing Input

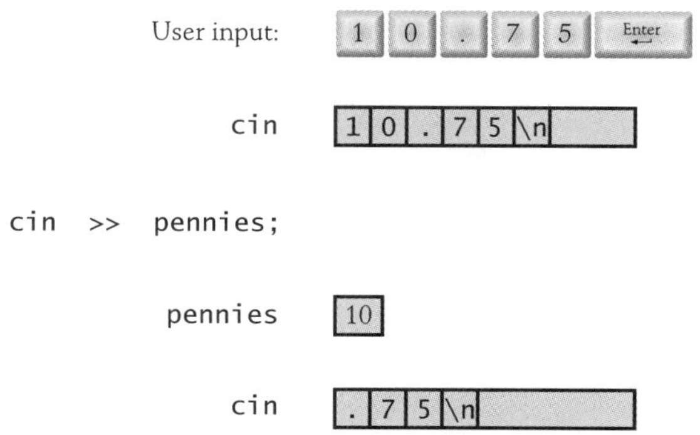

Reading a number into the variable `pennies` is achieved by the statement

```
cin >> pennies;
```

When this statement is executed, the program waits for the user to type in a number and press the Enter key. The number is then placed into the variable, and the program executes the next statement.

In this case, we did not initialize the variables that count the coins, because the input statements move values into these variables. We moved the variable definitions as close as possible to the input statements to indicate where the values are set.

You can read floating-point values as well:

```
float balance;
cin >> balance;
```

When an integer is read from the keyboard, zero and negative numbers are allowed as inputs, but floating-point numbers are not. For example, `-10` would be allowed as an input for the number of quarters, even though it makes no sense—you can't have a negative number of coins in your purse. Fractional numbers are not accepted. If you type `10.75` when an integer input is expected, the `10` will be read and placed into the variable in the input statement. The `.75` will not be skipped. It will be considered in the next input statement. (See Figure 1.) This is not intuitive and probably not what you expected.

Something even worse happens if you don't enter a number at all. For example, if you type `ten` or `help`, then the input-processing routine realizes that your answer isn't a number, so it does not set the variable in the input statement (that is, the old value of that variable is unchanged). What's more, it sets the `cin` input stream to a "failed" state. This means that `cin` has lost all confidence in the data it receives, so all subsequent input statements will be ignored. (See Figure 2.) Unfortunately, there is no warning beep or error message that alerts the user to this problem. We will learn later how to recognize and solve input problems. Of course, that is a necessary skill for building programs that can survive untrained or careless users. At this point we must just ask you to type in the right kind of responses to the input prompts.

Figure 2

Failed Input

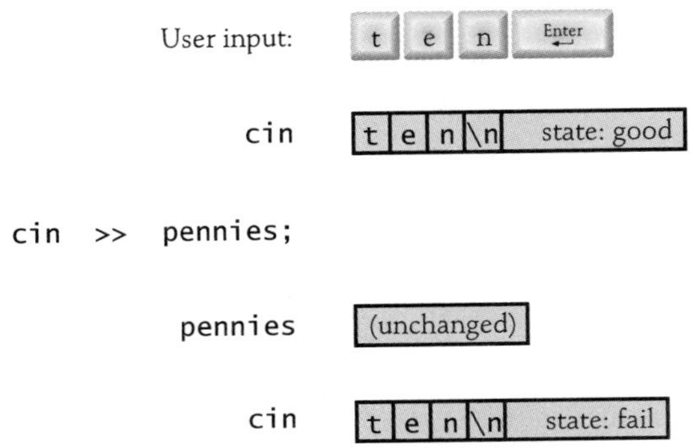

It is possible to read more than one value in at a time. For example, the input statement

```
cin >> pennies >> nickels >> dimes >> quarters;
```

reads four values from the keyboard. The values can be all on one line, such as

```
8 0 4 3
```

or on separate lines, such as

```
8
0
4
3
```

(See Figures 3 and 4.) All that matters is that the numbers are separated by *white space:* that is, blank spaces, tabs, or newlines. You enter a blank space by hitting the space bar, a tab by hitting the tab key (often marked with an arrow and vertical bar ⟶|), and a newline by hitting the Enter key. These keystrokes are used by the input reader to separate input.

Keyboard input is *buffered.* Lines of keystrokes are batched together, and the entire input line is processed when you hit the Enter key. For example, suppose the coin calculation program prompts you

```
How many pennies do you have?
```

As a response, you enter

```
8 0 4 3
```

Nothing happens until you hit the Enter key. Suppose you hit it. The line is now sent for processing by `cin`. The first input command reads the 8 and removes it from the input stream, and the other three numbers are left there for subsequent input operations. Then the prompt

```
How many nickels do you have?
```

Figure 3

Separating Input with Spaces

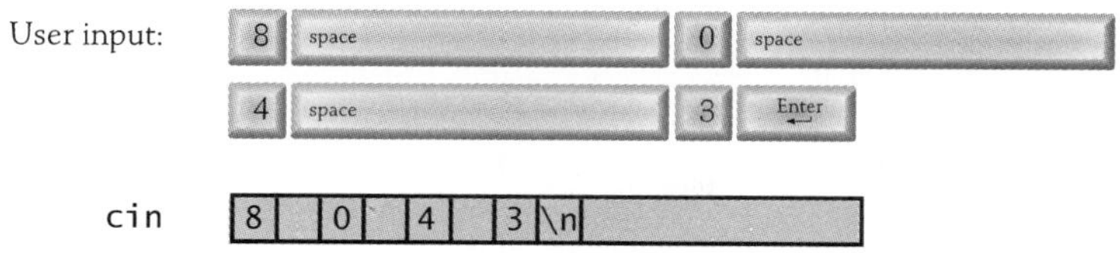

Figure 4

Separating Input with Newlines

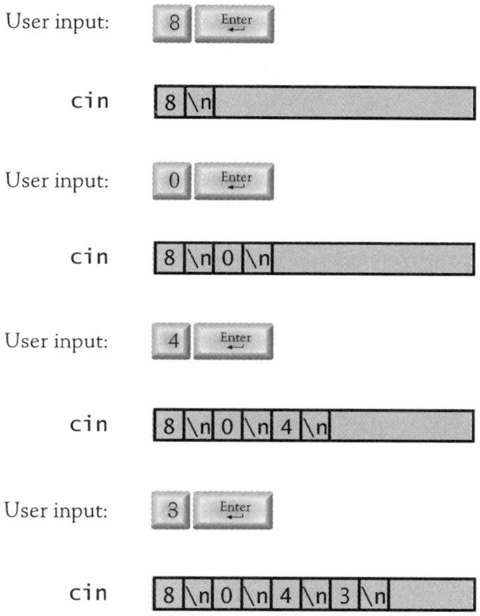

is displayed, and the program *immediately* reads the `0` from the partially processed line. You don't get a chance to type another number. Then the other two prompts are displayed, and the other two numbers are processed.

Of course, if you know what input the program wants, this type-ahead feature can be handy, but it is surprising to most users, who are used to more orderly input processing. Frankly, input from `cin` is not all that well suited for interaction with human users. It works well for reading data from a file, though, and it is very simple to program.

2.3 Assignment

All but the simplest programs use variables to store values. Variables are locations in memory that can hold values of a particular type. For example, the variable `total` holds values of type `float` because we declared it as `float total`. Up to now, the variables that we used were actually not very variable. Once we stored a value in them, either by initialization or by an input command, that value never varied.

Let us compute the value of the coins in a different way, by keeping a *running total.* First, we ask for the number of pennies and set the total to the value of the pennies. Then we ask for the number of nickels and *add* to the total the value of the nickels. Then we do the same to the dimes and quarters. Here is the program.

Program coins4.cpp

```
#include "iostream.h"
#include "stdlib.h"

int main()
{  cout << "How many pennies do you have? ";
   int count;
   cin >> count;
   float total = count * 0.01;

   cout << "How many nickels do you have? ";
   cin >> count;
   total = count * 0.05 + total;

   cout << "How many dimes do you have? ";
   cin >> count;
   total = count * 0.10 + total;

   cout << "How many quarters do you have? ";
   cin >> count;
   total = count * 0.25 + total;

   cout << "Total value = " << total << "\n";

   return EXIT_SUCCESS;
}
```

Rather than having four variables for each coin count, there now is just one variable, `count`. And the value of `count` really varies during program execution. Each input command `cin >> count` puts a new value into `count`, wiping out the prior contents.

In this program we only need one count variable, because we process the value right away, accumulating it into the total. The first processing statement, `total = pennies * 0.01`, is straightforward. The second statement is much more interesting:

```
total = count * 0.05 + total;
```

It means, "Compute the value of the nickel contribution (`count * 0.05`), add to it the value of the running total, *and place the result again into the memory location* `total`." (See Figure 5.)

Figure 5

Assignment

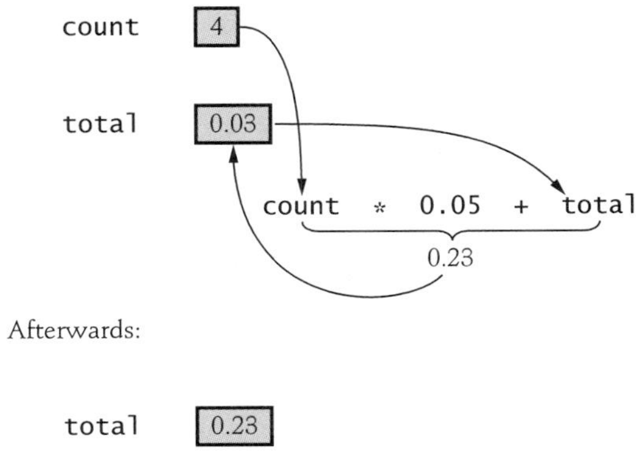

When you make an assignment of an expression into a variable, the *types* of the variable and the expression need to match. For example, it is an error to assign

```
total = "a lot";
```

because **total** is a floating-point variable and **"a lot"** is a string. It is, however, legal, to store an integer in a floating-point variable:

```
total = count;
```

If you assign a floating-point expression to an integer, the expression will be truncated to an integer. Unfortunately, that will not necessarily be the closest integer; Common Error 2.1 contains a dramatic example. Therefore it is never a good idea to make an assignment from floating-point to integer. In fact, many compilers emit a warning if you do. A better way of converting from floating-point to integer is to use the **round** function. That function is not part of standard C++, but it is included with the library that was developed for this book. Whenever you want to use the **round** function or another feature that is specific to this book, you must include the header file ccc.h (ccc stands for *Computing Concepts with C++*, the title of this book):

```
#include "ccc.h"
. . .
float total;
. . .
int pennies = round(100 * total);
```

There is a subtle difference between the statements

```
float total = count * 0.01;
```

and

```
total = count * 0.05 + total;
```

The first statement is the *definition* of **total**. It is a command to create a new variable of type **float**, to give it the name **total**, and to initialize it with **count**. The second statement is an *assignment statement:* an instruction to replace the contents of the existing variable **total** with another value.

It is not possible to have multiple definitions of the same variable. The sequence of statements

```
float total = count * 0.01;
...
float total = count * 0.05 + total; /* Error */
```

is illegal. The compiler will complain about an attempt to redefine `total`, because it thinks you want to define a new variable in the second statement. On the other hand, it is perfectly legal, and indeed very common, to make multiple assignments to the same variable:

```
total = count * 0.05 + total;
...
total = count * 0.10 + total;
```

The = sign doesn't mean that the left-hand side *is* equal to the right-hand-side but that the right-hand-side value is copied into the left-hand-side variable. You should not confuse this *assignment operation* with the = used in algebra to denote *equality*. The assignment operator is an instruction to do something, namely place a value into a variable. The mathematical equality states the fact that two values are equal. For example, in C++, it is perfectly legal to write

```
month = month + 1;
```

It means to look up the value stored in the variable `month`, to add 1 to it, and to stuff the sum back into `month`. (See Figure 6.) The net effect of executing this statement is to increment `month` by 1. Of course, in mathematics it would make no sense to write that month = month + 1; no value can equal itself plus 1.

The concepts of assignment and equality have no relationship with each other, and it is a bit unfortunate that the C++ language uses = to denote assignment. Other programming languages use a symbol such as ← or `:=`, which avoids the confusion.

Consider once more the statement `month = month + 1`. This statement increments the month counter. For example, if `month` was 3 before execution of the statement, it is set to 4 afterwards. This increment operation is so common when writing

Figure 6

Incrementing a Variable

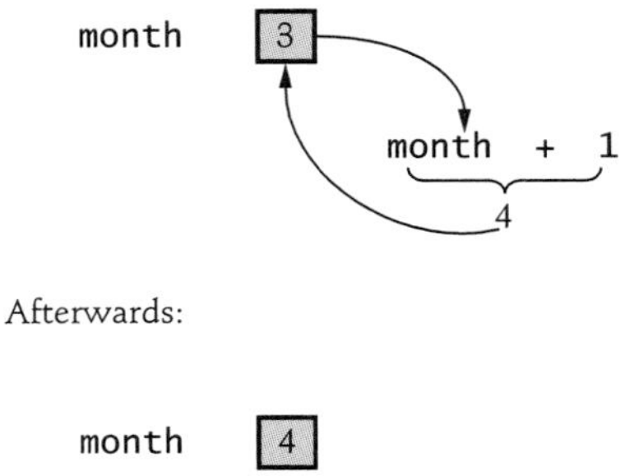

programs that there is a special shorthand for it, namely

```
month++;
```

This statement has exactly the same effect, namely to add 1 to `month`, but it is easier to type. As you might have guessed, there is also a decrement operator `--`. The statement

```
month--;
```

subtracts 1 from `month`.

The `++` increment operator gave the C++ programming language its name. C++ is the incremental improvement of the C language.

Common Error 2.1.

Roundoff Errors

Roundoff errors are a fact of life when calculating with floating-point numbers. You probably have encountered that phenomenon yourself with manual calculations. If you calculate 1/3 to two decimal places, you get 0.33. Multiplying again by 3, you obtain 0.99, not 1.00.

In the processor hardware, numbers are represented in the binary number system, not in decimal. You still get roundoff errors when binary digits are lost. They just may crop up at different places than you might expect. Here is an example:

```
float f = 10.13;
float g = 10.02;
int n = 100 * (f - g);
```

In the decimal system the difference between 10.13 and 10.02 is 0.11, so you would expect `n` to be $100 \times 0.11 = 11$. On many computers, however, this code sets `n` to 10, not to 11. In the binary system, there is no exact representation for 0.11, just as there is no exact representation for 1/3 in the decimal system. The representation used by the computer is just a little less than 0.11, so 100 times that value is just a little less than 11. When the floating-point value is converted to an integer, the entire fractional part, which is almost 1, is thrown away, and the integer 10 is stored in `n`.

To avoid this problem, you should never assign a floating-point expression to an integer. Always use the `round` function, which is guaranteed to round to the *nearest* integer.

```
int n = round(100 * (f - g));
```

The integer nearest to $100 \times$ (a little less than 0.11) is 11. This example shows that rounding is much less sensitive to roundoff errors than throwing away a fractional part.

The `round` function is not standard C++. It is part of the special library that was created for this book. You must place the line `#include "ccc.h"` at the top of any program that uses the `round` function.

Productivity Hint 2.1.

Avoid Unstable Layout

You should arrange program code and comments so that the program is easy to read. For example, you should not cram all statements on a single line, and you should make sure that braces {} line up.

However, you should embark on beautification efforts wisely. Some programmers like to line up the = signs in a series of assignments, like this:

```
pennies = 8;
nickels = 0;
dimes   = 4;
```

This looks very neat, but the layout is not *stable.* Suppose you add a line like the one at the bottom of this:

```
pennies = 8;
nickels = 0;
dimes   = 4;
quarters = 3;
```

Oops, now the = signs no longer line up, and you have the extra work of lining them up *again.*

Here is another example. Many teachers recommend the following style of comments.

```
/* In this program, we compute the value of a set of coins. The
** user enters the count of pennies, nickels, dimes, and quarters.
** The program then displays the total value.
*/
```

Sure, it looks pretty, and the column of ** makes it easy to see the extent of the comment block—but whoever recommends this style never updated a comment. Suppose the program is extended to work for half-dollar coins as well. Of course, we must modify the comment to reflect that change.

```
/* In this program, we compute the value of a set of coins. The
** user enters the count of pennies, nickels, dimes, half dollars
and quarters. ** The program then displays the total value.
*/
```

That didn't look so great. Now you, the highly paid software engineer, are supposed to rearrange the ** to tidy up the description? This scheme is a *disincentive* to keep comments up to date. Don't do it. Just block off the entire comment like this:

```
/*---------------------------------------
In this program, we compute the value of a set of coins. The
user enters the count of pennies, nickels, dimes, and quarters.
The program then displays the total value.
---------------------------------------*/
```

You may not care about these issues. Perhaps you plan to beautify your program just before it is finished, when you are about to turn in your homework. That is not a particularly useful approach. In practice, programs are never finished. They are continuously maintained and updated. It is better to develop the habit of laying out your programs well from the start, and keeping them legible at all times. As a consequence, you should avoid layout schemes that are hard to maintain.

Advanced Topic 2.4

Combining Assignment and Arithmetic

In C++ you can combine arithmetic and assignment. For example, the instruction

```
total += count * 0.05;
```

is a shortcut for

```
total = total + count * 0.05;
```

Similarly,

```
total -= count * 0.05;
```

means the same as

```
total = total - count * 0.05;
```

and

```
total *= 2;
```

is another way of writing

```
total = total * 2;
```

Many programmers find this a convenient shortcut. If you like it, go ahead and use it in your own code. For simplicity, we won't use it in this book, though.

2.4 Constants

We used variables such as `total` for two reasons. By using a name instead of just a formula, we make the program easier to read. Also, by reserving memory space for the variable, we can change its value during program execution. It is usually a good idea to give symbolic names to constants as well, to make programs easier to read and modify.

Consider the following program:

Program volume1.cpp

```
#include "iostream.h"
#include "stdlib.h"

int main()
{  float bottles;
   cout << "How many bottles do you have? ";
   cin >> bottles;

   float cans;
   cout << "How many cans do you have? ";
   cin >> cans;

   float total = bottles * 2 + cans * 0.355;

   cout << "The total volume is " << total << "\n";

   return EXIT_SUCCESS;
}
```

What is going on here? What is the significance of the `0.355`?

This formula computes the amount of soda in a refrigerator that is filled with two-liter bottles and 12-oz. cans. (See Table 1 for conversion factors between metric and nonmetric units.) Let us make the computation clearer by using constants:

Program volume2.cpp

```
#include "iostream.h"
#include "stdlib.h"

int main()
{  float bottles;
   cout << "How many bottles do you have? ";
   cin >> bottles;

   float cans;
   cout << "How many cans do you have? ";
   cin >> cans;

   const float BOTTLE_VOLUME = 2.0;
   const float CAN_VOLUME = 0.355;
   float total = bottles * BOTTLE_VOLUME
      + cans * CAN_VOLUME;
```

```
    cout << "The total volume is " << total
       << "liter.\n";

    return EXIT_SUCCESS;
}
```

Now CAN_VOLUME is a named entity. But unlike total, it is constant. After initialization with 0.355, it can never change.

In fact, we can do even better and explain where the value for the can volume came from:

```
const float LITER_PER_OZ = 0.029586;
const float CAN_VOLUME = 12 * LITER_PER_OZ;
   /* 12 oz. cans */
```

Sure, it is more trouble to type the constant definitions and use the constant names in the formulas. But it makes the code much more readable. It also makes the code much easier to change. Suppose our program does computations involving volumes in several different places. And suppose we need to switch from two-liter bottles to half-gallon bottles. If we simply multiply by 2 to get bottle volumes, we must now replace every 2 by 1.893 ... well, not *every* number 2. There may have been other uses of 2 in the program that had nothing to do with bottles. We have to *look* at every number 2 and see whether we need to change it. Did I mention the one formula that multiplied a case count by 36 because there were 18 bottles in every case? That number now needs to be turned into 18 × 1.893—we hope we were lucky enough to find it. If, on the other hand, the constant BOTTLE_VOLUME is conscientiously used throughout the program, we need only update it in *one location*. Named constants are very important for program maintenance. See Quality Tip 2.3 for more information.

Constants are commonly written using capital letters to distinguish them visually from variables.

Constants for the numbers π and e are predefined as M_PI and M_E if you include the file ccc.h. You must add the line #include "ccc.h" to the top of any program that uses these special constants. (The M_ is a reminder that these are mathematical quantities.)

Table 1 Conversion between Metric and Nonmetric Units

1 (fluid) ounce (oz.) = 29.586 milliliter (mL)
1 gallon = 3.785 liter (L)
1 ounce (oz.) = 28.3495 grams (g)
1 pound (lb.) = 453.6 grams
1 inch = 2.54 centimeter (cm)
1 foot = 30.5 centimeter
1 mile = 1.609 kilometer (km)

Quality Tip 2.3

Do Not Use Magic Numbers

A *magic number* is a numeric constant that appears in your code without explanation. For example,

```
if (col >= 66) . . .
```

Why 66? Maybe this program prints in a 12-point font on 8.5 × 11-inch paper with a 1-inch margin on the left- and right-hand sides? Indeed, then you can fit 65 characters on a line. Once we reach column 66, we are beyond the right margin and must do something special. However, these are awfully fragile assumptions. To make the program work for a different paper size, one must locate all values of 65 (and 66 and 64) and replace them, taking care not to touch those 65s (and 66s and 64s) that have nothing to do with paper size. In a program that is more than a few pages long, that is incredibly tedious and error-prone.

The remedy is to use a named constant instead:

```
const int RIGHT_MARGIN = 65;

if (col > RIGHT_MARGIN) . . .
```

Even the most reasonable cosmic constant is going to change one day. You think there are 365 days per year? Your customers on Mars are going to be pretty unhappy about your silly prejudice. Make a constant

```
const int DAYS_PER_YEAR = 365;
```

By the way, the device

```
const int THREE_HUNDRED_AND_SIXTY_FIVE = 365;
```

is counterproductive and frowned upon.

You should *never* use magic numbers in your code. Any number, with the possible exceptions of 0, 1, and 2, should be declared as named constants.

Advanced Topic 2.5

Enumerated Types

Sometimes, a variable should take values only from a finite set of possibilities. For example, a variable describing a weekday (Monday, Tuesday, . . . , Sunday) can have only one of seven states.

In C++, we can define such *enumerated types:*

```
enum Weekday { MONDAY, TUESDAY, WEDNESDAY, THURSDAY,
   FRIDAY, SATURDAY, SUNDAY };
```

This makes Weekday a type, similar to int. As with any type, we can declare variables of that type:

```
Weekday homework_due_day = WEDNESDAY;
   /* homework due every Wednesday */
```

Of course, you could have declared homework_due_day as an integer. Then you would need to encode the weekdays into numbers.

```
int homework_due_day = 2;
```

That violates our rule against "magic numbers." You could go on and define constants,

```
const int MONDAY = 0;
const int TUESDAY = 1;
const int WEDNESDAY = 2;
const int THURSDAY = 3;
const int FRIDAY = 4;
const int SATURDAY = 5;
const int SUNDAY = 6;
```

However, the Weekday enumerated type is clearer, and it is a convenience that you need not come up with the integer values yourself. It also allows the compiler to catch programming errors. For example, the following is a compile-time error:

```
Weekday homework_due_day = 10; /* compile-time error */
```

In contrast, the following statement will compile without complaint and create a logical problem when the program runs:

```
int homework_due_day = 10; /* logic error */
```

It is a good idea to use an enumerated type whenever a variable can have a finite set of values.

2.5 Arithmetic

We already saw how to add and multiply numbers and values stored in variables:

```
float t = p + d * 0.10 + q * 0.25;
```

All four basic arithmetic operations—addition, subtraction, multiplication, and division—are supported. You must write a * b to denote multiplication, not a b or a · b. Division is indicated with a /, not a fraction bar. For example,

$$\frac{a+b}{2}$$

becomes

```
(a + b) / 2
```

Parentheses are used just as in algebra: to indicate in which order the subexpressions should be computed. For example, in the expression `(a + b) / 2`, the sum `a + b` is computed first, and then the sum is divided by 2. In contrast, in the expression

```
a + b / 2
```

only `b` is divided by 2, and then the sum of `a` and `b / 2` is formed. Just as in regular algebraic notation, multiplication and division *bind more strongly* than addition and subtraction. For example, in the expression `a + b / 2`, the / is carried out first, even though the + operation occurs further to the left.

Division works as you would expect, as long as at least one of the numbers involved is a floating-point number. That is,

```
7.0 / 4.0
7 / 4.0
7.0 / 4
```

all yield 1.75. However, if *both* numbers are integers, then the result of the division is always an integer, with the remainder discarded. That is,

```
7 / 4
```

evaluates to 1, because 7 divided by 4 is 1 with a remainder of 3 (which is discarded). This can be a source of subtle programming errors—see Common Error 2.2.

If you are interested only in the remainder, use the % operator:

```
7 % 4
```

is 3, the remainder of the integer division of 7 by 4. The % operator can be applied only to integers, not to floating-point values. For example, `7.0 % 4` is an error. The % symbol has no analog in algebra. It was chosen because it looks similar to /, and the remainder operation is related to division.

Here is a typical use for the integer / and % operations. Suppose we want to know the value of the coins in a purse in dollars and cents. We can compute the value as an integer, denominated in cents, and then compute the whole dollar amount and the remaining change:

Program coins5.cpp

```
#include "iostream.h."
#include "stdlib.h"

int main()
{  cout << "How many pennies do you have? ";
   int pennies;
   cin >> pennies;

   cout << "How many nickels do you have? ";
   int nickels;
   cin >> nickels;
```

```
    cout << "How many dimes do you have? ";
    int dimes;
    cin >> dimes;

    cout << "How many quarters do you have? ";
    int quarters;
    cin >> quarters;

    int value = pennies + 5 * nickels + 10 * dimes
       + 25 * quarters;
    int dollar = value / 100;
    int cents = value % 100;

    cout << "Total value = " << dollar << " dollars and "
       << cents << " cents\n";

    return EXIT_SUCCESS;
}
```

For example, if `value` is 243, then the output statement will display

```
The value is 2 dollars and 43 cents.
```

To take the square root of a number, you use the `sqrt` function. For example, $\sqrt{x}$ is written as `sqrt(x)`. To compute x^n, you write `pow(x, n)`. But to compute x^2, it is significantly more efficient to simply write `x * x`. To use `sqrt` and `pow`, you must place the line `#include "math.h"` at the top of your program file. The header file math.h is a standard C++ header that is available with all C++ systems, just like iostream.h and stdlib.h.

As you can see, the effect of the /, `sqrt`, and `pow` operations is to flatten out mathematical terms. In algebra, you use fractions, exponents, and roots to arrange expressions in a compact two-dimensional form. In C++, you have to write all

Figure 7

Analyzing an Expression

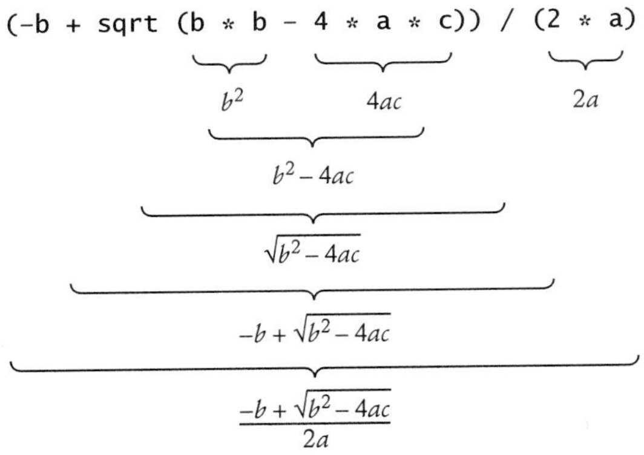

Table 2 Other Mathematical Functions

`sin(x)`	sine of x (x in radians)
`cos(x)`	cosine of x
`tan(x)`	tangent of x
`asin(x)`	(arc sine) $\sin^{-1} x \in [-\pi/2, \pi/2], x \in [-1, 1]$
`acos(x)`	(arc cosine) $\cos^{-1} x \in [0, \pi], x \in [-1, 1]$
`atan(x)`	(arc tangent) $\tan^{-1} x \in (-\pi/2, \pi/2)$
`atan2(y,x)`	(arc tangent) $\tan^{-1}(y/x) \in [-\pi/2, \pi/2]$, x may be 0
`exp(x)`	e^x
`log(x)`	(natural log) $\ln(x), x > 0$
`log10(x)`	(decimal log) $\lg(x), x > 0$
`sinh(x)`	hyperbolic sine of x
`cosh(x)`	hyperbolic cosine of x
`tanh(x)`	hyperbolic tangent of x
`ceil(x)`	smallest integer $\geq x$
`floor(x)`	largest integer $\leq x$
`fabs(x)`	absolute value $\|x\|$

expressions in a linear arrangement. For example, the subexpression

$$\frac{-b + \sqrt{b^2 - 4ac}}{2a}$$

of the quadratic formula becomes

```
(-b + sqrt(b * b - 4 * a * c)) / (2 * a)
```

Figure 7 shows how to analyze such an expression. With complicated expressions like these, it is not always easy to keep the parentheses `(...)` matched—see Common Error 2.3.

Table 2 shows additional functions declared in math.h. Inputs and outputs are floating-point numbers.

Common Error 2.2

Integer Division

It is unfortunate that C++ uses the same symbol, namely /, for both integer and floating-point division. These are really quite different operations. It is a common error to use integer division by accident. Consider this program segment that computes the average of three integers.

```
cout << "Please enter your last three test scores: ";
int s1;
int s2;
int s3;
cin >> s1 >> s2 >> s3;
float average = (s1 + s2 + s3) / 3; /* Error */
cout << "Your average score is " << average << "\n";
```

What could be wrong with that? Of course, the average of s1, s2, and s3 is

$$\frac{\mathtt{s1} + \mathtt{s2} + \mathtt{s3}}{3}$$

Here, however the / does not mean division in the mathematical sense. It denotes integer division, because both s1 + s2 + s3 and 3 are integers. For example, if the scores add up to 14, the average is computed to be 4, the result of the integer division of 14 by 3. That integer 4 is then moved into the floating-point variable average. The remedy is to make the numerator or denominator into a floating-point number:

```
float total = s1 + s2 + s3;
float average = total / 3;
```

or

```
float average = (s1 + s2 + s3) / 3.0;
```

Common Error 2.3

Unbalanced Parentheses

Consider the expression

```
1.5 * ((-(b - sqrt(b * b - 4 * a * c)) / (2 * a))
```

What is wrong with it? Count the parentheses. There are five (and four). The parentheses are *unbalanced.* This kind of typing error is very common with complicated expressions. Now consider this expression.

```
1.5 * (sqrt(b * b - 4 * a * c))) - ((b / (2 * a))
```

This expression has five (and five), but it is still not correct. In the middle of the expression,

```
1.5 * (sqrt(b * b - 4 * a * c))) - ((b / (2 * a))
                               ↑
```

there are only two (but three), which is an error. In the middle of an expression, the count of (must be greater than or equal to the count of), and at the end of the expression the two counts must be the same.

Here is a simple trick to make the counting easier without using pencil and paper. It is difficult for the brain to keep two counts simultaneously, so keep only one count when scanning the expression. Start with 1 at the first opening parenthesis; add 1 whenever you see an opening parenthesis; and subtract 1 whenever you see a closing parenthesis. Say the numbers aloud as you scan the expression. If the count ever drops below zero, or if it is not zero at the end, the parentheses are unbalanced. For example, when scanning the previous expression, you would mutter

```
1.5 * (sqrt(b * b - 4 * a * c) ) ) - ((b / (2 * a))
      1    2                  1 0 -1
```

and you would find the error.

Common Error 2.4

Forgetting Header Files

Every program that you write needs one header file at least, to include facilities for input and output; that file is normally iostream.h.

If you use mathematical functions such as `sqrt`, you need to include math.h. If you forget to include the appropriate header file, the compiler will not know symbols such as `sqrt` or `cout`. If the compiler complains about an undefined function or symbol, check your header files.

Sometimes you may not know which header file to include. Suppose you want to compute the absolute value of an integer using the `abs` function. As it happens, `abs` is not defined in math.h but in stdlib.h. How can you find the correct header file? You need to locate the documentation of the `abs` function, preferably using the on-line help of your editor (see Productivity Hint 2.2). Many programming editors have a hot key that summons help on the word under the cursor. Otherwise you can look into the library reference manual that came with the compiler, either in printed form or on a CD-ROM. The documentation includes a short description of the function and the name of the header file that you must include.

As an alternative, you can include the header file ccc.h, which was written especially for this book. It defines a number of special functions, and as an added convenience it automatically includes iostream.h, stdlib.h, and math.h.

Productivity Hint 2.2

On-Line Help

Today's integrated C++ programming environments contain sophisticated help systems. You should spend some time learning how to use the online help in your compiler. Help is available on compiler settings, keyboard shortcuts, and, most importantly, on library functions. If you are not sure how the pow function works, or cannot remember whether it was called pow

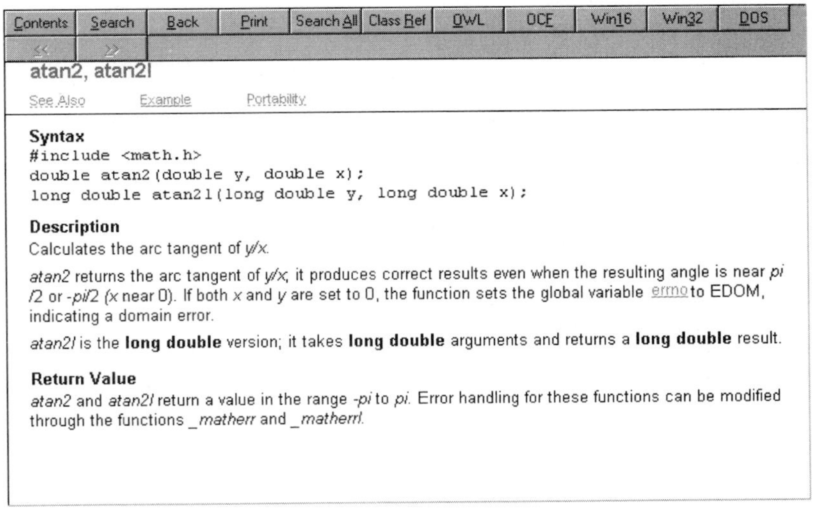

Figure 8

On-Line Help

or `power`, the online help can give you the answer quickly. Figure 8 shows a typical help screen.

Quality Tip 2.4

White Space

The compiler does not care whether you write your entire program onto a single line or place every symbol onto a separate line. The human reader, though, cares very much. You should use blank lines to group your code visually into sections. For example, you can signal to the reader that an output prompt and the corresponding input statement belong together by inserting a blank line before and after the group. You will find many examples in the source code listings in this book.

White space inside expressions is also important. It is easier to read

```
x1 = (-b + sqrt(b * b - 4 * a * c)) / (2 * a);
```

than

```
x1=(-b+sqrt(b*b-4*a*c))/(2*a);
```

Simply put spaces around all operators `+ - * / % =`. However, don't put a space after a *unary* minus: a `-` used to negate a single quantity, as in `-b`. That way, it can be easily distinguished from a *binary* minus, as in `a - b`. Don't put spaces between a function name and the parentheses, but do put a space after every C++ keyword. That makes it easy to see that the `sqrt` in `sqrt(x)` is a function name, whereas the `if` in `if (x > 0)...` is a keyword.

Quality Tip 2.5

Factor Out Common Code

Suppose we want to find both solutions of the quadratic equation $ax^2 + bx + c = 0$. The quadratic formula tells us that the solutions are

$$x_{1,2} = \frac{-b \pm \sqrt{b^2 - 4ac}}{2a}$$

In C++, there is no analog to the ± operation, which indicates how to obtain two solutions simultaneously. Both solutions must be computed separately:

```
x1 = (-b + sqrt(b * b - 4 * a * c)) / (2 * a);
x2 = (-b - sqrt(b * b - 4 * a * c)) / (2 * a);
```

This approach has two problems. First, the computation of `sqrt(b * b - 4 * a * c)` is carried out twice, which wastes time. Second, whenever the same code is replicated, the possibility of a typing error increases. The remedy is to *factor out* the common code:

```
float root = sqrt(b * b - 4 * a * c);
x1 = (-b + root) / (2 * a);
x2 = (-b - root) / (2 * a);
```

We could go even further and factor out the computation of `2 * a`, but the gain from factoring out very simple computations is small, and the resulting code can be hard to read.

2.6 Strings

2.6.1 String Variables

Next to numbers, *strings* are the most important data type that most programs use. A string is a sequence of characters, such as `"Hello"`. In C++ strings are enclosed in quotation marks which are not themselves part of the string.

You can declare variables that hold strings:

```
string name = "John";
```

The `string` type is a part of the ANSI standard for C++. To use it, simply include the header file ccc.h into all programs that use variables of type `string`. That header file either includes your compiler's string type or a compatible replacement if your compiler doesn't yet support ANSI C++ strings.

Use assignment to place a different string into the variable.

```
name = "Carl";
```

You can also read a string from the keyboard:

```
cout << "Please enter your name: ";
cin >> name;
```

When a string is read from an input stream, only one word is placed into the string variable. (Words are separated by white space.) For example, if the user types

```
Harry Hacker
```

as the response to the prompt, then only `Harry` is placed into `name`. To read the second string, another input statement must be used. This constraint makes it tricky to write an input statement that deals properly with user responses. Some users might type just their first names, others might type their first and last names, and others might even supply their middle initials.

To handle such a situation, use the `get_line` command. The statement

```
name = get_line(cin);
```

reads all keystrokes until the Enter key, makes a string containing all of the keystrokes, and places it into the `name` variable. With the preceding input example, `name` is set to the string `"Harry Hacker"`. This is a string containing 12 characters, one of which is a space. You should always use the `get_line` function if you are not sure that the user input consists of a single word.

You can also read a single character with the `get_char` command. A string containing a single character (which may be a space or newline), is returned:

```
string ch = get_char(cin);
```

If the user had typed `"Harry Hacker"`, `ch` would contain the string `"H"`.

The `get_line` and `get_char` functions are not part of standard C++. They are supplied in the ccc.h header file.

The number of characters in a string is called the *length* of the string. For example, the length of `"Harry Hacker"` is 12, and the length of `"Hello, World!\n"` is 14—the newline character counts as one character only. You can compute the length of a string with the `length` function. Unlike `sqrt` or `get_line`, the `length` function is invoked with the *dot notation:*

```
int n = name.length();
```

Many C++ functions require you to use this dot notation, and you must memorize (or look up) which do and which don't.

A string of length zero, containing no characters, is called the *empty string* and written as `""`. Unlike number variables, string variables are guaranteed to be initialized; they are initialized with the empty string:

```
string response; /* initialized as "" */
```

2.6.2 Substrings

Once you have a string, what can you do with it? You can extract substrings, and you can glue smaller strings together to form larger ones. To extract a substring, use the `substr` operation:

```
s.substr(start, length)
```

returns a string that is made up from the characters in the string `s`, starting at character `start`, and containing `length` characters. Just like `length`, `substr` uses the dot notation. You write first the variable name of the string from which you want to get a substring, then a period, then the parameters that describe which substring you want. Here is an example:

```
string greeting = "Hello, World!\n";
string sub = greeting.substr(0, 4);
   /* sub is "Hell" */
```

The `substr` operation makes a string that consists of four characters taken from the string `greeting`. Indeed, `"Hell"` is a string of length 4 that occurs inside `greeting`. The only curious aspect of the `substr` operation is the starting position. Starting position 0 means "start at the beginning of the string". For technical reasons that used to be important but are no longer relevant, C++ string position numbers start at 0. The first item in a sequence is labeled 0, the second one 1, and so on. For example, here are the position numbers in the `greeting` string:

H	e	l	l	o	,		W	o	r	l	d	!	\n
0	1	2	3	4	5	6	7	8	9	10	11	12	13

The position number of the last character (13) is always 1 less than the length of the string.

Let us figure out how to extract the substring `"World"`. Count characters starting at 0, not 1. You find that `w`, the 8th character, has position number 7. The string we want is 5 characters long. Therefore, the appropriate substring command is

```
string w = greeting.substr(7, 5);
```

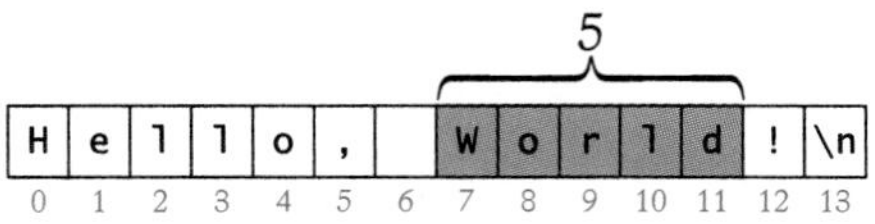

2.6.3 Concatenation

Now that we know how to take strings apart, let us see how to put them back together. Given two strings, such as "Harry" and "Hacker", we can *concatenate* them to one long string:

```
string fname = "Harry";
string lname = "Hacker";
string name = fname + lname;
```

The + operator concatenates two strings. The resulting string is "HarryHacker". Actually, that isn't really what we are after. We'd like the first and last name separated by a space. No problem:

```
string name = fname + " " + lname;
```

Now we concatenate three strings: "Harry", " ", and "Hacker". The result is "Harry Hacker".

You must be a bit careful when using + for strings. One or both of the strings surrounding the + must be a string *variable*. The expression `fname + " "` is OK, but the expression `"Harry" + " "` is not. This is not a big problem; in the second case, you can just write "Harry ".

Here is a simple program that puts these concepts to work. The program asks for your full name and prints out your initials. For example, if you give your name as "Harold Joseph Hacker", the program tells you that your initials are HJH.

Program initials.cpp

```
#include "ccc.h"

int main()
{  cout << "Enter your full name (first middle last): ";
   string first;
   string middle;
   string last;
   cin >> first >> middle >> last;
   string initials = first.substr(0, 1)
      + middle.substr(0, 1) + last.substr(0, 1);
   cout << "Your initials are " << initials << "\n";

   return EXIT_SUCCESS;
}
```

The operation `first.substr(0, 1)` makes a string consisting of one character, taken from the start of `first`. We do the same for the `middle` and `last` strings. Then we concatenate the three one-character strings to get a string of length 3: the `initials` string. (See Figure 9.)

Figure 9

Building the Initial String

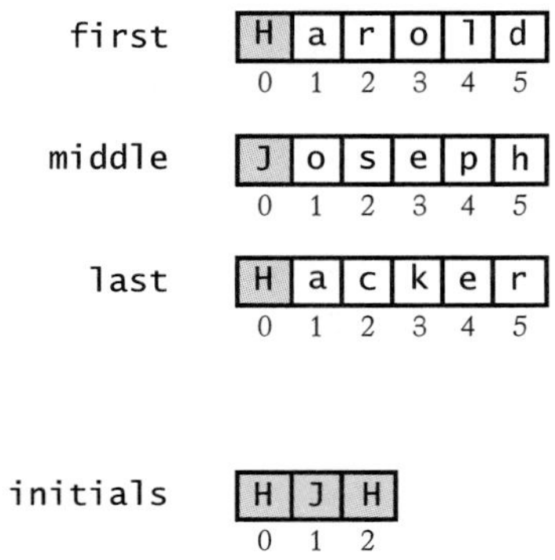

2.6.4 Converting between Numbers and Strings

Suppose we want to create passwords for user accounts. The password is to be the initials of the user name, converted to lowercase, followed by the age. If Harry is 19 years old, his password will be `hjh19`. (In practice, this would not be a good password. If Carl Cracker is familiar with the scheme, he can break into Harry's account. Even if he isn't sure about Harry's age, he just needs a few tries.)

First, we need to know how to change the initials to lowercase. The `uppercase` and `lowercase` functions make strings with only upper- or lowercase characters. For example,

```
string greeting = "Hello";
cout << uppercase(greeting) << " "
   << lowercase(greeting) << "\n";
```

displays `HELLO hello`. The original string `greeting` is not changed.

To generate the password, we ask users for their names and ages.

```
cout << "Enter your full name (first middle last): ";
string first;
string middle;
string last;
cin >> first >> middle >> last;
string initials = first.substr(0, 1)
   + middle.substr(0, 1) + last.substr(0, 1);

cout << "Please enter your age: ";
int age;
cin >> age;
```

Now we have a problem, however. We'd like to compute

```
string password = lowercase(initials) + age; /* Error */
```

That doesn't work. The expression `lowercase(initials)` is of type `string`, but the variable `age` is of type `int`. Just as you can't add the proverbial apples and oranges, you can't add strings and integers. There is a good reason. When you "add" two strings, the + denotes concatenation: Glue the two strings together. When you add numbers, + means to add them in the mathematical sense. These two meanings don't mix, and the compiler will not try to come up with a meaning if you add a string and a number.

Suppose `age` is 19. If we had a way of turning the number 19 into the string `"19"`, then we could take that string and concatenate it with the initials. The function `stringvalue` does just that. It makes a number (integer or floating point) into a string containing the same characters that would appear on the display if you printed the string. Here is an example.

```
int age = 19;
string output = "Age = " + stringvalue(age);
   /* output is the string "Age = 19" */
```

The `stringvalue` function solves our problem. We can compute the password string as

```
string password = lowercase(initials) + stringvalue(age);
```

Here is the complete program:

Program makepass.cpp

```
#include "ccc.h"

int main()
{  cout << "Enter your full name (first middle last): ";

   string first;
   string middle;
   string last;
   cin >> first >> middle >> last;
   string initials = first.substr(0, 1)
      + middle.substr(0, 1) + last.substr(0, 1);

   cout << "Please enter your age: ";
   int age;
   cin >> age;

   string password = lowercase(initials)
      + stringvalue(age);
   cout << "Your password is " << password << "\n";

   return EXIT_SUCCESS;
}
```

Occasionally, you have a string containing just digits, and you would like to know its numerical value. The `intvalue` and `floatvalue` functions perform the conversion from strings to numbers. For example, if `input` is the string `"10.5"`, then `floatvalue(input)` is the floating-point number 10.5. These functions are useful if you read a line of input with `get_line`, determine that the input is actually a number, and want to convert it to the numerical value.

2.6.5 Formatted Output

When you display several numbers, each of them is printed with the minimum number of digits needed to show the value. This often yields ugly output. Here is an example:

```
cout << pennies << " " << pennies * 0.01 << "\n";
cout << nickels << " " << nickels * 0.05 << "\n";
cout << dimes << " " << dimes * 0.10 << "\n";
cout << quarters << " " << quarters * 0.25 << "\n";
```

A typical output might look like this:

```
1 0.01
12 0.6
4 0.4
120 30
```

What a mess! The columns don't line up, and the money values don't show dollars and cents. We need to *format* the output. Let us make each column eight characters wide and use two digits of precision for the floating-point numbers. Use the `format` function to provide a pretty string representation:

```
cout << format("%8d", pennies)
   << format("%8.2f", pennies * 0.01) << "\n";
```

Now the output is

```
       1    0.01
      12    0.60
       4    0.40
     120   30.00
```

Use the format string `"%nd"` to format an integer in a column with n characters. Use the format string `"%n.pf"` to format a floating-point number in a column with n characters and p digits of precision.

To format a string, you should use `"%-ns"`. That makes the string *left aligned*. For example, to produce the output

```
Pennies   |        1      0.01
Nickels   |       12      0.60
Dimes     |        4      0.40
Quarters  |      120     30.00
```

you would write

```
cout << format("%-10s", "Pennies") << "|"
   << format("%8d", pennies)
   << format("%8.2f", pennies * 0.01) << "\n";
```

and the same for the other three lines. (See Figure 10.)

There are many more formatting options, to give you complete control over the appearance of the output. See Advanced Topic 2.7 for more information.

The string functions we have seen thus far are summarized in Table 3. The functions `get_line`, `uppercase`, `lowercase`, `stringvalue`, `intvalue`, `floatvalue`, and `format` are not part of standard C++. However, they are substantially easier to use than their standard C++ counterparts.

Figure 10

Formatting Output

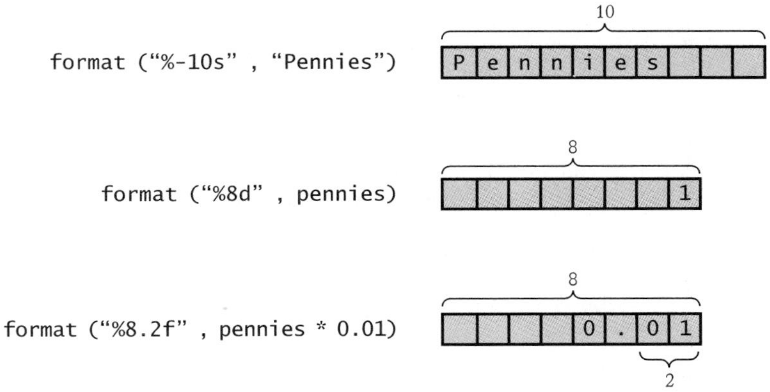

Table 3 String Functions

Name	Purpose
`s.length()`	The length of `s`
`s.substr(i, n)`	The substring of length `n` of `s` starting at index `i`
`get_line(f)`	Read a string from the input stream `f`
`get_char(f)`	Read a single character from the input stream `f`
`uppercase(s)`	`s` with all lowercase characters changed to uppercase
`lowercase(s)`	`s` with all uppercase characters changed to lowercase
`stringvalue(x)`	The string equivalent of the number `x`
`intvalue(s)`	The integer value represented by `s`
`floatvalue(s)`	The floating-point value represented by `s`
`format(s, x)`	The string representation of `x`, formatted as described in `s`

Advanced Topic 2.6

Locating Header Files

You must be careful that you give the compiler appropriate directions where to locate header files. That is not a problem with the *system header files,* such as iostream.h or math.h. This course, however, uses some header files that may not be generally available on your system, such as ccc.h. These files *may* have been placed into system directories, or your instructor may have told you to copy those files onto your personal directory.

It is a common convention to surround the names of header files that are kept in the system directories, such as iostream.h, with <. . .>.

```
#include <iostream.h>
```

That way, the compiler won't even look into your personal directory for a file iostream.h but will go straight to the system directories. You cannot do that with the nonstandard header files. For example, you must use `"..."` to locate ccc.h:

```
#include "ccc.h"
```

To complicate matters, the convention for specifying header files in C++ has recently changed. The new standard, which at the time of this writing is not yet supported by many compilers, will require that streams be included as

```
#include <iostream>
```

Note that the .h is dropped. Any code that uses `string` variables will need to contain the directive

```
#include <string>
```

This is *not* the same as

```
#include <string.h>
```

The `<string>` header defines C++-style strings; the `<string.h>` header defines C-style strings, which are completely different. To avoid any confusion, the file ccc.h contains the directive that is appropriate for your compiler. As long as you include ccc.h, you will be able to use strings.

Advanced Topic 2.7

Formatting Options

Here are the complete rules for the format string, which is the first parameter of the `format` function discussed in Section 2.6.5.

For historical reasons, the format string starts with a %. Then there are optional flags, which can come in any order:

- `-` Align the string left in its field.
- `+` Print + sign for positive numbers.
- `0` Pad the field with leading zeroes.

Next comes an optional field width (a number) and then an optional precision (a period followed by a number). Finally, there is a required *conversion character*. The following characters are valid:

`f`	Print floating-point number in fixed-point notation.
`e, E`	Print floating-point number in exponential notation, also often called scientific notation (such as `2.99793E+06`).
`g, G`	Use *general format,* which is either fixed or exponential, whichever is shorter.
`d`	Print integer in decimal (base 10).
`o`	Print integer in octal (base 8).
`x, X`	Print integer in hexadecimal (base 16).
`s`	Print a string.

The uppercase `E G X` cause the exponent indicator `E` and the hexadecimal digits `A B C D E F` to be printed in uppercase. Otherwise they are printed in lowercase.

For example, if you print a table of measurements in scientific notation, and you want a + sign for positive numbers, you can use

```
cout << format("%+14.6E", x);
```

The result of the `format` function is a string. You can print that string or process it further, just like any other string. The `format` function is not standard C++. See Advanced Topic 2.8 for more information on the standard C++ approach to formatted output.

Advanced Topic 2.8

Formatted Output in Standard C++

Standard C++ has its own method for producing formatted output. It is simple enough for simple situations.

Use `setw` to set the width of the next output field:

```
cout << setw(8) << pennies;
```

Use `setprecision` to set the number of digits after the decimal place:

```
cout << setw(8) << setprecision(2) << pennies * 0.01;
```

For the more advanced formatting options the syntax gets quite Byzantine. Here is how you select scientific notation and a plus sign for positive numbers:

```
cout << setiosflags(ios::showpos) << setw(8)
   << setprecision(2) << setiosflags(ios::scientific,
   ios::floatfield) << x;
```

To print a left-aligned string followed by a right-aligned floating-point number, you use

```
cout << setiosflags(ios::left, ios::alignfield)
   << setw(20) << name << setiosflags(ios::right,
   ios::alignfield) << setw(10) << setprecision(2)
   << setiosflags(ios::fixed, ios::floatfield) << salary
   << resetiosflags(ios::floatfield);
```

If you like this style, you can find more information in [2]. If not, use

```
cout << format("%-20s", name) << format("%10.2f", salary);
```

You need to include the file iomanip.h to use C++ output formatting.

Advanced Topic 2.9

Characters and C Strings

C++ has a data type `char` to denote individual characters. In the C language, the precursor to C++, the only way to implement strings was as sequences (so-called arrays) of individual characters. You can recognize C strings in C or C++ code by looking for types like `char *` or `char []`.

Using character sequences for strings puts the tremendous burden on the programmer to locate storage space for these sequences manually. In C, a common error is moving a string into an array variable that is too small to hold all of its characters. For efficiency's sake, there is no check against this possibility, and it is all too easy for the inexperienced programmer to corrupt adjacent variables.

The ANSI standard C++ strings handle all these chores completely automatically. We do not need the data type `char` at all. Instead, we just use strings of length 1 for individual characters. We supply you with a full collection of string-handling functions that are easier and much safer than their C equivalents. Our focus is to study programming—not housekeeping for character sequences.

There is just one slight problem with this approach. *Literal strings* (that is, strings enclosed in quotes) are actually C strings. Only `string` variables are proper C++ strings. Literal strings are automatically converted to C++ `string` values in almost all situations. There are just a few cases in which that automatic conversion fails. Here are two of them.

- The expression `"Hello, " + "World!"` does not compile at all. In particular, it does not concatenate the two strings. This is not a big problem. Just concatenate them by hand: `"Hello, World!"`.
- The expression `"Hello" + 3` compiles, even though it makes no sense. (It yields the string `"lo"`.) There is an arcane reason why the compiler attaches a legal but spurious interpretation to this expression.

In Appendix 3 you can learn how to use C strings if you have the misfortune to be involved in a programming project in which you cannot use the C++ string type.

Chapter Summary

1. C++ has several data types for numbers. The most common types are `float` and `int`. Floating-point numbers can have fractional values; integers cannot. Occasionally, other numeric types are required for larger values or higher precision.

2. Numbers, strings, and other values can be stored in *variables*. A variable has a name that indicates its function to the human reader. A variable can hold different values during program execution.

3. Numbers and strings can be read from an input stream with the >> operator. They are written to an output stream with the << operator. Output uses a general format; use the `format` function to achieve special formats.

4. When a variable is first filled with a value, it is *initialized.* The initial value can later be replaced with another by a process called *assignment.* In C++, assignment is denoted by the = operator—a somewhat unfortunate choice because the C++ meaning of = is not the same as mathematical equality.

5. Constants are values with a symbolic name. Constants cannot be changed once they are initialized. Named constants should be used instead of numbers to make programs easier to read and maintain.

6. All common arithmetic operations are provided in C++; however, the symbols are different from mathematical notation. In particular, * denotes multiplication. There is no horizontal fraction bar, and / must be used for division. To compute a power a^b or a square root $\sqrt{a}$, the `pow` and `root` functions must be used. Other functions, such as `sin` and `log`, are available as well. The % operator computes the remainder of an integer division.

7. Strings are sequences of characters. Strings can be *concatenated;* that is, put end to end to yield a new longer string. In C++, string concatenation is denoted by the + operator. The `substr` function extracts substrings. Strings containing digits are not the same as the numbers they represent; special functions (`intvalue`, `floatvalue`, `stringvalue`) convert between number and string data types.

Further Reading

[1] Franklin M. Fisher, John J. McGowan, and Joen E. Greenwood, *Folded, Spindled and Mutilated. Economic Analysis and* U.S. *vs.* IBM, MIT Press, 1983.

[2] Steve Teale, *C++ IOStreams Handbook,* Addison-Wesley, 1993.

Review Exercises

Exercise R2.1. Write the following mathematical expressions in C++.

$$s = s_0 + v_0 t + \frac{1}{2} g t^2$$

$$G = 4\pi^2 \frac{a^3}{P^2 m_1 + m_2}$$

$$\mathrm{FV} = \mathrm{PV} \cdot \left(1 + \frac{\mathrm{INT}}{100}\right)^{\mathrm{YRS}}$$

$$c = \sqrt{a^2 + b^2 - 2ab\cos\gamma}$$

Exercise R2.2. Write the following C++ expressions in mathematical notation.

```
dm = m * ((sqrt(1 + v / c) / sqrt(1 - v / c) - 1);
```

```
volume = M_PI * r * r * h;
```

```
volume = 4 * M_PI * pow(r, 3) / 3;
```

```
p = atan2(z, sqrt(x * x + y * y));
```

Exercise R2.3. What is wrong with this version of the quadratic formula?

```
x1 = (-b - sqrt(b * b - 4 * a * c)) / 2 * a;
x2 = (-b + sqrt(b * b - 4 * a * c)) / 2 * a;
```

Exercise R2.4. Give an example of integer overflow. Would the same example work correctly if you used floating-point? Give an example of a floating-point roundoff error. Would the same example work correctly if you used integers? When using integers, you would of course need to switch to a smaller unit, such as cents instead of dollars or milliliters instead of liters.

Exercise R2.5. Let n be an integer and x a floating-point number. Explain the difference between

```
n = x;
```

and

```
n = round(x);
```

For what values of x do they give the same result? For what values of x do they give different results? What happens if x is negative?

Exercise R2.6. Find at least five *syntax* errors in the following program.

```
#include iostream.h

int main();
{  cout << "Please enter two numbers:"
   cin >> x, y;
   cout << "The sum of << x << "and" << y
      << "is: " x + y << "\n";
   return exit_success;
}
```

Exercise R2.7. Find at least three *logic errors* in the following program.

```
#include "iostream.h"
#include "stdlib.h"

int main()
{  int total;
   int x1;
   cout << "Please enter a number:";
   cin >> x1;
   total = total + x1;
   cout << "Please enter another number:";
   int x2;
   cin >> x2;
   total = total + x1;
   float average = total / 2;
   cout << "The average of the two numbers is "
      << average << "\n"
   return EXIT_SUCCESS;
}
```

Exercise R2.8. Explain the differences between `2`, `2.0`, `"2"` and `"2.0"`.

Exercise R2.9. Explain what each of the following two program segments computes:

```
x = 2;
y = x + x;
```

and

```
s = "2";
t = s + s;
```

Exercise R2.10. Uninitialized number variables can be a serious problem. Should you *always* initialize every variable with zero? Explain the advantages and disadvantages of such a strategy.

Exercise R2.11. True or false?

(a) `intvalue(stringvalue(x))` is the same as `x`

(b) `stringvalue(intvalue(s))` is the same as `s`

(c) `s.substr(0, s.length())` is the same as `s`

Exercise R2.12. Explain the difference between *character-oriented, word-oriented,* and *line-oriented* input of strings. How do you achieve each in C++? When would you use which form?

Exercise R2.13. How do you get the first character of a string? The last character? How do you *remove* the first character? The last character?

Exercise R2.14. How do you get the last digit of a number? The first digit? That is, if `n` is `23456`, how do you find out `2` and `6`? Do not use `stringvalue`. *Hint:* `%, log`.

Exercise R2.15. This chapter contains a number of recommendations regarding variables and constants that make programs easier to read and maintain. Briefly summarize these recommendations.

Exercise R2.16. Suppose a C++ code contains the two input statements

```
cout << "Please enter your name: ";
string fname, lname;
cin >> fname >> lname;
```

and

```
cout << "Please enter your age: ";
int age;
cin >> age;
```

What is contained in the variables `fname`, `lname`, and `age` if the user enters the following inputs?

(a)
```
James Carter
56
```

(b)
```
Lyndon Johnson
49
```

(c)
```
Hodding Carter 3rd
44
```

(d)
```
Richard M. Nixon
62
```

Exercise R2.17. What are the values of the following expressions? In each line, assume that

```
float x = 2.5;
float y = -1.5;
int m = 18;
int n = 4;
string s = "Hello";
string t = "World";
```

(a) `x + n * y - (x + n) * y`

(b) `m / n + m % n`

(c) `5 * x - n / 5`

(d) `sqrt(sqrt(n));`

(e) `round(x)`

(f) `round(x) + round(y);`

(g) `s + t;`

(h) `s + n;`

(i) `1 - (1 - (1 - (1 - (1 - n))))`

(j) `s.substr(1, 2)`

(k) `s.length() + t.length()`

Programming Exercises

Exercise P2.1. Write a program that prints the values

```
1
10
100
1000
10000
100000
1000000
10000000
100000000
1000000000
10000000000
100000000000
```

as integers and as floating-point numbers. Explain the results.

Exercise P2.2. Write a program that displays the squares, cubes, and fourth powers of the numbers 1 through 5.

Exercise P2.3. Write a program that prompts the user for two integers and then prints

The sum
The difference
The product
The average
The distance (absolute value of the difference)
The maximum (the larger of the two)
The minimum (the smaller of the two)

It is tricky to compute the maximum and minimum if your compiler doesn't have `max` and `min` functions. *Hint:* Use the `abs` function and compute $|a - b| + a + b$.

Exercise P2.4. Write a program that prompts the user for a measurement in meters and then converts it into miles, feet, and inches.

Exercise P2.5. Write a program that prompts the user for a radius and then prints

The area and circumference of the circle with that radius
The volume and surface area of the sphere with that radius

Exercise P2.6. Write a program that asks the user for the lengths of the sides of a rectangle. Then print

The area and circumference of the rectangle
The length of the diagonal (use the Pythagorean theorem)

Exercise P2.7. Write a program that prompts the user for

The lengths of two sides of a triangle
The size of the angle between the two sides (in degrees)

Then the program displays

The length of the third side
The sizes of the other two angles.

Hint: Use the law of cosines.

Exercise P2.8. Write a program that prompts the user for

The length of a side of a triangle
The sizes of the two angles adjacent to that side (in degrees)

Then the program displays

The lengths of the other two sides
The size of the third angle

Hint: Use the law of sines.

Exercise P2.9. *Giving change.* Implement a program that directs a cashier how to give change. The program has two inputs: the amount due and the amount received from the customer. Compute the difference, and compute the dollar, quarters, dimes, nickels, and pennies that the customer should receive in return.

First transform the difference into an integer balance, denominated in pennies. Then compute the whole dollar amount. Subtract it from the balance. Compute the number of quarters needed. Repeat for dimes and nickels. Display the remaining pennies.

Exercise P2.10. Write a program that asks the user to input

The number of gallons of gas in the tank
The fuel efficiency in miles per gallon
The price of gas per gallon

Then print out how far the car can go with the gas in the tank and print the cost per 100 miles.

Exercise P2.11. *File names and extensions.* Write a program that prompts the user for the drive letter (C), the path (`\Windows\System`), the file name (`Readme`) and the extension (TXT). Then print the complete file name `C:\Windows\System\Readme.TXT`. (If you use Unix or a Macintosh, use / or `:` instead to separate directories.)

Exercise P2.12. Write a program that reads a number greater than or equal to 1000 from the user and prints it out *with a comma separating the thousands*. Here is a sample dialog; the user input is in color:

```
Please enter an integer >= 1000: 23456
23,456
```

Exercise P2.13. Write a program that reads a number greater than or equal to 1,000 from the user, where the user enters a comma in the input. Then print the number without a comma. Here is a sample dialog; the user input is in color:

```
Please enter an integer between 1,000 and 999,999:  23,456
23456
```

Hint: Read the input as a string. Measure the length of the string. Suppose it contains n characters. Then extract substrings consisting of the first $n - 4$ characters and the last three characters.

Exercise 2.14. *Printing a grid.* Write a program that prints the following grid to play tic-tac-toe.

```
+--+--+--+
|  |  |  |
+--+--+--+
|  |  |  |
+--+--+--+
|  |  |  |
+--+--+--+
```

Of course, you could simply write seven statements of the form

```
cout << "+--+--+--+\n";
```

You should do it the smart way, though. Define string variables to hold two kinds of patterns: a comb-shaped pattern and the bottom line. Print the comb three times and the bottom line once.

Exercise P2.15. Write a program that reads in an integer and breaks it into a sequence of individual digits. For example, the input 16384 is displayed as

```
1 6 3 8 4
```

You may assume that the input has no more than five digits and is not negative. *Hint:* There are two ways of solving this problem. You can use integer arithmetic and repeatedly divide by 10, or you can convert the number into a string and extract the digits from the string.

Exercise P2.16. The following program prints the values of sine and cosine for 0 degrees, 30 degrees, 45 degrees, 60 degrees, and 90 degrees. Rewrite the program for greater clarity by *factoring out common code.*

```
#include "iostream.h"
#include "stdlib.h"

int main()
{  cout << "0 degrees: " << sin(0) << " " << cos(0)
      << "\n");
   cout << "30 degrees: " << sin(30 * M_PI / 180) << " "
      << cos(30 * M_PI / 180) << "\n";
   cout << "45 degrees: " << sin(45 * M_PI / 180) << " "
      << cos(45 * M_PI / 180) << "\n";
   cout << "60 degrees: " << sin(60 * M_PI / 180) << " "
      << cos(60 * M_PI / 180) << "\n";
   cout << "90 degrees: " << sin(90 * M_PI / 180) << " "
      << cos(90 * M_PI / 180) << "\n";
   return EXIT_SUCCESS;
}
```

Exercise P2.17. Rewrite the program of the preceding exercise so that the three columns of the table line up. Use `format`.

Exercise P2.18. (*Hard.*) We don't yet know how to program decisions, but it turns out that there is a way to fake them using `substr`. Write a program that asks the user to input

The number of gallons of gas in the tank
The fuel efficiency in miles per gallon
The distance the user wants to travel

Then print out

```
You will make it
```

or

```
You will not make it
```

The trick here is to subtract the desired distance from the number of miles the user can drive. Suppose that that number is x. Suppose further that we find a way of setting a value n to 1 if $x \geq 0$ and to 0 if $x < 0$. Then we can solve our problem:

```
string answer = " not "; /* note the spaces before and after not */
cout << "You will" + answer.substr(0, 5 - 4 * n) + "make it";
```

It is more fun to figure this out by yourself, but here are a few hints. First note that $x + |x|$ is $2 \cdot x$ if $x \geq 0$, 0 if $x < 0$. If you didn't have to worry about the possibility that x is zero, then you could simply look at

$$\frac{x + |x|}{x} = \begin{cases} 2 & \text{if } |x| > 0 \\ 0 & \text{if } |x| < 0 \end{cases}$$

Dividing by x doesn't work, but you can safely divide by $|x| + 1$. That gives you a fractional part, and you should use the `floor` and `ceil` functions to cope with that.

Exercise P2.19. Write a program that reads two times in military format (0900, 1730) and prints the number of hours and minutes between the two times. Here is a sample run. User input is in color.

```
Please enter the first time: 0900
Please enter the second time: 1730
8 hours 30 minutes
```

Extra credit if you can deal with the case that the first time is later than the second time:

```
Please enter the first time: 1730
Please enter the second time: 0900
15 hours 30 minutes
```

Exercise P2.20. Run the following program, and explain the output you get.

```
#include "iostream.h"
#include "stdlib.h"

int main()
{  int total;
   cout << "Please enter a number: ";
   float x1;
   cin >> x1;
   cout << "total = " << total << "\n";
   total = total + x1;
   cout << "total = " << total << "\n";
   cout << "Please enter a number: ";
   float x1;
   cin >> x2;
   total = total + x2;
   cout << "total = " << total << "\n";
   total = total / 2;
   cout << "total = " << total << "\n";
   cout << "The average is " << total << "\n";
   return EXIT_SUCCESS;
}
```

Note the *trace messages,* which are inserted to show the current contents of the `total` variable. Then fix up the program, run it with the trace messages in place to verify that it works correctly, and remove the trace messages.

Exercise P2.21. *Writing large letters.* A large letter H can be produced like this:

```
*   *
*   *
*****
*   *
*   *
```

It can be declared as a string constant like this:

```
const string LETTER_H =
   "*   *\n*   *\n*****\n*   *\n*   *\n";
```

Do the same for the letters E, L, and O. Then write the message

```
H
E
L
L
O
```

in large letters.

Exercise P2.22. Write a program that transforms numbers `1`, `2`, `3`, ..., `12` into the corresponding month names `January`, `February`, `March`, ..., `December`. *Hint:* Make a very long string `"January February March ..."`, in which you add spaces such that each month name has *the same length.* Then use `substr` to extract the month you want.

Exercise P2.23. Change the password program to make it generate more secure passwords. Use the function call `rand_int(1, 1000)` to generate a random number between 1 and 1,000. Multiply the age with the random number. Then concatenate the initials with the *last four digits* of the product.

CHAPTER 3

Objects

Objectives

- To become familiar with objects
- To learn about the properties of several sample classes that were designed for this book
- To be able to construct objects and supply initial values
- To understand member functions and the dot notation
- To be able to modify and query the state of an object through member functions
- To write simple graphics programs containing points, lines, circles, and text
- To be able to select appropriate coordinate systems
- To learn how to process user input and mouse clicks in graphics programs
- To develop test cases that validate the correctness of your programs

We have learned about the basic data types of C++: numbers and strings. While it is possible to write interesting programs using nothing but numbers and strings, most useful programs need to manipulate data items that are more complex and more closely represent entities in the real world. Examples of these data items are employee records, graphical shapes, and so on.

The C++ language is ideally suited for designing and manipulating such data items, or, as they are usually called, *objects.* As it turns out, it requires a certain degree of technical mastery to design new object types, but it is quite easy to manipulate object types that have been designed by others. Therefore, we will split up our discussion of objects into two chapters. In this chapter, we will learn how to use objects that were specifically designed for use with this textbook. In Chapter 8 we will learn how to define these and other objects.

Some of the most interesting data structures that we consider are from the realm of graphics. In this chapter you will learn how to use objects that let you draw graphical shapes on the computer screen. To keep programming simple, we just introduce a few building blocks. You will find that the ability to draw simple graphs makes programming a lot more fun.

3.1 Constructing Objects

An *object* is a value that can be created, stored, and manipulated in a programming language. In that sense, the string `"Hello"` is an object. You can create it simply by using the C++ string notation `"Hello"`. You can store it in a variable, for example like this:

```
string greeting = "Hello";
```

You can manipulate it, for example by computing a substring:

```
cout << greeting.substr(0, 4);
```

This particular manipulation does not affect the object. After the substring is computed, the original string is unchanged. We will presently see object manipulations that do change objects.

In C++ every object must belong to a *class.* A class is a data type, just like `int` or `float`. However, classes are *programmer-defined,* whereas `int` and `float` are defined by the designers of the C++ language. At this point, you won't yet learn how to define your own classes, so the distinction between the built-in types and programmer-defined class types is not yet important.

In this chapter we will learn to work with the class `Time`, the class `Employee`, and four classes that represent graphical shapes. These classes are not part of standard C++; they have been created for use in this book.

Suppose you want to know how many seconds will elapse between now and the next millennium. This sounds like a major pain to compute by hand. Sure, every day has $24 \times 60 \times 60$ or 86,400 seconds. However, you would have to take into account that some months have 31 days and others have 30 days—except for February, which has 28 days, unless it is a leap year, when it has 29 days. It would take you quite a few seconds to compute this information by hand.

However, the `Time` class makes the job easy. We will see how, in this section and the next. First, let us learn how to specify an object of type `Time`. The beginning of the millennium is January 1, 2000, 0 hours, 0 minutes, and 0 seconds. Here is a `Time` object representing that time:

```
Time(2000, 1, 1, 0, 0, 0)
```

You specify a time object by giving six values: year, month, day, hours, minutes, and seconds. The hours are given in "military time": between 0 and 23 hours. The year must be 1970 or later.

You should think of this time object as an entity that is very similar to a number such as `7.5` or a string such as `"Hello"`. Just as floating-point values can be stored in `float` variables, `Time` objects can be stored in `Time` variables:

```
Time millennium = Time(2000, 1, 1, 0, 0, 0);
```

Think of this as the analog of

```
float interest_rate = 7.5;
```

or

```
string greeting = "Hello";
```

There is a shorthand for this very common situation. You can write

```
Time millennium(2000, 1, 1, 0, 0, 0);
```

This defines a variable `millennium` that is initialized to the `Time` object `Time(2000, 1, 1, 0, 0, 0)`; that is, January 1, 2000, 00:00:00. (See Figure 1.)

When a `Time` object is specified from six integer values such as 2000, 1, 1, 0, 0, and 0, we say that the object is *constructed* from these values, and the values used in the construction are the *construction parameters*. In general, an object value is constructed with the syntax

Class_name (*construction parameters*)

A variable of class type can be defined either as

Class_name variable_name = *Class_name* (*construction parameters*)

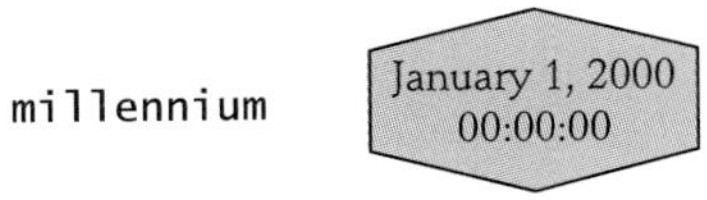

Figure 1

A `Time` Object

or

Class_name variable_name(*construction parameters*)

Many classes have more than one construction mechanism. For example, there are two methods for constructing times: by specifying year, month, day, hours, minutes, and seconds, and by specifying no parameters at all. The expression

```
Time()
```

creates an object representing the current time, that is, the time when the program is run. Making an object with no construction parameter is called *default construction.*

Of course, you can store a default `Time` object in a variable:

```
Time now = Time();
```

The shorthand notation for using default construction is slightly inconsistent:

```
Time now;
```

and not

```
Time now(); /* NO! This does not define a variable */
```

For strange historical reasons, you cannot use `()` when defining a variable with default construction.

3.2 Using Objects

Once we have a `Time` variable, what can we do with it? Here is one useful operation. We can add a certain number of seconds to the time:

```
now.add_seconds(1000);
```

Afterwards, the object in the variable `now` is changed. It is no longer the current time, but a time object representing a time that is exactly 1000 seconds from the time previously stored in `now`. (See Figure 2.)

Figure 2

Changing the State of an Object

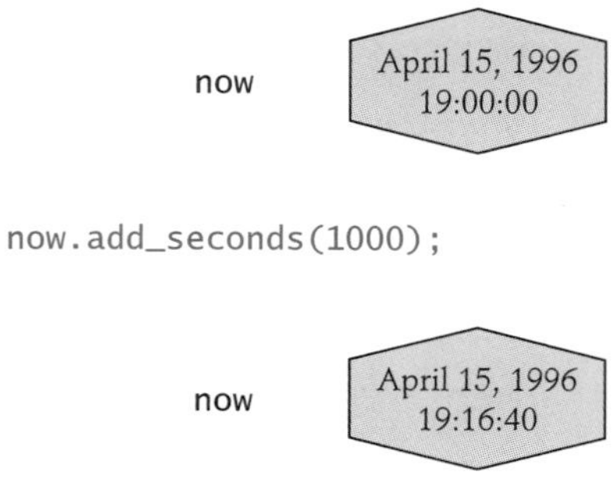

Whenever you apply a function (like **add_seconds**) to an object variable (like **now**), the syntax uses the "dot notation"

object.*function* (*parameters*)

This is the same dot notation that we already used for certain string functions:

```
int n = greeting.length();
cout <<  greeting.substr(0, 4);
```

A function that is applied to an object with the dot notation is called a *member function* in C++.

Now that we saw how to change the state of a time object, how can we find out the current time stored in the object? We have to ask it. There are six member functions for this purpose, called

```
get_seconds()
get_minutes()
get_hours()
get_day()
get_month()
get_year()
```

They too are applied to objects using the dot notation. (See Figure 3.)

Program time1.cpp

```
#include "ccc.h"

int main()
{  Time millennium(2000, 1, 1, 0, 0, 0);
   millennium.add_seconds(1000000.0); /* a million seconds later */
   cout << millennium.get_year() << " "
      << millennium.get_month() << " "
      << millennium.get_day() << "\n";

   return EXIT_SUCCESS;
}
```

This command prints out

```
2000 2 12
```

Figure 3

Querying the State of an Object

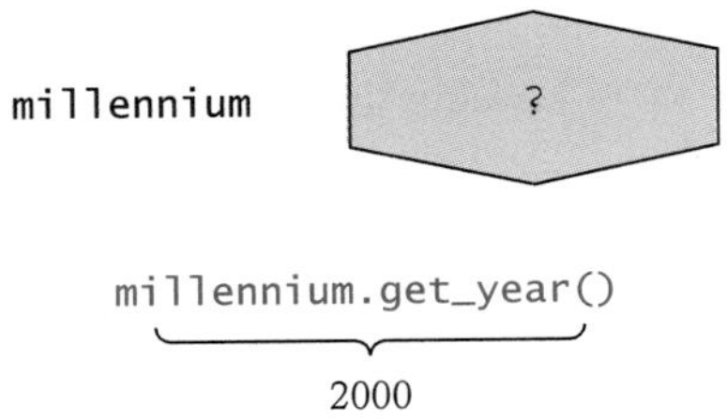

That is, February 12, 2000, is one million seconds into the new millennium. Note that the `add_seconds` function takes a parameter of type `float`. That allows us to represent very large numbers of seconds.

Since we can *get* the month of a time, it seems natural to suggest that we can *set* it as well:

```
homework_due.set_month(2); /* No! Not a supported member function */
```

Time objects do not support this member function. There is a good reason, of course. If the time before the `set_month` function was January 31, 2000, then it would be February 31, 2000 afterwards, and that would be an invalid time. To avoid these complications, the designer of the `Time` class decided not to support any "set" member functions.

Once a time object is created, you can modify it only with one member function: `add_seconds`. For example, to advance a time by one week, you can use

```
const float SECONDS_PER_WEEK = 7 * 24 * 60 * 60.0;
homework_due.add_seconds(SECONDS_PER_WEEK);
```

You can move the time back by a week:

```
homework_due.add_seconds(-SECONDS_PER_WEEK);
```

If you are entirely unhappy with the current object stored in a variable, you can overwrite it with another one:

```
homework_due = Time(2010, 4, 15, 19, 0, 0);
```

Figure 4 shows this replacement.

There is one final member function that a time variable can carry out: It can figure out the number of seconds between itself and another time. For example,

Figure 4

Replacing an Object with Another

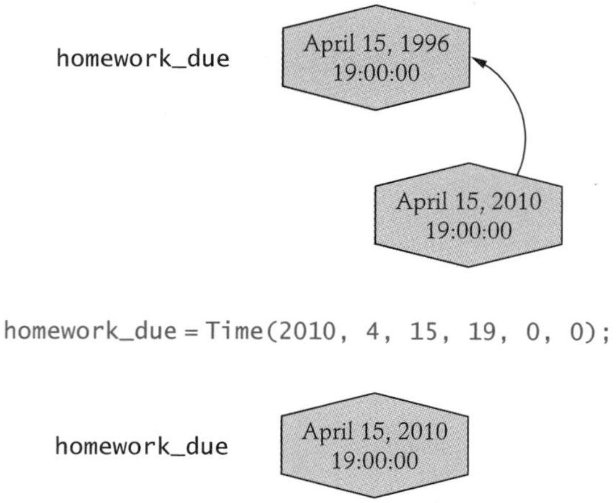

```
Time now;
Time homework_due(1996, 4, 15, 19, 0, 0);
float seconds = homework_due.seconds_from(now);
cout << "Homework is due " << seconds
   << " seconds from now!\n";
```

When you run the following program, you will find out how many seconds and how many days the new millennium is away from today.

Program time2.cpp

```
#include "ccc.h"

int main()
{  Time now;
   Time millennium(2000, 1, 1, 0, 0, 0);
   float seconds = millennium.seconds_from(now);
   const float SECONDS_PER_DAY = 24 * 60 * 60.0;

   cout << "The new millennium is " << seconds
      << " seconds or " << seconds / SECONDS_PER_DAY
      << " days from now.\n";

   return EXIT_SUCCESS;
}
```

If you run this program after January 1, 2000, you will get a negative result.

Let us summarize: In C++, objects are constructed by writing the class name, followed by construction parameters in parentheses. There is a shortcut notation for initializing an object variable. Member functions are applied to objects and object variables with the dot notation. The functions of the `Time` class are listed in Table 1.

Table 1 Functions of the `Time` Class

Name	Purpose
`Time()`	Constructs the current time
`Time(y, m, d, h, n, s)`	Constructs the time with year $y \geq 1970$, month `m`, day `d`, hours `h`, minutes `n`, seconds `s`
`t.get_seconds()`	Returns the seconds value of `t`
`t.get_minutes()`	Returns the minutes value of `t`
`t.get_hours()`	Returns the hours value of `t`
`t.get_day()`	Returns the day value of `t`
`t.get_month()`	Return the month value of `t`
`t.get_year()`	Return the year value of `t`
`t.add_seconds(n)`	Change `t` to move by `n` seconds
`t.seconds_from(t2)`	Compute the number of seconds between `t` and `t2`

Common Error 3.1

Trying to Call a Member Function Without a Variable

Suppose your code contains the instruction

```
add_seconds(30); /* Error */
```

The compiler will not know which time to advance. You need to supply a variable of type `Time`:

```
Time liftoff(1996, 4, 15, 19, 0, 0);
liftoff.add_seconds(30);
```

Productivity Hint 3.1

Keyboard Shortcuts for Mouse Operations

Programmers spend a lot of time with the keyboard and the mouse. Programs and documentation are many pages long and require a lot of typing. The constant switching among the editor, compiler, and debugger takes up quite a few mouse clicks. The designers of programs such as a C++ integrated development environment have added some features to make your work easier, but it is up to you to discover them.

Just about every program has a user interface with menus and dialog boxes. Click on a menu and click on a submenu to select a task. Click on each field in a dialog box, fill in the requested answer, and click Ok. These are great user interfaces for the beginner, because they are easy to master, but they are terrible user interfaces for the regular user. The constant switching between the keyboard and the mouse slows you down. You need to move a hand off the keyboard, locate the mouse, move the mouse, click the mouse, and move the hand back onto the keyboard. For that reason, most user interfaces have *keyboard shortcuts:* combinations of keystrokes that allow you to achieve the same tasks without having to switch to the mouse at all.

All Microsoft Windows applications use the following conventions:

- The Alt key plus the underlined key in a menu (as in "File") pulls down that menu. Inside a menu, just provide the underlined character in the submenu to activate it. For example, Alt+`F O` selects "File" "Open". Once your fingers know about this combination, you can open files faster than the fastest mouse artist.
- Inside dialog boxes, the Tab key is important; it moves from one option to the next. The arrow keys move within an option. The Enter key accepts the entire dialog, and Esc cancels it.
- In a program with multiple windows, Ctrl+Tab toggles through the windows managed by that program, for example between the source and error window.
- Alt+Tab toggles between applications, letting you quickly toggle between, for example, the compiler and a folder explorer program.

- Hold down the Shift key and press the arrow keys to highlight text. Then use Ctrl+X to cut the text, Ctrl+C to copy it, and Ctrl+V to paste it. These keys are easy to remember. The V looks like an insertion mark that an editor would use to insert text:

  Use the [Ctrl-C] V Key to copy text:

  The X should remind you of crossing out text. The C is just the first letter in "copy". (OK, so it is also the first letter in "cut"—no mnemonic rule is perfect.) You find these reminders in the Edit menu.

Of course, the mouse has its use in text processing: to locate or select text that is on the same screen but far away from the cursor.

Take a little bit of time to learn about the keyboard shortcuts that the designers of your programs provided for you, and the time investment will be repaid many times during your programming career. When you blaze through your work in the computer lab with keyboard shortcuts, you may find yourself surrounded by amazed onlookers who whisper, "I didn't know you could do *that.*"

3.3 Real-Life Objects

One reason for the popularity of object-oriented programming is that it is easy to *model* entities from real life in computer programs. That makes programs easy to understand and modify. Consider for example the following program:

Program employee.cpp

```
#include "ccc.h"

int main()
{  Employee harry("Hacker, Harry", 45000.00);

   float new_salary = harry.get_salary() + 3000;
   harry.set_salary(new_salary);

   cout << "Name: " << harry.get_name() << "\n";
   cout << "Salary: " << harry.get_salary() << "\n";

   return EXIT_SUCCESS;
}
```

This program creates a variable **harry** and initializes it with an object of type **Employee**. There are two construction parameters: the name of the employee and the starting salary.

Figure 5

An `Employee` Object

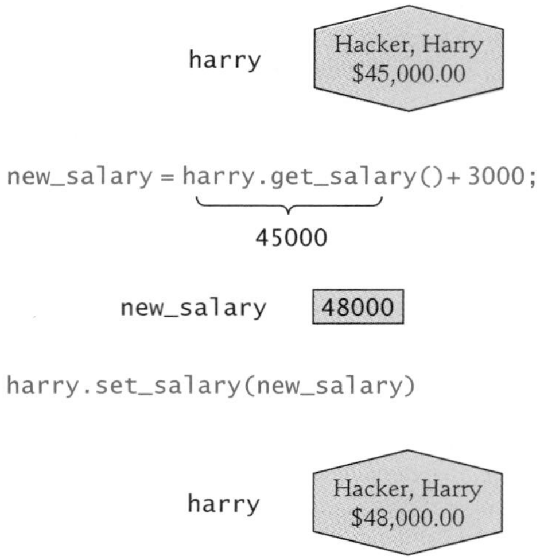

Table 2 Functions of the `Employee` Class

Name	Purpose
`Employee(n, s)`	Constructs an employee with name `n` and salary `s`
`e.get_name()`	Returns the name of `e`
`e.get_salary()`	Returns the salary of `e`
`e.set_salary(s)`	Sets salary of `e` to `s`

We then give Harry a $3,000 raise (see Figure 5). We first find his current salary with the **`get_salary`** member function. We determine the new salary by adding $3,000. We use the **`set_salary`** member function to set the new salary.

Finally, we print out the name and salary number of the employee object. We use the **`get_name`** and **`get_salary`** member functions to get the name and salary.

Note that you can change the salary of an employee with the **`set_salary`** member function. However, you cannot change the name of an employee object.

This `Employee` class, whose functions are listed in Table 2, is not very realistic. In real data-processing programs, employees also have ID numbers, addresses, job titles, and so on. To keep the sample programs in this book simple, this class has been stripped down to the most basic properties of employees.

Productivity Hint 3.2

Using the Command Line Effectively

If your programming environment lets you accomplish all routine tasks with menus and dialog boxes, you can skip this note. However, if you need to manually invoke the editor, the compiler, the linker, and the program to test, then it is well worth learning about *command line editing.*

Most operating systems (Unix, DOS, OS/2) have a *command line interface* to interact with the computer. (In Windows, you can use the DOS command line interface by double-clicking the "MS-DOS Prompt" icon.) You launch commands at a *prompt.* The command is executed, and upon completion you get another prompt.

When you develop a program, you find yourself executing the same commands over and over. Wouldn't it be nice if you didn't have to type beastly commands like

```
CC myprog.C -lm
```

more than once? Or if you could fix a mistake rather than having to retype the command in its entirety? Many command line interfaces have an option to do just that, but they don't always make it obvious. If you use DOS/Windows, you need to install a program called DOSKEY. If you use Unix, try to get the tcsh shell installed for you, not the standard csh shell, and also be sure the history feature is activated—ask a lab assistant or system administrator to help you with the setup. With the proper setup, the up arrow key ↑ is redefined to cycle through your old commands. You can edit lines with the left and right arrow keys. You can also perform *command completion.* For example, to reissue the same CC command, type CC and press F8 (DOS) or type !CC (Unix).

Random Fact 3.1

Mainframes—When Dinosaurs Ruled the Earth

When the International Business Machines Corporation, a successful manufacturer of punched-card equipment for tabulating data, first turned its attention to designing computers in the early 1950s, its planners assumed that there was a market of perhaps 50 such devices, for installation by the government, the military, and a few of the country's largest corporations. Instead, they sold about 1,500 machines of their System 650 model and went on to build and sell more powerful computers.

The so-called *mainframe* computers of the Fifties, Sixties, and Seventies were huge. They filled up a whole room, which had to be climate-controlled to protect the delicate equipment (see Figure 6). Today, because of miniaturization technology, even mainframes are getting smaller, but they are still very expensive. (At the time of this writing, the cost for a midrange IBM 3090 is approximately 4 million dollars.)

These huge and expensive systems were an immediate success when they first appeared, because they replaced many roomfuls of even more expensive employees, who had previously performed the tasks by hand. Few of these computers do any exciting computations. They keep mundane information, such as billing records or airline reservations; they just keep lots of them.

IBM was not the first company to build mainframe computers; that honor belongs to the Univac Corporation. However, IBM soon became the major player, partially because of technical excellence and attention to customer needs and partially because it exploited its strengths and structured its products and services in a way that made it difficult for customers to mix them with those of other vendors. In the Sixties its competitors, the so-called "Seven Dwarfs"—GE, RCA, Univac, Honeywell, Burroughs, Control Data, and NCR—fell on hard times. Some went out of the computer business altogether, while others tried unsuccessfully to combine their strengths by merging their computer operations. It was generally predicted

Figure 6

A Mainframe Computer

that they would eventually all fail. It was in this atmosphere that the U.S. government brought an antitrust suit against IBM in 1969. The suit went to trial in 1975 and dragged on until 1982, when the Reagan Administration abandoned it, declaring it "without merit".

Of course, by then the computing landscape had changed completely. Just as the dinosaurs gave way to smaller, nimbler creatures, three new waves of computers had appeared: the minicomputers, workstations, and microcomputers, all engineered by new companies, not the Seven Dwarfs. Today, the importance of mainframes in the marketplace has diminished, and IBM, while still a large and resourceful company, no longer dominates the computer market.

Mainframes are still in use today for two reasons. They still excel at handling large data volumes. More importantly, the programs that control the business data have been refined over the last 20 or more years, fixing one problem at a time. Moving these programs to less expensive computers, with different languages and operating systems, is difficult and error-prone. Sun Microsystems, a leading manufacturer of workstations, was eager to prove that its mainframe system could be "downsized" to its own equipment. Sun eventually succeeded, but it took over five years—far longer than it expected.

3.4 Displaying Graphical Shapes

In the remainder of this chapter you will learn how to use a number of useful classes to render simple graphics. The graphics classes will provide a basis for interesting programming examples.

There are two kinds of C++ programs that we will write in this course: *console* applications and *graphics* applications. Console applications read input from the keyboard (through `cin`) and display text output on the screen (through `cout`). Graphics programs read keystrokes and mouse clicks, and they display graphical shapes such as lines and circles, through a window object called `cwin`. Depending on your operating system, you need to close the program window or hit a key to terminate a graphics program.

You already know how to write console programs. You include the header file iostream.h and use the >> and << operators. To activate graphics for your programs, you must take two steps. First, you must place a special directive like

```
#define CCC_WIN
```

at the beginning of your program. The actual name of the directive depends on the graphics system that you use. If you use DOS graphics, a Macintosh, or Unix/Linux, then you must use `CCC_BGI`, `CCC_MAC` or `CCC_X11` instead of `CCC_WIN`. In this book, we will always use `CCC_WIN`, since Windows is the most commonly used graphics system. Just change the symbol to the one appropriate to your library. Admittedly, this sounds like magic. However, writing a graphics program from scratch is a complex task. The ccc.h header file includes the basic code framework for the graphics system of your computer when you define the appropriate identifier.

You must also include ccc.h. Unlike the iostream library, which is available on all C++ systems, this graphics library was created for use in this textbook.

To display a graphics object, you cannot just send it to `cout`:

```
Circle c;
. . .
cout << c; /* Won't display the circle */
```

The `cout` stream displays characters on the terminal, not pixels in a window. Instead, you must send the characters to a window called `cwin`:

```
cwin << c; /* The circle will appear in the graphics window */
```

In the next section we will learn how to make objects that represent graphical shapes.

3.5 Graphics Structures

A *point* has an *x*- and a *y*-coordinate. For example,

```
Point(1, 3)
```

is a point with *x*-coordinate 1 and *y*-coordinate 3. What can you do with a point?

You can display it in a graphics window.

Program point.cpp

```
#define  CCC_WIN
#include "ccc.h"

int main()
{  cwin << Point(1, 3);

   return EXIT_SUCCESS;
}
```

You frequently use points to make more complex graphical shapes.

```
Circle(Point(1, 3), 2.5);
```

This defines a circle whose center is the point with coordinates (1, 3) and whose radius is 2.5.

As always, you can store a `Point` object in a variable of type `Point`. The following code defines and initializes a `Point` variable and then displays the point. Then a circle with center `p` is created and also displayed (Figure 7).

Program circle.cpp

```
#define CCC_WIN
#include "ccc.h"

int main()
{  Point p(1, 3);
   cwin << p << Circle(p, 2.5);
   return EXIT_SUCCESS;
}
```

Figure 7

Output from point.cpp

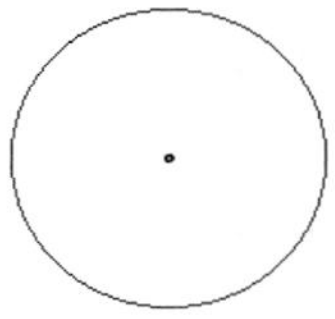

Figure 8

A Line

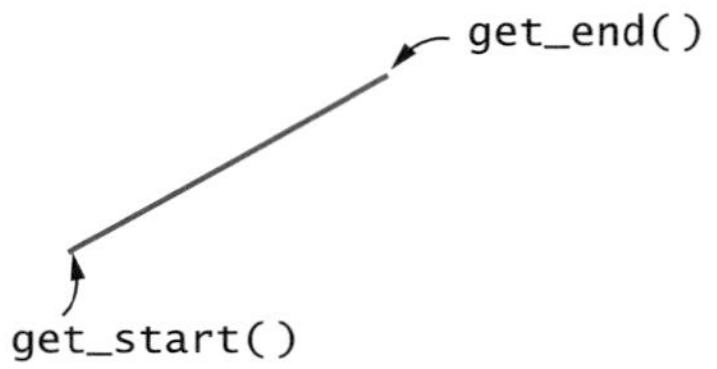

Figure 9

A Message

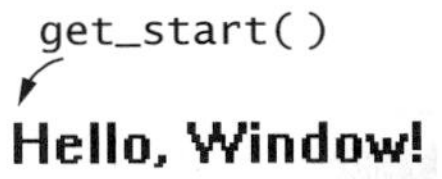

Two points can be joined by a *line* (Figure 8).

Program line.cpp

```
#define CCC_WIN
#include "ccc.h"

int main()
{  Point p(1, 3);
   Point q(4, 7);
   Line s(p, q);
   cwin << s;

   return EXIT_SUCCESS;
}
```

In a graphics window you can display *text* anywhere you like. You need to specify what you want to show and where it should appear (Figure 9).

Program hellowin.cpp

```
#define CCC_WIN
#include "ccc.h"

int main()
{  Point p(1, 3);
   Message greeting(p, "Hello, Window!");
   cwin << greeting;

   return EXIT_SUCCESS;
}
```

The point parameter specifies the *upper left corner* of the message. Points, circles, lines, and messages are the four graphical elements that we will use to create diagrams.

There is one member function that all our graphical classes implement: `move`. If `obj` is a point, circle, line, or message, then

```
obj.move(dx, dy)
```

changes the position of the object, moving the entire object by `dx` units in x-direction and `dy` units in y-direction. Either or both of `dx` and `dy` can be zero or negative (Figure 10). For example, the following code draws a square (see Figure 11).

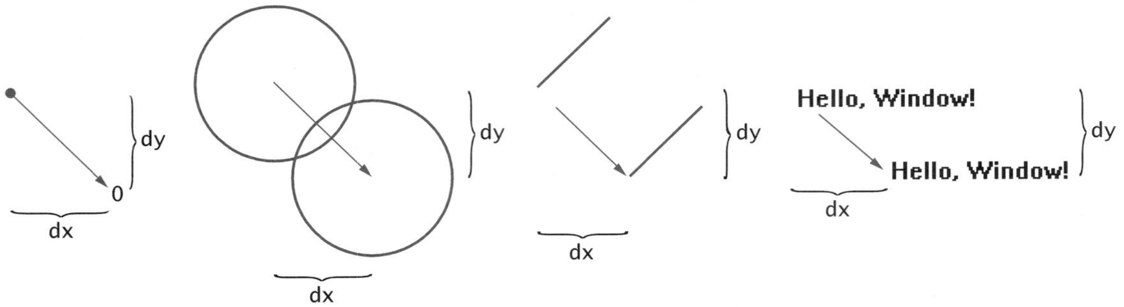

Figure 10

The move Operation

Figure 11

Square Drawn by square.cpp

Program square.cpp

```
#define CCC_WIN
#include "ccc.h"

int main()
{  Point p(1, 3);
   Point q = p;
   Point r = p;
   q.move(0, 1);
   r.move(1, 0);
   Line s(p, q);
   Line t(p, r);
   cwin << s << t;
   s.move(1, 0);
   t.move(0, 1);
   cwin << s << t;

   return EXIT_SUCCESS;
}
```

After a graphical object has been constructed and perhaps moved, we sometimes want to know where it is currently located. There are two member functions for `Point` objects: `get_x` and `get_y`. They get the x- and y-positions of the point.

The `get_center` and `get_radius` member functions return the center and radius of a circle. The `get_start` and `get_end` member functions return the starting point and end point of a line. The `get_start` and `get_text` member functions on a `Message` object return the starting point and the message text. Since `get_center`, `get_start`, and `get_end` return `Point` objects, you may need to apply `get_x` or `get_y` to them to find out their x- and y-coordinates. For example,

```
Circle c(. . .);
. . .
float cx = c.get_center().get_x();
```

You now know how to construct graphical objects, and you have seen all member functions for manipulating and querying them (summarized in Tables 3 through 6). We purposefully kept the design of these classes simple, but as a result some common tasks require a little ingenuity (See Productivity Hint 3.3).

Table 3 Functions of the `Point` Class

Name	Purpose
`Point(x, y)`	Constructs a point at location (x, y)
`p.get_x()`	Returns the x-coordinate of point p
`p.get_y()`	Returns the y-coordinate of point p
`p.move(dx, dy)`	Moves point p by (dx, dy)

Table 4 Functions of the `Circle` Class

Name	Purpose
`Circle(p, r)`	Constructs a circle with center p and radius r
`c.get_center()`	Returns the center point of circle c
`c.get_radius()`	Returns the radius of circle c
`c.move(dx, dy)`	Moves circle c by (dx, dy)

Table 5 Functions of the `Line` Class

Name	Purpose
`Line(p, q)`	Constructs a line joining points p and q
`l.get_start()`	Returns the starting point of line l
`l.get_end()`	Returns the ending point of line l
`l.move(dx, dy)`	Moves line l by (dx, dy)

Table 6 Functions of the `Message` Class

Name	Purpose
`Message(p, s)`	Constructs a message with starting point p and text string s
`m.get_start()`	Returns the starting point of message m
`m.get_text()`	Gets the text string of message m
`m.move(dx, dy)`	Moves message m by (dx, dy)

Common Error 3.2

Using Stream Output in Graphics Programs

You cannot use stream output on the graphics window to display text. Consider this program:

```
#define CCC_WIN
#include "iostream.h"
#include "stdlib.h"
#include "ccc.h"

int main()
{  cout << "Hello Graphical World!"; /* Error */
   cwin << Point(1, 3);

   return EXIT_SUCCESS;
}
```

Since the program defines `CCC_WIN` and then includes ccc.h, it is compiled into a graphics program, not a console program. Graphics programs have no well-defined support for `cin` and `cout`.

In some implementations the text will actually show up in the graphics window, overwriting the drawing and eventually scrolling it. In other implementations the text may not show up at all or may show up in a different window. Use the `Message` class to display text on the graphics window.

Productivity Hint 3.3

Think of Points as Objects, Not Pairs of Numbers

Suppose you want to draw a square starting with the point **p** as the upper left corner and with side length 1. If **p** has coordinates ($\mathbf{p}_x$, $\mathbf{p}_y$), then the upper right corner is the point with coordinates ($\mathbf{p}_x + 1$, $\mathbf{p}_y$). Of course, you can program that:

```
Point q(p.get_x() + 1, p.get_y()); /* Cumbersome */
```

We would like to encourage you instead to think about points as objects, not pairs of numbers. From that point of view, there is a more elegant solution: Initialize `q` to be the same point as `p`, then move it to where it belongs:

```
Point q = p;
q.move(1, 0); /* Simple */
```

Random Fact 3.2

Computer Graphics

The generation and manipulation of visual images is one of the most exciting applications of the computer. We distinguish between different kinds of graphics.

Diagrams, such as numeric charts or maps, are artifacts that convey information to the viewer (see Figure 12). They do not directly depict anything that occurs in the natural world, but are a tool for visualizing information.

Scenes are computer-generated images that attempt to depict images of the real or an imagined world (see Figure 13). It turns out to be quite challenging to render light and shadows accurately. Special effort must be taken so that the images do not look overly neat and simple;

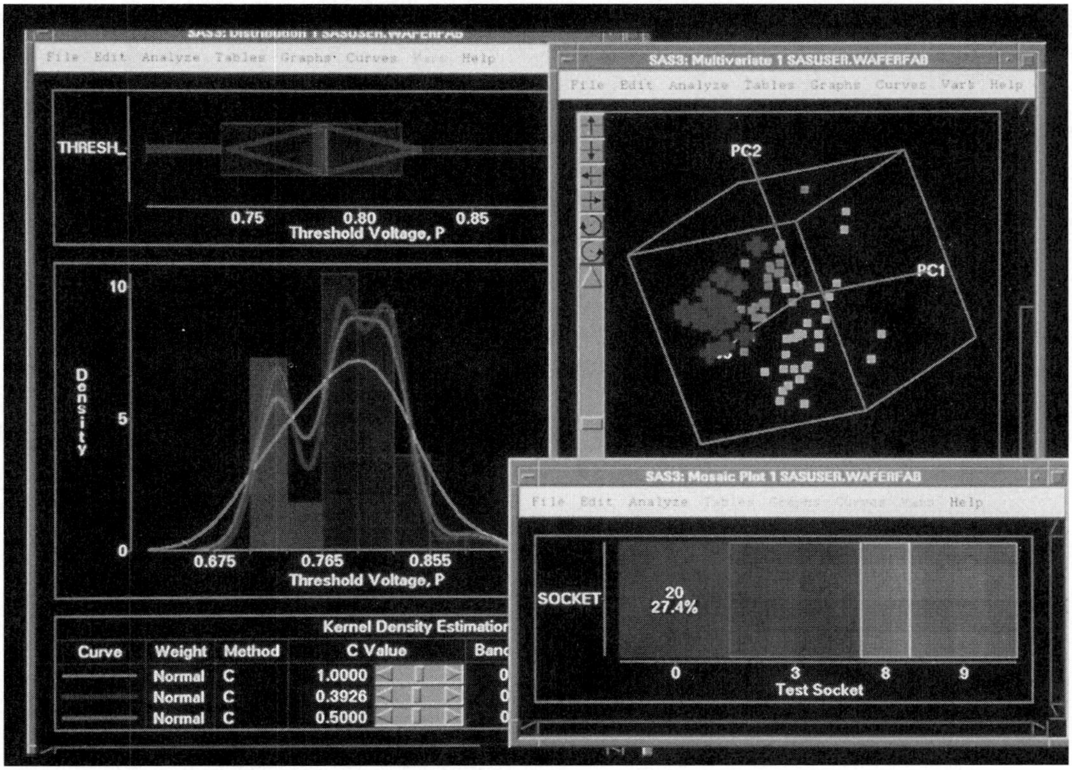

Figure 12

Diagrams

Figure 13

Scene

Figure 14

Manipulated Image (from DINOPIX by Teruhisa Tajima ©1995, published by Chronicle Books, San Francisco)

clouds, rocks, leaves, and dust in the real world have a complex and somewhat random appearance. The degree of realism in these images is constantly improving.

Manipulated images are photographs or film footage of actual events that have been converted to digital form and edited by the computer (see Figure 14). For example, film sequences of the movie *Apollo 13* were produced by starting from actual images and changing the perspective, showing the launch of the rocket from a more dramatic viewpoint.

Computer graphics is one of the most challenging fields in computer science. It requires processing of massive amounts of information at very high speed. New algorithms are constantly invented for this purpose. Viewing overlapping three-dimensional objects with curved boundaries requires advanced mathematical tools. Realistic modeling of textures and biological entities requires extensive knowledge of mathematics, physics, and biology.

3.6 Choosing a Coordinate System

We need to have an agreement on the meaning of particular coordinates. For example, where is the point with x coordinate 1 and y coordinate 3 located? Some graphics systems use pixels, the individual dots on the display, as coordinates, but different displays have different pixel counts and densities. Using pixels makes it difficult to write programs that look pleasant on every display screen. The library supplied with this book uses a coordinate system that is independent of the display.

Figure 15 shows the default coordinate system used by this book's library. The origin is at the center of the screen, and the x-axis and y-axis are 10 units long in either direction. The axes do not actually appear (unless you draw them yourself by drawing `Line` objects).

Figure 15

Default Coordinate System for Graphics Library

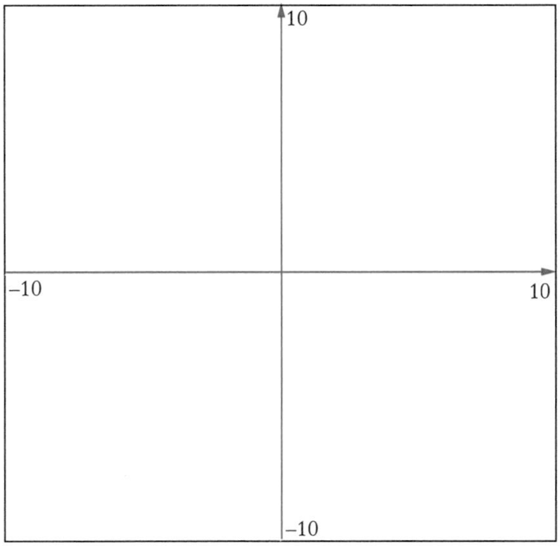

This default coordinate system is fine for simple test programs, but it is *useless* when dealing with real data. For example, suppose we want to show a graph plotting the average temperature (degrees Celsius) in Phoenix, Arizona, for every month of the year. The temperature ranges from 11°C in January to 33°C in July (See Table 7).

Even the January data

```
cwin << Point(1, 11);
```

won't show up in the window at all! In this situation, we need to change from the default coordinate system to one that makes sense for our particular program. Here, the x-coordinates range from 1 to 12 and the y-coordinates range from 11 to 33. Figure 16 shows the coordinate system that we need. As you can see, the top left corner is (1, 33) and the bottom right corner is (12, 11).

Table 7 Average Temperatures in Phoenix, Arizona

January	11°C	July	33°C
February	13°C	August	32°C
March	16°C	September	29°C
April	20°C	October	23°C
May	25°C	November	16°C
June	31°C	December	12°C

Figure 16

Coordinate System for Temperature Plot

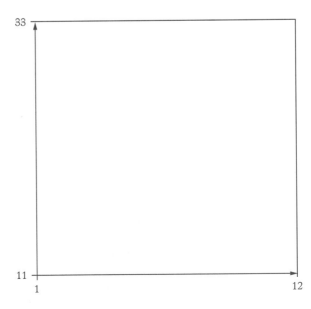

To select this coordinate system, we use the following instruction:

```
cwin.coord(1, 33, 12, 11);
```

Following a common convention in graphics systems, you must first specify the desired coordinates for the *top left* corner (which has x-coordinate 1 and y-coordinate 33), then the desired coordinates for the bottom right corner ($x = 12, y = 11$).

Here is the complete program:

Program phoenix.cpp

```
#define CCC_WIN
#include "ccc.h"

int main()
{  cwin.coord(1, 33, 12, 11);
   cwin << Point(1, 11);
   cwin << Point(2, 13);
   cwin << Point(3, 16);
   cwin << Point(4, 20);
   cwin << Point(5, 25);
   cwin << Point(6, 31);
   cwin << Point(7, 33);
   cwin << Point(8, 32);
   cwin << Point(9, 29);
   cwin << Point(10, 23);
   cwin << Point(11, 16);
   cwin << Point(12, 12);

   return EXIT_SUCCESS;
}
```

Figure 17 shows the output.

Figure 17

Average Temperatures in Phoenix, Arizona

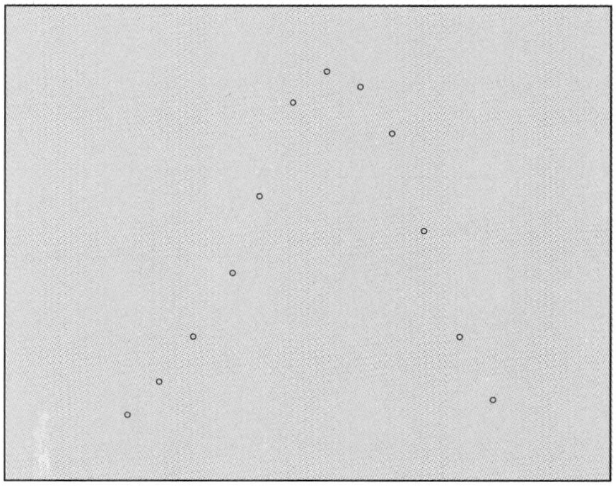

Productivity Hint 3.4

Choose a Convenient Coordinate System

Whenever you deal with real-world data, you should set a coordinate system that is matched to the data. Figure out which range of x- and y-coordinates is most convenient for you. For example, suppose you want to display a tic-tac-toe board (see Figure 18).

Of course, you could labor mightily and figure out where the lines are in relation to the default coordinate system. Or you can simply set your own coordinate system with (0, 0) in the top left corner and (3, 3) in the bottom right corner.

```
#define CCC_WIN
#include "ccc.h"

int main()
{  cwin.coord(0, 0, 3, 3);
   Line horizontal(Point(0, 1), Point(3, 1));
   cwin << horizontal;
   horizontal.move(0, 1);
   cwin << horizontal;
   Line vertical(Point(1, 0), Point(1, 3));
   cwin << vertical;
   vertical.move(1, 0);
   cwin << vertical;

   return EXIT_SUCCESS;
}
```

Some people have horrible memories about coordinate transformations from their high school geometry class and have taken a vow never to think about coordinates again for the remainder of their lives. If you are among them, you should reconsider. In C++ Lite, coordinate systems are your friend—they do all the horrible algebra for you, so you don't have to program it by hand.

Figure 18

Coordinate System for Tic-Tac-Toe Board

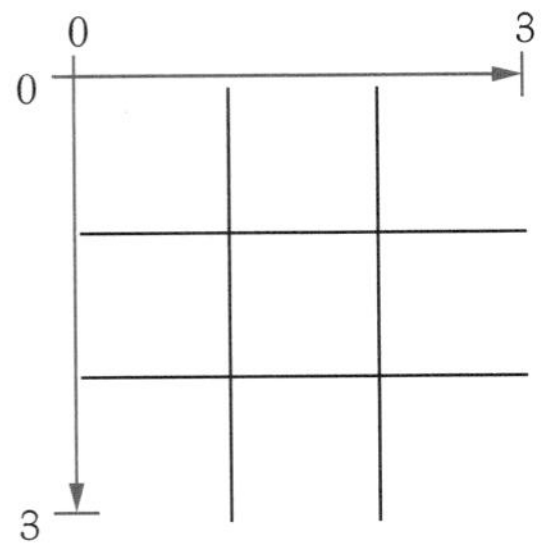

3.7 Getting Input from the Graphics Window

Just as stream output does not work with the graphics window, you cannot use stream input either. Instead, you must ask the window to get input for you. The command is

```
string response = cwin.get_string(prompt);
```

This is how you inquire about the user name:

```
string name = cwin.get_string("Please type your name:");
```

The prompt and a field for typing the input are displayed in a special input area. Depending on your computer system, the input area is in a dialog box or at the top or bottom of the graphics window. The user can then type input. After the user hits the Enter key, the user's keystrokes are placed into the `name` string. The message prompt is then removed from the screen.

The `get_string` function always returns a string. Use `get_int` or `get_float` to read an integer or floating-point number:

```
int age = cwin.get_int("Please enter your age:");
```

The user can specify a point with the mouse. To prompt the user for mouse input, use

```
Point response = cwin.get_mouse(prompt);
```

For example,

```
Point center = cwin.get_mouse("Enter center of circle");
```

The user can move the mouse to the desired location. Once the user clicks on the mouse button, the prompt is cleared and the selected point is returned.

Here is a program that puts these functions (summarized in Table 8) to work. It asks the user to enter a name and to try to click inside a circle. Then the program tests whether the point really lies inside the circle.

Table 8 Functions of the `GraphicsWindow` Class

Name	Purpose
`w.coord(x1, y1, x2, y2)`	Sets the coordinate system for subsequent drawing: (`x1, y1`) is the top left corner, (`x2, y2`) the bottom right corner
`w << x`	Displays the object `x` (a point, circle, line, or message) in window `w`
`w.clear()`	Clear window `w` (erase its contents)
`w.get_string(p)`	Displays prompt `p` in window `w` and returns the entered string
`w.get_int(p)`	Displays prompt `p` in window `w` and returns the entered integer
`w.get_float(p)`	Displays prompt `p` in window `w` and returns the entered value
`w.get_mouse(p)`	Displays prompt `p` in window `w` and returns the mouse click point

Program click.cpp

```
#define CCC_WIN
#include "ccc.h"

int main()
{  string name = cwin.get_string("Please type your name:");
   Circle c(Point(0, 0), 1);
   cwin << c;
   Point m = cwin.get_mouse("Please click inside the circle.");
   cwin << m << Message(m, "You clicked here");
   return EXIT_SUCCESS;
}
```

3.8 Comparing Visual and Numerical Information

The next example shows how one can look at the same problem both visually and numerically. We want to figure out the intersection between a line and a circle. The circle is centered on the screen. We ask the user to specify a radius of the circle and the y-intercept of a horizontal line. Then we draw the circle and the line.

Program intsect1.cpp

```
#define CCC_WIN
#include "ccc.h"

int main()
{  float radius = cwin.get_float("Radius: ");
   Circle c(Point(0, 0), radius);
   float b = cwin.get_float("Line position: ");
   Line s(Point(-10, b), Point(10, b));

   cwin << c << s;
   return EXIT_SUCCESS;
}
```

Figure 19 shows the output of this program.

Now suppose we would like to know the *exact* coordinates of the intersection points. The equation of the circle is

$$x^2 + y^2 = r^2$$

where r is the radius (which was given by the user). We also know y. A horizontal line

Figure 19

Intersection of a Line and a Circle

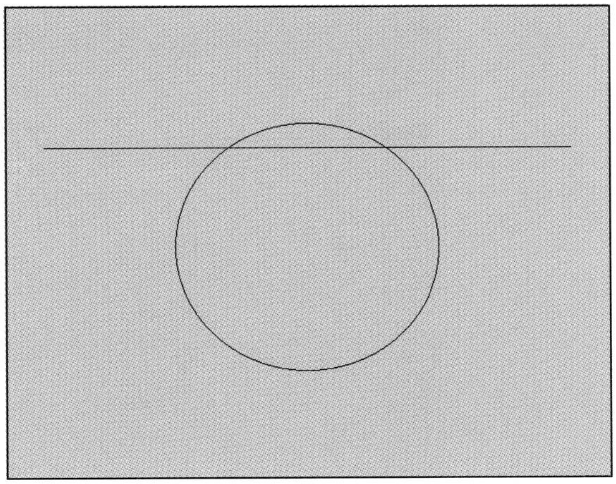

has equation $y = b$, and b is another user input. Thus x is the remaining unknown, and we can solve for it. We expect two solutions, corresponding to

$$x_{1,2} = \pm\sqrt{r^2 - b^2}$$

We then plot both points and label them with the numerical values. If we do it right, these two points will show up right on top of the actual intersections in the picture. If we don't, the two points will be at the wrong place.

Here is the code to compute and plot the intersection points.

Program intsect2.cpp

```
#define CCC_WIN
#include "ccc.h"

int main()
{  float radius = cwin.get_float("Radius: ");
   Circle c(Point(0, 0), radius)

   float b = cwin.get_float("Line position: ");
   Line s(Point(-10, b), Point(10, b));

   cwin << c << s;

   float root = sqrt(radius * radius - b * b);

   Point p1(root, b);
   Point p2(-root, b);
```

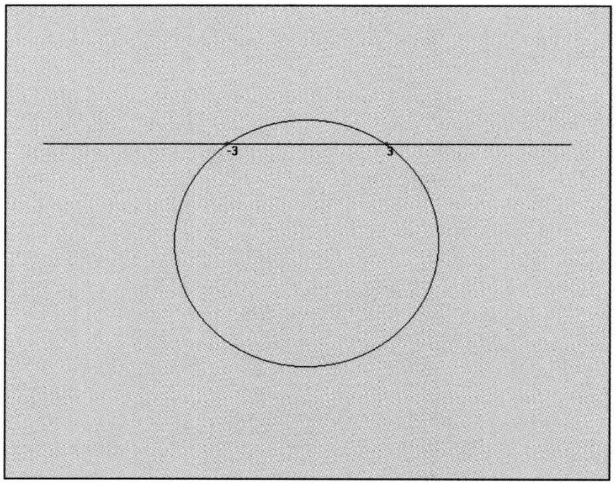

Figure 20

Computing the Intersection Points

```
    Message m1(p1, stringvalue(p1.get_x()));
    Message m2(p2, stringvalue(p2.get_x()));

    cwin << p1 << p2 << m1 << m2;

    return EXIT_SUCCESS;
}
```

Figure 20 shows the combined output. The results match perfectly, which gives us confidence that we did everything correctly. See Quality Tip 3.1 for more information on verifying that this program works correctly.

At this point you should be careful to specify only lines that intersect the circle. If the line doesn't meet the circle, then the program will attempt to compute a square root of a negative number, and it will terminate with a math error. We do not yet know how to implement a test to protect against this situation. That will be the topic of the next chapter.

Quality Tip 3.1

Calculate Sample Data Manually

It is difficult or impossible to prove that a given program functions correctly in all cases. For gaining confidence in the correctness of a program, or for understanding why it does not function as it should, manually calculated sample data are invaluable. If the program arrives at the same results as the manual calculation, our confidence in it is strengthened. If the manual results differ from the program results, we have a starting point for the debugging process.

Surprisingly, many programmers are reluctant to perform any manual calculations as soon as a program carries out the slightest bit of algebra. Their math phobia kicks in, and they irrationally hope that they can avoid the algebra and beat the program into submission by random tinkering, such as rearranging the + and - signs. Random tinkering is always a great time sink, but it rarely leads to useful results.

Figure 21

Three Test Cases

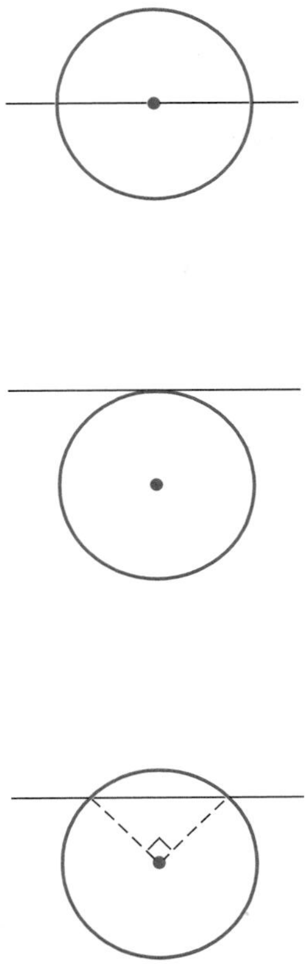

It is much smarter to look for test cases that are easy to compute and representative. In our example, let us look for three easy cases that we can compute by hand and then compare against program runs (see Figure 21).

First, let the horizontal line pass through the center of the circle. Then we expect the distance between the center and the intersection point to be the same as the radius of the circle. Let the radius be 2. The y position is 0 (the center of the window). We expect $x_1 = \sqrt{2^2 - 0^2} = 2 x_2 = -2$. Now, that wasn't so hard.

Next, let the horizontal line touch the circle on the top. Again let's fix the radius to be 2. Then the y position is also 2, and of course $x_1 = x_2 = 0$. That also was pretty easy.

The first two cases were *boundary cases* of the problem. A program may work correctly for several special cases but still fail for more typical input values. Therefore we must come up with an intermediate test case, even if it means a bit more computation. Let us choose a configuration where the center of the circle and the points of intersection form a right triangle. If the radius of the circle is again 2, then the height of the triangle is $\frac{1}{2}\sqrt{2}$. That looks complicated. So let's instead try choosing the height of the triangle to be 2. Thus, the base has length 4, and the radius of the circle is $2\sqrt{2}$. We therefore enter radius 2.828427, enter y-position 2, and expect $x_1 = 2, x_2 = -2$.

Running the program with these three inputs confirms the manual calculations. The computer calculations and the manual reasoning did not use the same formulas, so this gives us a great deal of confidence in the validity of the program.

Random Fact 3.3

Computer Networks and the Internet

Home computers and laptops are usually self-contained units with no permanent connection to other computers. Office and lab computers, however, are usually connected with each other and with larger computers: so-called *servers.* A server can store application programs and make them available on all computers on the network. Servers can also store data, such as schedules and mail messages, that everyone can retrieve. Networks that connect the computers in one building are called *local area networks,* or LANs.

Other networks connect computers in geographically dispersed locations. Such networks are called *wide area networks* or WANs. The most prominent wide area network is the *Internet.* At the time of this writing, the Internet is in a phase of explosive growth. In 1994 the Internet connected at least two million computers, and that number is estimated to double about every year. Nobody knows for certain how many users have access to the Internet, but the user population is estimated in the tens of millions. The Internet grew out of the ARPAnet, a network of computers at universities that was funded by the Advanced Research Planning Agency of the U.S. Department of Defense. The original motivation behind the creation of the network was the desire to run programs on remote computers. Using remote execution, a researcher at

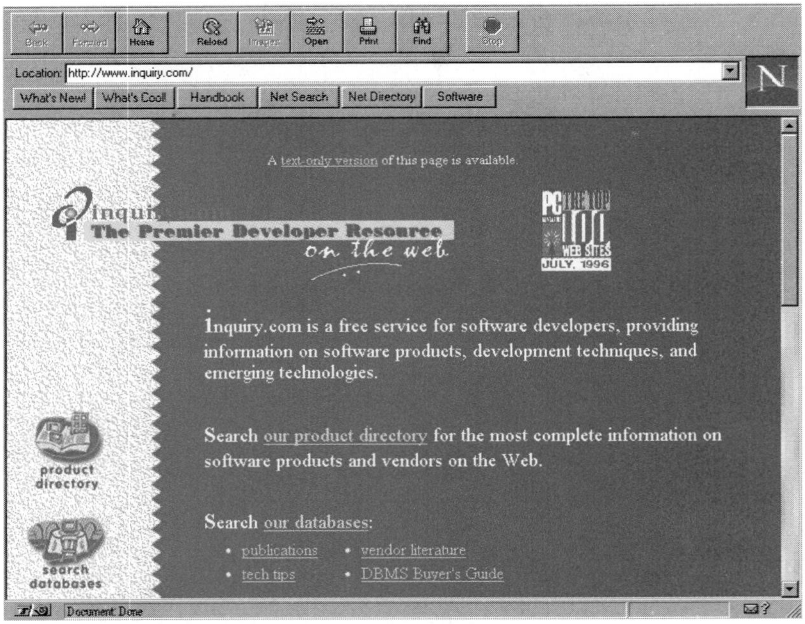

Figure 22

A WWW Browser

one institution would be able to access an underutilized computer at a different site. It quickly became apparent, though, that remote execution was not what the network was actually used for. The principal usage was *electronic mail:* the transfer of messages between computer users at different locations. To this day, electronic mail is one of the most compelling applications of the Internet.

Over time, more and more *information* became available on the Internet. The information was created by researchers and hobbyists and made freely available to anyone, either out the goodness of their hearts or for self-promotion. For example, the GNU project is producing a set of high-quality operating system utilities and program development tools that can be used freely by anyone (`ftp://prep.ai.mit.edu/pub/gnu`). The Project Gutenberg makes available the text of important classical books, whose copyright has expired, in computer-readable form (`http://jg.cso.uiuc.edu/pg`).

The first interfaces to retrieve this information were clumsy and hard to use. All that changed with the appearance of the *World Wide Web* (WWW). The World Wide Web brought two major advances to Internet information. The information could contain *graphics* and *fonts*—a great improvement over the older text-only format—and it became possible to embed *links* to other information pages. Using a *browser* such as *Mosaic* or *Netscape,* exploring the information becomes easy and fun (Figure 22).

Chapter Summary

1. We use objects in our program when we need to manipulate data that are more complex than just numbers and strings. Every object belongs to a class. A class determines the behavior of its objects. In this chapter we became familiar with objects from a number of classes that were predefined for use with this textbook. However, we must wait until Chapter 8 to be able to define our own classes.

2. Objects are constructed with the constructor notation. Once an object is constructed, member functions can be applied to it with the dot notation.

3. This book describes a library of graphical structures that are used for interesting and entertaining examples. Points, lines, circles, and messages can be displayed on a window in the computer screen. Programs can obtain both text and mouse input from the user. When writing programs that display data sets, you should select a coordinate system that fits the data points.

Further Reading

[1] C. Eames and R. Eames, *A Computer Perspective,* Harvard Press, Cambridge, MA, 1973. A pictorial based on an exhibition of the history and social impact of computing. It contains many entertaining and interesting pictures of historic computing devices, their inventors, and their impact on modern life.

Review Exercises

Exercise R3.1. Explain the difference between an object and a class.

Exercise R3.2. Give the C++ code for an *object* of class `Time` and for an *object variable* of class `Time`.

Exercise R3.3. Explain the differences between a member function and a nonmember function.

Exercise R3.4. Explain the difference between

```
Point(3, 4);
```

and

```
Point p(3, 4);
```

Exercise R3.5. What are the construction parameters for a `Circle` object?

Exercise R3.6. What is default construction?

Exercise R3.7. Give C++ code to construct the following objects:

- Your next birthday
- The current time
- The top right corner of the graphics window in the default coordinate system
- Your instructor as an employee (make a guess for the salary)
- A circle filling the entire graphics window in the default coordinate system
- A line representing the x-axis from -10 to 10.

Write just objects, not object variables.

Exercise R3.8. Repeat the preceding exercise, but now define variables that are initialized with the required values.

Exercise R3.9. Find the errors in the following statements:

```
Time now();
Point p = (3, 4);
p.set_x(-1);
cout << Time(1997, 5, 8, 0, 0, 0);
Time due_date(1997, 5, 31, 12, 0, 0);
Time birthday(1959, 6, 16, 5, 30, 0);
due_date.move(2, 12);
seconds_from(millennium);
Employee harry("Hacker", "Harry", 35000);
harry.set_name("Hacker, Harriet");
```

Exercise R3.10. Describe all constructors of the `Time` class. List all member functions that can be used to change a `Time` object. List all member functions that don't change the `Time` object.

Exercise R3.11. What is the value of `t` after the following operations?

```
Time t;
t = Time(1999, 12, 31, 20, 0, 0);
t.add_seconds(10000);
t.add_seconds(-2000);
```

Exercise R3.12. If `t1` and `t2` are objects of class `Time`, is the following true or false?

`t1.add_seconds(t2.seconds_from(t1))` is the same time as `t2`

Exercise R3.13. Which five classes are used in this book for graphics programming?

Exercise R3.14. What is the value of `c.get_center` and `c.get_radius` after the following operations?

```
Circle c(Point(1, 2), 3);
c.move(4, 5);
```

Exercise R3.15. You want to plot a bar chart showing the grade distribution of all students in your class (where A = 4.0, F = 0). What coordinate system would you choose to make the plotting as simple as possible?

Exercise R3.16. Let `c` be any circle. Write C++ code to plot the circle `c` and another circle that touches `c`. *Hint:* Use `move`.

Exercise R3.17. Write C++ instructions to display the letters X and T in a graphics window, by plotting line segments.

Exercise R3.18. Introduce an error in the program intsect2.cpp, by computing `root = sqrt(radius * radius + b * b)`. Run the program. What happens to the intersection points?

Exercise R3.19. Suppose you run the program intsect2.cpp and give a value of 5 for the radius of the circle and 4 for the line position. Without actually running the program, determine what values you will obtain for the intersection points.

Programming Exercises

Exercise P3.1. Write a program that asks for the due date of the next assignment (month, day, hour). Set the year of the due date to the current year, and the minutes and seconds to 0. Then print the number of hours between the current time and the due date.

Exercise P3.2. Write a graphics program that prompts the user to click on three points. Then draw a triangle joining the three points. *Hint:* To give the user feedback about the click, it is a nice touch to draw the point after each click:

```
Point p = cwin.get_mouse("Please click on the first point");
cwin << p; /* Feedback for the user */
```

Exercise P3.3. Write a graphics program that prompts the user to click on the center of a circle, then on one of the points on the boundary of the circle. Draw the circle that the user specified. *Hint:* The radius of the circle is the distance between the two points, which is computed as

$$\sqrt{(a_x - b_x)^2 + (a_y - b_y)^2}.$$

Exercise P3.4. Write a graphics program that prompts the user to click on two points. Then draw a line joining the points and write a message displaying the *slope* of the line; that is, the "rise over run" ratio. The message should be displayed at the *midpoint* of the line.

Exercise P3.5. Write a graphics program that prompts the user to click on two points. Then draw a line joining the points and write a message displaying the *length* of the line, as computed by the Pythagorean formula. The message should be displayed at the *midpoint* of the line.

Exercise P3.6. Write a graphics program that prompts the user to click on three points. Then draw a circle passing through the three points.

Exercise P3.7. Write a program that prompts the user for the first name and last name of an employee and a starting salary. Then give the employee a 5 percent raise, and print out the name and salary information stored in the employee object.

Exercise P3.8. Write a program that prompts the user for the names and salaries of three employees. Then print out the average salaries of the employees.

Exercise P3.9. Write a program to plot the following face.

Exercise P3.10. Write a program to plot the string "HELLO", using just lines and circles. Do not use the `Message` class, and do not use `cout`.

Exercise P3.11. Write a program that lets a user select two lines by prompting the user to click on both end points of the first segment, then on both end points of the second segment. Then compute the point of intersection of the lines extending through those segments, and plot it. (If the segments are parallel, then the lines don't intersect, or they are identical. In the formulas computing the intersection, this will manifest itself as a division by 0. Since you don't yet know how to write code involving decisions, your program will terminate when the division by 0 happens. Doing so is acceptable for *this* assignment.)

Here is the mathematics to compute the point of intersection. If **a** and **b** are the end points of the first line segment, then $t\mathbf{a} + (1 - t)\,\mathbf{b}$ runs through all points on the first line as t runs from $-\infty$ to ∞. If **c** and **d** are the end points of the second line segment, the second line is the collection of points $u\mathbf{c} + (1 - u)\mathbf{d}$. The point of intersection is the point lying on both lines. That is, it is the solution of both

$$t\mathbf{a} + (1 - t)\mathbf{b} = u\mathbf{c} + (1 - u)\mathbf{d}$$

and

$$(\mathbf{a} - \mathbf{b})t + (\mathbf{d} - \mathbf{c})u = \mathbf{d} - \mathbf{b}$$

Writing the x and y coordinates separately, we get a system of two linear equations

$$(\mathbf{a}_x - \mathbf{b}_x)t + (\mathbf{d}_x - \mathbf{c}_x)u = \mathbf{d}_x - \mathbf{b}_x$$

$$(\mathbf{a}_y - \mathbf{b}_y)t + (\mathbf{d}_y - \mathbf{c}_y)u = \mathbf{d}_y - \mathbf{b}_y$$

Find the solutions of this system. You just need the value for t. Then compute the point of intersection as $t\mathbf{a} + (1 - t)\mathbf{b}$.

Exercise P3.12. *Plotting a data set.* Make a bar chart to plot a data set like the following:

Name	**Longest span (ft)**
Golden Gate	4,200
Brooklyn	1,595
Delaware Memorial	2,150
Mackinaw	3,800

Prompt the user to type in four names and measurements. Then display a bar graph. Make the bars horizontal for easier labeling.

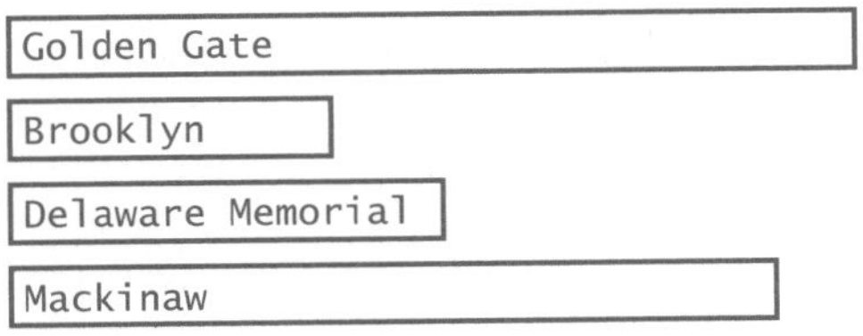

Hint: Set the window coordinates to 5,000 in the x-direction and 4 in the y-direction.

Exercise P3.13. Write a program that displays the Olympic rings. *Hint:* Construct and display the first circle, then call `move` four times.

Exercise P3.14. Write a graphics program that asks the user to enter the names of three employees and their salaries. Make three employee objects. Draw a stick chart showing the names and salaries of the employees.

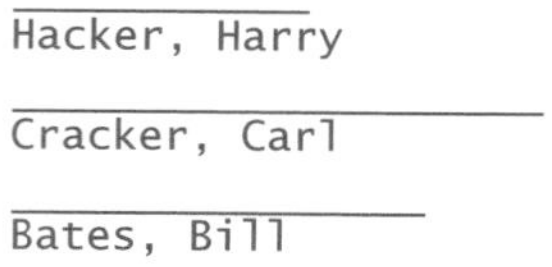

Exercise P3.15. Write a graphics program that asks the user to enter four data values. Then draw a pie chart showing the data values.

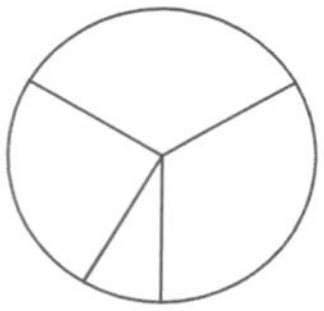

Exercise P3.16. Write a graphics program that draws a clock face with the current time:

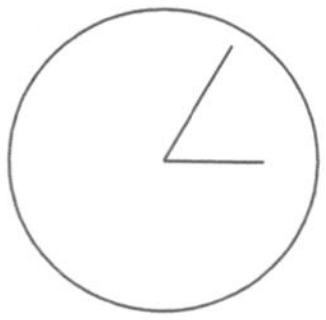

Hint: You need to find out the angles of the hour hand and the minute hand. The angle of the minute hand is easy: The minute hand travels 360 degrees in 60 minutes. The angle of the hour hand is harder; it travels 360 degrees in 12×60 minutes.

Exercise P3.17. Write a program that tests how fast a user can type. Get the time. Ask the user to type "The quick brown fox jumps over the lazy dog". Read a line of input. Get the current time again in another variable of type `Time`. Print out the seconds between the two times.

Exercise P3.18. Write a program that prints out how many days a month has. Ask the user for the month and year. Make a time describing the first day of the *next* month. Subtract one day's worth of seconds. That gets the last day of the month that the user entered. For example,

```
Please enter the month and year: 2 1996
29 days
```

Exercise P3.19. Your boss, Juliet Jones, is getting married and decides to change her name. Complete the following program so that you can type in the new name for the boss:

```
int main()
{  Employee boss("Jones, Juliet", 45000.00);
   your code goes here; leave the code above and below unchanged

   cout << "Name: " << boss.get_name() << "\n";
   cout << "Salary: " << boss.get_salary() << "\n";

   return EXIT_SUCCESS;
}
```

The problem is that there is no `set_name` member function for the `Employee` class. *Hint:* Make a new object of type `Employee` with the new name and the same salary. Then assign the new object to `boss`.

Exercise P3.20. Write a program that draws the picture of a house. It could be as simple as the figure below, or if you like, make it more elaborate (3-D, skyscraper, marble columns in the entryway, whatever).

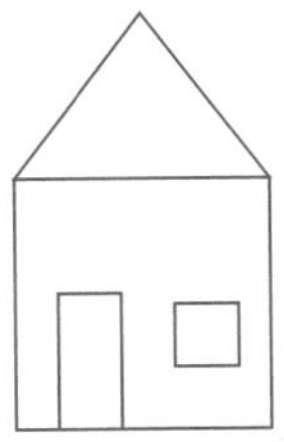

CHAPTER 4

Decisions

Objectives

- To be able to implement decisions using `if` statements
- To understand statement blocks and nesting
- To learn how to compare integers, floating-point numbers, and strings
- To develop strategies for processing input and handling input errors
- To recognize the correct ordering of decisions in multiple branches
- To program conditions using Boolean operators and variables

The programs we saw so far were able to do fast computations and render graphs, but they were very inflexible. Except for variations in the input, they worked the same way with every program run. One of the essential features of nontrivial computer programs is the ability to make decisions and to carry out different actions, depending on the nature of the inputs. The goal of this chapter is to learn how to program simple and complex decisions.

4.1 The `if` Statement

Consider the last program from the preceding chapter. That program computes the points of intersection between a line and a circle, as long as the line and circle actually meet. If the line and circle do not meet, the program crashes with a math error, because it is trying to compute a square root of a negative number.

Programs should never crash. It is the programmer's responsibility to anticipate problems. In this case, let us plot the intersection points only when the line and circle actually meet. Otherwise we simply don't plot anything.

The `if` statement is used to implement a decision. The `if` statement has two parts: a *test* and a *body*. If the test succeeds, the body of the statement is executed. The body of the `if` statement can consist of a single statement:

```
if (quarters > 0)
   cout << "Give the customer " << quarters
   << " quarters.\n";
```

The message "Give the customer . . . quarters" is printed only when the count of quarters is positive. That eliminates the annoying message "Give the customer 0 quarters." (See Figure 1.)

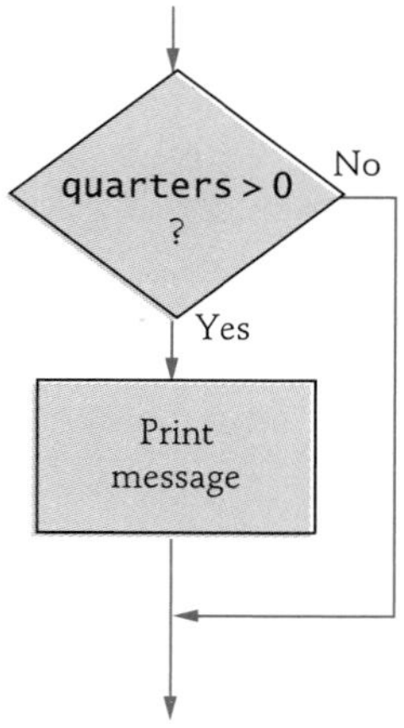

Figure 1

A Decision

Quite often, however, the body of the `if` statement consists of multiple statements that must be executed in sequence whenever the test is successful. These statements must be grouped together to form a *block statement* by enclosing them in braces {}.

Program intsect3.cpp

```
#define CCC_WIN
#include "ccc.h"

int main()
{  float radius = cwin.get_float("Radius: ");
   Circle c(Point(0, 0), radius);

   float b = cwin.get_float("Line position: ");
   Line s(Point(-10, b), Point(10, b));

   cwin << c << s;

   float r = radius * radius - b * b;
   if (r >= 0)
   {  float root = sqrt(r);

      Point p1(root, b);
      Point p2(-root, b);

      cwin << p1 << p2;
   }

   return EXIT_SUCCESS;
}
```

The purpose of the test is to compute the square root only if `r` is greater than or equal to (denoted as >=) 0. In that case, the intersection points also need to be be computed and plotted. If the test fails, the square root of the negative `r` is not computed—avoiding the crash—and no points are plotted either.

Quality Tip 4.1

Brace Layout

The compiler doesn't care where you place braces, but we strongly recommend that you follow the simple rule of making { and } line up.

```
int main()
{  float r;
   . . .
   if (r >= 0)
```

```
    {  float root = sqrt(r);
          . . .
    }
    . . .
    return EXIT_SUCCESS
}
```

This scheme makes it easy to spot matching braces. Some programmers put the opening brace on the same line as the `if`:

```
if (r >= 0) {
   float root = sqrt(r);
   . . .
}
```

That makes it harder to match the braces. Other programmers place the opening brace on a line by itself:

```
if (r >= 0)
{
   float root = sqrt(r);
   . . .
}
```

That seems a waste of precious screen space.

It is important that you pick a layout scheme and stick with it consistently. Which scheme you choose may depend on your personal preference or a coding style guide that you need to follow.

Productivity Hint 4.1

Tabs

Block-structured code has the property that nested statements are indented by one or more levels:

```
int main()

{  float r;
   . . .
   if (r >= 0)
   {  float root = sqrt(r);.
      . . .
   }
   . . .
   return EXIT_SUCCESS
}

↑  ↑  ↑
0  1  2
```

Indentation level

How many spaces should you use per indentation level? Some programmers use eight spaces per level, but that isn't a good choice:

```
int main()
{      float r;
       . . .
       if (r >= 0)
       {      float root = sqrt(r);
              . . .
       }
       . . .
       return EXIT_SUCCESS
}
```

It crowds the code too much to the right side of the screen. As a consequence, long expressions frequently must be broken into separate lines. More common values are 2, 3, or 4 spaces per indentation level.

How do you move the cursor from the leftmost column to the appropriate indentation level? A perfectly reasonable strategy is to hit the space bar a sufficient number of times. However, many programmers use the Tab key instead. A tab moves the cursor to the next tab stop. By default, there are tab stops every 8 columns, but most editors let you change that value; you should find out how to set your editor's tab stops to, say, every 3 columns. Note that the Tab key does not simply enter three spaces. It moves the cursor to the next tab column. For example, to enter the lines

```
if (r >= 0)
{  float root = sqrt(r);
   Point p1;
```

you type

```
Tab  if (r >= 0) Enter
Tab  { Tab float root = sqrt(r); Enter
Tab  Tab Point p1;
```

Some editors actually help you out with an *autoindent* feature. They automatically insert as many tabs or spaces as the preceding line had, because it is quite likely that the new line is supposed to be on the same indentation level. If it isn't, you must add or remove a tab, but that is still faster than tabbing all the way from the left margin.

As nice as tabs are for data entry, they have one disadvantage: They can mess up printouts. If you send a file with tabs to a printer, the printer may either ignore the tabs altogether or set tab stops every eight columns. It is therefore best to save and print your files with spaces instead of tabs. Some editors automatically convert tabs to spaces for printing. If yours does not, you need a *tab filter:* a program that performs that replacement.

4.2 Relational Operators

Every `if` statement performs a test. In many cases, the test compares two values. For example, in the previous examples we tested `quarters > 0` and `root >= 0`. The comparisons > and >= are called *relational operators.* C++ has six relational operators:

C++	Math notation	Description
>	$>$	Greater than
>=	$\geq$	Greater than or equal
<	$<$	Less than
<=	$\leq$	Less than or equal
==	$=$	Equal
!=	$\neq$	Not equal

As you can see, only two C++ relational operators (> and <) look as you would expect from the mathematical notation. Computer keyboards do not have keys for $\geq$, $\leq$ or $\neq$, but the >=, <= and != operators are easy to remember because they look similar. The == operator is initially confusing to most newcomers to C++. In C++, = already has a meaning, namely assignment. The == operator denotes equality testing:

```
a = 5; /* assign 5 to a */
if (a == 5) ...   /* test whether a equals 5 */
```

You will have to remember to use == always inside tests and to use = always outside tests. See Common Error 4.1 for more information.

You can compare strings as well:

```
if (name == "Harry")  ...
```

In C++ letter case matters. For example, "Harry" and "HARRY" are not the same string. To ignore the letter case, force the strings to uppercase and then compare them:

```
if (uppercase(name) != uppercase(boss.get_name())) ...
```

If you compare keys using < <= > >=, they are compared in dictionary order. For example, the test

```
string name = "Tom";
if (name < "Dick")  ...
```

fails because in the dictionary Dick comes before Tom. Actually, the dictionary ordering used by C++ is slightly different from that of a normal dictionary. C++ is case-sensitive and sorts characters by listing numbers first, then uppercase characters, then lowercase characters. For example, 1 comes before B, which comes before a. The space character comes before all other characters. Strictly speaking, the character sort order is implementation-dependent, but the majority of systems use the so-called *ASCII code* (American Standard Code for Information Interchange), or one of its extensions, whose characters are sorted as described.

Let us investigate the comparison process closely. When comparing two strings, corresponding letters are compared until one of the strings ends or the first difference

Figure 2

Lexicographic Ordering

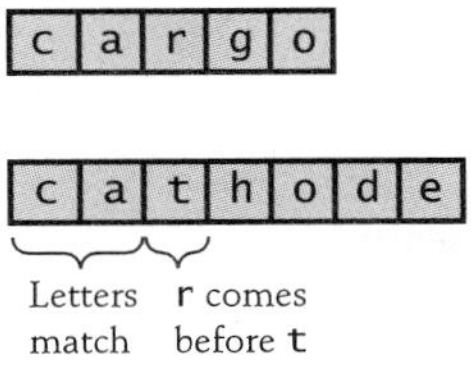

is encountered. If one of the strings ends, the longer string is considered the later one. If a character mismatch is found, compare the characters to determine which string comes later in the dictionary sequence. This process is called *lexicographic* comparison. For example, compare `"car"` with `"cargo"`. The first three letters match, and we reach the end of the first string. Therefore `"car"` comes before `"cargo"` in the lexicographic ordering. Now compare `"cathode"` with `"cargo"`. The first two letters match. Since `t` comes after `r`, the string `"cathode"` comes after `"cargo"` in lexicographic ordering. (See Figure 2.)

You can only compare numbers with numbers and strings with strings. The test

```
string name = "Harry";
if (name > 5)   . . .   /* Error */
```

is not valid.

You can use the relational operators only for numbers and strings. You cannot use them to compare objects. For example,

```
Point p(1, 1);
cwin << p;
Point q = cwin.get_mouse("Click on the point!");
. . .
if (p == q)  . . .  /* Error */
```

That is unfortunate. Instead, you must test that `p.get_x()` equals `q.get_x()` and that `p.get_y()` equals `q.get_y()`.

Common Error 4.1

Confusing = and ==

The rule for the correct usage of = and == is very simple: In tests, always use == and never use =. If it is so simple, why can't the compiler be helpful and flag any errors?

Actually, the C++ language allows the use of = inside tests. To understand this, we have to go back in time. For historical reasons, the expression inside an `if (...)` need not be a logical condition. Any numeric value can be used inside a condition, with the convention that 0 denotes false and any non-0 value denotes true. Furthermore, in C++ assignments are also expressions and have values. For example, the value of the expression `x = 5` is 5. That can be convenient—you can capture the value of an intermediate expression in a variable:

```
x1 = (-b - (r = sqrt(b * b - 4 * a * c))) / (2 * a);
x2 = (- b + r) / (2 * a);
```

The expression `r = sqrt(b * b - 4 * a * c)` has a value, namely the value that is assigned to `r`, and thus can be nested inside the larger expression. We don't recommend this style of programming, because it is not much more trouble to set `r` first and then set `x1` and `x2`, but there are situations in which the construction is useful.

These two features—namely that numbers can be used as truth values and that assignments are expressions with values—conspire to make a horrible pitfall. The test

```
if (x = y) ...
```

is legal C++, but it does not test whether `x` and `y` are equal. Instead, the code sets `x` to `y`, and if that value is not zero, the body of the `if` statement is executed.

Fortunately, most compilers issue a warning when they encounter such a statement. You should take such warnings extremely seriously. (See Quality Tip 4.2 for more advice about compiler warnings.)

Some shell-shocked programmers are so nervous about using = that they use == even when they want to make an assignment:

```
x2 == (- b + r) / (2 * a);
```

Again, this is legal C++. This statement tests whether `x2` equals the expression of the right-hand side. It doesn't do anything with the outcome of the test, but that is not an error. Some compilers will warn that "the code has no effect", but others will quietly accept the code.

Quality Tip 4.2

Compile with Zero Warnings

There are two kinds of messages that the compiler gives you: *errors* and *warnings*. Error messages are fatal; the compiler will not translate a program with one or more errors. Warning messages are advisory; the compiler will translate the program, but there is a good chance that the program will not do what you expect it to do.

You should make an effort to write code that emits no warnings at all. Usually, you can avoid warnings by convincing the compiler that you know what you are doing. For example, many compilers warn of a possible loss of information when you assign a floating-point expression to an integer variable:

```
int pennies = 100 * (amount_due - amount_paid);
```

Just use the `round` function to round properly to an integer, and the compiler will stop complaining:

```
int pennies = round(100 * (amount_due - amount_paid));
```

Some compilers emit warnings that cannot be avoided. For example, one popular PC compiler emits a warning "missing module definition file" whenever a console program is compiled. For a simple program, no such file is needed or useful, but the compiler warns nonetheless. Your instructor can tell you whether your compiler generates warnings that you can't avoid.

Common Error 4.2

Comparison of Floating-Point Numbers

Floating-point numbers have only a limited precision, and calculations can introduce roundoff errors. For example, the following code multiplies the square root of 2 by itself. We expect to get the answer 2:

```
float r = sqrt(2);
if (r * r == 2) cout << "sqrt(2) squared is 2\n";
else cout "sqrt(2) squared is not 2 but " <<  r * r << "\n".
```

Strangely enough, this program prints

```
sqrt(2) squared is not 2 but 2
```

To see what really happens, we need to see the output with higher precision and print `format("%.10f", r * r)` instead of just `r * r`. Then the answer is

```
sqrt(2) squared is not 2 but 1.9999998808
```

That certainly explains why `r * r` didn't compare to be equal to 2. Unfortunately, roundoff errors are unavoidable. It plainly does not make sense in most circumstances to compare floating-point numbers exactly. Instead, we should test whether they are *close enough*. That is, the magnitude of their difference should be less than some threshold. Mathematically, we would write that x and y are close enough if

$$|x - y| \leq \epsilon$$

for a very small number, ϵ. ϵ is the Greek letter epsilon, a letter commonly used to denote a very small quantity. It is common to set ϵ to 10^{-6} when comparing `float` numbers.

However, this is not quite good enough. Suppose x and y are rather large, say a few million each. Then one could be a roundoff error for the other even if their difference was quite a bit larger than 10^{-6}. To overcome this problem, we really need to test whether

$$\frac{|x - y|}{1 + \max(|x|, |y|)} \leq \epsilon$$

Similarly, if you want to test whether $x > y$, you must allow for the possibility that x and y are both slightly inaccurate. You only know for certain that $x > y$ if

$$\frac{x - y}{1 + \max(|x|, |y|)} > \epsilon$$

In C++, this code might look like this:

```
float denom = fabs(x);
if (fabs(y) > denom) denom = fabs(y);
if (fabs(x - y)/(1 + denom) <= EPSILON)   . . .
```

It would be tedious to program these comparisons every time. The header file ccc.h defines three functions, `float_equal`, `float_less`, and `float_greater`, which you should use instead.

Math notation	Floating-point test
$x = y$	`float_equal(x, y)`
$x \neq y$	`not float_equal(x, y)`
$x > y$	`float_greater(x, y)`
$x \leq y$	`not float_greater(x, y)`
$x < y$	`float_less(x, y)`
$x \geq y$	`not float_less(x, y)`

The meaning of the `not` operator is explained in Section 4.5.

4.3 Input Validation

An important application for the `if` statement is *input validation*. For simple programs, it is entirely acceptable to abort the program with an error message when the user specifies wrong input. (Of course, for more substantial programs the programmer must try harder. It wouldn't be acceptable if your spreadsheet program terminated without saving your work, just because you provided a bad input.)

The following code ensures that a value is positive:

Program readage1.cpp

```
#include "iostream.h"
#include "stdlib.h"
#include "math.h"

int main()
{  int age;
   cout << "Please enter your age: ";
   cin >> age;
   if (age < 0)
   {  cout << "Error: age cannot be negative\n";
      return EXIT_FAILURE;
   }
   /* now we know that age is ≥ 0 */

   cout << "The square root of your age is "
      << sqrt(age) << "\n";

   return EXIT_SUCCESS;
}
```

This program simply prints an error message and returns with a failure code if the input is invalid. (It is possible to test whether a program terminated successfully or with a failure, but the details are system-dependent. We simply follow the convention of having `main` return `EXIT_SUCCESS` when a program completes its task normally, `EXIT_FAILURE` otherwise.)

As we discussed previously, the program user must enter a sequence of digits when reading an integer from an input stream. If the user types in `five` when the program processes `cin >> age` for an integer `age`, then the variable `age` is not set and the stream is set to a failed state. You can test for that failed state.

```
if (cin.fail())
{  cout << "Error: bad input\n";
   return EXIT_FAILURE;
}
```

For practical programs it is important to carry out that test after *every* input. Users cannot be trusted to enter data with perfect consistency, and a serious program must validate every input. To validate the `age` input fully, we must first test that *some* integer was read successfully and then test whether that integer was positive.

Program readage2.cpp

```
#include "iostream.h"
#include "stdlib.h"
#include "math.h"

int main()
{  int age;
   cout << "Please enter your age: ";
   cin >> age;
   if (cin.fail())
   {  cout << "Error: bad input\n";
      return EXIT_FAILURE;
   }
   /* now we know that age is valid */
   if (age < 0)
   {  cout << "Error: age cannot be negative\n";
      return EXIT_FAILURE;
   }
   /* now we know that age is ≥ 0 */

   cout << "The square root of your age is "
      << sqrt(age) << "\n";

   return EXIT_SUCCESS;
}
```

The order of the `if` statements is important. Suppose we reversed the order:

```
int age;
cin >> age;

if (age < 0)
{  cout << "Error: age cannot be negative\n";
   return EXIT_FAILURE;
}
if (cin.fail())
{  cout << "Error: bad input\n";
   return EXIT_FAILURE;
}
```

If the user types an invalid input, such as `five`, then the statement `cin >> age` does not touch the value of `age`. However, `age` was never initialized, so it contains a random value. There is a 50 percent chance that the random value is negative. In that case, a confusing message "Error: age cannot be negative" is displayed.

Quality Tip 4.3

Avoid Conditions with Side Effects

As described in Common Error 4.1, it is legal to nest assignment statements inside test conditions:

```
if ((d = b * b - 4 * a * c) >= 0) r = sqrt(d);
```

It is also legal to read a number and then test the input stream:

```
if ((cin >> x).fail()) cout << "Error\n";
```

It is legal to use the increment operator inside other expressions:

```
if (n-- > 0)  . . .
```

All these are bad programming practice, because they mix a test with another activity. The other activity (setting the variable `d`, reading `x`, decrementing `n`) is called a *side effect* of the test.

As we will see in Advanced Topic 6.2, conditions with side effects can occasionally be helpful to simplify *loops*. For `if` statements, they should always be avoided.

4.4 The `if/else` Statement

Let us enhance the plotting program to give a message to the user when the line and circle do not intersect.

Of course, we could program two complementary `if` statements:

```
float r = c.radius * c.radius - b * b;
if (r >= 0)
{  float root = sqrt(r);

   Point p1(root, b);
   Point p2(-root, b);

   cwin << p1 << p2;
}

if (r < 0)
{  Message error(Point(0, 0), "No intersection");
   cwin << error;

}
```

There are two problems with this approach. First, if we need to modify the condition `r >= 0` for some reason, we must remember to update the condition `r < 0` as well. If we do not, then the logic of the program is no longer correct. And we must be careful not to modify the value of `r` in the body of the first `if` statement.

To implement a true alternative, use the `if/else` statement:

Program intsect4.cpp

```
#define CCC_WIN
#include "ccc.h"

int main()
{  float radius = cwin.get_float("Radius: ");
   Circle c(Point(0, 0), radius);

   float b = cwin.get_float("Line position: ");
   Line s(Point(-10, b), Point(10, b));

   cwin << c << s;
   float r = radius * radius - b * b;
   if (r >= 0)
   {  float root = sqrt(r);

      Point p1(root, b);
      Point p2(-root, b);

      cwin << p1  << p2;
   }
   else
```

Figure 3

Flowchart for `if/else` Statement

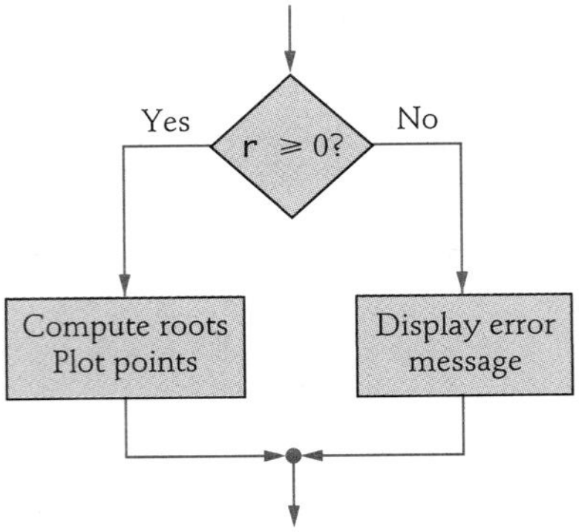


```
    {  Message error(Point(0, 0), "No intersection");
       cwin << error;
    }

    return EXIT_SUCCESS;
}
```

Now there is only one condition. If it is satisfied, the first block is executed. Otherwise, the second block is executed.

The flowchart in Figure 3 gives a graphical representation of the branching behavior.

A statement such as

```
y = x;
```

or

```
cout << x;
```

is called a *simple statement*. A group of statements, enclosed in braces, is called a *block*.

```
{  Message error(Point(0, 0), "No intersection");
   cwin << error;
}
```

A conditional statement is called a *compound statement*.

```
if (x >= 0) y = x;
else { y = -x; s = -1; }
```

In Chapter 6 we will encounter other compound statements: so-called *loops*.

If either of the alternatives consists of a *single* statement (either simple or compound), you do not need to enclose it in braces. For example, the following code sets `y` to the absolute value of `x`:

```
if (x >= 0) y = x;
else y = -x;
```

Advanced Topic 4.1

The Selection Operator

C++ has a selection operator of the form

test ? *value1* : *value2*

The value of that expression is either *value1* if the test passes or *value2* if it fails. For example, we can compute the absolute value as

```
y = x >= 0 ? x : -x;
```

which is a convenient shorthand for

```
if (x >= 0) y = x;
else y = -x;
```

The selection operator is similar to the `if/else` statement, but it works on a different syntactical level. The selection operator combines *expressions* and yields another expression. The `if/else` statement combines statements and yields another statement.

Expressions have values. For example, `-b + sqrt(r)` is an expression, as is `x >= 0 ? x : -x;`. Any expression can be made into a statement by adding a semicolon. For example, `y = x` is an expression (with value `x`), but `y = x;` is a statement. Statements do not have values. Since `if/else` forms a statement and does not have a value, you cannot write

```
y = if (x > 0) x; else -x; /* Error */
```

We don't use the selection operator in this book, but it is a convenient and legitimate construct that you will find in many C++ programs.

4.5 Multiple Alternatives

Consider a program that asks the user to specify a coin. The user will input "3 dimes" or "4 nickels". We only look at the first four characters in the input string. That way, we don't have to worry about singular or plural (1 penny, 3 pennies). Of course, if the user enters "4 dimetrodons", we will count that as dimes, not dinosaurs—a risk that we are willing to take in this program.

Program coins6.cpp

```
#include "ccc.h"

int main()
{  int n;
   string name;
   cin >> n >> name;
   name = name.substr(0, 4);
```

```
   float value = 0;

   if (name == "penn")
      value = n * 0.01;
   else if (name == "nick")
      value = n * 0.05;
   else if (name == "dime")
      value = n * 0.10;
   else if (name == "quar")
      value = value * 0.25;
   else
      cout << name << " is not a valid coin name\n";
   cout << "Value = " << value << "\n";

   return EXIT_SUCCESS;
}
```

This code distinguishes between five cases: The name can be "penn", "nick", "dime", or "quar", or something else. As soon as one of the first four tests succeeds, the appropriate variable is updated, and no further tests are attempted. If none of the four cases applies, an error message is printed. Figure 4 shows the flowchart for this multiple branch statement.

In this example the order of the tests was not important. Now let us consider a test where the order is important. The next program asks for a value describing the magnitude of an earthquake on the Richter scale and prints a description of the likely impact of the quake. The Richter scale is a measurement for the strength of an earthquake. Every step in the scale, for example from 6.0 to 7.0, signifies a tenfold increase in the strength of the quake. The 1989 Loma Prieta earthquake that damaged the Bay Bridge in San Francisco and destroyed many buildings in several Bay Area cities rated 7.1 on the Richter scale.

Program richter.cpp

```
#include "ccc.h"

int main()
{  cout << "Enter a magnitude on the Richter scale: ";
   float richter;
   cin >> richter;

   if (richter >= 8.0)
      cout << "Most structures fall\n";
   else if (richter >= 7.0)
      cout << "Many buildings destroyed\n";
   else if (richter >= 6.0)
      cout << "Many buildings considerably damaged;"
         << "some collapse\n";
```

Figure 4

Multiple Alternatives

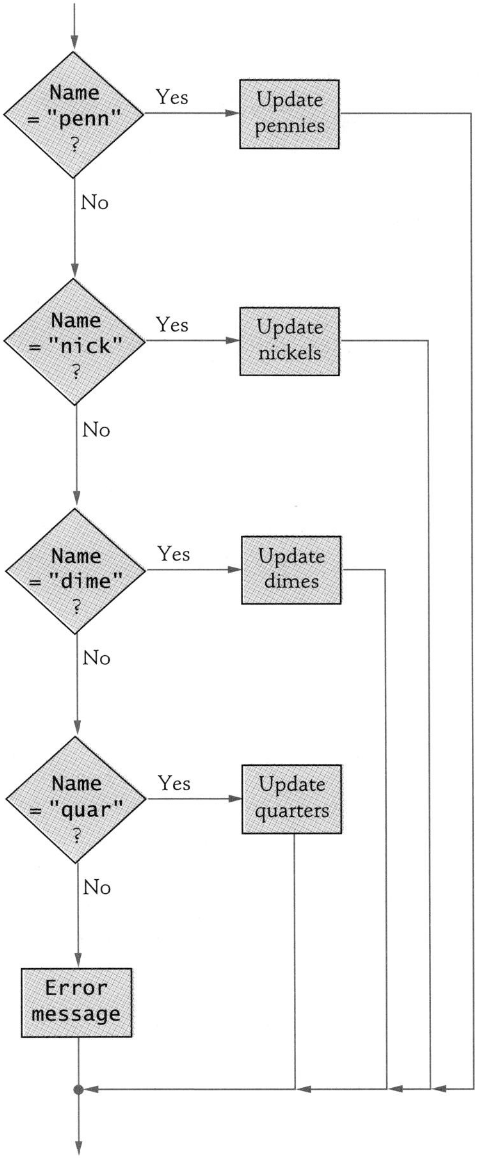

```
    else if (richter >= 4.5)
       cout << "Damage to poorly constructed buildings\n";
    else if (richter >= 3.5)
       cout << "Felt by many people, no destruction\n";
    else if (richter >= 0)
       cout << "Generally not felt by people\n";
    else
       cout << "Negative numbers are not valid\n";

    return EXIT_SUCCESS;
}
```

Here we must sort the conditions and test against the largest cutoff first. Suppose we reverse the order of tests:

```
if (richter >= 0) /* Tests in wrong order */
   cout << "Generally not felt by people\n";
else if (richter >= 3.5)
   cout << "Felt by many people, no destruction\n";
else if (richter >= 4.5)
   cout << "Damage to poorly constructed buildings\n";
else if (richter >= 6.0)
   cout << "Many buildings considerably damaged;"
      << "some collapse\n";
else if (richter >= 7.0)
   cout << "Many buildings destroyed\n";
else if (richter >= 8.0)
   cout << "Most structures fall\n";
```

This does not work. All positive values of `richter` fall into the first case, and the other tests will never be attempted.

In this example, it is also important that we use an `if/else/else` test, not just multiple independent `if` statements. Consider this sequence of independent tests:

```
if (richter >= 8.0) /* Didn't use else */
   cout << "Most structures fall\n";
if (richter >= 7.0)
   cout << "Many buildings destroyed\n";
if (richter >= 6.0)
   cout << "Many buildings considerably damaged;"
      << "some collapse\n";
if (richter >= 4.5)
   cout << "Damage to poorly constructed buildings\n";
if (richter >= 3.5)
   cout << "Felt by many people, no destruction\n";
if (richter >= 0)
   cout << "Generally not felt by people\n";
```

Now the alternatives are no longer exclusive. If `richter` is 5.0, then the first *four* tests all match, and four messages are printed.

Advanced Topic 4.2

The `switch` Statement

A sequence of `if/else/else` that compares a *single integer value* against several *constant* alternatives can be implemented as a `switch` statement. For example,

```
int digit;
...
switch(digit)
{  case 1: digit_name = "one"; break;
   case 2: digit_name = "two"; break;
   case 3: digit_name = "three"; break;
   case 4: digit_name = "four"; break;
   case 5: digit_name = "five"; break;
   case 6: digit_name = "six"; break;
   case 7: digit_name = "seven"; break;
   case 8: digit_name = "eight"; break;
   case 9: digit_name = "nine"; break;
   default: digit_name = ""; break;
}
```

This is a shortcut for

```
int digit;
...
if (digit == 1) digit_name = "one";
else if (digit == 2) digit_name = "two";
else if (digit == 3) digit_name = "three";
else if (digit == 4) digit_name = "four";
else if (digit == 5) digit_name = "five";
else if (digit == 6) digit_name = "six";
else if (digit == 7) digit_name = "seven";
else if (digit == 8) digit_name = "eight";
else if (digit == 9) digit_name = "nine";
else digit_name = "";
```

Well, it isn't much of a shortcut. It has one advantage—it is obvious that all branches test the *same* value, namely `digit`—but the `switch` statement can be applied only in narrow circumstances. The test cases must be constants, and they must be integers. You cannot use

```
switch(name)
{  case "penn": ... break; /* Error */
   ...
}
```

There is a reason for these limitations. The compiler can generate efficient test code (using so-called jump tables or binary searches) in just the situation that is permitted in a `switch` statement. Of course, modern compilers will be happy to perform the same optimization for a sequence of alternatives in an `if/else/else` statement, so the need for the `switch` has largely gone away.

We forgo the `switch` statement in this book for a different reason. Every branch of the switch must be terminated by a `break` instruction. If the `break` is missing, execution *falls through* to the next branch, and so on, until finally a `break` or the end of the `switch` is reached. There are a few cases in which this is actually useful, but they are very rare. Peter van der Linden [1, p. 38] describes an analysis of the `switch` statements in the Sun C compiler front end. Of the 244 `switch` statements, each of which had an average of 7 cases, only 3 percent used the fall-through behavior. That is, the default—falling through to the next case unless stopped by a `break`—is *wrong 97 percent of the time.* Forgetting to type the `break` is an exceedingly common error, yielding wrong code.

We leave it to you to use the `switch` statement for your own code or not. At any rate, you need to have a reading knowledge of `switch` in case you find it in the code of other programmers.

Productivity Hint 4.2

Copy and Paste in the Editor

When you see code like

```
if (richter >= 8.0)
   cout << "Most structures fall\n";
else if (richter >= 7.0)
   cout << "Many buildings destroyed\n";
else if (richter >= 6.0)
   cout << "Many buildings considerably damaged;"
      << "some collapse\n";
else if (richter >= 4.5)
   cout << "Damage to poorly constructed buildings\n";
else if (richter >= 3.5)
   cout << "Felt by many people, no destruction\n";
```

you should think “copy and paste”.

Make a template

```
else if (richter >= )
   cout << "";
```

and copy it. That is usually done by highlighting with the mouse and then selecting Edit and then Copy from the menu bar. (If you follow Productivity Hint 3.1, you are smart and use the keyboard. Hit Shift+ ↓ to highlight the entire line, then Ctrl + C to copy it. Then paste it multiple times (Ctrl + V) and fill the text into the copy. Of course, your editor may use different commands, but the concept is the same.)

The ability to copy and paste is always useful when you have code from an example or another project that is similar to your current needs. To copy, paste, and modify is faster than to type everything from scratch. You are also less likely to make typing errors.

Random Fact 4.1

Minicomputers and Workstations

Within 20 years after the first computers became operational, they had become indispensable for organizing the customer and financial data of every major corporation in America. Corporate data processing required a centralized computer installation and high staffing levels to ensure the round-the-clock availability of the data. These installations were enormously expensive, but they were vital to run a modern business. Major universities and large research institutions could also afford the installation of these expensive computers, but many scientific and engineering organizations and corporate divisions could not.

In the mid-1960s, when integrated circuits first became available, the cost of computers could be brought down for users who did not require as high a level of support and services (or data storage volume) as corporate data processing installations. Such users included scientists and engineers who had the expertise to operate computers. (At that time, to "operate" a computer did not just mean to turn it on. Computers came with little off-the-shelf software, and most tasks had to be programmed by the computer users.) In 1965 Digital Equipment Corporation introduced the PDP-8 *minicomputer,* housed in a single cabinet (see Figure 5) and thus small enough for departmental use. In 1978, the first 32-bit minicomputer, the VAX, was released, also by DEC. Other companies, such as Data General, brought out competing designs; the book [2] contains a fascinating description of the engineering work at Data General to bring out a machine that could compete with the VAX. Minicomputers were not just used for engineering applications, however. System integration companies would buy these machines, supply software, and resell them to smaller companies for business data processing. Minicomputers such as IBM's successful AS/400 line are still in use today, but they face stiff competition from workstations and personal computers, which are much less expensive and have increasingly powerful software.

In the early 1980s, engineering users became increasingly disenchanted with having to share computers with other users. Computers did divide up their attention among multiple users who were currently logged on, a process known as *time sharing.* However, graphical terminals were becoming available, and the fast processing of graphics was more than could be done in the allotted time slices. The technology had again advanced to the point where an entire computer could be put into a box that would fit on a desk. A new breed of manufacturers, such as Sun Microsystems, started producing *workstations* (Figure 6). These computers are used by individuals with high computing demands—for example, electronic-circuit designers, aerospace engineers, and, more recently, cartoon artists. Workstations typically run an operating system called *Unix.* While each workstation manufacturer has its own brand of Unix, with slight differences in each version, it became economical for software manufacturers to produce programs that could run on several hardware platforms. This was aided by the fact that most workstation manufacturers standardized on the *X Windows* system for displaying graphics.

Not all workstation manufacturers were successful. The book [3] tells the story of NeXT, a company that tried to build a workstation and failed, losing over $250 million of its investors' money in the process.

Nowadays workstations are used mainly for two distinct purposes: as fast graphics processors and as *servers* to store data such as electronic mail, sales information, or World Wide Web pages.

Figure 5

A Minicomputer

Figure 6

A Workstation

4.6 Nested Branches

In the United States different tax rates are used depending on the taxpayer's marital status. There are two main tax schedules, for single and for married taxpayers. Married taxpayers add their income together and pay taxes on the total. (In fact, there are two other schedules, "head of household" and "married filing separately", which we will ignore for simplicity.) Table 1 gives the tax rate computations for each of the filing categories, using the values for the 1992 federal tax return.

Now let us compute the taxes due, given a filing status and an income figure. The key point is that there are two *levels* of decision making. First, we must branch on the filing status. Then, for each filing status, we must have another branch on income level.

Program tax.cpp

```
#include "ccc.h"

int main()
{  float income;
   float tax;

   cout << "Please enter your income: ";
   cin >> income;

   cout << "Please enter S for single, M for married: ";
   string marital_status;
   cin >> marital_status;
   if (uppercase(marital_status) == "S")
   {  if (income <= 21450.00)
         tax = 0.15 * income;
      else if (income <= 51900.00)
         tax = 3217.50 + 0.28 * (income - 21450.00);
      else
         tax = 11743.50 + 0.31 * (income - 51900.00);
   }
   else
   {  if (income <= 35800.00)
         tax = 0.15 * income;
      else if (income <= 86500.00)
         tax = 5370.00 + 0.28 * (income - 35800.00);
      else
         tax = 19566.00 + 0.31 * (income - 86500.00);
   }
   cout  << "The tax is $" << tax << "\n";
   return EXIT_SUCCESS;
}
```

Table 1 Federal Tax Rate Schedule

If your filing status is Single

If the taxable income is over	But not over	The tax is	Of the amount over
$0	$21,450	15%	$0
21,450	51,900	$3,217.50+28%	21,450
51,900		11,743.50+31%	51,900

If your filing status is Married

If the taxable income is over	But not over	The tax is	Of the amount over
$0	$35,800	15%	$0
35,800	86,500	$5,370.00+28%	35,800
86,500		19,566.00+31%	86,500

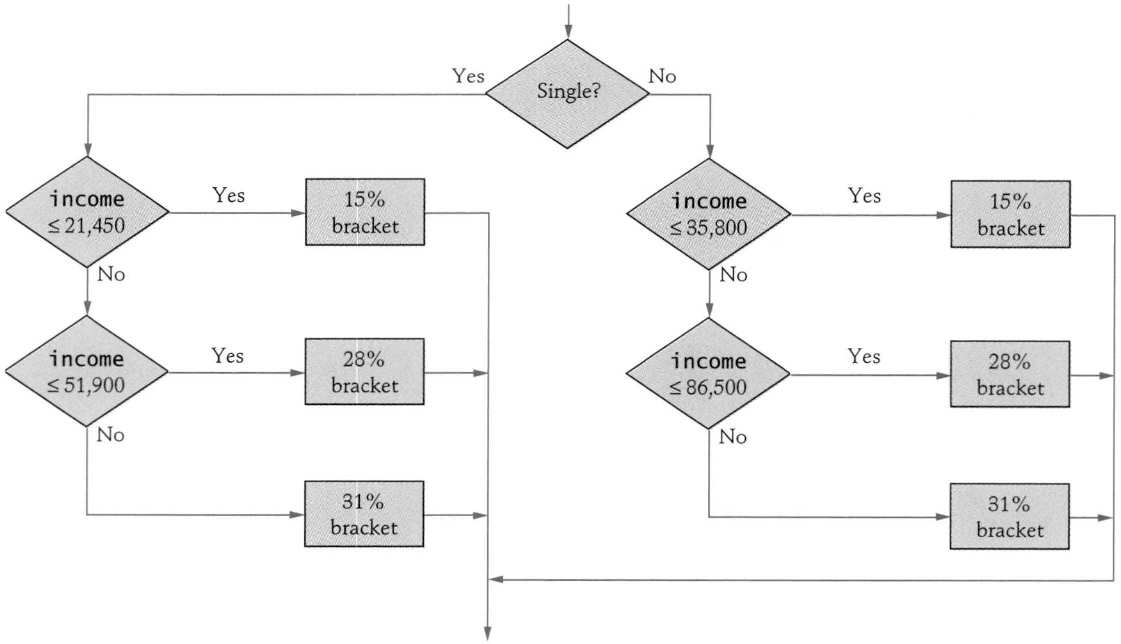

Figure 7

Income Tax Computation

The two-level decision process is reflected in two levels of `if` statements. We say that the income test is *nested* inside the test for filing status. (See Figure 7 for a flowchart.) In theory, nesting can go deeper than two levels. A three-level decision process (first by state, then by status, then by income level) requires three nesting levels.

Quality Tip 4.4

Prepare Test Cases Ahead of Time

Let us consider how we can test the tax computation program. Of course, we cannot try out all possible inputs of filing status and income level. Even if we could, there would be no point in trying them all. If the program correctly computes one or two tax amounts in a given bracket, then we have a good reason to believe that all amounts will be correct. We want to aim for complete *coverage* of all cases.

There are two possibilities for the filing status and three tax brackets for each status. That makes six test cases. Then we want to test a handful of *error conditions,* such as a negative income. That makes seven test cases. For the first six we need to compute manually what answer we expect. For the remaining one, we need to know what error reports we expect. We write down the test cases and then start coding.

Should you really test seven inputs for this simple program? You certainly should. Furthermore, if you find an error in the program that wasn't covered by one of the test cases, make another test case and add it to your collection. After you fix the known mistakes, *run all test cases again.* Experience has shown that the cases that you just tried to fix are probably working now, but that errors that you fixed two or three iterations ago have a good chance of coming back! If you find that an error keeps coming back, that is usually a reliable sign that you did not fully understand some subtle interaction between features of your program.

It is always a good idea to design test cases *before* starting to code. There are two reasons for this. Working through the test cases gives you a better understanding of the algorithm that you are about to program. Furthermore, it has been noted that programmers instinctively shy away from testing fragile parts of their code. That seems hard to believe, but you will often make that observation about your own work. Watch someone else test your program. There will be times when that person enters input that makes you very nervous because you are not sure that your program can handle it, and you never dared to test it yourself. This is a well-known phenomenon, and making the test plan before writing the code offers some protection.

Productivity Hint 4.3

Make a Schedule and Make Time for Unexpected Problems

Commercial software is notorious for being delivered later than promised. For example, Microsoft originally promised that the successor to its Windows 3 operating system would be available early in 1994, then late in 1994, then in March 1995; it finally was released in August

1995. Some of the early promises might not have been realistic. It was in Microsoft's interest to let prospective customers expect the imminent availability of the product. Had customers known the actual delivery date, they might have switched to a different product in the meantime. Undeniably, though, Microsoft had not anticipated the full complexity of the tasks it had set itself to solve.

Microsoft can delay the delivery of its product, but it is likely that you cannot. As a student or a programmer, you are expected to manage your time wisely and to finish your assignments on time. You can probably do simple programming exercises the night before the due date, but an assignment that looks twice as hard may well take four times as long, because more things can go wrong. You should therefore make a schedule whenever you start a programming project.

First, estimate realistically how much time it will take you to

- Design the program logic
- Develop test cases
- Type the program in and fix syntax errors
- Test and debug the program

For example, for the income tax program I might estimate 30 minutes for the design, because it is mostly done; 30 minutes for developing test cases; one hour for data entry and fixing syntax errors; and 2 hours for testing and debugging. That is a total of 4 hours. If I work 2 hours a day on this project, it will take me two days.

Then think of things that can go wrong. Your computer might break down. The lab might be crowded. You might be stumped by a problem with the computer system. (That is a particularly important concern for beginners. It is *very* common to lose a day over a trivial problem just because it takes time to track down a person who knows the magic command to overcome it.) As a rule of thumb, *double* the time of your estimate. That is, you should start four days, not two days, before the due date. If nothing went wrong, great; you have the program done two days early. When the inevitable problem occurs, you have a cushion of time that protects you from embarrassment and failure.

Common Error 4.3

The Dangling `else` Problem

When an `if` statement is nested inside another `if` statement, the following error may occur.

```
float shipping_charge = 5.00; /* $5 inside continental US */
if (country == "USA")
   if (state == "HI")
      shipping_charge = 10.00; /* Hawaii is more expensive */
else /* Pitfall! */
   shipping_charge = 20.00; /* as are foreign shipments */
```

The indentation level seems to suggest that the `else` is grouped with the test `country == "USA"`. Unfortunately, that is not the case. The compiler ignores all indentation and follows the rule that an `else` always belongs to the closest `if`. That is, the code is actually

```
float shipping_charge = 5.00; /* $5 inside continental US */
if (country == "USA")
   if (state == "HI")
      shipping_charge = 10.00; /* Hawaii is more expensive */
   else /* Pitfall! */
      shipping_charge = 20.00;
```

That isn't what we want. We want to group the `else` with the first `if`. For that, we must use braces.

```
float shipping_charge = 5.00; /* $5 inside continental US */
if (country == "USA")
{  if (state == "HI")
      shipping_charge = 10.00; /* Hawaii is more expensive */
}
else
   shipping_charge = 20.00; /* as are foreign shipments */
```

To avoid having to think about the pairing of the `else`, we recommend that you *always* use a set of braces when the body of an `if` contains another `if`. In the following example, the braces are not strictly necessary but they help clarify the code:

```
float shipping_charge = 20.00; /* $20 for foreign shipments */
if (country == "USA")
{  if (state == "HI")
      shipping_charge = 10.00; /* Hawaii is more expensive */
   else
      shipping_charge = 5.00; /* $5 inside continental US */
}
```

The ambiguous `else` is called a *dangling* `else`, and it is enough of a syntactical blemish that some programming language designers developed an improved syntax that avoids it altogether. For example, Algol 68 uses the construction

`if` *condition* `then` *statement* `else` *statement* `fi;`

The `else` part is optional, but since the end of the `if` statement is clearly marked, the grouping is unambiguous if there are two `if` and only one `else`. Here are the two possible cases:

`if` *c1* `then if` *c2* `then` *s1* `else` *s2* `fi fi;`

`if` *c1* `then if` *c2* `then` *s1* `fi else` *s2* `fi;`

By the way, `fi` is `if` written backwards. Other languages use `endif`, which has the same purpose but is less fun.

Common Error 4.4

Forgetting to Set a Variable in Some Branches

Consider the following code:

```
float shipping_charge;
if (country == "USA")
```

```
{  if (state == "HI")
      shipping_charge = 10.00;
   else if (state == "AK")
      shipping_charge = 8.00;
}
else
   shipping_charge = 20.00;
```

The variable `shipping_charge` is declared but left undefined because its value depends on several circumstances. It is then set in the various branches of the `if` statements. However, if the order is to be delivered inside the United States to a state other than Hawaii or Alaska, then the shipping charge is not set at all.

There are two remedies. Of course, we can check all branches of the `if` statements to make sure that each one of them sets the variable. In this example, we must add one case:

```
if (country == "USA")
{  if (state == "HI")
      shipping_charge = 10.00;
   else if (state == "AK")
      shipping_charge = 8.00;
   else
      shipping_charge = 5.00; /* within continental U.S. */
}
else
   shipping_charge = 20.00;
```

The safer way is to initialize the variable with the most likely value and then have that value overwritten in the less likely situations:

```
float shipping_charge = 5.00; /* within continental U.S. */
if (country == "USA")
{  if (state == "HI")
      shipping_charge = 10.00;
   else if (state == "AK")
      shipping_charge = 8.00;
}
else
   shipping_charge = 20.00;
```

That is slightly less efficient, but we are now assured that the variable is never left uninitialized.

4.7 Logical Operations

Suppose you want to test whether today is your brother's birthday. You need to compare the day and month fields of `today` and `birthday`. The test passes only if both fields match. In C++ we use the `and` operator to combine test conditions.

Program birthdy1.cpp

```
#include "ccc.h"

int main()
{  cout << "Enter your brother's birthday "
      << "(year month day): ";
   int year;
   int month;
   int day;
   cin >> year >> month >> day;
   Time birthday(year, month, day, 0, 0, 0);
   Time today;

   if (today.get_day() == birthday.get_day()
      and today.get_month() == birthday.get_month())
      cout << "His birthday is today!\n";

   return EXIT_SUCCESS;
}
```

The condition of the test has two parts, joined by the **and** operator. If the days are equal *and* the months are equal, then it is his birthday. If either one of the fields does not match, then the test fails.

The **and** operator combines several tests into a new test that passes only when all conditions are true. An operator that combines test conditions is called a *logical* operator.

The **or** logical operator also combines two or more conditions. The resulting test succeeds if at least one of the conditions is true. For example, in the following test we test whether an order is shipped to Alaska or Hawaii.

```
if (state == "HI" or state == "AK")
   shipping_charge = 10.00;
```

Figure 8 shows flowcharts for these examples.

You can combine both types of logical operations in one test. Here we test whether your brother's birthday already passed this year. That is the case if we are already past the birthday month, *or* if we are in that month *and* past the day.

Program birthdy2.cpp

```
#include "ccc.h"

int main()
{  cout << "Enter your brother's birthday"
      << "(year month day): ";
   int year;
   int month;
   int day;
   cin >> year >> month >> day;
```

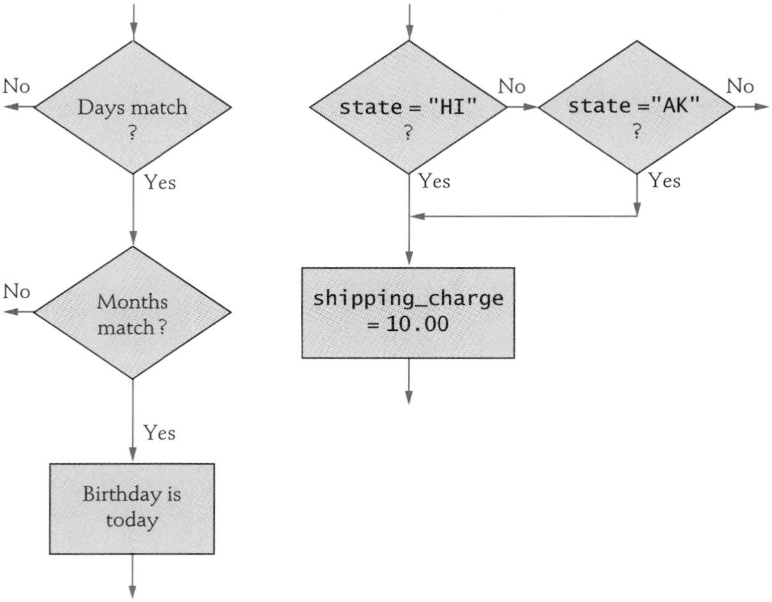

Figure 8

Flowcharts for **and** and **or** Combinations

```
   Time birthday(year, month, day, 0, 0, 0);
   Time today;

   if (today.get_month() > birthday.get_month() or
         (today.get_month() == birthday.get_month()
         and today.get_day() > birthday.get_day()))
      cout << "His birthday already passed this year.\n";
   else
      cout << "Still need to buy him a birthday gift.\n";
   return EXIT_SUCCESS;
}
```

The **and** and **or** operators are computed using *lazy evaluation.* In other words, logical expressions are evaluated from left to right, and evaluation stops as soon as the truth value is determined. When an *or* is evaluated and the first condition is true, the second condition is not evaluated, because it does not matter what the outcome of the second test is. Here is an example:

```
int age;
cin >> age;
if (cin.fail() or age < 0) cout << "Input error.\n";
```

If the input operation fails, the test `age < 0` is not evaluated, which is just as well, because `age` is then a random value. Here is another example of the benefit of lazy evaluation:

```
if (r > 0 and -b / 2 + sqrt(r) > 0) ...
```

If `r` is negative, then the first condition is false, and thus the combined statement is false, no matter what the outcome of the second test is. The second test is never evaluated for negative `r`, and there is no danger of computing the square root of a negative number.

Sometimes you need to *invert* a condition with the `not` logical operator. For example, we may want to carry out a certain action only if `cin` is not in a failed state:

```
cin >> n;
if (not cin.fail()) quarters = quarters + n;
```

The `not` operator takes a single condition and evaluates to `true` if that condition is false and to `false` if the condition is true.

Here is a summary of the three logical operations:

A	*B*	*A* and *B*
true	true	true
true	false	false
false	Any	false

A	*B*	*A* or *B*
true	Any	true
false	true	true
false	false	true

A	not *A*
true	false
false	true

Advanced Topic 4.3

&&, ||, and !

The ANSI C++ standard has introduced the keywords `and`, `or`, and `not`. Previously, C and C++ programmers had to use the following symbols:

```
and   &&
or    ||
not   !
```

The `!` symbol of the `not` operator is reminiscent of the not equal `!=` relational operator.

You will see `&&`, `||`, and `!` in many C++ programs. Before the ANSI committee permitted the use of the `and`, `or`, and `not` keywords, every programmer had to use those symbols. Many programmers still find the symbols more familiar or easier to type.

There are also so-called bit operations, `&` and `|`, which compute the *and* and *or* of every *bit* of their arguments. We will not cover bit operations at all in this book. If you do use `&&` and `||` in your own code, be sure never to confuse them with `&` and `|`.

Common Error 4.5

Multiple Relational Operators

Consider the expression

```
if (-0.5 <= x <= 0.5) .../* Error */
```

This looks just like the mathematical test $-0.5 \leq x \leq 0.5$. Unfortunately, it is not.

Let us dissect the expression `-0.5 <= x <= 0.5`. The first half, `-0.5 <= x`, is a test with outcome `true` or `false`, depending on the value of `x`. The outcome of that test (`true` or `false`) is then compared against 0.5. This seems to make no sense. Can one compare truth values and floating-point numbers? Is `true` larger than 0.5 or not? Unfortunately, to stay compatible with the C language, C++ converts `false` to 0 and `true` to 1.

You therefore must be careful not to mix logical and arithmetic expressions in your programs. Instead, use *and* to combine two separate tests:

```
if (-0.5 <= x and x <= 0.5) ...
```

Another common error, along the same lines, is to write

```
if (x and y > 0) ...   /* Error */
```

instead of

```
if (x > 0 and y > 0) ...
```

Unfortunately, the compiler will not issue an error message. Instead, it does the opposite conversion, converting `x` and `y` to `true` or `false`. Zero is converted to `false`, and any nonzero value is converted to `true`. It then computes the `and` of these two truth values, and finally it tests whether the result is greater than zero. Naturally, that computation makes no sense.

Common Error 4.6

Confusing and and or Conditions

It is a surprisingly common error to confuse *and* and *or* conditions. A value lies between 0 and 100 if it is at least 0 *and* at most 100. It lies outside that range if it is less than 0 *or* greater than 100. There is no golden rule; you just have to think carefully.

Often the *and* or *or* is clearly stated, and then it isn't too hard to implement it. But sometimes the wording isn't as explicit. It is quite common that the individual conditions are nicely set apart in a bulleted list, but with little indication how they should be combined. The instructions for the 1992 tax return say that you can claim single filing status if any one of the following is true:

- You were never married.
- You were legally separated or divorced on December 31, 1992.
- You were widowed before January 1, 1992 and did not remarry in 1992.

Since the test passes if *any one* of the conditions is true, you must combine the conditions with *or*. Elsewhere, the same instructions state that you may use the more advantageous status of married filing jointly if all five of the following conditions are true:

- Your spouse died in 1990 or 1991 and you did not remarry in 1992.
- You have a child whom you can claim as dependent.
- That child lived in your home of all of 1992.
- You paid over half the cost for keeping up your home for this child.
- You filed (or could have filed) a joint return with your spouse the year he or she died.

Because *all* of the conditions must be true for the test to pass, you must combine them with an *and*.

4.8 De Morgan's Law

Suppose we want to charge a higher shipping rate if we don't ship within the continental United States.

```
if (not (country = "USA"
        and state != "AK"
        and state != "HI"))
    shipping_charge = 20.00;
```

This test is a little bit complicated, and you have to think carefully through the logic. When it is *not* true that the country is USA *and* the state is not Alaska *and* the state is not Hawaii, then charge $20.00. Huh? It is not true that some people won't be confused by this code.

The computer doesn't care, but humans generally have a hard time comprehending logical conditions with *not* operators applied to *and/or* expressions. De Morgan's Law, named after the logician Augustus de Morgan (1806–1871), can be used to simplify these Boolean expressions. De Morgan's law has two forms: one for the negation of an *and* expression and one for the negation of an *or* expression:

`not` (A `and` B)	is the same as	`not` A `or` `not` B
`not` (A `or` B)	is the same as	`not` A `and` `not` B

Pay particular attention to the fact that the *and* and *or* operators are *reversed* by moving the *not* inwards. For example, the negation of "the state is Alaska *or* it is Hawaii",

```
not (state == "AK" or state == "HI")
```

is "the state is not Alaska *and* it is not Hawaii":

```
not (state == "AK") and not (state == "HI")
```

That is, of course, the same as

```
state != "AK" and state != "HI"
```

Let us apply the law to our shipping charge computation:

```
if (not (country = "USA"
        and state != "AK"
        and state != "HI"))
```

is equivalent to

```
if (not (country = "USA") or not (state != "AK") or
   not (state != "HI"))
```

That yields the simpler test

```
if (country != "USA"
   or state == "AK"
   or state == "HI"))
   shipping_charge = 20.00;
```

To simplify conditions with negations of *and* or *or* expressions, it is usually a good idea to apply De Morgan's Law to move the negations to the innermost level.

4.9 Using Boolean Variables

If a condition gets too complicated, it becomes difficult to understand. Because misunderstanding leads to program errors, it is helpful to simplify complex tests by breaking them up into steps. Intermediate steps are the outcomes of tests that can be true or false. To store the outcomes of these tests, you need so-called *Boolean* variables of a special data type `bool`. Boolean variables are named after the mathematician George Boole (1815–1864), a pioneer in the study of logic.

Variables of type `bool` can hold exactly two values, denoted `false` and `true`. These values are not strings or integers; they are special values, just for Boolean variables.

Here we decide whether we must use air freight or whether we can ship by truck:

```
bool ship_by_air = false;
if (country != "USA") ship_by_air = true;
else if (state == "AK" or state == "HI")
   ship_by_air = true;

if (ship_by_air)
   shipping_charge = 20.00;
else
   shipping_charge = 5.00;
```

There is an advantage of using a Boolean variable rather than a string. With a Boolean

variable we know with certainty that it holds either `false` or `true`. With a string variable we may intend that it hold either `"AIR"` or `"TRUCK"`, but there isn't an absolute guarantee that an overworked programmer hasn't accidentally set the string to a third value such as `"GROUND"`. It is also far more efficient to use Boolean variables than strings. Sometimes Boolean variables are called *flags* because they can have just two states: "up" and "down". (If there are three or more possible states, use an enumerated type—see Advanced Topic 2.5.)

It pays to think carefully about the naming of Boolean variables. In our example, it would not be a good idea to give the name `shipping_method` to the Boolean variable. What does it mean that the shipping method is `true`? With a name like `ship_by_air` there is no ambiguity; if `ship_by_air` is `true`, the order is shipped by air.

You can use Boolean variables to store the results of logical operations:

```
if (country != "USA") ship_by_air = true;
else ship_by_air = state == "AK" or state == "HI";
```

The result of the expression

```
state == "AK" or state == "HI"
```

is either `true` or `false`, and that truth value is stored in `ship_by_air`. Some people think this is a convenient shorthand; others find it confusing.

By the way, it is considered gauche to write a test such as

```
if (ship_by_air == true) .../* don't */
```

Just use the simpler test

```
if (ship_by_air) ...
```

In Chapter 6 we will use Boolean variables to control complex loops.

Random Fact 4.2

Artificial Intelligence

When one uses a sophisticated computer program such as a tax preparation package, one is bound to attribute some intelligence to the computer. The computer asks sensible questions and makes computations that we find a mental challenge. After all, if doing one's taxes were easy, we wouldn't need a computer to do it for us.

As programmers, however, we know that all this apparent intelligence is an illusion. Human programmers have carefully "coached" the software in all possible scenarios, and it simply replays the actions and decisions that were programmed into it.

Would it be possible to write computer programs that are genuinely intelligent in some sense? From the earliest days of computing, there was a sense that the human brain might be nothing but an immense computer, and that it might well be feasible to program computers to imitate some processes of human thought. Serious research into *artificial intelligence* began in the mid-1950s, and the first twenty years brought some impressive successes. Programs that play chess—surely an activity that appears to to require remarkable intellectual powers—have become so good that they now routinely beat all but the best human players. In 1975 an *expert-system* program called Mycin gained fame for being better in diagnosing meningitis in patients than the average physician. *Theorem-proving* programs produced logically correct mathematical proofs. *Optical character recognition* software can read pages from a scanner, recognize the character shapes, including those that are blurred or smudged, and reconstruct the original document text, even restoring fonts and layout.

However, there were serious setbacks as well. From the very outset, one of the stated goals of the AI community was to produce software that could translate text from one language to another, for example from English to Russian. That undertaking proved to be enormously complicated. Human language appears to be much more subtle and interwoven with the human experience than had originally been thought. Even the grammar-checking programs that come with many word processors today are more a gimmick than a useful tool, and analyzing grammar is just the first step in translating sentences.

From 1982 to 1992, the Japanese government embarked on a massive research project, funded at over 40 billion Japanese yen. It was known as the *Fifth-Generation Project.* Its goal was to develop new hard- and software to greatly improve the performance of expert system software. At its outset, the project created great fear in other countries that the Japanese computer industry was about to become the undisputed leader in the field. However, the end results were disappointing and did little to bring artificial intelligence applications to market.

Successful artificial intelligence programs, such as chess-playing programs, do not actually imitate human thinking. They are just very fast in exploring many scenarios and have been tuned to recognize those cases that do not warrant further investigation. One interesting exception are *neural networks:* coarse simulations of the neuron cells in animal and human brains. Suitably interconnected cells appear to be able to "learn". For example, if a network of cells is presented with letter shapes, it can be trained to identify them. After a lengthy training period, the network can recognize letters, even if they are slanted, distorted, or smudged.

A current AI project that has created great interest is the CYC (from en*cyc*lopedia) effort by Douglas Lenat and others at MCC in Austin, Texas. That project is trying to codify the implicit assumptions that underly human speech and writing. The team members started out analyzing news articles and asked themselves what unmentioned facts are necessary to actually understand the sentences. For example, consider the sentence "Last fall she enrolled in Michigan State." The reader automatically realizes that "fall" is not related to falling down in this context, but refers to the season. While there is a State of Michigan, here Michigan State denotes the university. A priori, a computer program has none of this knowledge. The goal of the CYC project is to extract and store the requisite facts—that is, (1) people enroll in universities; (2) Michigan is a state; (3) many states have universities named X State University, often abbreviated as X State; (4) most people enroll in a university in the fall. In 1995, the project had codified about 100,000 common-sense concepts and about a million facts of knowledge relating them. Even this massive amount of data has not proven sufficient for useful applications. It remains to be seen whether the CYC project will eventually lead to success or become another expensive AI failure.

Chapter Summary

1. The `if` statement lets a program carry out different actions depending on the nature of the data to be processed.

2. The `if` statement evaluates a *condition.* Conditions can contain comparisons of numbers or strings, Boolean values, and combinations thereof, using the **and**, **or**, and **not** Boolean operators.

3. Multiple conditions can be combined to evaluate complex decisions. The correct arrangement depends on the logic of the problem to be solved.

4. Complex combinations of conditions can be simplified by storing intermediate condition outcomes in Boolean variables, or by applying De Morgan's law.

Further Reading

[1] Peter van der Linden, *Expert C Programming,* Prentice-Hall, 1994.

[2] Tracy Kidder, *The Soul of a New Machine,* Little, Brown and Co., 1981.

[3] Randall E. Stross, *Steven Jobs and the NeXT Big Thing,* Atheneum, 1993.

[4] Cay Horstmann, *Mastering C++,* 2nd ed., John Wiley & Sons, 1995.

Review Exercises

Exercise R4.1. Find the errors in the following `if` statements.

```
if quarters > 0 then cout << quarters << " quarters\n";
```

```
if (1 + x > pow(x, sqrt(2)) y = y + x;
```

```
if (x = 1) y++; else if (x = 2) y = y + 2;
```

```
if (x and y == 0) cwin << Point(0, 0);
```

```
if (1 <= x <= 10) { cout << "Enter y: "; cin >> y; }
```

```
if (s != "nick" or s != "penn"
   or s != "dime" or s != "quar")
   cout << "Input error!";
```

```
if (uppercase(input) == "N" or "NO")
   return EXIT_SUCCESS;
```

```
cin >> x; if (cin.fail()) y = y + x;
```

```
language = "English"
if (country == "USA")
   if (state == "PR") language = "Spanish";
else if (country = "China")
   language = "Chinese";
```

Exercise R4.2. Explain the following terms, and give an example for each construct:

Expression
Condition
Statement
Simple statement
Compound statement
Block

Exercise R4.3. Explain the difference between an `if/else/else` statement and nested `if` statements. Give an example for each.

Exercise R4.4. Give an example for an `if/else/else` statement where the order of the tests does not matter. Give an example where the order of the tests matters.

Exercise R4.5. Of the following pairs of strings, which comes first in lexicographic order?

```
"Tom", "Dick"
"Tom", "Tomato"
"church", "Churchill"
```

```
"car manufacturer ", "carburetor"
"Harry", "hairy"
"C++", " Car"
"Tom", "Tom"
"Car", "Carl"
"car", "bar"
```

Exercise R4.6. Complete the following truth table by finding the truth values of the Boolean expressions for all combinations of the Boolean inputs `p`, `q`, and `r`.

p	q	r	p and q or not r	not (p and (q and not r))
false	false	false		
false	false	true		
false	true	false		
...				
5 more combinations				
...				

Exercise R4.7. Before implementing any complex algorithm, it is a good idea to understand and analyze it. The purpose of this exercise is to gain a better understanding of the tax computation algorithm.

Some people object to the fact that the tax rates increase with higher incomes, claiming that certain taxpayers are then better off *not* to work hard and get a raise, since they would then have to pay a higher tax rate and actually end up with less money after taxes. Can you find such an income level, and if not, why not?

Another feature of the tax code is the *marriage penalty.* Under certain circumstances, a married couple pays higher taxes than the sum of what the two partners would pay if they both were single. Find examples for such income levels.

Exercise R4.8. True or false? A **and** B is the same as B **and** A for any Boolean conditions A and B.

Exercise R4.9. Explain the difference between

```
s = 0;
if (x > 0) s++;
if (y > 0) s++;
```

and

```
s = 0;
if (x > 0) s++;
else if (y > 0) s++;
```

Exercise R4.10. Use De Morgan's Law to simplify the following Boolean expressions.

```
not (x > 0 and y > 0)

not (x != 0 or y != 0)

not (country == "USA" and state != "HI" and state != "AK")

not (x % 4 != 0 or not (x % 100 == 0 and x % 400 == 0))
```

Exercise R4.11. Make up another C++ code example that shows the dangling-`else` problem, using the following statement. A student with a GPA of at least 1.5, but less than 2, is on probation. With less than 1.5, the student is failing.

Exercise R4.12. When reading in a number, there are two possible ways for a stream to be set to the "failed" state. Give examples for both. How is the situation different when reading a string?

Exercise R4.13. What is wrong with the following program?

```
cout << "Enter the number of quarters: ";
cin >> quarters;
total = total + quarters * 0.25;
if (cin.fail()) cout << "Input error.";
```

Exercise R4.14. Reading numbers is surprisingly difficult, because a C++ input stream looks at the input one character at a time. First, white space is skipped. Then the stream consumes those input characters that can be a part of a number. Once the stream has recognized a number, it stops reading if it finds a character that cannot be a part of a number. However, if the first non–white space character is not a digit or a sign, or if the first character is a sign and the second one is not a digit, then the stream fails.

Consider a program reading an integer:

```
cout << "Enter the number of quarters: ";
int quarters;
cin >> quarters;
```

For each of the following user inputs, circle how many characters have been read and whether the stream is in the failed state or not.

```
15.9
15 9
+159
-15A9
Fifteen
-Fifteen
(end of file)
+ 15
1.5E3
+1+5
```

Exercise R4.15. When the stream state has been set to failed, it is possible to clear it again by calling the function `cin.clear()`. Some textbooks recommend clearing the input stream state and asking the user to try again. For example,

```
int quarters;
cin >> quarters;
if (cin.fail())
{  cout << "Bad input. Try again!";
   cin.clear();
   cin >> quarters;
   if (cin.fail()) /* hopeless */
      return EXIT_FAILURE;
}
```

Why is this a stupid suggestion? *Hint:* What happens if the user enters `four`? Could you think of an improvement? *Hint:* `get_line`.

Exercise R4.16. Explain how the lexicographic ordering of strings differs from the ordering of words in a dictionary or telephone book. *Hint:* Consider strings like `IBM`, `inquiry.com`, `Century 21`, `While-U-Wait`.

Exercise R4.17. Write C++ code to test whether two objects of type `Line` represent the same when displayed on the graphics screen.

```
Line a;
Line b;

if (your condition goes here)
   cwin << Message(Point(0, 0), "They look the same!");
```

Hint: If `p` and `q` are points, then `Line(p, q)` and `Line(q, p)` look the same.

Exercise R4.18. How can you test whether two objects `t1` and `t2` of type `Time` represent the same time, without comparing the year, month, day, hour, minute, and second values?

Exercise R4.19. Explain why it is more difficult to compare floating-point numbers than integers. Write C++ code to test whether an integer `n` equals 10 and whether a floating-point number `x` equals 10.

Exercise R4.20. Give an example for two floating-point numbers `x` and `y` such that `fabs(x - y)` is larger than 1000, but `x` and `y` are still identical except for a roundoff error.

Exercise R4.21. Give a set of test cases for the tax program in Section 4.6. Manually compute the expected results.

Exercise R4.22. Consider the following test to see whether a point falls inside a rectangle.

```
Point p = cwin.get_mouse("Click inside the rectangle");
bool x_inside = false;
if (x1 <= p.get_x() and p.get_x() <= x2)
   x_inside = true;
bool y_inside = false;
if (y1 <= p.get_y() and p.get_y() <= y2)
   y_inside = true;
if (x_inside and y_inside)
   cwin << Message(p, "Congratulations!");
```

Rewrite this code to eliminate the explicit `true` and `false` values, by setting `x_inside` and `y_inside` to the values of Boolean expressions.

Programming Exercises

Exercise P4.1. Write a program that prints all solutions to the quadratic equation $ax^2 + bx + c = 0$. Read in a, b, c and use the quadratic formula. If the *discriminant* $b^2 - 4ac$ is negative, display a message stating that there are no solutions.

Exercise P4.2. Write a program that takes user input describing a playing card in the following shorthand notation:

A	Ace
2 ... 10	Card values
J	Jack
Q	Queen
K	King
D	Diamonds
H	Hearts
S	Spades
C	Clubs

Your program should print the full description of the card. For example,

```
Enter the card notation: QS
Queen of spades
```

Exercise P4.3. According to [William H. Press et al., *Numerical Recipes in C*, Cambridge, 1988, p. 184], it is not smart to use the quadratic formula to find the solutions of $ax^2 + bx + c = 0$. If a, c, or both are small, then $\sqrt{b^2 - 4ac}$ is close to b, and one of $-b \pm \sqrt{b^2 - 4ac}$ involves subtraction of two nearly identical quantities, which can lose several digits of precision. They recommend to compute

$$q = -\frac{1}{2}\left(b + \text{sgn}(b)\sqrt{b^2 - 4ac}\right)$$

where

$$\operatorname{sgn}(b) = \begin{cases} 1 & \text{if } b \geq 0 \\ -1 & \text{if } b < 0 \end{cases}$$

Then the two solutions are

$$x_1 = q/a \quad \text{and} \quad x_2 = c/q$$

Implement this algorithm and verify that it gives more accurate solutions than the quadratic formula for small a or c.

Exercise P4.4. Find the solutions to the *cubic* equation $x^3 + ax^2 + bx + c = 0$. First compute

$$q = \frac{a^2 - 3b}{9} \quad \text{and} \quad r = \frac{2a^3 - 9ab + 27c}{54}$$

If $r^2 < q^3$, then there are three solutions. Compute

$$t = \cos^{-1}\left(r\sqrt{q^3}\right)$$

The three solutions are

$$x_1 = -2\sqrt{q}\cos\left(\frac{t}{3}\right) - \frac{a}{3}$$

$$x_2 = -2\sqrt{q}\cos\left(\frac{t + 2\pi}{3}\right) - \frac{a}{3}$$

$$x_3 = -2\sqrt{q}\cos\left(\frac{t - 2\pi}{3}\right) - \frac{a}{3}$$

Otherwise, there is a single solution

$$x_1 = u + v - \frac{a}{3}$$

where

$$u = -\operatorname{sgn}(r)\left(|r| + \sqrt{r^2 - q^3}\right)^{1/3}$$

and

$$v = \begin{cases} q/u & \text{if } u \neq 0 \\ 0 & \text{if } u = 0 \end{cases}$$

Exercise P4.5. *Intersection of lines.* As in Exercise P3.7, compute and plot the intersection of two lines, but now add error checking. If the two lines do not intersect, do not plot the point. There are two separate reasons the lines might not intersect. The lines might be parallel; in that case the determinant of the system of linear equations is zero. The point of intersection might not lie on either line; in that case, the value for t will be less than 0 or greater than 1.

Exercise P4.6. Write a program that reads in three floating-point numbers and prints the largest of the three inputs. For example:

```
Please enter three numbers: 4 9 2.5
The largest number is 9.
```

Exercise P4.7. Write a program that draws a square with corner points (0, 0) and (1, 1). Prompt the user for a mouse click. If the user clicked inside the square, then show a message "Congratulations." Otherwise, show a message "You missed."

Exercise P4.8. Write a graphics program that asks the user to specify two circles. Each circle is input by clicking on the center and typing in the radius. Draw the circles. If they intersect, then display a message "Circles intersect". Otherwise, display "Circles don't intersect". *Hint:* Compute the distance between the centers and compare it to the radii. Your program should terminate if the user enters a negative radius.

Exercise P4.9. Write a program that prints the question "Do you want to continue?" and reads a user input. If the user input is "Y," "Yes," "Ok," "Sure" or "Why not?", print out "Ok." If the user input is "N" or "No," then print out "Terminating." Otherwise, print "Bad input." The case of the user input should not matter. For example, "y" or "yes" are also valid inputs. *Hint:* Convert the user input to lowercase and then compare.

Exercise P4.10. Write a program that translates a letter grade into a number grade. Letter grades are `A B C D F`, possibly followed by `+` or `-`. Their numeric values are 4, 3, 2, 1, and 0. There is no `F+` or `F-`. A + increases the numeric value by 0.3, a - decreases it by 0.3. However, an `A+` has value 4.0.

```
Enter a letter grade: B-
The numeric value is 2.7.
```

Exercise P4.11. Write a program that translates a number between 0 and 4 into the closest letter grade. For example, the number 2.8 (which might have been the average of several grades) would be converted to `B-`. Break ties in favor of the better grade; for example 2.85 should be a `B`.

Exercise P4.12. *Roman numbers.* Write a program that converts a positive integer into the Roman number system. The Roman number system has digits

I	1
V	5
X	10
L	50
C	100
D	500
M	1000

Numbers are formed according to the following rules. (1) Only numbers up to 3999 are represented. (2) As in the decimal system, the thousands, hundreds, tens and ones are expressed separately. (3) The numbers 1 to 9 are expressed as

I	1
II	2
III	3
IV	4
V	5
VI	6
VII	7
VIII	8
IX	9

As you can see, an I preceding a V or X is subtracted from the value, and you can never have more than three I in a row. (4) Tens and hundreds are done the same way, except that the letters X, L, C and C, D, M are used instead of I, V, X, respectively.

Your program should take an input, such as 1978, and convert it to Roman numerals, MCMLXXVIII.

Exercise P4.13. Write a program that reads in three strings and sorts them lexicographically.

```
Enter three strings: Charlie Able Baker
Able
Baker
Charlie
```

Exercise P4.14. If you look at the tax tables in Section 4.6, you will note that the percentages 15%, 28%, and 31% are identical for both single and married taxpayers, but the cutoffs for the tax brackets are different. Married people get to pay 15% on their first $35,800, then pay 28% on the next $50,700, and 31% on the remainder. Single people pay 15% on their first $21,450, then pay 28% on the next $30,450, and 31% on the remainder. Write a tax program with the following logic. Set variables `cutoff15` and `cutoff28` that depend on the marital status. Then have a single formula that computes the tax, depending on the incomes and the cutoffs. Verify that your results are identical to that of the tax.cpp program.

Exercise P4.15. A year with 366 days is called a leap year. A year is a leap year if it is divisible by 4 (for example, 1980), except that it is not a leap year if it is divisible by 100 (for example, 1900); however, it is a leap year if it is divisible by 400 (for example, 2000); and there were no leap years before the introduction of the Gregorian calendar on October 15, 1582. Write a program that asks the user for a year and computes whether that year is a leap year.

Exercise P4.16. Write a program that asks the user to enter a month (1 = January, 2 = February, and so on) and then prints the number of days of a month. For February, print "28 or 29 days."

```
Enter a month: 5
30 days
```

Exercise P4.17. Write a program that reads in two floating-point numbers and tests whether they are the same up to two decimal places. Here are two sample runs.

```
Enter two floating-point numbers:  2.0 1.99998
They are the same up to two decimal places.

Enter two floating-point numbers:  2.0 1.98999
They are different.
```

Exercise P4.18. Write a program to simulate a bank transaction. There are two bank accounts: checking and saving. First, ask for the initial balances of the bank accounts; reject negative balances. Then ask for the transactions; options are deposit, withdrawal, and transfer. Then ask for the account; options are checking and saving. Then ask for the amount; reject transactions that overdraw an account. If the transaction was 0, print the balances of both accounts.

Exercise P4.19. Write a program that reads in the name and salary of an employee object. Here the salary will denote an *hourly* wage, such as $9.25. Then ask how many hours the employee worked in the past week. Be sure to accept fractional hours. Compute the pay. Any overtime work (over 40 hours per week) is paid at 150 percent of the regular wage. Print a paycheck for the employee.

Exercise P4.20. Write a unit conversion program using the conversion factors of Table 1 in Chapter 2. Ask the users from which unit they want to convert (fl.oz, gal, oz, lb, in, ft, mi) and which unit they want to convert to (ml, l, g, kg, mm, cm, m, km). Reject incompatible conversions (such as gal → km). Ask for the value to be converted; then display the result:

```
Convert from? gal
Convert to? ml
Value? 2.5
2.5 gal = 9462.5 ml
```

CHAPTER 5

Functions

Objectives

- To be able to program functions and procedures
- To become familiar with the concept of parameter passing
- To recognize when to use value and reference parameters
- To appreciate the importance of function comments
- To be able to determine the scope of variables
- To minimize the use of side effects and global variables
- To develop strategies for decomposing complex tasks into simpler ones
- To learn how to design programs that solve practical problems
- To document the responsibilities of functions and their callers with preconditions
- To be able to program recursive functions

5.1 Functions as Black Boxes

We have used a number of functions that were provided with the C++ system library or the library accompanying this book. Examples are

`sqrt`	Computes the square root of a floating-point number
`uppercase`	Computes an uppercase version of a string

We don't know how these functions perform their job. For example, how does `sqrt` compute square roots? By looking up values in a table? By repeated guessing of the answer? We will actually learn in Chapter 6 how to compute square roots using nothing more than basic arithmetic, but we don't need to know the internals of the computation to use the square root function. We can think of `sqrt` as a *black box*, as shown in Figure 1.

When we use `sqrt(x)` inside `main`, the *input value* or *parameter value* `x` is transferred, or *passed*, to the `sqrt` function. The execution of the `main` function is temporarily suspended. The `sqrt` function becomes active and computes the *output* or

Figure 1

The `sqrt` Function as a Black Box

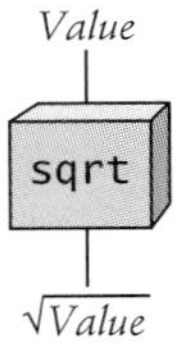

Figure 2

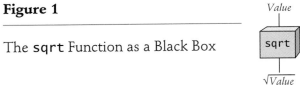

Execution Flow during a Function Call

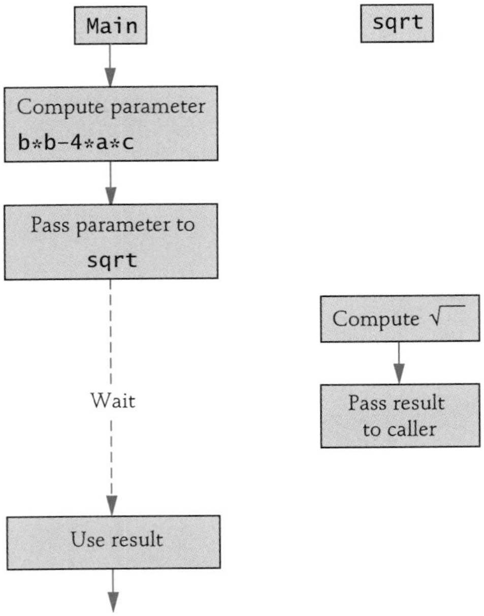

return value—the square root of the input value—using some method that (we trust) will yield the correct result. That return value is transferred back to `main`, which resumes the computation using the return value. The input value to a function need not be a single variable; it can be any expression, as in `sqrt(b * b - 4 * a * c)`. Figure 2 shows the flow of execution when a function is called.

Some functions have more than one input. For example, the `pow` function has two parameters: `pow(x, y)` computes x^y. Functions can have multiple inputs, but they only have one output.

Each function takes inputs of only particular types. For example, `sqrt` receives only numbers as parameters, whereas `uppercase` expects strings. It is an error to call `sqrt` with a string input.

Each function returns a value of a particular type: `sqrt` returns a floating-point number, `uppercase` returns a string, and `main` returns an integer.

5.2 Writing Functions

Let us compute the value of a savings account with an initial balance of \$1000 after 10 years, where interest is compounded monthly. If the annual interest rate is p percent, then the balance after 10 years is

$$b = 1000 \times (1 + p/(12 \times 100))^{12 \times 10}$$

For example, if the interest rate is 6 percent per year, then the the initial investment of \$1000 will have grown to \$1819.40 after ten years.

We will place this computation inside a function called `future_value`. Here is how we use the function:

```
int main()
{  cout << "Please enter the interest rate in percent: ";
   float rate;
   cin >> rate;

   float balance = future_value(rate);
   cout << "After 10 years, the balance is "
      << balance << "\n";

   return EXIT_SUCCESS;
}
```

Now let us write the function. The function receives a floating-point input and returns a floating-point value. We must give a *name* to the input value so that we can use it in the computation. Here we call it `p`.

```
float future_value(float p)
{  . . .
}
```

This declares a function **future_value** that returns a value of type **float** and that takes a parameter of type **float**. For the duration of the function, the parameter is stored in a *parameter variable* **p**. Just as with **main**, the body of the function is delimited by braces.

Next we need to compute the function result:

```
float future_value(float p)
{  float b = 1000 * pow(1 + p / (12 * 100), 12 * 10);
   . . .
}
```

Finally, we need to return that result to the caller of the function:

```
float future_value(float p)
{  float b = 1000 * pow(1 + p / (12 * 100), 12 * 10);
   return b;
}
```

This completes the definition of the **future_value** function. Figure 3 shows the flow of data into and out of the function.

The program is now composed of two functions: **future_value** and **main**. Both function definitions must be placed into the program file.

A function must be defined before it is used. Since **future_value** is used in **main**, its definition must come first. That means that **main** is always the last function in a program file.

Program futval.cpp

```
#include "iostream.h"
#include "stdlib.h"
#include "math.h"

float future_value(float p)
{  float b = 1000 * pow(1 + p / (12 * 100), 12 * 10);
   return b;
}

int main()
{  cout << "Please enter the interest rate in percent: ";
   float rate;
   cin >> rate;
   float balance = future_value(rate);

   cout << "After 10 years, the balance is "
      << balance << "\n";

   return EXIT_SUCCESS;
}
```

Figure 3

A Function Receiving a Parameter Value and Returning a Result

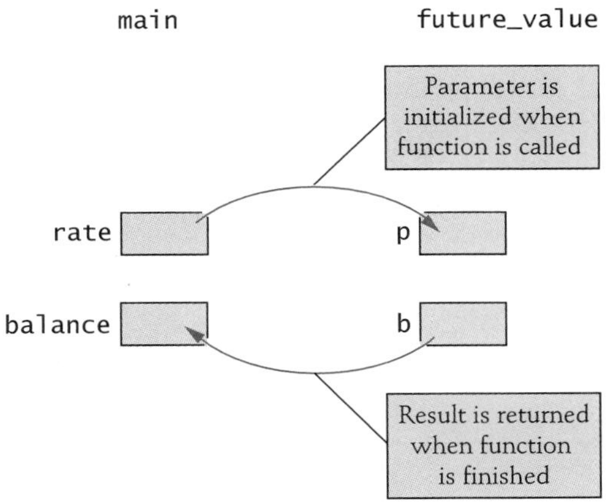

The **future_value** function has a major blemish: The starting amount of the investment ($1000) and the number of years (10) are *hard-wired* into the function code. It is not possible to use this function to compute the balance after 20 years. Of course, we could write a different function **future_value20**, but that would be a very clumsy solution. Instead, we will make the initial balance and the number of years into additional parameters:

```
float future_value(float initial_balance,
   float p, int nyear)
{  float b = initial_balance
      * pow(1 + p / (12 * 100), 12 * nyear);
   return b;
}
```

We now need to supply those values in the function call:

```
float b = future_value(1000, rate, 10);
```

Now our function is much more valuable, because it is *reusable*. For example, we can trivially modify `main` to print the balance after 10 and 20 years.

```
float b = future_value(1000, rate, 10);
cout << "After 10 years, the balance is" << b << "\n";

b = future_value(1000, rate, 20);
cout << "After 20 years, the balance is" << b << "\n";
```

Why are we using a function in the first place? We could have made the computations directly, without a function call.

```
float b = 1000 * pow(1 + p / (12 * 100), 12 * 10);
cout << "After 10 years, the balance is" << b << "\n";

b = 1000 * pow(1 + p / (12 * 100), 12 * 20);
cout << "After 20 years, the balance is" << b << "\n";
```

If you look at these two solutions in comparison, it should be quite apparent why functions are valuable. The function lets you abstract an *idea*, namely the computation of compound interest. Once you understand the idea, it is clear what the change from 10 to 20 means in the two function calls. Now compare the two expressions that compute the balances directly. To understand them, you have to look closely to find that they differ only in the last number, and then you have to remember the significance of that number.

When you find yourself coding the same computation more than once, or coding a computation that is likely to be useful in other programs, you should make it into a function.

Productivity Hint 5.1

Write Functions with Reuse in Mind

Functions are fundamental building blocks of C++ programs. When properly written, they can be reused from one project to the next. As you design the interface and implementation of a function, you should keep reuse in mind.

Keep the focus of the function specific enough that it does one task only, and solve that task completely. For example, when computing the future value of an investment, just compute the value; don't display it. A later programmer may need the computation but would not want the result displayed on the terminal.

Take the time to handle even those inputs that you may not need immediately. Now you understand the problem, and it will be easy for you to do this. If you or another programmer needs an extended version of the function later, that person must rethink the problem. That takes time, and misunderstandings can cause errors. We already eliminated all constants, except for the number of payments per year, which is fixed at 12. It would be a good idea to make that a variable too.

Then we need to check for the legal range of all inputs. Does it make sense to allow negative percentages? Negative investment amounts? Fractional years? Generalizations with clear benefits should be implemented.

5.3 Function Comments

There is one final important enhancement that we need to make to our `future_value` function. We must *comment* its behavior. Comments are for human readers, not compilers, and there is no universal standard for the layout of a function comment. In this book, we will always use the following layout:

```
float future_value(float initial_balance,
   float p, int nyear)
/* PURPOSE:   computes the value of an investment with compound
              interest
   RECEIVES:  initial_balance—the initial value of the investment
              p—the interest rate in percent
              nyear—the number of years the investment is held
   RETURNS:   the balance after nyear years
   REMARKS:   Interest is compounded monthly
*/
{  float b = initial_balance
      * pow(1 + p / (12 * 100), 12 * nyear);
   return b;
}
```

Whoa! The comment is longer than the function! Indeed it is, but that is irrelevant. We were just lucky that this particular function was easy to compute. The comment of the function does not document the implementation but the idea—ultimately a more valuable property.

According to our documentation style, every function (except `main`) must have a `PURPOSE` comment. As we will see later, some functions have no parameters or return values. For those functions, `RECEIVES` or `RETURNS` can be omitted. If you can't think of anything remarkable to document, omit the `REMARKS` section. Occasionally, you will find that these comments are silly to write. That is particularly true for general-purpose functions:

```
int max(int x, int y)
/* PURPOSE:   compute the maximum of two integers
   RECEIVES:  x, y—two integers
   RETURNS:   the larger of the two inputs
*/
{  if (x > y)
      return x;
   else
      return y;
}
```

It should be pretty clear that `max` computes the maximum, and it is perfectly obvious that the function receives two integers `x` and `y`. Indeed, in this case, the comment is somewhat overblown. We nevertheless strongly recommend writing the comment for every function. It is easy to spend more time pondering whether the comment is too trivial to write than it takes just to write it. In practical programming, very simple functions are rare. It is harmless to have a trivial function overcommented, whereas a complicated function without any comment can cause real grief to future maintenance programmers.

Practical experience has shown that comments for individual variables are rarely useful, provided the variable names are chosen to be self-documenting. Functions make up the most important logical division of a C++ program, and a large part of the documentation effort should be concentrated on explaining their black-box behavior.

It is always a good idea to write the function comment *first,* before writing the function code. This is an excellent test to see that you firmly understand what you need to program. If you can 't explain the function's inputs and outputs, you aren't ready to implement it.

Productivity Hint 5.2

Global Search and Replace

Suppose you chose an unfortunate name for a function, say `fv` instead of `future_value`, and you regret your choice. Of course, you can locate all occurrences of `fv` in your code and replace them manually. However, most programming editors have a command to search for the `fv`'s automatically and replace them with `future_value`.

You need to specify some details about the search.

- Do you want it to ignore case? That is, should `FV` be a match? In C++ you usually don't want that.
- Do you want it to match whole words only? If not, the `fv` in `Golfville` is also a match. In C++ you usually want to match whole words.
- Is this a regular expression search? No, but regular expressions can make searches even more powerful—see Productivity Hint 5.3.
- Do you want to confirm each replace or simply go ahead and replace all matches? I usually confirm the first three or four, and when I see that it works as expected, I give the go-ahead to replace the rest. (By the way, a *global* replace means to replace all occurrences in the document.) Good text editors can undo a global replace that has gone awry. Find out whether yours will.
- Do you want the search to go from the cursor to the rest of the program file, or should it search the currently selected text? Restricting replacement to a portion of the file can be very useful, but in this example you would want to move the cursor to the top of the file and then replace until the end of the file.

Not every editor has all these options. You should investigate what your editor offers.

Productivity Hint 5.3

Regular Expressions

Regular expressions describe character patterns. For example, numbers have a simple form. They contain one or more digits. The regular expression describing numbers is `[0-9]+`. The set `[0-9]` denotes any digit between 0 and 9, and the + means "one or more".

What good is it? A number of utility programs use regular expressions to locate matching text. Also, the search commands of some programming editors understand regular expressions. The most popular program that uses regular expressions is *grep* (which stands for "generalized regular expression pattern"). You can run grep from a command prompt or from inside some compilation environments. It needs a regular expression and one or more files to search. When grep runs, it displays a set of lines that match the regular expression.

Suppose we want to look for all magic numbers (see Quality Tip 2.3) in a file. The command

```
grep [0-9]+ homework.cpp
```

lists all lines in the file homework.cpp that contain sequences of digits. That isn't terribly useful; lines with variable names `x1` will be listed. OK, we want sequences of digits that do *not* immediately follow letters:

```
grep [^A-Za-z][0-9]+ homework.cpp
```

The set `[^A-Za-z]` denotes any characters that are *not* between A and Z or between a and z. This works much better, and it shows only lines that contain actual numbers.

There are a bewildering number of symbols (sometimes called *wildcards*) with special meanings in the regular expression syntax, and unfortunately, different programs use different styles of regular expressions. It is best to consult the program documentation for details.

5.4 Return Values

When the **return** statement is processed, the function exits *immediately*. This is convenient to handle exceptional cases at the beginning:

```
float future_value(float initial_balance, float p,
   int nyear)
{  if (nyear < 0) return 0;
   if (p < 0) return 0;
   float b = initial_balance
      * pow(1 + p / (12 * 100), 12 * nyear);
   return b;
}
```

If the function is called with a negative value for **nyear** or **p**, then the function returns 0 and the remainder of the function is not executed. (See Figure 4.)

In the preceding example each **return** statement returned a constant or a variable. Actually, the **return** statement can return any expression. Instead of saving the return value in a variable and returning the variable, it is often possible to eliminate the variable and return a more complex expression:

```
float future_value(float initial_balance,
   float p, int nyear)
{  return initial_balance
      * pow(1 + p / (12 * 100), 12 * nyear);
}
```

This is commonly done for very simple functions.

Figure 4

`return` Statements Exit a Function Immediately

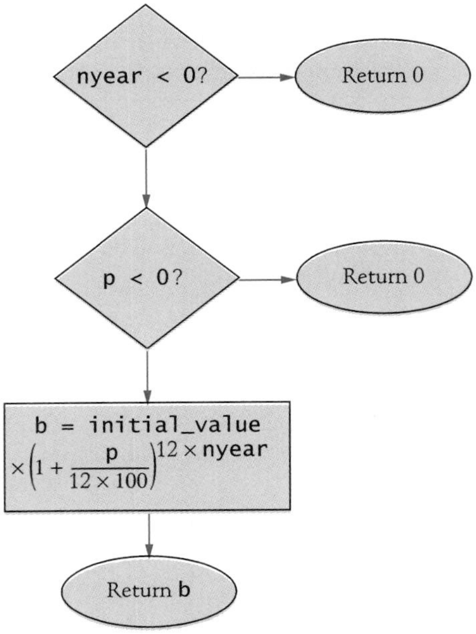

It is important that every branch of a function return a value. Consider the following incorrect version of the `future_value` function:

```
float future_value(float initial_balance,
   float p, int nyear)
{  if (nyear >= 0 and p >= 0)
      return initial_balance
         * pow(1 + p / (12 * 100), 12 * nyear);
   /* Error   */
}
```

Suppose we call `future_value` with a negative value for the year. Of course, we aren't supposed to call that, but it might happen as the result of a coding error. Since the `if` condition is not true, the `return` statement is not executed. However, the function must return *something*. Depending on circumstances, the compiler might flag this as an error, or a random value might be returned. This is always bad news, and we must protect against this by returning some safe value.

```
float future_value(float initial_balance,
   float p, int nyear)
{  if (nyear >= 0 and p >= 0)
      return initial_balance
         * pow(1 + p / (12 * 100), 12 * nyear);
   return 0;
}
```

The last statement of every function ought to be a `return` statement. That ensures that *some* value gets returned when the function reaches the end.

A function that returns a truth value is called a *predicate*. The following `is_inside` function tests whether a point lies within a circle. The function returns a value of type `bool`, which can be used inside a test.

Program inside.cpp

```
#define CCC_WIN
#include "ccc.h"

bool is_inside(Point p, Circle c)
{  float dx = p.get_x() - c.get_center().get_x();
   float dy = p.get_y() - c.get_center().get_y();
   float r = c.get_radius();

   return dx * dx + dy * dy <= r * r;
}

int main()
{  Circle c(Point(1, 1), 2);
   cwin << c;
   Point m =
      cwin.get_mouse("Please click inside the circle.");
   if (is_inside(m, c))
      cwin << Message(Point(3, 3), "Congratulations!");
   else
      cwin << Message(Point(3, 3), "You missed!");

   return EXIT_SUCCESS;
}
```

We have already seen another predicate function: the `fail` function to report on an input stream.

```
if (cin.fail()) cout << "Input error!\n";
```

Common Error 5.1

Missing Return Value

A function always needs to return something. If the code of the function contains several `if/else` branches, make sure that each one of them returns a value:

```
int sign(float x)
{  if (x < 0) return -1;
   if (x > 0) return +1;
   /* Error: missing return value if x equals 0 */
}
```

This function computes the sign of a number: −1 for negative numbers and +1 for positive numbers. If the parameter x is zero, however, no value is returned. Most compilers will issue a warning in this situation, but if you ignore the warning and the function is ever called with a parameter value of 0, a random quantity will be returned.

5.5 Parameters

When a function starts, its *parameter variables* are initialized with the expressions in the function call. Suppose we call

```
b = future_value(total / 2, rate, year2 - year1).
```

The `future_value` function has three parameter variables: `initial_balance`, `p`, and `nyear`. Before the function starts, the values of the expressions `total / 2` and `year2 - year1` are computed. Each parameter variable is initialized with the corresponding parameter value. Thus, `initial_balance` becomes `total / 2`, `p` becomes `rate` and `nyears` becomes `year2 - year1`. Figure 5 shows the parameter-passing process.

The term *parameter variable* is appropriate in C++. It is entirely legal to modify the values of the parameter variables later. Here is an example, where we use `p` as a variable:

```
float future_value(float initial_balance, float p, int nyear)
{  p = 1 + p / 12 / 100;
   int n = 12 * nyear;
   float b = initial_balance * pow(p, n);
   return b;
}
```

Actually, many programmers consider this practice bad style. It makes a lot of sense to separate the concept of a parameter (input to the function) from that of a variable (storage needed for computing the function result).

In this book we will always treat parameter variables as constants and never modify them.

Figure 5

Parameter Passing

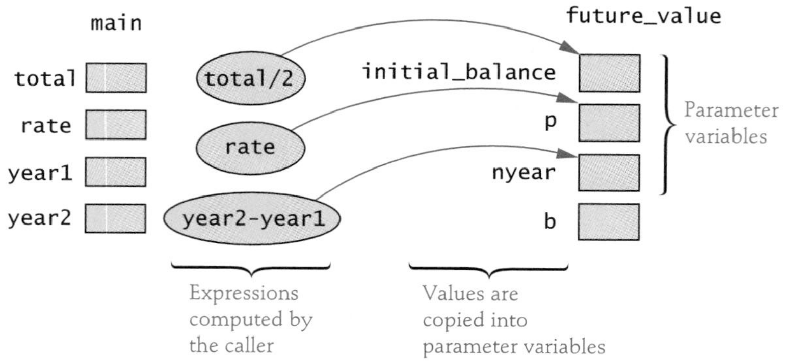

Quality Tip 5.1

Use Meaningful Names for Parameters

You can give any name you like to function parameters. Choose explicit names for parameters that have specific roles; choose simple names for those that are completely generic. The goal is to make the reader understand the purpose of the parameter without having to read the description.

`double sin(double x)` is not as good as `double sin(double radian)`. Naming the parameter `radian` gives additional information: namely, that the angle cannot be given in degrees.

The math library contains a function that is declared as

```
double atan2(double y, double x)
```

I can never remember whether it computes $\tan^{-1}(x/y)$ or $\tan^{-1}(y/x)$. I wish they had named the parameters more sensibly:

```
double atan2(double numerator, double denominator)
```

If a function is designed to take *any* parameter of a given type, then simple parameter names are appropriate.

```
bool is_inside(Point p, Circle c)
```

Common Error 5.2

Type Mismatch

The compiler takes the types of the function parameter and return values very seriously. It is an error to call a function with a value of an incompatible type. The compiler converts between integers and floating-point numbers, but it does not convert between numbers and strings or objects. For this reason, C++ is called a *strongly typed* language. This is a useful feature, because it lets the compiler find programming errors before they create havoc when the program runs.

For example, you cannot give a string to a numerical function, even if the string contains only digits:

```
string num = "1024";
float x = sqrt(num); /* Error */
```

You cannot store a numerical return value in a string variable:

```
string root = sqrt(2); /* Error */
```

Remedy: Use the `floatvalue` and `stringvalue` conversion functions:

```
float x = sqrt(floatvalue(num));
string root = stringvalue(sqrt(2));
```

Advanced Topic 5.1

Function Declarations

Functions need to be defined before they can be used. For that reason, you first define lower-level helper functions, then the midlevel workhorse functions, and finally `main` in your program.

Sometimes that ordering does not work. Suppose function `f` calls function `g`, and `g` calls `f` again. That is not a common setup, but it does happen. Another situation is much more common. The function `f` may use a function like `sqrt` that is defined in a separate file. To make `f` compile, it suffices to *declare* the functions `g` and `sqrt`. A declaration of a function lists the return value, function name, and parameters, but it contains no body:

```
int g(int n);
double sqrt(double x);
```

These are advertisements that promise that the function is implemented elsewhere, either later in the current file or in a separate file. It is easy to distinguish declarations from definitions: Declarations end in a semicolon, whereas definitions are followed by a `{ . . . }` block. Declarations are also called *prototypes*.

The declarations of common functions such as `sqrt` are contained in header files. If you have a look inside math.h, you will find the declaration of `sqrt` and the other math functions.

Some programmers like to list all function declarations at the top of the file and then write `main` and then the other functions. I don't recommend that style, because it is a hassle to maintain: Whenever you change the name of a function, or one of the parameter types, you would need to fix it in two places: the declaration and the definition.

5.6 Side Effects

Consider the `future_value` function. That function *returns* a number. Why didn't we have the function *print* the value at the same time?

```
float future_value(float initial_balance,
   float p, int nyear)
{  float b = initial_balance
      * pow(1 + p / (12 * 100), 12 * nyear);
   cout << "The balance is now " << b << "\n";
   return b;
}
```

It is a general design principle that a function had best leave no trace of its existence except for returning a value. If a function prints out a message, that function would be worthless in an environment that has no output stream, such as a graphics program or in the controller of a washing machine.

One particularly reprehensible practice is printing error messages inside functions. You should never do that:

```
float future_value(float initial_balance,
   float p, int nyear)
{  if (p < 0)
   {  cout << "Bad value of p.\n"; /* bad style */
      return 0;
   }

   float b = initial_balance
      * pow(1 + p / (12 * 100), 12 * nyear);

   return b;
}
```

Printing an error message severely limits the reusability of the **future_value** function. It can be used only in programs that can print to **cout**, eliminating graphics programs. It can be used only in applications in which a user actually reads the output, eliminating background processing. Also, it can be used only in applications where the user can understand an error message in the English language, eliminating the majority of your potential customers. Of course, your programs must contain some messages, but you should group all the input and output activity together—for example, in **main** if your program is short. Let the functions do just the computation, not the error report to the user.

An externally observable effect of a function is called a *side effect.* Displaying characters on the screen, updating variables outside the function, and terminating the program are examples of side effects.

In particular, a function that has no side effects can be run over and over with no surprises. Whenever it is given the same inputs, it will faithfully produce the same outputs. This is a desirable property, and indeed most functions have no side effects.

5.7 Procedures

Whenever a task needs to be done more than once, it makes sense to turn it into a function. Suppose you need to print an object of type **Time**:

```
Time now;
cout << now.get_year() << "/"
   << now.get_month() << "/"
   << now.get_day() << " "
   << now.get_hours() << ":"
   << format("%02d", now.get_minutes()) << ":"
   << format("%02d", now.get_seconds());
```

Of course, this is a pretty common task that may well occur again:

```
cout << liftoff.get_year() << "/"
   << liftoff.get_month() << "/"
```

```
     << liftoff.get_day() << " "
     << liftoff.get_hours() << ":"
     << format("%02d", liftoff.get_minutes()) << ":"
     << format("%02d", liftoff.get_seconds());
```

That is just the kind of repetition that functions are designed to handle.

Program printime.cpp

```
#include "ccc.h"

void print_time(Time t)
{  cout << t.get_year() << "/"
      << t.get_month() << "/"
      << t.get_day() << " "
      << t.get_hours() << ":"
      << format("%02d", t.get_minutes()) << ":"
      << format("%02d", t.get_seconds());
}

int main()
{  Time liftoff(2000, 1, 1, 7, 0, 15);
   Time now;

   cout << "Liftoff: ";
   print_time(liftoff);
   cout << "\n";

   cout << "Now: ";
   print_time(now);
   cout << "\n";

   return EXIT_SUCCESS;
}
```

Note that this code doesn't compute any value. It just performs some actions and then returns to the caller. A function without a return value is called a *procedure*. The missing return value is indicated by the keyword `void`. Procedures are called just as functions are, but there is no return value to use in an expression:

```
print_time(now);
```

Since a procedure does not return a value, it must have some other side effect; otherwise it would not be worth calling. This procedure has the side effect of printing the time.

Ideally, a function computes a single value and has no other observable effect. Calling the function multiple times with the same parameter returns the same value every time and leaves no other trace. Ideally, a procedure has only a side effect, such as setting variables or performing output, and returns no value.

Sometimes these ideals get muddied by the necessities of reality. Commonly, procedures return a status value. For example, a procedure `print_paycheck` might return a `bool` to indicate successful printing without a paper jam. However, computing that return value is not the principal purpose of calling the operation—you wouldn't print a check just to find out whether there is still paper in the printer. Hence, we would still call `print_paycheck` a procedure, not a function, even though it returns a value.

5.8 Reference Parameters

Let us write a procedure that raises the salary of an employee by `p` percent.

```
Employee harry;
. . .
raise_salary(harry, 5); /* now Harry earns 5% more */
```

Here is a first attempt:

```
void raise_salary(Employee e, float by) /* Does not work */
{  float new_salary = e.get_salary() * (1 + by / 100);
   e.set_salary(new_salary);
}
```

But this doesn't work. Let's walk through the procedure. As the procedure starts, the parameter variable `e` is set to the same value as `harry`, and `by` is set to 5. Then `e` is modified, but that modification had no effect on `harry`, because `e` is a separate variable. When the procedure exits, `e` is forgotten, and `harry` didn't get a raise.

A parameter like `e` or `by` is called a *value parameter,* because it is a variable that is initialized with a value supplied by the caller. All parameters in the functions and procedures that we have written so far have been value parameters. In this situation, though, we don't just want `e` to have the same value as `harry`. We want `e` to refer to the actual variable `harry` (or `joe` or whatever employee is supplied in the call). The salary of *that* variable should be updated. There is a second type of parameters, called *reference parameters,* with just that behavior. When we make `e` into a reference parameter, then `e` is not a new variable but a reference to an existing variable, and any change in `e` is actually a change in the variable to which `e` refers in that particular call. Figure 6 shows the difference between value and reference parameters.

Figure 6

Reference and Value Parameters

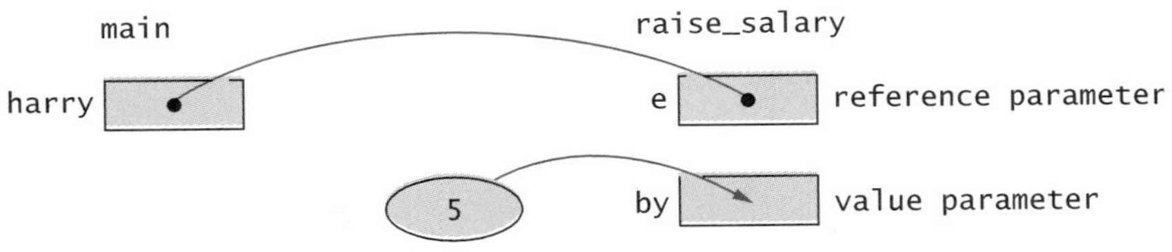

The syntax for a reference parameter is cryptic.

Program raisesal.cpp

```
#include "ccc.h"

void raise_salary(Employee& e, float by)
{  float new_salary = e.get_salary() * (1 + by / 100);
   e.set_salary(new_salary);
}

int main()
{  Employee harry("Hacker, Harry", 45000);
   raise_salary(harry, 5);
   cout << "New salary: " << harry.get_salary() << "\n";
   return EXIT_SUCCESS;
}
```

The & after the type name denotes a reference parameter. Employee& is read "employee reference" or, more briefly, "employee ref". The raise_salary function has two parameters, one of type, "employee ref" and the other a floating-point number.

The raise_salary procedure clearly has an observable side effect: It modifies the variable supplied in the call. Apart from producing output, reference parameters are the most common mechanism for achieving a side effect.

Of course, the parameter e refers to different variables in different procedure calls. If raise_salary is called twice,

```
raise_salary(harry, 5 + bonus);
raise_salary(charley, 1.5);
```

then e refers to harry in the first call, raising his salary by 5 percent plus the amount bonus. In the second call, e refers to charley, raising his salary by just 1.5 percent.

Should the second parameter be a reference?

```
void raise_salary(Employee& e, float& by) /* not desirable */
{  float new_salary = e.get_salary() * (1 + by / 100);
   e.set_salary(new_salary);
}
```

That is not desirable. The parameter by is never modified in the procedure; hence, we gain nothing from making it a reference parameter. All we accomplish is to restrict the call pattern. A reference parameter must be bound to a *variable* in the call, whereas a value parameter can be bound to any *expression*. With by a reference parameter, the call

```
raise_salary(harry, 5 + bonus)
```

becomes illegal, because you cannot have a reference to the expression `5 + bonus`. It makes no sense to change the value of an expression.

Advanced Topic 5.2

Constant References

As it happens, it is not very efficient to pass variables of type `Employee` to a subroutine by value. An employee record contains several data items, and all of them must be copied into the parameter variable. Reference parameters are more efficient. Only the location of the variable, not its value, needs to be communicated to the function.

You can instruct the compiler to give you the efficiency of call by reference together with the meaning of call by value, by using a *constant reference.* The procedure

```
void print_employee(Employee const& e)
{  cout << "Name: " << e.get_name()
      << " Salary: " << e.get_salary()  << "\n";
}
```

works exactly the same as the procedure

```
void print_employee(Employee e)
{  cout << "Name: "  << e.get_name()
      << " Salary: " << e.get_salary()  << "\n";
}
```

There is just one difference: Calls to the first procedure execute faster.

Adding `const&` to value parameters is generally worthwhile for objects but not for numbers. Using a constant reference for an integer or floating-point number is actually slower than using a value parameter. It would be nice if the compiler could perform this optimization on its own initiative, but there are unfortunate technical reasons why it cannot.

Adding `const&` to speed up the passing of structure values works only if the function or procedure never modifies its value parameters. While it is legal to modify a value parameter, changing a constant reference is an error. In Section 5.5 it was recommended to treat value parameters as constants. If you follow that recommendation, you can apply the `const&` speedup.

For simplicity, `const&` will not be used this book, but you will always find it in production code. Sometimes the `const` is written before the type name: `const Employee&`. It means the same thing.

Quality Tip 5.2

Keep Procedures Short

There is a certain cost for writing a procedure. The procedure needs to be documented; parameters need to be passed; the procedure must be tested. Some effort should be made to find whether the procedure can be made reusable rather than tied to a specific context. To avoid this cost, it is always tempting just to stuff more and more code in one place rather than going through the trouble of breaking up the code into separate procedures. It is quite common to see inexperienced programmers produce procedures that are several hundred lines long.

Ideally, each procedure should contain no more than one screenful of text. That makes it easy to read the code in the text editor. Of course, that is not always possible. As a rule of thumb, a procedure that is longer than 50 lines is usually suspect and should probably be broken up.

5.9 Variable Scope and Global Variables

It sometimes happens that the same variable name is used in two functions. Consider the variable `r` in the following example:

```
float future_value(float initial_balance,
   float p, int nyear)
{  float r = initial_balance
      * pow(1 + p / (12 * 100), 12 * nyear);
   return r;
}

int main()
{  cout << "Please enter the interest rate in percent: ";
   float r;
   cin >> r;

   float balance = future_value(r);
   cout << "After 10 years, the balance is "
      << balance << "\n";

   return EXIT_SUCCESS;
}
```

Perhaps the programmer chose `r` to denote the *return value* in the `future_value` function, and independently chose `r` to denote the *rate* in the main function. These variables are independent from each other. You can have variables with the same name `r` in different functions, just as you can have different motels with the same name "Bates' Motel" in different cities.

In a program, the part within which a variable is visible is known as the *scope* of the variable. In general, the scope of a variable extends from its definition to the end of the block in which it was defined. The scopes of the variables `r` is indicated by the brackets.

```
float future_value(float initial_balance, float p, int nyear)
{  float r = initial balance * pow(1 + p / (12 * 100), 12 * nyear);
   return r;
}

int main()
{  cout << "Please enter the interest rate in percent: ";
   float r;
   cin >> r;

   float balance = future value(r);
   cout << "After 10 years, the balance is" << balance << "\n";

   return EXIT SUCCESS;
}
```

C++ supports *global variables*, variables that are defined outside functions. A global variable is visible to all functions that are defined after it. Here is an example of a global variable.

Program global.cpp

```
#include "ccc.h"

float annual_raise;

void raise_salary(Employee& e)
{  float new_salary = e.get_salary()
      * (1 + annual_raise / 100);
   e.set_salary(new_salary);
}

int main()
{  Employee boss("Reindeer, Rudolf", 48000);
   Employee harry("Hacker, Harry", 35000);
   annual_raise = 5;
   raise_salary(boss);
   raise_salary(harry);
   cout << boss.get_name() << " "
      << boss.get_salary() << "\n";
   cout << harry.get_name() << " "
      << harry.get_salary() << "\n";
   return EXIT_SUCCESS;
}
```

In this case, `annual_raise` is a global variable. Note how it is set in `main` and read in `raise_salary`.

Actually, this is *not* considered a good way of transmitting data from one procedure to another. For example, suppose a programmer accidentally calls `raise_salary` before `annual_raise` is set. Then the procedure computes the wrong raise. Especially as a program gets long, these kinds of errors are extremely difficult to find. Of course, there is a simple remedy: Rewrite `raise_salary` and pass the percentage as a parameter.

Sometimes global variables cannot be avoided (for example, `cin`, `cout`, and `cwin` are global variables), but you should make every effort to avoid global variables in your program.

Quality Tip 5.3

Minimize Global Variables

There are a few cases where global variables are required, but they are quite rare. If you find yourself using many global variables, you are probably writing code that will be difficult to maintain and extend. As a rule of thumb, you should not have more than two global variables for every thousand lines of code.

How can you avoid global variables? Use *parameters* and use *classes*. You can always use function parameters to transfer information from one part of a program to another. If your program manipulates many variables, that can get tedious. In that case, you need to design classes that cluster related variables together. We will learn more about that process in Chapter 8.

5.10 Stepwise Refinement

One of the most powerful strategies for problem solving is the process of *stepwise refinement*. To solve a difficult task, break it down into simpler tasks. Then keep breaking down the simpler tasks into even simpler ones, until you are left with tasks that you know how to solve.

Let us apply that process to a problem of everyday life. You get up in the morning and simply must *get coffee*. How do you get coffee? You see whether you can get someone else, such as your mother or mate, to bring you some. If that fails, you must *make coffee*. How do you make coffee? If there is instant coffee available, you *boil water* and mix the boiling water with the instant coffee. How do you boil water? If there is a microwave, then you fill a cup with water, place it in the microwave and heat it for three minutes. Otherwise, you fill a kettle with water and heat it on the stove until the water comes to a boil. On the other hand, if you don't have instant coffee, you must *brew coffee*. How do you brew coffee? You add water to the coffee maker, put in a filter, *grind coffee*, put the coffee in the filter, and turn the coffee maker on. How do you grind coffee? You add coffee beans to the coffee grinder and push the button for 60 seconds.

The solution to the coffee problem breaks down tasks in two ways: with *decisions* and with *refinements*. We are already familiar with decisions: "*If* there is a microwave, use it, *else* use a kettle." Decisions are implemented as `if/else` in C++. A refinement gives a name to a composite task and later breaks that task down further: "... put in a filter, *grind coffee*, put the coffee in the filter... To grind coffee, add coffee beans to the coffee grinder..." Refinements are implemented as functions in C++. Figure 7 shows a flowchart view of the coffee-making solution. Decisions are shown as branches, refinements as expanding boxes.

Figure 8 shows a second view: a *call tree* of the tasks. The call tree shows which tasks are subdivided into which other tasks. It does not show decisions or loops, though. The name "call tree" is simple to explain: When you program each task as a C++ function, the call tree shows which functions call each other.

5.11 From Pseudocode to Code

When printing a check, it is customary to write the check amount both as a number ("$274.15") and as a text string ("two hundred seventy four dollars and 15 cents"). Doing so reduces the recipient's temptation to add a few digits in front of the amount (see Figure 9). For a human, this isn't particularly difficult, but how can a computer do this? There is no built-in function that turns 274 into `"two hundred seventy four"`. We need to program this function. Here is the description of the function we want to write:

```
string int_name(int n)
/* PURPOSE:   turn a number into its English name
   RECEIVES:  n—a positive integer < 1,000,000
   RETURNS:   the name of n (e.g., "two hundred seventy four")
*/
```

Before starting the programming, we need to have a plan. Consider a simple case. If the number is between 1 and 9, we need to compute `"one"` ... `"nine"`. In fact, we need the same computation *again* for the hundreds (`two hundred`). Any time you need something more than once, it is a good idea to turn that into a function. Rather than writing the entire function, let us just write the comment:

```
string digit_name(int n)
/* PURPOSE:   turn a digit into its English name
   RECEIVES:  n—an integer between 1 and 9
   RETURNS:   the name of n ("one" . . . "nine")
*/
```

This sounds simple enough to implement, using an `if/else` statement with nine branches, so we will worry about the implementation later.

Numbers between 10 and 19 are special cases. Let us have a separate function `teen_name` that converts them into strings `"eleven"`, `"twelve"`, `"thirteen"`, and so forth:

```
string teen_name(int n)
/* PURPOSE:   turn a number between 10 and 19 into its English name
   RECEIVES:  n—an integer between 10 and 19
   RETURNS:   the name of n ("ten" . . . "nineteen")
*/
```

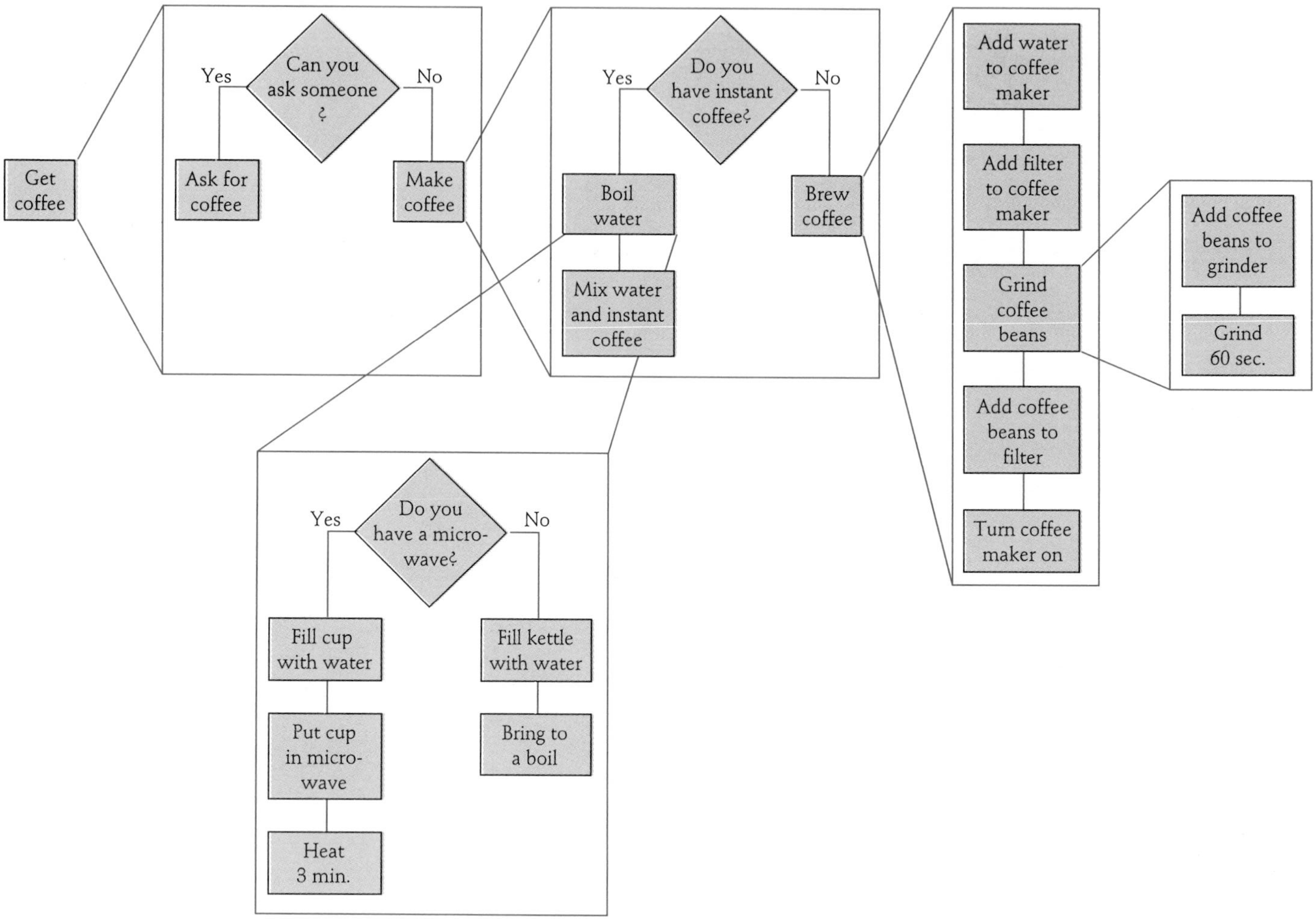

Figure 7

Flowchart of Coffee-Making Solution

Figure 8

Call Tree of Coffee-Making Procedure

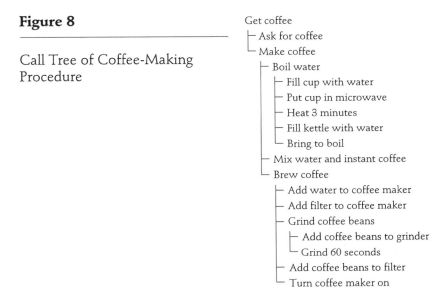

```
Get coffee
├─ Ask for coffee
└─ Make coffee
   ├─ Boil water
   │  ├─ Fill cup with water
   │  ├─ Put cup in microwave
   │  ├─ Heat 3 minutes
   │  ├─ Fill kettle with water
   │  └─ Bring to boil
   ├─ Mix water and instant coffee
   └─ Brew coffee
      ├─ Add water to coffee maker
      ├─ Add filter to coffee maker
      ├─ Grind coffee beans
      │  ├─ Add coffee beans to grinder
      │  └─ Grind 60 seconds
      ├─ Add coffee beans to filter
      └─ Turn coffee maker on
```

WILEY
John Wiley & Sons, Inc.
605 Third Avenue
New York, NY 10158_0012
Publishers' Bank Minnesota
2000 Prince Blvd
Jonesville, MN 55400
CHECK NUMBER
063331
74-39 / 311 567390
Date
Amount
PAY
4659484
04/29/96
$****10,974.79
TEN THOUSAND NINE HUNDRED SEVENTY FOUR AND 79 / 100 *************************
TO THE ORDER OF:
JOHN DOE
1009 Franklin Blvd
Sunnyvale, CA 95014

Figure 9

Check Showing the Amount as Both a Number and a String

Next, suppose that the number is between 20 and 99. Then we show the tens as `"twenty"`, `"thirty"`, `...`, `"ninety"`. For simplicity and consistency, let us also put that computation into a separate function:

```
string tens_name(int n)
/* PURPOSE:   give the English name of a multiple of 10
   RECEIVES: n—an integer between 2 and 9
   RETURNS:   the name of 10 * n ("twenty" . . . "ninety")
*/
```

Now suppose the number is at least 20 and at most 99. If the number is evenly divisible by 10, we use `tens_name`, and we are done. Otherwise, we print the teens with `teens_name` and the ones with `digit_name`. If the number is between 100 and 999, then we show a digit, the word `"hundred"`, and the remainder as described previously.

If the number is 1000 or larger, then we convert the multiples of thousand, in the same format, followed by the word `"thousand"`, then the remainder. For example, to convert 23,416, we first make 23 into a string `"twenty three"`, follow that with `"thousand"` and then convert 416.

This sounds complicated enough that it is worth turning it into *pseudocode.* Pseudocode is code that looks like C++, but the descriptions it contains are not explicit enough for the compiler to understand. Here is the pseudocode of the verbal description of the algorithm.

```
string int_name(int n)
{  int c = n; /* the part that still needs to be converted */
   string r; /* the return value */

   if (c >= 1000)
   {  r = name of thousands in c + "thousand"
      remove thousands from c;
   }

   if (c >= 100)
   {  r = r + name of hundreds in  c + "hundred"
      remove hundreds from c
   }

   if (c >= 20)
   {  r = r + name of tens in  c
      remove tens from c
   }

   else if (c >= 10)
   {  r = r + name of c
      c = 0
   }
```

```
    if (c > 0)
       r = r + name of c;

    return r;
}
```

This pseudocode has a number of important improvements over the verbal description. It shows how to arrange the tests, starting with the comparisons against the larger numbers, and it shows how the smaller number is subsequently processed in further `if` statements.

On the other hand, we were vague about the actual conversion of the pieces, just referring to "name of tens" and the like. Furthermore, we lied about spaces. As it stands, the code would produce strings with no spaces, `twohundredseventyfour`, for example. Compared to the complexity of the main problem, we would hope that spaces are a minor issue, and it is best not to muddy the pseudocode with that.

Some people like to write pseudocode on paper and use it as a guidance for the actual coding. Others type the pseudocode into the editor and then transform it into the final code. You may want to try out both methods and see which one works better for you.

Let us now turn the pseudocode into real code. The last three cases are easy, because we already developed helper functions for them:

```
if (c >= 20)
{  r = r + " " + tens_name(c / 10);
   c = c % 10;
}
else if (c >= 10)
{  r = r + " " + teen_name(c);
   c = 0;
}

if (c > 0)
   r = r + " " + digit_name(c);
```

The case of numbers between 100 and 999 is also easy, because we know that `c / 100` is a single digit:

```
if (c >= 100)
{  r = r + " " + digit_name(c / 100) + " hundred";
   c = c % 100;
}
```

Only the case of numbers larger than 1000 is somewhat vexing, because the number `c / 1000` is not necessarily a digit. If `c` is 23,416, then `c / 1000` is 23, and how are we going to obtain the name of *that*? We have helper functions for the ones, teens, and tens, but not for a value like 23. However, we know that `c / 1000` is less than 1000, because we assume that `c` is less than one million. We also have a perfectly good function that can convert any number < 1000 into a string—namely the function `int_name` itself.

```
if (c >= 1000)
{  r = int_name(c / 1000) + " thousand";
   c = c % 1000;
}
```

Here is the function in its entirety:

```
string int_name(int n)
/* PURPOSE:   Turn a number into its English name
   RECEIVES:  n—a positive integer < 1,000,000
   RETURNS:   The name of n (e.g., "two hundred seventy four")
*/
{  int c = n; /* the part that still needs to be converted */
   string r; /* the return value */

   if (c >= 1000)
   {  r = int_name(c / 1000) + " thousand";
      c = c % 1000;
   }

   if (c >= 100)
   {  r = r + " " + digit_name(c / 100) + " hundred";
      c = c % 100;
   }

   if (c >= 20)
   {  r = r + " " + tens_name(c / 10);
      c = c % 10;
   }
   else if (c >= 10)
   {  r = r + " " + teen_name(c);
      c = 0;
   }

   if (c > 0)
      r = r + " " + digit_name(c);

   return r;
}
```

You may find it odd that a function can call itself, not just other functions. That is actually not as far-fetched as it sounds at first glance. Here is an example from basic algebra. You probably learned in your algebra class how to compute a square of a number such as 25.4 without the benefit of a calculator. This is a handy trick if you are stuck on a desert island and need to find out how many square millimeters are in a square inch. (There are 25.4 millimeters in an inch.) Here is how you do it. You use the binomial formula

$$(a + b)^2 = a^2 + 2ab + b^2$$

with $a = 25$ and $b = 0.4$. To compute 25.4^2, you thus first *compute the simpler squares* 25^2 and 0.4^2: $25^2 = 625$ and $0.4^2 = 0.16$. Then you put everything together: $25.4^2 = 625 + 2 \times 25 \times 0.4 + 0.16 = 645.16$.

The same phenomenon happens with the `int_name` function. It gets a number like 23,456. It is stuck on the 23, so it suspends itself and calls a function to solve that task. It happens to be another copy of the same function. That function returns `"twenty three"`. The original function resumes, threads together `"twenty three thousand"`, and works on the remainder, 456.

There is one important caveat. When a function invokes itself, it must give a *simpler* assignment to the second copy of itself. For example, `int_name` couldn't just call itself with the value that it received or with 10 times that value. Then the calls would never stop. That is, of course, a general truth for solving problems by a series of functions. Each function must work on a simpler part of the whole.

Now we have seen all important building blocks for the `int_name` procedure. As already mentioned previously, the helper functions must be listed *before* the `int_name` function. Here is the complete program.

Program intname.cpp

```
#include "ccc.h"

string digit_name(int n)
/* PURPOSE:  Turn a digit into its English name
   RECEIVES: n—an integer between 1 and 9
   RETURNS:  The name of n ("one" . . . "nine")
*/
{  if (n == 1) return "one";
   else if (n == 2) return "two";
   else if (n == 3) return "three";
   else if (n == 4) return "four";
   else if (n == 5) return "five";
   else if (n == 6) return "six";
   else if (n == 7) return "seven";
   else if (n == 8) return "eight";
   else if (n == 9) return "nine";
   return "";
}

string teen_name(int n)
/* PURPOSE:  Turn a number between 10 and 19 into its English name
   RECEIVES: n—an integer between 10 and 19
   RETURNS:  The name of n ("ten" . . . "nineteen")
*/
{  if (n == 10) return "ten";
   else if (n == 11) return "eleven";
   else if (n == 12) return "twelve";
   else if (n == 13) return "thirteen";
   else if (n == 14) return "fourteen";
```

```
   else if (n == 15) return "fifteen";
   else if (n == 16) return "sixteen";
   else if (n == 17) return "seventeen";
   else if (n == 18) return "eighteen";
   else if (n == 19) return "nineteen";
   return "";
}

string tens_name(int n)
/* PURPOSE:   Give the English name of a multiple of 10
   RECEIVES:  n—an integer between 2 and 9
   RETURNS:   The name of 10 * n ("twenty" . . . "ninety")
*/
{  if (n == 2) return "twenty";
   else if (n == 3) return "thirty";
   else if (n == 4) return "forty";
   else if (n == 5) return "fifty";
   else if (n == 6) return "sixty";
   else if (n == 7) return "seventy";
   else if (n == 8) return "eighty";
   else if (n == 9) return "ninety";
   return "";
}

string int_name(int n)
/* PURPOSE:   Turn a number into its English name
   RECEIVES:  n—a positive integer < 1,000,000
   RETURNS:   The name of n (e.g. "two hundred seventy four")
*/
{  int c = n; /* the part that still needs to be converted */
   string r; /* the return value */

   if (c >= 1000)
   {  r = int_name(c / 1000) + " thousand";
      c = c % 1000;
   }

   if (c >= 100)
   {  r = r + " " + digit_name(c / 100) + " hundred";
      c = c % 100;
   }

   if (c >= 20)
   {  r = r + " " + tens_name(c / 10);
      c = c % 10;
   }
   else if (c >= 10)
   {  r = r + " " + teen_name(c);
      c = 0;
   }
```

```
    if (c > 0)
       r = r + " " + digit_name(c);

    return r;
}

int main()
{  int n;
   cout << "Please enter a positive integer: ";
   cin >> n;
   cout << int_name(n);
   return EXIT_SUCCESS;
}
```

5.12 Walkthroughs

The `int_name` function is sufficiently intricate that a dry run with it is a good idea, before we entrust it to the computer. Not only is there the issue with the call to itself; there are a number of other subtleties. For example, consider

```
if (c >= 20)
{  r = r + " " + tens_name(c);
   c = c % 10;
}
else if (c >= 10)
{  r = r + " " + teen_name(c);
   c = 0;
}
```

Why does the first branch set `c = c % 10` whereas the second branch sets `c = 0`? Actually, when I first wrote the code, both branches set `c = c % 10`, and then I realized my error when testing the code in my mind with a few examples. Such a mental test is called a *walkthrough*.

A walkthrough is done with pencil and paper. Take an index card, or some other piece of paper. Write down the function call that you want to study.

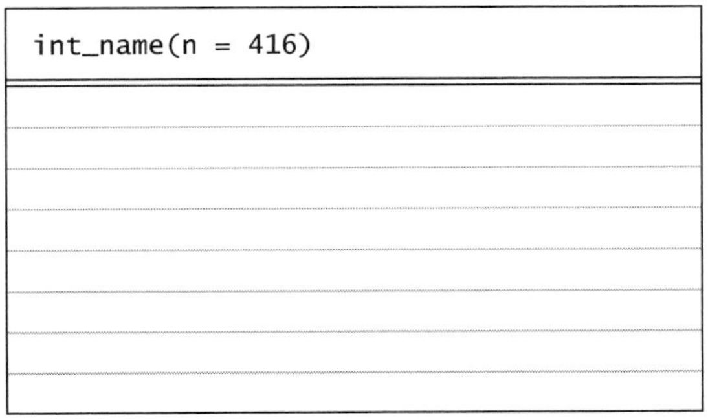

Then write the names of the function variables. Write them in a table, since you will update them as you walk through the code.

`int_name(n = 416)`	
`c`	`r`
`416`	`""`

We skip past the test `c >= 1000` and enter the test `c >= 100`. `c / 100` is 4 and `c % 100` is 16. `digit_name(4)` is easily seen to be `"four"`.

Had `digit_name` been complicated, you would have started another index card to figure out that function call. Actually, that can get out of hand if that function calls a third function. Computers have no trouble suspending one task, working on a second one, and coming back to the first, but people lose concentration when they have to switch their mental focus too often. So, instead of walking through subordinate function calls, you can just assume that they return the correct value. Write the value that you expect at the top of a separate index card.

`digit_name(n = 4)`
Returns `"four"`?

Set that card aside and walk through it later. You may of course accumulate a number of cards in this way. In practice, this procedure is necessary only for complex function calls, not simple ones like `digit_name`.

Now we are ready to update the variables. `r` has changed to `r + " " + digit_name(c / 100) + " hundred"`, that is `"four hundred"`, and `c` has changed to `c / 100` or 16. You can cross out the old values and write the new ones under them.

int_name(n = 416)	
c	r
~~416~~	~~""~~
16	"four hundred"

Now we enter the branch `c >= 10`. `teens_name(16)` is `sixteen`, so the variables now have the values

int_name(n = 416)	
c	r
~~416~~	~~""~~
~~16~~	~~"four hundred"~~
0	"four hundred sixteen"

Now it becomes clear why we need to set `c` to 0, not to `c / 10`. We don't want to get into the `c > 0` branch. If we did, the result would be `"four hundred sixteen six"`. However, if `c` is 36, we want to produce `"thirty"` first and then send the leftover 6 to the `c > 0` branch.

In this case the walkthrough was successful. However, you will very commonly find errors during walkthroughs. Then you just fix the code and try the walkthrough again. In a team with many programmers, regular walkthroughs through everyone's code are a useful method of improving code quality and understanding. (See [2].)

Productivity Hint 5.4

Commenting Out a Section of Code

Sometimes you are running tests on a long program, and a part of the program is incomplete or hopelessly messed up. You may want to ignore that part for some time and focus on getting the remainder of the code to work. Of course, you can cut out that text, paste it into another file, and paste it back later, but that is a hassle. Alternatively, you could just enclose the code to be ignored in comments.

The obvious method is to place a /* at the beginning of the offending code and a */ at the end. Unfortunately, that does not work in C++, because comments do not *nest.* That is, the /*

and */ do not pair up as parentheses or braces do:

```
/*

string teen_name(int n)
/* PURPOSE:   Turn a number between 10 and 19 into its English name
   RECEIVES: n—an integer between 10 and 19
   RETURNS:   The name of n ("ten" . . . "nineteen")
*/
{  if (n == 11) return "eleven";
   else . . .
}

*/
```

The */ closing delimiter after the RETURNS comment matches up with the /* opening delimiter at the top. All remaining code is compiled, and the */ at the end of the function causes an error message. This isn't very smart, of course. Some compilers do let you nest comments, but others don't. Some people recommend that you use only // comments. If you do, you can comment out a block of code with the /* ... */ comments—well, kind of: If you first comment out a small block and then a larger one, you run into the same problem.

There is another way of masking out a block of code: by using so-called *preprocessor directives.*

```
#if 0

string teen_name(int n)
/* PURPOSE:   Turn a number between 10 and 19 into its English name
   RECEIVES: n—an integer between 10 and 19
   RETURNS:   the name of n ("ten" . . . "nineteen")
*/
{  if (n == 11) return "eleven";
   else . . .
}

#endif
```

Preprocessing is the phase before compilation, in which `#include` files are included, macros are expanded, and portions of code are conditionally included or excluded. All lines starting with a # are instructions to the preprocessor. Selective inclusion of code with `#if`...`#endif` is useful if you need to write a program that has slight variations to run on different platforms. Here we use the feature to exclude the code. If you want to include it temporarily, change the `#if 0` to `#if 1`. Of course, once you have completed testing, you must clean it up and remove all `#if 0` directives and any unused code. Unlike /* ... */ comments, the `#if`...`#endif` directives can be nested.

Productivity Hint 5.5

Empty Stubs

Some people first write all code and then start compiling and testing. Others prefer to see some results quickly. If you are among the impatient, you will like the technique of *stubs.*

A stub is a function that is completely empty and returns a trivial value. The stub can be used to test that the code compiles and to debug the logic of other parts of the program.

```
string digit_name(int n)
/* PURPOSE:   Turn a digit into its English name
   RECEIVES:  n—an integer between 1 and 9
   RETURNS:   The name of n ("one" . . . "nine")
*/
{  return "mumble";
}

string teen_name(int n)
/* PURPOSE:   Turn a number between 10 and 19 into its English name
   RECEIVES:  n—an integer between 10 and 19
   RETURNS:   The name of n ("ten" . . . "nineteen")
*/
{  return "mumbleteen";
}

string tens_name(int n)
/* PURPOSE:   Give the English name of a multiple of 10
   RECEIVES:  n—an integer between 2 and 9
   RETURNS:   The name of 10 * n ("twenty" . . . "ninety")
*/
{  return "mumblety";
}
```

If you combine these stubs with the `int_name` function and test it with an input of 274, you will get an output of `"mumble hundred mumblety mumble"`, which shows you that you are on the right track. You can then flesh out one stub at a time.

This method is particularly helpful if you like composing your programs directly on the computer. Of course, the initial planning requires thought, not typing, and is best done at a desk. Once you know what functions you need, however, you can enter their interface descriptions and stubs, compile, implement one function, compile and test, implement the next function, compile and test, until you are done.

5.13 Preconditions

What should a function do when it is called with inappropriate inputs? For example, how should `sqrt(-1)` react? What should `digit_name(-1)` do? There are two choices.

- A function can fail safely. For example, the `digit_name` function simply returns an empty string when it is called with an unexpected input.
- A function can terminate. Many of the mathematical functions do that. The documentation states what inputs are legal and what inputs are not legal. If the function is called with an illegal input, it terminates in some way.

There are different ways of terminating a function. The mathematical functions choose the most brutal one: printing a message and terminating the entire program. C++ has a very sophisticated mechanism that allows a function to terminate and send a so-called *exception,* which signals to an appropriate receiver that something has gone very wrong. As long as such a receiver is in place, it can handle the problem and avoid termination of the program. However, exception handling is complex and beyond the scope of this book. We will choose a simpler method: using the **assert** macro, which is provided in the header file assert.h. (A *macro* is a special instruction to the compiler that inserts complex code into the program text.)

```
float future_value(float initial_balance,
   float p, int nyear)
{  assert(p >= 0 and nyear >= 0);

   return initial_balance
      * pow(1 + p / (12 * 100), 12 * nyear);
}
```

If the condition inside the macro is true when the macro is encountered, then nothing happens. However, when the condition is false, the program aborts with an error message

```
assertion failure in file fincalc.cpp line 49: p >= 0 and nyear = 0
```

This is a more useful message than that issued by a failing mathematical function. Those functions just state that an error has occurred *somewhere.* The **assert** message gives the exact line number of the trouble. The error message is displayed where the tester can see it: on the terminal screen for a text program or in a dialog box for a graphics program.

More importantly, it is possible to change the behavior of **assert** when a program has been fully tested. After a certain switch has been set in the compiler, **assert** statements are simply ignored. No time-consuming test takes place, no error message is generated, and the program never aborts.

When writing a function, how should you handle bad inputs? Should you terminate or should you fail safely? Consider **sqrt**. It would be an easy matter to implement a square root function that returns 0 for negative values and the actual square root for positive values. Suppose we use that function to compute the intersection points of a circle and a line. Suppose they don't intersect, but we forgot to take that possibility into account. Now the square root of a negative number will return a wrong value, namely 0, and we will obtain two bogus intersection points. (Actually, we will get the same point twice.) We may miss that during testing, and the faulty program may make it into production. This isn't a big deal for our graphics program, but suppose the program directs a dental drill robot. It would start drilling somewhere outside the tooth. This makes termination an attractive alternative. It is hard to overlook termination during testing, and it is better if the drill stops rather than boring through the patient's gums.

However, it is also easy to imagine situations where termination is not desirable. Suppose you do some complicated operation in your word processor, such as designing a table, and a minor program error is encountered. You will be pretty unhappy if the program terminates without even saving your work. You would probably prefer if the program just plodded along, in the hope that the minor problem does not break anything important. That is one reason why assertions can be turned off.

Here is what you should do when writing a function:

1. Establish clear *preconditions* for all inputs. Write in the `RECEIVES` comment what values you are not willing to handle.
2. Write `assert` statements that enforce the preconditions.
3. Be sure to supply correct results for all inputs that fulfill the precondition.

Let us apply that strategy to the `future_value` function:

```
float future_value(float initial_balance,
   float p, int nyear)
/* PURPOSE:   Computes the value of an investment with compound interest
   RECEIVES:  initial_balance—the initial value of the investment
              p—the interest rate in percent; must be ≥ 0
              nyear—the number of years the investment is held
   RETURNS:   The balance after nyear years
   REMARKS:   Interest is compounded monthly
*/
{  assert(p >= 0 and nyear >= 0);

   return initial_balance
      * pow(1 + p / (12 * 100), 12 * nyear);
}
```

We advertised that `p` must be ≥ 0. This is a *precondition* of the `future_value` function. The function is responsible only for handling inputs that conform to the precondition. It is free to do *anything* if the precondition is not fulfilled. It would be perfectly legal if the function reformatted the hard disk every time it was called with a wrong input. Naturally, that isn't reasonable. Instead, we check the precondition with an `assert` statement. If the function is called with a bad input, the program terminates. That may not be "nice", but it is legal. Remember that the function can do anything if the precondition is not fulfilled.

Another alternative is to let the function fail safely by returning a default value when the function is called with a negative interest rate:

```
float future_value(float initial_balance,
   float p, int nyear)
/* PURPOSE:   Computes the value of an investment with compound interest
   RECEIVES:  initial_balance—the initial value of the investment
              p—the interest rate in percent
              nyear—the number of years the investment is held
```

```
   RETURNS:  The balance after nyear years
   REMARKS:  Interest is compounded monthly
*/
{  if (p >= 0 and nyear >= 0)
      return initial_balance
         * pow(1 + p / (12 * 100), 12 * nyear);
   else
      return 0;
}
```

There are advantages and disadvantages to this approach. If the program calling the `future_value` function has a few bugs that cause it to pass a negative interest rate as an input value, then the version with the assertion will make the bugs very obvious during testing—it is hard to ignore if the program aborts. The fail-safe version, on the other hand, will quietly return 0, and you may not notice that it performs some wrong calculations as a consequence.

Bertrand Meyer [1] compares preconditions to contracts. The function promises to compute the correct answer for all inputs that fulfill the precondition. The caller promises never to call the function with illegal inputs. If the caller fulfills its promise and gets a wrong answer, it can take the function to programmer's court. If the caller doesn't fulfill its promise and something terrible happens as a consequence, it has no recourse.

5.14 Recursion

An important mathematical function is the *factorial*. $n!$ (read n factorial) is defined to be the product $1 \times 2 \times 3 \times \cdots \times n$. Also, by convention, $0! = 1$. Factorials for negative numbers are not defined. Here are the first few values of the factorial function:

n	$n!$
0	1
1	1
2	2
3	6
4	24
5	120
6	720
7	5040
8	40320

As you can see, these values get large very quickly. The factorial function is interesting, because it describes how many ways one can scramble or *permute* n distinct objects. For example, there are $3! = 6$ rearrangements of the letters in the string `"rum"`:

namely **mur**, **mru**, **umr**, **urm**, **rmu**, and **rum** itself. There are 24 permutations of the string **"drum"**.

How can we program this function? Of course we can 't write

```
float factorial(int n)
{  return 1 * 2 * 3 * ··· * n;
}
```

There is no magic "···" operation in C++ that fills in the details.

Consider how I filled in the table of factorials. When I computed 6! for the table, I did not multiply $1 \times 2 \times 3 \times 4 \times 5 \times 6$. I took the preceding entry, 120, and multiplied that by 6. That is, $6! = 6 \times 5!$. In general, $n! = n(n-1)!$ We can implement that. Recall that a function can call itself, as long as it calls itself with a simpler value:

```
float factorial(int n)
{  int result = n * factorial(n - 1);
   return result;
}
```

Let us walk through this function, computing **factorial(6)**. The first line asks to compute **6 * factorial(5)**. We don 't know what that is, so we take out another index card and walk through the computation of **factorial(5)**. It needs to compute **5 * factorial(4)**. We don't know what that is either, so we take out a third index card and work out **factorial(4)**, which needs **factorial(3)**. Eventually we are down to **factorial(2)**, **factorial(1)**, and **factorial(0)**. Now we should be getting nervous. That call returns **0 * factorial(-1)**, so something must be wrong. We really must handle 0! separately.

Program fac.cpp

```
#include "iostream.h"
#include "stdlib.h"

float factorial(int n)
{  if (n == 0)
      return 1;
   else
   {  float result = n * factorial(n - 1);
      return result;
   }
}

int main()
{  cout << "Please enter a number: ";
   int n;
   cin >> n;
   cout << n << "! = " << factorial(n) << "\n";
   return EXIT_SUCCESS;
}
```

With that fix, everything goes well. (It helps that $1! = 1 \times 0! = 1 \times 1$.) Here is an illustration of the sequence of calls and return values.

```
factorial(6) calls factorial(5)
   factorial(5) calls factorial(4)
      factorial(4) calls factorial(3)
         factorial(3) calls factorial(2)
            factorial(2) calls factorial(1)
               factorial(1) calls factorial(0)
                  factorial(0) returns 1
               factorial(1) returns 1 (1 × 1)
            factorial(2) returns 2 (2 × 1)
         factorial(3) returns 6 (3 × 2)
      factorial(4) returns 24 (4 × 6)
   factorial(5) returns 120 (5 × 24)
factorial(6) returns 720 (6 × 120)
```

The process of having a function call itself over and over is called *recursion*. The call pattern of a recursive function looks complicated, and the key to the successful design of a recursive function is *not to think about it.*

Instead, let us look at `factorial` again. The first part is utterly reasonable.

```
if (n == 0)
   return 1;
```

That just sets 0! to 1. The next part is actually also reasonable,

```
else
{  float result = n * factorial(n - 1);
   return result;
}
```

as long as you are willing to believe that the function works for simpler inputs. If `factorial` works as advertised, then `factorial(n - 1)` is $1 \times 2 \times 3 \times \cdots \times (n-1)$. Multiplying that number by n yields $n \times 1 \times 2 \times 3 \times \cdots \times (n-1) = n!$.

There are two key requirements to make sure that the recursion is successful:

1. Every recursive call must simplify the computation in some way.
2. There must be special cases to handle the simplest computations.

For the `factorial` function, "simpler" means "smaller parameter". In general, though, "simpler" does not necessarily mean smaller. It might mean shorter strings, or curves with fewer wiggles.

The `factorial` function calls itself again with smaller and smaller integers. Eventually the parameter value must reach 0, and there is a special case for computing 0!. Thus, the `factorial` function always succeeds.

Actually, we have to be careful. What happens when we call `factorial(-1)`? It calls `-1 * factorial(-2)`, so the parameter value gets bigger in magnitude. We never wanted to permit this case in the first place. Now is a good time to apply the lesson from Section 5.13 and spell out the precondition of the function:

```
float factorial(int n)

/* PURPOSE:  Compute the factorial of an integer
   RECEIVES: n—an integer ≥ 0
   RETURNS:  n!
*/
{  assert(n >= 0);

   if (n == 0)
      return 1;
   else
   {  float result = n * factorial(n - 1);
      return result;
   }
}
```

Common Error 5.3

Infinite Recursion

A common programming error is an infinite recursion: a function calling itself over and over with no end in sight. When you walk through a function call by hand, you need one index card for each call. Similarly, the computer needs some amount of memory for bookkeeping for each call. After some number of calls, all memory that is available for this purpose is exhausted. If you use a primitive operating system—in particular, DOS—you must then restart the computer (see Productivity Hint 5.6). More advanced operating systems shut down your program and report a "stack fault".

Infinite recursion happens either because the parameter values don't get simpler or because a special terminating case is missing.

Productivity Hint 5.6

Save Your Work Before Every Program Run

You now have learned enough about programming that you can write programs that "hang" the computer—that is, run forever without giving you the chance of using the keyboard or the mouse again. Congratulations are in order.

If you don't save your work and your program hangs the computer, there is nothing you can do. You must restart the computer and type it all again.

You should therefore get into the habit of *saving your work* before every program run. Some integrated environments can be configured to do this automatically, but it is not always the default behavior. You can configure your fingers to always issue a "File | Save All" command before running a program.

Random Fact 5.1

The Explosive Growth of Personal Computers

In 1971 an engineer at Intel Corporation was working on a chip for a manufacturer of electronic calculators. He realized that it would be a better idea to develop a *general-purpose* chip that could be *programmed* to interface with the keys and display of a calculator, rather than to do yet another custom design. Thus, the *microprocessor* was born. At the time, its primary application was as a controller for calculators, washing machines, and the like. It took years for the computer industry to notice that a genuine central processing unit was now available as a single chip.

Hobbyists were the first to catch on. In 1974 the first computer *kit,* the Altair 8800, was available from MITS Electronics for about $350. The kit consisted of the microprocessor, a circuit board, a very small amount of RAM memory, toggle switches, and a row of display lights. Purchasers had to solder and assemble it, then program it in machine language through the toggle switches. It was not a big hit.

The first big hit was the Apple II. It was a real computer with a keyboard, a monitor, and a floppy disk drive. When it was first released, users had a $3000 machine that could play Space Invaders, run a primitive bookkeeping program, or let users program it in BASIC. The original Apple II did not even support lowercase letters, making it worthless for word processing. The breakthrough came in 1979, with a new *spreadsheet* program, VisiCalc. In a spreadsheet, you enter financial data and their relationships into a grid of rows and columns (see Figure 10). Then you modify some of the data and watch in real time how the others change. For example, you can see how changing the mix of widgets in a manufacturing plant might affect estimated costs and profits. Middle managers in companies, who understood computers and were fed up with having to wait for hours or days to get their data runs back from the computing center, snapped up VisiCalc and the computer that was needed to run it. For them, the computer was a spreadsheet machine.

The next big hit was the IBM Personal Computer, ever after known as the PC. It was the first widely available personal computer that used Intel's 16-bit processor, the 8086, whose successors are still being used in personal computers today. The success of the PC was based not on any engineering breakthroughs but on the fact that it was easy to *clone.* IBM published specifications for plug-in cards, and it went one step further. It published the exact source code of the so-called BIOS (Basic Input/Output System), which controls the keyboard, monitor, ports, and disk drives and must be installed in ROM form in every PC. This allowed third-party vendors of plug-in cards to ensure that the BIOS code, and third-party extensions of it, interacted correctly with the equipment. Of course, the code itself was the property of IBM and could not be copied legally. Perhaps IBM did not foresee that functionally equivalent versions of the BIOS nevertheless could be recreated by others. Compaq, one of the first clone vendors, had fifteen engineers, who certified that they had never seen the original IBM code, write a new version that conformed precisely to the IBM specifications. Other companies did the same, and soon there were a number of vendors selling computers that ran the same software as IBM's PC but distinguished themselves by a lower price, increased portability, or better performance. In time, IBM lost its dominant position in the PC market. It is now one of many companies producing IBM PC-compatible computers.

IBM never produced an operating system for its PCs. An operating system organizes the interaction between the user and the computer, starts application programs, and manages disk

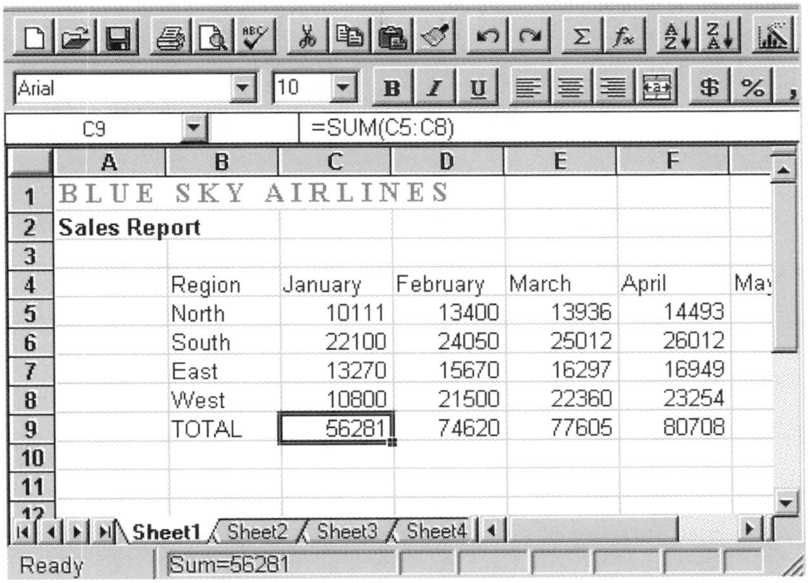

Figure 10

A Spreadsheet

storage and other resources. Instead, IBM offered customers the option of three separate operating systems. Most customers couldn't care less about the operating system. They chose the system that was able to launch most of the few applications that existed at the time. It happened to be DOS (Disk Operating System) by Microsoft. Microsoft cheerfully licensed the same operating system to other hardware vendors and encouraged software companies to write DOS applications. A huge number of useful application programs for PC-compatible machines was the result.

PC applications were certainly useful, but they were not easy to learn. Every vendor developed a different *user interface:* the collection of keystrokes, menu options, and settings that a user needed to master to use a software package effectively. Data exchange between applications was difficult, because each program used a different data format. The Apple Macintosh changed all that in 1984. The designers of the Macintosh had the vision to supply an intuitive user interface with the computer and to force software developers to adhere to it. It took Microsoft and PC-compatible manufacturers years to catch up.

The book [3] is highly recommended for an amusing and irreverent account of the emergence of personal computers.

At the time of this writing, it is estimated that one in four U.S. households own a personal computer and that one in ten use the Internet at least occasionally. Most personal computers are used for word processing, home finance (banking, budgeting, taxes), accessing information from CD-ROM and online sources, and entertainment. Some analysts predict that the personal computer will merge with the television set and cable network into an entertainment and information appliance.

Chapter Summary

1. A *function* receives input parameters and computes a result that depends on those inputs.

2. *Actual parameters* are supplied in the function call. They are stored in the *formal parameter* variables of the function. The types of the actual and formal parameters must match.

3. Once the function result has been computed, the `return` statement terminates the function and sends the result to the caller.

4. Function comments explain the purpose of the function and the meaning of the parameters and return value, as well as any special requirements.

5. Side effects are externally observable results caused by a function call, other than the returning of a result; for example, displaying a message. Generally, side effects should be avoided in functions that return values.

6. A *procedure* is a function that returns no value. Its return value usually has type `void`, and it accomplishes its purpose entirely through side effects.

7. A program consists of many functions and procedures. Just like variables, functions and procedures need to be defined before they can be used.

8. Use the process of *stepwise refinement* to decompose complex tasks into simpler ones.

9. *Preconditions* are restrictions on the function parameters. If a function is called in violation of a precondition, the function is not responsible for computing the right result. To check for conformance to preconditions, use the `assert` macro.

10. A function can call itself *recursively,* but it must provide a simpler parameter to itself in successive recursive calls. There must be special cases to handle the simplest parameter values.

Further Reading

[1] Bertrand Meyer, *Object-Oriented Software Construction,* Prentice-Hall, 1989, chapter 7.

[2] Daniel P. Freedman and Gerald M. Weinberg, *Handbook of Walkthroughs, Inspections and Technical Reviews,* Dorset House, 1990.

[3] Robert X. Cringely, *Accidental Empires,* Addison-Wesley, 1992.

Review Exercises

Exercise R5.1. Give realistic examples of the following:

A function with a `float` parameter and a `float` return value
A function with an `int` parameter and a `float` return value
A function with an `int` parameter and a `string` return value
A function with two `float` parameters and a `bool` return value
A procedure with two `int&` parameters and no return value
A function with no parameter and an `int` return value
A function with a `Circle` parameter and a `float` return value
A function with a `Line` parameter and a `Point` return value

Just describe what these functions do. Do not program them. For example, an answer to the first question is "sine" or "square root".

Exercise R5.2. True or false?

A function has exactly one `return` statement.
A function has at least one `return` statement.
A function has at most one return value.
A procedure (with return value `void`) never has a `return` statement.
When executing a `return` statement, the function exits immediately.
A function without parameters always has a side effect.
A procedure (with return value `void`) always has a side effect.
A function without side effects always returns the same value when called with the same parameters.

Exercise R5.3. Write detailed function comments for the following functions. Be sure to include a REMARKS section if there are conditions under which the function cannot compute its result. Just write the comments, not the functions.

```
float sqrt(float x)
Point midpoint(Point a, Point b)
float area(Circle c)
string roman_numeral(int n)
float slope(Line a)
bool is_leap_year(Time t)
string weekday(Time t)
```

Exercise R5.4. Consider these functions:

```
float f(float x) { return g(x) + sqrt(h(x)); }
float g(float x) { return 4 * h(x); }
float h(float x) { return x * x + k(x) - 1; }
float k(float x) { return 2 * (x + 1); }
```

Without actually compiling and running a program, determine the results of the following function calls.

```
float x1 = f(2);
float x2 = g(h(2));
float x3 = k(g(2) + h(2));
float x4 = f(0) + f(1) + f(2);
float x5 = f(-1) + g(-1) + h(-1) + k(-1);
```

Exercise R5.5. What is a predicate function? Give a definition, an example of a predicate function, and an example of how to use it.

Exercise R5.6. What is the difference between a parameter value and a return value? What is the difference between a parameter value and a parameter variable? What is the difference between a parameter value and a value parameter?

Exercise R5.7. Ideally, a function should have no side effect. Can you write a program in which no function has a side effect? Would such a program be useful?

Exercise R5.8. For the following functions and procedures, circle the parameters that must be implemented as reference parameters.

```
y = sin(x);
print_paycheck(harry, Time(1996, 10, 20, 12, 0, 0));
raise_salary(harry, 5.5);
make_uppercase(message);
key = uppercase(input);
change_name(harry, "Horton");
```

Exercise R5.9. For each of the variables in the following program, indicate the scope. Then determine what the program prints, without actually running the program.

```
int a;
int b;
int f(int c)
{  int i;
   int n = 0;
```

```
    for (i = 0; i < c; i++)
    {  int a = i;
       n = a + b;
    }
    return a;
}

int g(int c)
{  int i;
   int a;
   int n = 0;
   for (i = n; i > c; i--)
   {  int b = a;
      int a = i;
      n = a + b;
   }
}

int main()
{  int i = 1;
   int b = g(i);
   cout << a + b + i << "\n";
   return EXIT_SUCCESS;
}
```

Exercise R5.10. We have seen four kinds of variables in C++: global variables, parameter variables, local variables of a function, and local variables of a block. Classify the variables of the preceding exercise according to these categories.

Exercise R5.11. Use the process of stepwise refinement to describe the process of making scrambled eggs. Discuss what you do if you do not find eggs in the refrigerator. Produce a call tree.

Exercise R5.12. How many parameters does the following function have? How many return values does it have? *Hint:* The C++ notions of "parameter" and "return value" are not the same as the intuitive notions of "input" and "output".

```
void average(float& avg)
{  cout << "Please enter two numbers: ";
   float x;
   float y;
   cin >> x >> y;
   avg = (x + y) / 2;
}
```

Exercise R5.13. What is the difference between a function and a procedure? A function and a program? The `main` procedure and a program?

Exercise R5.14. Perform a walkthrough of the `int_name` function with the following inputs:

```
5
12
21
321
1024
11954
0
-2
```

Exercise R5.15. Perform a walkthrough of the `factorial` function with the following inputs:

```
5
2
1
0
-1
```

Exercise R5.16. What preconditions do the following functions from the standard C++ library have?

```
sqrt
tan
log
exp
pow
fabs
```

Exercise R5.17. When a function is called with parameters that violate its precondition, it can terminate or fail safely. Give two examples of library functions (ANSI standard or the library functions used in this book) that fail safely when called with invalid parameters, and give two examples of library functions that terminate.

Exercise R5.18. A *palindrome* is a string that is identical to its reverse, ignoring upper- and lowercase, spaces, and punctuation marks. Examples are "Radar", "A man, a plan, a canal: Panama", and of course, the world's first palindrome: "Madam, I'm Adam". Write the *pseudocode* for a predicate function

```
bool is_palindrome(string s)
```

Use the following logic: If the first character of `s` (that is, `s.substr(0, 1)`) is not a letter, simply ignore it by calling `is_palindrome(s.substr(1, s.length() - 1))`. Do the same for the last character. If both the first and last characters are letters, check whether they match. If they don't, the string is not a palindrome. If they do, it might be. Then remove both the first and the last character and call the function again. When should the recursion stop?

Exercise R5.19. Consider the following function:

```
int f(int n)
{  if (n <= 1) return 1;
   if (n % 2 == 0) /* n is even */
      return f(n / 2);
   else return f(3 * n + 1);
}
```

Perform walkthroughs of the computation `f(1)`, `f(2)`, `f(3)`, `f(4)`, `f(5)`, `f(6)`, `f(7)`, `f(8)`, `f(9)`, and `f(10)`. Can you conjecture what value this function computes for arbitrary `n`? Can you *prove* that the function always terminates? If so, please let the author know. At the time of this writing, this is an unsolved problem in mathematics, sometimes called the "$3n + 1$ problem" or the "Collatz problem".

Exercise R5.20. Consider the following procedure that is intended to swap the values of two integers:

```
void false_swap1(int& a, int& b)
{  a = b;
   b = a;
}

int main()
{  int x = 3;
   int y = 4;
   false_swap1(x, y);
   cout << x << " " y << "\n";
   return EXIT_SUCCESS;
}
```

Why doesn't the procedure swap the contents of `x` and `y`? How can you rewrite the procedure to work correctly?

Exercise R5.21. Consider the following procedure that is intended to swap the values of two integers:

```
void false_swap2(int a, int b)
{  int temp = a;
   a = b;
   b = temp;
}

int main()
{  int x = 3;
   int y = 4;
   false_swap2(x, y);
   cout << x << " " y << "\n";
   return EXIT_SUCCESS;
}
```

Why doesn't the procedure swap the contents of `x` and `y`? How can you rewrite the procedure to work correctly?

Exercise R5.22. Prove that the following procedure swaps two integers, without requiring a temporary variable!

```
void tricky_swap(int& a, int& b)
{  a = a - b;
   b = a + b;
   a = b - a;
}
```

Programming Exercises

Exercise P5.1. Enhance the program computing bank balances by prompting for the initial balance and the interest rate. Then print the balance after 10, 20, and 30 years.

Exercise P5.2. Write a procedure `void sort2(int& a, int& b)` that swaps the values of `a` and `b` if `a` is greater than `b` and leaves `a` and `b` unchanged. For example,

```
int u = 2;
int v = 3;
int w = 4;
int x = 1;
sort2(u, v); /* u is still 2, v is still 3 */
sort2(w, x); /* w is now 1, x is now 4 */
```

Exercise P5.3. Write a procedure `sort3(int& a, int& b, int& c)` that swaps its three inputs to arrange them in sorted order. For example,

```
int v = 3;
int w = 4;
int x = 1;
sort3(v, w, x); /* v is now 1, w is now 3, x is now 4 */
```

Hint: Use `sort2` of the preceding exercise.

Exercise P5.4. Enhance the `int_name` function so that it works correctly for values $\leq$ 2,000,000. (If your system uses 16-bit integers, change the `int` types to `long`.)

Exercise P5.5. Enhance the `int_name` function so that it works correctly for negative values and zero. *Caution:* Make sure the improved function doesn't print 20 as `"twenty zero"`.

Exercise P5.6. For some values (for example, 20), the `int_name` function returns a string with a leading space (`" twenty"`). Repair that blemish and ensure that spaces are inserted only when necessary. *Hint:* There are two ways of accomplishing this. Either ensure that leading spaces are never inserted, or remove leading spaces from the result before returning it.

Exercise P5.7. Write functions

```
float sphere_volume(float r);
float sphere_surface(float r);
float cylinder_volume(float r, float h);
float cylinder_surface(float r, float h);
float cone_volume(float r, float h);
float cone_surface(float r, float h);
```

that compute the volume and surface area of a sphere with radius `r`, a cylinder with circular base with radius `r` and height `h`, and a cone with circular base with radius `r` and height `h`. Then write a program that prompts the user for the values of `r` and `h`, calls the six functions, and prints the results.

Exercise P5.8. Write functions

```
float perimeter(Circle c);
float area(Circle c);
```

that compute the area and the perimeter of the triangle `t`. Use these functions in a graphics program that prompts the user to specify a circle. Then display messages with the perimeter and area of the circle.

Exercise P5.9. Write a function

```
distance(Point p, Point q)
```

that computes the distance between two points. Write a test program that asks the user to select two points. Then display the distance.

Exercise P5.10. Write the function

```
bool is_inside(Point p, Circle c)
```

that tests if a point is inside a circle. (You need to compute the distance between `p` and the center of the circle, and compare it to the radius.) Write a test program that asks the user to click on the center of the circle, then ask for the radius, then ask to click on any point on the screen. Display a message that indicates whether the user clicked inside the circle.

Exercise P5.11. Write a function

```
float get_float(string prompt)
```

that displays the prompt string, followed by a space, reads a floating-point number in, and returns it. (In other words, write a console version of `cwin.get_float`.) Here is a typical usage:

```
salary = get_float("Please enter your salary:");
perc_raise =
   get_float("What percentage raise would you like?");
```

If there is an input error, abort the program by calling `exit(EXIT_FAILURE)`. (We will see in Chapter 6 how to improve this behavior.)

Exercise P5.12. Write functions

```
display_H(Point p);
display_E(Point p);
display_L(Point p);
display_O(Point p);
```

that show the letters H, E, L, O on the graphics window, where the point `p` is the top left corner of the letter. Fit the letter in a 1×1 square. Then call the functions to draw the words "HELLO" and "HOLE" on the graphics display. Draw lines and circles. Do not use the `Message` class. Do not use `cout`.

Exercise P5.13. *Leap years.* Write a predicate function

```
bool leap_year(int year)
```

that tests whether a year is a leap year: that is, a year with 366 days. Leap years are necessary to keep the calendar synchronized with the sun because the earth revolves around the sun once every 365.25 days. Actually, that figure is not entirely precise, and for all dates after 1582 the *Gregorian correction* applies. Usually years that are divisible by 4 are leap years, for example 1996. However, years that are divisible by 100 (for example, 1900) are not leap years, but years that are divisible by 400 are leap years (for example, 2000).

Exercise P5.14. *Julian dates.* Suppose you would like to know how many days ago Columbus was born. It is tedious to figure this out by hand, because months have different lengths and because you have to worry about leap years. Many people, such as astronomers, who deal with dates a lot have become tired of dealing with the craziness of the calendar and instead represent days in a completely different way: the so-called Julian day number. That value is defined as the number of days that have elapsed since Jan. 1, 4713 B.C. A convenient reference point is that October 9, 1995, is Julian day 2,450,000.

Here is an algorithm to compute the Julian day number: Set `jd`, `jm`, `jy` to the day, month, and year. If the year is negative, add 1 to `jy`. (There was no year 0. Year 1 B.C. was immediately followed by year 1 A.D.) If the month is larger than February, add 1 to `jm`. Otherwise, add 13 to `jm` and subtract 1 from `jy`. Then compute

```
long jul = floor(365.25 * jy) + floor(30.6001 * jm) + d
          + 1720995.0
```

We store the result in a variable of type `long`; simple integers may not have enough digits to hold the value. If the date was before October 15, 1582, return this value. Otherwise, perform the following correction:

```
int ja = 0.01 * jy;
jul = jul + 2 - ja + 0.25 * ja;
```

Now write a function

```
long julian(int year, int month, int day)
```

that converts a date into a Julian day number. Use that function in a program that prompts the user for a date in the past, then prints out how many days that is away from today's date.

Exercise P5.15. Write a function

```
void jul_to_date(long jul, int& year,
                 int& month, int& day)
```

that performs the opposite conversion, from Julian day numbers to dates. Here is the algorithm. Starting with October 15, 1582 (Julian day number 2,299,161), apply the correction

```
long jalpha = ((jul - 1867216) - 0.25) / 36524.25;
jul = jul + 1 + jalpha - 0.25 * jalpha;
```

Then compute

```
long jb = ja + 1524;
long jc = 6680.0 + (jb - 2439870 - 122.1)/365.25;
long jd = 365 * jc + (0.25 * jc);
int je = (jb - jd)/30.6001;
```

The day, month, and year are computed as

```
day = jb - jd - (long)(30.6001 * je);
month = je - 1;
year = (int)(jc - 4715);
```

If the month is greater than 12, subtract 12. If the month is greater than 2, subtract one from the year. If the year is not positive, subtract 1.

Use the function to write the following program. Ask the user for a date and a number `n`. Then print the date that is `n` days away from the input date. You can use that program to find out the exact day that was 100,000 days ago. The computation is simple. First convert the input date to the Julian day number, using the function of the preceding exercise, then subtract `n`, and then convert back using `jul_to_date`.

Exercise P5.16. In exercise P4.12 you were asked to write a program to convert a number to its representation in Roman numerals. At the time, you did not know how to factor out common code, and as a consequence the resulting program was rather long. Rewrite that program by implementing and using the following function:

```
string roman_digit(int n, string one, string five,
                   string ten)
```

That function translates one digit, using the strings specified for the one, five, and ten values. You would call the function as follows:

```
roman_ones = roman_digit(n % 10, "I", "V", "X");
n = n / 10;
roman_tens = roman_digit(n % 10, "X", "L", "C");
. . .
```

Exercise P5.17. Write a program that converts a Roman number such as MCM-LXXVIII to its decimal number representation. *Hint:* First write a function that yields the numeric value of each of the letters. Then convert a string as follows: Look at the first *two* characters. If the first has a larger value than the second, then simply convert the first, call the conversion function again for the substring starting with the second character, and add both values. If the first one has a smaller value than the second, compute the difference and add to it the conversion of the tail. This algorithm will convert "Pig Roman" numbers like "IC". Extra credit if you can modify it to process only genuine Roman numbers.

Exercise P5.18. *Postal bar codes.* For faster sorting of letters, the United States Postal Service encourages companies that send large volumes of mail to use a bar code denoting the zip code (see Figure 11).

The encoding scheme for a five-digit zip code is shown in Figure 12. There are full-height frame bars on each side. The five encoded digits are followed by a correction digit, which is computed as follows: Add up all digits, and choose the correction digit to make the sum a multiple of 10. For example, the zip code 95014 has sum of digits 19, so the correction digit is 1 to make the sum equal to 20.

Figure 11

A Postal Bar Code

```
*************** ECRLOT ** CO57

CODE C671RTS2
JOHN DOE                            CO57
1009 FRANKLIN BLVD
SUNNYVALE     CA 95014 – 5143
```

Figure 12

Encoding for 5-Digit Bar Codes

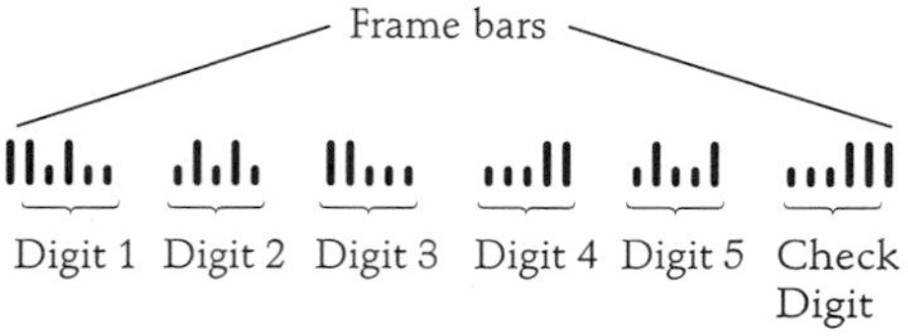

Each digit of the zip code, and the correction digit, is encoded according to the following table.

	7	4	2	1	0
1	0	0	0	1	1
2	0	0	1	0	1
3	0	0	1	1	0
4	0	1	0	0	1
5	0	1	0	1	0
6	0	1	1	0	0
7	1	0	0	0	1
8	1	0	0	1	0
9	1	0	1	0	0
0	1	1	0	0	0

where 0 denotes a half bar and 1 a full bar. Note that they represent all combinations of two full and three half bars. The digit can be easily computed from the bar code using the column weights 7, 4, 2, 1, 0. For example, 01100 is $0 \times 7 + 1 \times 4 + 1 \times 2 + 0 \times 1 + 0 \times 0 = 6$. The only exception is 0, which would yield 11 according to the weight formula.

Write a program that asks the user for a zip code and prints the bar code. Use `:` for half bars, `|` for full bars. For example, 95014 becomes

```
||:|:::|:|:||::::::||:|::|:::|||
```

Exercise P5.19. Write a program that displays the bar code, using actual bars, on your graphic screen. *Hint:* Write functions `half_bar(Point start)` and `full_bar (Point start)`.

Exercise P5.20. Write a program that reads in a bar code (with `:` denoting half bars and `|` denoting full bars) and prints out the zip code it represents. Print an error message if the bar code is not correct.

Exercise P5.21. The *Fibonacci sequence* is defined by the following rule. The first two values in the sequence are 1 and 1. All other values are the sum of the preceding two. For example, the third value is $1 + 1 = 2$, the fourth value is $1 + 2 = 3$, and the fifth $2 + 3 = 5$. If f_n denotes the nth value in the Fibonacci sequence, then

$$f_n = \begin{cases} 1 & \text{if } n \text{ is 1 or 2} \\ f_{n-1} + f_{n-2} & \text{if } n > 2 \end{cases}$$

Write a program that prompts the user for `n` and prints the `n`th value in the Fibonacci sequence. *Hint:* Write a recursive function `fibonacci`.

This is actually *not* a very efficient method of computing the Fibonacci numbers. We will discuss this issue in Chapter 12.

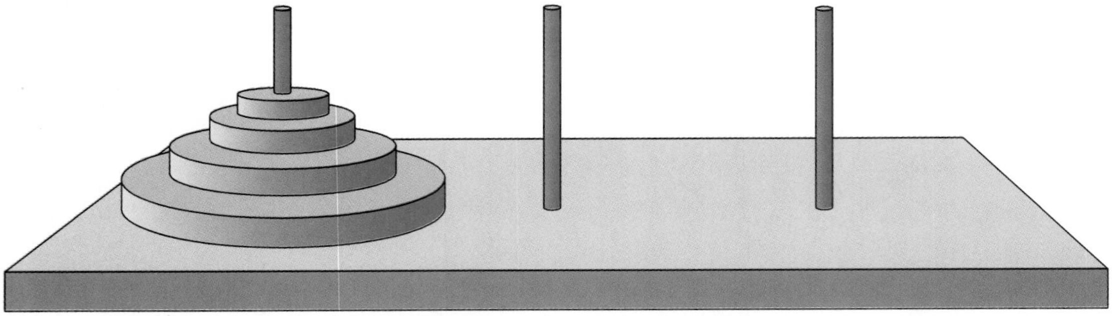

Figure 13

Towers of Hanoi

Exercise P5.22. Consider the following algorithm for computing x^n for integer n. If $n < 0$, x^n is $1/(x^n)$. x^0 is 1. If n is positive and even, then $x^n = (x^{n/2})^2$. If n is positive and odd, then $x^n = x^{n-1}x$. Implement a function `int_power(float x, int n)` that uses this algorithm.

Exercise P5.23. *Towers of Hanoi.* This is a well-known puzzle. A stack of disks of decreasing size is to be transported from the leftmost peg to the rightmost peg. The middle peg can be used as a temporary storage. (See Figure 13.)

One disk can be moved at one time, from any peg to any other peg. You can only place smaller disks on top of larger ones, not the other way around. Write a procedure that prints the moves necessary to solve the puzzle for n disks. (Ask the user for n at the beginning of the program.) Print moves in the form

```
Move disk from peg 1 to peg 3
```

Hint: Rather than writing a procedure `hanoi()` without parameters, write a procedure

```
void hanoi(int from, int to, int n)
```

that moves the top `n` disks from the peg `from` to the peg `to`. Then figure out how you can achieve that by first moving the pile of the top `n`−1 disks to the third peg, moving the `n`th disk to the destination, and then moving the pile from the third peg to the destination peg, this time using the original peg as the temporary storage. Extra credit if you write the program to actually draw the moves on the graphic screen!

Exercise P5.24. Write a program that prints instructions to get coffee, asking the user for input whenever a decision needs to be made. Decompose each task into a procedure, for example:

```
void brew_coffee()
{  cout << "Add water to the coffee maker.\n";
   cout << "Put a filter in the coffee maker.n";
   grind_coffee();
   cout << "Put the coffee in the filter.\n";
   . . .
}
```

Exercise P5.25. Write procedures to rotate and scale a point.

```
void rotate(Point& p, float angle);
void scale(Point& p, float scale);
```

Here are the equations for the transformations. If **p** is the original point, α the angle of the rotation, and **q** the point after rotation, then

$$\mathbf{q}_x = \mathbf{p}_x \cos\alpha + \mathbf{p}_y \sin\alpha$$
$$\mathbf{q}_y = -\mathbf{p}_x \sin\alpha + \mathbf{p}_y \cos\alpha$$

If **p** is the original point, s the scale factor, and **q** the point after scaling, then

$$\mathbf{q}_x = s\mathbf{p}_x$$
$$\mathbf{q}_y = s\mathbf{p}_y$$

However, note that your functions need to *replace* the point with its rotated or scaled image.

Now write the following graphics program. Start out with the point (5, 5). Rotate it five times by 10 degrees, then scale it five times by 0.95. Then start with the point (−5, −5). Repeat the following five times.

```
rotate(b, 10 * M_PI / 180);
scale(b, 0.95);
```

That is, interleave the rotation and scaling five times.

We don't yet know how to program "do this five times", so you should just use cut and paste and make five copies of the procedure calls.

Exercise P5.26. Write a procedure

```
int find(string s, string t)
```

that tests if the string `t` is contained in the string `s`. If so, it returns the offset of the first match. If not, it returns −1. For example,

`find("Mississippi", "is")` returns 1.

`find("Mississippi", "Miss")` returns 0.

`find("Mississippi", "pi")` returns 9.

`find("Mississippi", "hip")` returns −1.

Hint: If `t` is longer than `s`, you can return −1 with confidence. Otherwise, compare `t` and the initial substring of `s` with `t.length()` characters. If those are the same strings, then return 0. Otherwise call the function recursively with the tail of `s` (that is, `s` without the first character).

CHAPTER 6

Iteration

Objectives

- To be able to program loops with the `while`, `for`, and `do/while` statements
- To learn how to read input from a file through redirection
- To learn how to process character, word, and line input
- To implement approximations and simulations
- To avoid infinite loops and off-by-one errors
- To understand nested loops and nested variable scopes

6.1 Simple Loops

6.1.1 Doubling an Investment

Recall the investment problem from Chapter 1. You put $10,000 into a bank account that earns 6 percent interest per year. Interest is compounded monthly. How many years does it take for the account balance to be double the original?

In Chapter 1 we developed an algorithm for this problem, but we did not know enough C++ to implement it. Here is the algorithm.

Step 1. Start with the table

After month	Balance
0	$10,000.00

Step 2. Repeat steps 2a . . . 2c while the balance is less than $20,000.

Step 2a. Add a new row to the table.
Step 2b. In column 1 of the new row, put one more than the preceding month value.
Step 2c. In column 2 of the new row, place the preceding balance value multiplied by 1.005 (0.5%).

Step 3. Divide the last number in the month column by 12, and report it as the number of years required to double the investment.

We now know that each column in that table corresponds to a C++ variable, and we know how to update and print the variables. What we don't yet know is how to carry out "Repeat steps 2a . . . 2c while the balance is less than $20,000."

In C++, the `while` statement implements such a repetition. The code

```
while (condition)
{  statements
}
```

keeps executing the statements in the block delimited by {. . .} while the condition is true.

Here is the program that solves our investment problem:

Program doublinv.cpp

```
#include "iostream.h"
#include "stdlib.h"
```

```
int main()
{  float rate = 6;
   float balance = 10000;
   int month = 0;

   while (balance < 20000)
   {  month++;
      balance = balance * (1 + rate / 12 / 100);
   }

   cout << "The investment doubled after "
      << month / 12.0  << " years.\n";

   return EXIT_SUCCESS;
}
```

A `while` statement is often called a *loop*. If you draw a flowchart, the control loops backwards to the test after every iteration (see Figure 1).

6.1.2 Factorial

In Chapter 5 we encountered the factorial $n! = 1 \times 2 \times 3 \times \cdots \times n$ and developed a recursive function to compute it. However, the $\cdots$ in the formula is a good indication that a loop can also be used to compute the result:

Program whilefac.cpp

```
#include "iostream.h"
#include "stdlib.h"

float factorial(int n)
{  float product = 1;
   int factor = 1;
   while (factor <= n)
   {  product = product * factor;
        factor++;
   }

   return product;
}

int main()
{  cout << "Please enter a number: ";
   int n;
   cin >> n;
   cout << n << "! = " << factorial(n) << "\n";
   return EXIT_SUCCESS;
}
```

Figure 1

Flowchart of a `while` Loop

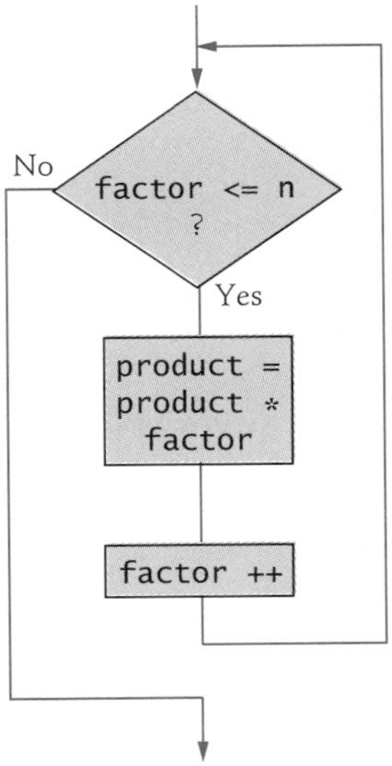

When the `while` statement is entered, the test condition is evaluated. If the test succeeds, the body is executed. Then the test is performed again. As long as it is successful, the body of the `while` statement is executed. As soon as the test fails, the next statement after the end of the body is executed. The following index card shows the computation of 4!.

factorial (n=4)	
product	factor
1	1
1	2
2	3
6	4
24	5

It is possible that the body of the `while` statement is never executed at all: namely, if the test fails the first time. In the factorial function, that happens when computing 0!. Since `factor` is 1 and `n` is 0 at the outset, the test `factor <= n` fails right away, and the body of the `while` statement is skipped.

6.1.3 Maximum Value

Here is a third example: a loop that reads in employee records from the keyboard and prints the employee with the highest salary. The loop stops at the end of the file.

The input data has the format

```
Hacker, Harry
35000
Reindeer, Rudolf R.
64700
Lam, Larry
63100
```

That is, one line contains the employee name and the next line contains the salary. You must force the end of the input file (for example, by typing Ctrl + Z on a DOS/Windows system or Ctrl + D on Unix) when you have entered all records.

To find the largest salary value in a sequence of values, we use the following logic: We keep the maximum value of all data that we have encountered so far—initially, the value 0. Whenever we read in a new element, we compare it with that tentative maximum. If the new value is larger, then it becomes the new maximum; otherwise, we ignore it. When we have read all data, we know the maximum value of all of them.

Program maxsal.cpp

```
#include "ccc.h"

Employee read_employee()
{  cout  << "Name: ";
   string name = get_line(cin);
   cout  << "Salary: ";
   float salary = floatvalue(get_line(cin));
   return Employee(name, salary);
}

int main()
{  Employee emax("", 0);
   bool done = false;

   while (not done)
   {  Employee e = read_employee();
      if (cin.fail())
         done = true;
      else
      {  if (e.get_salary() > emax.get_salary())
         emax = e;
      }
   }

   cout << "The best-paid employee is " <<  emax.get_name()
      << " with salary "  << emax.get_salary() << "\n.";

   return EXIT_SUCCESS;
}
```

This loop is a little different, because the test condition is a variable **done**. That variable stays **false** until an input fails. Then it is set to **true**; the next time the loop starts at the top, **not done** is false, and the loop exits.

There is a reason for using a variable. The test for loop termination, **cin.fail()**, occurs in the *middle* of the loop, not at the top. We must first try to read a number before we know whether the test succeeds. There isn't a ready-made control structure for the pattern "do work, then test, then do more work". Therefore we use a combination of a **while** loop and a **bool** variable. This pattern is sometimes called "loop-and-a-half"; see Advanced Topics 6.2.

Common Error 6.1

Infinite Loops

The most annoying loop error is an infinite loop: a loop that runs forever and can be stopped only by killing the program or restarting the computer. If there are output statements in the loop, then reams and reams of output flash by the screen. Otherwise, the program just sits there and *hangs,* seeming to do nothing. On some systems, you can kill a hanging program by hitting Ctrl + Break or Ctrl + C. On others, you can close the window in which the program runs. On DOS machines your only recourse may be to restart the computer.

A common reason for infinite loops is forgetting to advance the variable that controls the loop:

```
int factorial(int n)
{  int product = 1;
   int factor = 1;

   while (factor <= n)
   {  product = product * factor;
   }
   return product;
}
```

Here the programmer forgot to add a `factor++` command in the loop. As a result, the factor always stays 1, and the loop never comes to an end.

Another common reason for an infinite loop is accidentally to increment a counter that should be decremented (or vice versa). Consider this example:

```
int factorial(int n)
{  int product = 1;
   int factor = n;

   while (factor > 1)
   {  product = product * factor;
      factor++;
   }
   return product;
}
```

The `factor` variable really should have been decremented, not incremented. This is a common error because incrementing counters is so much more common than decrementing that your fingers may type the ++ on autopilot. As a consequence, `factor` is always larger than 1, and the loop never terminates. (Actually, eventually `factor` may exceed the largest representable positive integer and *wrap around* to a negative number. Then the loop exits—of course, with a completely wrong result.)

Common Error 6.2

Line-Oriented Input

It is tricky to mix `get_line` and `cin >> x` commands. Consider the case of the `read_employee` procedure:

```
Employee read_employee()
{  cout << "Name: ";
   string name = get_line(cin);
   cout << "Salary: ";
   float salary = floatvalue(get_line(cin));
   return Employee(name, salary);
}
```

It would appear simpler to read the salary with the >> operator:

```
Employee read_employee()
{  cout << "Name: ";
   string name = get_line(cin);
   cout << "Salary: ";
   float salary;
   cin >> salary;
   return Employee(name, salary);
}
```

That would indeed be simpler. It would also be wrong. Consider the sample input

H	a	c	k	e	r	,		H	a	r	r	y	\n	3	5	0	0	0	\n

R	e	i	n	d	e	e	r	,		R	u	d	o	l	f		R	.	\n	6	4	7	0	0	\n	...

After the call to `get_line`, the input stream is

3	5	0	0	0	\n

R	e	i	n	d	e	e	r	,		R	u	d	o	l	f		R	.	\n	6	4	7	0	0	\n	...

After the call to `cin >> salary`, the input stream is

\n

R	e	i	n	d	e	e	r	,		R	u	d	o	l	f		R	.	\n	6	4	7	0	0	\n	...

The >> operator eats up all *leading* white space, but it leaves all *trailing* white space in place. Thus, the next call to `get_line` yields just an empty line!

This is an unpleasant error, which you can avoid in two ways. The easier strategy is not to mix `get_line` and `cin >> x`. If you need `get_line` for some input, use it for all input and combine it with `floatvalue` or `intvalue` when necessary. Alternatively, you can add calls to `get_line` that eat up extraneous newline characters, as in the following example:

```
Employee read_employee()
{  cout << "Name: ";
   string name = get_line(cin);
   cout << "Salary: ";
   float salary;
   cin >> salary;
   get_line(cin); /* eat up trailing newline */
   return Employee(name, salary);
}
```

6.2 Other Loop Statements

6.2.1 for Loops

Far and away the most common loop has the form

```
i = start;
while (i <= end)
{  . . .
   i++;
}
```

Because this loop is so common, there is a special form for it that amplifies the pattern:

```
for (i = start ; i <= end ; i++)
{  . . .
}
```

Here is the factorial function, rewritten to use the `for` loop.

Program forfac.cpp

```
#include "iostream.h"
#include "stdlib.h"

float factorial(int n)
{  float product = 1;
   int factor;

   for ( factor = 1; factor <= n; factor++)
   {  product = product * factor;
   }
```

```
return product;
}

int main()
{  cout << "Please enter a number: ";
   int n;
   cin >> n;
   cout << n << "! = " << factorial(n)  << "\n";
   return EXIT_SUCCESS;
}
```

Figure 2 shows the corresponding flowchart.

The three slots in the `for` header can contain any three expressions. We can count down instead of up:

```
int factorial(int n)
{  int product = 1;
   int factor;

   for (factor = n; factor > 0; factor--)
   {  product = product * factor;
   }

   return product;
}
```

The increment or decrement need not be in steps of 1:

```
for (x = -10; x <= 10; x = x + 0.5) . . .
```

Figure 2

Flowchart of a `for` Loop

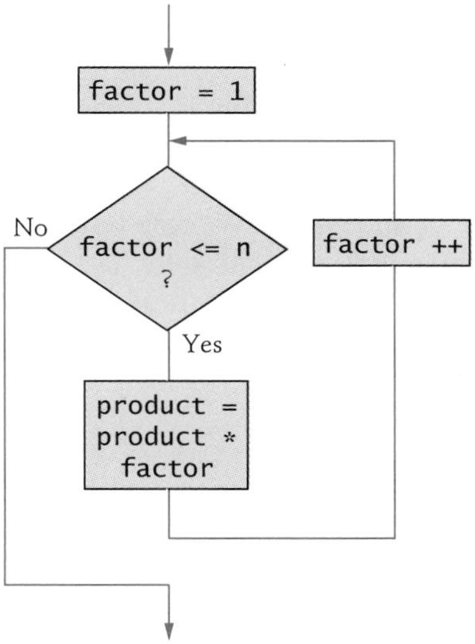

It is possible—but a sign of unbelievably bad taste—to put unrelated conditions into the loop:

```
for (rate = 6; month--; cout >> balance) . . . /* bad taste */
```

We won't even begin to decipher what that might mean; look in Feuer [1] for puzzles of this kind. You should stick with `for` loops that initialize, test, and update a single variable.

If the body of a loop consists of a single statement, you can omit the braces. For example, you can replace

```
for (factor = 1; factor <= n; factor++)
{  product = product * factor;
}
```

with

```
for (factor = 1;  factor <= n; factor++)
   product = product * factor;
```

6.2.2 do Loops

Sometimes we want to execute the body of a loop at least once and perform the loop test after the body was executed. The `do/while` loop serves that purpose:

```
do
{  statements
}  while (condition );
```

Here is an example of such a loop. The ancient Greeks were aware of a simple approximation algorithm to compute square roots. The algorithm starts by guessing a value x that might be somewhat close to the desired square root $\sqrt{a}$. The initial value doesn't have to be very close; $x = a/2$ is a perfectly good choice. Now consider the quantities x and a/x. If $x < \sqrt{a}$, then $a/x > a/\sqrt{a} = \sqrt{a}$. Similarly, if $x > \sqrt{a}$, then $a/x < a/\sqrt{a} = \sqrt{a}$. That is, $\sqrt{a}$ lies between x and a/x. We make the *midpoint* of that interval our improved guess of the the square root, as shown in Figure 3. We therefore set $x_{\text{new}} = (x + a/x)/2$ and repeat the procedure—that is, compute the average of x_{new} and a/x_{new}. We stop when two successive approximations differ from each other by a very small amount.

The method converges very rapidly. To compute $\sqrt{300}$, only 8 steps are required:

```
150.000000
 76.000000
 39.973682
 23.739309
 18.188288
 17.341209
 17.320520
 17.320509
```

Figure 3

Approximation of the Square Root

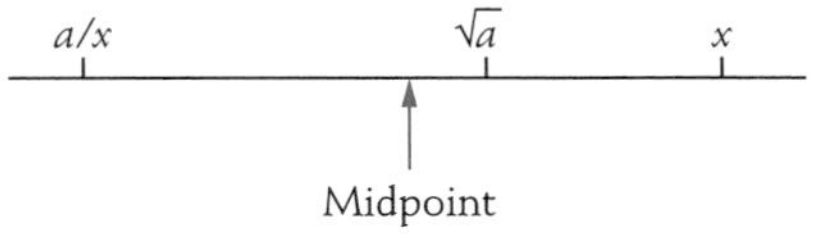

The following function implements that algorithm:

Program sqroot.cpp

```
#include "ccc.h"

float squareroot(float a)
{  float xnew = a / 2;
   float xold;

   do
   {   xold = xnew;
       xnew = (xold + a / xold) / 2;
   }
   while (not float_equal(xnew, xold));

   return xnew;
}

int main()
{  cout << "Please enter a number: ";
   float x;
   cin >> x;
   cout << "The square root is " << squareroot(x) << "\n";
   return EXIT_SUCCESS;
}
```

Here the `do...while` loop is a good choice. We want to enter the loop at least once so that we can compute the difference between two approximations.

Like a `for` loop, a `do...while` loop can always be replaced by a `while` loop. Here we initialize `xold` with an artificial value that is sufficiently distant from `xnew` to ensure that the test passes the first time around:

```
float squareroot(float a)
{  float xnew = a / 2;
   float xold = xnew + 1;

   while (not float_equal(xnew, xold))
   {  xold = xnew;
      xnew = (xold + a / xold) / 2;
   }

   return xnew;
}
```

6.2.3 Looping Forever

The loop

```
while (true)
{  body
}
```

executes the body over and over, without ever terminating. Whoa! Why would we want that? The program would never stop. There are two reasons. Some programs indeed never stop; the software controlling an automated teller machine, a telephone switch, or a microwave oven doesn't ever stop (at least not until the device is turned off). Our programs are not usually of that kind, but even if we can't terminate the loop, we can exit from the function that contains it.

This can be helpful when the termination test naturally falls into the middle of the loop, as it does with the iterative algorithm for square roots:

```
float squareroot(float a)
{  float xnew = a / 2;

   while (true)
   {  float xold = xnew;
      xnew = (xold + a / xold) / 2;
      if (float_equal(xnew, xold)) return xnew;
   }
}
```

Common Error 6.3

Off-by-1 Errors

Consider the binomial coefficient

$$\binom{n}{k} = \frac{n}{1} \times \frac{n-1}{2} \times \cdots \times \frac{n-k+1}{k}$$

computed as follows:

```
int binomial(int n, int k)
{  int b = 1; /* the binomial coefficient   */
   int i;
   for (i = 1; i <= k; i++)
      b = b * (n + 1 - i) / i;
   return b;
}
```

Should `i` go from 1 to `k`, or perhaps to `k + 1`? Is the correct factor really `(n + 1 - i)`, or should it be `(n - i)` or even `(n - 1 - i)`? It is easy to be *off by 1* in these expressions.

Some people try to solve off-by-1 errors by randomly inserting `+ 1` or `- 1` until the program seems to work. That is, of course, a terrible strategy. It can take a long time to compile and test all the various possibilities. Expending a small amount of mental effort is a real time saver.

There are two useful strategies to check that you are not off by 1. *Count iterations,* and *check boundary conditions.* Counting iterations is simple in this case. The loop makes `k` iterations, which is correct, as you can see from the formula by looking at the denominators. (Getting a count from looking at the numerators is confusing, but it can be done as well. Quality Tip 6.4 explains that the count of numerators is $high - low + 1 = (n - k + 1) - n + 1 = k$).

Now look at the *boundary conditions.* That is, test the first and last iteration of the loop. When `i` is 1, the first factor is

```
(n + 1 - 1)/1
```

which is correct. The last factor is

```
(n - k + 1)/k
```

which also checks out.

Common Error 6.4

Forgetting a Semicolon

It occasionally happens that all the work of a loop is already done in the loop header. This code looks for the position of the first period in a filename:

```
string filename; /* e.g., hello.cpp */
string name;
. . .
for (i = 0; filename.substr(i, 1) != '.'; i++)
    ;

name = filename.substr(0, i); /* e.g., hello */
```

The body of the `for` loop is completely empty, containing just one empty statement terminated by a semicolon.

We are not advocating this strategy. This loop doesn't work correctly if `filename` doesn't happen to contain a period. Such an anemic loop is often a sign of poor error handling.

If you do run into a loop without a body, it is important that you really make sure the semicolon is not forgotten. If the semicolon is accidentally omitted, then the code

```
for (i = 0; filename.substr(i, 1) != '.'; i++)

name = filename.substr(0, i); /* e.g., hello */
```

repeats the statement `name = filename.substr(0, i)` until a period is found, and then it doesn't execute it again. (If `filename` is `"hello.cpp"`, the last assignment into `name` is, quite appropriately, `"hell"`.)

To make the semicolon really stand out, place it on a line all by itself, as shown in the first example.

Quality Tip 6.1

Use for Loops for Their Intended Purpose Only

A for loop is an *idiom* for a while loop of a particular form. A counter runs from the start to the end, with the constant increment:

```
for (i = start; i <  (or <=)  end; i = i + increment)
{  . . .
   /* i, start, end, increment not changed here  */
}
```

If your loop doesn't match this pattern, don't use the for construction. The compiler won't prevent you from writing idiotic for loops:

```
/* bad style—unrelated header expressions */
for (cout << "Inputs: "; not (cin >> x).fail(); sum = sum + x)
   count++;

for (i = 0; i < s.length(); i++)
{  /* bad style—modifies counter */
   if (s.substr(i, 1) == ".") i++;
   count++;
}
```

These loops will work, but they are plainly bad style. Use a while loop for iterations that do not fit into the for pattern.

Quality Tip 6.2

Don't Use != to Test the End of a Range

Here is a loop with a hidden danger:

```
for (i = 1; i != nyear; i++)
{  . . .
}
```

The test i != nyear is a poor idea. What would happen if nyear happened to be negative? Of course, nyear should never be negative, because it makes no sense to have a negative number of years—but the impossible and unthinkable do happen with distressing regularity. If nyear is negative, the test i != nyear is never true, because i starts at 1 and increases with every step. The program dies in an infinite loop.

The remedy is simple. Test

```
for (i = 0; i < nyear; i++) . . .
```

For floating-point values there is another reason not to use !=: Because of roundoff errors, the exact termination point may never be reached.

Of course, you would never write

```
for (rate = 5; rate != 10; rate = rate + 0.3333333) . . .
```

because it is looks highly unlikely that `rate` would match 10 exactly after 15 steps. But the same problem may happen for the harmless-looking

```
for (rate = 5; rate != 10; rate = rate + 0.1) . . .
```

The number 0.1 is exactly representable in the decimal system, but the computer represents floating-point numbers in binary. There is a slight error in any finite binary representation of 1/10, just as there is a slight error in a decimal representation 0.3333333 of 1/3. Maybe `rate` is exactly 10 after 50 steps; maybe it is off by a tiny amount. There is no point in taking chances. Just use < instead of !=:

```
for (rate = 5; rate < 10; rate = rate + 0.1) . . .
```

Random Fact 6.1

Spaghetti Code

In this chapter we used flowcharts to illustrate the behavior of the loop statements. It used to be common to draw flowcharts for every function, on the theory that flowcharts are easier to read and write than the actual code. Nowadays, flowcharts are no longer routinely used for program development and documentation.

Flowcharts have one fatal flaw. While it is possible to express the `while`, `for`, and `do/while` loops with flowcharts, it is also possible to draw flowcharts that cannot be programmed with loops. Consider the chart in Figure 4.

The lower half is a `do/while` loop:

```
do
{  xold = xnew;
   xnew = (xold + a/xold) / 2;
}  while (not float_equal(xnew, xold));
```

The top is an input statement and an assignment:

```
cin >> a;
xold = a / 2;
```

However, now we are supposed to continue in the middle of the loop, skipping the first statement.

```
cin >> a;
xold = a / 2;
goto a;

do
{  xold = xnew;
   a: xnew = (xold + a/xold) / 2;
}  while (not float_equal(xnew, xold));
```

Figure 4

Flowchart That Cannot Be Implemented with Loops

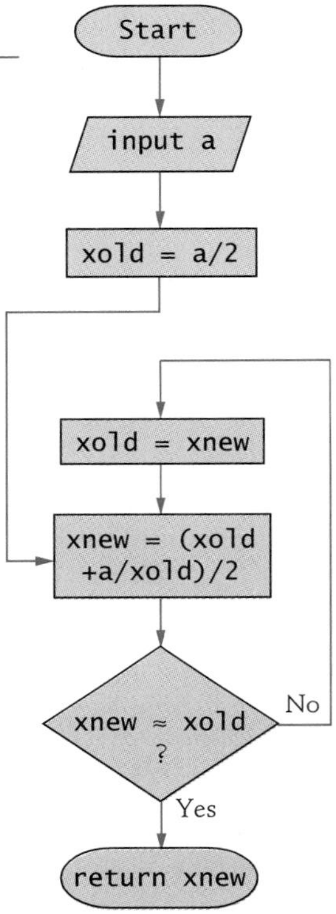

In fact, why even bother with the `do/while`? Here is a faithful interpretation of the flowchart:

```
cin >> a;
xold = a / 2;
goto a;
b: xold = xnew;
a: xnew = (xold + a/xold) / 2;
if (not float_equal(xnew, xold)) goto b:
```

This *nonlinear* control flow turns out to be extremely hard to read and understand if you have more than one or two `goto` statements. Because the lines denoting the `goto` statements weave back and forth in complex flowcharts, the resulting code is named *spaghetti code.* The `while` loop was invented to untangle it.

In the 1960s the influential computer scientist Edsger Dijkstra wrote a famous note, entitled "Goto statements considered harmful" [2], in which he argued for the use of loops instead of unstructured jumps. Initially, many programmers who had been using `goto` for years were mortally insulted and dug out examples where the use of `goto` does lead to clearer or faster code. Some languages started offering weaker forms of `goto`, such as the `break` statement in C++ discussed in Advanced Topics 6.2, that are less harmful. Nowadays, most computer scientists accept Dijkstra's argument and fight bigger battles than optimal loop design.

If you like to draw pictures of your code, you may consider so-called *structure charts* (see Figure 5). They avoid the problem of flow charts and are directly translatable to C++. Figure 6 shows a structure chart for the loop computing a square root.

Figure 5

Structure Charts

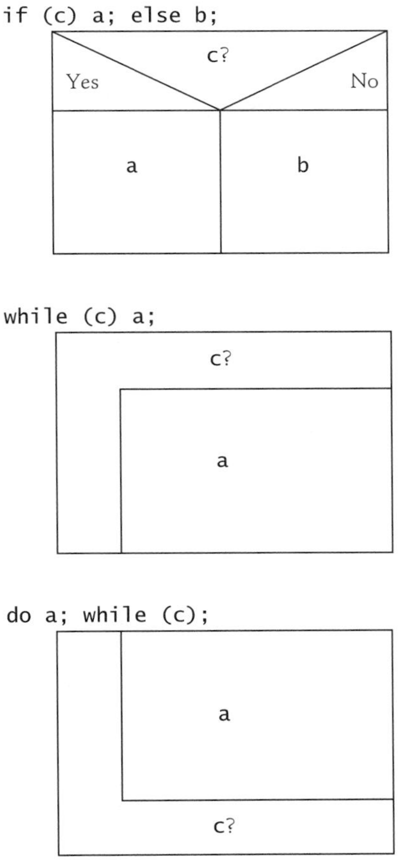

Figure 6

Structure Chart for Square Root Loop

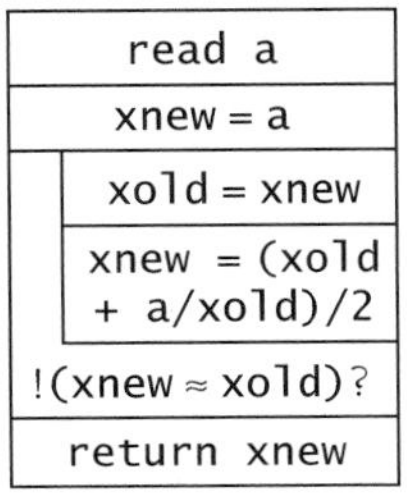

6.3 Common Loop Types

In this section we discuss common loop patterns. You can just follow these models if you need to solve a related problem.

6.3.1 Reading Data

This loop reads through input data:

```
bool done = false;
while (not done)
{  read data
   if (cin.fail())
      done = true;
   else
   {  process data
   }
}
```

This is an extremely common pattern that is well worth committing to memory. We have already had an example of this pattern in the average.cpp program in Section 6.1.3.

The *read data* is frequently one of the following:

Read an integer	`cin >> n`
Read a floating-point number	`cin >> x`
Read a character	`ch = get_char(cin)`
Read a word	`cin >> w`
Read a line	`line = get_line(cin)`

A *word* is any sequence of characters surrounded by white space (spaces, tabs, or newlines).

For example, here is a program that counts the number of words in an input file. This program is useful if you are a writer who is paid by the word.

Program words.cpp

```
#include "ccc.h"

int main()
{  int count = 0;
   bool done = false;
   while (not done)
   {  string word;
      cin >> word;
```

```
         if (cin.fail())
            done = true;
         else
            count++;
      }
      cout << count << " words.\n";

      return EXIT_SUCCESS;
   }
```

6.3.2 Detecting a Sentinel

Suppose you need to read in *two* sets of data from a file. You can't just use the end of the file as the termination criterion. There must be some indication where the first data set ends and the second one begins.

Sometimes you are lucky and no input value can be zero. Then you can prompt the user to keep entering numbers, or 0 to finish that data set. If zero is allowed but negative numbers are not, you can use −1 to indicate termination. Such a value, which is not an actual input but serves as a signal for termination, is called a *sentinel*.

Program sentinl1.cpp

```
#include "ccc.h"

int main()
{  float sum = 0;
   int count = 0;
   bool done = false;
   while (not done)
   {  float x;
      cout << "Enter a number, 0 to finish: ";
      cin >> x;
      if (cin.fail() or x == 0) /* test for sentinel */
         done = true;
      else
      {  sum = sum + x;
         count++;
      }
   }
   if (count > 0)
      cout << "Average: " << sum / count  << "\n";
   return EXIT_SUCCESS;
}
```

That works if there is some restriction on the input. In many cases, though, there isn't. Suppose you want to compute the average of a data set that may contain 0 or negative values. You can't use −13 as a sentinel, even if it is your lucky number. That number just might occur as a legitimate value in some data set, and you wouldn't be so lucky. In that case, we might prompt the user "Enter a number, Q to finish". But now we must be careful reading the input. If the "Q" is encountered in a command `cin >> x`, where `x` is a number, then the state of `cin` turns to fail, and we don't know how to reset it. (There is a way, but it is not particularly convenient). Instead, we must read in the input as a string and then convert it to a number if it is not "Q".

Program sentinl2.cpp

```
#include "ccc.h"

int main()
{  float sum = 0;
   int count = 0;
   bool done = false;
   while (not done)
   {  string s;
      cout << "Enter a number, Q to finish:";
      cin >> s;
      if (cin.fail() or uppercase(s) == "Q")
      /* test for sentinel */
         done = true;
      else
      {  float x = floatvalue(s);
         sum = sum + x;
         count++;
      }
   }
   if (count > 0)
      cout << "Average: " << sum / count << "\n";
   return EXIT_SUCCESS;
}
```

6.3.3 Displaying a Table of Values

Let us print a table that shows the account balance of an account with initial investment of $10,000 after 10 years under a variety of interest rates, from 5 percent to 10 percent in increments of 0.5 percent.

Program baltable.cpp

```
#define CCC_WIN
#include "ccc.h"

float future_value(float initial_balance, float p,
   int nyear)
{  float b = initial_balance
      * pow(1 + p / 12 / 100, 12 * nyear);
```

```
   return b;
}

int main()
{  cout  << " Rate Balance\n\n";

   float rate;
   float initial_amount = 10000;
   int nyear = 10;

   for (rate = 5; rate <= 10; rate = rate + 0.5)
   {  float balance = future_value(initial_amount, rate,
         nyear);
      cout << format("%10.2f", rate)
         << format("%10.2f", balance) << "\n";
   }
   return EXIT_SUCCESS;
}
```

This program displays the following table:

```
 Rate  Balance

 5.00  16470.10
 5.50  17310.76
 6.00  18193.97
 6.50  19121.84
 7.00  20096.61
 7.50  21120.65
 8.00  22196.40
 8.50  23326.47
 9.00  24513.57
 9.50  25760.55
10.00  27070.41
```

We can show the same information graphically by plotting a series of dots, one for each value:

Program balgraph.cpp

```
#define  CCC_WIN
#include "ccc.h"

float future_value(float initial_balance,
   float p, int nyear)
{  float b = initial_balance
      * pow(1 + p / 12 / 100, 12 * nyear);
   return b;
}
```

Figure 7

Growth of an Investment

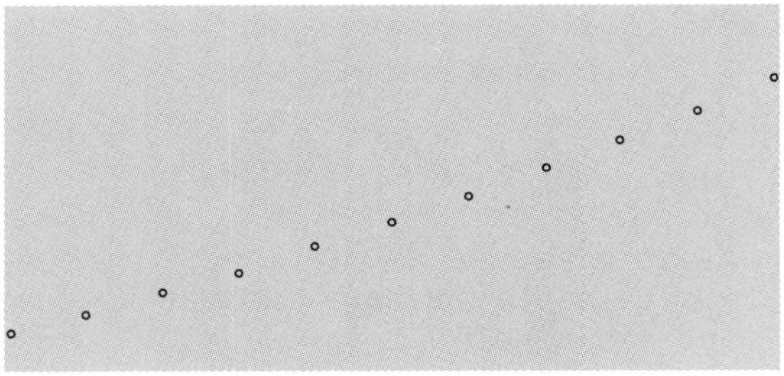

```
int main()
{  float rate;
   float initial_amount = 10000;
   int nyear = 10;
   cwin.coord(5, 3 * initial_amount, 10, 0);
   for (rate = 5; rate <= 10; rate = rate + 0.5)
   {  float balance = future_value(initial_amount,
         rate, nyear);
      cwin << Point(rate, balance);
   }

   return EXIT_SUCCESS;
}
```

This program generates the picture shown in Figure 7.

6.3.4 Iterating through the Characters in a String

The general pattern to traverse all characters in a string is

```
int i;
for (i = 0; i < s.length(); i++)
{  string c = s.substr(i, 1);
   do something with c
}
```

Let us use this pattern to write a function that computes the *reverse* of a string. For example, the reverse of `"Hello"` is `"olleH"`. We compute the reverse by looking at all characters, one at a time, and concatenating them together in the opposite order.

Program reverse.cpp

```
#include "ccc.h"

string reverse(string s)
{  string r = "";
```

```
   int i;
   for (i = 0; i < s.length(); i++)
   {  string ch = s.substr(i, 1);
      r = ch + r; /* add ch in front */
   }
   return r;
}

int main()
{  cout << "Please enter a string:";
   string s;
   cin >> s;
   cout << s << " reversed is"  << reverse(s) << "\n";
   return EXIT_SUCCESS;
}
```

This loop is somewhat subtle. To clarify how it works, look at this walkthrough when `reverse` is called with `s = "Hello"`.

reverse("Hello")		
i	ch	r
0	"H"	"H"
1	"e"	"eH"
2	"l"	"leH"
3	"l"	"lleH"
4	"o"	"olleH"

6.3.5 Convergence

Many iterative algorithms compute better and better approximations until two successive approximations are very close together. There is usually the possibility that the values refuse to get closer to another, and we must be prepared for that as well. If the values do not converge after a certain number of iterations, then we exit the loop.

```
new_value = initial value;
int iteration = 0;
const int MAX_ITERATIONS = 10000;

do
{  old_value = new_value;
   new_value = better approximation computed from old_value
   iteration++;
}  while (new_value and old_value aren't close enough
   and iteration < MAX_ITERATION);
```

Here we graphically show the convergence of computing a square root. To give a dynamic view of the process, the y-position of the first point is at the top of the screen and moves down with further iterations. The x-position converges to the actual root.

Program converge.cpp

```
#include CCC_WIN
#include "ccc.h"

int main()
{  float a = cwin.get_float("Please enter a number");
   float xnew = a / 2;
   float xold;
   int iteration = 0;
   const int MAX_ITERATIONS = 20;

   cwin.coord(0, 0, a, MAX_ITERATIONS);
   do
   {  xold = xnew;
      xnew = (xold + a / xold) / 2;
      cwin << Point(xnew, iteration);
      iteration++;
   }  while (not float_equal(xnew, xold)
         and iteration < MAX_ITERATIONS);

   return EXIT_SUCCESS;
}
```

Figure 8 shows the convergence.

Figure 8

Convergence of the Square Root Algorithm

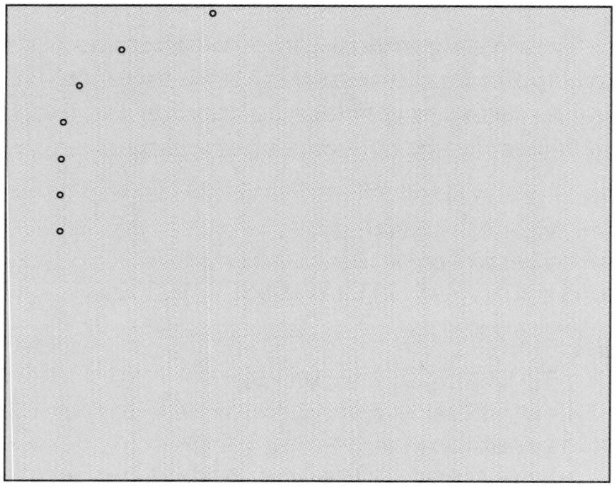

Productivity Hint 6.1

Redirection of Input and Output

Consider the word-counting program of Section 6.3.2. How would you use it? You would type text in, and at the end of the input the program would tell you how many words you typed. However, none of the words would be saved for posterity. That is truly dumb—you would never want to use such a program.

Such programs are not intended for keyboard input. The program makes a lot of sense if input is read from a *file*. The command line interfaces of most operating systems provide a way to link a file to the input of a program, as if all the characters in the file had actually been typed by a user. If you type

```
wcount < article.txt
```

the word-counting program is executed. Its input instructions no longer expect input from the keyboard. All input commands (>>, `get_line`, `get_char`) get their input from the file article.txt.

This mechanism works for any program that reads its input from the standard input stream `cin`. By default, `cin` is tied to the keyboard, but it can be tied to any file by specifying *input redirection* on the command line.

If you have always launched your program from the integrated environment, you need to find out whether your environment supports input redirection. If it does not, you need to learn how to open a command window (often called a *shell*) and launch the program in the command window by typing its name and redirection instructions.

You can also redirect output. In this program, that is not terribly useful. If you run

```
words < article.txt > output.txt
```

the file output.txt contains a single line like "513 words." However, redirecting output is obviously useful for programs that produce lots of it. You can print the file containing the output or edit it before you turn it in for grading.

Advanced Topic 6.1

Pipes

Output of one program can become the input of another program. Here is a simple program that writes each word of the input file onto a separate line:

```
int main()
{  while (true)
   {  string word;
      cin >> word;
      if (cin.fail())
         return EXIT_SUCCESS;
```

```
         else
            cout << word << "\n";
      }
   }
```

Let us call this program *split.* Then

```
split < article.txt
```

lists the words in the file article.txt, one on each line. That isn't too exciting, but it becomes useful when combined with another program: *sort.* We don't yet know how to write a program that sorts strings, but most operating systems have a sort program. A sorted list of the words in a file would be quite useful—for example, for making an index. We can save the unsorted words in a temporary file.

```
split < article.txt > temp.txt
sort < temp.txt > sorted.txt
```

Now the sorted words are in the file sorted.txt. Because this operation is so common, there is a command line shorthand for it.

```
split < article.txt | sort > sorted.txt
```

The split program runs first, reading input from article.txt. Its output becomes the input of the sort program. The output of sort is saved in the file sorted.txt. The | operator instructs the operating system to construct a *pipe* linking the output of the first program to the input of the second.

The file sorted.txt has one blemish. It is likely to contain runs of repeated words, like

```
a
a
a
an
an
anteater
asia
```

This is easy to fix with another program that removes *adjacent* duplicates. Removing duplicates in arbitrary positions is quite hard, but adjacent duplicates are easy to handle:

```
int main()
{  string last;
   while (true)
   {  string word;
      cin >> word;
      if (cin.fail())
         return EXIT_SUCCESS;
      else if (word != last)
         cout << word << "\n";
      last = word;
   }
}
```

Figure 9

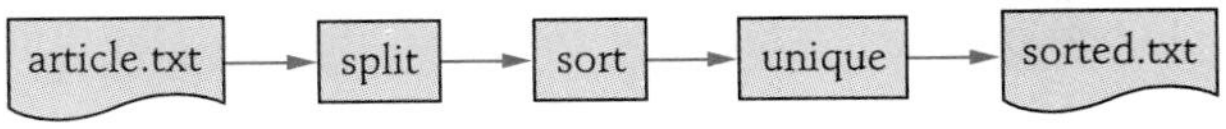

A Series of Pipes

Let us call this program *unique*. The sorted word list, with duplicates removed, is obtained as the series of pipes

```
split < article.txt | sort | unique > sorted.txt
```

(See Figure 9.)

Redirection and pipes make it possible to combine simple programs to do useful work. This approach was pioneered by the Unix operating system. Unix comes with dozens of commands that perform common tasks and are designed to be combined with each other.

Quality Tip 6.3

Symmetric and Asymmetric Bounds

It is easy to write a loop with `i` going from 1 to `n`.

```
for (i = 1; i <= n; i++) . . .
```

The values for `i` are bounded by the relation $1 \le$ `i` $\le$ `n`. Because there are $\le$ on both bounds, the bounds are called *symmetric*.

When traversing the characters in a string, the bounds are *asymmetric*.

```
for (i = 0; i < s.length(); i++) . . .
```

The values for `i` are bounded by $0 \le$ `i` $<$ `s.length()`, with a $\le$ to the left and a $<$ to the right. That is appropriate, because `s.length()` is not a valid position.

It is not a good idea to force symmetry artificially:

```
for (i = 0; i <= s.length() - 1; i++) . . .
```

That is more difficult to read and understand.

For every loop, consider which form is most natural according to the needs of the problem and use that.

Quality Tip 6.4

Count Iterations

Finding the correct lower and upper bounds for an iteration can be confusing. Should I start at 0? Should I use `<= b` or `< b` as a termination condition?

Counting the number of iterations is a very useful device for better understanding a loop. Counting is easier for loops with asymmetric bounds. The loop

```
for (i = a; i < b; i++) . . .
```

is executed b − a times. For example, the loop traversing the characters in a string,

```
for (i = 0; i < s.length(); i++) . . .
```

runs `s.length()` times. That makes perfect sense, since there are `s.length()` characters in a string.

The loop with symmetric bounds,

```
for (i = a; i <= b; i++)
```

is executed b − a +1 times. That "+1" is the source for many programming errors. For example,

```
for (x = 0; x <= 10; x++)
```

runs 11 times. Maybe that is what you want; if not, start at 1 or use < 10.

If the increment is a value c other than 1, then the counts are

(b − a)/c	for the asymmetric loop
(b − a)/c + 1	for the symmetric loop

For example, the loop `for (i=10; i<=40; i+=5)` executes (40 − 10)/5 + 1 = 7 times.

Advanced Topic 6.2

The "Loop and a Half" Problem

When reading data from input, we always needed to use a somewhat unsightly loop

```
bool done = false;
while (not done)
{  read data
   if (cin.fail())
      done = true;
   else
   {  process data
   }
}
```

The true test for loop termination is in the middle of the loop, not at the top. This is called a "loop and a half" because one must go halfway into the loop before knowing whether one needs to terminate.

Some programmers very much dislike the introduction of an additional Boolean variable for loop control. Two C++ language features can be used to alleviate the "loop and a half" problem. I don't think either is a superior solution, but since both approaches are fairly common, it is worth knowing about them when reading other people's code.

The expression `cin >> word` has a value, namely `cin`. That makes it possible to write `cin >> word >> x`. It also makes it possible to write

```
while (not (cin >> word).fail())
{  process data
}
```

The expression `not (cin >> word).fail()` means, "First read a word; then test whether `cin` failed." This is an expression with a side effect. The primary purpose of the expression is to serve as a test for the `while` loop, but it also actually does some work—namely, reading the input. In general, it is always a bad idea to use side effects, because they make a program hard to read and maintain. In this case, however, it is somewhat seductive, because it eliminates the control variable `done`, which also makes the code hard to read and maintain.

The other solution is to use the `break` keyword. If you read the description of the `switch` statement in Advanced Topic 4.2, you have encountered `break` already. Using `break` is necessary to leave the switch. It is also possible to use `break` to leave a loop:

```
while (true)
{  read data
   if (cin.fail()) break;
   process data
}
```

In general, a `break` is a very poor way of exiting a loop. Misusing a `break` caused the failure of an AT&T 4ESS telephone switch on January 15, 1990. The failure propagated through the entire U.S. network, rendering it nearly unusable for about nine hours. A programmer had used a `break` to terminate an `if` statement. Unfortunately, `break` cannot be used with `if`, so the program execution broke out of the enclosing `switch` statement, skipping some variable initializations and running into chaos [3, p. 38]. Using `break` statements also makes it difficult to use *correctness proof* techniques (see Advanced Topic 6.4).

Side effects in conditions and `break` statements are beneficial in the "loop and a half" case, but it is difficult to lay down clear rules as to when they are safe and when they should be avoided. To keep things simple, we will not use them in this book. Instead, we suggest the following remedy: Put the loop inside a separate function and use a `return` statement to exit the loop and the function. For example,

```
void read_words()
{  while(true)
   {  string word;
      cin >> word;
      if (cin.fail()) return;
      process data
   }
}
```

6.4 Simulations

In a simulation we generate random events and evaluate their outcomes. Here is a typical problem that can be decided by running a simulation, the *Buffon needle experiment,* devised by Comte Georges-Louis Leclerc de Buffon (1707–1788), a French naturalist. A needle of length 1 inch is dropped onto paper that is ruled with lines 2 inches apart. If the needle drops onto a line, we count it as a *hit.* Buffon conjectured that the quotient *tries/hits* approximates π. (See Figure 10.)

Figure 10

The Buffon Needle Experiment

Now, how can we run this experiment in the computer? We don't actually want to build a robot that drops needles on paper. The C++ library has a *random number generator,* which produces numbers that appear to be completely random. The library for this book supplies two functions that make the random number generator a little easier to use:

`rand_int(a, b)`	returns a random integer between `a` and `b`
`rand_float(a, b)`	returns a random floating point number between `a` and `b`

For example, we can simulate the throwing of dice by calling `rand_int(1, 6)`. To give you a feeling for the random numbers, run the following program a few times:

Program dice.cpp

```
#include "ccc.h"

int main()
{  int i;
   for (i = 1; i <= 10; i++)
   {  int d = rand_int(1, 6);
      cout << d << "";
   }
   cout << "\n";
   return EXIT_SUCCESS;
}
```

Here are a few typical program runs.

```
6 5 6 3 2 6 3 4 4 1
3 2 2 1 6 5 3 4 1 2
4 1 3 2 6 2 4 3 3 5
```

As you can see, this program produces a different stream of simulated dice throws every time it is run. Actually, the numbers are not completely random. They are drawn from very long sequences of numbers that don't repeat for a long time. These sequences are actually computed from fairly simple formulas; they just behave like random numbers. For that reason, they are often called *pseudorandom* numbers. How to generate good sequences of numbers that behave like truly random sequences is an important and well-studied problem in computer science. We won't investigate this issue further, though; we'll just use the random numbers produced by `rand_int` and `rand_float`.

To run the Buffon needle experiment we have to work a little harder. When we throw a die, it has to come up with one of six faces. When throwing a needle, however, there are many possible outcomes. We must generate *two* random numbers: one to describe the starting position and one to describe the angle of the needle with the x-axis. Then we need to test whether the needle touches a grid line. We stop after 10,000 tries.

Let us agree to generate the *lower* point of the needle. Its x-coordinate is irrelevant, and we may assume its y-coordinate y_{low} to be any random number between 0 and 2. The angle α between the needle and the x-axis can be any value between -90 degrees and 90 degrees. The upper end of the needle has y-coordinate

$$y_{\text{high}} = y_{\text{low}} + \cos\alpha$$

The needle is a hit if y_{high} is at least 2.

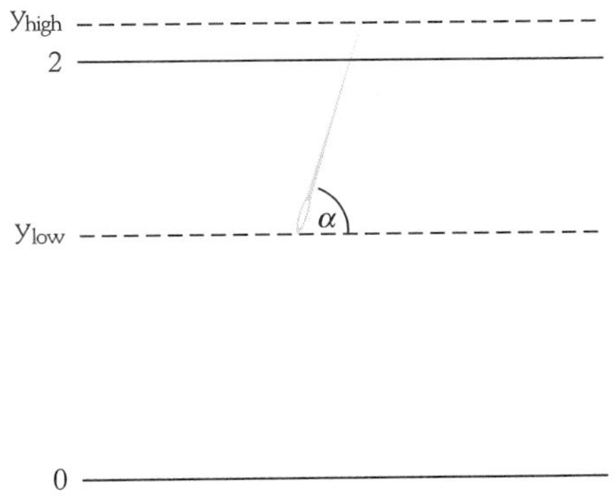

Here is the program carrying out the simulation of the needle experiment.

Program buffon.cpp

```
#include "ccc.h"

float deg2rad(float alpha)
/* PURPOSE:   Convert an angle from degrees to radians
   RECEIVES: alpha—the angle in degrees
   RETURNS:   The angle in radians
*/
```

```
{  return alpha * M_PI / 180;
}

int main()
{  int NTRIES = 10000;
   int i;
   int hits = 0;
   for (i = 1; i <= NTRIES; i++)
   {  float ylow = rand_float(0, 2);
      float angle = rand_float(-90, 90);
      float yhigh = ylow + cos(deg2rad(angle));
      if (yhigh >= 2) hit++;
   }
   cout << "Tries / Hits ="
      << (NTRIES * 1.0) / hits  << "\n";
   return EXIT_SUCCESS;
}
```

On one computer I obtained the result 3.10 when running 10,000 iterations and 3.1429 when running 100,000 iterations.

The point of this program is *not* to compute π (after all, we needed the value of π in the `deg2rad` function). Rather, the point is to show how a physical experiment can be simulated on the computer. Buffon had to drop the needle physically thousands of times and record the results, which must have been a rather dull activity. We can have the computer execute the experiment quickly and accurately.

Simulations are very common computer applications. All simulations use essentially the same pattern as the code of this example: In a loop, a large number of sample values are generated; the values of certain observations are recorded for each sample; when the simulation is completed, the averages of the observed values are printed out.

A typical example of a simulation is the modeling of customer queues at a bank or a supermarket. Rather than observing real customers, one simulates their arrival and their transactions at the teller window or checkout stand in the computer. One can try out different staffing or building layout patterns in the computer simply by making changes in the program. In the real world, making many such changes and measuring their effect would be impossible, or at least very expensive.

6.5 Nested Loops

Let us print a table that tells us the fate of our \$10,000 investment under various interest rate scenarios if we keep the money for 5, 10, 15, 20, 25, and 30 years. (Note that the investment grows to almost \$200,000 if we keep the money for 30 years at 10% interest!)

Rate	5 years	10 years	15 years	20 years	25 years	30 years
5.00	12833.59	16470.10	21137.04	27126.40	34812.91	44677.44
5.50	13157.04	17310.76	22775.84	29966.26	39426.71	51873.88
6.00	13488.50	18193.97	24540.94	33102.04	44649.70	60225.75
6.50	13828.17	19121.84	26442.01	36564.47	50561.98	69917.98
7.00	14176.25	20096.61	28489.47	40387.39	57254.18	81164.98
7.50	14532.94	21120.65	30694.52	44608.17	64828.80	94215.34
8.00	14898.46	22196.40	33069.21	49268.03	73401.76	109357.30
8.50	15273.01	23326.47	35626.54	54412.43	83104.13	126924.98
9.00	15656.81	24513.57	38380.43	60091.52	94084.15	147305.77
9.50	16050.09	25760.55	41345.93	66360.62	106509.41	170948.62
10.00	16453.09	27070.41	44539.20	73280.73	120569.45	198374.00

Of course, the basic idea is simple. Here is the pseudocode:

```
print table header

float rate;
for (rate = RATE_MIN; rate <= RATE_MAX;
      rate = rate + RATE_INCR)
{     print table row
}
```

How do we print a table row? We need to print values for 5, 10, . . . , 30 years. There are the dots again, so we need to program a loop.

```
cout << format(" %10.2f", rate);
int year;
for (year = YEAR_MIN; year <= YEAR_MAX;
      year = year + YEAR_INCR)
{  balance = future_value(initial_balance, rate, year);
   cout << format("%10.2f", balance);
}
cout << "\n";
```

This loop prints a table row, including the newline at the end. Next, let us print the table header. We could print a long string

```
"Rate  5 years 10 years 15 years 20 years 25 years 30 years"
```

Since the header needs to change if we change the year range or increment, it is better to program a loop:

```
cout << "Rate     ";
int year;
for (year = YEAR_MIN; year <= YEAR_MAX;
      year = year + YEAR_INCR)
```

```
{  cout << format("%2d", year) << " years ";
}
cout << "\n";
```

Now we put everything together:

Program table.cpp

```
#include "ccc.h"

float future_value(float initial_balance, float p,
   int nyear)
{  float b = initial_balance
      * pow(1 + p / 12 / 100, 12 * nyear);
   return b;
}

int main()
{  const float RATE_MIN = 5;
   const float RATE_MAX = 10;
   const float RATE_INCR = 0.5;
   const int YEAR_MIN = 5;
   const int YEAR_MAX = 30;
   const int YEAR_INCR = 5;

   /* print table header  */

   cout << " Rate";
   int year;
   for (year = YEAR_MIN; year <= YEAR_MAX;
        year = year + YEAR_INCR)
   {  cout << format("%2d", year) << " years";
   }
   cout << "\n";

   float rate;
   float initial_balance = 10000;
   for (rate = RATE_MIN; rate <= RATE_MAX;
        rate = rate + RATE_INCR)
   {  /* print table row */
      int year;
      cout << format("%5.2f", rate);
      for (year = YEAR_MIN; year <= YEAR_MAX;
           year = year + YEAR_INCR)
      {  float balance =
            future_value(initial_balance, rate, year);
         cout << format("%10.2f", balance);
      }
      cout << "\n";
```

```
    }
    return EXIT_SUCCESS;
}
```

Now we have a total of three `for` loops! The first one is harmless; it just prints six columns in the table header. The other two loops are more interesting. The loop printing a single row is *nested* in the loop that traverses the interest rates. There are a total of 11 rates in the outer loop ($11 = (10-5)/0.5+1$, see Quality Tip 6.4). For each rate we print six columns of balances in the inner loop. Thus, a total of $11 \times 6 = 66$ balances are printed.

You put a loop after another if all iterations of the first loop need to be carried out before the first iteration of the second loop. If the first loop has m iterations and the second loop has n iterations, there are a total of $m + n$ iterations. You nest a loop inside another if all cases of the inner loop must be repeated for each iteration of the outer loop. That yields a total of $m \times n$ iterations.

Sometimes the iteration count of the inner block depends on the outer block. Let us print *Pascal's triangle,* an arrangement of the so-called *binomial coefficients*

$$\binom{n}{k} = \frac{n!}{k!(n-k)!}$$

The Pascal triangle is the arrangement

$$\begin{array}{ccccc}
\binom{0}{0} & & & & \\
\binom{1}{0} & \binom{1}{1} & & & \\
\binom{2}{0} & \binom{2}{1} & \binom{2}{2} & & \\
\binom{3}{0} & \binom{3}{1} & \binom{3}{2} & \binom{3}{3} & \\
\binom{4}{0} & \binom{4}{1} & \binom{4}{2} & \binom{4}{3} & \binom{4}{4} \\
. & . & . & . & .
\end{array}$$

or

$$\begin{array}{ccccc}
1 & & & & \\
1 & 1 & & & \\
1 & 2 & 1 & & \\
1 & 3 & 3 & 1 & \\
1 & 4 & 6 & 4 & 1 \\
. & . & . & . & .
\end{array}$$

These numbers are very common in mathematics. They are called the binomial coefficients because they make up the sequence of coefficients in the expansion of $(x + y)^n$. For example,

$$(x+y)^4 = \mathbf{1} \times x^4 + \mathbf{4} \times x^3y + \mathbf{6} \times x^2y^2 + \mathbf{4} \times xy^3 + \mathbf{1} \times y^4$$

Just as factorials count the number of permutations of a sequence, binomial coefficients count the number of subsets of a set. For example, you can take $\binom{4}{2} = 6$ subsets of 2 elements each out of a set of 4 elements. If the set is $\{d, r, u, m\}$, the subsets are $\{d, r\}$, $\{d, u\}$, $\{d, m\}$, $\{r, u\}$, $\{r, m\}$, and $\{u, m\}$.

Pascal's triangle has an interesting property: Except for the fringe of 1's, every number is the sum of the number immediately above it and the number above and on the left.

```
1
1 1
 \|
1 2 1
 \|\|
1 3 3 1
 \|\|\|
1 4 6 4 1
. . . . .
```

However, this property is not very useful for computing the values of the binomial coefficients. Neither is the original formula $n!/k!(n-k)!$, because the factorials overflow for even moderate values of n. Instead, we cancel $(n-k)!$ and compute

$$\frac{n}{1} \times \frac{n-1}{2} \times \cdots \times \frac{n-k+1}{k}$$

which we do with the following C++ function:

```
int binomial(int n, int k)
{  int b = 1; /*  the binomial coefficient */
   int i;
   for (i = 1; i <= k; i++)
      b = b * (n + 1 - i) / i;
   return b;
}
```

If you remember Common Error 2.2, this should make you nervous. The / denotes integer division because the numerator `b * (n + 1 - i)` and the denominator `i` are both integers. It looks as if the remainder of the division would be lost in every step. Fortunately, in this computation there is never a remainder (see Exercise R6.14), so we are justified in using the faster integer arithmetic.

Now let us print Pascal's triangle. The key to printing the triangle is to note that the inner loop gets longer with every iteration of the outer loop.

Program pascal.cpp

```
#include "ccc.h"

int binomial(int n, int k)
{  int b = 1; /* the binomial coefficient */
   int i;
   for (i = 1; i <= k; i++)
      b = b * (n + 1 - i) / i;
   return b;
}

int main()
{  const int NROWS = 10;
   /* print the first 10 rows of Pascal's triangle */
   int n;
   for (n = 0; n < NROWS; n++)
   { int k;
     for (k = 0; k <= n; k++)
        cout << format("%7d", binomial(n, k));
      cout << "\n";
   }
   return EXIT_SUCCESS;
}
```

6.6 Block Scope

In the preceding code examples that involved nested loops, it often happened that a variable was declared in an inner loop; for example,

```
int main()
{  float rate;
   for (. . .)
   {  int year;
      . . .
      for (. . .)
      {  float balance;
         . . .
      }
      . . .
   }
}
```

The general rule of thumb is to define a variable as closely as possible to its first use. So it should come as no surprise that variables are often declared in inner loops.

A variable is known only inside the block in which it is defined. The region in which a variable is known is called its *scope*. The following picture shows the scope of the three variables:

```
int main()
{  . . .
   float rate;
   for (. . .)
   {  int year;
      . . .
      for (. . .)
      {  float balance;
         . . .
      }
      . . .
   }
   . . .
   return EXIT_SUCCESS;
}
```

We cannot refer to `balance` outside the innermost `for` loop. In this case we had no need to do so. If we wanted to use the last computed balance elsewhere, however, we would need to move the definition of `balance` to an outer block.

Consider this version of the square root approximation loop:

```
float xnew = a / 2;

do
{  float xold;
   xold = xnew;
   xnew = (x + a / x) / 2;
}
while (not float_equal(xnew, xold)); /* Error */
```

The variable `xold` is defined and initialized at the same time, which is generally considered the ideal situation. However, its scope extends only until the end of the closing brace, before the test condition. The compiler will complain that `xold` is an undefined name in the expression `fabs(xnew - xold)`. The variable must therefore be defined outside the loop:

```
float xnew = a / 2;
float xold;

do
{  xold = xnew;
   xnew = (x + a / x) / 2;
}
while (not float_equal(xnew, xold));
```

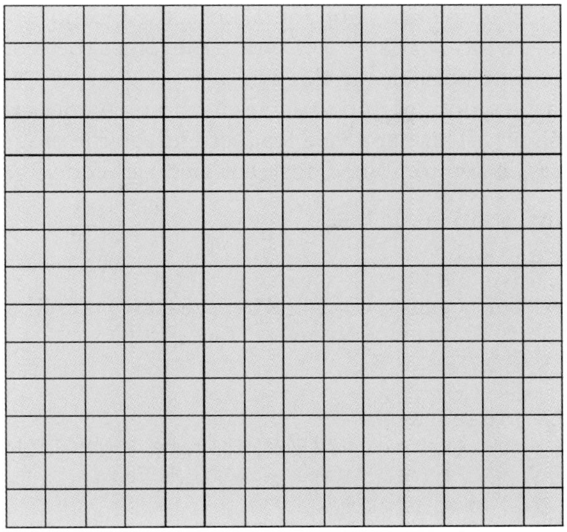

Figure 11

Output for grid.cpp

It is possible to have two variables with the same name defined in different blocks. If the blocks are disjoint, that is not a problem. Consider this code to draw a grid of horizontal and vertical lines on the screen (see Figure 11):

Program grid.cpp

```
#define CCC_WIN
#include "ccc.h"

int main()
{  float x;
   for (x = -10; x <= 10; x++)
   {  Line g(Point(x, -10), Point(x, 10));
      cwin << g;
   }
   float y;
   for (y = -10; y <= 10; y++)
   {  Line g(Point(-10, y), Point(10, y));
      cwin << g;
   }
   return EXIT_SUCCESS;
}
```

The first loop draws horizontal lines, the second loop draws vertical lines. Each loop defines a local variable `g` of type `Line`. Since the scopes of the variables do not meet, there is no possible ambiguity.

If the scopes of two variables with two names are nested, then there is a possible ambiguity. This happened inadvertently in the program that printed a table of future values, as we combined different pieces of code:

```
int main()
{  . . .
   int year;
   for (year = YEAR_MIN; year <= YEAR_MAX;
        year = year + YEAR_INCR)
   {  . . .
   }
   float rate;
   for (rate = RATE_MIN; rate <= RATE_MAX;
        rate = rate + RATE_INCR)
   {  int year;
      for (year = YEAR_MIN; year <= YEAR_MAX;
           year = year + YEAR_INCR)
      {  . . .
      }
   }
   . . .
}
```

This is not an error, although it is not terribly good programming practice either. The name `year` always refers to the closest definition. It denotes the first integer everywhere except in the second `for` loop. In that scope the inner `year` *masks* the outer one, since there is no way of accessing the value of the variable in the outer scope.

In this case, we can just drop the definition of the second `year`, because they are both of the same type and the value of the first one is no longer needed. Otherwise we should rename the second one.

Common Error 6.5

End-of-File Detection

When reading an indeterminate amount of data from a stream, you can either read until a sentinel value (see Section 6.3.3) or read until the end of file.

If the data are stored in a file and supplied to the program through input redirection (see Productivity Hint 6.1), then the end of the file is reached when all data in the file have been read. If the data are supplied through keyboard input, then the user must hit a special key combination (such as Ctrl+`Z` under DOS or Ctrl+`D` under Unix) to indicate the end of the file. That special code is *not* appended to the input file. It just tells the operating system to stop collecting keyboard input. End-of-file detection is a little tricky. There is a function `eof` that reports the end of the file, but you can call it with reliable results only *after the input stream has failed*. The following loop does not work:

```
while (not cin.eof()) /* Don't! */
{  cin >> x;
   sum = sum + x;
   n++;
}
```

If the stream input fails for another reason (usually because a non-number was encountered in the input), then all further input operations fail, and the end of the file is never reached. The loop then becomes an infinite loop. For example, consider the input

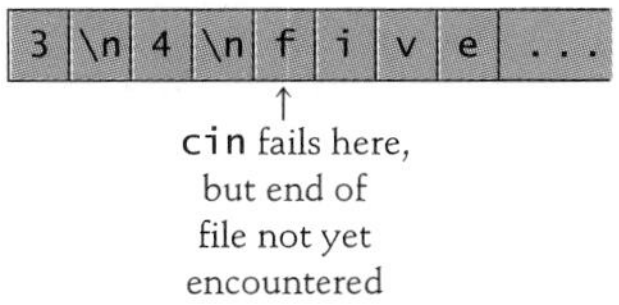

Instead, first test for failure and then test for `eof`:

```
bool done = false;
while (not done)
{  cin >> x;
   if (cin.fail())
   {  done = true;
      if (not cin.eof())
         cout << "Bad input data";
   }
   else
   {  sum = sum + x;
      n++;
   }
}
```

Here is another common error.

```
while (not cin.fail())
{  cin >> x;
   sum = sum + x; /* Don't! */
   n++;
}
if (not cin.eof()) cout << "Bad input data";
```

You must test for failure *after every input.* If the last item in the file were succeeded by white space (and it usually is followed by a newline), then that white space would mask the end of the file. Consider the following sample input:

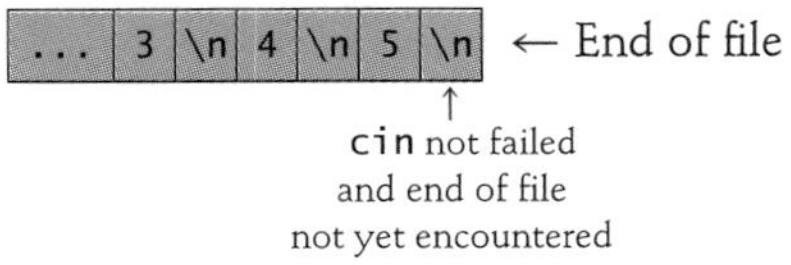

Only when another input is attempted after the last value has been read is the end of the file recognized, and input fails. Then `x` should not be added again to `sum`.

Common Error 6.6

Underestimating the Size of a Data Set

It is a common programming error to underestimate the amount of input data that a user will pour into an unsuspecting program. A program that was designed to handle input lines that are at most 255 characters long will surely fail when the first user runs it with a file whose lines are 1000 characters long. Your text editor may or may not be able to generate such long lines, but it is easy enough to write a program that produces output with very long lines. That program just won't print a newline between outputs. The output of such a program may well become the input of your program, and you should never make any assumptions that input lines are short.

Here is another common problem. In Section 6.3.2 we wrote a program that counted the number of words in a file. How many words might be in an input file? If you enter a test file by hand, surely no more than a few dozen. If you take another convenient file from your hard disk, say a readme.txt file from some software package, there may be a few thousand words. If you feed in the entire text of *Alice in Wonderland* or *War and Peace* (which are available on the Internet), you all of a sudden have to count a few hundred thousand words. The `int` data type on your computer may not be able to count that high, and you may need to switch to `long`.

A famous article [4] analyzed how several Unix programs reacted when they were fed large or random data sets. Sadly, about a quarter didn't do well at all, crashing or hanging without a reasonable error message. For example, in some versions of Unix the tape backup program *tar* cannot handle file names that are longer than 100 characters, which is a pretty unreasonable limitation. Many of these shortcomings are caused by features of the C language that this book neatly sidesteps with the `string` and `vector` types. Others are caused by integer overflow, a problem that we face as well.

Advanced Topic 6.3

Scope of Variables Defined in a Loop Header

It is legal in C++ to define a variable in the header of a branch or loop. Here is the most common form of this syntax:

```
int main()
{  for (int i  = -10; i <= 10; i++)

   {  Line g(Point(i, -10), Point(i, 10));
      cwin << g;
   }
   . . .
   return EXIT_SUCCESS;
}
```

This is undeniably neat, and many C++ programmers like and use this feature. We don't use it in this book, for two reasons. First, it is yet another syntax element that is not essential for learning how to program. Second, there is considerable confusion among compilers about the scope of the loop variable.

The ANSI standard demands that the scope of the variable extend only up to the end of the loop. That is, after the loop the variable `i` is no longer defined. The following code is legal; the two variables `i` have nonoverlapping scope.

```
int main()
{  for (int i  = -10; i <= 10; i++)
   {  Line g(Point(i, -10), Point(i, 10));
      cwin << g;
   }
   /* ANSI C++: i no longer defined here */
   for (int i  = -10; i <= 10; i++)
   {  Line g(Point(-10, i), Point(10, i));
      cwin << g;
   }
   return EXIT_SUCCESS;
}
```

However, in older versions of C++ the scope of the first variable `i` extended from the point of definition until the end of the block containing the `for` statement. Those compilers give a "variable defined twice" error when they encounter the second definition of `i`. When using such a compiler, you would need to write

```
int main()
{  for (int i  = -10; i <= 10; i++)
   {  Line g(Point(i, -10), Point(i, 10));
      cwin << g;
   }
   /* Older C++: i still defined here */
   for (i  = -10; i <= 10; i++)
   {  Line g(Point(-10, i), Point(10, i));
      cwin << g;
   }
   return EXIT_SUCCESS;
}
```

Naturally, this won't compile with an ANSI C++ compiler, which will complain that `i` is undefined in the second loop. Right now, the easiest way to avoid this problem is not to define variables in loop headers.

Advanced Topic 6.4

Loop Invariants

Consider the task of computing a^n, where a is a floating-point number and n is a positive integer. Of course, you can multiply $a \times a \cdots \times a$, n times, but if n is large, you'll end up doing a lot of multiplications. The following function computes a^n in far fewer steps:

```
float power(float a, int n)
{  float r = 1;
   float b = a;
```

```
    int i = n;
    while (i > 0)
    {  if (i % 2 == 0) /* n is even */
       {  b = b * b;
          i = i / 2;
       }
       else
       {  r = r * b;
          i--;
       }
    }
    return r;
}
```

Consider the case n = 100. The function performs the following steps.

power(a, 100)		
b	i	r
a	100	1
a^2	50	
a^4	25	
	24	a^4
a^8	12	a^4
a^{16}	6	
a^{32}	3	
	2	a^{36}
a^{64}	1	
	0	a^{100}

Amazingly enough, the algorithm yields exactly a^{100}. Do you understand why? Are you convinced it will work for all values of n? Here is a clever argument to show that the function always computes the correct result. We will demonstrate that whenever the program reaches the top of the `while` loop, it is true that

$$r \cdot b^{i} = a^{n} \tag{I}$$

Certainly, it is true the first time around, because b = a and i = n. Suppose that (I) holds at the beginning of the loop. We label the values of r, b, and i as "old" when entering the loop, as "new" when exiting the loop. We assume that upon entry

$$r_{old} \cdot b_{old}^{i_{old}} = a^{n}$$

In the loop we have to distinguish two cases: i even and i odd. If n is even, the loop performs the following transformations:

$$r_{new} = r_{old}$$

$$b_{new} = b_{old}^{2}$$

$$i_{new} = i_{old}/2$$

Therefore,

$$\begin{aligned} r_{new} \cdot b_{new}^{\ i_{new}} &= r_{old} \cdot (b_{old})^{2 \cdot i_{old}/2} \\ &= r_{old} \cdot b_{old}^{i_{old}} \\ &= a^n \end{aligned}$$

On the other hand, if i is odd, then

$$\begin{aligned} r_{new} &= r_{old} \cdot a_{old} \\ b_{new} &= b_{old} \\ i_{new} &= i_{old} - 1 \end{aligned}$$

Therefore,

$$\begin{aligned} r_{new} \cdot b_{new}^{\ i_{new}} &= r_{old} \cdot b_{old} \cdot b_{old}^{i_{old}-1} \\ &= r_{old} \cdot b_{old}^{\ i_{old}} \\ &= a^n \end{aligned}$$

In either case, the new values for r, b, and i fulfill the *loop invariant* (I). So what? When the loop finally exits, (I) holds again:

$$r \cdot b^i = a^n$$

Furthermore, we know that $i = 0$ since the loop is terminating. But because $i = 0$, $r \cdot b^i = r \cdot b^0 = r$. Hence $r = a^n$, and the function really does compute the nth power of a.

This technique is quite useful because it can explain an algorithm that is not at all obvious. The condition (I) is called a loop invariant because it is true when the loop is entered, at the top of each pass, and when the loop is exited. If a loop invariant is chosen skillfully, we may be able to deduce correctness of a computation. See [5] for another nice example.

Random Fact 6.2

Correctness Proofs

In Advanced Topic 6.3 we introduced the technique of loop invariants. If you skipped that note, have a glance at it now. That technique can be used to prove rigorously that a function returns exactly the value that it is supposed to compute. Such a proof is far more valuable than any testing. No matter how many test cases you try, you always worry whether another case that you haven't tried yet might show a bug. A proof settles the correctness for *all* possible inputs.

For some time, programmers were very hopeful that proof techniques such as loop invariants would greatly reduce the need of testing. You would prove that each simple function and procedure is correct, and then put the proven components together and prove that they work together as they should. Once it is proved that main works correctly, no testing is required at all! Some researchers were so excited about these techniques that they tried to omit the programming step altogether. The designer would write down the program requirements, using the notation of formal logic. An automatic prover would prove that such a program could be written and generate the program as part of its proof.

Unfortunately, in practice these methods never worked very well. The logical notation to describe program behavior is complex. Even simple scenarios require many formulas. It is easy enough to express the idea that a function is supposed to compute a^n, but the logical formulas describing all procedures in a program controlling an airplane, for instance, would fill many pages. These formulas are created by humans, and humans make errors when they deal with difficult and tedious tasks. Experiments showed that instead of buggy programs, programmers wrote buggy logic specifications and buggy program proofs.

Van der Linden [3], p. 287, gives some examples of complicated proofs that are much harder to verify than the programs they are trying to prove.

Program proof techniques are valuable for proving the correctness of individual procedures that make computations in nonobvious ways. At this time, though, there is no hope to prove any but the most trivial programs correct in such a way that the specification and the proof can be trusted more than the program.

Chapter Summary

1. Loops execute a block of code repeatedly. A termination condition controls how many times the loop is executed.

2. There are three kinds of loops: `while`, `for`, and `do/while` loops. The `while` loop is the most common; `for` loops are used when an integer runs from a starting to an ending value with a constant increment or decrement; `do/while` loops are appropriate when the loop body must be executed at least once.

3. There are a number of common loop patterns. It is helpful to be familiar with sample programs that involve these patterns and to be able to adapt them to similar problems.

4. Loops can be nested.

5. The body of a loop, and in fact any pair of `{}`, introduces a new *block scope*. Variables defined inside the block are not visible outside the block.

Further Reading

[1] Alan Feuer, *The C Puzzle Book,* Prentice-Hall, 1989.

[2] E. W. Dijkstra, "Goto Statements Considered Harmful", *Communications of the ACM.,* vol. 11, no. 3 (March 1968), pp. 147–148.

[3] Peter van der Linden, *Expert C Programming,* Prentice-Hall 1994.

[4] Barton P. Miller, Louis Fericksen, and Bryan So, "An Empirical Study of the Reliability of Unix Utilities", *Communications of the ACM,* vol. 33, no. 12 (December 1990), pp. 32–44.

[5] Jon Bentley, *Programming Pearls,* Addison-Wesley, 1986, Chapter 4, "Writing Correct Programs".

[6] Kai Lai Chung, *Elementary Probability Theory with Stochastic Processes,* Undergraduate Texts in Mathematics, Springer-Verlag, 1974.

[7] Rudolf Flesch, *How to Write Plain English,* Barnes & Noble Books, 1979.

Review Exercises

Exercise R6.1. Which loop statements does C++ support? Give simple rules when to use each loop type.

Exercise 6.2. Is the following code legal?

```
int i;
for (i = 0; i < 10; i++)
{  int i;
   for (i = 0; i < 10; i++)
      cout << i;
   cout << "\n";
}
```

What does it print? Is it good coding style? If not, how would you improve it?

Exercise 6.3. How often do the following loops execute? Assume that `i` is not changed in the loop body.

```
for (i = 1; i <= 10; i++) . . .
for (i = 0; i < 10; i++) . . .
for (i = 10; i > 0; i--) . . .
for (i = -10; i <= 10; i++) . . .
for (i = 10; i >= 0; i++) . . .
for (i = -10; i <= 10; i = i + 2) . . .
for (i = -10; i <= 10; i = i + 3) . . .
```

Exercise R6.4. Rewrite the following `for` loop into a `while` loop.

```
int i;
int s = 0;
for (i = 1; i <= 10; i++) s = s + i;
```

Exercise R6.5. Rewrite the following `do/while` loop into a `while` loop.

```
int n;
cin >> n;
float x = 0;
float s;
do
{  s = 1 / (1 + 1.0/(n * n));
   x = x + s;
}  while (s > 0.01);
```

Exercise R6.6. What is an infinite loop? On your computer, how can you terminate a program that executes an infinite loop?

Exercise R6.7. There are two methods to supply input to `cin`. Describe both methods. Explain how the "end of file" is signaled in both cases.

Exercise R6.8. In DOS/Windows and Unix, there is no special "end of file" character stored in a file. Verify that statement by producing a file with known character count—for example, a file consisting of the following three lines

```
Hello
cruel
world
```

Then look at the directory listing. How many characters does the file contain? Remember to count the newline characters. (In DOS, you may be surprised that the count is not what you expect. DOS text files store each newline as a two-character sequence. The input and output streams automatically translate between this carriage return/line feed sequence used by files and the "`\n`" character used by C++ programs, so you don't need to worry about it.) Why does this prove that there is no "end of file" character? Why do you nevertheless need to type Ctrl + `Z`/Ctrl + `D` to end console input?

Exercise R6.9. There are three kinds of input: character-oriented, word-oriented, and line-oriented. Explain the differences between them, show how to implement each in C++, and give simple rules when to use which kind.

Exercise R6.10. Explain why it is problematic to mix word-oriented input (`cin >> x`) and line-oriented input (`get_line(cin)`). Give two strategies for reading multiple input values of the form

name of bridge
length of bridge

Here the name of the bridge can be "Brooklyn" or "Golden Gate". The length is a floating-point number.

Exercise R6.11. What are the values of `s` and `n` after the following loops?

```
int s = 1;
int n = 1;
while (s < 10) { s = s + n; n++; }

int s = 1;
int n;
for (n = 1; n < 5; n++) s = s + n;

int s = 1;
int n = 1;
do { s = s + n; n++; } while (s < 10 * n);
```

Exercise R6.12. What do the following loops print? Work out the answer without using the computer.

```
int s = 1;
int n;
for (n = 1; n <= 5; n++)
{  s = s + n;
   cout << s;
}
```

```
int s = 1;
int n;
for (n = 1; n <= 5; cout << s)
{  n = n + 2;
   s = s + n;
}
```

```
int s = 1;
int n;
for (n = 1; n <= 5; n++)
{  s = s + n;
   n++;
}
cout << s << " " << n;
```

Exercise R6.13. What do the following program segments print? Find the answers by hand, not by using the computer.

```
int i;
int n = 1;
for (i = 2; i < 5; i++) n = n + i;
cout << n;
int i;
float n = 1 / 2;
for (i = 2; i <= 5; i++) n = n + 1.0 / i;
cout << i;
```

```
float x = 1;
float y = 1;
int i = 0;
do
{  y = y / 2;
   x = x + y;
   i++;
}  while (x < 1.8);
cout << i;
```

```
float x = 1;
float y = 1;
int i = 0;
while (y >= 1.5)
{  x = x / 2;
   y = x + y;
   i++;
}
cout << i;
```

Exercise R6.14. Show that in the computation of $\binom{n}{k}$, the division

$$\frac{n}{1} \times \frac{n-1}{2} \times \cdots \times \frac{n-i+1}{i}$$

never leaves a remainder.

Exercise R6.15. What is a "loop and a half"? Give four strategies to implement the following "loop and a half":

loop
{ *read employee name*
  if not OK, exit loop
  read employee salary
  if not OK, exit loop
  give employee 5 percent raise
  print employee data
}

Use a Boolean variable, a `break` statement, a `goto` statement, and a separate function with multiple `return` statements. Which of these four approaches do you find clearest?

Exercise R6.16. What is a sentinel value? Give simple rules when it is better to use a sentinel value and when it is better to use the end of the input file to denote the end of a data sequence. *Hint:* Consider the number of data sets and the origin of the data (keyboard input vs. file input).

Exercise R6.17. Write pseudocode for a predicate function that tests whether a string such as `"-3.145E+01"` is actually a legal floating-point number or not.

Exercise R6.18. What is an "off by one" error? Give an example from your own programming experience.

Exercise R6.19. Give an example of a `for` loop where symmetric bounds are more natural. Give an example of a `for` loop where asymmetric bounds are more natural.

Exercise R6.20. What are nested loops? Give an example where a nested loop is typically used.

Exercise R6.21. Suppose you didn't know about the method for computing square roots that was introduced in Section 6.2.2. If you had to compute square roots by hand, you would probably use a different approximation method. For example, suppose you need to compute the square root of 300. You would first find that $17^2 = 289$ is smaller than 300 and $18^2 = 324$ is larger than 300. Then you would try 17.1^2, 17.2^2, and so on. Write pseudocode for an algorithm that uses this strategy. Be precise about the progression from one step to the next and the termination criterion.

Exercise R6.22. If two variables *with the same name* are defined in a function, their scopes can be disjoint or they can overlap. Give examples of both situations. If the scopes overlap, then one variable *masks* the other. Explain.

Programming Exercises

Exercise P6.1. The series of pipes in Advanced Topic 6.1 has one final problem: The output file contains upper- and lowercase versions of the same word, such as "The" and "the". Modify the procedure, either by changing one of the programs or, in the true spirit of piping, by writing another short program and adding it to the series.

Exercise P6.2. *Currency conversion.* Write a program that asks the user to type today's exchange rate between U.S. dollars and Japanese yen. Then the program reads U.S. dollar values and converts each to yen. Use 0 or a negative input as a sentinel.

Exercise P6.3. Write a program that asks the user to type in today's exchange rate between U.S. dollars and Japanese yen. Then the program reads U.S. dollar values and converts each to Japanese yen. Use 0 as the sentinel value to denote the end of dollar inputs. Then the program reads a sequence of yen amounts and converts them to dollars. The second sequence is terminated by the end of the input file.

Exercise P6.4. *Random walk.* Simulate the walk of a drunkard in a square street grid. Draw a grid of 10 streets horizontally and 10 streets vertically. Place a simulated inebriated person in the middle of the grid, denoted by a point. For 100 times, have the simulated person randomly pick a direction (east, west, north, south), move one block in the chosen direction, and redraw the dot. After the iterations, display the distance that the drunkard has covered. (One might expect that on average the person might not get anywhere because the moves to different directions cancel another out in the long run, but in fact it can be shown that with probability 1 the person eventually moves outside any finite region. See, for example, [6], chapter 8, for more details.)

Exercise P6.5. *Projectile flight.* Suppose a cannonball is propelled straight into the air with a starting velocity v_0. Then any calculus book will be proud to tell us that the position of the ball after t seconds is $s(t) = -\frac{1}{2}gt^2 + v_0t$, where $g = 9.81 m/sec^2$ is the gravitational force of the earth. No calculus book ever mentions why someone would want to carry out such an obviously dangerous experiment, so we will do it in the safety of the computer.

In fact, we will confirm the theorem from calculus by a simulation. In our simulation, we will consider how the ball moves in very short time intervals Δt. In a short time interval the velocity v is nearly constant, and we can compute the distance the ball moves as $\Delta s = v \, \Delta t$. In our program, we will simply set

```
const float delta_t = 0.01;
```

and update the position by

```
s = s + v * delta_t;
```

The velocity changes constantly—in fact, it is reduced by the gravitational force of the earth. In a short time interval, $\Delta v = -g \, \Delta t$, and we must keep the velocity updated as

```
v = v - g * delta_t;
```

In the next iteration the new velocity is used to update the distance.

Now run the simulation until the cannonball falls back onto the earth. Get the initial velocity as an input (100 m/sec is a good value.) Update the position and velocity 100 times per second, but print out the position only every full second. Also print out the values from the exact formula $s(t) = -\frac{1}{2}gt^2 + v_0t$ for comparison.

What is the benefit of this kind of simulation when an exact formula is available? Well, the formula from the calculus book is *not* exact. Actually, the gravitational force diminishes the further the cannonball is away from the surface of the earth. This complicates the algebra sufficiently that it is not possible to give an exact formula for the actual motion, but the computer simulation can simply be extended to apply a variable gravitational force. For cannonballs, the calculus-book formula is actually good enough, but computers are necessary to compute accurate trajectories for higher-flying objects such as ballistic missiles.

Exercise P6.6. Most cannonballs are not shot upright but at an angle. If the starting velocity has magnitude v and the starting angle is α, then the velocity is actually a vector with components $v_x = v \cos \alpha$, $v_y = v \sin \alpha$. In x-direction the velocity does not change. In the y-direction the gravitational force takes its toll. Repeat the simulation from the previous exercise, but store the position of the cannonball as a `Point` variable. Update the x-and-y positions separately, and also update the x-and-y components of the velocity separately. Every full second, plot the location of the cannonball on the graphics display. Repeat until the cannonball has reached the earth again.

This kind of problem is of historical interest. The first computers were designed to carry out just such ballistic calculations, taking into account the diminishing gravity for high-flying projectiles and wind speeds.

Exercise P6.7. *Fast computation of Fibonacci numbers.* In Chapter 5, we computed Fibonacci numbers using a *recursive* algorithm. Actually, that was not an efficient method. In this exercise you will compute the Fibonacci numbers using an *iterative* algorithm. When asked to compute a particular f_n, we will simply compute *all* numbers and stop at the nth one. Recall the formula

$$\begin{aligned} f_1 &= 1 \\ f_2 &= 1 \\ f_n &= f_{n-1} + f_{n-2} \end{aligned}$$

As in the algorithm to compute the square root of a number, we will reformulate that as

```
fold1 = 1;
fold2 = 1;
fnew = fold1 + fold2;
```

After that, discard `fold2`, which is no longer needed, and set `fold2` to `fold1` and `fold1` to `fnew`. Repeat computing `fnew` for an appropriate number of times.

Implement a program that computes the Fibonacci numbers in that way. Note that it performs approximately `n` additions. Then go back to the recursive program in Exercise P5.21. Have it print a message in every recursive function call that carries out an addition. Compare the results. Why is the recursive function much busier?

Exercise P6.8. Write a program that prints a *bar chart* from a data set. The program should be a graphics application that prompts the user first for the number of bars, then for the actual values. Assume all values are between 0 and 100. Then draw a bar chart like this.

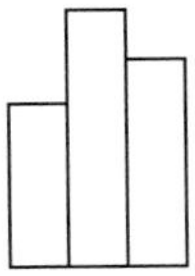

Exercise P6.9. Mean and standard deviation. Write a program that reads a set of floating-point data values from the input. When the end of file is reached, print out the count of the values, the average, and the standard deviation. The average of a data set $\{x_1, \ldots, x_n\}$ is $\overline{x} = \sum x_i/n$, where $\sum x_i = x_1, \ldots, x_n$ is the sum of the input values. The standard deviation is

$$s = \sqrt{\frac{\sum (x_i - \overline{x})^2}{n - 1}}$$

However, that formula is not suitable for our task. By the time that we have computed $\overline{x}$, the individual x_i are long gone. Until we know how to save these values, use the numerically less stable formula

$$s = \sqrt{\frac{\sum x_i^2 - \frac{1}{n}\sum x_i}{n - 1}}$$

You can compute this quantity by keeping track of the count, the sum, and the sum of squares as you process the input values.

Exercise P6.10. Write a program that plots a *regression line:* that is, the line with the best fit through a collection of points. First ask the user to specify the data points by clicking on them in the graphics window. To find the end of the input, place a small rectangle labeled "Stop" at the bottom of the screen; when the user clicks inside that rectangle, then stop gathering input. The regression line is the line with equation

$$y = \overline{y} + m(x - \overline{x}), \qquad \text{where } m = \frac{\sum x_i y_i - n\overline{x}\,\overline{y}}{\sum x_i^2 - n\overline{x}^2}$$

$\overline{x}$ is the mean of the x-values and $\overline{y}$ is the mean of the y-values.

As in Exercise P6.9, you need to keep track of

- The count of input values
- The sum of x, y, x^2, and xy values

To draw the regression line, compute its endpoints at the left and right edge of the screen, and draw a segment.

Exercise P6.11. *Flesch Readability Index.* The following index [7] was invented by Flesch as a simple tool to gauge the legibility of a document without linguistic analysis.

1. Count all words in the file. A *word* is any sequence of characters delimited by white space, whether or not it is an actual English word.
2. Count all syllables in each word. To make this simple, use the following rules: Each *group* of adjacent vowels (a,e,i,o,u,y) counts as one syllable (for example, the "ea" in "real" contributes one syllable, but the "e..a" in "regal" count as two syllables). However, an "e" at the end of a word doesn't count as a syllable. Also each word has at least one syllable, even if the previous rules give a count of 0.
3. Count all sentences. A sentence is ended by a period, colon, semicolon, question mark, or exclamation mark.

4. The index is computed by

$$\text{Index} = 206.835 - 84.6 \times \frac{\text{Number of syllables}}{\text{Number of words}} - 1.015 \times \frac{\text{Number of words}}{\text{Number of sentences}}$$

rounded to the nearest integer.

This index is a number, usually between 0 and 100, indicating how difficult the text is to read. Some examples for random material for various publications are

Comics	95
Consumer ads	82
Sports Illustrated	65
Time	57
New York Times	39
Auto insurance policy	10
Internal Revenue Code	−6

Translated into educational levels, the indices are

91–100	5th grader
81–90	6th grader
71–80	7th grader
66–70	8th grader
61–65	9th grader
51–60	High school student
31–50	College student
0–30	College graduate
Less than 0	Law school graduate

The purpose of the index is to force authors to rewrite their text until the index is high enough. This is achieved by reducing the length of sentences and by removing long words. For example, the sentence

> The following index was invented by Flesch as a simple tool to estimate the legibility of a document without linguistic analysis.

can be rewritten as

> Flesch invented an index to check whether a document is easy to read. To compute the index, you need not look at the meaning of the words.

His book [7] contains delightful examples of translating government regulations into "plain English".

Your program should read in a text file, a word at a time, and compute the legibility index.

Exercise P6.12. *Factoring of integers.* Write a program that asks the user for an integer and then prints out all its factors. For example, when the user enters 150, the program should print

```
2
3
5
5
```

Exercise P6.13. *Prime numbers.* Write a program that prompts the user for an integer and then prints out all prime numbers up to that integer. For example, when the user enters 20, the program should print

```
2
3
5
7
11
13
17
19
```

Recall that a number is a prime number if it is not divisible by any number except 1 and itself.

Exercise P6.14. The best known iterative method for computing roots is *Newton–Raphson approximation.* To find the zero of a function whose derivative is also known, compute

$$x_{\text{new}} = x_{\text{old}} - \frac{f(x_{\text{old}})}{f'(x_{\text{old}})}.$$

This method actually yields the same algorithm for finding square roots as does the classical Greek method. Finding $\sqrt{a}$ is the same as finding a zero of $f(x) = x^2 - a$. Thus,

$$x_{\text{new}} = x_{\text{old}} - \frac{f(x_{\text{old}})}{f'(x_{\text{old}})} = x_{\text{old}} - \frac{x_{\text{old}}^2 - a}{2x_{\text{old}}}$$

Clearly this method generalizes to find cube roots and nth roots. For this exercise, write a program to compute nth roots of floating-point numbers. Prompt the user for a and n, then obtain $\sqrt[n]{a}$ by computing a zero of the function $f(x) = x^n - a$.

Exercise P6.15. Write a program that reads a file from standard input and rewrites the file to standard output, replacing all tab characters `\t` with the *appropriate* number of spaces. Make the distance between tab columns a constant and set it to 3, the value we use in this book for C++ programs. Then expand tabs to the number of spaces necessary to move to the next tab column. *That may be less than three spaces.*

For example, the line

\t	{	\t	n	=	0	;	\n	...

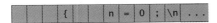

must be converted to

			{			n	=	0	;	\n	...	

Exercise P6.16. Write a program that reads a series of floating-point numbers and prints

- The maximum value
- The minimum value
- The average value

Exercise P6.17. *The game of Nim.* This is a well-known game with a number of variants. We will consider the following variant, which has an interesting winning strategy. Two players alternately take marbles from a pile. In each move, a player chooses how many marbles to take. The player must take at least one but at most half of the marbles. Then the other player takes a turn. The player who takes the last marble loses.

You will write a program in which the computer plays against a human opponent. Generate a random integer between 10 and 100 to denote the initial size of the pile. Generate a random integer between 0 and 1 to decide whether the computer or the human takes the first turn. Generate a random integer between 0 and 1 to decide whether the computer plays *smart* or *stupid.* In stupid mode the computer simply takes a random legal value (between 1 and n/2) from the pile whenever it has a turn. In smart mode the computer takes off enough marbles to make the size of the pile a power of two minus 1—that is, 3, 7, 15, 31, or 63. That is always a legal move, except if the size of the pile is currently one less than a power of two. In that case, the computer makes a random legal move.

You will note that the computer cannot be beaten in smart mode when it has the first move, unless the pile size happens to be 15, 31, or 63. Of course, a human player who has the first turn and knows the winning strategy can win against the computer.

Exercise P6.18. The value of e^x can be computed as the power series

$$e^x = \sum_{n=0}^{\infty} \frac{x^n}{n!} = 1 + x + \frac{x^2}{2!} + \frac{x^3}{3!} + \cdots$$

Write a function **`exponential(x)`** that computes e^x using this formula. Of course, you can't compute an infinite sum. Just keep adding values until an individual summand (term) is less than a certain threshold. At each step, you need to compute the new term and add it to the total. It would be a poor idea to compute

```
summand = pow(x, n)/factorial(n).
```

Instead, update the summand in each step:

```
summand = summand * x / n;
```

Exercise P6.19. Program the following simulation: Darts are thrown at random points onto the square with corners (1, 1) and (−1, −1). If the dart lands inside the unit circle (that is, the circle with center (0, 0) and radius 1), it is a hit. Otherwise it is a miss. Run this simulation and use it to determine an approximate value for π. Explain why this is a better method for estimating π than the Buffon needle program.

Exercise P6.20. It is easy and fun to draw graphs of curves with the C++ graphics library. Simply draw a hundred line segments joining the points $(x, f(x))$ and $(x + d, f(x + d))$, where x ranges from x_{min} to x_{max} and $d = (x_{max} - x_{min})/100$. Draw the curve $f(x) = x^3/100 - x + 10$, where x ranges from -10 to 10 in this fashion.

Exercise P6.21. Draw a picture of the "four-leaved rose" whose equation in polar coordinates is $r = \cos 2\theta$, $0 \leq \theta \leq 2\pi$. Let θ go from 0 to 2π in 100 steps. Each time, compute r and then compute the (x, y) coordinates from the polar coordinates by using the formula

$$x = r \cos \theta$$
$$y = r \sin \theta$$

You can get extra credit if you can vary the number of petals.

CHAPTER 7

Testing and Debugging

Objectives

- To learn how to design test stubs for testing components of your programs in isolation
- To understand the principles of test case selection and evaluation
- To be able to use assertions to document program assumptions
- To become familiar with the debugger
- To learn strategies for effective debugging

A complex program never works right the first time; it needs to be tested. It is easier to test a program if it has been designed with testing in mind. This is a common engineering practice: On television circuit boards or in the wiring of an automobile, you will find lights and wire connectors that serve no direct purpose for the TV or car but are put in place for the repair person in case something goes wrong. In the first part of this chapter we will learn how to instrument our programs in a similar way. It is a little more work up-front, but that work is amply repaid by shortened debugging times.

In the second part of this chapter we will learn how to run the debugger to cope with programs that don't do the right thing.

7.1 Unit Tests

The single most important testing tool is the unit test of a function or procedure. For this test, the procedure is compiled outside the program in which it will be used, together with a *test stub* that feeds arguments to the procedure.

The test arguments can come from one of three sources: from user input, by running through a range of values in a loop, and as random values.

Here is a test stub for the `squareroot` procedure of Chapter 6:

Program sqrtest1.cpp

```
#include "ccc.h"

/* Function to be tested */

float squareroot(float a)
{  float xnew = a / 2;
   float xold;
   do
   {  xold = xnew;
      xnew = (xold + a / xold) / 2;
   }
   while (not float_equal(xnew, xold));
   return xnew;
}

/* Test stub */

int main()
{  int done = false;
   while (not done)
   {  float x;
      cin >> x;
      if (cin.fail()) done = true;
      else
```

```
      {  float y = squareroot(x);
         cout << "squareroot of  " << x << " = "
            << y << "\n";
      }
   }
   return EXIT_SUCCESS;
}
```

When you run this test stub, you need to enter inputs and to force an end of input when you are done, by typing a key such as Ctrl+`Z` or Ctrl+`D` (see Section 6.1.3). You can also store the test data in a file and use redirection:

```
sqrtest1 < test1.in
```

For each test case, the stub code runs the **`squareroot`** procedure and prints the result. You can then manually check the computations. Once you have confidence that the function works correctly, you can plug it into your program.

It is also possible to generate test cases automatically. If there are few possible inputs, it is feasible to run through a representative number of them with a loop:

Program sqrtest2.cpp

```
#include "ccc.h"

/* Function to be tested */

float squareroot(float a)
{  float xnew = a / 2;
   float xold;
   do
   {  xold = xnew;
      xnew = (xold + a / xold) / 2;
   }
   while (not float_equal(xnew, xold));
   return xnew;
}

/* Test stub */


int main()
{  float x;
   for (x = 0; x <= 10; x = x + 0.5)
   {  float y = squareroot(x);
      cout << "squareroot of  " << x << " = " << y << "\n";
   }

   return EXIT_SUCCESS;
}
```

Note that we purposefully test boundary cases (zero) and fractional numbers.

Unfortunately, this test is only restricted to a small subset of values. To overcome that limitation, random generation of test cases can be useful.

Program sqrtest3.cpp

```
#include "ccc.h"

/* Function to be tested */

float squareroot(float a)
{  float xnew = a / 2;
   float xold;
   do
   {  xold = xnew;
      xnew = (xold + a / xold) / 2;
   }
   while (not float_equal(xnew, xold));
   return xnew;
}

/* Test stub */

int main()
{  int i;
   for (i = 1; i <= 100; i++)
   {  float x = rand_float(0, 1E6);
      float y = squareroot(x);
      cout << "squareroot of "  << x << " = " << y << "\n";
   }
   return EXIT_SUCCESS;
}
```

No matter how you generate the test cases, the important point is that you test the procedure thoroughly before you put it into the program. If you ever put together a computer or fixed a car, you probably followed a similar process. Rather than simply throwing all the parts together and hoping for the best, you probably first tested each part in isolation. It takes a little longer, but it greatly reduces the possibility of complete failure once the parts are put together.

7.2 Selecting Test Cases

Selecting good test cases is an important skill for debugging programs. Of course, you want to test your program with inputs that a typical user might supply.

You should test all program features. In the program that prints English names of numbers, you should check typical test cases such as 5, 19, 29, 1093, 1728, 30000.

These tests are *positive* tests. They consist of legitimate inputs, and you expect the program to handle them correctly.

Next, you should include *boundary cases.* Test what happens if the input is `0` or `-1`. Boundary cases are still legitimate inputs, and you expect that the program will handle them correctly, usually in some trivial way.

Finally, gather *negative* test cases. These are inputs that you expect the program to reject. Examples are inputs in the wrong format such as `five`.

How should you collect test cases? This is easy for programs that get all their input from standard input. Just make each test case into a file—say, test1.in, test2.in, test3.in. These files contain the keystrokes that you would normally type at the keyboard when the program runs. Feed the files into the program to be tested by using redirection:

```
program < test1.in > test1.out
program < test2.in > test2.out
program < test3.in > test3.out
```

Then study the outputs and see if they are correct.

Keeping a test case in a file is smart, because you can then use it to test every version of the program. In fact, it is a common and useful practice to make a test file whenever you find a program bug. You can use that file to verify that your bug fix really works. Don't throw it away; feed it to the next version after that and all subsequent versions. Such a collection of test cases is called a *test suite.*

You will be surprised how often a bug that you fixed will reappear in a future version. This is a phenomenon known as *cycling.* Sometimes you don't quite understand the reason for a bug and apply a quick fix that appears to work. Later, you apply a different quick fix that solves a second problem but makes the first problem appear again. Of course, it is always best to really think through what causes a bug and fix the root cause instead of doing a sequence of "Band-Aid" solutions. If you don't succeed in doing that, however, at least you want to have an honest appraisal of how well the program works. By keeping all old test cases around and testing them all against every new version, you get that feedback. The process of testing against a set of past failures is called *regression testing.*

Testing the functionality of the program without consideration of its internal structure is called *black-box testing.* That is an important part of testing, because, after all, the users of a program do not know its internal structure. If a program works perfectly on all positive inputs and fails gracefully on all negative ones, then it does its job.

However, it is impossible to ensure absolutely that a program will work correctly on all inputs, just by supplying a finite number of test cases. As the famous computer scientist Edsger Dijkstra pointed out, testing can only show the presence of bugs—not their absence. To gain more confidence in the correctness of a program, it is useful to consider its internal structure. Testing strategies that look inside a program are called *white-box testing.* Performing unit tests of each procedure and function is a part of white-box testing.

You want to make sure that each part of your program is exercised at least once by one of your test cases. This is called *test coverage.* If some code is never executed by any of your test cases, you have no way of knowing whether that code would perform correctly if it ever were executed by user input. That means that you need to look at every `if/else` branch to see that each of them is reached by some test case. Many conditional branches are in the code only to take care of strange and abnormal inputs, but they still do something. It is a common phenomenon that they end up doing something incorrect but that those faults are never discovered during testing because nobody supplied the strange and abnormal inputs. Of course, these flaws become immediately apparent when the program is released and the first idiot user types in a bad input and is incensed when the program crashes. A test suite should ensure that each part of the code is covered by some input.

For example, in testing the `int_name` function you want to make sure that every `if` statement is entered for at least one test case and that it is skipped for another test case. For example, you might to test the inputs 1234 and 1034 to see what happens if the test `if (c >= 100)` is entered and what happens if it is skipped.

It is a good idea to write the first test cases *before* the program is written completely. Designing a few test cases can give you insight into what the program should do, which is valuable for implementing it. You will also have something to throw at the program when it compiles for the first time. Of course, the initial set of test cases will be augmented as the debugging process progresses.

Modern programs can be quite challenging to test. In a program with a graphical user interface, the user can click random buttons with a mouse and supply input in random order. Programs that receive their data through a network connection need to be tested by simulating occasional network delays and failures. All this is much harder, since you cannot simply place keystrokes in a file. We need not worry about these complexities in this course, and there are tools to automate testing in these scenarios. The basic principles of regression testing (never throwing a test case away) and complete coverage (executing all code at least once) still hold.

7.3 Test Case Evaluation

In the last section, we worried about how to get test *inputs*. Now let us consider what to do with the *outputs*.

How do you know whether the output is correct? Sometimes you can verify the output by calculating the correct values by hand. For example, for a payroll program you can compute taxes manually.

Sometimes a computation does a lot of work, and it is not practical to do the computation manually. That is the case with many approximation algorithms, which may run through dozens or hundreds of iterations before they arrive at the final answer. The square root function of Section 6.2.2 is an example of such an approximation.

How can we test that the square root function works correctly? We can supply test inputs for which we know the answer, such as 4 and 900, and also $\frac{25}{4}$, so that we don't just restrict the inputs to integers.

Alternatively, we can write a test stub program that verifies that the output values fulfill certain properties. For the square root program we can compute the square root, compute the square of the result, and verify that we obtain the original input:

Program sqrtest4.cpp

```
#include "ccc.h"

/* Function to be tested */

float squareroot(float a)
{  float xnew = a / 2;
   float xold;
   do
   {  xold = xnew;
      xnew = (xold + a / xold) / 2;
   }
   while (not float_equal(xnew, xold));
   return xnew;
}

/* Test stub */

int main()
{  int i;
   for (i = 1; i <= 100; i++)
   {  float x = rand_float(0, 1E6);
      float y = squareroot(x);
      if (float_equal(y * y, x)) cout << "Test passed. ";
      else cout << "Test failed. ";
      cout << "squareroot of "  << x << " = " << y << "\n";
   }

   return EXIT _SUCCESS;
}
```

Finally, there may be a less efficient way of computing the same value that a function produces. We can then run a test stub that computes the function to be tested, together with the slower process, and compares the answers. For example, $\sqrt{x} = x^{1/2}$, so we can use the slower pow function to generate the same value. Such a slower but reliable procedure is called an *oracle.*

Program sqrtest5.cpp

```
#include "ccc.h"

/* Function to be tested */
```

```
float squareroot(float a)
{  float xnew = a / 2;
   float xold;
   do
   {  xold = xnew;
      xnew = (xold + a / xold) / 2;
   }
   while (not float_equal(xnew, xold));
   return xnew;
}

/* Test stub */

int main()
{  int i;
   for (i = 1; i <= 100; i++)
   {  float x = rand_float(0, 1E6);
      float y = squareroot(x);
      if (float_equal(y, pow(x, 0.5)))
         cout << "Test passed. ";
      else cout << "Test failed. ";
      cout << "squareroot of " << x << " = " << y << "\n";
   }

   return EXIT_SUCCESS;
}
```

Productivity Hint 7.1

Batch Files and Shell Scripts

If you need to perform the same tasks repeatedly on the command line, then it is worth learning about the automation features offered by your operating system.

Under DOS, you use *batch files* to execute a number of commands automatically. For example, suppose you need to test a program with three inputs:

```
program < test1.in
program < test2.in
program < test3.in
```

Then you find a bug, fix it, and run the tests again. Now you need to type the three commands once more. There has to be a better way. Under DOS, put the commands in a text file and call it test.bat. Then you just type

```
test
```

and the three commands in the batch file execute automatically.

It is easy to make the batch file more useful. If you are done with program and start working on program2, you can of course write a batch file test2.bat, but you can do better than that.

Give the test batch file a *parameter*. That is, call it with

```
test program
```

or

```
test program2
```

You need to change the batch file to make this work. In a batch file, %1 denotes the first string that you type after the name of the batch file, %2 the second string, and so on:

File test.bat

```
%1 < test1.in
%1 < test2.in
%1 < test3.in
```

What if you have more than three test files? DOS batch files have a very primitive `for` loop:

File test.bat

```
for %%f in (test*.in) do %1 < %%f
```

If you work in a computer lab, you will want a batch file that copies all your files onto a floppy disk when you are ready to go home. Put the following lines in a file gohome.bat:

File gohome.bat

```
copy *.cpp a:
copy *.h a:
copy *.txt a:
copy *.in a:
```

There are lots of uses for batch files, and it is well worth it to learn more about them.

Batch files are a feature of the DOS operating system, not of C++. On a Unix system, *shell scripts* are used for the same purpose.

7.4 Assertions

We covered assertions previously in Section 5.13, but this is a good place to remind you of their power again.

Programs often contain implicit assumptions. For example, denominators need to be nonzero; salaries should not be negative. Sometimes the iron force of logic ensures that these conditions are satisfied. If you divide by `1 + x * x`, then that value will never be zero, and you need not worry. Negative salaries, however, are not necessarily ruled out by logic but merely by convention. Surely nobody would ever work for a negative salary, but such a value might creep into a program due to an input or processing error. In practice the "impossible" happens with distressing regularity.

Assertions provide a valuable sanity check.

```
void raise_salary(Employee& e, float by)
{  assert(e.get_salary() >= 0);
   assert(by >= -100);
   float new_salary = e.get_salary() * (1 + by / 100);
   e.set_salary(new_salary);
}
```

If an assertion is not satisfied, the program terminates with a useful error message showing the line number and the code of the failed assertion:

```
assertion failure in file fincalc.cpp line 61: by >= -1000
```

That is a powerful signal that something went wrong elsewhere and that the program needs further testing.

7.5 Program Traces

Sometimes you run a program and you are not sure where it spends its time. To get a printout of the program flow, you can insert trace messages into the beginning and end of every procedure:

```
string digit_name(int n)
{  cout << "Entering digit_name\n";
   . . .
   cout << "Exiting digit_name\n";
}
```

It is also useful to print the input parameters when a procedure is entered and to print return values when a function is exited:

```
string digit_name(int n)
{  cout << "Entering digit_name. n = " << n << "\n";
   . . .
   cout << "Exiting digit_name. Return value = "
      << s << "\n";
   return s;
}
```

To get a proper trace, you must locate *each* function exit point. Place a trace message before every `return` statement and at the end of the function.

You aren't restricted to "enter/exit" messages. You can report on progress inside a function:

```
string int_name(int n)
{  . . .
   cout << "Inside int_name. Thousands\n";
   . . .
   cout << "Inside int_name. Hundreds\n";
   . . .
   cout << "Inside int_name. Tens\n";
   . . .
   cout << "Inside int_name. Ones\n");
   . . .
}
```

Here is a trace of a call to `int_name` and all the functions that it calls. The input is `n` = 12305.

```
Inside int_name. Thousands
Entering int_name. n = 12
Inside int_name. Teens
Entering teen_name. n = 12
Exiting teen_name. Return value = twelve
Exiting digit_name. Return value =  twelve
Inside int_name. Hundreds
Entering digit_name. n = 3
Exiting digit_name. Return value = three
Inside int_name. Ones
Entering digit_name. n = 5
Exiting digit_name. Return value = five
Exiting digit_name. Return value =  twelve thousand three hundred five
```

Program traces can be useful to analyze the behavior of a program, but they have a number of definite disadvantages. It can be quite time-consuming to find out which trace messages to insert. If you insert too many messages, you produce a flurry of output that is hard to analyze; if you insert too few, you may not have enough information to spot the cause of the error. When you are done with the program, you need to remove all trace messages. If you find another error, however, you need to stick the print statements back in. If you find that a hassle, you are not alone. Most professional programmers use a *debugger,* not trace messages, to locate errors in their code. The debugger is the topic of the remainder of this chapter.

7.6 The Debugger

As you have undoubtedly realized by now, computer programs rarely run perfectly the first time. At times, it can be quite frustrating to find the errors, or *bugs* as they are called by programmers. Of course, you can insert trace messages to show the program flow as well as the values of key variables, run the program, and try to analyze the printout. If the printout does not clearly point to the problem, you may need to add and remove print commands and run the program again. That can be a time-consuming process.

Modern development environments contain special programs, so-called *debuggers,* that help you locate bugs by letting you follow the execution of a program. You can stop and restart your program and see the contents of variables whenever your program is temporarily stopped. At each stop, you have the choice of what variables to inspect and how many program steps to run until the next stop.

Some people feel that debuggers are just a tool to make programmers lazy. Admittedly some people write sloppy programs and then fix them up with the debugger, but the majority of programmers make an honest effort to write the best program they can before trying to run it through the debugger. These programmers realize that the debugger, while more convenient than print statements, is not cost-free. It does take time to set up and carry out an effective debugging session.

In actual practice, you cannot avoid using the debugger. The larger your programs get, the harder it is to debug them simply by inserting print statements. You will find that the time investment to learn about the debugger is amply repaid in your programming career.

Random Fact 7.1

The First Bug

According to legend, the first bug was found in the Mark II, a huge electromechanical computer at Harvard University. It really was caused by a bug—a moth was trapped in a relay switch. Actually, from the note that the operator left in the log book next to the moth (see Figure 1), it appears as if the term "bug" had already been in active use at the time.

The pioneering computer scientist Maurice Wilkes wrote: "Somehow, at the Moore School and afterwards, one had always assumed there would be no particular difficulty in getting programs right. I can remember the exact instant in time at which it dawned on me that a great part of my future life would be spent finding mistakes in my own programs."

Figure 1

The First Bug

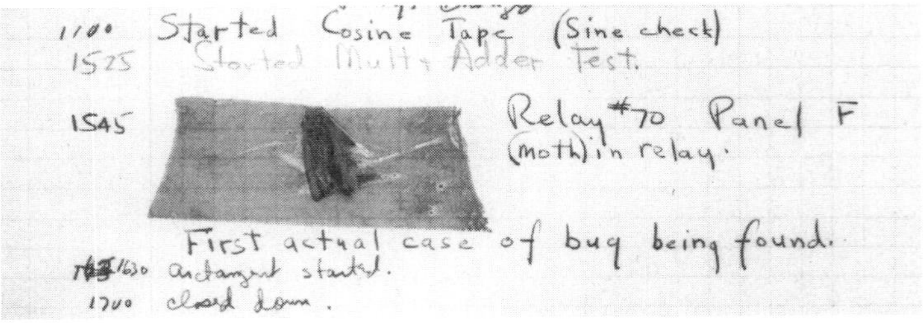

7.6.1 Using a Debugger

Like compilers, debuggers vary widely from one system to another. On some systems they are quite primitive and require you to memorize a small set of arcane commands; on others they have an intuitive window interface.

You will have to find out how to prepare a program for debugging and how to start the debugger on your system. If you use an integrated development environment, which contains an editor, compiler, and debugger, this step is usually very easy. You just build the program in the usual way and pick a menu command to start debugging. On many Unix systems, you must manually build a debug version of your program and invoke the debugger.

Once you have started the debugger, you can go a long way with just three debugging commands: "run until this line", "step to next line", and "inspect variable". The names and keystrokes or mouse clicks for these commands differ widely between debuggers, but all debuggers support these basic commands. You can find out how, either from the documentation or a lab manual, or by asking someone who has used the debugger before.

The "run until this line" command is the most important. Many debuggers show you the source code of the current program in a window. Select a line with the mouse or cursor keys. Then hit a key or select a menu command to run the program to the selected line. On other debuggers, you have to type in a command or a line number. In either case, the program starts execution and stops as soon as it reaches the line you selected (see Figure 2). Of course, you may have selected a line that will not be

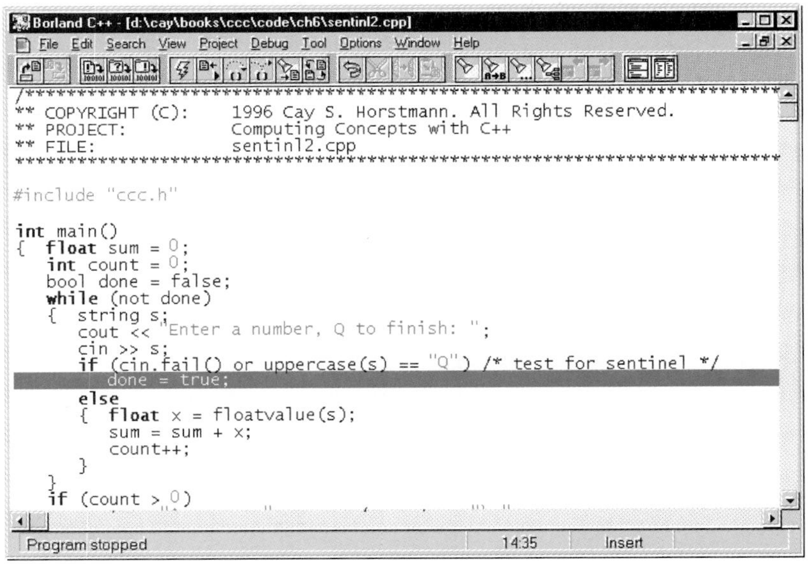

Figure 2

Debugger Stopped at Selected Line

reached at all during a particular program run. Then the program terminates in the normal way. The very fact that the program has or has not reached a particular line can be valuable information.

The "step to next line" command executes the current line and stops at the next program line.

Once the program has stopped, you can look at the current values of variables. Again, the method for selecting the variables differs among debuggers. On some debuggers you select the variable name with the mouse or cursor keys and then issue a menu command such as "inspect variable". In other debuggers you must type the name of the variable into a dialog box. The debugger then displays the contents of the variable (Figure 3). If all variables contain what you expected, you can run the program until the next point where you want to stop.

The program also stops to read data, just as it does when you run it without the debugger. Just enter the inputs in the normal way, and the program will continue running.

Finally, when the program has completed running, the debug session is also finished. You can no longer inspect variables. To run the program again, you may be able to reset the debugger, or you may need to exit the debugging program and start over. Details depend on the particular debugger.

7.6.2 A Sample Debugging Session

Consider the following program, whose purpose is to compute all prime numbers up to a number n. An integer is defined to be prime if it is not evenly divisible by any

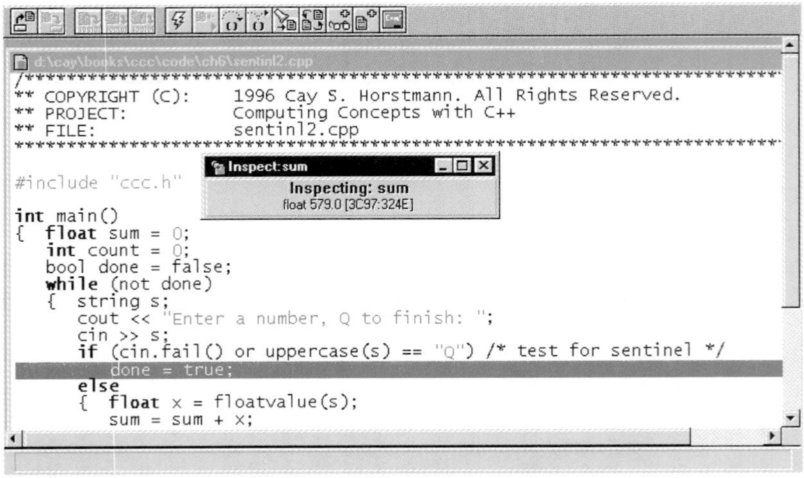

Figure 3

Inspecting a Variable in the Debugger

number except by 1 and itself. Also, mathematicians find it convenient not to call 1 a prime. Thus, the first few prime numbers are 2, 3, 5, 7, 11, 13, 17, 19.

Program primebug.cpp

```
                #include "ccc.h"

/*   1 */   bool isprime(int n)
            /* PURPOSE:  Tests whether an integer is a prime
               RECEIVES: n—any positive integer
               RETURNS:  true iff n is a prime
            */
/*   2 */   {  if (n == 2) return true;
/*   3 */      if (n % 2 == 0) return false;
/*   4 */      int k = 3;
/*   5 */      while (k * k < n)
/*   6 */      {  if (n % k == 0) return false;
/*   7 */         k = k + 2;
/*   8 */      }
/*   9 */      return true;
/*  10 */   }

/*  11 */   int main()
/*  12 */   {  int n;
/*  13 */      cout << "Please enter the upper limit: ";
/*  14 */      cin >> n;
/*  15 */      int i;
/*  16 */      for (i = 1; i <= n; i = i + 2)
/*  17 */      {  if (isprime(i))
/*  18 */            cout << i << "\n";
/*  19 */      }
/*  20 */      return EXIT_SUCCESS;
/*  21 */   }
```

We numbered the lines (except for blank lines, comments, and **#include** directives) so we can refer to them in this example. Probably your debugger won't actually number them.

When you run this program with an input of 10, then the output is

```
1
3
5
7
9
```

That is not very promising; it looks as if the program just prints all odd numbers. Let us find out what it does wrong by using the debugger. Actually, for such a simple program, it is easy to correct mistakes simply by looking at the faulty output and the program code. However, we want to learn to use the debugger.

Let us first go to line 17. On the way, the program will stop to read the input into n. Supply the input value 10.

```
/*  11 */    int main()
/*  12 */    {  int n;
/*  13 */       cout << "Please enter the upper limit: ";
/*  14 */       cin >> n;
/*  15 */       int i;
/*  16 */       for (i = 1; i <= n; i = i + 2)
/*  17 */       {  if (isprime(i))
/*  18 */             cout << i << "\n";
/*  19 */       }
/*  20 */       return EXIT_SUCCESS;
/*  21 */    }
```

Now we wonder why the program treats 1 as a prime. Go to line 2.

```
/*  1 */    bool isprime(int n)
            /* PURPOSE:    Tests whether an integer is a prime
               RECEIVES:   n—any positive integer
               RETURNS:    true iff n is a prime
            */
/*  2 */    {  if (n == 2) return true;
/*  3 */       if (n % 2 == 0) return false;
/*  4 */       int k = 3;
/*  5 */       while (k * k < n)
/*  6 */       {  if (n % k == 0) return false;
/*  7 */          k = k + 2;
/*  8 */       }
/*  9 */       return true;
/* 10 */    }
```

Convince yourself that the argument of `isprime` is currently 1 by inspecting `n`. Then execute the "run to next line" command. You will notice that the program goes to lines 3 and 4 and then directly to line 9.

```
/*  1 */    bool isprime(int n)
            /* PURPOSE:    Tests whether an integer is a prime
               RECEIVES:   n—any positive integer
               RETURNS:    true iff n is a prime
            */
/*  2 */    {  if (n == 2) return true;
/*  3 */       if (n % 2 == 0) return false;
/*  4 */       int k = 3;
/*  5 */       while (k * k < n)
/*  6 */       {  if (n % k == 0) return false;
/*  7 */          k = k + 2;
/*  8 */       }
/*  9 */       return true;
/* 10 */    }
```

Inspect the value of `k`. It is 3, and therefore the `while` loop was never entered. It looks like the `isprime` function needs to be rewritten to treat 1 as a special case.

Next, we would like to know why the program doesn't print 2 as a prime even though the `isprime` function does recognize that 2 is a prime, whereas all other even numbers are not. Go again to line 2, the next call of `isprime`. Inspect `n`; you will note that `n` is 3. Now it becomes clear: The `for` loop in `main` tests only odd numbers. The `main` should either test both odd and even numbers or, better, just handle 2 as a special case.

Finally, we would like to find out why the program believes 9 is a prime. Go again to line 2 and inspect `n`; it should be 5. Repeat that step twice until `n` is 9. (With some debuggers, you may need to go from line 2 to line 3 before you can go back to line 2.) Now use the "run to next line" command repeatedly. You will notice that the program again skips past the `while` loop; inspect `k` to find out why. You will find that `k` is 3. Look at the condition in the `while` loop. It tests whether `k * k < n`. Now `k * k` is 9 and `n` is also 9, so the test fails. Actually, it does make sense to test divisors only up to $\sqrt{n}$; if `n` has any divisors except 1 and itself, at least one of them must be less than $\sqrt{n}$. However, actually that isn't quite true; if `n` is a perfect square of a prime, then its sole nontrivial divisor is *equal* to $\sqrt{n}$. That is exactly the case for $9 = 3^2$.

By running the debugger, we have now discovered three bugs in the program:

- `isprime` falsely claims 1 to be a prime.
- `main` doesn't handle 2.
- The test in `isprime` should be `while (k * k <= n)`.

Here is the improved program:

Program goodprim.cpp

```
#include "ccc.h"

bool isprime(int n)
/* PURPOSE:   Tests whether an integer is a prime
   RECEIVES: n—any positive integer
   RETURNS:  true iff n is a prime
*/
{  if (n == 1) return false;
   if (n == 2) return true;
   if (n % 2 == 0) return false;
   int k = 3;
   while (k * k <= n)
   {  if (n % k == 0) return false;
      k = k + 2;
   }
   return true;
}
```

```
int main()
{  int n;
   cout << "Please enter the upper limit: ";
   cin >> n;
   int i;
   if (n >= 2) cout << "2\n";
   for (i = 3; i <= n; i = i + 2)
   {  if (isprime(i))
         cout << i << "\n";
   }
   return EXIT_SUCCESS;
}
```

Is our program now free from bugs? That is not a question the debugger can answer. Remember: Testing can only show the presence of bugs, not their absence.

7.6.3 Stepping through a Program

We have learned how to run a program until it reaches a particular line. Variations of this strategy are often useful.

There are two methods of running the program in the debugger. We can tell it to run to a particular line; then it gets speedily to that line, but we don't know how it got there. We can also *single-step* with the "run to next line" command. Then we know how the program flows, but it can take a long time to step through it.

Actually, there are two kinds of single-stepping commands, often called "step over" and "step into." The "step over" command always goes to the next program line. The "step into" command steps into function calls. For example, suppose the current line is

```
r = future_value(balance, p, n);
cout << format("%10.2f", r);
```

When you "step over" function calls, you get to the next line:

```
r = future_value(balance, p, n);
cout << format("%10.2f", r);
```

However, if you "step into" function calls, you enter the first line of the `future_value` function.

```
float future_value(float initial_balance,
   float p, int nyear)
{  float b = initial_balance * pow(1+p/(12*100), 12*nyear);
   return b;
}
```

You should step into a function to check whether it carries out its job correctly. You should step over a function if you know it works correctly.

If you single-step past the last line of a function, either with the "step over" or the "step into" command, you return to the line in which the function was called.

You should not step into system functions like `format`. It is easy to get lost in them, and there is no benefit in stepping through system code. If you do get lost, there are three ways out. You can just choose "step over" until you are finally again in familiar territory. Many debuggers have a command "run until function return" that executes to the end of the current function, and then you can select "step over" to get out of the function. Finally, most debuggers can show you a *call stack:* a listing of all currently pending function calls. On the one end of the call stack is `main`, on the other the function that is currently executing (see Figure 4).

By selecting another function in the middle of the call stack, you can jump to the code line containing that function call. Then move the cursor to the next line and choose "run until this line." That way, you get out of any nested morass of function calls.

The techniques we saw so far let you trace through the code in various increments. All debuggers support a second navigational approach: You can set so-called *breakpoints* in the code. Breakpoints are set at specific code lines, with a command "add breakpoint here"; again, the exact command depends on the debugger. You can set as many breakpoints as you like. When the program reaches any one of them, execution stops and the breakpoint that causes the stop is displayed.

Breakpoints are particularly useful when you know at which point your program starts doing the wrong thing. You can set a breakpoint, have the program run at full speed to the breakpoint, and then start tracing slowly to observe the program's behavior.

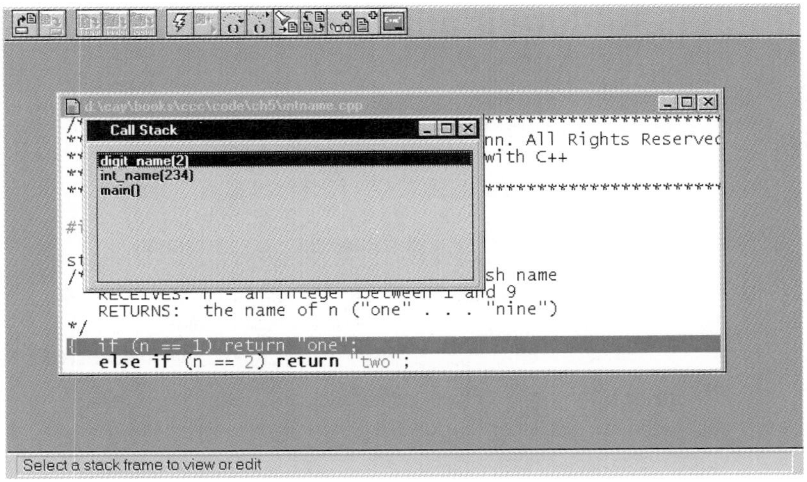

Figure 4

Call Stack Display

Some debuggers let you set *conditional breakpoints.* A conditional breakpoint stops the program only when a certain condition is met. You could stop at a particular line only if a variable `n` has reached 0, or if that line has been executed for the twentieth time. Conditional breakpoints are an advanced feature that can be indispensable in knotty debugging problems.

7.6.4 Inspecting Data

We have learned how to inspect variables in the debugger with the "inspect" command. The "inspect" command works well to show numeric values. When inspecting an object variable, all fields are displayed (see Figure 5).

To inspect a string, you need to select the so-called pointer variable (called `_str` in the code accompanying this book) that points to the actual character sequence in memory. Display its contents, typically by double-clicking or by highlighting it and hitting the Enter key (see Figure 6).

Most debuggers offer two kinds of display commands: "inspect" and "watch." When you inspect a variable, its contents are displayed and it goes away when you continue debugging. When you watch a variable, it is placed into a separate window and its value is continuously updated as you trace through the program (see Figure 7).

It is helpful that watched variables stay visible and are updated, but there are drawbacks. The size of the watch window is limited, and objects don't show up well in the watch window. Use the watch window only for those variables that you need to monitor for an extended amount of time.

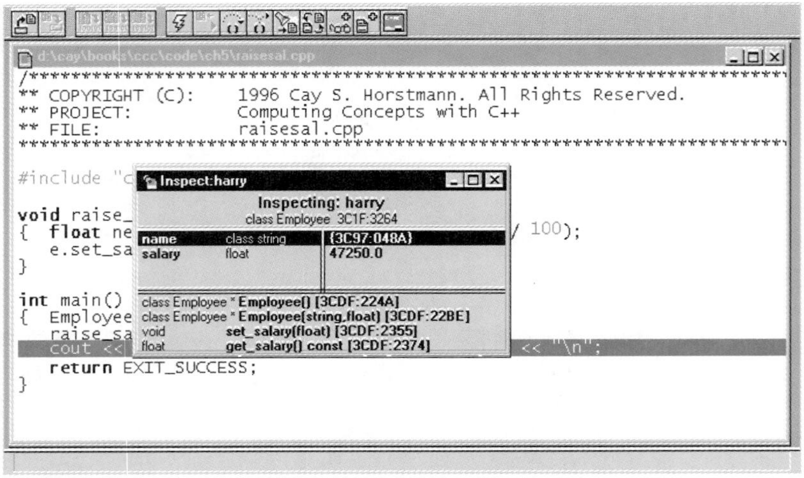

Figure 5

Inspecting an Object

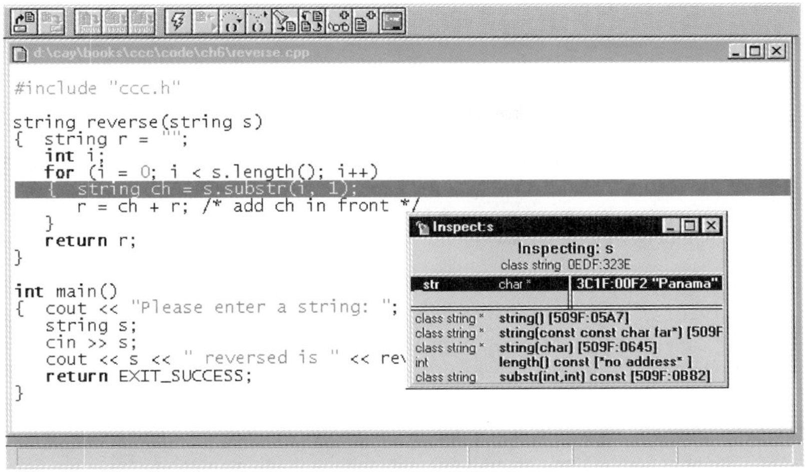

Figure 6

Inspecting a String

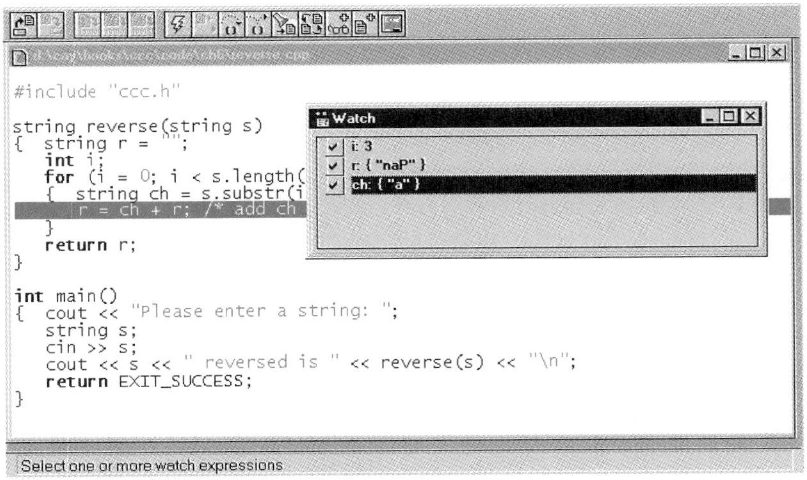

Figure 7

Watching Variables While Tracing

7.7 Strategies

Now you know about the mechanics of debugging, but all that knowledge may still leave you helpless when you fire up the debugger to look at a sick program. There are a number of strategies that you can use to recognize bugs and their causes.

7.7.1 Reproduce the Error

As you test your program, you notice that your program sometimes does something wrong. It gives the wrong output, it seems to print something completely random, it goes in an infinite loop, or it crashes. Find out exactly how to *reproduce* that behavior. What numbers did you enter? Where did you click with the mouse?

Run the program again; type in exactly the same answers and click with the mouse on the same spots (or as close as you can get). Does the program exhibit the same behavior? If so, then you are ready to fire up the debugger to study this particular problem. Debuggers are good for analyzing particular failures. They aren't terribly useful for studying a program in general.

7.7.2 Divide and Conquer

Now that you have a particular failure, you want to get as close to the failure as possible. Suppose your program dies with a division by 0. Since there are many division operations in a typical program, it is often not feasible to set breakpoints to all of them. Instead, use a technique of *divide and conquer.* Step over the procedures in `main`, but don't step inside them. Eventually, the failure will happen again. Now you know which procedure contains the bug: It is the last procedure that was called from `main` before the program died. Restart the debugger and go back to that line in `main`, then step inside that procedure. Repeat the process.

Eventually, you will have pinpointed the line that contains the bad division. Maybe it is completely obvious from the code why the denominator is not correct. If not, you need to find the location where it is computed. Unfortunately, you can't go *back* in the debugger. You need to restart the program and move to the point where the denominator computation happens.

7.7.3 Know What Your Program Should Do

The debugger shows you what the program *does* do. You must know what the program *should* do, or you will not be able to find bugs. Before you trace through a loop, ask yourself how many iterations you *expect* the program to make. Before you inspect a variable, ask yourself what you expect to see. If you have no clue, set aside some time and think first. Have a calculator handy to make independent computations. When you know what the value should be, inspect the variable. This is the moment of truth. If the program is still on the right track, then that value is what you expected, and you must look further for the bug. If the value is different, you may be on to something. Double-check your computation. If you are sure your value is correct, find out why your program comes up with a different value.

In many cases, program bugs are the result of simple errors such as loop termination conditions that are off by 1. Quite often, however, programs make computational errors. Maybe they are supposed to add two numbers, but by accident the code was written to subtract them. Unlike your calculus instructor, programs don't make a special effort to ensure that everything is a simple integer. You will need to make some calculations with large integers or nasty floating-point numbers. Sometimes these calculations can be avoided if you just ask yourself, "Should this quantity be positive? Should it be larger than that value?" Then inspect variables to verify those theories.

7.7.4 Look at All Details

When you debug a program, you often have a theory about what the problem is. Nevertheless, keep an open mind and look around at all details. What strange messages are displayed? Why does the program take another unexpected action? These details count. When you run a debugging session, you really are a detective who needs to look at every clue available.

If you notice another failure on the way to the problem that you are about to pin down, don't just say, "I'll come back to it later". That very failure may be the original cause for your current problem. It is better to make a note of the current problem, fix what you just found, and then return to the original mission.

7.7.5 Understand Each Error Before You Fix It

Once you find that a loop makes too many iterations, it is very tempting to apply a "Band-Aid" solution and subtract 1 from a variable so that the particular problem doesn't appear again. Such a quick fix has an overwhelming probability of creating trouble elsewhere. You really need to have a thorough understanding of how the program should be written before you apply a fix.

It does occasionally happen that you find bug after bug and apply fix after fix, and the problem just moves around. That usually is a symptom of a larger problem with the program logic. There is little you can do with the debugger. You must rethink the program design and reorganize it.

7.8 Debugger Limitations

A debugger is a tool, and like every tool, you can't expect it to be good at everything. Here are some problems that you will encounter in your use of the debugger.

7.8.1 Recursive Procedures

When you set a breakpoint into a recursive procedure, then the program stops as soon as that program line is encountered in *any* call to the recursive procedure. Suppose we want to debug the `int_name` function.

```
/*  1 */   string int_name(int n)
/*  2 */   {  int c = n;
/*  3 */      string r;

/*  4 */      if (c >= 1000)
/*  5 */      {  r = int_name(c / 1000) + "thousand";
/*  6 */         c = c % 1000;
/*  7 */      }

/*  8 */      if (c >= 100)
/*  9 */      {  r = r + " " + digit_name(c / 100)
                     + "hundred";
/* 10 */         c = c % 100;
/* 11 */      }
              . . .
```

Suppose we inspect `c` in line 4 and it is 23405. We tell the debugger to run until line 8. When we inspect c again, its value is 23! That makes no sense. The instruction `c = c % 1000` should have set `c` to 405! Is that a bug?

No. The program stopped in the first recursive invocation of `int_name` that reached line 8. You can see from the call stack that two calls to `int_name` were pending (see Figure 8).

You can debug recursive functions with the debugger. You just need to be particularly careful, and watch the call stack frequently.

7.8.2 Register Variables

Sometimes, the compiler realizes that it can generate faster code by keeping a variable in a processor register rather than reserving a memory location for it. This is common for loop counters and other short-lived integer variables, but it is hard on the debugger. It may happen that the debugger cannot find that variable, or that it displays the wrong value for it.

There is not too much you can do. You can try to turn off all compiler optimizations and recompile. You can open a special register window that shows the status of all processor registers, but that is definitely an advanced technique.

7.8.3 Errors That Go Away under the Debugger

Sometimes your program shows an error when you run it normally, but the error goes away when you run the program under the debugger. This is, of course, extremely annoying.

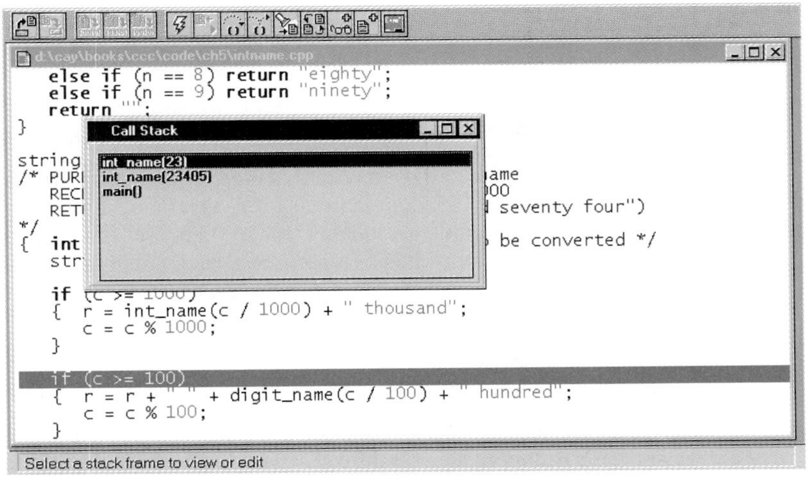

Figure 8

Call Stack Display during Recursive Call

The cause for such flaky behavior is usually an uninitialized variable. Suppose you forgot to initialize a loop counter `i` and you use it.

```
int main()
{  string s;
   . . .
   int i; /* Bug: forgot to initialize */
   while (i < s.length())
   {  string ch = s.substr(i, 1);
      . . .
   }
   . . .
}
```

If `i` happens to be zero, then the code will run correctly, but if `i` is negative, then the call to `s.substr(i, 1)` will crash the program. There is a chance that the variable `i` happens to contain a negative value when the program is run by itself, but that it is zero when the debugger launches it. (In fact, there is at least one debugger that goes through the trouble of zeroing out all program memory areas before launching the debugging session, thereby making many bugs go away.) In that case, you cannot use the debugger to solve your problem. Inspect all variables manually and check that they are initialized, or go back to inserting print statements if you are desperate.

Random Fact 7.2

The Therac-25 Incidents

The Therac-25 is a computerized device to deliver radiation treatment to cancer patients (see Figure 9). Between June 1985 and January 1987, several of these machines delivered serious overdoses to at least six patients, killing some of them and seriously maiming the others.

The machines were controlled by a computer program. Bugs in the program were directly responsible for the overdoses. According to [1], the program was written by a single programmer, who had since left the manufacturing company producing the device and could not be located. None of the company employees interviewed could say anything about the educational level or qualifications of the programmer.

The investigation by the federal Food and Drug Administration (FDA) found that the program was poorly documented and that there was neither a specification document nor a formal test plan. (This should make you think. Do you have a formal test plan for your programs?)

The overdoses were caused by an amateurish design of the software that had to control different devices concurrently, namely the keyboard, the display, the printer, and of course the radiation device itself. Synchronization and data sharing between the tasks were done in an ad hoc way, even though safe multitasking techniques were known at the time. Had the programmer enjoyed a formal education that involved these techniques, or taken the effort to

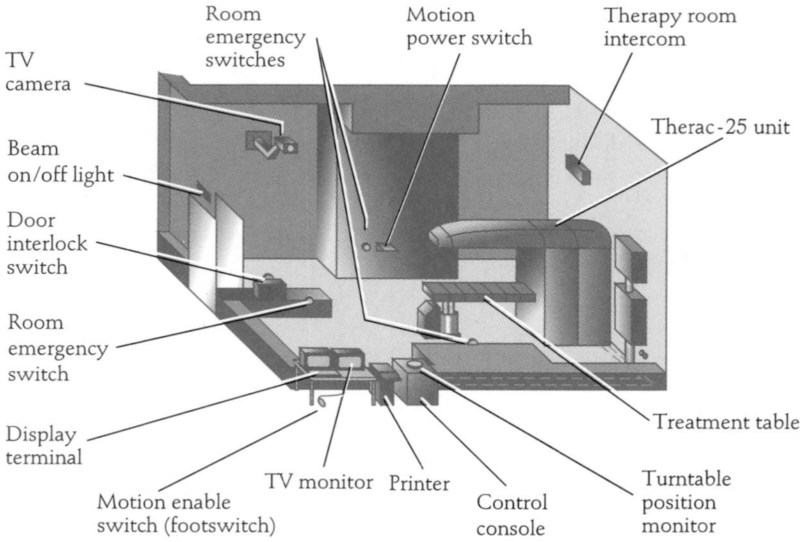

Figure 9

Typical Therac-25 Facility

study the literature, a safer machine could have been built. Such a machine would have probably involved a commercial multitasking system, which might have required a more expensive computer.

The same flaws were present in the software controlling the predecessor model, the Therac-20, but that machine had hardware interlocks that mechanically prevented overdoses. The hardware safety devices were removed in the Therac-25 and replaced by checks in the software, presumably to save cost.

Frank Houston of the FDA wrote in 1985[1]: "A significant amount of software for life-critical systems comes from small firms, especially in the medical device industry; firms that fit the profile of those resistant to or uninformed of the principles of either system safety or software engineering."

Who is to blame? The programmer? The manager who not only failed to ensure that the programmer was up to the task but also didn't insist on comprehensive testing? The hospitals that installed the device, or the FDA, for not reviewing the design process? Unfortunately, even today there are no firm standards of what constitutes a safe software design process.

Chapter Summary

1. Use *unit tests* to test each key function in isolation. Write a *test stub* to feed test data to the function being tested. Select test cases that cover each branch of the function.

2. You can debug a program by inserting trace printouts, but that gets quite tedious for even moderately complex debugging situations. You should learn to use the debugger.

3. You can make effective use of the debugger by mastering just three commands: "run until this line", "step to next line", and "inspect variable". The names and keystrokes or mouse clicks for these commands differ between debuggers.

4. Use the "divide-and-conquer" technique to locate the point of failure of a program. Inspect variables and compare their actual contents against the values that you know they should have.

5. The debugger can be used only to analyze the presence of bugs, not to show that a program is bug-free.

Further Reading

[1] Nancy G. Leveson and Clark S. Turner, "An Investigation of the Therac-25 Accidents," *IEEE Computer,* July 1993, pp. 18–41.

Review Exercises

Exercise R7.1. Define the terms *unit test* and *test stub.*

Exercise R7.2. If you want to test a program that is made up of four different procedures, one of which is `main`, how many test stubs do you need?

Exercise R7.3. What is an oracle?

Exercise R7.4. Define the terms *regression testing* and *test suite.*

Exercise R7.5. What is the debugging phenomenon known as "cycling"? What can you do to avoid it?

Exercise R7.6. The arc sine function is the inverse of the sine function. That is, $y = \arcsin x$ *if* $x = \sin y$. It is only defined if $-1 \leq x \leq 1$. Suppose you need to write a C++ function to compute the arc sine. List five positive test cases with their expected return values and two negative test cases with their expected outcomes.

Exercise R7.7. What is a program trace? When does it make sense to use a program trace, and when does it make more sense to use a debugger?

Exercise R7.8. Explain the differences between these debugger operations:

- Stepping into a function
- Stepping over a function

Exercise R7.9. Explain the differences between these debugger operations:

- Running until the current line
- Setting a breakpoint to the current line

Exercise R7.10. Explain the differences between these debugger operations:

- Inspecting a variable
- Watching a variable

Exercise R7.11. What is a call stack display in the debugger? Give two debugging scenarios in which the call stack display is useful.

Exercise R7.12. Explain in detail how to inspect the information stored in a `Point` object in your debugger.

Exercise R7.13. Explain in detail how to inspect the string stored in a `string` object in your debugger.

Exercise R7.14. Explain in detail how to inspect a string stored in an `Employee` object in your debugger.

Exercise R7.15. Explain the "divide-and-conquer" strategy to get close to a bug in the debugger.

Exercise R7.16. True or false:

(a) If a program has passed all tests in the test suite, it has no more bugs.
(b) If a program has a bug, that bug always shows up when running the program through the debugger.
(c) If all functions in a program were proven correct, then the program has no bugs.

Programming Exercises

Exercise P7.1. The arc sine function is the inverse of the sine function. That is,

$$y = \arcsin x$$

if

$$x = \sin y$$

For example,

$$\begin{aligned}
\arcsin(0) &= 0 \\
\arcsin(0.5) &= \pi/6 \\
\arcsin(\sqrt{2}/2) &= \pi/4 \\
\arcsin(\sqrt{3}/2) &= \pi/3 \\
\arcsin(1) &= \pi/2 \\
\arcsin(-1) &= \pi/2
\end{aligned}$$

The arc sine is defined only for values between -1 and 1. This function is also often called $\sin^{-1} x$. Note, however, that it is not at all the same as $1/\sin x$. There is no C++ standard library function to compute the arc sine. For this exercise, write a C++ function that computes the arc sine from its Taylor series expansion

$$\arcsin x = x + x^3/3! + x^5 \cdot 3^2/5! + x^7 \cdot 3^2 \cdot 5^2/7! + x^9 \cdot 3^2 \cdot 5^2 \cdot 7^2/9! + \cdots$$

You should compute the sum until a new term is $< 10^{-6}$. This function will be used in subsequent exercises.

Exercise P7.2. Write a simple test stub for the `arcsin` function that reads floating-point numbers from `cin` and computes their arc sines, until the end of the input is reached. Then run that program and verify its outputs against the arc sine function of a scientific calculator.

Exercise P7.3. Write a test stub that automatically generates test cases for the `arcsin` function, namely numbers between -1 and 1 in a step size of 0.1.

Exercise P7.4. Write a test stub that generates 10 random floating-point numbers between -1 and 1 and feeds them to `arcsin`.

Exercise P7.5. Write a test stub that automatically tests the validity of the `arcsin` function by verifying that `sin(arcsin(x))` is approximately equal to `x`. Test with 100 random inputs.

Exercise P7.6. There is a reason that the standard C++ library does not provide an arc sine function: It can be computed from the arc tangent function, according to the formula

$$\arcsin x = \arctan\left(x/\sqrt{1 - x^2}\right)$$

Use that expression as an *oracle* to test that your arc sine function works correctly. Test both functions with 100 random inputs.

Exercise P7.7. The domain of the arc sine function is $-1 \leq x \leq 1$. Supply an assertion to your `arcsin` function that checks that the input is valid. Test your function by computing `arcsin(1.1)`. What happens?

Exercise P7.8. Place trace messages into the loop of the arc sine function that computes the power series. Print the value of `n`, of the current term and the current approximation to the result. What trace output do you get when you compute `arcsin(0.5)`?

Exercise P7.9. Add trace messages to the beginning and end of all functions in the program that computes the English names of integers. What trace output do you get when converting the number 12,345?

Exercise P7.10. Add trace messages to the beginning and end of the `isprime` function in the buggy prime program. Also put a trace message as the first statement of the `while` loop in the `isprime` function. Print relevant values such as function parameters, return values and loop counters. What trace do you get when you compute all primes up to 20? Are the messages informative enough to spot the bug?

Exercise P7.11. Run a test stub of the `arcsin` function through the debugger. Step inside the computation of `arcsin(0.5)`. Step through the computation until the x^7 term has been computed and added to the sum. What is the value of the current term and of the sum at this point?

Exercise P7.12. Run a test stub of the `arcsin` function through the debugger. Step inside the computation of `arcsin(0.5)`. Step through the computation until the x^n term has become smaller than 10^{-6}. Then inspect `n`. How large is it?

Exercise P7.13. Consider the following buggy function:

```
Employee read_employee()
{  cout << "Please enter the name: ";
   string name = get_line(cin);
   cout << "Please enter the salary: ";
   float salary;
   cin >> salary;
   Employee r(name, salary);
   return r;
}
```

When you call this function once, it works fine. When you call it again in the same program, it won't return the second employee record correctly. Write a test stub that verifies the problem. Then step through the function. Inspect the contents of the string `name` and the `Employee` object `r` after the second call. What values do you get?

Exercise P7.14. Write a program that tests the recursive factorial function from Chapter 5. Compute `factorial(6)`. Step inside recursive calls until you arrive at `factorial(3)`. Then display the call stack. Which calls are currently pending?

CHAPTER 8

Classes

Objectives

- To be able to implement your own classes
- To master the separation of interface and implementation
- To understand the concept of encapsulation
- To design and implement accessor and mutator member functions
- To understand object construction
- To learn how to discover new classes and member functions
- To learn how to use object-oriented design to build complex programs

In Chapter 3 you learned how to use objects from existing classes. By now, you have used employee records and graphical shapes in many programs and are probably quite familiar with them. Recall how objects differ from numerical data types. Objects are *constructed* by specifying construction parameters, such as

```
Employee harry("Hacker, Harry", 35000);
```

To use objects, either to inquire about their state or to modify them, you apply *member functions* with the *dot notation.*

```
harry.set_salary(38000);
cout << harry.get_name();
```

In this chapter you will learn how to design your own classes and member functions. Together with the mechanics of defining classes, constructors, and member functions, you will learn how to discover useful classes that help you solve programming problems.

8.1 Discovering Classes

If you find yourself defining a number of related variables that all refer to the same concept, stop coding and think about that concept for a while. Then define a class that abstracts the concept and contains these variables as data fields.

Suppose you read in information about computers. Each information record contains the model name, the price, and a score between 0 and 100. Here are some sample data:

```
ACMA P100               $3,995  75
Alaris Nx586            $2,798  57
AMAX Powerstation 100   $3,999  75
AMS Infogold P100       $2,995  69
AST Premmia             $5,080  80
Austin 100              $3,499  95
Blackship NX-100        $2,495  60
Compaq 590              $4,598  60
```

You are trying to find the "best bang for the buck": the product with the highest score/price ratio. The following program finds this information for you.

Program bangbuck.cpp

```
#include "ccc.h"

int main()
{  string best_name = "";
   float best_price = 0;
   int best_score = 0;
```

```
   bool done = false;
   while (not done)
   {  string next_name;
      float next_price;
      int next_score;

      cout << "Please enter the model name: ";
      next_name = get_line(cin);
      cout << "Please enter the price: ";
      next_price = floatvalue(get_line(cin));
      cout << "Please enter the score: ";
      next_score = intvalue(get_line(cin));

      if (next_price != 0)
      {  if (best_price == 0 or
               next_score / next_price
                  > best_score / best_price)
         {  best_name = next_name;
            best_score = next_score;
            best_price = next_price;
         }
      }
      string answer;
      cout << "More data? (Y/N) ";
      answer = get_line(cin);
      if (uppercase(answer) != "Y") done = true;
   }

   cout << "The best bang for the buck is "  << best_name
      << " (Score: " << best_score
      << " Price: " << best_price << ")\n";

   return EXIT_SUCCESS;
}
```

Pay special attention to the two sets of variables: **best_name**, **best_price**, **best_score** and **next_name**, **next_price**, **next_score**. The very fact that you have two sets of these variables suggests that a common concept is lurking just under the surface.

Each of these two sets of variables describes a *product.* One of them describes the best product, the other one the next product to be read in. In the following sections we will develop a **Product** class to simplify this program.

8.2 Interfaces

To define a class, we first need to specify an *interface.* The interface of the **Product** class consists of all functions that we want to apply to product objects. Looking at the program of the preceding section, we need to be able to perform the following:

- Make a new product object
- Read in a product object
- Compare two products and find out which one is better
- Print a product

The interface is specified in the *class definition*. Here is the C++ syntax for the interface part of the definition of the Product class:

```
class Product
{
public:
   Product();

   void read();

   bool is_better_than(Product b) const;
   void print() const;
private:
   implementation details—see Section 8.2
};
```

The interface is made up from three parts. First we list the *constructors*: the functions that are used to initialize new objects. Constructors always have the same name as the class. The Product class has one constructor, with no parameters. Such a constructor is called a *default constructor.* It is used when you define an object without construction parameters, like this:

```
Product best; /* uses default constructor Product() */
```

As a general rule of thumb, every class should have a default constructor. All classes used in this book do.

Then we list the *mutator functions.* A mutator is an operation that modifies the object. The Product class has a single mutator: read. After you call

```
p.read();
```

the contents of p have changed.

Finally, we list the *accessor functions.* Accessors just query the object for some information without changing it. The Product class has two accessors: is_better_than and print. Applying one of these functions to a product object does not modify the object. In C++, accessor operations are tagged as const. Note the position of the const keyword: after the closing parenthesis of the parameter list, but before the semicolon that terminates the function declaration. See Common Error 8.2 for the importance of the const keyword.

Now we know *what* a Product object can do, but not *how* it does it. Of course, to use objects in our programs, we only need to use the interface. To enable any function to access the interface functions, they are placed in the public section of the class definition. As we will see in the next section, the variables used in the implementa-

Figure 1

The Interface of the **Product** Class

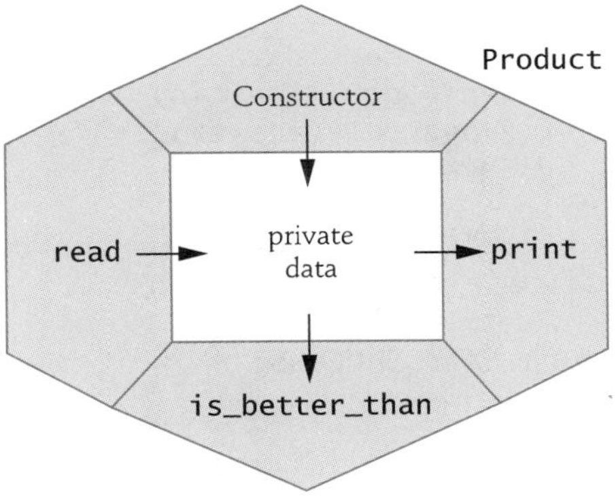

tion will be placed in the **private** section. That makes them inaccessible to the users of the objects.

Figure 1 shows the interface of the **Product** class. The mutator functions are shown with arrows pointing inside the private data to indicate that they modify the data. The accessor functions are shown with arrows pointing the other way to indicate that they just read the data.

Now that we have this interface, let us put it to work to simplify the program of the preceding section.

Program product1.cpp

(compiles but doesn't run):

```
#include "ccc.h"

class Product
{
public:
   Product();

   void read();

   bool is_better_than(Product b) const;
   void print() const;
private:
};

int main()
{  Product best;
   bool done = false;
   while (not done)
   {  Product next;
      next.read();
      if (next.is_better_than(best)) best = next;
```

```
      string answer;
      cout << "More data? (Y/N) ";
      answer = get_line(cin);
      if (uppercase(answer) != "Y") done = true;
   }

   cout << "The best bang for the buck is ";
   best.print();

   return EXIT_SUCCESS;
}
```

Wouldn't you agree that this program is much easier to read than the first version? Making `Product` into a class really pays off.

However, this program will not yet run. The interface definition of the class just *declares* the constructors and member functions. The actual code for these functions must be supplied separately. We will see how in Section 8.3.

Common Error 8.1

Forgetting a Semicolon

Braces `{ }` are common in C++ code, and usually you do not place a semicolon after the closing brace. However, `class` definitions always end in `};`. A common error is to forget that semicolon:

```
class Product
{
public:
   . . .
private:
   . . .
} /* forgot semicolon */

int main()
{  Product best; /* many compilers report error in this line */
   . . .
}
```

This can be extremely confusing to many compilers. There is syntax, now obsolete but supported for compatibility with old code, to define class types and variables of that type simultaneously. Because the compiler doesn't know that you don't use that obsolete construction, it tries to analyze the code wrongly and ultimately reports an error. Unfortunately, it may report the error *several lines away* from the line in which you forgot the semicolon.

If the compiler reports bizarre errors in lines that you are sure are correct, check that each of the preceding `class` definitions is terminated by a semicolon.

8.3 Encapsulation

Each **Product** object must store the name, price, and score of the product. These data items are defined in the private section of the class definition.

```
class Product
{
public:
   Product();

   void read();

   bool is_better_than(Product b) const;
   void print() const;
private:
   string name;
   float price;
   int score;
};
```

Every product object has a name field, a price field, and a score field (see Figure 2). However, there is a catch. Because these fields are defined to be private, only the constructors and member functions of the class can access them. You cannot access the fields directly:

```
int main()
{
   . . .
   cout << best.name; /* Error—use print() instead */
   . . .
}
```

All data access must occur through the public interface (see Figure 3). Thus, the data fields of an object are effectively hidden from the programmer. The act of hiding data is called *encapsulation*. While it is theoretically possible in C++ to leave data fields

Figure 2

An Object of Type **product**

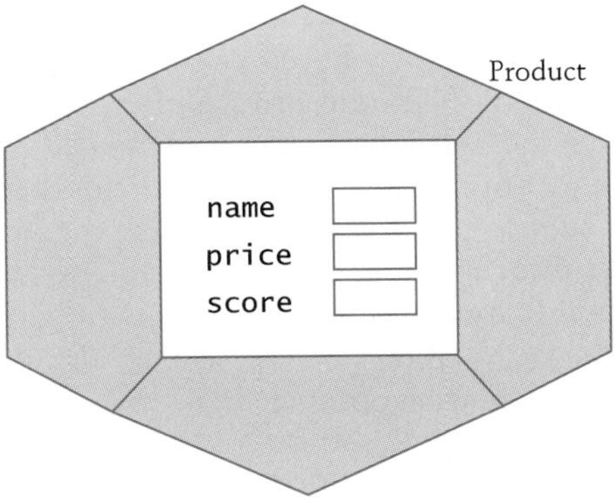

Figure 3

Encapsulation

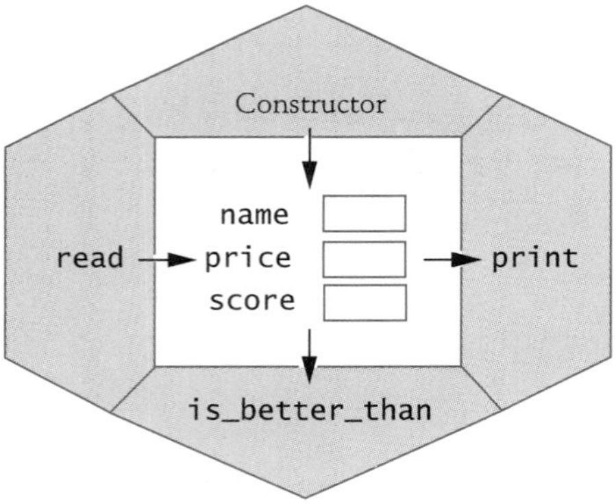

unencapsulated (by placing them into the public section), this is very uncommon in practice. We will always make all data fields private in this book.

The `Product` class is so simple that it is not obvious what benefit we gain from the encapsulation. The primary benefit of the encapsulation mechanism is the guarantee that the object data cannot accidentally be put in an incorrect state. To understand the benefit better, consider the `Time` class:

```
class Time
{
public:
   Time();
   Time(int y, int m, int d, int hrs, int min, int sec);

   void add_seconds(float s);

   int get_seconds() const;
   int get_minutes() const;
   int get_hours() const;
   int get_day() const;
   int get_month() const;
   int get_year() const;
   float seconds_from() const;
private:
   . . . /* hidden data representation */
};
```

Because the data fields are private, there are only three functions that can change these fields: the two constructors and the `add_seconds` mutator function. The seven accessor functions cannot modify the fields, because they are declared as `const`.

Let us suppose for the moment that programmers could access data fields of the `Time` class directly. This would open the possibility of a whole type of bug, namely the creation of invalid times:

```
Time release_date(1997, 1, 31, 0, 0, 0);
/* release date of product */
. . .
/* looks like the product is getting delayed by another month */
release_date.month++; /* won't compile, but suppose it did */
```

At first glance, there appears to be nothing wrong with this code. But if you look carefully, **release_date** happens to be January 31 before the month is incremented. Thus, it is February 31 after the increment—an invalid date.

Fortunately, this error cannot happen with the **Time** class. The constructor that makes a time out of six integers checks that the construction parameters denote a valid date. If not, an error message is displayed and the program terminates. The **Time()** constructor sets a date object to the current date, which is always valid, and the **add_seconds** function knows about the lengths of the months and always produces a valid result. Since no other function can mess up the private data fields, we can *guarantee* that all dates are always valid, thanks to the encapsulation mechanism.

8.4 Member Functions

Every member function that is advertised in the class interface must be implemented separately. Here is an example: the **read** function of the **Product** class.

```
class Product
{
public:
   Product();

   void read();

   bool is_better_than(Product b) const;
   void print() const;
private:
   string name;
   float price;
   int score;
};

void Product::read()
{  cout << "Please enter the model name: ";
   name = get_line(cin);
   cout << "Please enter the price: ";
   price = floatvalue(get_line(cin));
   cout << "Please enter the score: ";
   score = intvalue(get_line(cin));
}
```

The **Product::** prefix makes it clear that we are defining the **read** function of the **Product** class. In C++ it is perfectly legal to have **read** functions in other classes as well, and it is important to be specific which **read** function we are defining. You use the *Class_name*::**read()** syntax only when defining the function, not when calling it. When you call the **read** member function, the call has the form *object*.**read()**.

When defining an accessor member function, you must supply the keyword **const** following the closing brace of the parameter list. For example, the call **a.is_better_than(b)** only inspects the object **a** without modifying it. Hence `is_better_than` is an accessor function that should be tagged as `const`:

```
bool Product::is_better_than(Product b) const
{  if (price == 0) return false;
   if (b.price == 0) return true;
   if (score / price > b.score / b.price)
      return true;
   return false;
}

void Product::print() const
{  cout << name
      << " Price: " << price
      << " Score: " << score << "\n"
}
```

Whenever you refer to a data field, such as `name` or `price`, in a member function, it denotes that data field *of the object for which the member function was called.* For example, when called with

```
best.print();
```

the `Product.print()` function prints `best.name`, `best.score`, and `best.price`. (See Figure 4.)

The code for the member function makes no mention at all of the object to which a member function is applied. It is called the *implicit parameter* of the member function. You can visualize the code of the `print` function like this:

```
void Product::print() const
{  cout << implicit_parameter.name
      << " Price: " << implicit_parameter.price
      << " Score: " << implicit_parameter.score  << "\n"
 }
```

In contrast, a parameter that is explicitly mentioned in the function definition, such as the `b` parameter of the `is_better_than` function, is called an *explicit* parameter. Every member function has exactly one implicit parameter and zero or more explicit parameters.

For example, the `is_better_than` function has one implicit parameter and one explicit parameter. In the call

```
if (next.is_better_than(best))
```

`next` is the implicit parameter and `best` is the explicit parameter (see Figure 5). Again, you may find it helpful to visualize the code of `Product::is_better_than` in the following way:

```
bool Product::is_better_than(Product b) const
{  if (implicit_parameter.price == 0) return false;
   if (b.price == 0) return true;
   if (implicit_parameter.score  / implicit_parameter.price
         > b.score / b.price)
      return true;
   return false;
}
```

Figure 4

The Member Function Call `best.print()`

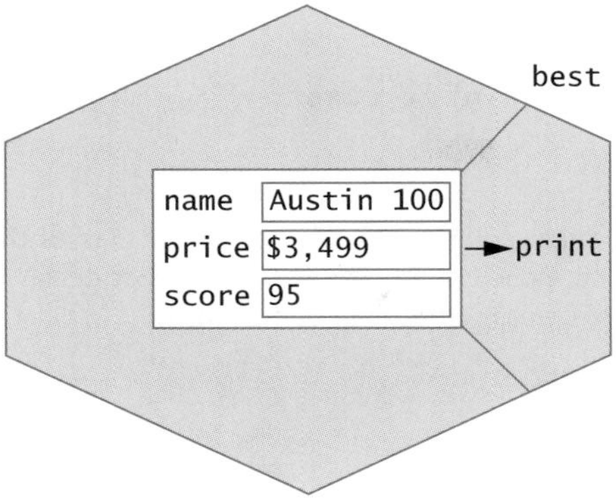

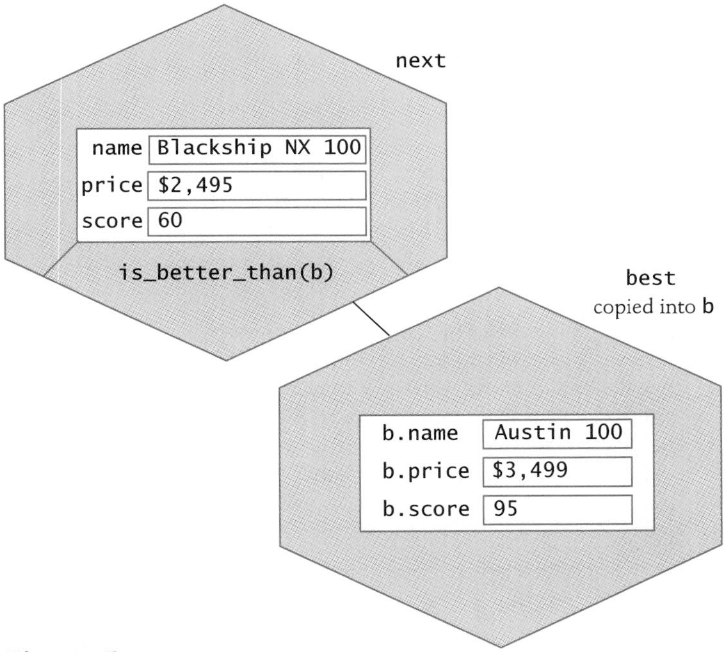

Figure 5

Implicit and Explicit Parameters of the Call `next_is_better_than(best)`

Common Error 8.2

`const` Correctness

You must declare all accessor functions in C++ with the `const` keyword. (Recall that an accessor function is a member function that does not modify its implicit parameter.) For example,

```
class Product
{  . . .
   void print() const;
   . . .
};
```

If you fail to follow this rule, you build classes that other programmers cannot reuse. For example, suppose `Product::print` was not declared `const`, and another programmer used the `Product` class to build an `Order` class.

```
class Order
{
public:
   . . .
   void print() const;
private:
   string customer;
   Product article;
   . . .
};

void Order::print() const
{  cout << customer << "\n";
   article.print(); /* Error */
   . . .
}
```

The compiler refuses to compile the expression `article.print()`. Why? Because `article` is an object of class `Product`, and `Product::print` is not tagged as `const`, the compiler suspects that the call `article.print()` may modify `article`. But `article` is a data field of `Order`, and `Order::print` promises not to modify any data fields of the order. The programmer of the `Order` class uses `const` correctly and must rely on all other programmers to do the same.

If you write a program with other team members who do use `const` correctly, it is very important that you do your part as well. You should therefore get into the habit of using the `const` keyword for all member functions that do not modify their implicit parameter.

8.5 Default Constructors

There is only one remaining issue with the `Product` class. We need to define the default constructor.

The code for a constructor sets all data fields of the object. *The purpose of a constructor is to initialize the data fields of an object.*

```
Product::Product()
{  price = 0;
   score = 0;
}
```

Note the curious name of the constructor function: **Product::Product**. The **Product::** indicates that we are about to define a member function of the **Product** class. The second **Product** is the name of that member function. Constructors always have the same name as their class.

Most default constructors set all data fields to a default value. The **Product** default constructor sets the price and score to 0. The product name is automatically set to the empty string, as will be explained shortly. Not all default constructors act like that. For example, the **Time** default constructor sets the time object to the current time.

In the code for the default constructor, you need to worry about initializing only *numeric* data fields. For example, in the **Product** class you must set **price** and **score** to zero, because numeric types are not classes and have no constructors. But the **name** field is automatically set to the empty string by the default constructor of the string class. In general, all data fields of class type are automatically constructed when an object is created, but the numeric fields must be set in the class constructors.

We now have all the pieces for the version of the product comparison program that uses the **Product** class. Here is the program:

Program product2.cpp:

```
#include "ccc.h"

class Product
{
public:
   Product();

   void read();

   bool is_better_than(Product b) const;
   void print() const;
private:
   string name;
   float price;
   int score;
};

Product::Product()
{  price = 0;
   score = 0;
}

void Product::read()
{  cout << "Please enter the model name: ";
   name = get_line(cin);
   cout << "Please enter the price: ";
   price = floatvalue(get_line(cin));
   cout << "Please enter the score: ";
```

```
   score = intvalue(get_line(cin));
}

bool Product::is_better_than(Product b) const
{  if (price == 0) return false;
   if (b.price == 0) return true;
   if (score / price > b.score / b.price)
      return true;
   return false;
}

void Product::print() const
{  cout << name
      << " Price: " << price
      << " Score: " << score << "\n";
}

int main()
{  Product best;

   bool done = false;
   while (not done)
   {  Product next;
      next.read();
      if (next.is_better_than(best)) best = next;

      string answer;
      cout << "More data? (Y/N) ";
      answer = get_line(cin);
      if (uppercase(answer) != "Y") done = true;
   }

   cout << "The best bang for the buck is ";
   best.print();

   return EXIT_SUCCESS;
}
```

8.6 Constructors with Parameters

The **Product** class of the preceding section had only one constructor—the default constructor. In contrast, the **Employee** class has two constructors:

```
class Employee
{
public:
   Employee();
   Employee(string employee_name, float initial_salary);
```

```
      void set_salary(float new_salary);

      string get_name() const;
      float get_salary() const;
   private:
      string name;
      float salary;
   };
```

Both constructors have the same name as the class, `Employee`. But the default constructor has no parameters, whereas the second constructor has a `string` and a `float` parameter. Whenever two functions have the same name but are distinguished by their parameter types, the function name is *overloaded*. (See Advanced Topic 8.2 for more information on overloading in C++.)

Here is the implementation of the constructor that makes an employee object from a name string and a starting salary.

```
Employee::Employee(string employee_name,
   float initial_salary)
{  name = employee_name;
   salary = initial_salary;
}
```

This is a straightforward situation; the constructor simply sets all data fields. Sometimes a constructor gets more complex because one of the data fields is itself an object of another class with its own constructor.

To see how to cope this situation, suppose the `Employee` class stores the hire date of the employee:

```
class Employee
{
public:
   Employee(string employee_name,
      int hire_year, int hire_month, int hire_day);
   . . .
private:
   string name;
   float salary;
   Time hiredate;
};
```

This constructor must set the `name`, `salary`, and `hiredate` fields. Since `hiredate` is itself an object of a class, it must be initialized with an object of that class.

```
Employee::Employee(string employee_name,
   int hire_year, int hire_month, int hire_day)
{  name = employee_name;
   salary = 0;
   hiredate = Time(hire_year, hire_month,
      hire_day, 0, 0, 0);
}
```

The `Employee` class in the library of this book does not actually store a hire date. This is just an illustration to show how to construct a data field that is itself an object of a class.

Common Error 8.3

Forgetting to Initialize All Fields in a Constructor

Just as it is a common error to forget the initialization of a variable, it easy to forget about data fields. Every constructor needs to ensure that all data fields are set to appropriate values.

Here is a variation on the `Employee` class. The constructor receives only the name of the employee. The class user is supposed to call `set_salary` explicitly to set the salary.

```
class Employee
{
public:
   Employee(string n);
   void set_salary(float s);
   float get_salary() const;
      . . .
private:
   string name;
   float salary;
};

Employee::Employee(string n)
{  name = n;
   /* oops—salary not initialized */
}
```

If someone calls `get_salary` before `set_salary` has been called, a random salary will be returned. The remedy is simple: Just set `salary` to 0 in the constructor.

Common Error 8.4

Trying to Reset an Object by Calling a Constructor

The constructor is invoked only when an object is first created. You cannot call the constructor to reset an object:

```
Time homework_due(2010, 4, 15, 19, 0, 0);
. . .
homework_due.Time(); /* Error */
```

It is true that the default constructor sets a *new* time object to the current time, but you cannot invoke a constructor on an *existing* object.

The remedy is simple: Make a new time object and overwrite the current one.

```
homework_due = Time(); /* OK */
```

Advanced Topic 8.1

Calling Constructors from Constructors

Consider again the variation of the Employee class with a hire date field of type Time. There is an unfortunate inefficiency in the constructor:

```
Employee::Employee(string employee_name,
   int hire_year, int hire_month, int hire_day)
{  name = employee_name;
   salary = 0;
   hiredate = Time(hire_year, hire_month, hire_day, 0, 0, 0);
}
```

Before the constructor code starts executing, the default constructors are automatically invoked on all data fields that are objects. In particular, the hiredate field is initialized with the current time through the default constructor of the Time class. Immediately afterwards, that value is overwritten with the object Time(hire_year, hire_month, hire_day, 0, 0, 0).

It would be more efficient to construct the hiredate field with the correct values right away. That is achieved with the following syntax:

```
Employee::Employee(string employee_name,
   int hire_year, int hire_month, int hire_day)
:  hiredate(hire_year, hire_month, hire_day, 0, 0, 0)
{  name = employee_name;
   salary = 0;
}
```

Most people find this syntax confusing, and we won't use it in this book to initialize data fields. The price we pay is inefficient initialization. Note, however, that this syntax is necessary when using inheritance, an advanced feature of C++ that we discuss in Chapter 14.

Advanced Topic 8.2

Overloading

When the same function name is used for more than one function, then the name is *overloaded.* In C++ you can overload function names provided the parameter types are different. For example, you can define two functions, both called print, one to print an employee record and one to print a time object:

```
void print (Employee e) {/* ... */}
void print (Time t) {/* ... */}
```

When the `print` function is called,

```
print(x);
```

the compiler looks at the type of `x`. If `x` is an `Employee` object, the first function is called. If `x` is a `Time` object, the second function is called. If `x` is neither, the compiler generates an error.

We have not used the overloading feature in this book. Instead, we gave each function a unique name, such as `print_employee` or `print_time`. However, we have no choice with constructors. C++ demands that the name of a constructor equals the name of the class. If a class has more than one constructor, then that name must be overloaded.

In addition to name overloading, C++ also supports *operator overloading*. You can define new meanings to the familiar C++ operators such as +, ==, and <<, provided at least one of the arguments is an object of some class. For example, we could overload the > operator to test whether one product is better than another. Then the test

```
if (next.is_better_than(best)) ...
```

could instead be written as

```
if (next > best) ...
```

To teach the compiler this new meaning of the > operator, we need to implement a function called `operator>` with two parameters of type `Product`:

```
bool Product::operator>(Product b) const
{  if (price == 0) return false;
   if (b.price == 0) return true;
   if (score / price > b.score / b.price) return true;
   return false;
}
```

Operator overloading can make programs easier to read. In particular, it is quite common to overload the <<, >>, and == operators. Unfortunately, programming overloaded operators is somewhat complex, and we do not cover it further in this book. See [1] for more details.

8.7 Accessing Data Fields

Only member functions of a class are allowed to access the private data fields of objects of that class. All other functions—that is, member functions of other classes and functions that are not member functions of any class—must go through the public interface of the class.

For example, the `raise_salary` function of Chapter 5 cannot read and set the `salary` field directly:

```
void raise_salary(Employee& e, float percent)
{  e.salary = e.salary * (1 + percent / 100); /* Error */
}
```

Instead, it must use the `get_salary` and `set_salary` functions:

```
void raise_salary(Employee& e, float percent)
{  float new_salary = e.get_salary()
```

```
        * (1 + percent / 100);
    e.set_salary(new_salary);
}
```

These two member functions are extremely simple:

```
float Employee::get_salary() const
{  return salary;
}

void Employee::set_salary(float salary) const
{  salary = new_salary;
}
```

In your own classes you should not automatically write accessor functions for *all* data fields. The less implementation detail you reveal, the more flexibility you have to improve the class. Consider, for example, the `Product` class. There was no need to supply functions such as `get_score` or `set_price`. Also, if you have a `get_...` function, don't feel obliged to implement a matching `set_...` function. For example, the `Time` class has a `get_month` function but not a `set_month` function.

8.8 Comparing Member Functions with Nonmember Functions

Consider again the `raise_salary` function of Chapter 5.

```
void raise_salary(Employee& e, float percent)
{  float new_salary = e.get_salary()
      * (1 + percent / 100);
   e.set_salary(new_salary);
}
```

This function is not a member function of the `Employee` class. It is not a member function of any class, in fact. Thus, the dot notation is not used when the function is called. There are two explicit arguments and no implicit argument.

```
raise_salary(harry, 7); /* raise Harry's salary by 7 percent */
```

Let us turn `raise_salary` into a member function:

```
class Employee
{
public:
   void raise_salary(float percent);
   . . .
};

void Employee::raise_salary(float percent)
{  salary = salary * (1 + percent / 100);
}
```

Now the function must be called with the dot notation:

```
harry.raise_salary(7); /* raise Harry's salary by 7 percent */
```

Which of these two solutions is better? It depends on the *ownership* of the class. If you are designing a class, you should make useful operations into member functions. However, if you are using a class designed by someone else, then you should not add your own member functions. The author of the class that you are using may improve the class and periodically give you a new version of the code. It would be a nuisance if you had to keep adding your own modifications back into the class definition every time that happened.

Inside `main` or another nonmember function, it is easy to differentiate between member function calls and other function calls. Member functions are invoked using the dot notation; nonmember functions don't have an "*object*." preceding them. Inside member functions, however, it isn't as simple.

One member function can invoke another member function on its implicit parameter. Suppose we add a member function `print` to our `Employee` class:

```
class Employee
{
public:
   void print() const;
   . . .
};

void Employee::print() const
{  cout << "Name: " << get_name()
      << "Salary: " << get_salary()
      << "\n";
}
```

Now consider the call `harry.print()`, with implicit parameter `harry`. The call `get_name()` inside the `Employee::print` function really means `harry.get_name()`. Again, you may find it helpful to visualize the function like this:

```
void Employee::print() const
{  cout << "Name: " << implicit_parameter.get_name()
      << "Salary: " << implicit_parameter.get_salary()
      <<"\n";
}
```

In this simple situation we could equally well have accessed the `name` and `salary` data fields directly in the `Employee::print` function. In more complex situations it is very common for one member function to call another.

If you see a function call without the dot notation inside a member function, you first need to check whether that function is actually another member function of the same class. If so, it means "call this member function with the same implicit parameter".

If you compare the member and nonmember versions of `raise_salary`, you can see an important difference. The member function is allowed to modify the `salary` data field of the `Employee` object, even though it was not defined as a reference parameter.

Recall that by default, function parameters are value parameters, which the function cannot modify. You must supply an ampersand `&` to indicate that a parameter is a reference parameter, which can be modified by the function. For example, the first parameter of the nonmember version of `raise_salary` is a reference parameter (`Employee&`), because the `raise_salary` function changes the employee record.

The situation is exactly opposite for the implicit parameter of member functions. By default, the implicit parameter *can* be modified. Only if the member function is tagged as `const` must the default parameter be left unchanged.

The following table summarizes these differences.

	Explicit parameter	Implicit parameter
Reference parameter (can be changed)	Use &	Default
Value parameter (not changed)	Default	Use `const`

Productivity Hint 8.1

Inspecting an Object in the Debugger

In C++ the expression `*this` denotes the implicit parameter of a member function. We have not discussed that notation, because we do not need it for programming and because it requires

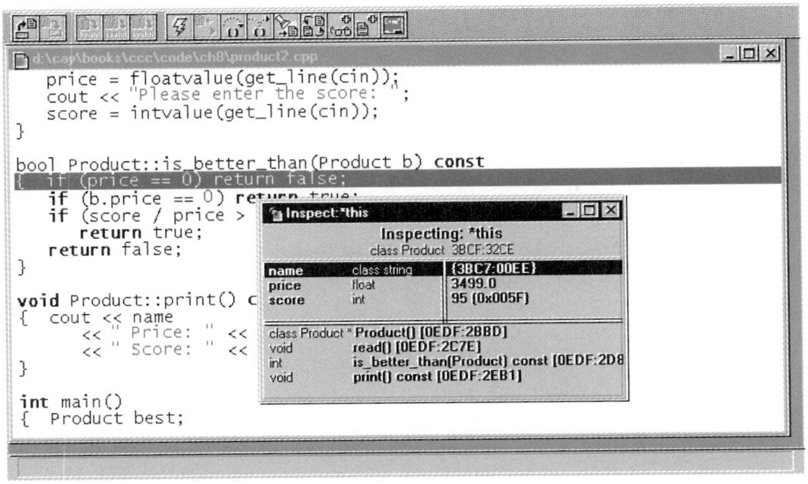

Figure 6

Implicit Parameter Display

knowledge of pointers, which we won't cover until Chapter 13. However, inspecting `*this` in the debugger is a very handy trick.

When you trace inside a member function, tell the debugger you want to inspect a variable, and then type `*this`. You will see all data fields of the implicit parameter (see Figure 6).

You can even put `*this` in the watch window. Then the implicit parameter is always displayed. It changes automatically as you step from one member function to another.

Quality Tip 8.1

File Layout

By now we have learned quite a few C++ features, all of which can occur in a C++ source file. Keep your source files neat and organize items in the following order:

- Header files
- Constants
- Classes
- Global variables
- Functions

The member functions can come in any order. Sort the nonmember functions so that every function is defined before it is used. In particular, `main` comes last.

Random Fact 8.1

Programmer Productivity

If you talk to your friends in this programming class, you will find that some of them consistently complete their assignments much more quickly than others. Perhaps they have more experience. Even when comparing programmers with the same education and experience, however, wide variations in competence are routinely observed and measured. It is not uncommon to have the best programmer in a team be five to ten times as productive as the worst, using any of a number of reasonable measures of productivity [2].

That is a staggering range of performance among trained professionals. In a marathon race, the best runner will not run five to ten times faster than the slowest one. Software product managers are acutely aware of these disparities. The obvious solution is, of course, to hire only the best programmers, but even in recent periods of economic slowdown the demand for good programmers has greatly outstripped the supply.

Fortunately for all of us, joining the rank of the best is not necessarily a question of raw intellectual power. Good judgment, experience, broad knowledge, attention to detail, and superior planning are at least as important as mental brilliance. These skills can be acquired by individuals who are genuinely interested in improving themselves.

Even the most gifted programmer can deal with only a finite number of details in a given time period. Suppose a programmer can implement and debug one procedure every two hours, or one hundred procedures per month. (This is a generous estimate. Few programmers are this productive.) If a task requires 10,000 procedures (which is typical for a medium-sized program), then a single programmer would need 100 months to complete the job. Such a project is sometimes expressed as a "100-man-month" project. But as Brooks explains in his famous book [3], the concept of "man-month" is a myth. One cannot trade months for programmers. One hundred programmers cannot finish the task in one month. In fact, 10 programmers probably couldn't finish it in 10 months. First of all, the 10 programmers need to learn about the project before they can get productive. Whenever there is a problem with a particular procedure, both the author and its users need to meet and discuss it, taking time away from all of them. A bug in one procedure may have all of its users twiddling their thumbs until it is fixed.

It is difficult to estimate these inevitable delays. They are one reason why software is often released later than originally promised. What is a manager to do when the delays mount? As Brooks points out, adding more manpower will make a late project even later, because the productive people have to stop working and train the newcomers.

You will experience these problems when you work on your first team project with other students. Be prepared for a major drop in productivity, and be sure to set ample time aside for team communications.

There is, however, no alternative to teamwork. Most important and worthwhile projects transcend the ability of one single individual. Learning to function well in a team is as important for your education as it is to be a competent programmer.

8.9 Object-Oriented Design

In the beginning of this chapter we designed a `Product` class, which made the code of the product comparison program both easy to understand and safe. Designing your own classes is an essential skill for writing complex programs. The key question is, of course, how do you know what classes and member functions to program?

The process of *object-oriented design* gives you some guidance how to make the progression from a problem description to an implementation in C++. In its simplest form, the process has the following steps:

1. Find objects and classes.
2. Define interfaces for these classes.
3. Implement the interfaces.
4. Combine objects to solve the problem.

Let us take these steps one at a time.

A class represents some useful concept. We have seen classes for concrete entities such as employees, times, and products. Other classes represent abstract concepts such as points and windows. A simple rule for finding classes is to look for *nouns* in the task description. For example, if your job is to implement a student registration database, then obvious classes that come to mind are `Student` and `Course`.

Once a set of classes has been identified, we need to define the interfaces for each class. That is, we need to find out what functions each object needs to carry out to

Figure 7

The Screen Display of the Clock Program

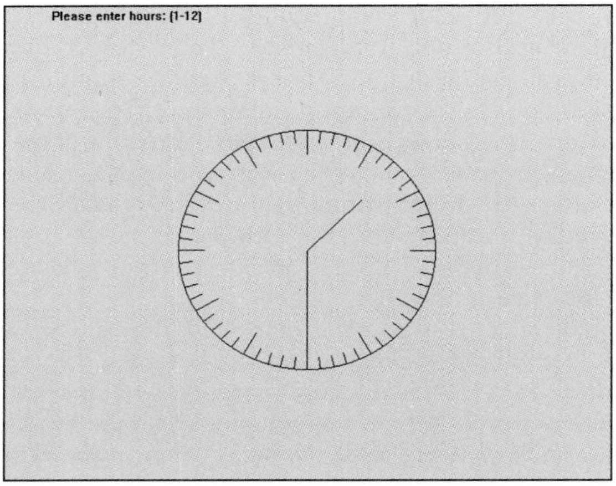

solve the programming problem. A simple rule for finding these functions is to look for *verbs* in the task description, and then match the verbs to the appropriate objects. For example, in a program that registers students for courses, someone needs to carry out the `register` function. Now we need to figure out *who* is responsible for this function. Do student objects register themselves for courses? Do course objects add students to themselves?

Once we know what each class needs to do, we need to add private data fields and implement the functions that we discovered.

Finally, we write a `main` function that creates objects and starts their activities.

Let us explore this process with a practical assignment of some complexity. Your task is to write a game program that teaches your baby sister how to read the clock (see Figure 7). The game should do the following: randomly generate a time, draw a clock face with that time, and ask the player to type in the time. The player gets two tries before the game displays the correct time. Whenever the player gets the right answer, the score increases by one point. There are four levels of difficulty. Level 1 teaches full hours, level 2 teaches 15-minute intervals, level 3 teaches 5-minute intervals, and level 4 displays all times. When the player has reached a score of five points on one level, the game advances to the next level.

At the beginning, the game asks the player for the name and the desired starting level. After every round, the player is asked whether he or she wants to play more. The game ends when the player decides to quit.

8.9.1 Finding Classes

What classes can we find? We need to look at nouns in the problem description. Here are several that come to mind:

```
Player
Clock
```

```
Time
Level
Game
Round
```

Not all nouns that you find make useful objects. For example, the `Level` is just an integer between 1 and 4; it doesn't really do anything. At this time, the best course of action is to leave it in the list of possible classes and to abandon it later if it turns out not to have any useful actions.

8.9.2 Finding Interfaces

As a warm-up, let us look at a simple class first: the `Clock` class. The clock object has one important responsibility: to draw the clock face.

Many programmers use paper index cards to write down the classes and interfaces they discover. Here is what such a card looks like when we decide that a clock should be able to draw itself:

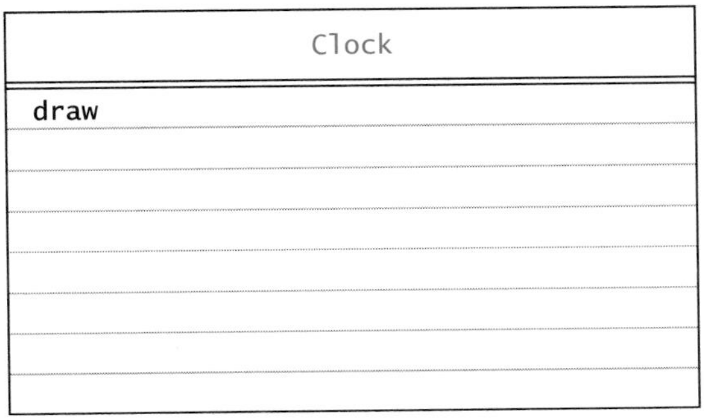

When a clock draws itself, it must draw the hour and minute hands to show the current times. How does the clock know what time it is? We need to tell it:

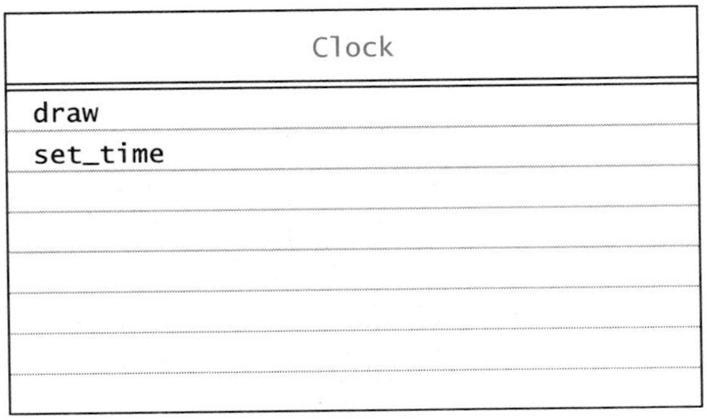

Next, let us take up the `Time` class. We need to construct time objects, given hours and minutes. We need to be able to tell when two times are the same:

Time
Time(hours, minutes)
get_hours
get_minutes
is_same_as(Time)

Let's look at the player. A player has a name, a level, and a score. The name and initial level are set when the player is first created:

Player
Player(name, initial level)

Every time the player gets a correct answer, the score must be incremented.

Player
Player(name, initial level)
increment_score

After every five score increments, the level is incremented as well. We'll let the `increment_score` function take care of that. Of course, then we have to find out what the current level is:

Player
Player(name, initial level)
increment_score
get_score

Now we are in a fairly typical situation. We have a mess of classes, each of which seems to do interesting things, but we don't know how they will all work together. A good plan is to introduce a class that represents the entire program—in our case, the game:

Game
play

Unlike the previously discovered functions, it is not at all obvious how this function works. We must use the process of stepwise refinement, which we discussed in Chapter 5. What does it mean to play the game? The game starts by asking the player's name and level. Then the player plays a round, the game asks if the player wants to play again, and so on.

Play the game

```
read player information
do
{  play a round
   ask whether player wants to play again
}  while(player wants to play again);
```

Now we have found a couple of new actions: to get player information and to play a round. Let's add "get player information" to the **Game** class:

Game
`play`
`read_player_information`

Now, how about "play a round"? Should the **Game** class or the **Player** class implement this function? What is involved in playing a round? We need to make a time, depending on the level of the player. We need to draw the clock, ask for input, check whether the input is correct, play again if it is not, and increment the player's score if it is.

We can assign the responsibility either way. In this discussion, we will let the **Game** class take care of playing the round:

Game
`play`
`start_game`
`play_round`

We have seen no need for the classes **Round** and **Level** that we tentatively noted in the class discovery step, so we will not implement them.

Now we have a set of classes, with reasonably complete interfaces. Are we done? In practice, that is not always an easy question to answer. It is quite common to find during the implementation phase that a particular task cannot be carried out with the interface functions. Then one needs to go back and revise the classes and interfaces.

8.9.3 Implementing Interfaces

Here is the `Clock` class that we discovered:

Clock
draw
set_time

The clock must remember the time that is set with `set_time` so that it can draw the clock face.

```
class Clock
{
public:
   Clock();
   Clock(Point c, float r);

   void set_time(Time t);
   void draw() const;
private:
   Time current_time;
   Point center;
   float radius;
};

void Clock::set_time(Time t)
{  current_time = t;
}
```

The `draw` function is more complex. Let us use the process of stepwise refinement to simplify it:

Draw the clock

draw a circle
draw the hour "ticks"
draw the minute "ticks"
draw the hour hand
draw the minute hand

We need a function to draw a tick and a function to draw a hand. Each of these functions takes two parameters: the angle of the line segment to draw and its length. The angle is measured clockwise, starting from the 12 o'clock position. For convenience, it is measured in multiples of 6 degrees (the angle between two minute ticks).

```
void Clock::draw_tick(float angle, float length) const
{  float alpha = M_PI / 2 - 6 * angle * M_PI / 180;
   Point from(center.get_x() + cos(alpha) * radius
      * (1 - length), center.get_y() + sin(alpha)
      * radius * (1 - length));
   Point to(center.get_x() + cos(alpha) * radius * length,
      center.get_y() + sin(alpha) * radius * length);
   cwin << Line(from, to);
}

void Clock::draw_hand(float angle, float length) const
{  float alpha = M_PI / 2 - 6 * angle * M_PI / 180;
   Point from = center;
   Point to(center.get_x() + cos(alpha) * radius * length,
      center.get_y() + sin(alpha) * radius * length);
   cwin << Line(from, to);
}
```

Then the function to draw the clock face is relatively simple:

```
void Clock::draw()
{  cwin << Circle(center, radius);
   int i;
   for (i = 0; i < 12; i++)
   {  draw_tick(i * 5, HOUR_TICK_LENGTH);
      int j;
      for (j = 1; j <= 4; j++)
         draw_tick(i * 5 + j, MINUTE_TICK_LENGTH);
   }
   draw_hand(current_time.get_minutes(),
      MINUTE_HAND_LENGTH);
   draw_hand((current_time.get_hours() +
      current_time.get_minutes() / 60.0) * 5,
      HOUR_HAND_LENGTH);
}
```

The `draw` function illustrates an important point. Object-oriented design does not replace the process of stepwise refinement. It is quite common to have member functions that are complex and need to be refined further. Because the helper functions `draw_tick` and `draw_hand` are only meant to be called by `draw`, they should be placed in the private section of the class.

Let us next turn to the `Time` class. This class is actually quite similar to the `Time` class that is a part of the library of this book (see Chapter 3). Rather than reinventing the wheel, let's see whether we can use that class. We need the following functionality:

Time
Time(hours, minutes)
get_hours
get_minutes
is_same_as(Time)

If we want to use the existing Time class, we also need to specify a year, month, day, and seconds, but we can choose any convenient date and set the seconds to zero. To see whether two times are identical, we can just check whether there are zero seconds from the first to the second time. Thus, to everyone's relief, we can just use the library class and don't need to write a new one.

Now we turn to the Player class:

Player
Player(name, initial level)
increment_score
get_level

The constructor and the get_level function are straightforward:

```
class Player
{
public:
   Player(string player_name, int initial_level);

   void increment_score();
   int get_level() const;
private:
   string name;
   int score;
   int level;
};
```

```
Player::Player(string player_name, int initial_level)
{  name = player_name;
   level = initial_level;
   score = 0;
}

int Player::get_level() const
{  return level;
}
```

The `increment_score` function is more interesting. Of course, it increments the score. When the score becomes a multiple of five, and the level is less than four, the level is also incremented:

```
void Player::increment_score()
{  score++;
   if (score % 5 == 0 and level < 4)
      level++;
}
```

The last class we need to consider is the **Game** class.

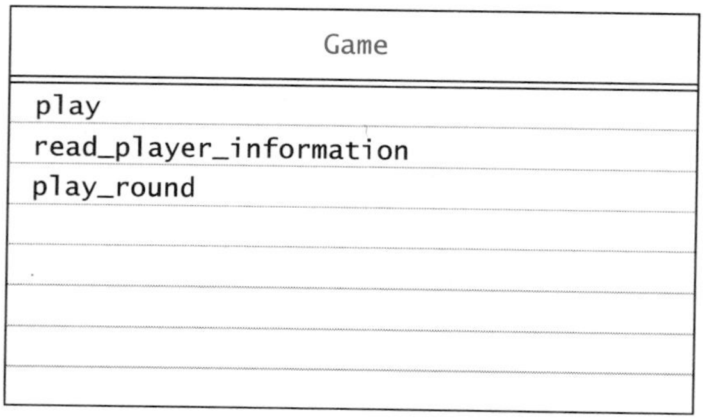

What data fields does the game need? It needs a player. How about the clock and the time? Each round generates a new random time, and the time is not needed in the other functions. Therefore, we won't make the clock and time data fields of the **Game** class. They will just be local variables of the `play_round` function:

```
class Game
{
public:
   Game();

   void play();
   void read_player_information();
   void play_round();
private:
   Player player;
};
```

```
Game::Game()
{
}
```

We already saw the pseudocode for the `play` procedure. Here is the full C++ code:

```
void Game::play()
{  read_player_information();
   string response;
   do
   {  play_round();
      response = cwin.get_string(
         "Do you want to play again? (Y/N)");
   }  while (uppercase(response) == "Y");
}
```

The `read_player_information` function is straightforward:

```
void Game::read_player_information()
{  string name = cwin.get_string("What is your name?");
   int initial_level;
   do
   {  initial_level = get_int(
         "At what level do you want to start? (1-4)");
   }  while (initial_level < 1 or initial_level > 4);
   p = Player(name, initial_level);
}
```

Not unexpectedly, the `play_round` function is the hardest. Here is a refinement:

Play a round

```
make a random time
show the time
get a guess
if (guess is not correct)
   get a guess
if (guess is correct)
{  congratulate player
   increment score
}

else
   give correct answer
```

The *random time* depends on the level. If the level is 1, then the time must be a full hour—that is, a multiple of 60. If the level is 2, then the number of minutes is a multiple of 15. If the level is 3, then the number of minutes is a multiple of 5. Otherwise, it can be any number.

```
Time Game::random_time()
{  int level = player.level();
   int minutes;
   if (level == 1) minutes = 0;
   else if (level == 2) minutes = 15 * rand_int(0, 3);
   else if (level == 3) minutes = 5 * rand_int(0, 11);
   else minutes = rand_int(0, 59);
   int hours = rand_int(1, 12);
   return Time(1970, 1, 1, hours, minutes, 0);
}
```

Since *get a guess* occurs twice, let us make that into a separate procedure:

```
Time Game::get_guess()
{  int hours;
   do
   {  hours = get_int("Please enter hours: (1-12)");
   }  while (hours < 1 or hours > 12);
   int minutes;
   do
   {  minutes = get_int("Please enter minutes: (0-59)");
   }  while (minutes < 0 or minutes > 59);

   return Time(1970, 1, 1, hours, minutes, 0);
}
```

Now we are ready to implement the `play_round` function.

```
void Game::play_round()
{  Time t = random_time();
   Clock clock(Point(0,0), CLOCK_RADIUS);
   clock.set_time(t);
   clock.draw();

   Time guess = get_guess();
   if (t.seconds_from(guess) != 0)
      guess = get_guess();

   string text;
   if (t.seconds_from(guess) == 0)
   {  text = "Congratulations, " + player.get_name()
         + "! That is correct.";
      player.increment_score();
   }
   else
      text = "Sorry, " + player.get_name()
         + "The correct answer is " + t.get_hours()
         + ":" + t.get_minutes();
   cwin << Message(Point(0, CLOCK_RADIUS), text);
}
```

There is, however, a slight problem. We want to be friendly and congratulate the player by name:

```
Congratulations, Susan! That is correct.
```

However, if you look at the `Player` class, you won't find a `get_name` function. That was an oversight; we had not anticipated that we would need the function. It is easy to remedy:

```
class Player
{
public:
   Player(string player_name, int initial_level);

   void increment_score();

   int get_level() const;
   string get_name() const;

private:
   string name;
   int score;
   int level;
};

string Player::get_name() const
{ return name;
}
```

When we design a collection of collaborating classes, as we are doing to implement this game, it is quite common to discover imperfections in some of the classes. This is not a problem. Revisiting a class to add more member functions is perfectly acceptable.

8.9.4 Combining the Classes into a Program

The `main` program is now quite short. We just need to make a `Game` object and call `play`:

```
int main()
{  Game clock_game;
   clock_game.play();

   return EXIT_SUCCESS;
}
```

This is actually quite anticlimactic after the complicated development of the classes and member functions. As a consistency check, let us write down a call tree that shows how the program unfolds. We won't write down constructors and very simple accessor functions such as `get_minutes`.

```
main
 ├── Game::play
 ├── Game::get_player_information
 └── Game::play_round
      ├── Game::random_time
      ├── Game::get_guess
      ├── Clock::set_time
      ├── Clock::draw
      ├── Game::get_guess
      └── Player::increment_score
```

This example shows the power of the methods of finding objects and stepwise refinement. It also shows that designing and implementing even a moderately complex program is a lot of work.

Here is the entire program—by far the longest program we have developed in this book:

Program clock.cpp

```
#define CCC_WIN
#include "ccc.h"

class Clock
{
public:
   Clock();
   Clock(Point c, float r);

   void set_time(Time t);

   void draw() const;
private:
   void draw_tick(float angle, float length) const;
   void draw_hand(float angle, float length) const;

   Time current_time;
   Point center;
   float radius;
};

class Player
{
public:
   Player();
   Player(string player_name, int initial_level);

   void increment_score();
```

```
   int get_level() const;
   string get_name() const;
private:
   string name;
   int score;
   int level;
};

class Game
{
public:
   Game();

   void play();
   void read_player_information();
   void play_round();
   Time random_time();
   Time get_guess();
private:
   Player player;
};

Clock::Clock()
{
}

Clock::Clock(Point c, float r)
{  center = c;
   radius = r;
}

void Clock::set_time(Time t)
{  current_time = t;
}

void Clock::draw_tick(float angle, float length) const
{  float alpha = M_PI / 2 - 6 * angle * M_PI / 180;
   Point from(center.get_x() +
      cos(alpha) * radius * (1 - length),
      center.get_y() + sin(alpha) * radius * (1 - length));
   Point to(center.get_x() + cos(alpha) * radius,
      center.get_y() + sin(alpha) * radius);
   cwin << Line(from, to);
}

void Clock::draw_hand(float angle, float length) const
{  float alpha = M_PI / 2 - 6 * angle * M_PI / 180;
   Point from = center;
   Point to(center.get_x() + cos(alpha) * radius * length,
      center.get_y() + sin(alpha) * radius * length);
```

```
   cwin << Line(from, to);
}

void Clock::draw() const
{  cwin << Circle(center, radius);
   int i;
   const float HOUR_TICK_LENGTH = 0.2;
   const float MINUTE_TICK_LENGTH = 0.1;
   const float HOUR_HAND_LENGTH = 0.6;
   const float MINUTE_HAND_LENGTH = 0.75;
   for (i = 0; i < 12; i++)
   {  draw_tick(i * 5, HOUR_TICK_LENGTH);
      int j;
      for (j = 1; j <= 4; j++)
         draw_tick(i * 5 + j, MINUTE_TICK_LENGTH);
   }
   draw_hand(current_time.get_minutes(), MINUTE_HAND_LENGTH);
   draw_hand((current_time.get_hours() +
      current_time.get_minutes() / 60.0) * 5,
      HOUR_HAND_LENGTH);
}

Player::Player()
{  level = 1;
   score = 0;
}

Player::Player(string player_name, int initial_level)
{  name = player_name;
   level = initial_level;
   score = 0;
}

int Player::get_level() const
{  return level;
}

string Player::get_name() const
{  return name;
}

void Player::increment_score()
{  score++;
   if (score % 5 == 0 and level < 4)
      level++;
}

Game::Game()
{
}
```

```
void Game::play()
{  read_player_information();
   string response;
   do
   {  play_round();
      response = cwin.get_string
         ("Do you want to play again? (Y/N)");
   } while (uppercase(response) == "Y");
}

void Game::read_player_information()
{  string name = cwin.get_string("What is your name?");
   int initial_level;
   do
   {  initial_level = cwin.get_int(
         "At what level do you want to start? (1-4)");
   } while (initial_level < 1 or initial_level > 4);
   player = Player(name, initial_level);
}

Time Game::random_time()
{  int level = player.get_level();
   int minutes;
   if (level == 1) minutes = 0;
   else if (level == 2) minutes = 15 * rand_int(0, 3);
   else if (level == 3) minutes = 5 * rand_int(0, 11);
   else minutes = rand_int(0, 59);
   int hours = rand_int(1, 12);
   return Time(1970, 1, 1, hours, minutes, 0);
}

Time Game::get_guess()
{  int hours;
   do
   {  hours = cwin.get_int("Please enter hours: (1-12)");
   }  while (hours < 1 or hours > 12);
   int minutes;
   do
   {  minutes = cwin.get_int(
      "Please enter minutes: (0-59)");
   } while (minutes < 0 or minutes > 59);

   return Time(1970, 1, 1, hours, minutes, 0);
}

void Game::play_round()
{  cwin.clear();
   Time t = random_time();
   const float CLOCK_RADIUS = 5;
```

```
    Clock clock(Point(0, 0), CLOCK_RADIUS);
    clock.set_time(t);
    clock.draw();

    Time guess = get_guess();
    if (t.seconds_from(guess) != 0)
       guess = get_guess();

    string text;
    if (t.seconds_from(guess) == 0)
    {  text = "Congratulations, " + player.get_name()
          + "! That is correct.";
       player.increment_score();
    }
    else
       text = "Sorry, " + player.get_name()
          + ". The correct answer is "
          + format("%2d", t.get_hours()) + ":"
          + format("%02d", t.get_minutes());
    cwin << Message(Point(-CLOCK_RADIUS, CLOCK_RADIUS + 1), text);
}

int main()
{  Game clock_game;
   clock_game.play();

   return EXIT_SUCCESS;
}
```

Random Fact 8.2

Programming—Art or Science?

There has been a long discussion whether the discipline of computing is a science or not. We call the field "computer science", but that doesn't mean much. Except possibly for librarians and sociologists, few people believe that library science and social science are scientific endeavors.

A scientific discipline aims to discover certain fundamental principles dictated by the laws of nature. It operates on the *scientific method*: by posing hypotheses and testing them with experiments that are repeatable by other workers in the field. For example, a physicist may have a theory on the makeup of nuclear particles and attempt to verify or falsify that theory by running experiments in a particle collider. If an experiment cannot be verified, such as the "cold fusion" research at the University of Utah in the early 1990s, then the theory dies a quick death.

Some programmers indeed run experiments. They try out various methods of computing certain results, or of configuring computer systems, and measure the differences in performance. However, their aim is not to discover laws of nature.

Some computer scientists discover fundamental principles. One class of fundamental results, for instance, states that it impossible to write certain kinds of computer programs, no matter how powerful the computing equipment is. For example, it is impossible to write a program that takes as its input any two C++ program files and as its output prints whether or not these two programs always compute the same results. Such a program would be very handy for grading student homework, but nobody, no matter how clever, will ever be able to write one that works for all input files. The majority of programmers write programs, however, instead of researching the limits of computation.

Some people view programming as an *art* or *craft.* A programmer who writes elegant code that is easy to understand and runs with optimum efficiency can indeed be considered a good craftsman. Calling it an art is perhaps far-fetched, because an art object requires an audience to appreciate it, whereas the program code is generally hidden from the program user.

Others call computing an *engineering discipline.* Just as mechanical engineering is based on the fundamental mathematical principles of statics, computing has certain mathematical foundations. There is more to mechanical engineering than mathematics, though, such as knowledge of materials and of project planning. The same is true for computing.

In one somewhat worrisome aspect, computing does not have the same standing as other engineering disciplines. There is little agreement as to what constitutes professional conduct in the computer field. Unlike the scientist, whose main responsibility is the search for truth, the engineer must strive for the conflicting demands of quality, safety, and economy. Engineering disciplines have professional organizations that hold their members to standards of conduct. The computer field is so new that in many cases we simply don't know the correct method for achieving certain tasks. That makes it difficult to set professional standards.

What do you think? From your limited experience, do you consider the discipline of computing an art, a craft, a science, or an engineering activity?

Chapter Summary

1. Classes represent *concepts*, either derived from the problem that the program is supposed to solve or representing a construct that is useful for the computation.

2. Every class has a public *interface*: a collection of *member functions* through which the objects of the class can be manipulated.

3. Every class has a private *implementation*: data fields that store the state of an object. By keeping the implementation private, we protect it from being accidentally corrupted. Furthermore, the implementation can be changed easily without affecting the users of the class.

4. A *mutator* member function changes the state of the object on which it operates. An *accessor* member function does not modify the object. In C++, accessors must be tagged with `const`.

5. A *constructor* is used to initialize objects when they are created. A constructor with no parameters is called a *default constructor.*

6. The process of *object-oriented design* aims to decompose a programming problem into classes and member functions. For discovering relevant classes, a good rule of thumb is to look for nouns in the problem description. For member functions, look for verbs. For each function, you must find a class that is responsible for carrying it out.

Further Reading

[1] Cay S. Horstmann, *Mastering Object-Oriented Design,* John Wiley & Sons, 1995.

[2] W.H. Sackmann, W.J. Erikson, and E.E. Grant, "Exploratory Experimental Studies Comparing Online and Offline Programming Performance", *Communications of the ACM,* vol. 11, no. 1 (January 1968), pp. 3–11.

[3] F. Brooks, *The Mythical Man-Month,* Addison-Wesley, 1975.

Review Exercises

Exercise R8.1. List all classes that we have used so far in this book. Categorize them as

- Real-world entities
- Mathematical abstractions
- System services

Exercise R8.2. What is the *interface* of a class? What is the *implementation* of a class?

Exercise R8.3. What is a member function, and how does it differ from a nonmember function?

Exercise R8.4. What is a mutator function? What is an accessor function?

Exercise R8.5. What happens if you forget the `const` in an accessor function? What happens if you accidentally supply a `const` in a mutator function?

Exercise R8.6. What is an implicit parameter? How does it differ from an explicit parameter?

Exercise R8.7. How many implicit parameters can a member function have? How many implicit parameters can a nonmember function have? How many explicit parameters can a function have?

Exercise R8.8. What is a constructor?

Exercise R8.9. What is a default constructor? What is the consequence if a class does not have a default constructor?

Exercise R8.10. How many constructors can a class have? Can you have a class with no constructors? If a class has more than one, which of them gets called?

Exercise R8.11. How can you define an object variable that is not initialized with a constructor?

Exercise R8.12. How are member functions declared? How are they defined?

Exercise R8.13. What is encapsulation? Why is it useful?

Exercise R8.14. Data fields are hidden in the private section of a class, but they aren't hidden very well at all. Anyone can read the private section. Explain to what extent the `private` keyword hides the private members of a class.

Exercise R8.15. An accessor function accessing a single data field is sometimes called a *field accessor.* For example, the `get_salary` function of the `Employee` class just reads the value of the `salary` field. Similarly, a function such as `set_salary` is sometimes called a *field mutator.* Should every data field of a class have associated field accessors and mutators? Explain why or why not.

Exercise R8.16. What changes to the `Product` class would be necessary if you wanted to make `is_better_than` into a nonmember function? (*Hint:* You would need to introduce field accessors.) Write the class definition of the changed `Product` class, the definitions of the new member functions and the definition of the changed `is_better_than` function.

Exercise R8.17. What changes to the `Product` class would be necessary if you wanted to make the `read` function into a nonmember function? (*Hint:* You would need to read in the name, price, and score and then construct a product with these properties.) Write the class definition of the changed `Product` class, the definition of the new constructor, and the definition of the changed `read` function.

Exercise R8.18. In a nonmember function, it is easy to differentiate between calls to member functions and calls to nonmember functions. How do you tell them apart? Why is it not as easy for functions that are called from a member function?

Exercise R8.19. How do you indicate whether the implicit parameter is passed by value or by reference? How do you indicate whether an explicit parameter is passed by value or by reference?

Exercise R8.20. Explain the process of object-oriented design.

Exercise R8.21. Give a rule of thumb for how to find classes when designing a program.

Exercise R8.22. Give a rule of thumb for how to find member functions when designing a program.

Exercise R8.23. After discovering a function, why is it important to identify the object that is *responsible* for carrying out the action?

Exercise R8.24. Consider the following "nonsense class". Identify the constructors, mutator functions, and accessor functions.

```
class A
{
public:
   A();
   A(int a);
   void f();
   void g();
   int h() const;
   void k() const;
private:
   int n;
};

A::A() { n = 0; }
A::A(int a) { n = a; }
void A::f() { n++; }
void A::g() { f(); n = 2 * n; f(); }
int h() const { return n; }
void k() const { cout << n << "\n";  }
```

Exercise R8.25. With the nonsense class of the preceding exercise, determine what the following program prints. Work through this problem by hand. Do not actually compile and run the program.

```
int main()
{  A x;
   A y(2);
   A z = y;
   A d = A(3);
   a.f(); b.g(); c.f(); d.g();
   d.k();
   A e(a.h() + b.h() + c.h());
   e.k();
   return EXIT_SUCCESS;
}
```

Exercise R8.26. Add a constructor to the nonsense class of the preceding exercises that constructs an `A` object from a string that specifies a number, for example `A x("12")`.

Exercise R8.27. Add a member function `c()` to the nonsense class of the preceding exercises that divides `n` by 2 if `n` is even and replaces it with `3 * n + 1` if `n` is odd. Pay attention to `const`.

Exercise R8.28. Add a member function `e(A b)` to the nonsense class of the preceding exercises that returns true if the implicit parameter and the explicit parameter `b` are equal. Pay attention to `const`.

Programming Exercises

Exercise P8.1. Implement all member functions of the following class:

```
class Person
{
public:
   Person();
   Person(string pname, Time pbirthday);
   void get_name() const;
   void get_age() const;
private:
   string name;
   string birthday;
}
```

Exercise P8.2. Implement a class `PEmployee` that is just like the `Employee` class except that it stores an object of type `Person` as developed in the preceding exercise.

```
class PEmployee
{
public:
   PEmployee();
   PEmployee(string employee_name, float initial_salary);
   void set_salary(float new_salary);
   float get_salary() const;
   string get_name() const;
private:
   Person person_data;
   float salary;
};
```

Exercise P8.3. Implement a class `Address`. An address has a house number, a street, an optional apartment number, a city, a state, and a postal code. Supply two constructors: one with an apartment number and one without. Supply a `print` function that prints the address with the street on one line and the city, state, and postal code on the next line. Supply a member function `comes_before` that tests whether one address comes before another when the addresses are compared by postal code.

Exercise P8.4. Implement a class `Account`. An account has a balance, functions to add and withdraw money, and a function to inquire the current balance. Charge a $5 penalty if an attempt is made to withdraw more money than available in the account.

Exercise P8.5. Enhance the `Account` class to compute interest on the current balance. Then use the `Account` class to implement the problem from the beginning of the book: An account has an initial balance of $10,000, and 6 percent annual interest is compounded monthly until the investment doubles.

Exercise P8.6. Implement a class `Bank`. This bank has two objects, `checking` and `savings`, of the type `Account` that was developed in the preceding exercise. Implement four member functions:

```
deposit(float amount, string account)
withdraw(float amount, string account)
transfer(float amount, string account)
print_balances()
```

Here the account string is `"S"` or `"C"`. For the deposit or withdrawal, it indicates which account is affected. For a transfer it indicates the account from which the money is taken; the money is automatically transferred to the other account.

Exercise P8.7. Implement a class `Rectangle` that works just like the other graphics classes such as `Circle` or `Line`. A rectangle is constructed from two corner points. The sides of the rectangle are parallel to the coordinate axes:

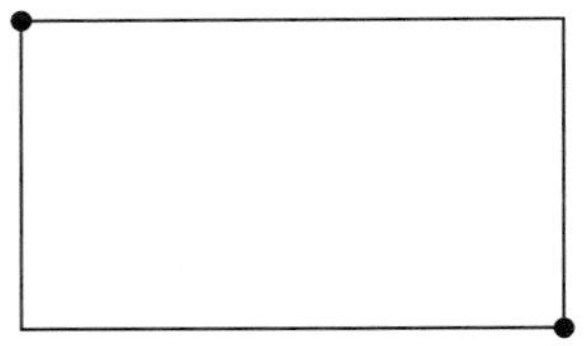

You do not yet know how to define a << operator to plot a rectangle. Instead, define a member function `plot`. Supply a function `move`. Pay attention to `const`. Then write a sample program that constructs and plots a few rectangles.

Exercise P8.8. Enhance the `Rectangle` class of the preceding exercise by adding member functions `circumference` and `area` that compute the circumference and area of the rectangle.

Exercise P8.9. Implement a class `Triangle` that works just like the other graphics classes such as `Circle` or `Line`. A triangle is constructed from three corner points. You do not yet know how to define a << operator to plot a triangle. Instead, define a member function `plot`. Supply a function `move`. Pay attention to `const`. Then write a sample program that constructs and plots a few triangles.

Exercise P8.10. Enhance the `Triangle` class of the preceding exercise by adding member functions `circumference` and `area` that compute the circumference and area of the triangle.

Exercise P8.11. Implement a class `GPA` to compute grade point averages. Member functions are needed to add a grade, change a grade, and get current GPA. Specify grades as strings, such as `"B+"`. You will also need a function that translates those strings into their numeric values (for example, `"B+"` becomes 3.3). Should that function be a member function? Test your function by adding a few grades and computing the resulting GPA.

Exercise P8.12. Write a program that implements a different game, to teach arithmetic to your baby sister. The program tests addition and subtraction. In level 1 it tests only addition of numbers less than 10 whose sum is less than 10. In level 2 it tests addition of arbitrary one-digit numbers. In level 3 it tests subtraction of one-digit numbers with a nonnegative difference. Generate random problems and get the player input. The player gets up to two tries per problem. As in the clock game, advance from one level to the next when the player has achieved a score of five points.

Exercise P8.13. Write a bumper car game with the following rules. Bumper cars are located in grid points (x, y), where x and y are integers between -10 and 10. A bumper car starts moving in a random direction, either left, right, up, or down. If it reaches the boundary of its track (that is, x or y is 10 or -10), then it reverses direction. If it is about to bump into another bumper car, it reverses direction. Model a track with two bumper cars. Make each of them move 100 times, alternating between the two cars. Display the movement on the graphics screen. Use at least two classes in your program. There should be no global variables.

Exercise P8.14. Define a class `Country` that stores the name of the country, its population, and its area. Using that class, write a program that reads in a set of countries and prints

- The country with the largest area
- The country with the largest population
- The country with the largest population density (people per square kilometer)

Think through the problem that you need to solve. What member functions will you need? Then design the class and implement the member function. Then write the program. Did you need to add member functions later? Did you supply member functions that you never needed?

Exercise P8.15. In the clock game program, we assigned the `play_round` function to the `Game` class. That choice was somewhat arbitrary. Modify the clock program so that the `Player` class is responsible for `play_round`.

Exercise P8.16. Design a class `House` that defines a house in a street. A house has a house number and an (x, y) location, where x and y are numbers between -10 and 10. The key member function is `plot`, which plots the house.

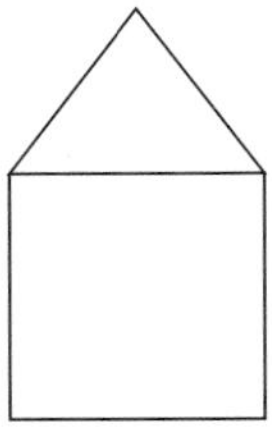

Next, design a class `Street` that contains a number of equally spaced houses. An object of type `Street` stores the first house, the last house (which can be anywhere on the screen), and the number of houses in the street. The `Street::plot` function needs to make the intermediate house objects on the fly, because we don't yet know how to store an arbitrary number of objects.

Use these classes in a graphics program in which the user clicks with the mouse on the locations of the first and last house, then enters the house numbers of the first and last house, and the number of houses on the street. Then the entire street is plotted.

Exercise P8.17. Design a class `Message` that models an email message. A message has a recipient, a sender, a time stamp, and a message text. Support the following member functions:

- A constructor that takes the sender and recipient and sets the time stamp to the current time
- A member function `append` that appends a line of text to the message body
- A member function `to_string` that makes the message into one long string like this:

  `"From: Harry Hacker\nTo: Rudolf Reindeer\nTime: ... \n ..."`
- A member function `print` that prints the message text. *Hint:* Use `to_string`.

Write a program that uses this class to make a message and print it.

Exercise P8.18. Design a class `Mailbox` that stores mail messages, using the `Message` class of the preceding exercise. We don't yet know how to store a collection of message objects. Instead we will use the following brute force approach: The mailbox contains one very long string, which is the concatenation of all messages. You can tell where a new message starts by searching for a `From:` at the beginning of a line. This may sound like a dumb strategy, but surprisingly, many email systems do just that.

Implement the following member functions:

```
void Mailbox::add_message(Message m);
Message Mailbox::get_message(int i) const;
void remove_message(int i) const;
```

What do you do if the message body happens to have a line starting with `"From: "`? Then the `to_string` function of the `Message` class should really insert a > in front of the `From:` so that it reads `>From:` . Again, this sounds dumb, but it is a strategy used by real email systems. Extra credit if you implement this enhancement.

Exercise P8.19. Design a class `Cannonball` to model a cannonball that is fired into the air. A ball has

- An x- and a y-position
- An x- and a y-velocity

Supply the following member functions:

- A constructor with a weight and an x-position (the y-position is initially 0)
- A member function `move(float sec)` that moves the ball to the next position (first compute the distance traveled in `sec` seconds, using the current velocities, then update the x- and y-positions; then update the y-velocity by taking into account the gravitational acceleration of -9.81 m/sec^2; the x-velocity is unchanged)
- A member function `plot` that plots the current location of the cannonball
- A member function `shoot` whose parameters are the angle α and initial velocity v (compute the x-velocity as $v \cos \alpha$ and the y-velocity as $v \sin \alpha$; then keep calling `move` with a time interval of 0.1 seconds until the x-position is 0; call `plot` after every move)

Use this class in a program that prompts the user for the starting angle and the initial velocity. Then call `shoot`.

CHAPTER 9

Vectors and Matrices

Objectives

- To become familiar with using ANSI standard vectors to collect objects
- To be able to access vector elements and resize vectors
- To be able to pass vectors to functions
- To learn about common array algorithms
- To be able to build classes containing vectors
- To learn how to use matrices for two-dimensional collections

9.1 Using Vectors to Collect Data Items

Suppose we write a program that graphs the salaries of all employees of a company or department, as in Figure 1.

The program needs to read the employee salaries and then plot a series of lines. To make the graph fill the screen, we need to know how many employees there are and what the highest salary is. If we make an assumption such as "the highest salary will be $100,000", then the graph will look pretty silly if we are plotting the graphs of either a law firm or a hamburger joint.

In Chapter 6 we saw a program that read salary values in and computed the maximum salary. To determine the maximum, all data values must be read in. Then we are ready to plot the lines. We can't very well ask the user to input all the data values a second time, so we must store them somewhere.

If we knew that there were just ten employees, then we could store the data in ten variables `staff1`, `staff2`, `staff3`, . . . , `staff10`. Such a sequence of variables

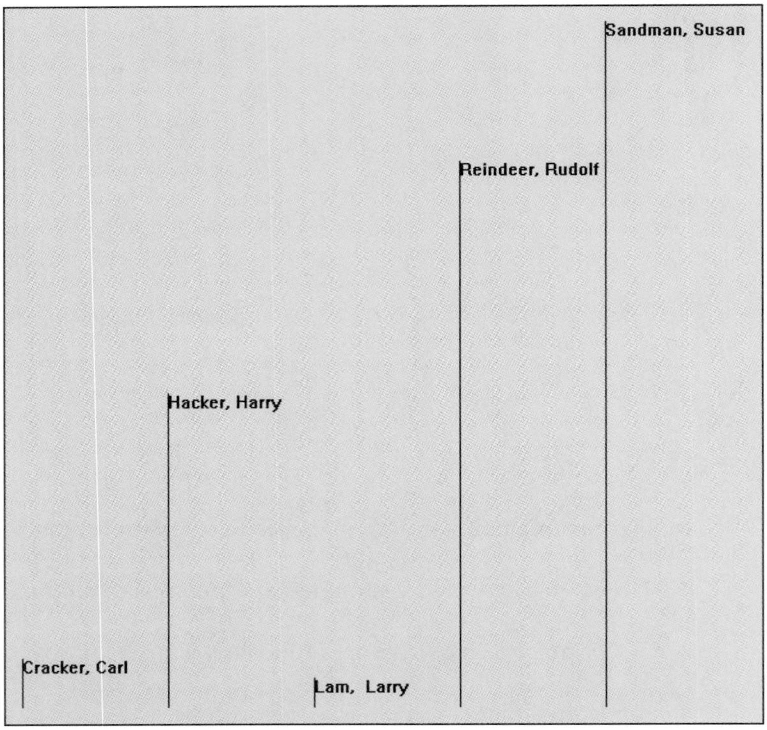

Figure 1

Graph of Employee Salaries

is not very practical to use. We would have to write quite a bit of code ten times, once for each of the variables. There might also be a hundred employees on the staff. In C++ there is a better way of implementing a sequence of data items: the vector construct.

A *vector* is a collection of data items of the same type. Every element of the collection can be accessed separately. Here we define a vector of ten employees:

```
vector<Employee> staff(10);
```

This is the definition of a variable `staff` whose type is `vector<Employee>`. That is, `staff` stores a sequence of employees. The `(10)` indicates that the vector holds 10 employee records. (See Figure 2.)

To get some data into `staff`, we need to specify which slot in the vector we want to use. That is done with the `[]` operator:

```
Employee harry("Hacker, Harry", 35000);

staff[4] = harry;
```

Figure 2

Vector of `Employees`

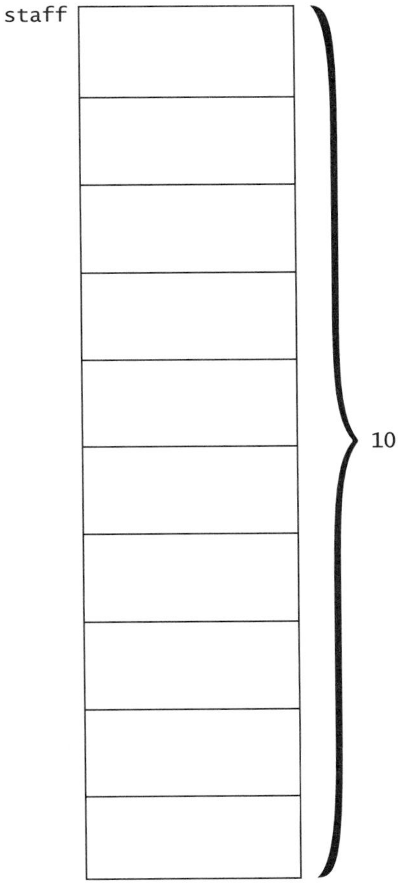

Now the slot with index 4 of `staff` is filled with the same data as `harry`. (See Figure 3).

Because `staff` is a vector of `Employees`, a slot such as `staff[4]` can be used just like any variable of type `Employee`:

```
cout << staff[4].get_name() << "\n";
```

Before we go on, we must take care of one unpleasant detail of C++ vectors. If you look carefully at Figure 3, you will find that the *fifth* slot was filled with data when we changed `staff[4]`. Unfortunately, in C++, the slots of vectors are numbered *starting at 0.* That is, the legal slots for the `staff` vector are

`staff[0]`, the first slot
`staff[1]`, the second slot
`staff[2]`, the third slot

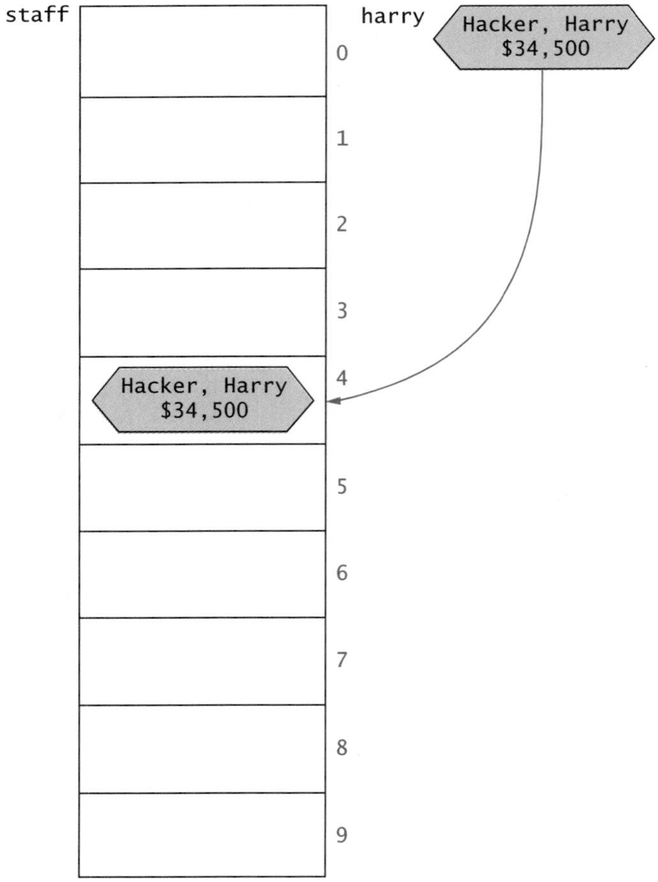

Figure 3

Vector Slot Filled with `Employee` Object

`staff[3]`, the fourth slot
`staff[4]`, the fifth slot
. . .
`staff[9]`, the tenth slot

In "ancient" times there was a technical reason why this setup was a good idea. Because so many programmers got used to it, the `vector` construction imitates it. It is, however, a major source of grief for the newcomer.

The name `vector` is also somewhat unconventional. Most other programming languages call a sequence of values an *array,* and we will sometimes use that term in this book as well. The name *vector* comes from mathematics. You can have a vector in the plane, with (x, y) coordinates; a vector in space with (x, y, z) coordinates; or a vector in a space with more than three dimensions, in which case the coordinates are no longer given separate letters x, y, z, but a single letter with subscripts $(x_1, x_2, x_3, \ldots, x_{10})$. In C++ this would be implemented by a

```
vector<float> x(10);
```

Of course, in C++ the subscripts go from 0 to 9, not from 1 to 10. There is no easy way of writing subscripts x_4 on the computer screen, so the bracket operator `x[4]` is used instead. A vector of floating-point numbers really has the same meaning as the mathematical construct. A vector of employees, on the other hand, has no mathematical meaning; it is just a sequence of individual employee data, each of which can be accessed with the `[]` operator. In mathematics the subscript i selecting a vector element x_i is often called an *index.* In C++ the value `i` of the expression `x[i]` is also called an index.

We now know how to fill a vector with values: by filling each slot. Now let us find the employee with the highest salary.

```
Employee highest_paid = staff[0];
for (i = 1; i < 10; i++)
   if (staff[i].get_salary() > highest_paid.get_salary())
      highest_paid = staff[i];
```

The key observation is that we can use a variable index `staff[i]` to analyze the contents of the vector one element at a time.

Advanced Topic 9.1

C Arrays

The vectors that we cover in this book are a part of the ANSI C++ standard, and they are convenient to use. There is a lower-level construct in C and C++ that can be used instead of vectors: namely, *arrays.* An array of employees is defined as

```
Employee staff[10];
```

The size of the array must be a constant, known at compile time. A programmer cannot change the size of the array later. The individual elements of the array are accessed just like those of a vector: `staff[i]` is the `i`th element.

Veteran C and C++ programmers will be surprised that we use vectors, not C arrays, in this book. There is a good reason. Compared to vectors, C arrays are enormously inconvenient.

- You must know the exact size of a C array when you compile the program; you cannot later grow or shrink the array. Vectors can grow and shrink on demand.
- A C array is usually partially filled, and you must keep a companion variable to know which elements are in use. Vectors are objects that can tell you how full they are.
- You need a loop to make a copy of a C array. Vectors can be copied with a single assignment.
- C arrays turn into pointers when you pass them to functions. Vectors stay objects.

Of course, C arrays are more efficient, and they are needed to implement other data structures. For example, the vector template uses C arrays in its implementation. Appendix 3 covers C arrays in detail.

9.2 Vector Subscripts

A C++ program accesses slots of a vector with the `[]` operator. Recall that the value of `n` in the expression `v[n]` is called an index or subscript. This subscript has an important restriction: trying to access a slot that does not exist in the vector is an error.

For example, if `staff` holds ten employees, then the statement

```
int i = 20;
cout << staff[i].get_salary();
```

is an error. There is no `staff[20]`. The compiler does not catch this error. Generally, it is too difficult for the compiler to follow the current contents of `staff` and `i`. If you use the `vector` implementation that is supplied with this book, an error message is printed at run time and the program aborts. Unfortunately, the error message states only that a *vector index is out of bounds,* and it prints the size of the array (10) and the value of the offending index (20). The error message does not contain the name of the array or the line number of the code causing the error. See Productivity Hint 9.2 for more information on how to locate the cause of such an error. Note that many `vector` implementations generate *no* error message and silently overwrite another memory location.

The most common bounds error is the following:

```
vector<Employee> staff(10);
cout << staff[10].get_salary();
```

There is no `staff[10]` in a vector with ten elements—the legal subscripts are `staff[0]` until `staff[9]`.

Another common error is to forget to size the vector.

```
vector<Employee> staff; /* no size given */
staff[0] = Employee("Hacker, Harry", 35000);
```

When a vector is defined without a size parameter, it is empty and can hold *no* elements.

You can find out the size of a vector by calling the `size` function. For example, the loop of the preceding section,

```
for (i = 1; i < 10; i++)
   if (staff[i].get_salary() > highest_paid.get_salary())
      highest_paid = staff[i];
```

can be written as

```
for (i = 1; i < staff.size(); i++)
   if (staff[i].get_salary() > highest_paid.get_salary())
      highest_paid = staff[i];
```

Using `size` is actually a better idea than using the number 10. If the program changes, such as by allocating space for 20 employees in the `staff` vector, the first loop is no longer correct, but the second loop automatically stays valid. This principle is another way to avoid magic numbers, as discussed in Quality Tip 2.3.

Note that `i` is a legal index for the vector `v` if $0 \leq$ `i` and `i` $<$ `v.size()`. Therefore the `for` loop

```
for (i = 0; i < v.size(); i++)
   do something with v[i];
```

is extremely common to visit all elements in a vector. By the way, don't write it as

```
for (i = 0; i <= v.size() - 1; i++)
```

The condition `i <= v.size() - 1` means the same thing as `i < v.size()`, but it is harder to read.

It is often difficult to know initially how many elements you need to store. For example, we want to store all employee records that are entered in the salary chart program. We have no idea how many records the program user will enter. The function `push_back` allows us to start out with an empty vector and grow the vector whenever another employee is added:

```
vector<Employee> staff;
. . .
string name = cwin.get_string("Employee name:");
float salary = cwin.get_float("Salary:");
Employee e(name, salary);
staff.push_back(e);
```

The `push_back` command resizes the vector `staff` by adding one element to its end; then it sets that element to `e`. The strange name `push_back` indicates that `e` is *pushed* onto the *back* end of the array.

Although it is undeniably convenient to grow a vector on demand with **push_back**, it is also inefficient. More memory must be found to hold the longer vector, and all elements must be copied into the larger space. If you already know how many elements you need in a vector, you should specify that size when you define it, and then fill it.

Another member function, **pop_back**, removes the last element of a vector, shrinking its size by one.

```
vector<Employee> staff(10);
. . .
staff.pop_back(); /* Now staff has size 9 */
```

Note that the **pop_back** function does not return the element that is being removed. If you want to know what that element is, you need to capture it first.

```
Employee last = staff[staff.size() - 1];
staff.pop_back(); /* removes last from the vector */
```

This is not very intuitive if you are familiar with the so-called *stack* data structure, whose **pop** operation returns the top value of the stack. Intuitive or not, the names **push_back** and **pop_back** are part of the ANSI standard for C++. The ANSI standard defines many more useful functions for vectors; in this book, we only use **push_back** and **pop_back**.

We now have all the pieces together to implement the program outlined at the beginning of the chapter. This program reads employee records and displays a bar graph of the salaries, scaled to fit the window.

Program bargraph.cpp

```
#define CCC_WIN
#include "ccc.h"

int main()
{  vector<Employee> staff;
   string more;
   do
   {  string name = cwin.get_string("Employee name:");
      float salary = cwin.get_float("Salary:");
      staff.push_back(Employee(name, salary));
      more = cwin.get_string("More data? (Y/N)");
   }  while (uppercase(more) == "Y");

   int i;

   Employee highest_paid = staff[0];
   for (i = 1; i < staff.size(); i++)
      if (staff[i].get_salary() > highest_paid.get_salary())
         highest_paid = staff[i];
```

```
    cwin.coord(0, highest_paid.get_salary(),
    staff.size(), 0);

    for (i = 0; i < staff.size(); i++)
    {  Line bar(Point(i, 0), Point(i, staff[i].get_salary());
       cwin << bar << Message(bar.get_end(),
          staff[i].get_name()));
    }

    return EXIT_SUCCESS;
}
```

Common Error 9.1

Bounds Errors

The most common vector error is accessing a nonexistent slot.

```
vector<float> data(10);
data[10] = 5.4;
   /* Error—data has 10 elements with subscripts 0 to 9 */
```

If you use the `vector` that is included with the code for this book, an out-of-bounds subscript simply generates an error message when the program runs. If you use the `vector` type that comes with your compiler, however, or if you use C-style arrays, there is no error message. Instead, the program will quietly (or not so quietly) corrupt some memory. Except for very short programs, in which the problem may go unnoticed, that corruption will make the program act flaky or cause a horrible death many instructions later. These are serious errors that can be difficult to detect. I therefore strongly recommend that you use vectors with bounds checking, such as the `vector` implementation of this book.

Quality Tip 9.1

Don't Combine Array Access and Index Increment

It is possible to increment a variable that is used as an array index, for example

```
x = v[i++];
```

That is a shortcut for

```
x = v[i];
i++;
```

Many years ago, when compilers were not very powerful, the `v[i++]` shortcut was useful, because it made the compiler generate faster code. Nowadays, the compiler generates the same efficient code for both versions. You should therefore use the second version, because it is clearer and less confusing.

Productivity Hint 9.1

Inspecting Vectors in the Debugger

Vectors are more difficult to inspect in the debugger than numbers or objects. Suppose you are running a program and want to inspect the contents of

```
vector<Employee> staff;
```

First, you tell the debugger to inspect the vector variable `staff`. It just shows you the inner details of an object. You need to find the data field that points to the vector elements (called `_elements` in the code accompanying this book). Then tell the debugger to inspect that variable. Depending on your debugger, you may need to click on it or select it and hit Enter. That shows you the *first* element in the array. Then you must expand the range to show you as many elements as you would like to see. The commands to do so differ widely among debuggers; on one popular debugger, you must click on the field with the *right* mouse button and select "Range" from the menu. You will then get a display of all array elements that you selected (see Figure 4).

Inspecting vectors is an important debugging skill. Read the debugger documentation, or ask someone who knows, such as your lab assistant or instructor, for details.

Figure 4

Display of Vector Elements

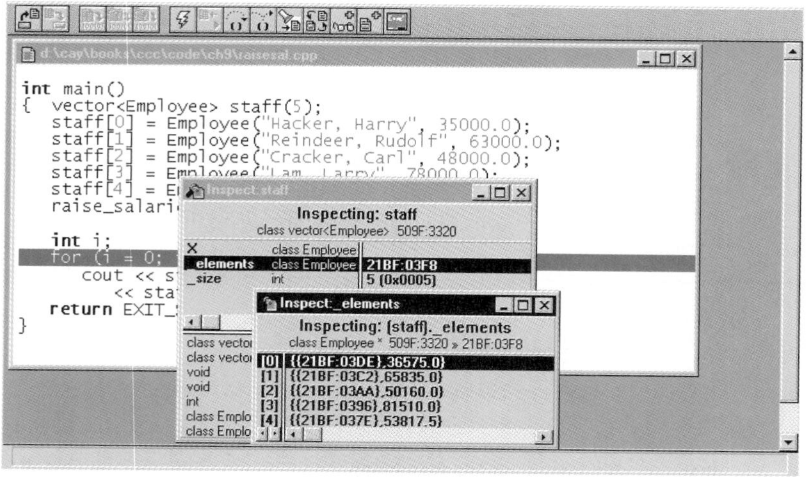

Productivity Hint 9.2

Debugging Bounds Errors

When your program dies with a bounds error, the program reports the size of the vector and the index that was out of bounds. The error message might state that the vector size was 10 and the index was also 10. Unfortunately, the error report cannot tell you the name of the vector or the line number of the illegal code.

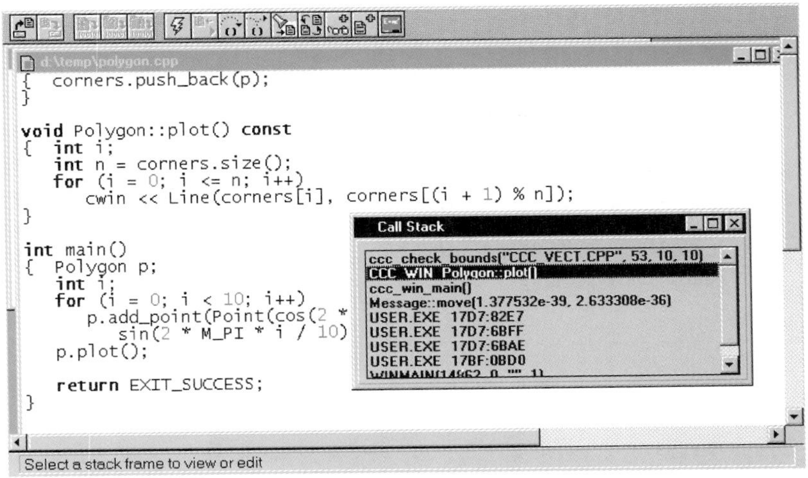

Figure 5

Debugging a Bounds Error

Of course, you can use the debugger and step through the code until it dies; the last index access before the death was the culprit.

That stepping through can be pretty tedious. Here is another method (which takes a little extra time to set up and it works only with the vectors from the library accompanying this book, not the vector class supplied by your compiler): Set a breakpoint in the `ccc_check_bounds` function in ccc_util.cpp. If a bounds error occurs, that breakpoint will be triggered. Then inspect the call stack. The last function in the call stack that belongs to your code, and not the library code, is the culprit (see Figure 5).

Advanced Topic 9.2

Strings Are Vectors of Characters

A `string` variable is essentially a vector of characters. C++ has a basic data type `char` to denote individual characters. For example, the string `greeting` defined by

```
string greeting = "Hello";
```

can be considered a vector of five characters `'H'`, `'e'`, `'l'`, `'l'`, `'o'`. Note that values of type `char` are enclosed in *single* quotes. `'H'` denotes the individual character, `"H"` a string containing one character. An individual character can be stored in one byte. A string, even if it has length 1, needs to store both the contents and the length, which requires several bytes.

You can modify the characters in a string:

```
greeting[3] = 'p';
greeting[4] = '!';
```

Now the string is "Help!". Of course, the same effect can be achieved using string operations rather than direct character manipulation.

```
greeting = greeting.substr(0, 3) + "p!";
```

Manipulating the characters directly is more efficient than extracting substrings and concatenating strings, but it is a hassle to have to worry about bounds errors. For example, accessing `greeting[6]` without first resizing the string is an error. In this book, we will consider strings as fundamental types, just like integers or floating-point numbers. Just as we won't edit individual bits of a floating-point number, we won't edit individual characters of a string. However, many C++ programs and all C programs manipulate strings a character at a time.

Random Fact 9.1

The Internet Worm

In November 1988, a college student from Cornell University launched a so-called virus program that infected about 6,000 computers connected to the Internet across the United States. Tens of thousands of computer users were unable to read their email or otherwise use their computers. All major universities and many high-tech companies were affected. (The Internet was much smaller then than it is now.)

The particular kind of virus used in this attack is called a *worm*. The virus program crawled from one computer on the Internet to the next. The entire program is quite complex; its major parts are explained in [1]. However, one of the methods used in the attack is of interest here. The worm would attempt to connect to the `finger` program of its remote victim. Some versions of that program are known to contain sloppy C code that places characters into an array without checking that the array overflows. The worm program purposefully filled the 512-character array with 536 bytes, replacing the return address of the function reading the string. When that function was finished, it didn't return to its caller but to code supplied by the worm. That code ran under the same super-user privileges as `finger`, allowing the worm to gain entry into the remote system.

Had the programmer who wrote `finger` been more conscientious, this particular attack would not be possible. In C++, as in C, all programmers must be very careful not to overrun array boundaries. The `vector` template that is included with this book checks against bounds errors, but other implementations do not.

One may well speculate what would possess a skilled programmer to spend many weeks or months to plan the antisocial act of breaking into thousands of computers and disabling them. It appears that the break-in was fully intended by the author, but the disabling of the computers was a side effect of continuous reinfection and efforts by the worm to avoid being killed. It is not clear whether the author was aware that these moves would cripple the attacked machines.

In recent years, the novelty of vandalizing other people's computers has worn off, and there are fewer jerks with programming skills who write new viruses. Other attacks by individuals with more criminal energy, whose intent has been to steal information or money, have surfaced. Reference [2] gives a very readable account of the discovery and apprehension of one such person.

9.3 Vector Parameters and Return Values

Functions and procedures often have vector parameters. This function computes the average salary of a vector of employees:

Program avgsal.cpp

```
#include "ccc.h"

float average_salary(vector<Employee> s)
/* PURPOSE:   Computes the average salary of a vector of employees
   RECEIVES: s—a vector of employees
   RETURNS:   The average salary
*/
{  if (s.size() == 0) return 0;
   int i;
   float salary_sum = 0;
   for (i = 0; i < s.size(); i++)
     salary_sum = salary_sum + s[i].get_salary();
   return salary_sum / s.size();
}

int main()
{  vector<Employee> staff(5);
   staff[0] = Employee("Hacker, Harry", 35000.0);
   staff[1] = Employee("Reindeer, Rudolf", 63000.0);
   staff[2] = Employee("Cracker, Carl", 48000.0);
   staff[3] = Employee("Lam, Larry", 78000.0);
   staff[4] = Employee("Sandman, Susan", 51500.0);

   float avgsal = average_salary(staff);

   cout << "The average salary is " << avgsal << "\n";
   return EXIT_SUCCESS;
}
```

To visit each element of the vector `s`, the function needs to determine the size of `s`. It inspects all elements, with index starting at 0 and going up to, but not including, `s.size()`.

A function can modify a vector. Two kinds of modifications are common. The elements in a vector can be rearranged; for example, a vector of employee records can be sorted by name or salary:

```
void sort_by_name(vector<Employee>& s)
```

(We will study algorithms for sorting a vector in Chapter 12.)

The individual elements of an array can also be modified:

Program raisesal.cpp

```
#include "ccc.h"

void raise_salaries(vector<Employee>& s, float p)
/* PURPOSE:   Give a raise to all employees in a vector
   RECEIVES: s—vector of employees
             p—percentage to raise salary by
*/
{  int i;
   for (i = 0; i < s.size(); i++)
   {  float new_salary = s[i].get_salary()
         * (1 + p / 100);
      s[i].set_salary(new_salary);
   }
}

int main()
{  vector<Employee> staff(5);
   staff[0] = Employee("Hacker, Harry", 35000.0);
   staff[1] = Employee("Reindeer, Rudolf", 63000.0);
   staff[2] = Employee("Cracker, Carl", 48000.0);
   staff[3] = Employee("Lam, Larry", 78000.0);
   staff[4] = Employee("Sandman, Susan", 51500.0);

   raise_salaries(staff, 4.5);

   int i;
   for (i = 0; i < staff.size(); i++)
      cout << staff[i].get_name() << " "
         << staff[i].get_salary() << "\n";
   return EXIT_SUCCESS;
}
```

In both cases of modification, the vector must be passed by reference (`vector<Employee>&`). If a vector is passed by value, and a function modifies the vector, the modification affects the local copy of that value only, not the call parameter. That either is a programming error, or, if done intentionally, is considered bad style.

A function can return a vector. This is useful if a function computes a result that consists of a collection of values of the same type. Here is a function that collects employees whose salary falls within a certain range:

Program salbetw.cpp

```
#include "ccc.h"

vector<Employee> salary_between(vector<Employee> s,
   float low, float high)
/* PURPOSE:  Returns all employees with salary within a range
```

```
   RECEIVES: s—a vector of employees
             low—the low end of the range
             high—the high end of the range
   RETURNS:  A vector of employees from s with low ≤ salary ≤ high
*/
{  vector<Employee> result;
   int i;
   for (i = 0; i < s.size(); i++)
   if (low <= s[i].get_salary()
       and s[i].get_salary() <= high)
      result.push_back(s[i]);
   return result;
}

int main()
{  vector<Employee> staff(5);
   staff[0] = Employee("Hacker, Harry", 35000.0);
   staff[1] = Employee("Reindeer, Rudolf", 63000.0);
   staff[2] = Employee("Cracker, Carl", 48000.0);
   staff[3] = Employee("Lam, Larry", 78000.0);
   staff[4] = Employee("Sandman, Susan", 51500.0);

   vector<Employee> result
      = salary_between(staff, 45000.0, 65000.0);

   int i;
   for (i = 0; i < result.size(); i++)
      cout << result[i].get_name() << "\n";
   return EXIT_SUCCESS;
}
```

Advanced Topic 9.3

Passing Vectors by Constant Reference

Passing a vector into a function by value is unfortunately somewhat inefficient, because the function must make a copy of all elements. As explained in Advanced Topic 5.2, the cost of a copy can be avoided by using a constant reference.

```
float average_salary(vector<Employee> const& s)
```

instead of

```
float average_salary(vector<Employee> s)
```

This is a useful optimization that greatly increases performance.

9.4 Simple Vector Algorithms

In this section we discuss several very common and important vector algorithms. More complex algorithms will be the topic of Chapter 12.

9.4.1 Finding a Value

Suppose we want to find the first employee with a salary > $50,000. We can simply inspect each element until we find a match or reach the end of the vector:

Program find.cpp

```
#include "ccc.h".

int main()
{  vector<Employee> staff(5);
   staff[0] = Employee("Hacker, Harry", 35000.0);
   staff[1] = Employee("Reindeer, Rudolf", 63000.0);
   staff[2] = Employee("Cracker, Carl", 48000.0);
   staff[3] = Employee("Lam, Larry", 78000.0);
   staff[4] = Employee("Sandman, Susan", 51500.0);

   int i = 0;
   bool found = false;
   while (i < staff.size() and not found)
   {  if (staff[i].get_salary() > 50000.0)
         found = true;
      else
         i++;
   }

   if (found)
      cout << staff[i].get_name() << "\n";
   return EXIT_SUCCESS;
}
```

At the end of this loop, either `found` is true, in which case `data[i]` is the first computer fulfilling our requirements, or `i` is `data.size()`, which means that we searched the entire list without finding a match. Note that we do *not* increment `i` if we had a match.

9.4.2 Counting

Suppose we want to find *how many* employees have a salary > $50,000.

Program count.cpp

```
#include "ccc.h".

int main()
```

```
{  vector<Employee> staff(5);
   staff[0] = Employee("Hacker, Harry", 35000.0);
   staff[1] = Employee("Reindeer, Rudolf", 63000.0);
   staff[2] = Employee("Cracker, Carl", 48000.0);
   staff[3] = Employee("Lam, Larry", 78000.0);
   staff[4] = Employee("Sandman, Susan", 51500.0);

   int i;
   int count = 0;
   for (i = 0; i < staff.size(); i++)
   {  if (staff[i].get_salary() > 50000.0)
         count++;
   }

   cout << count << "employees\n";
   return EXIT_SUCCESS;
}
```

Now we don't stop on the first match but keep going to the end of the list, counting how many entries match.

9.4.3 Collecting Matches

Suppose we want to know the names of *all* the employees who have a salary > $50,000. Maybe there is exactly one such employee; then the find algorithm will locate it. Or maybe there is no match. Then the count algorithm will return 0. But perhaps there are several matches, and we would like to know them all.

We can collect the subscripts of all matching employees in a vector of integers. For example, if `staff[1]`, `staff[3]`, and `staff[4]` are employees matching our criterion, we would end up with a vector containing the integers 1, 3, and 4. Once we know where all matches occur, we can print just those:

Program matches.cpp

```
#include "ccc.h".

int main()
{  vector<Employee> staff(5);
   staff[0] = Employee("Hacker, Harry", 35000.0);
   staff[1] = Employee("Reindeer, Rudolf", 63000.0);
   staff[2] = Employee("Cracker, Carl", 48000.0);
   staff[3] = Employee("Lam, Larry", 78000.0);
   staff[4] = Employee("Sandman, Susan", 51500.0);

   vector<int> matches;
   int i;
   for (i = 0; i < staff.size(); i++)
   {  if (staff[i].get_salary() > 50000.0)
         matches.push_back(i);
   }
```

```
   int j;
   for (j = 0; j < matches.size(); j++)
      cout << staff[matches[j]].get_name() << "\n";
   return EXIT_SUCCESS;
}
```

Note the nested subscripts, `staff[matches[j]]`. Here `matches[j]` is the subscript of the `j`th match. In our example, `matches[0]` is 1, `matches[1]` is 3, and `matches[2]` is 4. Thus, `staff[1]`, `staff[3]`, and `staff[4]` are printed.

9.4.4 Removing an Element

Suppose we want to *remove* an element from a vector. If the elements in the vector are not in any particular order, that task is easy to accomplish. Simply overwrite the element to be removed with the *last* element of the vector, then shrink the size of the vector. (See Figure 6.)

Program remove1.cpp

```
#include "ccc.h".

int main()
{  vector<Employee> staff(5);
   staff[0] = Employee("Hacker, Harry", 35000.0);
   staff[1] = Employee("Reindeer, Rudolf", 63000.0);
   staff[2] = Employee("Cracker, Carl", 48000.0);
   staff[3] = Employee("Lam, Larry", 78000.0);
   staff[4] = Employee("Sandman, Susan", 51500.0);

   int pos;
   cout << "Remove which element? (0 - 4) ";
   cin >> pos;
   int last_pos = staff.size() - 1;
   staff[pos] = staff[last_pos];
   staff.pop_back();
```

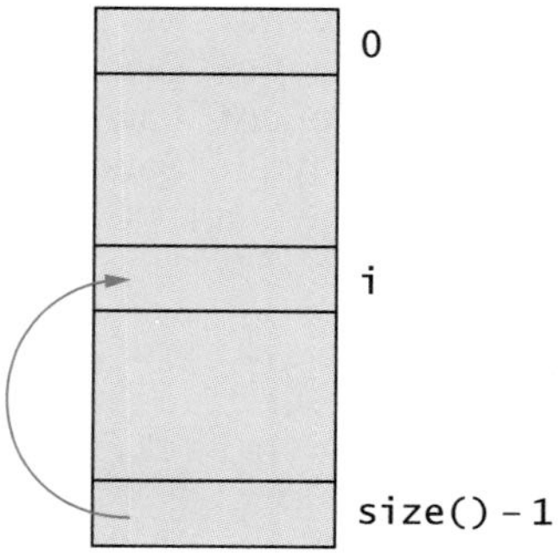

Figure 6

Removing an Element in an Unordered Vector

```
   int i;
   for (i = 0; i < staff.size(); i++)
      cout << staff[i].get_name() << "\n";
   return EXIT_SUCCESS;
}
```

The situation is more complex if the order of the elements matters. Then we must move all elements above the element to be removed down by one slot, and then shrink the size of the vector. (See Figure 7.)

Program remove2.cpp

```
#include "ccc.h".

int main()
{  vector<Employee> staff(5);
   staff[0] = Employee("Cracker, Carl", 48000.0);
   staff[1] = Employee("Hacker, Harry", 35000.0);
   staff[2] = Employee("Lam, Larry", 78000.0);
   staff[3] = Employee("Reindeer, Rudolf", 63000.0);
   staff[4] = Employee("Sandman, Susan", 51500.0);

   int pos;
   cout << "Remove which element? (0 - 4) ";
   cin >> pos;

   int i;

   for (i = pos; i < staff.size() - 1; i++)
      staff[i] = staff[i + 1];
   staff.pop_back();

   for (i = 0; i < staff.size(); i++)
      cout << staff[i].get_name() << "\n";
   return EXIT_SUCCESS;
}
```

Figure 7

Removing an Element in an Ordered Element

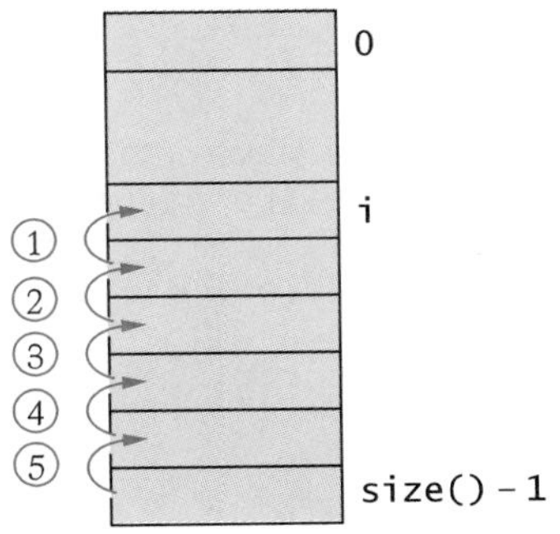

9.5 Parallel Vectors

Consider the graph in Figure 8. It shows a set of data points of prices and performance scores of computers. Prices grow in the x-direction, performance in the y-direction.

Such a graph is useful to get a quick visual impression of the data set. The computer with the highest score may be very expensive and thus not a good buy. Savvy buyers will look for computers that give good performance at a low price; those are the ones in the upper left corner of the diagram. On the other hand, the computers in the lower right corner of the diagram have a comparatively high price for the performance they offer. Unless there are other factors, such as exceptional service, one would be less inclined to choose those models.

Here is a simple program that reads the computer data in and plots the graph:

Program plot1.cpp

```
#define CCC_WIN
#include "ccc.h"

int main()
{  vector<string> names;
   vector<float> prices;
   vector<int> scores;
   string more;

   do
   {  string n = cwin.get_string("Product name:");
      names.push_back(n);
      float p = cwin.get_float("Price:");
      prices.push_back(p);
      int s = cwin.get_int("Score:");
      scores.push_back(s);
      more = cwin.get_string("More data? (Y/N)");
   }  while (uppercase(more) == "Y");

   const float MAX_PRICE = 10000;
   const float MAX_SCORE = 100;

   cwin.coord(0, 0, MAX_PRICE, MAX_SCORE);

   int i;
   for (i = 0; i < names.size(); i++)
   {  Message label(Point(prices[i],
         scores[i]), names[i]);
      cwin << label.get_start() << label;
   }
   return EXIT_SUCCESS;
}
```

The problem with this program is that it contains three vectors (`names`, `prices`, `scores`) of the same length, where the `i`th *slice* `names[i]`, `prices[i]`, `scores[i]`,

Figure 8

Computer Performance versus Price

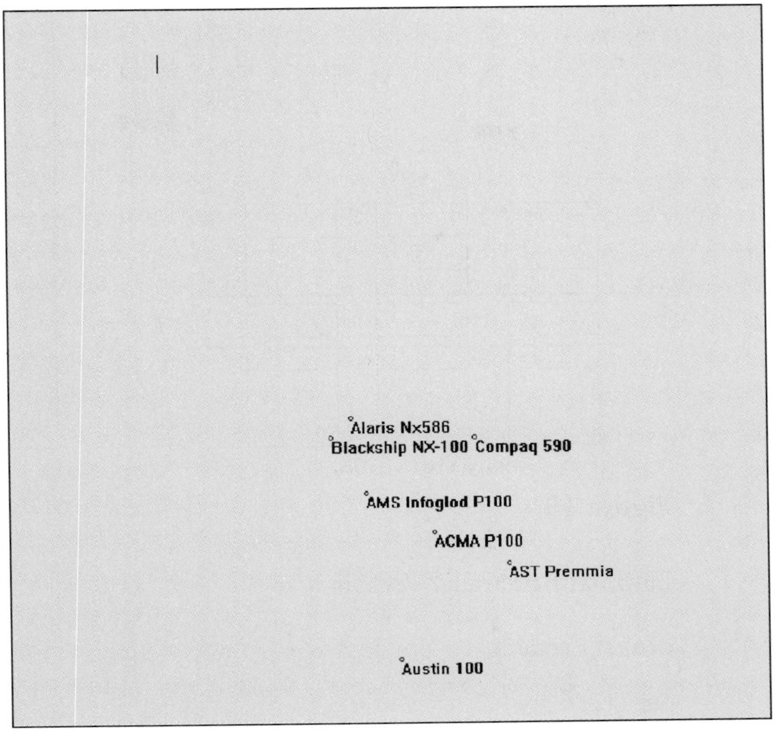

Figure 9

Parallel Vectors

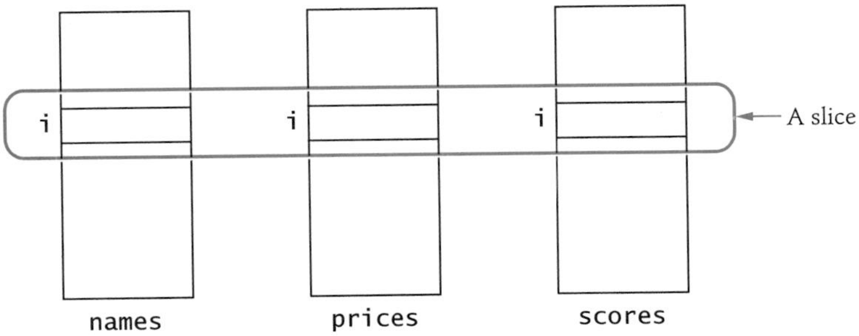

contains data that needs to be processed together. These vectors are called *parallel vectors* (Figure 9).

Parallel vectors become a headache in larger programs. The programmer must ensure that the vectors always have the same length and that each slice is filled with values that actually belong together. Most importantly, any function that operates on a slice must get all vectors as parameters, which is tedious to program.

The remedy is simple. Look at the slice and find the *concept* that it represents. Then make the concept into a class. In our example each slice contains a name, a price, and a score, describing a *product*. Let's turn this into a class.

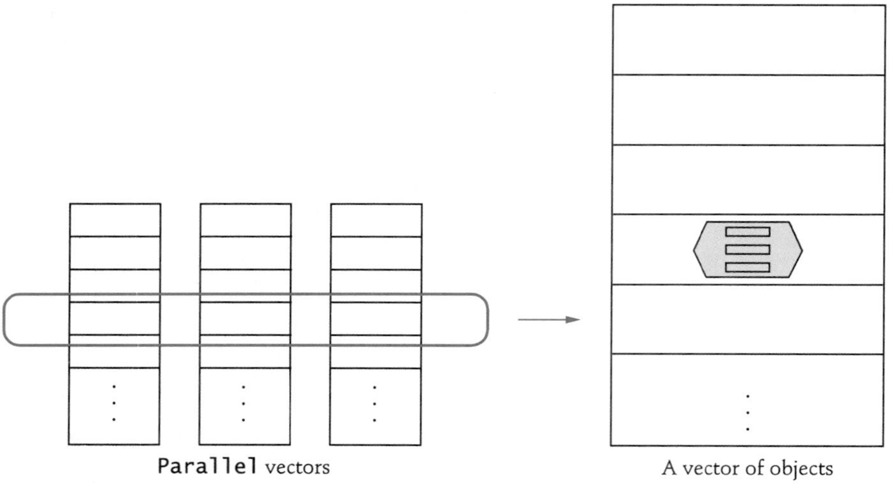

Figure 10

Eliminating Parallel Vectors

```
class Product
{
public:
   . . .
private:
   float price;
   int score;
   string name;
};
```

This is, of course, very similar to the `Product` class in Chapter 8. However, the member functions for product input and output are slightly different.

Note that the `main` function now has a single vector of product data. This shows that the process of eliminating parallel vectors was successful. The set of parallel vectors is replaced by a single vector. Each slot in the resulting vector corresponds to a slice in the set of parallel vectors (see Figure 10).

Program plotdat2.cpp

```
#define CCC_WIN
#include "ccc.h"

class Product
{
public:
   Product();
   void read();
   void get_price() const;
   void plot() const;
```

```
private:
   float price;
   int score;
   string name;
};

Product::Product()
{  price = 0;
   score = 0;
}

void Product::read()
{  name = cwin.get_string("Product name:");
   price = cwin.get_float("Price:");
   score = cwin.get_int("Score:");
}

void Product::plot() const
{  Message label(Point(price, score), name);
   cwin << label.get_start() << label;
}

int main()
{  vector<Product> data;
   string more;

   do
   {  Product c;
      c.read();
      data.push_back(c);
      more = cwin.get_string("More data? (Y/N)");
   }  while (uppercase(more) == "Y");

   const float MAX_PRICE = 10000;
   const float MAX_SCORE = 100;

   cwin.coord(0, 0, MAX_PRICE, MAX_SCORE);

   int i;
   for (i = 0; i < data.size(); i++)
      data[i].plot();
   return EXIT_SUCCESS;
}
```

Quality Tip 9.2

Make Parallel Vectors into Vectors of Objects

If you find yourself using two vectors that have the same length, ask yourself if you couldn't replace them with a single vector of a class type. For example,

```
vector<string> name;
vector<float> salary;
```

could become

```
vector<Employee> staff;
```

Parallel vectors are evil because they lead to a greater evil: namely, global variables. It is tedious to write functions that work on a set of parallel vectors. Each of those functions would need all parallel vectors as parameters. Programmers using parallel vectors are therefore tempted to make the parallel vectors into global variables.

9.6 Vectors as Object Data

A *polygon* is a closed sequence of lines (Figure 11). To describe a polygon, we need to store the sequence of its corner points. Because the number of points is variable, we use a vector.

```
class Polygon
{
public:
   Polygon();
   void add_point(Point p);
   void plot() const;
private:
   vector<Point> corners;
};

Polygon::Polygon()
{
}

void Polygon::add_point(Point p)
{  corners.push_back(p);
}
```

Figure 11

Polygon

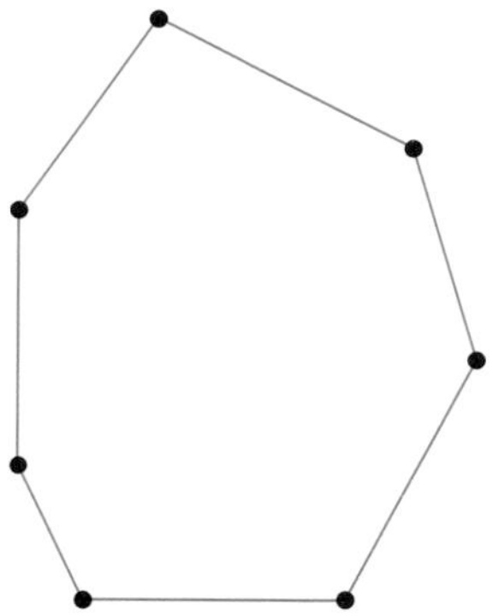

Figure 12

Two Polygons

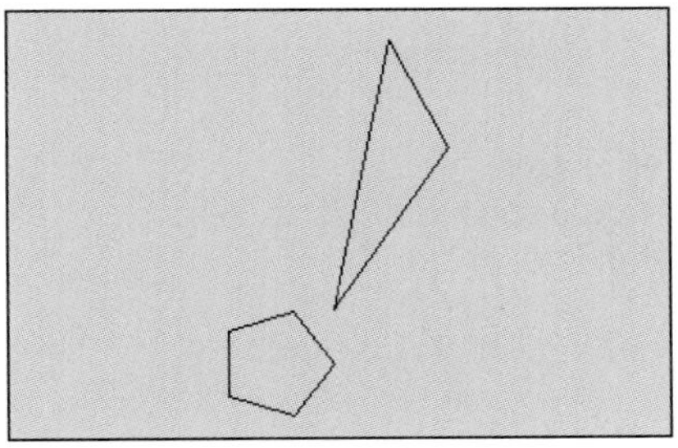

Here are two examples of polygons. First, a triangle:

```
Polygon triangle;
triangle.add_point(Point(1, 1));
triangle.add_point(Point(3, 4));
triangle.add_point(Point(2, 6));
```

A *regular* polygon has all sides of the same length. It is easy to generate a regular polygon. A regular n-gon with center (0, 0) and radius 1 has n corners, $v_0, \ldots, v_{n-1}$, where

$$v_i = (\cos(2\pi i/n), \sin(2\pi i/n))$$

Here is a fragment of code that generates a regular pentagon.

```
Polygon pentagon;
for (i = 0; i < 5; i++)
   pentagon.add_point(Point(cos(2 * M_PI * i / 5),
      sin(2 * M_PI * i / 5)));
```

Of course, we would like to see what the polygon looks like. To plot a polygon, we need to draw the lines joining adjacent corners, and then close up the path by joining the last and first corner.

```
void Polygon::plot() const
{  int i;
   int n = corners.size();
   for (i = 0; i < n; i++)
      cwin << Line(corners[i], corners[(i + 1) % n]);
}
```

Here is a complete program. Figure 12 shows the plot.

Program polygon.cpp

```
#define CCC_WIN
#include "ccc.h"
```

```
class Polygon
{
public:
   Polygon();
   void add_point(Point p);
   void plot() const;
private:
   vector<Point> corners;
};

Polygon::Polygon()
{
}

void Polygon::add_point(Point p)
{  corners.push_back(p);
}

void Polygon::plot() const
{  int i;
   int n = corners.size();
   for (i = 0; i < n; i++)
      cwin << Line(corners[i], corners[(i + 1) % n]);
}

int main()

{  Polygon triangle;
   triangle.add_point(Point(1, 1));
   triangle.add_point(Point(3, 4));
   triangle.add_point(Point(2, 6));
   triangle.plot();

   Polygon pentagon;
   int i;
   for (i = 0; i < 5; i++)
      pentagon.add_point(Point(cos(2 * M_PI * i / 5),
         sin(2 * M_PI * i / 5)));
   pentagon.plot();

   return EXIT_SUCCESS;
}
```

We modeled a polygon as a class containing a vector of points. It is a certain amount of trouble to define a new class. Why didn't we just write a polygon plot function with a `vector<Point>` parameter?

```
plot_polygon(vector<Point> v)
{  int i;
   int n = v.size();
```

```
      for (i = 0; i < n; i++)
         cwin << Line(v[i], v[(i + 1) % n]);
}
```

Indeed, this is simpler than defining a new class to represent polygons. Conceptually, however, it is wrong to say that a vector of points and a polygon are one and the same thing.

Consider another geometric configuration: a *cloud* of points, as in Figure 13. A cloud is a set of dots that are not connected by lines. Like a polygon, it too is described by a vector of points, but, of course, the code for plotting a cloud is completely different from the code for plotting a polygon.

Program cloud.cpp

```
#define CCC_WIN
#include "ccc.h"

class Cloud
{
public:
   Cloud();
   void add_point(Point p);
   void plot() const;
private:
   vector<Point> dots;
};
Cloud::Cloud()
{
}

void Cloud::add_point(Point p)
{  dots.push_back(p);
}
```

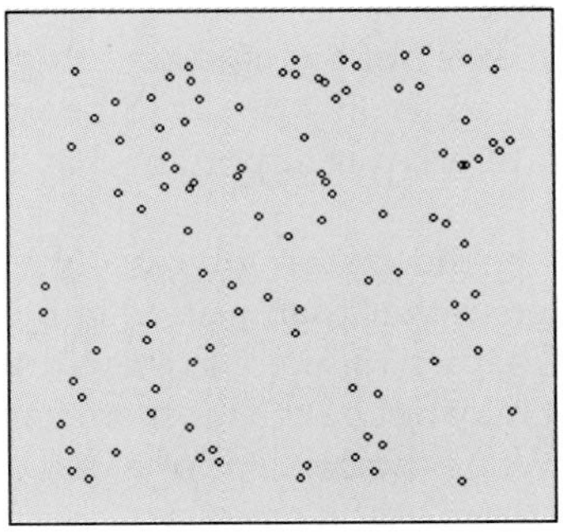

Figure 13

Cloud of Points

```
void Cloud::plot() const
{  int i;
   for (i = 0; i < dots.size(); i++)
      cwin << dots[i];
}

int main()
{  Cloud random_cloud;
   int i;
   for (i = 1; i <= 100; i++)
      random_cloud.add_point(Point(rand_float(-4, 4),
         rand_float(-4, 4)));
   random_cloud.plot();

   return EXIT_SUCCESS;
}
```

Again, it would be simpler to omit the `Cloud` class and pass the array of points directly to a `plot_cloud` function:

```
void plot_cloud(vector<Point> d)
{  int i;
   for (i = 0; i < d.size(); i++)
      cwin << d[i];
}
```

Then we have two functions to plot a `vector<Point>`, namely `plot_polygon` and `plot_cloud`. For a given vector of points, we have to know which one is appropriate.

```
vector<Point> v; /* Is it a polygon or a cloud? */
```

Making separate classes for polygons and clouds clarifies the code using the geometric objects.

```
Cloud v; /* It is a cloud */
```

As a beginning programmer you usually spend a lot of effort implementing procedures that operate on simple data types, such as plotting clouds or computing the area of a polygon, and you would naturally like to simplify your life as much as possible. In most larger programs, however, where the focus is on using these procedures on actual data, it is not so important that the data type is a little more complicated to define. After all, it only needs to be written once, but if it is at all useful, it will be used many times. It is important that one can see at a glance what every variable stands for.

There is a second reason why we like to declare a polygon class that contains a vector of points rather than just equating polygons with vectors of points. As we will learn in Chapter 13, there is more than one way of collecting points. A *vector* of points may or may not be the most efficient container. Perhaps a *list* of points is more appropriate. When the concept of a polygon is made explicit, it is easy to carry out a change to a more useful container structure.

9.7 Matrices

9.7.1 Defining and Using Matrices

Vectors can store linear sequences of numbers. It often happens that we want to store collections of numbers that have a two-dimensional layout. For example, in Section 6.5 we wrote a program that produces a table of values:

12833.59	16470.10	21137.04	27126.40	34812.91	44677.44
13157.04	17310.76	22775.84	29966.26	39426.71	51873.88
13488.50	18193.97	24540.94	33102.04	44649.70	60225.75
13828.17	19121.84	26442.01	36564.47	50561.98	69917.98
14176.25	20096.61	28489.47	40387.39	57254.18	81164.98
14532.94	21120.65	30694.52	44608.17	64828.80	94215.34
14898.46	22196.40	33069.21	49268.03	73401.76	109357.30
15273.01	23326.47	35626.54	54412.43	83104.13	126924.98
15656.81	24513.57	38380.43	60091.52	94084.15	147305.77
16050.09	25760.55	41345.93	66360.62	106509.41	170948.62
16453.90	27070.41	44539.20	73280.73	120569.45	198374.00

Such an arrangement, consisting of rows and columns of values, is called a *matrix*. In C++ a matrix of floating-point numbers is obtained as

```
matrix<float> balances(11, 6);
```

Just as we specify the size of vectors when we define them, we must specify how many rows and columns we need. In this case, we ask for 11 rows and 6 columns.

To set a particular element in the matrix, we need to specify two subscripts in separate brackets:

```
balances[3][4] = future_value(10000, 6.5, 20);
```

To find out how large a matrix is, use the `rows` and `columns` functions. We use these functions in the following code sample, which prints all values stored in a matrix:

Program matrix.cpp

```
#include "ccc.h"

float future_value(float initial_balance, float p,
   int nyear)
{  float b = initial_balance * pow(1 + p / 12 / 100,
      12 * nyear);
   return b;
}
```

```
void print_matrix(matrix<float> m)
{  int i;
   for (i = 0; i < m.rows(); i++)
   {  int j;
      for (j = 0; j < m.columns(); j++)
         cout << format("%10.2f", m[i][j]);
      cout << "\n";
   }
}

int main()
{  matrix<float> balances(11, 6);
   int i;
   int j;
   for (i = 0; i < balances.rows(); i++)
      for (j = 0; j < balances.columns(); j++)
         balances[i][j] = future_value(10000,
            5 + i * 0.5, 5 + j * 5);

   print_matrix(balances);

   return EXIT_SUCCESS;
}
```

9.7.2 Matrix Multiplication

In linear algebra, matrices are used to describe transformations of vectors: A vector is *transformed* by forming the product of the transformation matrix with the vector. To multiply a matrix with a vector, you must first master the multiplication of a row of numbers with a column of numbers. The row and column must have the same length, and their product is the sum of products in the same position. For example,

$$\begin{pmatrix} 1 & 2 & 3 \end{pmatrix} \cdot \begin{pmatrix} 4 \\ 5 \\ 6 \end{pmatrix} = 1 \cdot 4 + 2 \cdot 5 + 3 \cdot 6 = 4 + 10 + 18 = 32$$

Multiplying a matrix with a vector, you form a new vector. Each of its entries is the product of a row of the matrix with the original vector. For example,

$$\begin{pmatrix} 1 & 2 & 3 \\ 0 & 1 & -1 \\ 2 & 1 & 0 \end{pmatrix} \cdot \begin{pmatrix} 4 \\ 5 \\ 6 \end{pmatrix} = \begin{pmatrix} 1 \cdot 4 + 2 \cdot 5 + 3 \cdot 6 \\ 0 \cdot 4 + 1 \cdot 5 - 1 \cdot 6 \\ 2 \cdot 4 + 1 \cdot 5 + 0 \cdot 6 \end{pmatrix} = \begin{pmatrix} 32 \\ -1 \\ 13 \end{pmatrix}$$

This operation is tedious to carry out by hand, but it is easy to program:

Program vproduct.cpp

```
#include "ccc.h"
```

```
vector<float> vproduct(matrix<float> a, vector<float> v)
{  assert(a.columns() == v.size());
   vector<float> r(a.rows());
   int i;
   for (i = 0; i < a.rows(); i++)
   {  int k;
      float sum = 0;
      for (k = 0; k < a.columns(); k++)
         sum = sum + a[i][k] * v[k];
      r[i] = sum;
   }
   return r;
}

int main()
{  matrix<float> m(3, 3);
   m[0][0] = 1; m[0][1] = 2; m[0][2] = 3;
   m[1][0] = 0; m[1][1] = 1; m[1][2] = - 1;
   m[2][0] = 2; m[2][1] = 1; m[2][2] = 0;

   vector<float> v(3);

   v[0] = 4; v[1] = 5; v[2] = 6;
   vector<float> r = vproduct(m, v);

   int i;
   for (i = 0; i < r.size(); i++)
      cout << r[i] << "\n";

   return EXIT_SUCCESS;
}
```

We will be concerned with vectors that describe points on the screen. The point with coordinates (x, y) will be represented as the vector

$$\begin{pmatrix} x \\ y \\ 1 \end{pmatrix}$$

The transformation matrices we will consider all have the special form

$$\begin{pmatrix} a & b & e \\ c & d & f \\ 0 & 0 & 1 \end{pmatrix}$$

Multiplying such a matrix with a vector whose third coefficient is 1 again yields a vector with third coefficient equal to 1.

Figure 14

Rotation of a Point

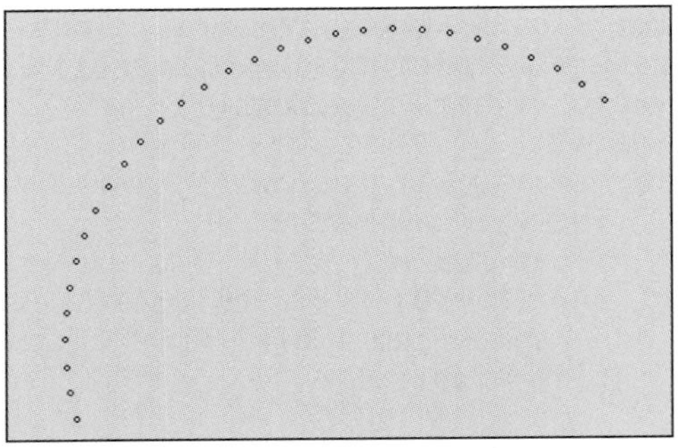

A vector in the plane is *rotated* about the origin by an angle α by multiplying it with the matrix

$$\begin{pmatrix} \cos\alpha & -\sin\alpha & 0 \\ \sin\alpha & \cos\alpha & 0 \\ 0 & 0 & 1 \end{pmatrix}$$

The following program rotates the point with coordinates (5, 5) thirty times by 5 degrees. (See Figure 14.)

Program rotate.cpp

```
#define CCC_WIN
#include "ccc.h"

vector<float> vproduct(matrix<float> a, vector<float> v)

{  assert(a.columns() == v.size());
   vector<float> r(a.rows());
   int i;
   for (i = 0; i < a.rows(); i++)
   {  int k;
      float sum = 0;
      for (k = 0; k < a.columns(); k++)
         sum = sum + a[i][k] * v[k];
      r[i] = sum;
   }
   return r;
}

int main()
{  matrix<float> rot(3, 3);
   float alpha = 5 * M_PI / 180; /* 5 degrees */
   rot[0][0] = cos(alpha);
   rot[0][1] = - sin(alpha);
   rot[0][2] = 0;
   rot[1][0] = sin(alpha);
```

```
    rot[1][1] = cos(alpha);
    rot[1][2] = 0;
    rot[2][0] = 0;
    rot[2][1] = 0;
    rot[2][2] = 1;

    vector<float> v(3);
    v[0] = 5; v[1] = 5; v[2] = 1;
    int i;
    for (i = 1; i <= 30; i++)
    {  v = vproduct(rot, v);
       cwin << Point(v[0], v[1]);
    }

    return EXIT_SUCCESS;
}
```

A vector is *translated,* or moved on the plane, by multiplying it with the matrix

$$\begin{pmatrix} 1 & 0 & t \\ 0 & 1 & u \\ 0 & 0 & 1 \end{pmatrix}.$$

That statement is easy to verify:

$$\begin{pmatrix} 1 & 0 & t \\ 0 & 1 & u \\ 0 & 0 & 1 \end{pmatrix} \cdot \begin{pmatrix} x \\ y \\ 1 \end{pmatrix} = \begin{pmatrix} x + t \\ y + u \\ 1 \end{pmatrix}$$

Suppose we want to calculate a rotation by 45 degrees whose center is not the origin but the point (4, 3). Rather than trying to find a complicated equation, we can put the transformations that we know to work. We first translate so that the point (4, 3) falls on the origin; then we rotate; then we translate back. That is, we carry out

$$\begin{pmatrix} 1 & 0 & 4 \\ 0 & 1 & 3 \\ 0 & 0 & 1 \end{pmatrix} \begin{pmatrix} \cos(\pi/4) & -\sin(\pi/4) & 0 \\ \sin(\pi/4) & \cos(\pi/4) & 0 \\ 0 & 0 & 1 \end{pmatrix} \begin{pmatrix} 1 & 0 & -4 \\ 0 & 1 & -3 \\ 0 & 0 & 1 \end{pmatrix} \begin{pmatrix} x \\ y \\ 1 \end{pmatrix}$$

Suppose we want to apply this compound transformation to a number of vectors. We can compute the product

```
vproduct(t2, vproduct(rot, vproduct(t1, v)))
```

for a number of vectors `v`, or we can determine the coefficients of the compound transformation by multiplying the matrices.

Two matrices are multiplied with the same row-by-column operation used to multiply a matrix with a vector. However, now there are many more combinations of rows and columns. The (i, j) coefficient of the product matrix is the product of the ith row of the first factor and the jth column of the second factor. In this example we compute the (1,3) element of the product of `rot` and `t1`.

$$\begin{pmatrix} \cos(\pi/4) & -\sin(\pi/4) & 0 \\ \sin(\pi/4) & \cos(\pi/4) & 0 \\ 0 & 0 & 1 \end{pmatrix} \begin{pmatrix} 1 & 0 & -4 \\ 0 & 1 & -3 \\ 0 & 0 & 1 \end{pmatrix} = \begin{pmatrix} \text{¿} & \text{¿} & \text{¿} \\ \text{¿} & \text{¿} & \sin(\pi/4) \cdot -4 + \cos(\pi/4) \cdot -3 + 0 \cdot 1 \\ \text{¿} & \text{¿} & \text{¿} \end{pmatrix}$$

This is an even more tedious computation than the product of a matrix with a vector. To multiply two 3 by 3 matrices, we need to form 9 row-by-column products, each of which consists of three multiplications and additions. Fortunately, this operation is easy to program. Note that the matrices to be multiplied need not have the same size, but the number of columns in the first factor must match the number of rows in the second factor.

In our rotation problem we can therefore first compute the product of the three transformation matrices, store it, and use it to transform all vectors.

```
matrix<float> a = mproduct(t2, mproduct(rot, t1));
```

Program mproduct.cpp

```
#include "ccc.h"

matrix<float> mproduct(matrix<float> a, matrix<float> b)
{  assert(a.columns() == b.rows());
   matrix<float> r(a.rows(), b.columns());
   int i;
   for (i = 0; i < a.rows(); i++)
   {  int j;
      for (j = 0; j < b.columns(); j++)
      {  int k;
         float sum = 0;
         for (k = 0; k < a.columns(); k++)
            sum = sum + a[i][k] * b[k][j];
         r[i][j] = sum;
      }
   }
   return r;
}

void print_matrix(matrix<float> m)
{  int i;
   for (i = 0; i < m.rows(); i++)
   {  int j;
      for (j = 0; j < m.columns(); j++)
         cout << format("%10.2f", m[i][j]);
      cout << "\n";
   }
}

int main()
{  matrix<float> rot(3, 3);
   float alpha = M_PI / 2; /* 45 degrees */
```

```
    rot[0][0] = cos(alpha);
    rot[0][1] = -sin(alpha);
    rot[0][2] = 0;
    rot[1][0] = sin(alpha);
    rot[1][1] = cos(alpha);
    rot[1][2] = 0;
    rot[2][0] = 0;
    rot[2][1] = 0;
    rot[2][2] = 1;

    matrix<float> t1(3, 3);
    t1[0][0] = 1; t1[0][1] = 0; t1[0][2] = - 4;
    t1[1][0] = 0; t1[1][1] = 1; t1[1][2] = - 3;
    t1[2][0] = 0; t1[2][1] = 0; t1[2][2] = 1;

    matrix<float> t2 = t1;
    t2[0][2] = 4;
    t2[1][2] = 3;

    matrix<float> a = mproduct(t2, mproduct(rot, t1));
    print_matrix(a);

    return EXIT_SUCCESS;
}
```

9.7.3 Fractals

Matrix multiplication is an extremely important operation in many areas of mathematics. Here we will show one amazing application: to generate strangely lifelike pictures, so-called *fractals*. Figure 15 shows a typical example.

To generate a fractal, we need several transformation matrices. For example, the fern in Figure 15 is generated by the four matrices

$$\begin{pmatrix} 0.05 & 0 & 0 \\ 0 & 0.16 & -4.20 \\ 0 & 0 & 1 \end{pmatrix}, \begin{pmatrix} 0.85 & 0.04 & 0.20 \\ -0.04 & 0.85 & 0.85 \\ 0 & 0 & 1 \end{pmatrix},$$

$$\begin{pmatrix} 0.2 & -0.26 & -1.3 \\ 0.23 & 0.22 & -2.3 \\ 0 & 0 & 1 \end{pmatrix}, \begin{pmatrix} -0.15 & 0.28 & 1.4 \\ 0.26 & 0.24 & -3.36 \\ 0 & 0 & 1 \end{pmatrix}$$

Start with any point on the plane; plot it. Pick one of the transformations at random; apply it to the point; plot the new point. Pick another transformation at random; apply it to the new point; plot the resulting point. Repeat the process a few thousand times. The resulting cloud of points approximates the fern.

There is one technicality. We cannot pick each of the matrices with equal probability. Instead, we must pick them with a probability proportional to the absolute value of their determinant. In general, it is not easy to compute the determinant of a matrix, but in our special case that is not a problem.

Figure 15

Fractal Pattern

$$\det\begin{pmatrix} a & b & e \\ c & d & f \\ 0 & 0 & 1 \end{pmatrix} = ad - bc$$

We now compute the absolute values of the determinants. In our example, we get the values

0.008	1%
0.7241	77%
0.1038	11%
0.1088	11%

The percentages are the ratios of the individual determinants by the sum of all four. That means, we must pick the third and fourth matrix with an approximately equal probability (11%), but the second one should be picked about 7 times as often as either of them. The first one should be applied only rarely.

Program fractal.cpp

```
#define CCC_WIN
#include "ccc.h"

float determinant(matrix<float> m)
{  assert(m.rows() == 3 and m.columns() == 3);
   assert(m[2][0] == 0 and m[2][1] == 0 and m[2][2] == 1);
   return m[0][0] * m[1][1] - m[0][1] * m[1][0];
}

vector<float> vproduct(matrix<float> a, vector<float> v)
{  assert(a.columns() == v.size());
```

```
    vector<float> r(a.rows());
    int i;
    for (i = 0; i < a.rows(); i++)
    {  int k;
       float sum = 0;
       for (k = 0; k < a.columns(); k++)
          sum = sum + a[i][k] * v[k];
       r[i] = sum;
    }
    return r;
}

int main()
{  vector<matrix<float> > transforms;

   /* set up transforms */
   matrix<float> a(3, 3);
   a[0][0] = 0.05; a[0][1] = 0; a[0][2] = 0;
   a[1][0] = 0; a[1][1] = 0.16; a[1][2] = -4.2;
   a[2][0] = 0; a[2][1] = 0; a[2][2] = 1;
   transforms.push_back(a);

   a[0][0] = 0.85; a[0][1] = 0.04; a[0][2] = 0.20;
   a[1][0] = -0.04; a[1][1] = 0.85; a[1][2] = 0.85;
   transforms.push_back(a);

   a[0][0] = 0.2; a[0][1] = -0.26; a[0][2] = -1.3;
   a[1][0] = 0.23; a[1][1] = 0.22; a[1][2] = -2.3;
   transforms.push_back(a);

   a[0][0] = -0.15; a[0][1] = 0.28; a[0][2] = 1.4;
   a[1][0] = 0.26; a[1][1] = 0.24; a[1][2] = -3.36;
   transforms.push_back(a);

   /* compute probabilities */
   vector<float> prob(transforms.size());
      /* probability to select the ith transformation */
   int i;
   float sum = 0;
   for (i = 0; i < transforms.size(); i++)
   {  prob[i] = fabs(determinant(transforms[i]));
      sum = sum + prob[i];
   }
   for (i = 0; i < transforms.size(); i++)
      prob[i] = prob[i] / sum;

   const int NTRIES = 2000;
   vector<float> p(3); /* the point to be transformed */
   p[0] = 1; p[1] = 1; p[2] = 1;
```

```
    /* compute and plot transforms of p */
    int t;
    for (t = 1; t <= NTRIES; t++)
    {  float r = rand_float(0, 1);
       i = 0;
       while (r > prob[i] and i < transforms.size() - 1)
       {  r = r - prob[i];
          i++;
       }
       /* now pick the ith transform */
       p = vproduct(transforms[i], p);
       cwin << Point(p[0], p[1]);
    }
    return EXIT_SUCCESS;
}
```

Since we have a sequence of matrices, the matrices are stored as a vector

```
vector<matrix<float> > transforms;
```

(The space between the the two >> is necessary so the compiler won't mistake >> for an "input" token.) Then `transforms[i]` is the `i`th matrix in that sequence. It looks forbidding, but there is nothing special about this. You can collect vectors of any type. If the need arises to collect a sequence of matrices, then a vector of matrices is the appropriate data type.

Advanced Topic 9.4

Multidimensional Arrays

Standard C++ has one-dimensional vectors. The library for this book adds two-dimensional matrices. In theory, there ought to be arrays with more dimensions. For example, a three-dimensional array would have three subscripts, `a[i][j][k]`. In practice, such arrays are comparatively rare. You need to use C arrays for arrays of more than two dimensions.

For example, suppose that we want to allocate a three-dimensional grid for a spatial graph of investment returns:

```
const int GRID_SIZE = 20;
float grid [GRID_SIZE][GRID_SIZE][GRID_SIZE];
```

Then we can access `grid[i][j][k]`, provided `i`, `j`, and `k` are between 0 and `GRID_SIZE-1`.

Random Fact 9.2

International Alphabets

The English alphabet is pretty simple: upper- and lowercase *a* to *z*. Other European languages have accent marks and special characters. For example, German has three so-called *umlaut*

Figure 16

German Keyboard

characters, ä, ö, ü, and a *double-s* character ß. These are not optional frills; you couldn't write a page of German text without using these characters a few times. German computer keyboards have keys for these characters (see Figure 16).

This poses a problem for computer users and designers. The American standard character encoding (called ASCII, for American Standard Code for Information Interchange) specifies 128 codes: 52 upper- and lowercase characters, 10 digits, 32 typographical symbols, and 34 control characters (such as space, newline, and 32 others for controlling printers and other devices). The umlaut and double-s are not among them. Some German data processing systems replace seldom-used ASCII characters with German letters: [\ ] { | } ~ are replaced with Ä Ö Ü ä ö ü ß. While most people can live without these characters, C++ programmers definitely cannot. Other encoding schemes take advantage of the fact that one byte can encode 256 different characters, of which only 128 are standardized by ASCII. Unfortunately, there are multiple incompatible standards for such encodings, resulting in a certain amount of aggravation among European computer users.

Many countries don't use the Roman script at all. Russian, Greek, Hebrew, Arabic, and Thai letters, to name just a few, have completely different shapes (see Figure 17). To complicate matters, Hebrew and Arabic are typed from right to left. Each of these alphabets has between 30 and 100 letters, and the countries using them have established encoding standards for them.

The situation is much more dramatic in languages that use the Chinese script: the Chinese dialects, Japanese, and Korean. The Chinese script is not alphabetic but *ideographic* (see Figure 18). A character represents an idea or thing. Most words are made up of one, two, or three of these ideographic characters. Over 50,000 ideographs are known, of which about 20,000 are in active use. Therefore, two bytes are needed to encode them. China, Taiwan, Japan, and Korea have incompatible encoding standards for them. (Japanese and Korean writing use a mixture of native syllabic and Chinese ideographic characters.)

The inconsistencies among character encodings have been a major nuisance for international electronic communication and for software manufacturers vying for a global market. Between 1988 and 1991 a consortium of hardware and software manufacturers developed a uniform 16-bit encoding scheme that is capable of encoding text in essentially all written languages of the world [3]. About 28,000 characters are given codes, including 21,000 Chinese ideographs. Since a 16-bit code can incorporate 65,000 codes, there is ample space for expansion. There are plans to add codes for American Indian languages and Egyptian hieroglyphs.

Figure 17

The Thai Script

	ฐ	ภ	ะ	เ	๐		เ◌
ก	ฑ	ม	◌ั	แ	๑		แ◌
ข	ฒ	ย	า	โ	๒		โ◌
ฃ	ณ	ร	◌ำ	ใ	๓		ใ◌
ค	ด	ฤ	◌ิ	ไ	๔		ไ◌
ฅ	ต	ล	◌ี	ๅ	๕		
ฆ	ถ	ฦ	◌ึ	ๆ	๖		
ง	ท	ว	◌ื	◌็	๗		
จ	ธ	ศ	◌ุ	◌่	๘		
ฉ	น	ษ	◌ู	◌้	๙		
ช	บ	ส	◌ฺ	◌๊	๚		
ซ	ป	ห		◌๋	๛		
ฌ	ผ	ฬ		◌์			
ญ	ฝ	อ		◌ํ			
ฎ	พ	ฮ		๎			
ฏ	ฟ	ฯ					

		CLASSIC SOUPS	Sm.	Lg.
清燉雞湯	57.	House Chicken Soup (Chicken, Celery, Potato, Onion, Carrot)	1.50	2.75
雞飯湯	58.	Chicken Rice Soup	1.85	3.25
雞麵湯	59.	Chicken Noodle Soup	1.85	3.25
廣東雲呑	60.	Cantonese Wonton Soup	1.50	2.75
蕃茄蛋湯	61.	Tomato Clear Egg Drop Soup	1.65	2.95
雲呑湯	62.	Regular Wonton Soup	1.10	2.10
酸辣湯	63.	❧ Hot & Sour Soup	1.10	2.10
蛋花湯	64.	Egg Drop Soup	1.10	2.10
雲蛋湯	65.	Egg Drop Wonton Mix	1.10	2.10
豆腐菜湯	66.	Tofu Vegetable Soup	NA	3.50
雞玉米湯	67.	Chicken Corn Cream Soup	NA	3.50
蟹肉玉米湯	68.	Crab Meat Corn Cream Soup	NA	3.50
海鮮湯	69.	Seafood Soup	NA	3.50

Figure 18

The Chinese Script

Chapter Summary

1. Use a vector to collect multiple values of the same type. Individual values are accessed by an integer index or subscript: `v[i]`. Valid values for the index range from 0 to one less than the size of the array. Supplying an invalid index is a common programming error that has serious consequences.

2. When creating a vector, you can set it to a certain size, or you can start out with an empty vector. Use the **push_back** procedure to add more elements to a vector. Use **pop_back** to reduce the size. Use the **size** function to inquire the current size.

3. Vectors can occur as the parameters and return values of functions and procedures. Classes can have data fields that are vectors of values.

4. Avoid parallel vectors by changing them into vectors of objects.

5. Many common algorithms on vectors traverse the elements of a vector from 0 either to the end of the vector or until a specific element has been found. Common algorithms include finding a particular element and counting elements with a certain property.

6. Vectors form a linear, one-dimensional sequence of values. Matrices form a tabular, two-dimensional arrangement. Individual elements are accessed by double subscripts `m[i][j]`.

Further Reading

[1] Peter J. Denning, *Computers under Attack,* Addison-Wesley, 1990.

[2] Cliff Stoll, *The Cuckoo's Egg,* Doubleday, 1989.

[3] The Unicode Consortium, *The Unicode Standard Worldwide Character Encoding, Version 1.0,* Addison-Wesley, 1991.

Review Exercises

Exercise R9.1. Write code that fills a vector v with the values

1	2	3	4	5	6	7	8	9	10	
0	2	4	6	8	10	12	14	16	18	20
1	4	9	16	25	36	49	64	81	100	
0	0	0	0	0	0	0	0	0	0	
1	4	9	16	9	7	4	9	11		

Exercise R9.2. Write a loop that fills a vector v with ten random numbers between 1 and 100. Write code for two nested loops that fill v with ten *different* random numbers between 1 and 100.

Exercise R9.3. Write C++ code for a loop that simultaneously computes the maximum and minimum of a vector.

Exercise R9.4. What is wrong with the following loop?

```
vector<int> v(10);
int i;
for (i = 1; i <= 10; i++) v[i] = i * i;
```

Explain two ways of fixing the error.

Exercise R9.5. What is an array index? What are the bounds of an array? What is a bounds error?

Exercise R9.6. Write a program that contains a bounds error. Run the program. What happens on your computer? If you use the C++ Lite implementation of `vector`, you will get an error message, but no line number pointing to the error.

Set a breakpoint in `check_bounds` in the file ccc_util.cpp. Take a screen snapshot of the call stack. Why does it help you locate the error?

Exercise R9.7. Write a program that fills a vector with the numbers 1, 4, 9, ..., 100. Compile it and launch the debugger. After the vector has been filled with three numbers, *inspect it.* Take a screen snapshot of the display that shows the ten slots of the vector.

Exercise R9.8. Write a loop that reads ten numbers and a second loop that prints them out in the opposite order from which they were entered.

Exercise R9.9. Give an example of

- A useful function that has a vector of integers as a value parameter
- A useful function that has a vector of integers as a reference parameter
- A useful function that has a vector of integers as a return value

Just describe each function. Don't implement the functions.

Exercise R9.10. A function that has a vector as a reference parameter can change the vector in two ways. It can change the contents of individual vector elements, or it can rearrange the elements. Describe two useful functions with `vector<Product>&` parameters that change a vector of products in each of the two ways just described.

Exercise R9.11. What are parallel vectors? Why are parallel vectors indications of poor programming? How can they be avoided?

Exercise R9.12. Design a class `Staff` that stores a collection of employees. What public member functions should you support? What advantages and disadvantages does a `Staff` class have over a `vector<Employee>`?

Exercise R9.13. Suppose `v` is a *sorted* vector of employees. Give pseudocode that describes how a new employee can be inserted in its proper position so that the resulting vector stays sorted.

Exercise R9.14. In many programming languages it is not possible to grow a vector. That is, there is no analog to `push_back` in those languages. Write code that reads a sequence of numbers into a vector without using `push_back`. First create a vector of a reasonable size (say 20). Also, use an integer variable `length` that tests how *full* the vector currently is. Whenever a new element is read in, increase `length`. When `length` reaches the *size* of the vector (20 at the outset), create a new vector of twice the size and copy all existing elements into the new vector. Write C++ code that performs this task.

Exercise R9.15. How do you perform the following tasks with vectors in C++?

- Test that two vectors contain the same elements in the same order
- Copy one vector to another (*Hint:* You need not copy one element at a time)
- Fill a vector with zeroes, overwriting all elements in it
- Remove all elements from a vector (*Hint:* You need not remove them one by one)

Exercise R9.16. True or false?

- All elements of a vector are of the same type.
- Vector subscripts must be integers.
- Vectors cannot contain strings as elements.
- Vectors cannot use strings as subscripts.
- Parallel vectors must have equal length.
- Matrices always have the same numbers of rows and columns.
- Two parallel arrays can be replaced by a matrix.
- Elements of different columns in a matrix can have different types.

Exercise R9.17. True or false?

- All vector parameters are reference parameters.
- A function cannot return a matrix.
- A procedure cannot change the dimensions of a matrix that is passed by value.
- A procedure cannot change the length of a vector that is passed by reference.
- A procedure can only reorder the elements of a vector, not change the elements.

Programming Exercises

Exercise P9.1. Write a function

```
float scalar_product(vector<float> a, vector<float> b)
```

that computes the scalar product of two vectors. The scalar product is

$$a_0 b_0 + a_1 b_1 + \cdots + a_{n-1} b_{n-1}$$

Exercise P9.2. Write a function that computes the *alternating sum* of all elements in a vector. For example, if `alternating_sum` is called with a vector containing

1 4 9 16 9 7 4 9 11

then it computes

$$1 - 4 + 9 - 16 + 9 - 7 + 4 - 9 + 11 = -2$$

Exercise P9.3. Write a procedure `reverse` that reverses the sequence of elements in a vector. For example, if `reverse` is called with a vector containing

1 4 9 16 9 7 4 9 11

then the vector is changed to

11 9 4 7 9 16 9 4 1

Exercise P9.4. Write a function

```
vector<int> append(vector<int> a, vector<int> b)
```

that appends one vector after another. For example, if `a` is

1 4 9 16

and `b` is

9 7 4 9 11

then `append` returns the vector

1 4 9 16 9 7 4 9 11

Exercise P9.5. Write a function

```
vector<int> merge(vector<int> a, vector<int> b)
```

that merges two arrays, alternating elements from both arrays. If one array is shorter than the other, then alternate as long as you can and then append the remaining elements from the longer array. For example, if `a` is

1 4 9 16

and `b` is

9 7 4 9 11

then `merge` returns the array

1 9 4 7 9 4 16 9 11

Exercise P9.6. Write a function

```
vector<int> merge_sorted(vector<int> a, vector<int> b)
```

that merges two *sorted* arrays, producing a new sorted array. Keep an index into each array, indicating how much of it has been processed already. Each time, append the smallest unprocessed element from either array, then advance the index. For example, if a is

1 4 9 16

and b is

4 7 9 9 11

then merge_sorted returns the array

1 4 4 7 9 9 9 11 16

Exercise P9.7. Write a predicate function

```
bool equals(vector<int> a, vector<int> b)
```

that checks whether two vectors have the same elements in the same order.

Exercise P9.8. Write a predicate function

```
bool same_set(vector<int> a, vector<int> b)
```

that checks whether two vectors have the same elements in some order, ignoring multiplicities. For example, the two vectors

1 4 9 16 9 7 4 9 11

and

11 11 7 9 16 4 1

would be considered identical. You will probably need one or more helper functions.

Exercise P9.9. Write a predicate function

```
bool same_elements(vector<int> a, vector<int> b)
```

that checks whether two vectors have the same elements in some order, with the same multiplicities. For example,

1 4 9 16 9 7 4 9 11

and

11 1 4 9 16 9 7 4 9

would be considered identical, but

1 4 9 16 9 7 4 9 11

and

11 11 7 9 16 4 1

would not. You will probably need one or more helper functions.

Exercise P9.10. Write a function that removes duplicates from a vector. For example, if `remove_duplicates` is called with a vector containing

1 4 9 16 9 7 4 9 11

then the vector is changed to

1 4 9 16 7 11

Exercise P9.11. Write functions

```
float Polygon::circumference() const
```

and

```
float Polygon::area() const
```

that compute the circumference and the area of a polygon. To compute the perimeter, compute the distance between adjacent points, and total up the distances.

The area of a polygon with corners $(x_0, y_0), \ldots, (x_{n-1}, y_{n-1})$ is

$$\frac{1}{2}|x_1y_2 + x_2y_3 + \cdots + x_{n-1}y_0 - y_1x_2 - y_2x_3 - \cdots - y_{n-1}x_0|$$

As test cases, compute the perimeter and area of a rectangle and of a regular hexagon.

Exercise P9.12. Write member functions

```
void Polygon::move(float dx, float dy);
void Polygon::rotate(float angle);
void Polygon::scale(float factor);
```

The first procedure moves all points of a polygon by the specified amounts in the x- and y-directions. The second procedure performs a rotation around the origin and updates the coordinates of the points of the polygon accordingly. The third procedure performs a scaling with the given scale factor and updates the coordinates of the points of the polygon accordingly. *Hint:* Use the `move` member function of the `Point` class. For rotation, see Section 9.7.2. To scale a point, multiply both the x- and y-coordinate with the scale factor.

Exercise P9.13. Write a program that asks the user to input a number n and prints all permutations of the sequence of numbers $1, 2, 3, \ldots, n$. For example, if n is 3, the program should print

```
1 2 3
1 3 2
2 1 3
2 3 1
3 1 2
3 2 1
```

Hint: Write a function

```
permutation_helper(vector<int> prefix,
   vector<int> to_permute)
```

that computes all the permutations in the array `to_permute` and prints each permutation, prefixed by all numbers in the array `prefix`. For example, if `prefix` contains the number 2 and `to_permute` the numbers 1 and 3, then `permutation_helper` prints

```
2 1 3
2 3 1
```

The `permutation_helper` function does the following: If `to_permute` has no elements, print the elements in `prefix`. Otherwise, for each element `e` in `to_permute`, make an array `to_permute2` that is equal to `permute` except for `e` and an array `prefix2` consisting of `prefix` and `e`. Then call `permutation_helper` with `prefix2` and `to_permute2`.

Exercise P9.14. Write a program that produces 10 random permutations of the numbers 1 to 10. To generate a random permutation, you need to fill a vector with the numbers 1 to 10 so that no two entries of the vector have the same contents. You can do it by brute force, by calling `rand_int` until it produces a value that is not yet in the vector. Instead, you should implement a smart method. Make a second array and fill it with the numbers 1 to 10. Then pick one of those at random, *remove it,* and append it to the permutation vector. Repeat ten times.

Exercise P9.15. Write a procedure

```
void bar_chart(vector<float> data)
```

that displays a bar chart of the values in `data`. You may assume that all values in `data` are positive. *Hint:* You must figure out the maximum of the values in `data`. Set the coordinate system so that the x-range equals the number of bars and the y-range goes from 0 to the maximum.

Exercise P9.16. Improve the `bar_chart` procedure of the preceding exercise to work correctly when `data` contains negative values.

Exercise P9.17. Write a procedure

```
void pie_chart(vector<float> data)
```

that displays a pie chart of the values in `data`. You may assume that all values in `data` are positive.

Exercise P9.18. Write a program that prints out a bank statement. The program input is a sequence of transactions. Each transaction has the form

date *amount* *description*

For example,

```
12/15/1995 -224 Check 2140
12/16/1995 1200 ATM deposit
```

Your program should read in the descriptions and then print out a statement listing all deposits, withdrawals, and the daily balance for each day. You should then compute the interest earned by the account. Use both the *minimum daily balance* and the *average daily balance* methods for computing interest, and print out both values. Assume that the interest rate is 5 percent per month. You may assume that the input data are sorted by the date and that they span only one month (for example `12/1/1995` to `12/31/1995`). You may also assume that the first entry is of the form

```
12/1/1995 1143.24 Initial balance
```

Exercise P9.19. Define a class

```
class Staff
{
public:
   . . .
private:
   vector<Employee> members;
};
```

and implement the `find` and `raise_salary` procedures for the `Staff` data type.

Exercise P9.20. Design a class `Student`, or use one from a previous exercise. A student has a name and a birthday. Make a vector

```
vector<Student> friends;
```

Read a set of names and birthdays in from a file or type them in, thus populating the `friends` vector. Then print out all friends whose birthday falls in the current month.

Exercise P9.21. Design a class `Appointment` that describes an appointment including the starting time, ending time and a description; for example,

```
Dentist
1996/10/1 17:30:00 1996/10/1 18:30:00
CS1 class
1996/10/2 08:30:00 1996/10/2 10:00:00
```

Design a class `Schedule` that holds a vector of appointments. Supply the following member functions:

```
void Schedule::read()
void Schedule::print()
void Schedule::print_conflicts()
```

The last function prints out all appointments that overlap; for example,

```
Dentist
1996/10/1 12:30:00 1996/10/1 13:30:00
CS1 class
1996/10/1 13:30:00 1996/10/1 14:00:00
```

Exercise P9.22. Write a program that plays tic-tac-toe. The tic-tac-toe game is played on an 3×3 grid as in

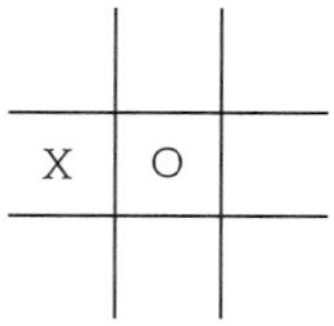

The game is played by two players, who take turns. The first player marks moves with a circle, the second with a cross. The player who has formed a horizontal, vertical, or diagonal sequence of 3 marks wins. Your program should draw the game board, accept mouse clicks into empty squares, change the players after every successful move, and pronounce the winner.

Exercise P9.23. Write a tic-tac-toe game that plays against the computer. Your program will play many turns against a human opponent, and it will learn. Process human inputs as in the preceding exercise. When it is the computer's turn, the computer randomly selects an empty field, except that it won't ever choose a losing combination. For that purpose, your program must keep a vector of losing combinations. Whenever the human wins, the immediately preceding combination is stored as losing. For example, suppose that x = computer and o = human. Suppose the current combination is

O	X	X
	O	

Now it is the human's turn, who will of course choose

O	X	X
	O	
		O

The computer should then remember the preceding combination

O	X	X
	O	

as a losing combination. As a result, the computer will never again choose that combination from

O	X	
	O	

or

O		X
	O	

Hints: Make a class Combination that contains matrix<int>. Each element in that matrix is 0 = empty, 1 = x, or 2 = o. Write a function that tests whether two combinations are identical. Write a function that tests whether a combination is present in a vector<Combination>.

Exercise P9.24. *Magic squares.* An $n \times n$ matrix that is filled with the numbers $1, 2, 3, \ldots, n^2$ is a magic square if the sum of the elements in each row, in each column, and in the two diagonals is the same value. For example,

16	3	2	13
5	10	11	8
9	6	7	12
4	15	14	1

Write a program that reads in n^2 values from the keyboard and tests whether they form a magic square when put into array form. You need to test three features:

1. Did the user enter n^2 numbers for some n?
2. Does each of the numbers $1, 2, \ldots, n^2$ occur exactly once in the user input?
3. When the numbers are put into a square, are the sums of the rows, columns, and diagonals equal to each other?

Hint: First read the numbers into a vector. If the size of that vector is a square, test whether all numbers between 1 and n are present. Then fill the numbers into a matrix and compute the row, column, and diagonal sums.

Exercise P9.25. Implement the following algorithm to construct magic n by n squares; it works only if n is odd. Place a 1 in the middle of the bottom row. After k has been placed in the (i, j) square, place $k + 1$ into the square to the right and down, wrapping around the borders. However, if you reach a square that has already been filled, or if you reach the lower right corner, then you must move to the square to the right and up instead. Here is the 5 by 5 square that you get if you follow this method:

11	18	25	2	9
10	12	19	21	3
4	6	13	20	22
23	5	7	14	16
17	24	1	8	15

Write a program whose input is the number n and whose output is the magic square of order n if n is odd.

Exercise P9.26. *Airline seating.* Write a program that assigns seats on an airplane. Assume the airplane has 20 seats in first class (5 rows of 4 seats each, separated by an aisle) and 180 seats in economy class (30 rows of 6 seats each, separated by an aisle). Your program should take three commands, add passengers, show seating, and quit. When passengers are added, ask for the class (first or economy), the number of passengers traveling together (1 or 2 in first class; 1 to 3 in economy), and the seating

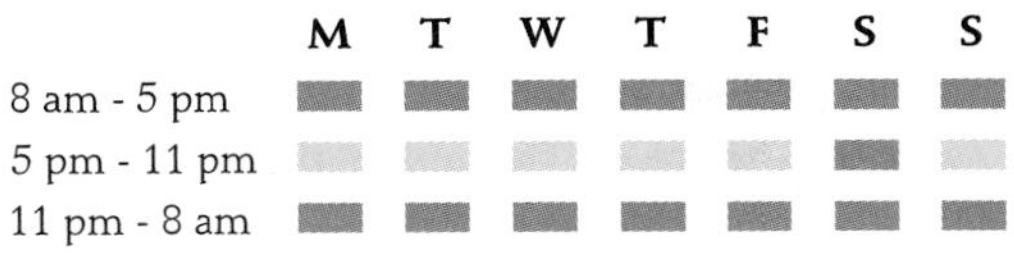

Dial direct

Sample rates from city of **Waltham** to:	**Mileage bands** Airline miles	**Weekday full rate** First minute	Each additional minute	**Evening 35% discount** First minute	Each additional minute	**Night & Weekend 60% discount** First minute	Each additional minute
Sudbury	0–10	.19	.09	.12	.05	.07	.03
Framingham	11–14	.26	.12	.16	.07	.10	.04
Lowell	15–19	.32	.14	.20	.09	.12	.05
Brockton	20–25	.38	.15	.24	.09	.15	.06
Worcester	26–33	.43	.17	.27	.11	.17	.06
Rockport	34–43	.48	.19	.31	.12	.19	.07
Fall River	44–55	.51	.20	.33	.13	.20	.08
Falmouth	56–70	.53	.21	.34	.13	.21	.08
Hyannis	71–85	.54	.22	.35	.14	.21	.08

preference (aisle or window in first class; aisle, center, or window in economy). Then try to find a match and assign the seats. If no match exists, print a message.

Exercise P9.27. *Pretty-printing tables.* Write a function that prints a table with aligned columns, column titles, and lines between the columns when requested. The function receives a matrix of floating-point values and two vectors of column descriptors, containing for each column the title of the column and the format description to be used for that column. The format description contains a format string like `"%10.2f"` used by `format`. Here is an example table:

```
 Rate 5 years  10 years

 5.00 12833.59 16470.10
 5.50 13157.04 17310.76
 6.00 13488.50 18193.97
 6.50 13828.17 19121.84
 7.00 14176.25 20096.61
 7.50 14532.94 21120.65
 8.00 14898.46 22196.40
 8.50 15273.01 23326.47
 9.00 15656.81 24513.57
 9.50 16050.09 25760.55
10.00 16453.09 27070.41
```

To print this table, you call `print_table` with three parameters: an 11 by 3 matrix containing the table values; a vector of the three strings `" Rate"`, `"   5 years"`, `"  10 years"`; and a vector of the three format descriptors `"5.2f"`, `"%10.2f"` and `"%10.2f"`.

Exercise P9.28. The table shown on page 423 can be found in the "West Suburban Boston, Area Code 617, 1990–1991" telephone book. Write a program that asks the user

The destination of the call
The starting time
The length of the call
The weekday

The program should compute and print the charge. Note that the rate may vary. If the call starts at 4:50 pm and ends at 5:10 pm, then half of it falls into the day rate and half of it into the evening rate.

Exercise P9.29. The *Game of Life* is a well-known mathematical game that gives rise to amazingly complex behavior, although it can be specified by a few simple rules. (It is not actually a game in the traditional sense, with players competing for a win.) Here are the rules. The game is played on a rectangular board. Each square can either be empty or occupied. At the beginning, you can specify empty and full cells in some way; then the game runs automatically. In each *generation,* the next generation is computed. A new cell is born on an empty square if it is surrounded by exactly three neighbor cells. A cell dies out of overcrowding if it is surrounded by four or more neighbors, and it dies of loneliness if it is surrounded by zero or one neighbors. A neighbor is an inhabitant of an adjacent square to the left, right, top, or bottom or in a diagonal direction. The following shows a cell and its neighbors.

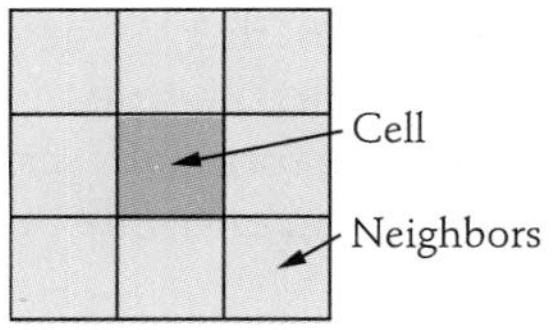

Many configurations show interesting behavior when subjected to these rules. Figure 19 shows a *glider,* observed over five generations. Note how it moves. After

Figure 19

Glider

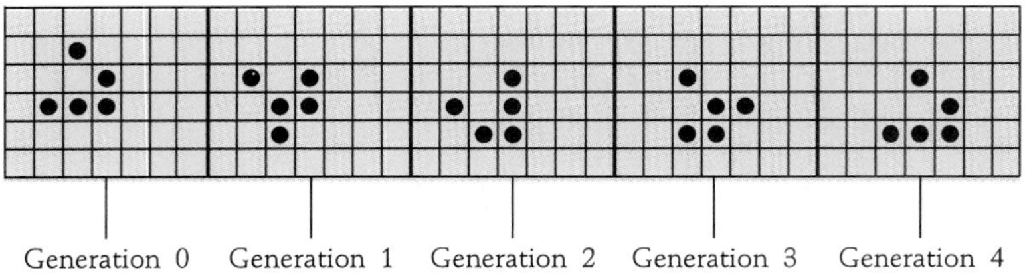

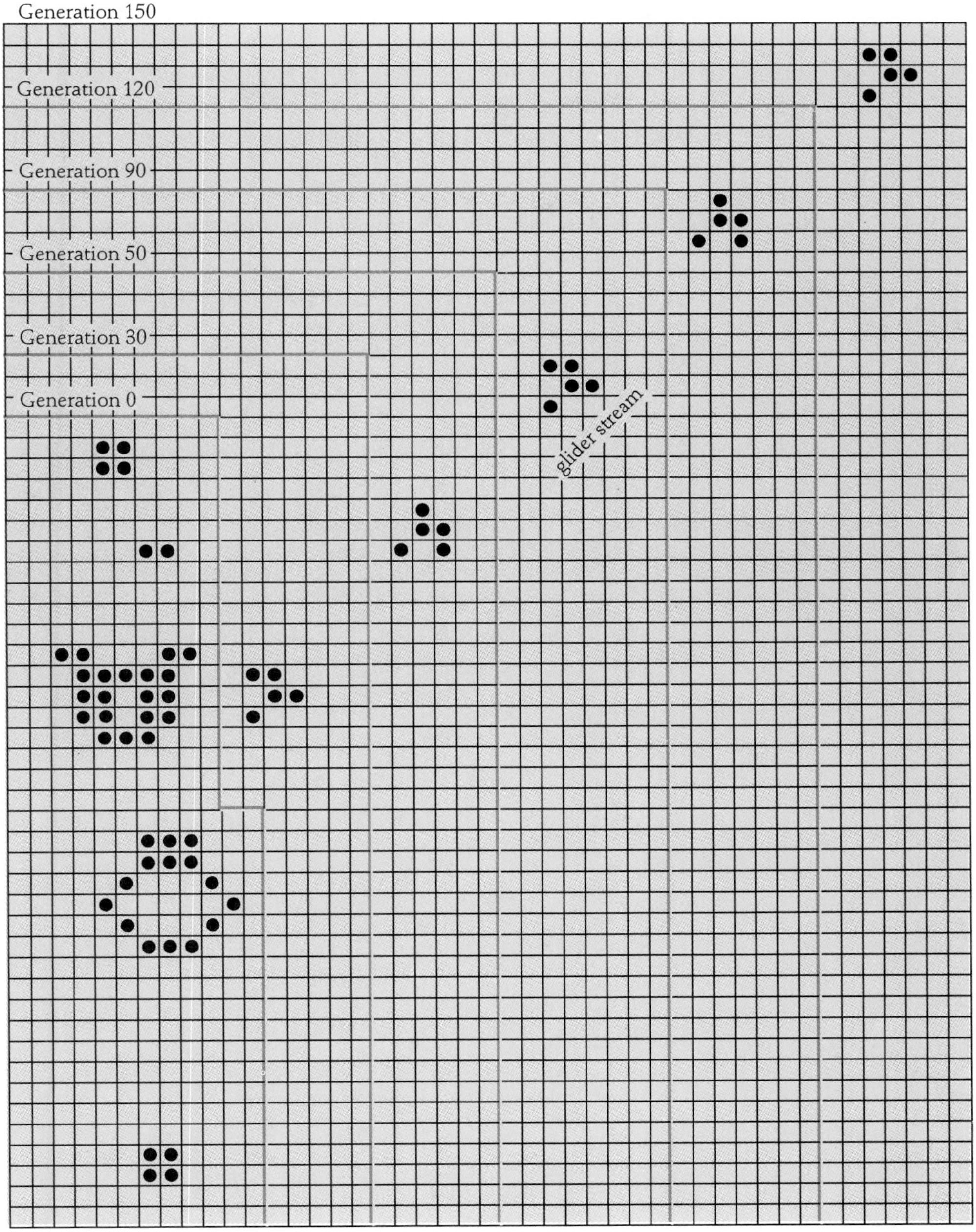

Figure 20

Glider Gun

five generations, it is transformed into the identical shape, but located one square to the right and below.

One of the more amazing configurations is the *glider gun:* a complex collection of cells that, after 30 moves, turns back into itself and a glider. (See Figure 20.)

We will want to program the game to eliminate the drudgery of computing successive generations. Use a matrix to store the rectangular configuration. Write a program that shows successive generations of the game on the graphics screen. Extra credit if you let the user add or remove cells by clicking with the mouse.

CHAPTER 10

Files

Objectives

- To be able to read and write files
- To learn how to process the command line
- To understand the concepts of sequential and random access
- To be able to build simple random-access database files
- To learn about encryption

10.1 Reading and Writing Text Files

All programs that we have written until now read their input from the keyboard and displayed their output on the screen. For text mode programs, we can change the source of the input and the destination of the output through redirection (see Productivity Hint 6.1). That is not possible for graphics programs, which do not have standard input and output. Furthermore, both text and graphics programs frequently need to read or write two or more files.

To access a disk file, you need to open a file variable. File variables are variables of type `fstream`. For example,

```
fstream input_data;
```

If you don't use the ccc.h header file, you must include the header file fstream.h to use file variables.

To read anything from a file, you need to *open* it. When you open a file, you give the name of the disk file and an *open mode* that describes what you want to do with the file. Suppose we want to read data from a file named input.dat, located in the same directory as the program. Then you use the following command to open the file:

```
input_data.open("input.dat", ios::in);
```

The first explicit parameter of the `open` procedure is the name of the file. The second parameter is the open mode. Use `ios::in` to read from the file, `ios::out` to write the file, or `ios::in + ios::out` to do both. This procedure call associates the file variable `input_data` with the disk file named input.dat. Reading from the file is now completely straightforward: You simply use the same functions that you have always used.

```
int n;
float x;
input_data >> n >> x;
```

You read strings and characters in the same way:

```
string s;
input_data >> s; /* read a word */
s = get_line(input_data); /* read a line */
s = get_char(input_data); /* read an individual character */
```

The `fail` function tells you whether input has failed. Just as for standard input, the file can be in a failed state because you reached the end of file or because of a formatting error. There can be yet another reason for a failed state: If you open a file and the name is invalid, or if there is no file of that name, then the file is also in a failed state. It is a good idea to test for failure whenever you open a file.

When you are done reading from a file, you should *close* it:

```
input_data.close();
```

Writing to a file is just as simple. You open the file for writing:

```
fstream output_data;
output_data.open("output.dat", ios::out);
```

Now you send information to the output file in the usual way.

```
output_data << n << " " << x << "\n";
```

When you are finished with the output, remember to close the file.

```
output_data.close();
```

The file name that you give to the `open` command may be a string constant:

```
fstream input_data;
input_data.open("input.dat", ios::in);
```

It may also be a string variable that contains a file name supplied by the program user:

```
string input_name =
   cwin.get_string("Please enter the file name:");
fstream input_data;
input_data.open(input_name, ios::in);
```

Actually, many compilers don't yet support `string` parameters for the `fstream::open` function. If yours does not support it, use the following command instead throughout this chapter.

```
input_data.open(input_name.c_str(), ios::in);
   /*use if open doesn't work with string parameter */
```

File names can contain directory path information, as in

```
c:\homework\input.dat     (Windows)
~/homework/input.dat      (Unix)
```

When you specify the file name as a constant string, and the name contains backslash characters (as in a Windows filename), you must supply each backslash *twice*:

```
input_data.open("c:\\homework\\input.dat", ios::in);
```

Recall that a single backslash inside quoted strings is an *escape character* that is combined with another character to form a special meaning, such as `\n` for a newline character. The \\ combination denotes a single backslash. When the file name is entered into a string variable by the user, the user should not type the backslash twice.

10.2 Example: Reading Input Data in a Graphics Program

Recall the program in Section 9.1, which reads in employee data and then plots the data on the screen. That program is a graphics program, and it prompts the user to enter all data points. Of course, if the user makes a single mistake in a data value, then there is no going back, and all data values must be entered again.

It makes more sense for the user to place the data values into a file using a text editor and then to specify the name of that file when the data values are to be used.

Here is the modified program that incorporates this improvement. The program queries the user for an input file name, opens a file variable, and passes that variable to the `read_employee` procedure:

Program emplfile.cpp

```
#define CCC_WIN
#include "ccc.h"

void read_employee(Employee& e, fstream& fs)
{  string name = get_line(fs);
   float salary;
   fs >> salary;
   get_line(fs);
   e = Employee(name, salary);
}

int main()
{  string filename =
      cwin.get_string("Please enter the data file name: ");
   fstream fs;
   fs.open(filename.c_str(), ios::in);

   vector<Employee> staff;
   bool done = false;
   while (not done)
   {  Employee e;
      read_employee(e, fs);
      if (fs.fail()) done = true;
      else staff.push_back(e);
   };

   int i;

   Employee highest_paid = staff[0];
   for (i = 1; i < staff.size(); i++)
      if (staff[i].get_salary() > highest_paid.get_salary())
         highest_paid = staff[i];

   cwin.coord(0, highest_paid.get_salary(), staff.size(), 0);
   for (i = 0; i < staff.size(); i++)
   {  Line bar(Point(i, 0), Point(i, staff[i].get_salary()));
      cwin << bar
         << Message(bar.get_end(), staff[i].get_name());
   }
```

```
    return EXIT_SUCCESS;
}
```

The input file has the following format:

```
Hacker, Harry
34500
Cracker, Carl V.
61820.75
. . .
```

The employee name must be in a line all by itself, because it contains spaces and a variable number of words.

Note that the `fstream` parameter of the `read` procedure is passed by *reference.* Reading from a file modifies the file variable. The file variable monitors how many characters have been read or written so far. Any read or write operation changes that data. For that reason, you must always pass file variables by reference.

10.3 Command Line Arguments

Depending on the operating system and C++ development system used, there are different methods of starting a program—for example, by selecting "Run" in the compilation environment, by clicking on an icon, or by typing the name of the program at a prompt in a terminal or shell window. The latter method is called "invoking the program from the command line". When you use this method, you must of course type the name of the program, but you can also type in additional information that the program can use. These additional strings are called *command line arguments.* For example, if you start a program with the command line

```
prog -v input.dat
```

then the program receives two command line arguments: the strings `"-v"` and `"input.dat"`. It is entirely up to the program what to do with these strings. It is customary to interpret strings starting with a `-` as options and other strings as file names.

Only text mode programs receive command line arguments; the graphics library that comes with this book does not collect them.

To receive command line arguments, you need to define the `main` function in a different way. You define two parameters: one integer and one with a type called `char*[]`, which denotes a C-style array of C strings.

```
int main(int argc, char* argv[])
{
    . . .
}
```

Here `argc` is the count of arguments, and `argv` contains the values of the arguments. Because they are C strings, you need to convert them to C++ strings. `string(argv[i])` is the `i`th command line argument, ready to use in C++. You must be careful to access `argv[i]`only if `i` is not negative and less than `argv`.

Figure 1

Caesar Cipher

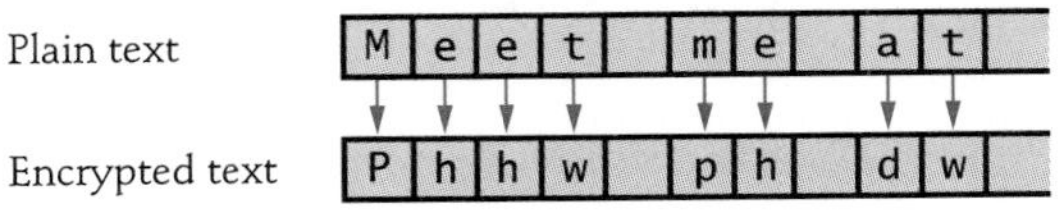

In our example, **argc** is 3, and **argv** contains the three strings

```
string(argv[0]):   "prog"
string(argv[1]):   "-v"
string(argv[2]):   "input.dat"
```

Note that `string(argv[0])` is always the name of the program and that **argc** is always at least 1.

Let us write a program that *encrypts* a file—that is, scrambles it so that it is unreadable except to those who know the decryption method and the secret keyword. Ignoring 2000 years of progress in the field of encryption, we will use a method familiar to Julius Caesar. The person performing any encryption chooses an *encryption key;* here the key is a number between 1 and 25 that indicates the shift to be used in encrypting each letter. For example, if the key is 3, we will replace A with a D, B with an E, and so on (see Figure 1).

The program takes the following command line arguments:

An optional **-d** flag to indicate decryption instead of encryption

An optional encryption key, specified with a **-k** flag

The input file name

The output file name

If no key is specified, then 3 is used. For example,

```
crypt input.txt encrypt.txt
```

encrypts the file input.txt with a key of 3 and places the result into encrypt.txt.

```
crypt -d -k11 encrypt.txt output.txt
```

decrypts the file encrypt.txt with a key of 11 and places the result into output.txt.

Here is the program:

Program caesar.cpp

```
#include "ccc.h"

void usage(string program_name)
{  cout << "Usage: "  << program_name
      << "[-d] [-kn] infile outfile\n";
   exit(EXIT_FAILURE);
}
```

```
void open_file_error(string filename)
{  cout << "Error opening file " << filename << "\n";
   exit(EXIT_FAILURE);
}

string encrypt(string s, int k)
{  string letters = "abcdefghijklmnopqrstuvwxyz";
   int i;
   for (i = 0; i < letters.length(); i++)
   {  if (lowercase(s) == letters.substr(i, 1))
      {  int j = (i + k) % letters.length();
         string es = letters.substr(j, 1);
         if (s == lowercase(s)) /* s is lowercase   */
            return es;
         else
            return uppercase(es);
      }
   }
   return s;
}

void encrypt_file(fstream& in, fstream& out, int k)
{  while (true)
   {  string s;
      s = get_char(in);
      if (in.fail()) return;
      out << encrypt(s, k);
   }
}

int main(int argc, char* argv[])
{  bool decrypt = false;
   int key = 3;
   int nfile = 0; /* the number of files specified   */
   fstream infile;
   fstream outfile;

   if (argc < 3 or argc > 5) usage(string(argv[0]));

   int i;
   for (i = 1; i < argc; i++)
   {  string arg = string(argv[i]);
      if (arg.substr(0, 1) == "-")
         /* it is a command line option */
      {  string option = arg.substr(1, 1);
         if (option == "d")
            decrypt = true;
         else if (option == "k")
            key = intvalue(arg.substr(2,
               arg.length() - 2));
      }
```

```
            else
            {  nfile++;
               if (nfile == 1)
               {  infile.open(arg.c_str(), ios::in);
                  if (infile.fail()) open_file_error(arg);
               }
               else if (nfile == 2)
               {  outfile.open(arg.c_str(), ios::out);
                  if (outfile.fail()) open_file_error(arg);
               }
            }
         }

         if(nfile != 2) usage(string(argv[0]));

         if (decrypt) key = 26 - key;

         encrypt_file(infile, outfile, key);
         infile.close();
         outfile.close();
         return EXIT_SUCCESS;
      }
```

Random Fact 10.1

Encryption Algorithms

The exercises at the end of this chapter give a few algorithms to encrypt text. Don't actually use any of those methods to send secret messages to your lover. Any skilled cryptographer can *break* these schemes in a very short time—that is, reconstruct the original text without knowing the secret keyword.

In 1978 Ron Rivest, Adi Shamir, and Leonard Adleman introduced an encryption method that is much more powerful. The method is called *RSA* encryption, after the last names of its inventors. The exact scheme is too complicated to present here, but it is not actually difficult to follow. You can find the details in [1].

RSA is a remarkable encryption method. There are two keys: a public key and a private key. (See Figure 2.) You can print the public key on your business card (or in your email signature block) and give it to anyone. Then anyone can send you messages that only you can decrypt. Even though everyone else knows the public key, and even if they intercept all the messages coming to you, they cannot break the scheme and actually read the messages. In almost 20 years nobody has discovered any method of breaking the scheme, even with the most massive computer power.

The inventors of the algorithm obtained a *patent* for it. That means that anyone using it must seek a license from the inventors. They have given permission for most noncommercial usage, but if you implement RSA in a product that you sell, you must get their permission and probably pay them some amount of money.

A patent is a deal that society makes with an inventor. For a period of 17 years after the patent is awarded, the inventor has an exclusive right for its commercialization, may collect

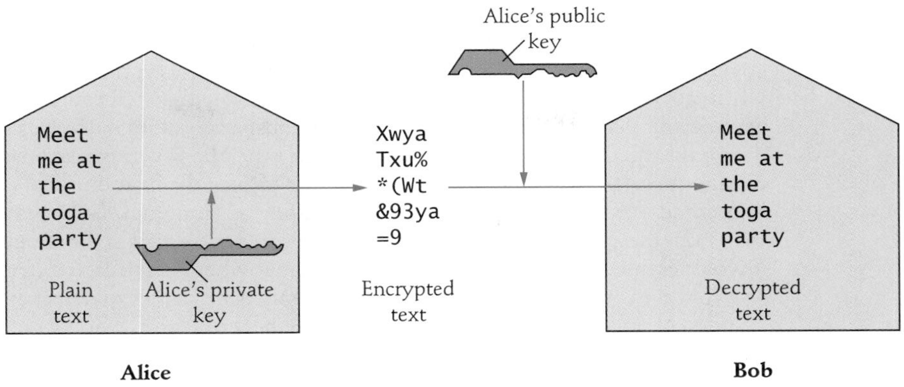

Figure 2

Public-Key Encryption

royalties from others wishing to manufacture the invention, and may even stop competitors from marketing it altogether. In return, the inventor must publish the invention, so that others may learn from it, and must relinquish all claim to it after the protection period ends. The presumption is that in the absence of patent law, inventors would be reluctant to go through the trouble of inventing, or they would try to cloak their techniques to prevent others from copying their devices. The RSA patent expires on September 20, 2000.

What do you think? Are patents a fair deal? Unquestionably, some companies have chosen not to implement RSA, and instead chose a less capable method, because they could not or would not pay the royalties. Thus, it seems that the patent may have hindered, rather than advanced, commerce. Had there not been patent protection, would the inventors have published the method anyway, thereby giving the benefit for society without the cost of the 17-year monopoly? In this case, the answer is probably yes; the inventors were academic researchers, who live on salaries rather than sales receipts and are usually rewarded for their discoveries by a boost in their reputation and careers. Would their followers have been as active in discovering (and patenting) improvements? There is no way of knowing, of course. Is an algorithm even patentable, or is it a mathematical fact that belongs to nobody? The patent office did take the latter attitude for a long time. The RSA inventors and many others described their inventions in terms of imaginary electronic devices, rather than algorithms, to circumvent that restriction. Nowadays, the patent office will award software patents.

There is another fascinating aspect to the RSA story. A programmer, Phil Zimmermann, developed a program called PGP (for *Pretty Good Privacy*) [2]. PGP implements RSA. That is, you can have it generate a pair of public and private keys, publish the public key, receive encrypted messages from others who use their copy of PGP and your public key, and decrypt them with your private key. Even though the encryption can be performed on any personal computer, decryption is not feasible even with the most powerful computers. You can get a copy of PGP by anonymous ftp (Internet file transfer protocol) from `net-dist.mit.edu` in the directory `/pub/PGP`. As long as it is for personal use, there is no charge, courtesy of Phil Zimmermann and the folks at RSA.

The existence of PGP bothers the government to no end. They worry that criminals use the package to correspond by email and that the police cannot tap those "conversations". Foreign governments can send communications that the National Security Agency (the premier electronic spy organization of the United States) cannot decipher. At the time of this writing, the government is attempting to standardize on a different encryption scheme, called *Skipjack*, to which government organizations hold a decryption key that—of course—they promise not to use without a court order. There have been serious proposals to make it illegal to use any other encryption method in the United States. At one time, the government considered charging Mr. Zimmermann with breaching another law that forbids the unauthorized export of munitions as a crime and defines cryptographic technology as "munitions". They made the argument that, even though Mr. Zimmermann never exported the program, he should have known that it would immediately spread through the Internet when he released it in the United States.

What do you think? Will criminals and terrorists be harder to detect and convict once encryption of email and phone conversations is widely available? Should the government therefore have a backdoor key to any legal encryption method? Or is this a gross violation of our civil liberties? Is it even possible to put the genie back into the bottle at this time?

10.4 Random Access

Consider a file that contains a set of employee data. We want to give some of the employees a raise. Of course, we can read all data into an array, update the information that has changed, and save the data out again. If the data set in the file is very large, we may end up doing a lot of reading and writing just to update a handful of records. It would be better if we could locate the changed information in the file and just replace it.

This is quite different from the file access that we programmed up to now. In the past, we read from a file an item at a time and wrote to a file an item at a time. That access pattern is called *sequential access.* Now we would like to access specific locations in a file and change just those locations. This access pattern is called *random access* (see Figure 3). There is nothing "random" about random access—the term just means that you can read and modify any character stored at any location in the file.

Only disk files support random access; the `cin` and `cout` streams, which are attached to the keyboard and the terminal, do not. Each disk file has two special positions: the *get* position and the *put* position (see Figure 4). Normally, the put position is at the end of the file, and any output is appended to the end. However, if you move the put position to the middle of the file and write to the file, the output over-

Figure 3

Sequential and Random Access

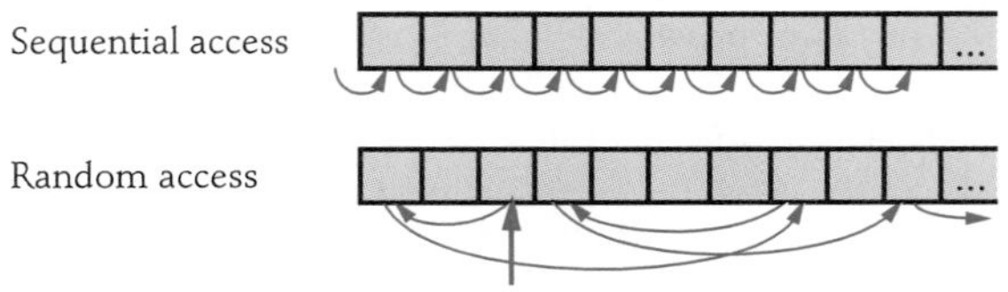

Figure 4

Get and Put Positions

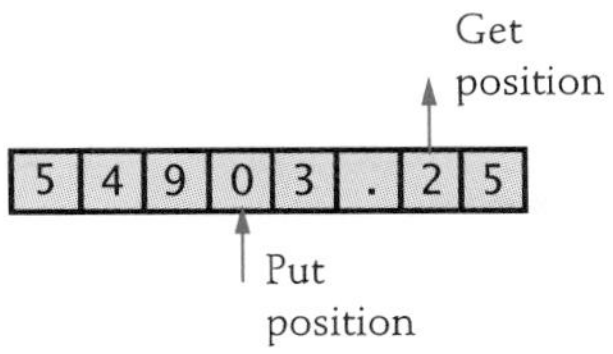

writes what is already there. Normally, the get position starts at the beginning of the file and is moved toward the end as you read from the file. However, if you move the get position to another location, the next read command starts reading input at that location. Of course, you cannot move the get or put position beyond the last character currently in the file.

The procedure calls

```
fs.seekg(n, ios::beg);
fs.seekp(n, ios::beg);
```

move the get and put positions to character `n` counted from the beginning of the file `fs`. To move to the position `n` characters away from the end of the file or the current position, use `ios::end` or `ios::cur`, respectively, instead of `ios::beg`. To find out the current position of the get and put positions (counted from the beginning of the file), use

```
n = fs.tellg();
n = fs.tellp();
```

Because files can be very large, the file positions are `long` integers. To find out the number of characters in a file, move the get position to the end and then find out the distance from the beginning of the file:

```
fs.seekg(0, ios::end);
long file_length = fs.tellg();
```

If we want to manipulate a data set in a file, we have to pay special attention to the formatting of the data. Suppose we just store the data as text:

If Harry's salary is increased by 5.5 percent, the new salary is $36,397.50. If one places the put position to the first character of the old value and simply writes out the new value, the result is

That is not working too well. The update is overwriting some characters in the next field.

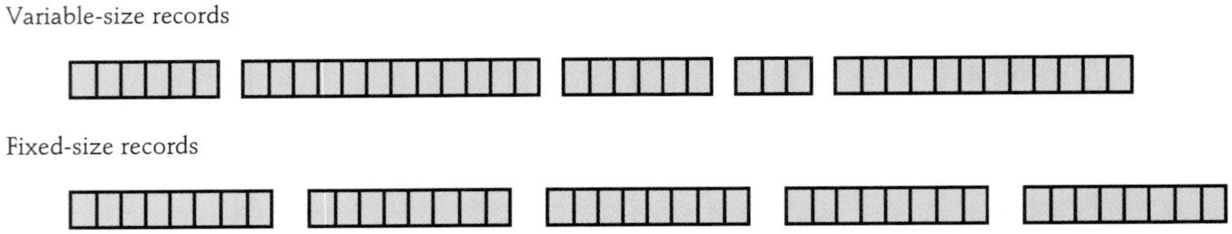

Figure 5

Variable-Size and Fixed-Size Records

In order to be able to update a file, we must give each field a *fixed* size that is sufficiently large. As a result, every record in the file has the same size. That has another advantage: It is then easy to quickly skip to, say, the 50th record, without having to read in the first 49 records. Because records can be accessed at random when they all have the same size, a file with that structure is called a *random-access file.* (See Figure 5.)

To structure the data file in our example for random access, we set the field lengths to the following dimensions:

Name: 30 characters
Salary: 10 characters

The file then looks as follows:

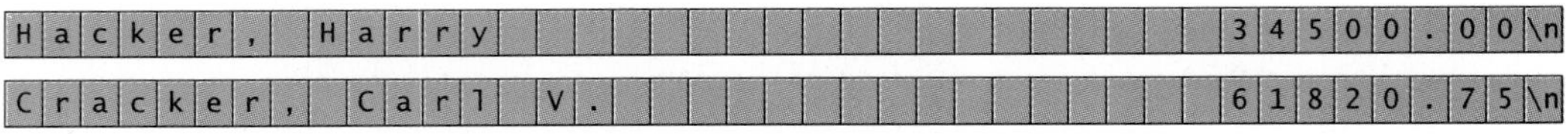

How large is each record? It would appear to be 30 + 10 = 40 characters long. However, we must also count the newline character at the end of each line. Unfortunately, some operating systems—in particular DOS/Windows—store a newline as two separate characters (a so-called *carriage return* and a so-called *line feed*). Our programs never see that, because the input and output functions automatically convert between the `'\n'` character in strings and the carriage return/line feed combination in files. When counting file positions, though, we must take both characters into account. An alternative is not to separate lines at all but simply to store the entire data set as one huge line, but then it is hard to look at the data file with a text editor.

The fact that the newline character may occupy one or two characters on disk, depending on the operating system, is an annoyance. To write programs that work on either platform, we define a constant `NEWLINE_LENGTH` and set it to the appropriate value for the operating system:

```
const int NEWLINE_LENGTH = 1; /* or 2 on DOS/Windows */
```

Now that we have agreed on the file layout, we can implement our random-access file functions. The following program asks the user to enter the position of the record that should be updated, and the price increase.

Program database.cpp

```
#include "ccc.h"

const int NEWLINE_LENGTH = 2; /* or 1 on Unix */
const int RECORD_SIZE = 30 + 10 + NEWLINE_LENGTH;

void raise salary(Employee& e, float percent)
{  float new_salary = e.get_salary() * (1 + percent/100);
   e.set_salary(new_salary);
}

void read_employee(Employee& e, fstream& fs)
{  string line = get_line(fs);
   if (fs.fail()) return;
   string name = line.substr(0, 30);
   float salary = floatvalue(line.substr(30, 10));
   e = Employee(name, salary);
}

void write_employee(Employee e, fstream& fs)
{  fs << format("%-30s", e.get_name())
      << format("%10.2f", e.get_salary())
      << "\n";
}

int main()
{  cout << "Please enter the data file name: ";
   string filename;
   cin >> filename;
   fstream fs;
   fs.open(filename.c_str(), ios::in + ios::out);
   fs.seekg(0, ios::end); /* go to end of file */
   int nrecord = fs.tellg() / RECORD_SIZE;

   cout << "Please enter the record to update: (0 - "
      << nrecord - 1 << ")";
   int pos;
   cin >> pos;

   cout << "Please enter the salary change in percent: ";
   float salary_change;
   cin >> salary_change;

   Employee e;
   fs.seekg(pos * RECORD_SIZE, ios::beg);
```

```
    read_employee(e, fs);
    raise_salary(e, salary_change);
    fs.seekp(pos * RECORD_SIZE, ios::beg);
    write_employee(e, fs);

    fs.close();
    return EXIT_SUCCESS;
}
```

Advanced Topics 10.1

Binary Files

When a program saves numeric data to disk with the << operation, the data is saved in text format. For example, the floating-point number 314.7 is saved as `314.7` or perhaps `3.147E2`. Actually, it is more efficient to save the number in the same format in which it is represented in the computer: as a set of four bytes. That has the added advantage that the number automatically occupies a fixed size in the file, making random access easier.

When saving large data sets, it makes a lot of sense to use a binary format. We have not done that in this book, because it requires a little more technical overhead in C++.

Another disadvantage of binary format is that it makes debugging *much* harder. When you look into a text file with a text editor, you can see exactly what is inside. To look inside a binary file, or to make a minor modification, you need special tools. We recommend using text files for saving data until an application is fully debugged. If the added efficiency of binary files is crucial, then rewrite just the input/output procedures to switch to binary format.

Random Fact 10.2

Databases and Privacy

Most companies use computers to keep huge data files of customer records and other business information. Special *database* programs are used to rapidly search and update that information. This sounds like a straightforward extension of the techniques we learned in this chapter, but it does take special skills to handle truly massive amounts of data. You will likely take a course in database programming as part of your computer science education.

Databases not only lower the cost of doing business; they improve the quality of service that companies can offer. Nowadays it is almost unimaginable how time-consuming it used to be to withdraw money from a bank branch or to make travel reservations.

Today most databases are organized according to the *relational model.* Suppose a company stores your orders and payments. They will probably not repeat your name and address on every order; that would take unnecessary space. Instead, they will keep one file of all their customer names and identify each customer by a unique customer number. Only that customer number, not the entire customer information, is kept with an order record. (See Figure 6.)

To print an invoice, the database program must issue a *query* against both the customer and order files and pull the necessary information (name, address, articles ordered) from both.

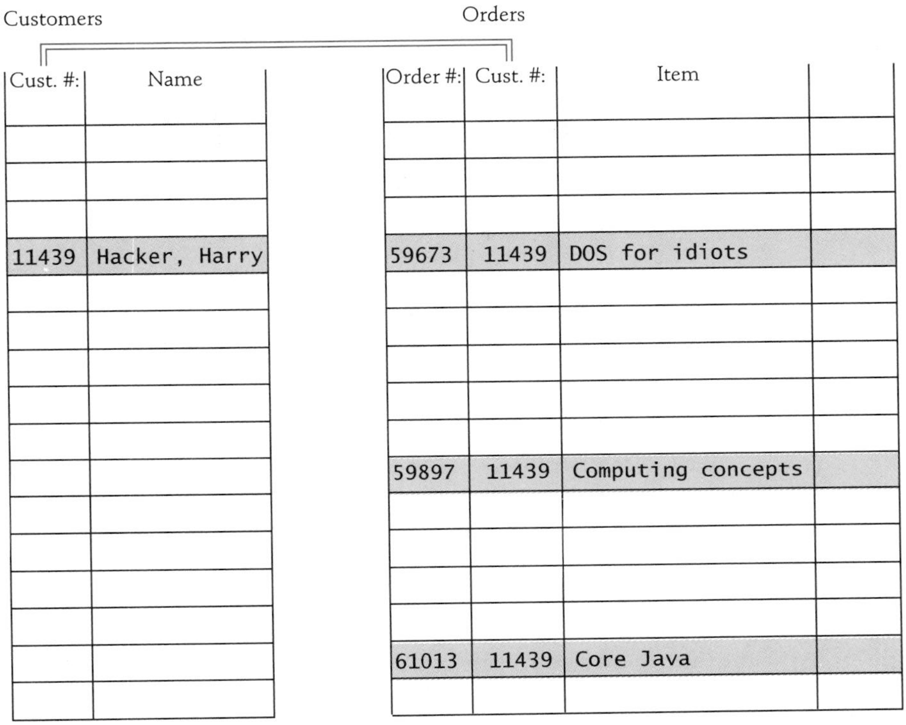
Customers
Orders
Cust. #:
Name
Order #:
Cust. #:
Item
11439
Hacker, Harry
59673
11439
DOS for idiots
59897
11439
Computing concepts
61013
11439
Core Java

Figure 6

Relational Database Files

Frequently, queries involve more than two files. For example, the company may have a file of addresses of car owners and a file of people with good payment history and may want to find all of its customers who placed an order in the last month, drive an expensive car, and pay their bills, to send them another catalog. This kind of query is, of course, much faster if all customer files use the *same* key, which is why so many organizations in the United States try to collect the Social Security number of their customers.

The Social Security Act of 1935 provided that each contributor be assigned a Social Security number to track contributions into the Social Security Fund. These numbers have a distinctive format, such as 078-05-1120. (This particular number is not actually a Social Security number belonging to any person. It was printed on sample cards that were inserted in wallets in the 1940s and 1950s.) Figure 7 shows a Social Security card.

Although they had not originally been intended for use as a universal identification number, Social Security numbers have become just that in the last 60 years. The tax authorities and many other government agencies are required to collect the numbers, as are banks (for the reporting of interest income) and, of course, employers. Many other organizations find it convenient to use the number as well.

Figure 7

Social Security Card

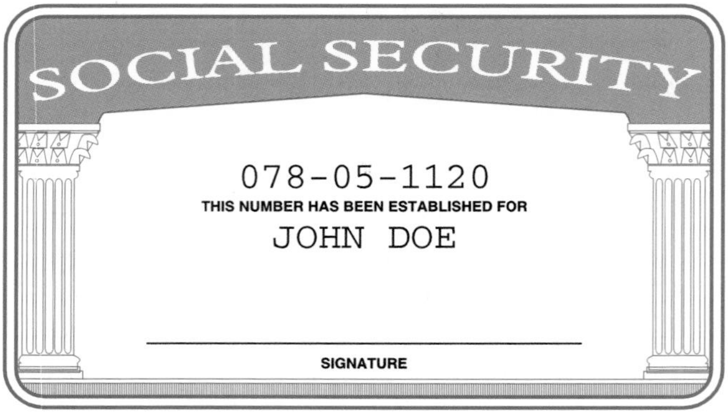

From a technical standpoint, Social Security numbers are a lousy method for indexing a database. There is a risk of having two records with the same number, because many illegal immigrants use fake numbers. Not everyone has a number—in particular, foreign customers. Because there is no checksum, a clerical error (such as transposing two digits) cannot be detected. (Credit card numbers have a checksum.) For the same reason, it is easy for anyone to make up a number.

Some people are very concerned about the fact that just about every organization wants to store their Social Security number. Unless there is a legal requirement, such as for banks, one can usually fight it or take one's business elsewhere. Even when an organization is required to collect the number, such as an employer, one can insist that the number be used only on tax and Social Security paperwork, not on the face of an ID card. Unfortunately, it usually takes near-superhuman effort to climb the organizational ladder to find someone with the authority to process paperwork with no Social Security number or to assign another identification number.

The discomfort that many people have about the computerization of their personal information is understandable. There is the possibility that companies and the government can merge multiple databases and derive information about us that we may wish they did not have or that simply may be untrue. An insurance company may deny coverage, or charge a higher premium, if it finds that you have too many relatives with a certain disease. You may be denied a job because of an inaccurate credit or medical report, and you may not even know the reason. These are very disturbing developments that have had a very negative impact for a small but growing number of people. See [3] for more information.

Chapter Summary

1. To read or write disk files, you need to use objects of type `fstream`. When opening the file object, you supply the name of the disk file. When you are done using the file, you should close the file object.

2. To read and write data, use the operations <<, >>, `get_char`, `get_line`, and `fail` in the same way they are used with `cin` and `cout`.

3. Programs that start from the command line can retrieve the name of the program and the command line arguments in the `main` procedure.

4. You can access any position in a file by moving the *file pointer* prior to a read or write operation. That is particularly useful if all records in a file have the same size.

Further Reading

[1] Bruce Schneier, *Applied Cryptography,* John Wiley & Sons, 1994.
[2] Phillip R. Zimmermann, *The Official PGP User's Guide,* MIT Press, 1995.
[3] David F. Linowes, *Privacy in America,* University of Illinois Press, 1989.
[4] Abraham Sinkov, *Elementary Cryptanalysis,* Mathematical Association of America, 1966.
[5] Don Libes, *Obfuscated C and Other Mysteries,* John Wiley & Sons, 1993.

Review Exercises

Exercise R10.1. Write C++ code to open a file with the name Hello.txt, store the message "Hello, World!" in the file, and close the file. Then open the same file again and read the message into a string variable. Close the file again.

Exercise R10.2. When do you open a file with `ios::in`, `ios::out` or `ios::in + ios::out`? Could you simply open all files with `ios::in + ios::out`?

Exercise R10.3. What happens if you write to a file that you only opened for reading? Try it out if you don't know.

Exercise R10.4. What happens if you try to open a file for reading that doesn't exist? What happens if you try to open a file for writing that doesn't exist?

Exercise R10.5. What happens if you try to open a file for writing, but the file or device is write-protected (sometimes called read-only)? Try it out with a short test program!

Exercise R10.6. Some operating systems have a limit on the number of files that an application can open at the same time. Find out if your operating system has such a limitation, by opening files file1.txt, file2.txt, . . . , file1000.txt, until the call to `open` fails.

Exercise R10.7. How do you open a file name that contains a backslash, like temp\output.dat or c:\temp\output.dat?

Exercise R10.8. Why is the `fstream` parameter of the `read` procedure in Section 10.2 a reference parameter and not a value parameter?

Exercise R10.9. Why does the `read` procedure in Section 10.2 call `get_line(fs)` after reading the salary?

Exercise R10.10. What is a command line? How can a program read its command line?

Exercise R10.11. If a program `woozle` is started with the command

```
woozle -DNAME=Piglet -I\eeyore -v heff.cpp a.cpp lump.cpp
```

what is the value of `argc`, and what are the values of `string(argv[0])`, `string(argv[1])`, and so on?

Exercise R10.12. How can you break the Caesar cipher? That is, how can you read a letter that was encrypted with the Caesar cipher, even though you don't know the key?

Exercise R10.13. What is the difference between sequential access and random access?

Exercise R10.14. What is the difference between a text file and a binary file?

Exercise R10.15. Some operating systems, in particular MS-DOS, convert a `'\n'` character into a two-character sequence (carriage return/line feed) whenever writing a text file and convert the two-character sequence back into a newline when reading the text file back in. This is normally transparent to the C++ programmer. Why do we need to consider this issue in the database program of Section 10.4?

Exercise R10.16. What are the get and put positions in a file? How do you move them? How do you tell their current positions? Why are they long integers?

Exercise R10.17. How do you move the get position to the first byte of a file? To the last byte? To the exact middle of the file?

Exercise R10.18. What happens if you try to move the get or put position past the end of a file? What happens if you try to move the get or put position of `cin` or `cout`? Try it out and report your results.

Programming Exercises

Exercise P10.1. Write a program that asks the user for a file name and that prints the number of characters, words and lines in that file. Then the program asks for the name of the next file. When the user enters a file that doesn't exist (such as the empty string), the program exits.

Exercise P10.2. *Random monoalphabet cipher.* The Caesar cipher, to shift all letters by a fixed amount, is ridiculously easy to crack—just try out all 25 possible keys. Here is a better idea. As key, we don't use numbers but words. Suppose the key word is FEATHER. Then we first remove duplicate letters, yielding FEATHR, and append the other letters of the alphabet in reverse order:

F	E	A	T	H	R	Z	Y	X	W	V	U	S	Q	P	O	N	M	L	K	J	I	G	D	C	B

We now encrypt the letters as follows:

A	B	C	D	E	F	G	H	I	J	K	L	M	N	O	P	Q	R	S	T	U	V	W	X	Y	Z
↓	↓	↓	↓	↓	↓	↓	↓	↓	↓	↓	↓	↓	↓	↓	↓	↓	↓	↓	↓	↓	↓	↓	↓	↓	↓
F	E	A	T	H	R	Z	Y	X	W	V	U	S	Q	P	O	N	M	L	K	J	I	G	D	C	B

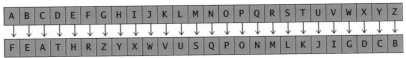

Write a program that encrypts or decrypts a file using this cipher. For example,

```
crypt -d -kFEATHER encrypt.txt output.txt
```

decrypts a file using the keyword FEATHER. It is an error not to supply a keyword.

Exercise P10.3. *Letter frequencies.* If you encrypt a file using the cipher of the preceding exercise, it will have all of its letters jumbled up, and it doesn't look as if there was any hope of decrypting it without knowing the keyword. Guessing the keyword seems hopeless too. There are just too many possible keywords. However, someone who is trained in decryption will be able to break this cipher in no time at all. The average letter frequencies of English letters are well known. The most common letter is E, which occurs about 13% of the time. Here are the average frequencies of the letters (see [4]).

A	8%	N	8%
B	< 1%	O	7%
C	3%	P	3%
D	4%	Q	< 1%
E	13%	R	8%
F	3%	S	6%
G	2%	T	9%
H	4%	U	3%
I	7%	V	1%
J	< 1%	W	2%
K	< 1%	X	< 1%
L	4%	Y	2%
M	3%	Z	< 1%

Write a program that reads an input file and prints the letter frequencies in that file. Such a tool will help a code breaker. If the most frequent letters in an encrypted file are H and K, then there is an excellent chance that they are the encryptions of E and T.

Exercise P10.4. *Vigenère cipher.* The trouble with a monoalphabetic cipher is that it can be easily broken by frequency analysis. The so-called Vigenère cipher overcomes this problem by encoding a letter into one of several cipher letters, depending on its position in the input document. Choose a keyword, for example TIGER. Then encode the first letter of the input text like this:

A	B	C	D	E	F	G	H	I	J	K	L	M	N	O	P	Q	R	S	T	U	V	W	X	Y	Z
↓	↓	↓	↓	↓	↓	↓	↓	↓	↓	↓	↓	↓	↓	↓	↓	↓	↓	↓	↓	↓	↓	↓	↓	↓	↓
T	U	V	W	X	Y	Z	A	B	C	D	E	F	G	H	I	J	K	L	M	N	O	P	Q	R	S

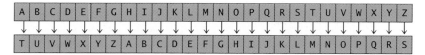

The encoded alphabet is just the regular alphabet shifted to start at T, the first letter of the keyword TIGER. The second letter is encrypted according to the map

A	B	C	D	E	F	G	H	I	J	K	L	M	N	O	P	Q	R	S	T	U	V	W	X	Y	Z
↓	↓	↓	↓	↓	↓	↓	↓	↓	↓	↓	↓	↓	↓	↓	↓	↓	↓	↓	↓	↓	↓	↓	↓	↓	↓
I	J	K	L	M	N	O	P	Q	R	S	T	U	V	W	X	Y	Z	A	B	C	D	E	F	G	H

The third, fourth, and fifth letters in the input text are encrypted using the alphabet sequences beginning with characters G, E, and R, and so on. Because the key is only five letters long, the sixth letter of the input text is encrypted in the same way as the first.

Write a program that encrypts or decrypts an input text according to this cipher.

Exercise P10.5. *Playfair cipher.* Another way of thwarting a simple letter frequency analysis of an encrypted text is to encrypt *pairs* of letters together. A simple scheme to do this is the Playfair cipher. You pick a keyword and remove duplicate letters from it. Then you fill the keyword, and the remaining letters of the alphabet, into a 5×5 square. (Since there are only 25 squares, I and J are considered the same letter.)

Here is such an arrangement with the keyword PLAYFAIR.

```
P L A Y F
I R C D E
G H K M N
O Q R S T
U V W X Z
```

To encrypt a letter pair, say AM, look at the rectangle with corners A and M:

```
P L A-Y F
I R C D E
G H K-M N
O Q R S T
U V W X Z
```

The encoding of this pair is formed by looking at the other two corners of the rectangle, in this case, YK. If both letters happen to be in the same row or column, such as GO, simply swap the two letters. Decryption is done in the same way.

Write a program that encrypts or decrypts an input text according to this cipher.

Exercise P10.6. *Junk mail.* Write a program that reads in two files: a *template* and a *database*. The template file contains text and tags. The tags have the form |1| |2| |3|... and need to be replaced with the first, second, third, ... field in the current database record.

A typical database looks like this:

```
Mr.|Harry|Hacker|1105 Torre Ave. |Cupertino|CA|95014
Dr.|John|Lee|702 Ninth Street Apt. 4|San Jose|CA|95109
Miss|Evelyn|Garcia|1101 S. University Place|Ann Arbor|MI|48105
```

And here is a typical form letter:

```
To:
|1| |2| |3|
|4|
|5|, |6| |7|

Dear |1| |3|:
You and the |3| family may be the lucky winners of
$10,000,000 in the C++ compiler clearinghouse
sweepstakes! . . .
```

Exercise P10.7. The program in Section 10.4 only locates one record and updates the price. Write a program that raises or lowers the salaries of all employees by a given percentage.

Exercise P10.8. The program in Section 10.4 asks the user to specify the record number. More likely than not, a user has no way of knowing the record number. Write a program that asks the user for the name of an employee, finds the record with that name, and displays the record. Then the program should give the following options to the user:

- Change the salary of this record
- View the next record
- Find another employee
- Quit

Exercise P10.9. To find a particular employee in a database file, the program needs to search one record at a time. If the records are *sorted,* there is a faster way. Count the number of records in the file, by dividing the length of the file by the length of each record. Set a variable `first` to 1, `last` to `nrecords`. Compute `mid = (first + last)/2`. Read the record at `mid`. Maybe you are lucky, and you actually found the record you wanted. If so, print it and exit. Is its name before or after the name that you are searching? Adjust either `last` to `mid - 1` or `first` to `mid + 1` and repeat the search. This searching method is called a *binary* search, and it is much faster than a sequential search through all records. Implement this searching method.

Exercise P10.10. It is unpleasant that we have to use the constant `NEWLINE_LENGTH`. We must remember to change the constant when porting the database program from Unix to DOS. Implement the following strategy that avoids the problem. Write a function

```
int newline_length(fstream& fs)
```

Remember the current get position. Reset it to the beginning of the file. Keep calling `tellg` and reading characters. When the character is a `"\n"`, check whether the get position jumps by 1 or 2. Return that value. If you don't find a newline in the entire file, then report 0. Before exiting, restore the get position to its original value.

Write this function and put it inside the database program.

Exercise P10.11. Write a program that keeps an employee database in a random-access file. Implement functions for adding and removing employees. You need not keep employees in sorted order. To remove an employee, just fill the entire record with spaces. When adding an employee, try to add it into one of those empty spots first before appending it to the end of the file.

Exercise P10.12. Write a program that manipulates three database files. The first file contains the names and telephone numbers of a group of people. The second file contains the names and Social Security numbers of a group of people. The third file contains the Social Security numbers and annual salaries of a group of people. The groups of people should overlap but need not be completely identical. Your program should ask the user for a telephone number and then print the name, Social Security number, and annual income, if it can determine that information.

Exercise P10.13. Write a program that prints out a student grade report. There is a file, classes.txt, that contains the names of all classes taught at a college, such as

File classes.txt

```
CSC1
CSC2
CSC46
CSC151
MTH121
. . .
```

For each class, there is a file with student numbers and grades:

File csc2.txt

```
11234 A-
12547 B
16753 B+
21886 C
. . .
```

Write a program that asks for a student ID and prints out a grade report for that student, by searching all class files. Here is a sample report

```
Student ID 16753
CSC2 B+
MTH121 C+
CHN1 A
PHY50 A-
```

Exercise P10.14. A bank keeps all bank accounts in a random access file in which each line has the format

account_number balance

Write a program that simulates an automatic teller machine. A user can deposit money to an account by specifying the account number and amount, withdraw money, query the account balance, or transfer money from one account to another.

Exercise P10.15. Write a program `copyfile` that copies one file to another. The file names are specified on the command line. For example,

```
copyfile report.txt report.sav
```

Exercise P10.16. Write a program that *concatenates* the contents of several files into one file. For example,

```
catfiles chapter1.txt chapter2.txt chapter3.txt book.txt
```

makes a long file book.txt that contains the contents of the files chapter1.txt, chapter2.txt, and chapter3.txt. The target file is always the last file specified on the command line.

Exercise P10.17. Write a program `find` that searches all files specified on the command line and prints out all lines containing a keyword. For example, if you call

```
find Tim report.txt address.txt homework.cpp
```

then the program might print

```
report.txt: discussed the results of my meeting with Tim T
address.txt: Torrey, Tim|11801 Trenton Court|Dallas|TX
address.txt: Walters, Winnie|59 Timothy Circle|Detroit|MI
homework.cpp: Time now;
```

The keyword is always the first command line argument.

Exercise P10.18. Write a program that checks the spelling of all words in a file. It should read each word of a file and check whether it is contained in a word list. A word list is available on most Unix systems in the file /usr/dict/words. (If you don't have access to a Unix system, your instructor should be able to get you a copy.) The program should print out all words that it cannot find in the word list.

Exercise P10.19. Write a program that opens a file for reading and writing, and replaces each line with its reverse. For example, if you run

```
reverse hello.cpp
```

then the contents of hello.cpp is changed to

```
"h.maertsoi" edulcni#
"h.bildts" edulcni#
```

```
()niam tni
;"n\!dlroW ,olleH" << tuoc }
;SSECCUS_TIXE nruter
}
```

Of course, if you run **reverse** twice on the same file, then you get back the original file.

Exercise P10.20. The preceding exercise shows a limitation of the hello.cpp program. If you reverse every line, it no longer is a legal C++ program. You may not think that this is much to worry about, but there are people who try hard to write programs that can be scrambled in various ways. For example, a winner of the 1989 Obfuscated C Contest wrote a program that can be reversed and still does something useful. The grand prize winner of the 1990 contest wrote a C program that can be sorted! The unsorted version solves a differential equation, whereas the version in which the lines are sorted in alphabetical order prints Fibonacci numbers. Look at [5] for a highly entertaining account of these contests.

Your task is to write a C++ program that turns into another legal C++ program when you reverse each line.

CHAPTER 11

Modules

Objectives

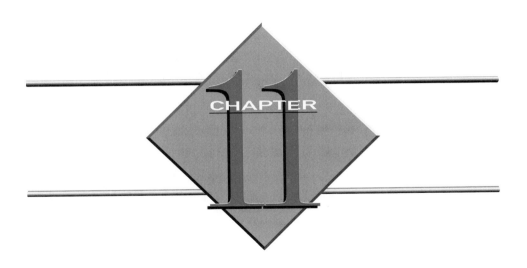

- To learn how to distribute program code over multiple source and header files
- To understand the roles of the compiler and the linker in building executable programs
- To understand where to place declarations and definitions that are used by multiple source files
- To be able to build programs that are composed of multiple files
- To understand projects and make files
- To study an application of the stack data structure to parse arithmetic expressions

11.1 Separate Compilation

When you write and compile small programs, you naturally place all your code into a single source file. When your programs get larger or you work in a team, that situation changes; you will need to split your code into separate source files. There are two primary reasons why this split-up is necessary. First, it takes time to compile a file, and it seems silly to wait for the compiler to translate code over and over that doesn't change. If your code is distributed over several source files, then only those files that you changed need to be recompiled. The second reason becomes apparent when you work with other programmers in a team. It would be very difficult for multiple programmers to edit a single source file simultaneously. Therefore, the program code is broken up so that each programmer is solely responsible for one or more files.

If a program is composed of multiple files, then you need to be able to tell the compilation system how to compile and build the program. The simple procedure of choosing "build program" from the menu no longer works. Section 11.3 explains how to combine multiple source files to make a program.

If a program is composed of multiple files, some of these files will define data types or functions that are needed in other files. There must be a path of communication between the files. In C++ that communication happens through the inclusion of header files, as shown in Figure 1. You have already used this process whenever you included a header file such as iostream.h or ccc.h. Section 11.2 explains how to design header files and what information to place into them.

11.2 Designing Header Files

When you write a source file that is to be used in a project consisting of multiple source files, you must always design an associated header file. Suppose you are im-

Figure 1

Header Files

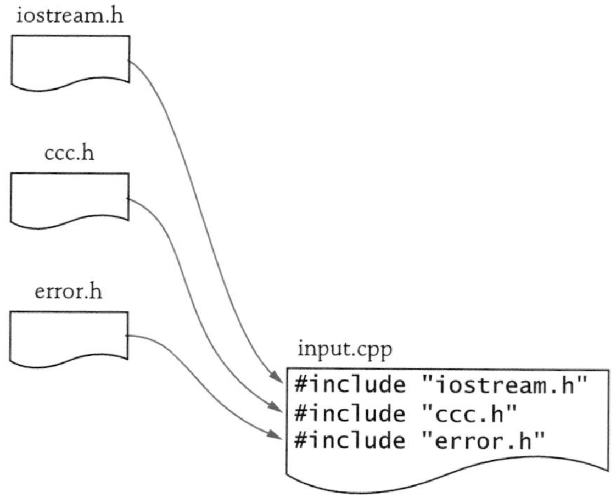

plementing a file stack.cpp. Then you must also supply a file stack.h that explains to other source files what services the file stack.cpp provides.

Let us do just that. We first need to define what a *stack* is. A stack is a special data structure that allows insertion and removal only at one end, the so-called top of the stack. Insertion and removal follow a *last in/first out* (LIFO) discipline. The last item inserted becomes the first item that is removed. Inserting a value into a stack is called *pushing* it *onto* the stack. The operation of retrieval and removal is called *popping* a value *off* the stack (see Figure 2). It is an error to try to pop an element off a stack that is *empty*.

Here is an example of a sequence of push and pop actions.

```
s.push("Able")
s.push("Baker")
s.push("Charlie")
s.pop() ⇛ returns "Charlie"
s.push("Delta")
s.pop() ⇛ returns "Delta"
s.pop() ⇛ returns "Baker"
s.pop() ⇛ returns "Able"
```

You can think of a stack as a pile of values, where items are only inserted and removed at the top of the pile. The action sequence in the example becomes

		"Charlie"		"Delta"			
	"Baker"	"Baker"	"Baker"	"Baker"	"Baker"		
"Able"	"Able"	"Able"	"Able"	"Able"	"Able"	"Able"	Empty

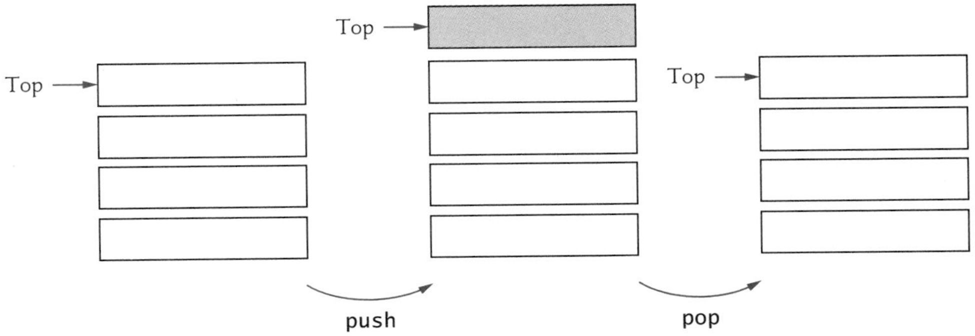

Figure 2

A Stack

Here is an implementation of a stack class:

```
class Stack
{
public:
   Stack();
   void push(string s);
   string pop();
   bool is_empty() const;
private:
   vector<string> data;
   int top;
};

Stack::Stack()
{  top = 0;
}

void Stack::push(string s)
{  if (top < data.size()) data[top] = s;
   else data.push_back(s);
   top++;
}

string Stack::pop(string s)
{  assert(top >= 0);
   string r = data[top];
   top--;
   return r;
}

bool Stack::is_empty() const
{  return top == 0;
}
```

How should this information be distributed among stack.cpp and stack.h? The header file stack.h is included into any source file that uses stacks. The header file must therefore contain the definition of the stack class. That automatically includes the properties of the functions that operate on stacks.

On the other hand, the implementations of the functions must be in the stack.cpp source file. They need to be translated to machine code exactly once. If any code of functions is placed into a header file, and that header file is included in two source files, then the function is translated twice, and the linker (the tool that combines the translated code of the various source files into the executable file) will complain about a duplicate definition of the function. (It does not check that the code for both versions is identical.)

Thus we see that the header files contain declarations that explain the features that the source file implements. The source file contains those instructions that are actually translated into machine code or variable allocations.

In the stack example, the information is split up as follows:

File stack.h

```
#include "ccc_vect.h"
#include "ccc_strg.h"

class Stack
{
public:
   Stack();
   void push(string s);
   string pop();
   bool is_empty() const;
private:
   vector<string> data;
   int top;
};
```

File stack.cpp

```
#include "stack.h"
#include "assert.h"

Stack::Stack()
{  top = 0;
}

void Stack::push(string s)
{  if (top < data.size()) data[top] = s;
   else data.push_back(s);
   top++;
}

string Stack::pop()
{  assert(top > 0);
   top --;
   return data[top];
}

bool Stack::is_empty() const
{  return top == 0;
}
```

That is, the class definition is placed in the header file and the implementation of the member functions is placed in the source file.

Note that stack.cpp includes the file stack.h. If you don't include it, then the compiler won't know what a stack is, and it will complain that it isn't prepared to translate functions referring to stacks. Some programmers don't include stack.h in stack.cpp but, instead, place identical copies of the class definition into both files. That is not a good idea; if you do that and change the class in any way, you must always remember to update both files.

Note that stack.h includes the header file ccc_vect.h. That is necessary because the stack class itself relies on another feature, namely the vector construct. In the past, we obtained vectors by including the special file ccc.h, but that file can be included only in the source file containing `main`. All other files must include only the component headers that they actually use. Those headers are

ccc_strg.h	for strings
ccc_vect.h	for vectors and matrices
ccc_graf.h	for graphics
ccc_misc.h	for miscellaneous declarations (see Appendix A2)
ccc_empl.h	for employee records
ccc_time.h	for the `Time` class

Because header files commonly include other header files, it could easily happen that one header file is included twice. For example, both stack.h and ccc.h include ccc_vect.h.

If a file calc.cpp includes both stack.h and ccc.h, the file ccc_vect.h is included twice. The compiler is not smart enough to realize that a header file has already been encountered and should not be read again. In fact, it will read the contents of the file twice, and because it isn't smart enough to compare the definitions from the first and second reading, it will complain that you are trying to redefine vectors. You must take a special precaution to avoid this. If you look inside ccc_vect.h, you will find that it starts out with the magic commands

```
#ifndef CCC_VECT_H
#define CCC_VECT_H
```

and ends with a matching

```
#endif
```

When ccc_vect.h is read for the first time, the preprocessor variable `CCC_VECT_H` is defined. When the file is read for the second time, the entire contents are skipped. You need to repeat the same magic for your own header files. For example,

File stack.h

```
#ifndef STACK_H
#define STACK_H

#include "ccc_vect.h"

class Stack
{
public:
   Stack();
   void push(string s);
```

```
    string pop();
    bool is_empty() const;
private:
    vector<string> data;
    int top;
};

#endif
```

11.3 Breaking Up a Program into Multiple Source Files

We will write a program called `calc` that evaluates arithmetic expressions. The user of the program types an expression like

```
10 + 2 ^ 10 =
2 ^ (10 + 2) =
2 ^ 10 / 10 ^ 2 =
1 - (1 - (1 - (1 - 2))) =
```

The program prints the result. (Here $a \wedge b$ denotes raising a to the power of b. We must translate that into a call to `pow`.) We must write a program that understands parentheses and the *precedence of operators.* For example, the program must know that * *binds more strongly* than +. That is, when processing the expression `1 + 2 * 3`, the `1` must be set aside until `2 * 3` is evaluated. To implement the setting aside of intermediate values, we need a stack.

Here is the algorithm. We keep two stacks: one for numbers and one for operators.

- When a number is encountered, it is pushed onto the number stack.
- When an opening parenthesis `(` is encountered, it is pushed onto the operator stack.
- When an operator is encountered in the input, its precedence is compared with the precedence of the topmost operator of the stack. Precedence values are as follows:

Operator	Precedence
+ -	1
* /	2
^	3

  If the new operator has higher precedence than the operator on the stack, it is pushed. Otherwise, pop the old operator from the operator stack, push two numbers of the number stack, evaluate the result, and push it back onto the number stack. Then push the new operator.

- When a closing parenthesis) is encountered, pop off all operators and evaluate them until an opening parenthesis is encountered.
- When an = is read in, empty the operator stack and evaluate the operators. Then print the element on the top of the number stack; there should be exactly one remaining.

Consider this example:

```
3 * (1 + 2 ^ 10) =
```

It leads to the following sequences of stacks.

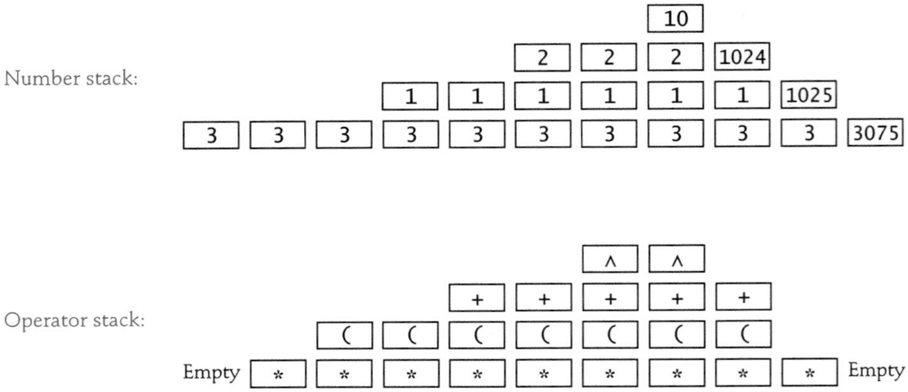

Let us implement this algorithm. Here is the `main` function, to be placed in the file calc.cpp. We will include stack.h in calc.cpp because the `main` function defines and uses two stacks.

File calc.cpp

```
#include "ccc.h"
#include "stack.h"
#include "input.h"
#include "eval.h"
#include "error.h"

int main()
{  Stack numstack;
   Stack opstack;

   while (true)
   {  string s = next_token();
      if (is_operator(s))
      {  if (opstack.is_empty())
            opstack.push(s);
```

```
            else
            {  string old_op = opstack.pop();
               if (precedence(s) > precedence(old_op))
                  opstack.push(old_op);
               else
                  evaluate(numstack, old_op);
               opstack.push(s);
            }
         }
         else if (s == "(")
            opstack.push(s);
         else if (s == ")")
         {  bool more = true;
            while (more)
            {  if (opstack.is_empty()) error("No matching (");
               string old_op = opstack.pop();
               if (old_op == "(") more = false;
               else evaluate(numstack, old_op);
            }
         }
         else if (s == "=")
         {  while (not opstack.is_empty())
            {  string old_op = opstack.pop();
               if (old_op == "(") error("No matching )");
               else evaluate(numstack, old_op);
            }
            if (numstack.is_empty())
               error("Syntax error");
            cout << numstack.pop() << "\n";
            if (not numstack.is_empty())
               error("Syntax error");
         }
         else if (s == "") /* end of input */
            return EXIT_SUCCESS;
         else /* must be a number */
            numstack.push(s);
      }
   }
```

If any files of a program use features of the library accompanying this book, you must include ccc.h into the same file that contains `main`. Therefore, calc.cpp includes ccc.h.

In this implementation, we have liberally used several functions that have yet to be implemented:

```
string next_token();
bool is_operator(string s);
int precedence(string s);
```

```
void error(string message);
void evaluate(Stack& num, string op);
```

In which file should we implement these functions: in calc.cpp, stack.cpp, or a third source file? Certainly, we should leave stack.cpp alone; it implements a stack of strings that may well be useful in other programs. We don't want to limit that reusability by cluttering it up with unrelated details.

The procedures `precedence` and `evaluate` have to do with evaluating expressions. We will place them into a file eval.cpp.

The `next_token` procedure deals with processing user input. We will place it into a third file: input.cpp. Of course, then calc.cpp must include input.h. The `is_operator` function tests whether a string denotes an operator or another token. Is that related more to calculation or to processing user input? Let us decide, perhaps somewhat arbitrarily, that it is a user input task, because the user input routine must already know something about operators.

Finally, the `error` procedure has nothing to do with user input or calculation. We could put it into a fifth file, error.cpp. That would then be a very short file, but it would be quite useful in many programs, not just this one, so let us decide to do just that.

We now have five source files,

calc.cpp
stack.cpp
input.cpp
eval.cpp
error.cpp

and four header files,

stack.h
input.h
eval.h
error.h

We already know what must be in the header files. They must contain the functions that we are using in calc.cpp.

File error.h

```
#ifndef ERROR_H
#define ERROR_H

#include "ccc_strg.h"

void error(string message);

#endif
```

File input.h

```
#ifndef INPUT_H
#define INPUT_H

#include "ccc_strg.h"

bool is_operator(string s);
string next_token();

#endif
```

File eval.h

```
#ifndef EVAL_H
#define EVAL_H

#include "ccc_strg.h"
#include "stack.h"

int precedence(string s);
void evaluate(Stack& num, string op);

#endif
```

Here are the source files.

File error.cpp

```
#include "stdlib.h"
#include "iostream.h"
#include "ccc_strg.h"
#include "error.h"

void error(string message)
{  cout << "ERROR: " << message  << ".\n";
   exit(EXIT_FAILURE);
}
```

File eval.cpp

```
#include "ccc_strg.h"
#include "stack.h"
#include "error.h"
#include "eval.h"

int precedence(string s)
{  if (s == "+" or s == "-")
      return 1;
```

```
   else if (s == "*" or s == "/")
      return 2;
   else if (s == "^")
      return 3;
   else return 0;
}

void evaluate(Stack& num, string op)
{  if (num.is_empty()) error("Syntax error");
   float y = floatvalue(num.pop());
   if (num.is_empty()) error("Syntax error");
   float x = floatvalue(num.pop());
   float z;
   if (op == "^") z = pow(x, y);
   else if (op == "*") z = x * y;
   else if (op == "/")
   {  if (y == 0) error("Divide by 0");
      else z = x / y;
   }
   else if (op == "+") z = x + y;
   else if (op == "-") z = x - y;
   else error("Syntax error");
   num.push(stringvalue(z));
}
```

File input.cpp

```
#include "iostream.h"
#include "ccc_strg.h"
#include "ccc_util.h"
#include "error.h"
#include "input.h"

bool is_digit(string s)
{  return "0" <= s and s <= "9" and s.length() == 1);
}

bool is_space(string s)
{  return s == " " or s == "\n" or s == "t";
}

bool is_operator(string s)
{  return s == "+" or s == "-" or s == "*" or s == "/"
      or s == "^";
}

void skip_whitespace()
{  while (true)
   {  string ch = get_char(cin);
```

```
            if (not is_space(ch))
            {  putback_char(cin, ch);
               return;
            }
         }
      }

      string next_number()
      {  string r = "";
         while (true)
         {  string ch = get_char(cin);
            if (not is_digit(ch))
            {  putback_char(cin, ch);
               return r;
            }
            r = r + ch;
         }
      }

      string next_token()
      {  skip_whitespace();
         string ch = get_char(cin);
         if (is_digit(ch))
         {  putback_char(cin, ch);
            return next_number();
         }
         else if (is_operator(ch) or ch == "(" or ch == ")"
                 or ch == "=" or ch == "")
            return ch;
         else
         {  error("Unexpected input " + ch);
            return "";
         }
      }
```

Note that the declarations of the `skip_whitespace` and `next_number` functions are not included in the input.h header file. These functions are not called from other modules.

11.4 Sharing Variables and Constants between Modules

In this example, we need to share only classes (such as `Stack`) and the functions (such as `next_token`) between modules.

Next, let us consider global variables and constants. As we mentioned several times, it is undesirable to have global variables. It is even less desirable to have global variables that are shared among modules, because it is then really difficult to control who modifies them.

Suppose that a module user.cpp has a global variable `user_name`. If functions in another module need to be able to read or set that variable, a declaration of the variable must be placed in the header file. To denote the fact that the variable is defined elsewhere, you must use the keyword `extern` in the header file.

File user.h

```
. . .
extern string user_name;
. . .
```

File user.cpp

```
. . .
string user_name = guest;
. . .
```

Finally, constants that need to be shared among source files are placed in a header file. For example,

File display.h

```
const int MAX_SCORE = 100;
const float MAX_PRICE = 10000;
. . .
```

The constants should *not* be redefined in display.cpp. Instead, display.cpp should include display.h.

File display.cpp

```
. . .
#include "display.h"
. . .
```

Common Error 11.1

Name Clashes

What happens if you have two global integers, both called `counter`, in two different modules? The linker will refuse to build the program, complaining about a multiple definition.

With functions the situation is not as simple. It is legal in C++ (but not in C) to define many functions with the same name, provided the argument types are different. (See Advanced Topic 8.2.) You can have a function

```
void print(Employee e)
```

and another function

```
void print(string greeting)
```

The compiler can tell the difference. If you call

```
print(harry);
```

it uses the first function. If you call

```
print("Hello Harry!");
```

it uses the second. But if another module defines a function

```
void print(string warning)
```

then the linker will complain that there are multiple definitions of `print(string)`.

Many functions that you use, such as `sqrt` or `fabs`, are defined in the standard library. While it is legal to redefine a library function, it is always a bad idea. Not only will your code call your new function (which is what you want), but existing code in the library will also call your function instead of the library function that you replaced. Since you didn't write the code for those library functions, you don't know whether that is what you want or not. An example is described in [1]. A programmer at Sun wrote a function `mktemp`. Unbeknownst to him, there was already a library function `mktemp` that worked differently, and another library function now called his version, causing a failure that was extremely difficult to track down.

Advanced Topic 11.1

Static Functions and Global Variables

Any nonmember function or global variable in a module can be accessed from any other module, provided its declaration is contained in the header file. C and older versions of C++ had a mechanism to indicate that a nonmember function or global variable should not be accessible from functions outside its own module. Such functions and variables were tagged with the keyword `static`.

```
static void skip_whitespace()
{ . . .
}

static string user_name = "guest";
```

In this situation, `static` has the same meaning for a module as `private` has for a class. Although you will see that keyword in existing code, it has been slated for eventual removal from the language. With the advent of classes, there should be fewer reasons to use global variables and nonmember functions.

Be warned that the keyword `static` has four entirely unrelated meanings in C++:

1. A `static` global variable or a nonmember function is private to its module.
2. A `static` local variable is not abandoned after its block exits.

3. A `static` data field of a class is shared among all objects of that class.
4. A `static` member function of a class has no implicit argument.

All four meanings are rather technical and are not covered in this book.

Random Fact 11.1

Software Piracy

As you read this, you have written a few computer programs, and you have experienced first-hand how much effort it takes to write even the humblest of programs. Writing a real software product, such as a financial application or a computer game, takes a lot of time and money. Few people, and fewer companies, are going to spend that kind of time and money if they don't have a reasonable chance to make more money from their effort. (Actually, there are some companies that give away their software in the hope that users will upgrade to more elaborate paid versions. There are also individuals who donate their time, out of enthusiasm, and produce programs that you can copy freely.)

When selling software, a company must rely on the honesty of its customers. It is an easy matter for an unscrupulous person to make copies of computer programs without paying for them. In most countries that is illegal. Most governments provide legal protection, such as copyright laws and patents, to encourage the development of new products. Countries that tolerate widespread piracy have found that they have an ample cheap supply of foreign software, but that no local manufacturer is stupid enough to design good software for their own citizens, such as word processors in the local script or financial programs adapted to the local tax laws.

When a mass market for software first appeared, vendors were enraged by the money they lost through piracy. They tried to fight back by various schemes to ensure that only the legitimate owner could use the software. Some manufacturers used *key disks:* floppy disks with a special pattern of holes burned in by a laser, which couldn't be copied. Others used *dongles:* devices that are attached between the computer and a printer port. Legitimate users hated these measures. They paid for the software, but they had to suffer through the inconvenience of inserting a key disk every time they started the software, or having a meter's worth of dongles stick out from the back of their computer. In the United States, market pressures forced vendors to give up on these copy protection schemes, but they are still commonplace in other parts of the world.

Because it is so easy and inexpensive to pirate software, and the chance of being found out is minimal, you have to make a moral choice for yourself. If a package that you would really like to have is too expensive for your budget, do you steal it, or do you stay honest and get by with a more affordable product?

11.5 Projects

Now that we have broken up our application into multiple source files, we can compile each of them. If you have each file in a separate window of your programming environment, you can then select "Compile" in the menu for each file. If you use a compiler that you invoke from the command line, you can type

```
CC -c calc.cpp
CC -c error.cpp
CC -c eval.cpp
CC -c input.cpp
CC -c stack.cpp
```

(Depending on your compiler, you may need to substitute a different name for CC, such as bcc, cl, or g++.)

The compiler has now translated the five source files into an intermediate format: so-called *object files*. It has not yet built the application program. The application is obtained by *linking* the five object files together into a single executable file (see Figure 3). A special program called the *linker* is responsible for this task. From the command

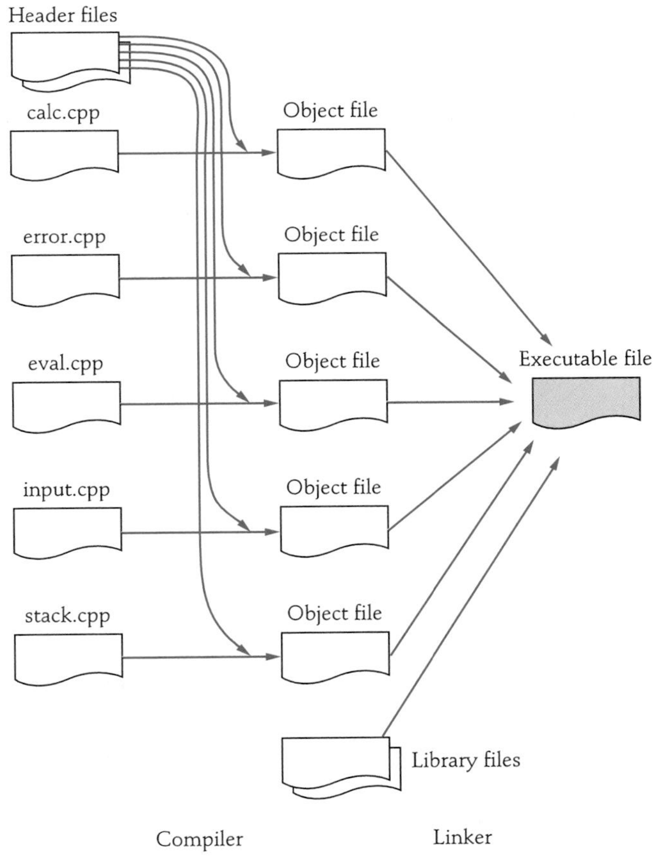

Figure 3

Separate Compilation

line, we can invoke the linker with the command

```
CC calc.obj error.obj eval.obj input.obj stack.obj
```

(On Unix systems, substitute `.o` for `.obj`.) This produces an *executable* file (called `stack.exe` on Windows or `a.out` on Unix) that you can run.

If you work in an integrated environment, the process is quite different. You must tell the environment the component files for the executable. You usually do so by creating a *project*. Give the project the same name as the executable, in this case, `calc`. Then add the five files

calc.cpp
error.cpp
eval.cpp
input.cpp
stack.cpp

to the project. Different vendors implement this in different ways, but they all show the project in some form. Figure 4 shows a typical screen display.

Now select "Make" or "Build" (instead of "Compile") from the menu. Then the application program is linked together. You can now start it from the compilation environment by selecting "Run" from the menu or by typing the name `calc` in a command line window.

Now suppose one of the input files changes. For example, go ahead and edit the error message in error.cpp to read `"Fatal error"` instead of `"Error"`. When

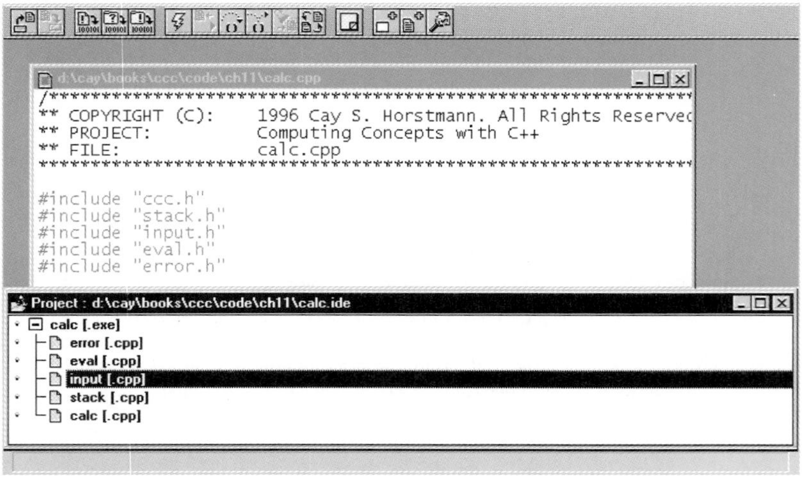

Figure 4

Source Files Added to a Project

you are done with the change, select "Make" again. If you watch closely, you will find that only error.cpp is recompiled. The other object files are already up to date. That is a major benefit of separate compilation. By recompiling only those files that have changed since the last program build, the time needed to rebuild the program can be cut dramatically, especially if the program consists of many source files. The compilation environment finds out which files need to be recompiled by looking at the time stamp of each file. If the source file is newer than the object file, then the object file is out of date and must be rebuilt.

If you invoke the compiler from the command line, you can still enjoy the benefit of recompiling only the needed files. You need to place program building instructions into a special file, called a *make file.* Use a text editor to write a file like this:

File calc.mak

```
CC = bcc
# substitute your compiler command if it is different

.cpp.obj
      CC -c $<

OBJS = calc.obj error.obj eval.obj input.obj stack.obj
PROG = calc.exe
# update the object files and the program name for other projects

$(PROG): $(OBJS)
      CC -e $(PROG) $(OBJS)
```

Call the file calc.mak. Then you type the command

```
make -f calc.mak
```

(With some systems, you need to type a slightly different command, such as `nmake`.) The make utility program uses the make file to deduce that files with extension .obj depend on files with extension .cpp and that calc.exe depends on calc.obj, input.obj, error.obj, and stack.obj. It then checks the time stamps of all files. If it finds that error.cpp is newer than error.obj, it invokes the compiler to regenerate error.obj. Assuming that all other object files are newer than their corresponding source files, the make utility calls the linker to rebuild the executable.

Unfortunately, the exact syntax of make files is not standardized, and your version of make may require a slightly different format. In particular, Unix make is infamous for its requirement that certain lines start with a tab, not with spaces!

There is also a potential problem with header files. If you modify a header file, then all source files that include the header file need to be changed. Some versions of make do this automatically; others force you to add the dependencies to the make file.

Even if you normally use an integrated environment and projects, knowing about make files is a useful skill. Project files are notoriously difficult to move from one machine to the next. They often differ from one compiler version to the next and usually depend on the exact directory layout of the current machine. That makes it difficult to share project files when you work with several team members. Unless all team members can standardize on one version of the compiler and the same directory layout, using make files will preserve your sanity.

Productivity Hint 11.1

Personal Libraries

In this book we use several functions that make standard library functions more convenient, such as `rand_int`. Sure, we could use `rand() % 6 + 1`, but `rand_int(1, 6)` is simpler and easier to understand.

You may find that you write certain convenience functions in many programs. A typical candidate would be

```
void error(string message)
{  cout << "ERROR: " << message << ".\n";
   exit(EXIT_FAILURE);
}
```

If you want to avoid the hassle of copying and pasting such functions from one assignment to the next, then you can make a file mystuff.cpp containing all your useful functions, and a header file mystuff.h with their declarations.

Productivity Hint 11.2

Using grep to Locate Header Files

Sometimes you may need to know which header file defines a function that you want to use. For many standard functions you can use on-line help. But for lesser-known functions, or those that are in header files of your teammates, you can use grep (see Productivity Hint 5.3). If you run the following command from a command prompt,

```
grep print_customer *.h
```

prints all lines in all header files in the current directory that contain the string `print_customer`. To look inside the system header files, you must know where they are.

```
grep seek /usr/include/*.h
```

Of course, you will get some number of mismatches, because grep stupidly copies all lines containing the search string. For example,

```
grep size \borlandc\include\*.h
```

will give you a few hundred lines of gibberish like

```
void qsort(void*, size_t, size_t, void(*)(const void*, const void*));
```

Try looking for `size(` or `size[^A-Za-z_]` instead.

Some compilation environments have a convenient method of running grep and collecting all matches in a window. Find out whether yours does!

Random Fact 11.2

Software Engineering

The major topic of this book is to teach you *programming:* the ability to translate informal plans into code and fix the inevitable errors that arise in the process. In Chapters 12 and 13 we touch upon the *analysis of algorithms and data structures.* In your studies you will learn about *operating systems, computer networks,* and *graphics.* Unfortunately, putting together a team of programmers well trained in all these topics has proved to be insufficient to ensure that they can produce working software.

The goal of the discipline of *software engineering* is to identify processes that *ensure* the timely delivery of functioning software. This is a difficult task. It is one thing to describe an algorithm that sorts an array, quite another to set down rules that guarantee that a project will be successful, provided the team members follow those rules.

There is no question that the professionalism of many programming teams is not what it should be. The Software Engineering Institute (SEI) of Carnegie-Mellon University defines the following rating scheme for organizations:

Level 1	Initial	Task execution unpredictable and poorly controlled
Level 2	Repeatable	Previously mastered tasks can be repeated
Level 3	Defined	Tasks are formally characterized
Level 4	Managed	Tasks are measured and controlled
Level 5	Optimizing	Focus on task improvement

Here a "task" is not simply "get the program to run", but all the myriad subtasks: "define requirements", "plan data structures", "draw up test plan", "perform unit testing", "process bug reports", and so on. At level 3 an organization has a breakdown of what these tasks are.

At level 4 the organization understands how to measure progress. That is no easy feat. How do you know that you are 50% done with debugging a particular module? You don't know when you have found half of your bugs, because you don't know how many bugs you have in the first place. Fortunately, for larger programs the laws of averages help us out, and it does become possible to use the techniques of statistical quality control with some degree of precision.

At level 5 the effort is not just on fixing bugs but on fixing the problem that caused the bug in the first place. Developments in this area have been fairly promising. Many organizations that took the time to analyze their development process subsequently improved their track record.

In some other areas progress has been disappointing. In the last 10 years, a lot of attention has been focused on CASE (Computer-Aided Software Engineering). Specialized CASE was to organize the information needed by a programming team to finish its task. Such software typically produces graphs depicting the relationships among different variables, functions, and modules. Conversely, it encourages developers to draw the graphs showing the desired relationships and then translates them into code. Quite a few vendors of these tools vastly exaggerated their impact, touting them as the "silver bullet" that would magically fix the development process. The improvements turned out to be far more more modest than promised.

Another technology that has not yet lived up to its promise is that of *reusable components.* The idea is tempting. Just as you purchase standard-size water pipe at the hardware store, or a computer designer uses standardized computer chips, software manufacturers would buy components and put them together. You'd take a linked list here, a sorting algorithm there, and . . . then what? Let's work backwards from an actual application, say a program that computes a tax return. Sure, you need data structures to hold the transactions and algorithms to find them again, but they are just a small part of the problem. You can't buy a software component that shows a tax form on the screen, or pulls the totals from some schedules and feeds them into others. Anyone writing those components would find it more profitable to sell another tax package rather than serving the handful of vendors in the tax preparation market. This situation is slowly changing. It may actually make sense for a vendor to provide a component that can display, print, and link any form, be it a tax form or a loan application form. Standard interfaces for such entities are beginning to appear, and a more viable component market may yet emerge.

Chapter Summary

1. Larger programs are split up into separate source files. Any information that needs to be accessible by more than one source file is placed in a header file. Each source file includes those header files that it needs to compile.

2. The definitions of classes that are shared among modules belong in header files. The definitions of the member functions belong in the source file implementing the class. That source file needs to include its own header file.

3. Function definitions belong in source files, but those functions that are called from other modules must have a declaration or prototype in the header file. Global variables that are used in more than one source file must have an `extern` declaration in the header file.

4. To combine multiple source files into a program, use the *project* or *make* feature of your development environment.

Further Reading

[1] Peter van der Linden, *Expert C Programming*, Prentice Hall, 1994, pp. 123–128.

Review Exercises

Exercise R11.1. Define the term *separate compilation*. Why is separate compilation necessary for larger programs?

Exercise R11.2. What is the difference between a header file and a source file?

Exercise R11.3. Of the following items, which belong in header files and which belong in source files? Assume that the item is to be shared among separate source files.

- Function declarations
- Function definitions
- Structure definitions
- Constant definitions

Exercise R11.4. If you place a structure or a constant definition into a source file, it cannot be accessed by another source file. When is that desirable?

Exercise R11.5. What happens if you include a function definition in a header file and include that header file in two source files?

Exercise R11.6. What happens if you include a function declaration in a header file, but you forget to place the matching function definition into the corresponding source file?

Exercise R11.7. Why should every source file include its own header file?

Exercise R11.8. When should one header file include another header file?

Exercise R11.9. How do you protect a header file against multiple scanning of its contents?

Exercise R11.10. When you build a program out of multiple files, does each file have a `main` function?

Exercise R11.11. Explain the difference between

```
int counter;
```

and

```
extern int counter;
```

Exercise R11.12. Explain the difference between

```
void do_nothing();
```

and

```
void do_nothing() {}
```

Exercise R11.13. What is a name clash?

Exercise R11.14. If you use an integrated environment, find out what information the compiler keeps about your project. Exit and reenter the program and reload the project. Does the compiler remember which programs are a part of the project? Does it remember which files were open when you left the project?

Exercise R11.15. Write a make file for the calculator project and try it out on your system. Your make utility might use a slightly different syntax. Check the documentation, or look at a sample make file that your compiler vendor provided.

Programming Exercises

Exercise P11.1. Make a project consisting of three modules: student.cpp, class.cpp, and register.cpp. Write source and header files for a program that registers students for courses. Design a class `Student` that stores the name of the student, the ID number, and a vector of all course numbers for which the student is registered. Design a class `Course` that stores the course number and a vector of the ID numbers of all students who are registered. In the register.cpp file, implement functions that add and drop students and print course lists.

Exercise P11.2. Rewrite the intname program of Chapter 5. Put all helper functions into one file and the `int_name` and `main` functions in another file.

Exercise P11.3. Rewrite the clock program of Chapter 8. Make a separate file for each class.

Exercise P11.4. Rewrite the program in Section 9.5 that produces a product data plot. Distribute the code over three files: product.cpp, input.cpp, and dataplot.cpp. Distribute the functionality such that the product class knows neither about `fstream` nor about `cwin`. That means that you will need to make `read` and `plot` into nonmember functions. Only the input.cpp module should know about `fstream`, and only the dataplot.cpp module should deal with `cwin`. The `main` procedure should be in dataplot.cpp.

Exercise P11.5. Add functions `sin`, `cos`, `log`, `exp`, `sqrt` to the calculator program. For example, `cos 0 + sqrt(2 + 2)` evaluates to 3. Push the operators `cos`, `sqrt`, `log`, and so on onto the operator stack and give them a higher precedence than the binary operators.

Exercise P11.6. Modify the calculator program so that it reads its input from a string, not the standard input. For example, `calculate("1.5 + 2 * 3")` returns 7.5. You should be able to leave most of the program intact, except for the input.cpp file.

Exercise P11.7. Modify the calculator program so that it can handle a variable `x`. For example, `calculate("x^2 - 1", 5)` returns the value 24. Every time you read in the special variable `x`, simply replace it with the value for the second parameter of the `calculate` function. Use this enhancement to write a program that can print a table of function values. Here is a sample run.

```
Please enter the function: x^2 - 1
xmin = 0
xmax = 5
number of values = 6

x    x^2 - 1
------------------
0    -1
1    0
2    3
3    8
4    15
5    24
```

Exercise P11.8. Modify the program of the preceding run so that it *plots* the function on the graphic screen. Call `calculate` with a hundred values, and plot the graph as a sequence of lines joining adjacent data points. Put the graphing code into another source file, graph.cpp.

Exercise P11.9. Write a program that can graph data sets. The program reads in a data set. Each data item in the data set consists of a name and a value, such as

```
San Jose
775000
```

The user can choose among five different graph types: bar chart, pie chart, curve plot, stick plot, and dot plot (see Figure 5). Put the code for each kind of plot into a separate source file.

Exercise P11.10. Write a program that keeps an appointment calendar and shows the appointments in three views: a day view, a week view, and a month view. Make

Figure 5

Graph Types

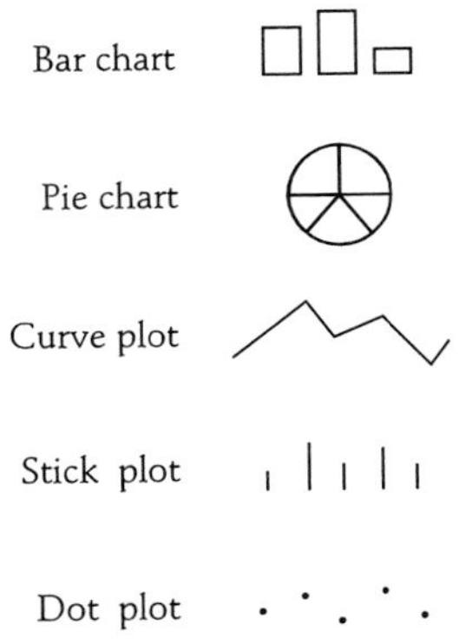

a class `Appointment` that stores a description of the appointment, the starting time, and the ending time. The day view should list all appointments on a particular day, with starting and ending times. The week view should show all appointments in a week, without starting and ending times. The month view should show all days in a month and just mark the days that have appointments. Put the code for each kind of view into a separate source file.

CHAPTER 12

Algorithms

Objectives

- To study the selection sort, merge sort, linear search, and binary search algorithms
- To appreciate that algorithms for the same task can differ widely in performance
- To understand the big-Oh notation
- To learn how to estimate and compare the performance of algorithms
- To learn how to measure the running time of a program
- To understand when the use of recursion makes an algorithm more efficient

One of the most common tasks in data processing is sorting. For example, a collection of employees needs to be printed out in alphabetical order, or sorted by salary. We will study several sorting methods in this chapter and compare their performance. This is by no means an exhaustive treatment on the subject of sorting. You will revisit this topic at a later time in your computer science studies. Reference [1] gives a good overview of the many sorting methods available.

Once a sequence of records is sorted, one can locate individual records rapidly, We will study the *binary search* algorithm that carries out this fast lookup.

The fast sorting and searching algorithms that we discuss in this chapter are recursive. However, not all recursive algorithms are fast. We end the chapter with a discussion of when recursion is appropriate.

12.1 Selection Sort

To keep the examples simple, we will discuss how to sort a vector of integers before going on to sorting strings or employee data. Consider the following vector **a**:

11	9	17	5	12

An obvious first step is to find the smallest element. In this case the smallest element is 5, stored in `a[3]`. We should move the 5 to the beginning of the vector. Of course, there is already an element stored in `a[0]`, namely 11. Therefore we cannot simply move `a[3]` into `a[0]` without moving the 11 somewhere else. We don't yet know where the 11 should end up, but we know for certain that it should not be in `a[0]`. We simply get it out of the way by *swapping it* with `a[3]`.

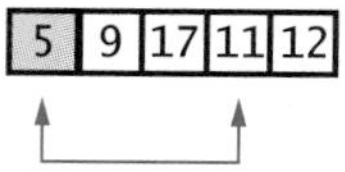

Now the first element is in the correct place. In the foregoing figure, the color indicates the portion of the array that is already sorted from the unsorted remainder.

Next we take the minimum of the remaining entries `a[1] ... a[4]`. That minimum value, 9, is already in the correct place. We don't need to anything in this case and can simply extend the sorted area by one to the right:

5	9	17	11	12

We repeat the process. The minimum value of the unsorted region is 11, which needs to be swapped with the first value of the unsorted region, 17.

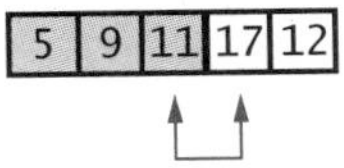

Now the unsorted region is only two elements long, but we keep to the same successful strategy. The minimum element is 12 and we swap it with the first value, 17.

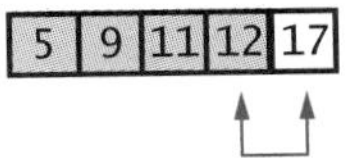

That leaves us with an unprocessed region of length 1, but of course a region of length 1 is always sorted. We are done.

Let us program this algorithm.

Program selsort.cpp

```
#include "ccc.h"

void swap(int& x, int& y)
{  int temp = x;
   x = y;
   y = temp;
}

void selection_sort(vector<int>& a)
{  int next; /* the next position to be set to the minimum */

   for (next = 0; next < a.size() - 1; next++)
   {  /* find the position of the minimum   */
      int min_pos = next;
      int i;
      for (i = next + 1; i < a.size(); i++)
         if (a[i] < a[min_pos]) min_pos = i;

      if (min_pos != next)
         swap(a[min_pos], a[next]);
   }
}

void print(vector<int> a)
{  int i;
   for (i = 0; i < a.size(); i++)
      cout << a[i] << " ";
   cout << "\n";
}
```

```
int main()
{  vector<int> v(20);
   int i;
   for (i = 0; i < v.size(); i++)
      v[i] = rand_int(1, 100);
   print(v);
   selection_sort(v);
   print(v);
   return EXIT_SUCCESS;
}
```

The algorithm will sort any array of integers. If speed were not an issue for us, or if there simply were no better sorting method available, we could stop the discussion of sorting right here. As the next section shows, however, this algorithm, while entirely correct, shows disappointing performance when run on a large data set.

12.2 Profiling the Selection Sort Algorithm

To measure the performance of a program, we could simply run it and measure how long it takes by using a stopwatch. However, most of our programs run very quickly, and it is not easy to time them accurately in this way. Furthermore, when a program does take a noticeable time to run, a certain amount of that time may simply be used for loading the program from disk into memory (for which we should not penalize it) or for screen output (whose speed depends on the computer model, even for computers with identical CPUs). We will instead use the `Time` class. Recall that

```
Time now;
```

sets `now` to the current time.

Here is how we will use the timer to measure the performance of the sorting algorithm.

Program sorttime.cpp

```
#include "ccc.h"

void swap(int& x, int& y)
{  int temp = x;
   x = y;
   y = temp;
}

void selection_sort(vector<int>& a)
{  int next; /* the next position to be set to the minimum */
```

```
      for (next = 0; next < a.size() - 1; next++)
      {  /* find the position of the minimum   */
         int min_pos = next;
         int i;
         for (i = next + 1; i < a.size(); i++)
            if (a[i] < a[min_pos]) min_pos = i;

         if (min_pos != next)
            swap(a[min_pos], a[next]);
      }
   }

   int main()
   {  cout << "Enter vector size: ";
      int n;
      cin >> n;
      vector<int> v(n);
      int i;
      for (i = 0; i < v.size(); i++)
         v[i] = rand_int(1, 200);

      Time before;
      selection_sort(v);

      Time after;
      cout  << "Elapsed time = " << after.seconds_from(before)
         << " seconds\n";
      return EXIT_SUCCESS;
   }
```

By measuring the time just before the sorting and stopping it just afterwards, we don't count the time it takes to initialize the vector or the time during which the program waits for the user to type in n.

Here are the results of some sample runs.

n	Seconds
1000	11
2000	45
3000	101
4000	179
5000	279
6000	403

These measurements were obtained on a 486 processor with a clock speed of 50 MHz running Windows 95. On another computer, the actual numbers will look different,

Figure 1

Time Taken by Selection Sort

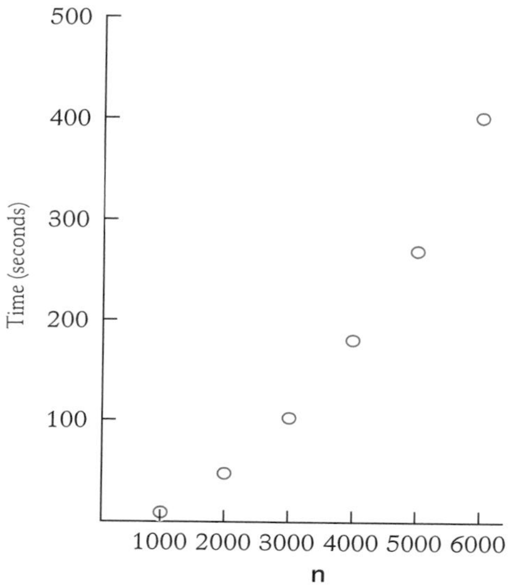

but the relationship between the numbers will be the same. Figure 1 shows a plot of the measurements.

As you can see, doubling the size of the data set more than doubles the time needed to sort it.

12.3 Analyzing the Performance of the Selection Sort Algorithm

Let us count the number of operations that the program must carry out to sort an array by the selection sort algorithm. Actually, we don't know how many machine operations are generated for each C++ instruction or which of those instructions are more time-consuming than others, but we can make a simplification. We will simply count how often an array element is *visited*. Each visit requires about the same amount of work by other operations, such as incrementing subscripts and comparing values.

Let n be size of the array. First, we must find the smallest of n numbers. To achieve that, we must visit n array elements. Then we swap the elements, which takes 2 visits. (You may argue that there is a certain probability that we don't need to swap the values. That is true, and one can refine the computation to reflect that observation. As we will soon see, doing so would not affect the overall conclusion.) In the next step, we need to visit only $n - 1$ elements to find the minimum and then visit two of them to swap them. In the following step, $n - 2$ elements are visited to find the minimum. The last run visits two elements to find the minimum and requires 2 visits to swap the elements. Therefore, the total number of visits is

$$\begin{aligned} & n + 2 + (n-1) + 2 + \cdots + 2 + 2 \\ &= n + (n-1) + \cdots + 2 + (n-1) \cdot 2 \\ &= 2 + \cdots + (n-1) + n + (n-1) \cdot 2 \\ &= \frac{n(n+1)}{2} - 1 + (n-1) \cdot 2 \end{aligned}$$

because

$$1 + 2 + \cdots + (n-1) + n = \frac{n(n+1)}{2}$$

After multiplying out and collecting terms of n, we find that the number of visits is

$$\tfrac{1}{2}n^2 + \tfrac{5}{2}n - 3$$

We obtain a quadratic equation in n. That explains why the graph of Figure 1 looks approximately like a parabola.

Now let us simplify the analysis further. When you plug in a large value for n (for example, 1000 or 2000), then $\frac{1}{2}n^2$ is 500,000 or 2,000,000. The lower term, $\frac{5}{2}n - 3$, doesn't contribute much at all; it is just 2,497 or 4,997, a drop in the bucket compared to the hundreds of thousands or even millions of comparisons specified by the $\frac{1}{2}n^2$ term. We will just ignore these lower-level terms. Next, we will ignore the constant factor $\frac{1}{2}$. We are not interested in the actual count of visits for a single n. We want to compare the ratios of counts for different values of n. For example, we can say that sorting an array of 2000 numbers requires 4 times as many visits as sorting an array of 1000 numbers:

$$\left(\tfrac{1}{2} \times 2000^2\right) / \left(\tfrac{1}{2} \times 1000^2\right) = 4$$

The factor $\frac{1}{2}$ cancels out in comparisons of this kind. We will simply say, "The number of visits is of order n^2". That way, we can easily see that the number of comparisons increases fourfold when the size of the vector doubles: $(2n)^2 = 4n^2$.

To indicate that the number of visits is of order n^2, computer scientists often use *big-Oh notation*: The number of visits is $O(n^2)$. This is a convenient shorthand.

To turn an exact expression like

$$\tfrac{1}{2}n^2 + \tfrac{5}{2}n - 3$$

into big-Oh notation, simply locate the fastest-growing term, n^2, and ignore the constant coefficient $\frac{1}{2}$.

We observed before that the actual number of machine operations, and the actual number of microseconds that the computer spends on them, is approximately proportional to the number of element visits. Maybe there are about 10 machine operations (increments, comparisons, memory loads and stores) for every element visit. The number of machine operations is then approximately $10 \times \frac{1}{2}n^2$. Again, we aren't interested in the coefficient and can say that the number of machine operations, and hence the time spent on the sorting, is of the order of n^2 or $O(n^2)$. The sad fact remains that doubling the size of the vector causes a fourfold increase in the time required for sorting it. To sort a vector of 100,000 entries, for example to create a telephone directory, takes 10,000 times as long as sorting 1000 entries. If 1000 entries can be sorted in 11 seconds (as in our example), then 100,000 entries require over 30 hours. That is a problem. We will see in the next section how one can dramatically improve the performance of the sorting process by choosing a more sophisticated algorithm.

12.4 Merge Sort

Suppose we have a vector of 10 integers. Let us engage in a bit of wishful thinking and hope that the first half of the vector is already perfectly sorted, and the second half is too, like this:

Now it is an easy matter to *merge* the two sorted arrays into a sorted array, simply by taking taking a new element from either the first or the second subvector and choosing the smaller of the elements each time:

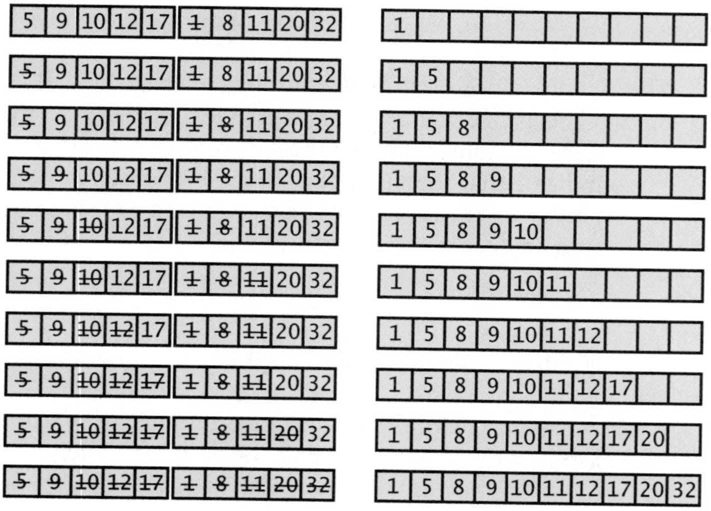

In fact, you probably performed this merging before when you and a friend had to sort a pile of papers. You and the friend split up the pile in the middle, each of you sorted your half, and then you merged the results together.

That is all good and well, but it doesn't seem to solve the problem for the computer. It still has to sort the first and the second half of the array, because it can't very well ask a few buddies to pitch in. As it turns out, though, if the computer keeps dividing the vector into smaller and smaller subvectors, sorting each half and merging them back together, it carries out dramatically fewer steps than the selection sort requires.

Let us write a program that implements this idea. Because we will call the sort procedure multiple times to sort portions of the array, we will supply the range of elements that we would like to have sorted.

```
void merge_sort(vector<int>& a, int from, int to)
{  if (from == to) return;
   int mid = (from + to) / 2;

   /* sort the first and the second half */
   merge_sort(a, from, mid);
   merge_sort(a, mid + 1, to);
   merge(a, from, mid, to);
}
```

The `merge` procedure is somewhat long but actually straightforward.

Program mergsort.cpp

```
#include "ccc.h."

void merge(vector<int>& a, int from, int mid, int to)
{  int n = to - from + 1; /* size of the range to be merged */
   /* merge both halves into a temporary vector b */
   vector<int> b(n);

   int i1 = from;
   /* next element to consider in the first half */
   int i2 = mid + 1;
   /* next element to consider in the second half  */
   int j = 0; /* next open position in b */

   /* as long as neither i1 nor i2 past the end, move the smaller
      element into b */
   while (i1 <= mid && i2 <= to)
   {  if (a[i1] < a[i2])
      {  b[j] = a[i1];
         i1++;
      }
      else
      {  b[j] = a[i2];
         i2++;
```

```
      }
      j++;
   }

   /* note that only one of the two while loops below is executed */

   /* copy any remaining entries of the first half */
   while (i1 <= mid)
   {  b[j] = a[i1];
      i1++;
      j++;

   }
   /* copy any remaining entries of the second half */
   while (i2 <= to)
   {  b[j] = a[i2];
      i2++;
      j++;
   }
   /* copy back from the temporary vector */
   for (j = 0; j < n; j++)
      a[from + j] = b[j];
}

void merge_sort(vector<int>& a, int from, int to)
{  if (from == to) return;
   int mid = (from + to) / 2;

   /* sort the first and the second half */
   merge_sort(a, from, mid);
   merge_sort(a, mid + 1, to);

   merge(a, from, mid, to);
}

void print(vector<int> a)
{  int i;
   for (i = 0; i < a.size(); i++)
      cout << a[i] << " ";
   cout << "\n";
}

int main()
{  vector<int> v(20);
   int i;
   for (i = 0; i < v.size(); i++)
      v[i] = rand_int(1, 100);
   print(v);
   merge_sort(v, 0, v.size() - 1);
   print(v);
```

```
    return EXIT_SUCCESS;
}
```

12.5 Analyzing the Merge Sort Algorithm

This algorithm looks a lot more complicated than the selection sort algorithm, and it appears that it may well take much longer to carry out these repeated subdivisions. However, the timing results for merge sort look much better than those for selection sort:

n	Merge sort (seconds)	Selection sort (seconds)
1000	1	11
2000	2	45
3000	3	101
4000	3	179
5000	4	279
6000	5	403

Figure 2 shows a graph comparing both performance data. That is a tremendous improvement. To understand why, let us estimate the number of array element visits

Figure 2

Merge Sort Timing (Rectangles)versus Selection Sort (Circles)

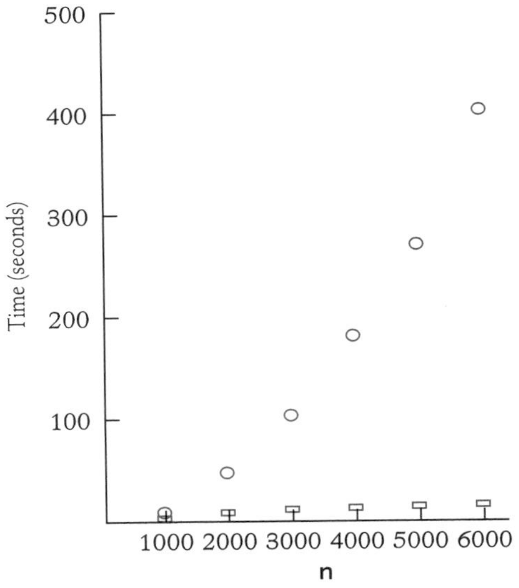

that are required to sort an array with the merge sort algorithm. First, let us tackle the merge process that happens after the first and second half have been sorted.

Each step in the merge process adds one more element to b. There are n elements in b. That element may come from the first or second half, and in most cases the elements from the two halves must be compared to see which one to take. Let us count that as 3 visits (one for b and one each for the two halves of a) per element, or 3n visits total. Then we must copy back from b to a, yielding another 2n visits, for a total of 5n.

If we let $v(n)$ denote the number of visits required to sort a range of n elements through the merge sort process, then we obtain

$$v(n) = v\left(\frac{n}{2}\right) + v\left(\frac{n}{2}\right) + 5n$$

because sorting each half takes $v(n/2)$ visits. (Actually, if n is not even, then we have one subarray of size $(n - 1)/2$ and one of size $(n + 1)/2$. While it turns out that this detail does not affect the outcome of the computation, we will nevertheless assume for now that n is a power of 2, say $n = 2^m$. That way, all subarrays can be evenly divided into two parts.)

Unfortunately, the formula

$$v(n) = 2v\left(\frac{n}{2}\right) + 5n$$

does not clearly tell us the relationship between n and $v(n)$. To understand the relationship, let us evaluate $v(n/2)$, using the same formula:

$$v\left(\frac{n}{2}\right) = 2v\left(\frac{n}{4}\right) + 5\frac{n}{2}$$

Therefore

$$v(n) = 2 \times 2v\left(\frac{n}{4}\right) + 5n + 5n$$

Let us do that again:

$$v\left(\frac{n}{4}\right) = 2v\left(\frac{n}{8}\right) + 5\frac{n}{4}$$

hence

$$v(n) = 2 \times 2 \times 2v\left(\frac{n}{8}\right) + 5n + 5n + 5n$$

This generalizes from 2, 4, 8, to arbitrary powers of 2:

$$v(n) = 2^k v\left(\frac{n}{2^k}\right) + 5nk$$

Recall that we assume that $n = 2^m$; hence, for $k = m$,

$$\begin{aligned} v(n) &= 2^m v\left(\frac{n}{2^m}\right) + 5nm \\ &= nv(1) + 5nm \\ &= n + 5n \log_2 n \end{aligned}$$

(Because $n = 2^m$, we have $m = \log_2 n$.) To establish the growth order, we drop the lower order term n and are left with $5n \log_2 n$. We drop the constant factor 5. It is also customary to drop the base of the logarithm because all logarithms are related by a constant factor. For example,

$$\log_2 x = \log_{10} x / \log_{10} 2 \approx \log_{10} x \times 3.32193$$

Hence we say that merge sort is an $O(n \log n)$ algorithm.

Is an $O(n \log n)$ algorithm better than an $O(n^2)$ algorithm? You bet it is. Recall that it took $100^2 = 10{,}000$ times longer to sort 100,000 records than it takes to sort 1000 records with an $O(n^2)$ algorithm. With an $O(n \log n)$ algorithm, the ratio is

$$\frac{100{,}000 \log 100{,}000}{1000 \log 1000} = 100\left(\frac{5}{3}\right) \approx 167$$

Suppose for the moment that merge sort takes the same time as selection sort to sort an array of 1000 integers, that is, 11 seconds on the test machine. (Actually, it is much faster than that.) Then it would take about 11 × 167 seconds, or about 30 minutes, to sort 100,000 integers. Contrast that with selection sort, which would take over 30 *hours* for the same task. As you can see, even if it takes you 30 hours to learn about a better algorithm, that can be time well spent.

In this chapter we have barely begun to scratch the surface of this interesting topic. There are many sort algorithms, some with even better performance than the merge sort algorithm, and the analysis of these algorithms can be quite challenging. You will revisit these important issues in a later computer science class.

Random Fact 12.1

Ada

In the early 1970s the U.S. Department of Defense (DoD) was seriously concerned about the high cost of the software components of its weapons equipment. It was estimated that more than half of the total DoD budget was spent on the development of this *embedded-systems* software—that is, the software that is embedded in some machinery, such as an airplane or missile, to control it. One of the perceived problems was the great diversity of programming languages that were used to produce that software. Many of these languages, such as TACPOL, CMS-2, SPL/1, and JOVIAL, were virtually unknown outside the defense sector.

In 1976 a committee of computer scientists and defense industry representatives was asked to evaluate existing programming languages. The committee was to determine whether any of them could be made the DoD standard for all future military programming. To nobody's surprise, the committee decided that a new language would need to be created. Contractors were then invited to submit designs for such a new language. Of 17 initial proposals, four were chosen to develop their languages. To ensure an unbiased evaluation, the languages received code names: Red (by Intermetrics), Green (by CII Honeywell Bull) , Blue (by Softech), and Yellow (by SRI International). All four languages were based on Pascal.

The Green language emerged as the winner in 1979. It was named Ada, after Ada Augusta, Countess of Lovelace (1815–1852), a sponsor of Charles Babbage, the 19th century pioneer who built several enormous programmable mechanical calculators (see Figure 3). Ada Lovelace was one of the first people to realize the potential of such a machine, not just for computing mathematical tables but for nonnumerical data processing. She is considered by many the world's first programmer.

In 1983 the Ada standard was finalized. Besides the usual unreadable reference manual that is *de rigueur* for most language standards, the Ada standard had one major innovation:

Figure 3

Babbage's Analytical Engine

a huge *validation suite* of test cases that a compiler had to pass in order to be labeled conformant. Because of this validation suite, Ada compilers from different vendors are highly compatible with one another. In 1995, a second generation of Ada was standardized that supports object-oriented programming and an improved definition of parallel execution of functions.

Ada was not an immediate success. It was a complex language, laden with every feature imaginable that was perceived to be useful for embedded-systems programming. Initial versions of compilers and development systems were slow, unreliable, and expensive. The language was roundly derided by academics as a typical bloated Defense Department product. Military contractors routinely sought, and obtained, exemptions from the requirement that they had to use Ada on their projects. Outside the defense industry, few companies used Ada. This has slowly changed. Ada is now established as the principal language for military software, and it has found application in other large projects.

In hindsight, many of the criticisms leveled against Ada are unfair. C++ has become a language that is every bit as complex and difficult to compile as Ada, but Ada has a more strictly defined standard and a cleaner interaction between language constructs. Ada was ahead of its time in realizing that a modern programming language requires a large number of built-in features to free programmers from having to reinvent these mechanisms.

12.6 Searching

Suppose you need to find the telephone number of your friend. You look up his name in the telephone book, and naturally you can find it quickly, because the telephone book is sorted alphabetically. Quite possibly, you may never have thought how important it is that the telephone book is sorted. To see that, think of the following problem: Suppose you have a telephone number and you must know to what party it belongs. You could of course call that number, but suppose nobody picks up on the other end, or you just get a recording. You could look through the telephone book, a number at a time, until you find the number. That would obviously be a tremendous amount of work, and you would have to be desperate to attempt that.

This thought experiment shows the difference between a search through an unsorted data set and a search through a sorted data set. The following two sections will analyze the difference formally.

If you want to find a number in a sequence of values that occur in arbitrary order, there is nothing you can do to speed up the search. You must simply look through all elements until you have found a match or until you reach the end. This is called a *linear* or *sequential search*.

Here is a procedure that performs a linear search through a vector `v` of integers for the value `a`. The procedure then returns the index of the match, or −1 if `a` does not occur in `v`.

Program lsearch.cpp

```
int linear_search(vector<int> v, int a)
{  int i;
   for (i = 0; i < v.size(); i++)
```

```
   {  if (v[i] == a)
         return i;
   }
   return -1;
}

void print(vector<int> a)
{  int i;
   for (i = 0; i < a.size(); i++)
      cout << a[i] << " ";
   cout << "\n";
}

int main()
{  vector<int> v(20);
   int i;
   for (i = 0; i < v.size(); i++)
      v[i] = rand_int(1, 100);
   print(v);
   cout << "Enter number to search for: ";
   int n;
   cin >> n;
   int j = linear_search(v, n);
   cout << "Found in position " << j << "\n";
   return EXIT_SUCCESS;
}
```

How long does a linear search take? If we assume that the element **a** is present in the vector **v**, then the average search visits $n/2$ elements. If it is not present, then all n elements must be inspected to verify the absence. Either way, a linear search is an $O(n)$ algorithm.

12.7 Binary Search

Now let us search an item in a data sequence that had been previously sorted. Of course, we could still do a linear search, but it turns out we can do much better than that.

Consider the following example: The data set is

v[0]	v[1]	v[2]	v[3]	v[4]	v[5]	v[6]	v[7]
14	43	76	100	115	290	400	511

and we would like to see if the value 123 is in the data set. The last point in the first half of the data set, **v[3]**, is 100. It is smaller than the value we are looking for; hence, we should look in the second half of the data set for a match, that is, in the sequence

v[4]	v[5]	v[6]	v[7]
115	290	400	411

Now the last value of the first half of this sequence is 290; hence, the value must be located in the sequence

v[4]	v[5]
115	290

The last value of the first half of this very short sequence is 115, which is smaller than the value that we are searching, so we must look in the second half:

v[5]
290

It is trivial to see that we don't have a match, because $123 \neq 290$. If we wanted to insert 123 into the sequence, we would need to insert it just before **v[5]**.

This search process is called a *binary search*, because we cut the size of the search in half in each step. That cutting in half works only because we know that the sequence of values is sorted.

The following procedure implements a binary search in a sorted array of integers. It returns the position of the match if the search succeeds, or -1 if **a** is not found in v:

Program bsearch.cpp

```
#include "ccc.h"

int binary_search(vector<int> v, int from, int to, int a)
{  if (from > to)
      return -1;
   int mid = (from + to) / 2;
   int diff = v[mid] - a;
   if (diff == 0) /* v[mid] == a */
      return mid;
   else if (diff < 0) /* v[mid] > a */
      return binary_search(v, mid + 1, to, a);
   else
      return binary_search(v, from, mid - 1, a);
}

void print(vector<int> a)
{  int i;
   for (i = 0; i < a.size(); i++)
      cout << a[i] << " ";
```

```
      cout << "\n";
}

int main()
{  vector<int> v(20);
   int i;
   v[0] = 1;
   for (i = 1; i < v.size(); i++)
      v[i] = v[i - 1] + rand_int(1, 10);
   print(v);
   cout << "Enter number to search for: ";
   int n;
   cin >> n;
   int j = binary_search(v, 0, v.size() - 1, n);
   cout << "Found in position " << j << "\n";
   return EXIT_SUCCESS;
}
```

Let us determine the number of visits of array elements required to carry out a search. We can use the same technique as in the analysis of merge sort and observe that

$$v(n) = v\left(\frac{n}{2}\right) + 1$$

since we look at the middle element, which counts as one comparison, and then search either the left or the right subarray. Using the same equation,

$$v\left(\frac{n}{2}\right) = v\left(\frac{n}{4}\right) + 1$$

and, by plugging it into the original equation, we get

$$v(n) = v\left(\frac{n}{4}\right) + 2$$

That generalizes to

$$v(n) = v\left(\frac{n}{2^k}\right) + k$$

As in the analysis of merge sort, we make the simplifying assumption that n is a power of 2, $n = 2^m$, where $m = \log_2 n$. Then we obtain

$$v(n) = 1 + \log_2 n$$

Therefore, binary search is an $O(\log n)$ algorithm.

That result makes intuitive sense. Suppose that n is 100. Then after each search, the size of the search range is cut in half, to 50, 25, 12, 6, 3, and 1. After seven comparisons we are done.This agrees with our formula since $\log_2 100 \approx 6.64386$, and indeed the next larger power of 2 is $2^7 = 128$.

Since a binary search is so much faster than a linear search, is it worthwhile to sort an array first and then use a binary search? It depends. If you only search the array once, then it is more efficient to pay for an $O(n)$ linear search than for an $O(n \log n)$ sort and and $O(\log n)$ binary search. But if one makes a number of searches in the same array, then sorting it is definitely worthwhile.

12.8 Searching and Sorting Real Data

In this chapter, we have studied how to search and sort vectors of integers. Of course, in real programming there is rarely a need to search through a collection of integers. However, the procedures can be modified easily to search through real data. Here is a procedure that applies the binary search algorithm to find an employee by name. Of course, we must assume that the vector is currently sorted on the name field!

Program esearch.cpp

```
#include "ccc.h"

int binary_search(vector<Employee> v, int from, int to,
   string n)
{  if (from > to)
      return -1;
   int mid = (from + to) / 2;
   if (v[mid].get_name() == n)
      return mid;
   else if (v[mid].get_name() < n)
      return binary_search(v, mid + 1, to, n);
   else
      return binary_search(v, from, mid - 1, n);
}

int main()
{  vector<Employee> staff(5);
   staff[0] = Employee("Cracker, Carl", 48000.0);
   staff[1] = Employee("Hacker, Harry", 35000.0);
   staff[2] = Employee("Lam, Larry", 78000.0);
   staff[3] = Employee("Reindeer, Rudolf", 63000.0);
   staff[4] = Employee("Sandman, Susan", 51500.0);
```

```
    cout << "Enter name of employee to search for: ";
    string name = get_line(cin);
    int i = binary_search(staff, 0, staff.size() - 1,
       name);

    if (i >= 0)
       cout << staff[i].get_name() << " "
          <<staff[i].get_salary() << "\n";
       else
          cout << "Not found.\n";

    return EXIT_SUCCESS;
}
```

Random Fact 12.2

Cataloging Your Necktie Collection

People and companies use computers to organize just about every aspect of our lives. On the whole, computers are tremendously good for collecting and analyzing data. In fact, the power offered by computers and their software makes them seductive solutions for just about any organizational problem. It is easy to lose sight of the fact that using a computer is not always the best solution to a problem.

John Bear [2] describes a home computer user who wrote him to describe how he uses a personal computer. That user catalogs his necktie collection, putting descriptions of the ties into a database and generating reports that list them by color, price, or style. Hopefully that person had another use to justify the purchase of a piece of equipment worth several thousand dollars, but that application was so dear to his heart that he wanted to share it. Perhaps not surprisingly, few other users share that excitement, and you don't find the store shelves of your local software store lined with necktie-cataloging software.

The phenomenon of using technology for its own sake is quite widespread. At the time of this writing, several large corporations show great enthusiasm for using computer networks to deliver movies to home viewers on demand. With today's technology, that is an expensive way of getting a movie to a person's home. Fast network connections and new receiving equipment are required. It sounds like a lot of trouble just to eliminate the trip to the video rental store. Indeed, initial field experiments were sobering. In these experiments, the network lines and computers are simulated by employees putting tapes into remote video tape players. Few customers were willing to pay a sufficient premium for this service to warrant the huge investments needed. At some point in the future, it may well be economical to send movies over computer networks, but at this time the $200 VCR and $3 rental tapes do a better job more cheaply.

As computer programmers, it is our desire to program everything. As computer professionals, though, we owe it to our employers and clients to understand their work process and to deploy computers and software only where they add more value than cost.

12.9 The Efficiency of Recursion

As we have seen in this chapter, recursion can be a powerful tool to implement efficient algorithms. On the other hand, recursion can lead to algorithms that perform poorly. In this section, we will analyze the question of when recursion is beneficial and when it is inefficient.

Consider the Fibonacci sequence introduced in Chapter 5: a sequence of numbers defined by the equation

$$f_1 = 1$$
$$f_2 = 1$$
$$f_n = f_{n-1} + f_{n-2}$$

That is, each value of the sequence is the sum of the two preceding values. The first ten terms of the sequence are

1, 1, 2, 3, 5, 8, 13, 21, 34, 55

It is easy to extend this sequence indefinitely. Just keep appending the sum of the last two values of the sequence. For example, the next entry is 34 + 55 = 89.

We would like to write a function that computes f_n for any value of n. Suppose we translate the definition directly into a recursive function.

Program fibtime.cpp

```
#include "ccc.h"

int fib(int n)
{  if (n <= 2) return 1;
   else return f(n - 1) + f(n - 2);
}

int main()
{  cout << "Enter n: ";
   int n;
   cin >> n;
   Time before;
   int f = fib(n);
   Time after;
   cout << "fib(" << n << ") = " << f << "\n";
   cout << "Elapsed time = " << after.seconds_from(before)
      << " seconds\n";
   return EXIT_SUCCESS;
}
```

That is certainly simple, and the function will work correctly. However, consider the following timing data. They indicate that the function runs quite slowly, even for moderate values of *n*:

n	Seconds
30	3
31	4
32	7
33	12
34	21
35	33
36	53
37	85

That makes no sense. Armed with pencil, paper, and a pocket calculator you could calculate f_{37} in under a minute, so it shouldn't take the computer so long. (Try it out: Extend the sequence to its 37th term. It is 24,157,817.)

To find out the problem, let us insert trace messages into the function.

Program fibtrace.cpp

```
#include "iostream.h"
#include "stdlib.h"

int fib(int n)
{  cout << "Entering fib: n = " << n << "\n";
   int f;
   if (n <= 2) f = 1;
   else f = fib(n - 1) + fib(n - 2);
   cout << "Exiting fib: n = " << n
      << " return value = " << f << "\n";
   return f;
}

int main()
{  cout << "Enter n: ";
   int n;
   cin >> n;
   int f = fib(n);
   cout << "fib(" << n << ") = " << f << "\n";
   return EXIT_SUCCESS;
}
```

Here is the trace for computing `fib(7)`:

```
Entering fib: n = 7
Entering fib: n = 6
Entering fib: n = 5
Entering fib: n = 4
Entering fib: n = 3
Entering fib: n = 2
Exiting fib: n = 2 return value = 1
Entering fib: n = 1
Exiting fib: n = 1 return value = 1
Exiting fib: n = 3 return value = 2
Entering fib: n = 2
Exiting fib: n = 2 return value = 1
Exiting fib: n = 4 return value = 3
Entering fib: n = 3
Entering fib: n = 2
Exiting fib: n = 2 return value = 1
Entering fib: n = 1
Exiting fib: n = 1 return value = 1
Exiting fib: n = 3 return value = 2
Exiting fib: n = 5 return value = 5
Entering fib: n = 4
Entering fib: n = 3
Entering fib: n = 2
Exiting fib: n = 2 return value = 1
Entering fib: n = 1
Exiting fib: n = 1 return value = 1
Exiting fib: n = 3 return value = 2
Entering fib: n = 2
Exiting fib: n = 2 return value = 1
Exiting fib: n = 4 return value = 3
Exiting fib: n = 6 return value = 8
Entering fib: n = 5
Entering fib: n = 4
Entering fib: n = 3
Entering fib: n = 2
Exiting fib: n = 2 return value = 1
Entering fib: n = 1
Exiting fib: n = 1 return value = 1
Exiting fib: n = 3 return value = 2
Entering fib: n = 2
Exiting fib: n = 2 return value = 1
Exiting fib: n = 4 return value = 3
Entering fib: n = 3
Entering fib: n = 2
Exiting fib: n = 2 return value = 1
Entering fib: n = 1
Exiting fib: n = 1 return value = 1
Exiting fib: n = 3 return value = 2
Exiting fib: n = 5 return value = 5
Exiting fib: n = 7 return value = 13
```

Now it is becoming apparent why the function takes so long. It is computing the same values over and over. For example, the computation of `fib(7)` calls `fib(4)` three times and `fib(3)` five times. That is very different from the computation we would do with pencil and paper. There we would just write down the values as they were computed and add up the last two to get the next one until we reached the desired entry; no sequence value would ever be computed twice.

If we exactly imitate the pencil-and-paper process, then we get the following program.

Program fibloop.cpp

```
#include "ccc.h"

int fib(int n)
{  if (n <= 2) return 1;
   int fold = 1;
   int fold2 = 1;
   int i;
   int fnew;
   for (i = 3; i <= n; i++)
   {  fnew = fold + fold2;
      fold2 = fold;
      fold = fnew;
   }
   return fnew;
}

int main()
{  cout << "Enter n: ";
   int n;
   cin >> n;
   Time before;
   int f = fib(n);
   Time after;
   cout << "fib(" << n << ") = " << f << "\n";
   cout  << "Elapsed time = " <<
      after.seconds_from(before) << " seconds\n";
   return EXIT_SUCCESS;
}
```

This function runs *much* faster than the recursive version.

In this example of the `fib` function, the recursive solution was easy to program because it exactly followed the mathematical definition, but it ran far more slowly than the iterative solution, because it computed many intermediate results multiple times.

Let $T(n)$ denote the number of times the recursive `fib` function calls itself when computing the nth Fibonacci number. It can be shown that $T(n)$ is of the same order as f_n, and that f_n is equal to the integer closest to $g^n/\sqrt{5}$, where $g = (1 + \sqrt{5})/2$ is the so-called *golden ratio number*. (See [3] for a proof.) Hence the running time of the recursive `fib` function is $O(g^n)$. This is an example of *exponential growth*. When n gets larger, the exponential term g^n grows very rapidly—much more rapidly than a polynomial such as n^2.

It is not always true that the recursive solution to a problem is slower than a nonrecursive one. Frequently, the iterative and recursive solution have essentially the same performance. For example, the computation of $n!$ can be equally well performed with a recursive function

```
int factorial(int n)
{  if (n <= 0) return 1;
   else return n * factorial(n - 1);
}
```

or a simple loop,

```
int factorial(int n)
{  int r = 1;
   int i;
   for (i = 1; i <= n; i++)
      r = r * i;
   return r;
}
```

There is a good reason to choose the loop over the recursion. Each function call takes a certain amount of processor time. Nested function calls also consume a small amount of space for the return address and the local variables of the nested functions. It is in principle possible to exhaust the space set aside for these data values (the so-called run-time stack).

Let us reconsider the binary search function from Section 12.7. Is it possible to remove the recursion? After we compare `a` with the middle element, we can just reset the boundaries of the range to the selected subrange and recompute its middle. This can be done in a loop.

```
int binary_search(vector<int> v, int a)
{  int from = 0;
   int to = v.size() - 1;
   while (from <= to)
   {  int mid = (from + to) / 2;
      int diff = v[mid] - a;
      if (diff == 0) /* v[mid] == a */
         return mid;
      else if (diff > 0) /* v[mid] > a */
         from = mid + 1;
      else
         to = mid - 1;
   }
   return -1;
}
```

Can we rewrite the merge sort algorithm in the same way? There is an essential difference between the recursive calls in binary search and merge sort. In binary search, the range was cut in half and only one of the two subranges was further considered. In merge sort, *both* subranges are again subdivided. There is no easy way to capture this in a simple loop. While it is possible to write a nonrecursive version of merge sort, such a procedure would be extremely complex. In this situation, the recursive procedure is an example of the effective use of recursion.

Chapter Summary

1. Algorithms that perform the same task can have significant differences in performance. We analyzed two sorting algorithms: selection sort and merge sort. Both rearrange an array in sorted order, but merge sort is much faster on large data sets.

2. Computer scientists use big-Oh notation to give approximate descriptions of the efficiency of algorithms. In big-Oh notation only the fastest-growing term is important; constant factors are ignored. Selection sort is an $O(n^2)$ algorithm; merge sort is an $O(n \log n)$ algorithm.

3. Searching a value in an unsorted data set requires $O(n)$ steps. If the data set is sorted, binary search can find it in $O(\log n)$ steps.

4. Recursive algorithms are often more convenient to program, but they can be slower than iterative algorithms. They are, however, essential for algorithms, such as merge sort, that cannot easily be rewritten as an iteration.

Further Reading

[1] Robert Sedgwick, *Algorithms in C++,* Addison-Wesley, 1992.

[2] John Bear, *Computer Wimp,* Ten Speed Press, 1983.

[3] Donald E. Knuth, *The Art of Computer Programing, Vol. 1: Fundamental Algorithms,* Addison-Wesley, 1973.

Review Exercises

Exercise R12.1. *Checking against off-by-1 errors.* When writing the selection sort algorithm of Section 12.1, a programmer must make the usual choices of < against

`<=`, `a.size()` against `a.size() - 1`, and `next` against `next + 1`. This is a fertile ground for off-by-1 errors. Make code walkthroughs of the algorithm with arrays of length 0, 1, 2, and 3 and check carefully that all index values are correct.

Exercise R12.2. What is the difference between searching and sorting?

Exercise R12.3. For the following expressions, what is the order of the growth of each?

$$n^2 + 2n + 1$$
$$n^{10} + 9n^9 + 20n^8 + 145n^7$$
$$(n + 1)^4$$
$$(n^2 + n)^2$$
$$n + 0.001n^3$$
$$n^3 - 1000n^2 + 10^9$$
$$n + \log n$$
$$n^2 + n \log n$$
$$2^n + n^2$$
$$(n^3 + 2n)/(n^2 + 0.75)$$

Exercise R12.4. We determined that the actual number of visits in the selection sort algorithm is

$$v(n) = \tfrac{1}{2}n^2 + \tfrac{5}{2}n - 3$$

We then characterized this function as having $O(n^2)$ growth. Compute the actual ratios

$$v(2000)/v(1000)$$
$$v(2000)/v(1000)$$
$$v(10000)/v(1000)$$

and compare them with

$$f(2000)/f(1000)$$
$$f(2000)/f(1000)$$
$$f(10000)/f(1000)$$

where $f(n) = n^2$.

Exercise R12.5. Suppose algorithm A takes 5 seconds to handle a data set of 1000 records. If the algorithm A is an $O(n)$ algorithm, how long will it take to handle a data set of 2000 records? Of 10,000 records?

Exercise R12.6. Suppose an algorithm takes 5 seconds to handle a data set of 1,000 records. Fill in the following table, which shows the approximate growth of the execution times depending on the complexity of the algorithm.

	$O(n)$	$O(n^2)$	$O(n^3)$	$O(n \log n)$	$O(2^n)$
1000	5	5	5	5	5
2000					
3000		45			
10000					

For example, since $3000^2/1000^2 = 9$, the algorithm would take 9 times as long, or 45 seconds, to handle a data set of 3000 records.

Exercise R12.7. Sort the following growth rates from slowest growth to fastest growth.

$$O(n)$$
$$O(n^3)$$
$$O(n^n)$$
$$O(\log n)$$
$$O(n^2 \log n)$$
$$O(n \log n)$$
$$O(2^n)$$
$$O(\sqrt{n})$$
$$O(n\sqrt{n})$$
$$O(n^{\log n})$$

Exercise R12.8. What is the order of complexity of the standard algorithm to find the minimum value of an array? Of finding both the minimum and the maximum?

Exercise R12.9. What is the order of complexity of the following function?

```
int count(vector<int> a, int c)
{  int i;
   int count = 0;
```

```
    for (i = 0; i < a.size(); i++)
    {  if (a[i] == c) count++;
    }
    return count;
}
```

Exercise R12.10. Your task is to remove all duplicates from an array. For example, if the array has the values

4 7 11 4 9 5 11 7 3 5

then the array should be changed to

4 7 11 9 5 3

Here is a simple algorithm. Look at `a[i]`. Count how many times it occurs in `a`. If the count is larger than 1, remove it. What is the order of complexity of this algorithm?

Exercise R12.11. Consider the following algorithm to remove all duplicates from an array. Sort the array. For each element in the array, look at its two neighbors to decide whether it is present more than once. If so, remove it. Is this a faster algorithm than the one in the preceding exercise?

Exercise R12.12. Develop a fast algorithm for removing duplicates from an array if the resulting array must have the same ordering as the original array.

Exercise R12.13. Consider the following sorting algorithm. To sort `a`, make a second array `b` of the same size. Then insert elements from `a` into `b`, keeping `b` in sorted order. For each element, call the binary search function of Exercise P12.7 to determine where it needs to be inserted. To insert an element into the middle of an array, you need to move all elements above the insert location up.

Is this an efficient algorithm? Estimate the number of array element visits in the sorting process. Assume that on average half of the elements of `b` need to be moved to insert a new element.

Exercise R12.14. Make a walkthrough of selection sort with the following data sets.

4 7 11 4 9 5 11 7 3 5

−7 6 8 7 5 9 0 11 10 5 8

Exercise R12.15. Make a walkthrough of merge sort with the following data sets.

5 11 7 3 5 4 7 11 4 9

9 0 11 10 5 8 −7 6 8 7 5

Exercise R12.16. Make a walkthrough of the following:

Linear search for 7 in −7 1 3 3 4 7 11 13

Binary search for 8 in −7 2 2 3 4 7 8 11 13

Binary search for 8 in −7 1 2 3 5 7 10 13

Programming Exercises

Exercise P12.1. Modify the selection sort algorithm to sort a vector of integers in descending order.

Exercise P12.2. Modify the selection sort algorithm to sort a vector of employees by salary.

Exercise P12.3. Write a program that generates the table of sample runs of the selection sort times automatically. The program should ask for the smallest and largest value of `n` and the number of measurements and then make all sample runs.

Exercise P12.4. Modify the merge sort algorithm to sort a vector of employees by salary.

Exercise P12.5. Write a telephone lookup program. Read a data set of 1000 names and telephone numbers from a file that contains the numbers in random order. Handle lookups by name and also reverse lookups by phone number. Use a binary search for both lookups.

Exercise P12.6. Modify the binary search algorithm so that you can search the records stored in a *database file* without actually reading them into a vector. Use the employee database of Chapter 10, sort it by product name, and make lookups for products.

Exercise P12.7. Consider the binary search function in Section 12.2.2. If no match is found, the function returns −1. Modify the function so that it returns a `bool` value indicating whether a match was found. Add a reference parameter `m`, which is set to the location of the match if the search was successful. If `a` was not found, set `m` to the index of the next larger value instead, or to `a.size()` if `a` is larger than all the elements of the vector.

Exercise P12.8. Use the modification of the binary search function of the preceding exercise to sort an array. Make a second array of the same size as the array to be sorted. For each element in the first array, call binary search on the second array to find out where the new element should be inserted. Then move all elements above

Figure 4

Graphical Animation

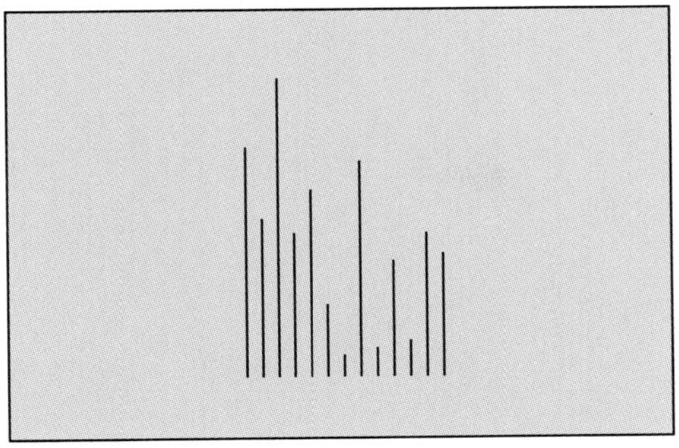

the insertion point up by one slot and insert the new element. Thus, the second array is always kept sorted. Implement this algorithm and measure its performance.

Exercise P12.9. Implement the `merge_sort` procedure without recursion, where the size of the vector is a power of 2. First merge adjacent regions of size 1, then adjacent regions of size 2, then adjacent regions of size 4, and so on.

Exercise P12.10. Implement the `merge_sort` procedure without recursion, where the size of the vector is an arbitrary number. *Hint:* Use a stack to keep track of which subarrays have been sorted.

Exercise P12.11. Give a *graphical animation* of selection sort as follows: Fill an array with a set of random numbers between 1 and 100. Set the window coordinate system to `a.size()` by 100. Draw each array element as a stick, as in Figure 4. Whenever you change the array, clear the screen and redraw.

Exercise P12.12. Write a graphical animation of merge sort.

Exercise P12.13. Write a graphical animation of binary search. Highlight the currently inspected element.

Exercise 12.14. Find out how often the recursive version of `fib` calls itself. Keep a global variable `fib_count` and increment it once in every call of `fib`. What is the relationship between `fib(n)` and `fib_count`?

Exercise 12.15. Write a program that keeps an appointment book. Make a class `Appointment` that stores a description of the appointment, the starting time, and the ending time. Your program should keep the appointments in a sorted vector. Users can add appointments and print out all appointments for a given day. When a new appointment is added, use binary search to find where it should be inserted in the vector. Do not add it if it conflicts with another appointment.

CHAPTER 13

An Introduction to Data Structures

Objectives

- To learn about linked lists and binary trees
- To understand about pointers and dynamic memory allocation
- To be able to program linked lists
- To be able to program insertion and removal of list and tree elements
- To learn about ANSI standard lists and iterators

13.1 Vector-Based Linked Lists

Imagine a program that maintains a vector of employee records, sorted by the last name of the employees. When a new employee is hired, a record needs to be inserted into the vector. Unless the name of the new employee begins with Z, it is likely to need to be inserted into the middle of the vector; then all other employee records must be moved downwards.

Before:

Index	Employee
0	`Cracker, Carl`
1	`Hacker, Harry`
2	`Lam, Larry`
3	`Sandman, Susan`

After:

Index	Employee
0	`Cracker, Carl`
1	`Hacker, Harry`
2	`Lam, Larry`
3	`Reindeer, Rudolf`
4	`Sandman, Susan`

Conversely, if an employee leaves the company, the hole in the sequence needs to be closed up by moving all employee records that came after it.

Employee records contain the name and salary of the employee. In a realistic application, they also contain the address, telephone extension and other information. These can be fairly substantial data sets. When an employee record is moved, all those data need to be copied from the old location to the new location. Moving a large number of employee records can involve a substantial amount of computer time. We would like to discover a method that minimizes this cost.

Suppose we simply inserted every newly hired employee at the end of the vector of employees. Of course, that would minimize movement of records, but unless the company managed to hire employees in dictionary order, the vector would not be sorted. Let us therefore enhance the records so that each record remembers the position of the next employee in the sequence.

Index	Employee	Next
0	`Lam, Larry`	1
1	`Sandman, Susan`	−1
2	`Cracker, Carl`	3
3	`Hacker, Harry`	0

We also need to remember where the first record is stored. In the example, it is located at index 2.

Now it is easy to print out the sequence of employees in sorted order. Start with the first one, at position 2 and print `Cracker, Carl`. Then look up the index of the next employee; it is 3. Print that employee, `Hacker, Harry`, and find the index of the next employee, 0. Print `Lam, Larry` and move to the next one at index 1. After printing `Sandman, Susan`, we are done, because the next index is −1, the signal that we reached the last employee.

Let us add a new employee: `Reindeer, Rudolf`. As promised, the record is appended at the end of the array, at position 4, without moving any of the existing records. In the sort order, it comes after `Lam, Larry` at position 0 and before `Sandman, Susan` at position 1. We must therefore update the next position of `Lam, Larry` to point to the new record, and the next field of the new record must point to position 1.

Index	Employee	Next
0	`Lam, Larry`	4
1	`Sandman, Susan`	−1
2	`Cracker, Carl`	3
3	`Hacker, Harry`	0
4	`Reindeer, Rudolf`	2

Such a data organization is called a *linked list.* Each record has a *link* to the next record, namely the index through which the next record can be located.

The actual position of the records in the vector is completely accidental. When drawing a picture of the data organization, it is customary to draw each record as a separate rectangle, and to draw the links as arrows. For example, the linked list of employees in our example is rendered as in Figure 1.

Let us now implement the linked list in C++. We don't want to mess with the employee class definition, so we define a helper class that contains the employee record and the position of the next record:

```
class EmployeeLink
{
private:
   Employee data;
   int next;
friend class EmployeeList;
};
```

Note the `friend` declaration. It indicates that the `EmployeeList` member functions are allowed to inspect and modify the data members of the `EmployeeLink` class, which we will write presently.

A class should not grant friendship to another class lightly, because it breaks the privacy protection. In this case it makes sense, though, since the list code does all the

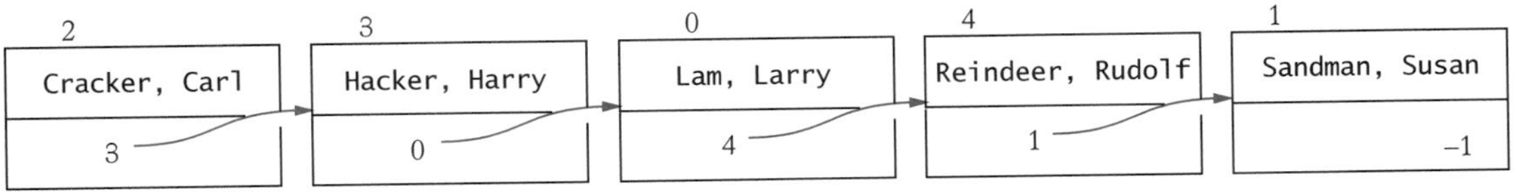

Figure 1

Linked List

necessary work and the link class is just an artifact of the implementation. Note that no other code besides the list member functions can access the link fields.

The list consists of a sequence of links, and the index of the first link in the list:

```
class EmployeeList
{
public:
   EmployeeList();
   void insert(Employee e);
   void print() const;
private:
   vector<EmployeeLink> links;
   int first;
};

EmployeeList::EmployeeList()
{  first = -1;
}
```

Here is the code to print all records in the list in sorted order.

```
void EmployeeList::print() const
{  int current = first;
   while (current != -1)
   {  cout << links[current].data.get_name() << "\n";
      current = links[current].next;
   }
}
```

Now let us write the code to insert a new employee into the list. The basic idea is straightforward: We must find the predecessor of the new record. Its next value must point to the new record, and the next value of the new record must point to the predecessor's successor. (See Figure 2.)

```
links[new_record].next = links[pre].next;
links[pre].next = new_record;
```

Figure 2

Inserting a Record into a Linked List

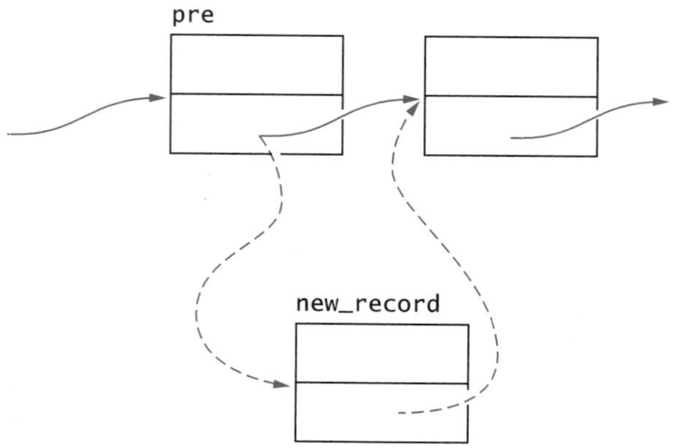

Figure 3

Inserting a Record at the First Position

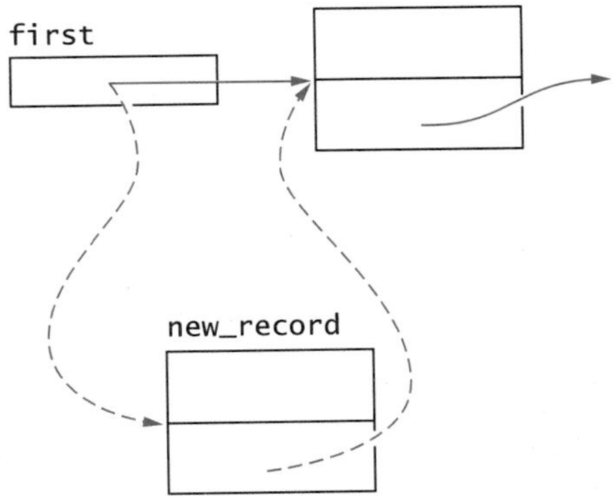

There is one special case. Suppose the new record comes before *all* other records in the list. Then we must update `first` to point to the new record, and the next field of the new record points to the record that used to be the first one. (See Figure 3.)

```
links[new_record].next = first;
first = new_record;
```

The following program contains the complete insert procedure.

Program elist1.cpp

```
#include "ccc.h"

class EmployeeLink
{
private:
   Employee data;
   int next;
friend class EmployeeList;
};

class EmployeeList
{
public:
   EmployeeList();
   void insert(Employee e);
   void print() const;
private:
   vector<EmployeeLink> links;
   int first;
};

void EmployeeList::insert(Employee e)
{  EmployeeLink new_link;
   new_link.data = e;
```

```
   new_link.next = -1;
   links.push_back(new_link);
   int new_record = links.size() - 1;
   if (first == -1
      or links[first].data.get_name() > e.get_name())
   {  /* make e the first record*/
      links[new_record].next = first;
      first = new_record;
   }
   else
   {  /* find the predecessor of e */
      int pre = first;
      int succ = links[pre].next;
      /* the next position after pre */
      while (succ != -1
         and links[succ].data.get_name() < e.get_name())
      {  pre = succ;
         succ = links[pre].next;
      }
      links[new_record].next = succ;
      links[pre].next = new_record;
   }
}

EmployeeList::EmployeeList()
{  first = -1;
}

void EmployeeList::print() const
{  int current = first;
   while (current != -1)
   {  cout << links[current].data.get_name() << "\n";
      current = links[current].next;
   }
}

int main()
{  EmployeeList staff;
   bool done = false;
   while (not done)
   {  cout << "Enter name: ";
      string name = get_line(cin);
      if (cin.fail()) done = true;
      else staff.insert(Employee(name, 0));
   }
   staff.print();
   return EXIT_SUCCESS;

}
```

What do we do when an employee leaves the company? Even if we make an effort to fire employees in reverse order of hiring, there may be employees who leave on their own initiative or who retire or die. We would then have a gap in our sequence of employees. Of course, we could fill the gap by moving the last employee from the vector into the gap and adjusting the links, but that gets a little complicated. It turns out that obtaining and releasing space for data records is such a common task that there is special support for it. We will discuss that in the next section.

To build a linked list, it really isn't necessary to store all elements in a vector. A vector is useful to store elements in a particular sequence, but the sequence in which the employee records are stored is entirely random. We use the links to keep them in order. All we actually need is some space for the records and a way of locating them. In the next section we will see how to allocate objects without using a vector.

13.2 Dynamic Memory Allocation

The C++run-time system can create new objects for us. When we ask for a

```
new Employee
```

then the *memory allocator* finds a storage location for a new employee record. The memory allocator keeps a large storage area, called the *heap,* for that purpose. The heap is a very flexible pool for memory. It can hold values of any type. We can equally well ask for

```
new Time
new Circle
```

When allocating a new heap value, the storage manager also tells us where the value is located, by giving us the *memory address* for it. To manipulate memory addresses, we need to learn about a new C++ data type: the *pointer.* A pointer to an employee record,

```
Employee* boss;
```

contains the location or memory address for the employee object. A pointer to a circle,

```
Circle* bubble;
```

stores the memory address for a circle object. The types `Employee*` and `Circle*` denote pointers to employees and circles. Variables of type `Employee*` and `Circle*` can store the location or memory address of link and circle objects. They cannot store actual employees and circles, however (see Figure 4).

When a new object is created on the heap, you may want to initialize it. You can supply construction parameters, using the familiar syntax.

```
Circle* bubble = new Circle(Point(1, 2), 3);
```

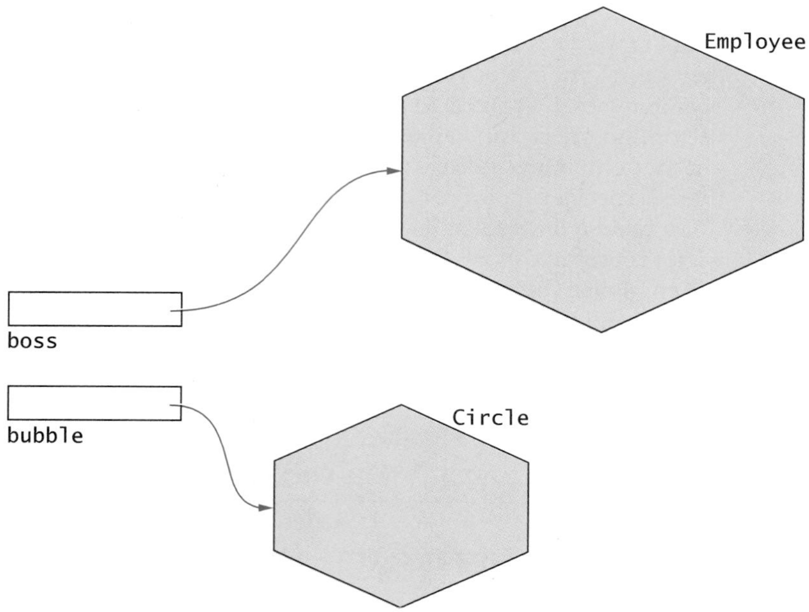

Figure 4

Pointers and the Objects to Which They Point

When we have a pointer to a value, we need to be able to access the value to which it points. That action—to go from the pointer to the value—is called *dereferencing*. In C++, the * operator is used to indicate the value associated with a pointer. For example, if `bubble` is a `Circle*`, then `*bubble` is a `Circle` value:

```
Circle* bubble = new Circle(Point(1, 2), 3);
cwin << *bubble;
```

When you make a variable of type `Circle`, then the memory for the Circle is allocated on the so-called *run-time stack*. The memory automatically goes away when the program leaves the block in which the variable is allocated.

```
void f()
{  Circle c; ← memory for c allocated on the stack
   . . .
}  ← memory for c automatically reclaimed
```

Values that are allocated on a heap do not follow this automatic allocation and reclamation discipline. You allocate values on the heap with **new**, and you must reclaim them using the **delete** operator.

```
void g()
{  Circle* bubble;
   bubble = new Circle;  ← memory for circle
                           allocated on the heap
   . . .
   delete bubble;  ← memory for circle manually reclaimed
}
```

Actually, the foregoing example is a little more complex than that. There are two allocations: one on the stack and one on the heap. The variable **bubble** is allocated on the stack. It is of type **Circle***; that is, **bubble** can hold the address of a circle object. At the end of the block, the storage space for the variable **bubble** on the stack is automatically reclaimed. After **bubble** is declared, a value of type **Circle** is manually allocated on the heap, and it is manually reclaimed before exit.

Note that the pointer variable on the stack has a *name,* namely **bubble**. But the circle value, allocated on the heap with **new Circle**, has no name! It can be reached only through the **bubble** pointer. Values on the stack always have names; heap values do not.

When a pointer variable is first defined, it contains a random address. Using that random address is very dangerous and will very likely crash the program or corrupt data:

```
Circle* bubble;
cwin << *bubble; /* NO!!! bubble contains a random address */
```

You must always make a pointer point to an actual value before you can use it:

```
Circle* bubble = new Circle(Point(1, 2), 3);
cwin << *bubble; /* OK */
```

After you delete the value attached to the pointer, you can no longer use that address. It may already be given out to someone else!

```
delete bubble;
cwin << *bubble; /* NO!!! next points to a deleted element */
```

There is one special value **NULL** that can be used to indicate a pointer that doesn't point anywhere. You should always set pointer variables to **NULL** when they are defined and not immediately filled with an actual memory address.

```
Circle* bubble = NULL; /* will fill later */
. . .
if (bubble != NULL) cwin << *next;
```

You cannot dereference a null pointer, either; the purpose of a null pointer is to test that it doesn't point to any valid object.

Common Error 13.1

Dangling Pointers

The most common pointer error is to use a pointer that has not been initialized or that has already been deleted. Such a pointer is called a *dangling* pointer, because it does point somewhere. You can create real damage by writing to the location to which it points.

An uninitialized pointer has a good chance of pointing to an address that your program does not own. On most operating systems, attempting to read from that location or to write to it causes a processor error and the operating system shuts down the program. You may have seen that happen to other programs—a dialog with a bomb icon or a message such as "general protection fault" or "segmentation fault" comes up, and the program is shut down. Less sophisticated operating systems—in particular, DOS—are not so helpful. You can read from all pointers and get random garbage back when one points to a random location. If you write to a random pointer, you can create random damage, such as disabling the computer keyboard or crashing the operating system.

If the dangling pointer does point to a valid memory location, then writing to it will damage *your* program. You will change the value of one of your variables, or perhaps damage the control structures of the heap so that after several calls to new, something crazy happens.

When your program crashes and you restart it, the problem may not reappear, or it may manifest itself in different ways because the random pointer is now initialized with a different random address. Programming with pointers requires iron discipline, because you can create true damage with dangling pointers.

Always initialize pointer variables. If you can't initialize them with the return value of new, initialize with NULL.

Never use a pointer that has been deleted. Some people immediately set every pointer to NULL after deleting it. That is certainly helpful:

```
delete first;
first = NULL;
```

Unfortunately, it is not a complete solution.

```
second = first;
. . .
delete first;
first = NULL;
/* must still remember that second is now invalid */
```

On a PC, consider running under Windows, not DOS. Windows traps some invalid pointers, DOS does not.

Common Error 13.2

Confusing Pointers with the Data to Which They Point

A pointer is a memory address—essentially a long integer telling where a variable is stored in memory. You don't ever do anything with a pointer except store it so that you can remember where some important piece of information is located. Confusing the pointer with the data to which it points is a common error.

```
Circle* bubble = new Circle(Point(1, 2), 3);
cwin << bubble; /* Error */
```

Remember that the pointer `bubble` only describes *where* the circle object is. To actually refer to the circle object, use `*bubble`.

```
cwin << *bubble; /* OK */
```

Common Error 13.3

Declaring Two Pointers on the Same Line

It is legal in C++ to define multiple variables together, like this:

```
int i = 0, j = 1;
```

This style will *not* work with pointers:

```
Circle* p, q;
```

For historical reasons, the * associates only with the first variable. That is, `p` is a circle pointer, but `q` is a circle.

In this book we never define multiple variables in one line. If you follow that style, you won't have any problems with pointer definitions either.

Advanced Topic 13.1

The -> Operator

Suppose `bubble` is a pointer to a circle, and we want to find out the center to the circle:

```
Circle* bubble;
. . .
Point p = *bubble.get_center(); /* Error */
```

Unfortunately, that is a syntax error. The dot operator has a higher precedence than the * operator. That is, the compiler thinks that you mean

```
Circle* bubble;
. . .
Point p = *(bubble.get_center()); /* Error */
```

However, `circle` is a pointer, not an object. You can't apply `.` to a pointer, and the compiler reports an error.

You must make it clear that you first want to apply the *, then the dot:

```
Circle* bubble;
. . .
Point p = (*bubble).get_center(); /* OK */
```

Because it is such a common situation, the designers of C++ supply an operator to abbreviate the "dereference and take member" operation. That operator is written -> and usually pronounced as "arrow".

```
Point p = bubble->get_center(); /* OK */
```

Many programmers prefer the compact

pointer->*member*

notation. However, in this book, we will use the explicit

(**pointer*).*member*

construction. There are two reasons. Beginners generally find it clearer, and the ANSI C++ iterators (pointerlike objects for container traversal) do not support the -> notation. Using the * operator for both pointers and iterators seems more consistent.

13.3 Linked Lists with Dynamic Memory Allocation

We will now implement linked lists that allocate the links on the heap, not in a vector. We must modify the vector-based implementation in four ways:

1. Remove the vector `links` from the `EmployeeList` class.
2. Change the integer positions `first` and `next` that point inside the `vector<EmployeeLink>` and make them into `EmployeeLink*` pointers.
3. Change the call to `push_back` into a call to `new EmployeeLink`.
4. Use `NULL`, not −1, for pointers that point nowhere.

The data structures become

```
class EmployeeLink
{
private:
   Employee data;
   EmployeeLink* next;
friend class EmployeeList;
};

class EmployeeList
{
public:
   EmployeeList();
   void insert(Employee e);
   void print() const;
private:
   EmployeeLink* first;
};
```

Figure 5

Inserting into a Linked List on the Heap

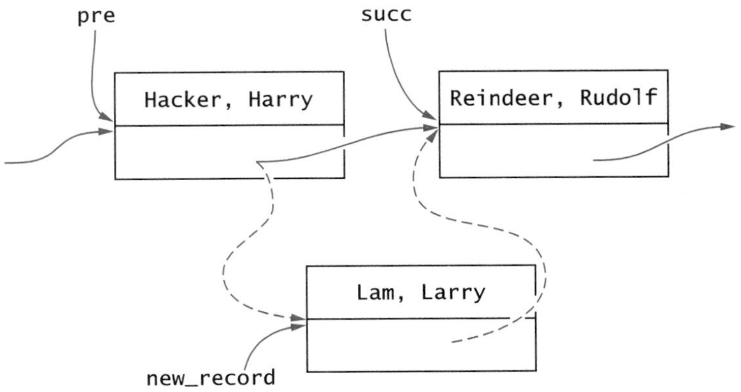

To see how the pointers are used, we will first look at the code to print the contents of the list:

```
void EmployeeList::print() const
{  EmployeeLink* current = first;
   while (current != NULL)
   {  cout << (*current).data.get_name() << "\n";
      current = (*current).next;
   }
}
```

This code is actually a little simpler than the code in Section 13.1, because the array `links` has gone away. It is simpler to think of the current link (`*current`) instead of the element `links[current]`.

You will need to study the `insert` procedure quite closely. Note how the new link is obtained from the heap. Figure 5 shows the pointer variables `pre` and `succ` when the new link is inserted into the list.

Program elist2.cpp

```
#include "ccc.h"

class EmployeeLink
{
private:
   Employee data;
   EmployeeLink* next;
friend class EmployeeList;
};

class EmployeeList
{
public:
   EmployeeList();
```

```
   void insert(Employee e);
   void print() const;
private:
   EmployeeLink* first;
};

EmployeeList::EmployeeList()
{  first = NULL;
}

void EmployeeList::insert(Employee e)
{  EmployeeLink* new_record = new EmployeeLink;
   (*new_record).data = e;
   if (first == NULL
      or (*first).data.get_name() > e.get_name())
   {  /* make  e the first record */
      (*new_record).next = first;
      first = new_record;
   }
   else
   {  /* find the predecessor of e */
      EmployeeLink* pre = first;
      EmployeeLink* succ = (*pre).next;
      /* the next position after pre */
      while (succ != NULL
         and (*succ).data.get_name() < e.get_name())
      {  pre = succ;
         succ = (*pre).next;
      }
      (*new_record).next = succ;
      (*pre).next = new_record;
   }
}

void EmployeeList::print() const
{  EmployeeLink* current = first;
   while (current != NULL)
   {  cout << (*current).data.get_name() <<  "\n";
      current = (*current).next;
   }
}

int main()
{  EmployeeList staff;
   bool done = false;
   while (not done)
   {  cout << "Enter name: ";
      string name = get_line(cin);
```

```
        if (cin.fail()) done = true;
        else staff.insert(Employee(name, 0));
    }
    staff.print();
    return EXIT_SUCCESS;
}
```

Random Fact 13.1

Garbage Collection

Managing heap memory is a tedious and error-prone activity. You have to allocate memory (for example for the links of a list) when you need it. That is usually not a problem. The problem is that you must remember to get rid of it again when you don't need it any more. If you don't ever delete heap memory and your program runs for a long time, it will exhaust all available memory. If you delete it too early and continue using it, your program will crash or act flaky.

Heap allocation bugs are among the most insidious bugs in C++ programs. They are quite common but extremely difficult and time-consuming to track down. Many modern languages, but unfortunately not C++, offer a better way: *garbage collection.* A garbage collector periodically identifies which heap objects are still pointed at by some pointer, and reclaims those that are no longer in use. There is a problem with garbage collection: It is slow. It takes time to track all pointers and the locations to which they point. However, garbage collection algorithms have improved in recent years, and the cost is now tolerable for many applications.

13.4 List Element Access with a Cursor

We have now seen how elements are inserted into a linked list. Once they are in the list, we can print the contents. But suppose we want to analyze the data in the list. We have no access functions at all.

Accessing an element in an array is simple: You just use an integer index. To allow access to any element in a linked list, we will come up with a similar mechanism that is suitable for this data structure. We will add a *cursor position* to the list, a pointer to a particular link (see Figure 6). The programmer can move the cursor position from the beginning of the list to the end and inspect each list element.

There are four cursor manipulation functions that we will provide:

`void EmployeeList::reset()`—reset cursor to first element

`Employee EmployeeList::current() const`—the value stored at the cursor position

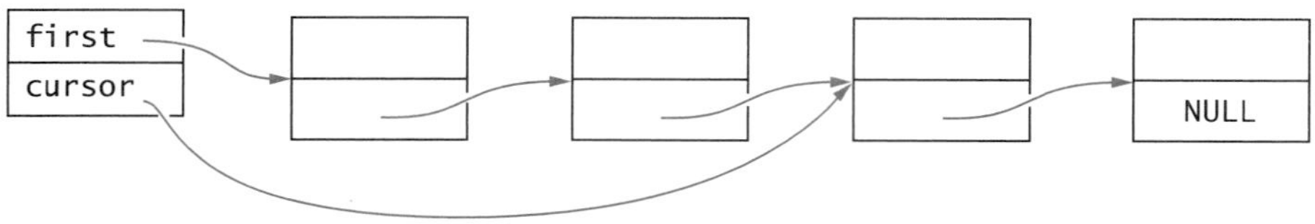

Figure 6

Access to List Link with Cursor

`void EmployeeList::next()`—moves the cursor to the next position

`bool EmployeeList::at_end() const`—tests if the cursor is at the end of the list

Here is an example of how you can use these functions to locate an employee in the list:

```
EmployeeList staff;
. . .
string name = "Hacker, Harry";
staff.reset();
bool found = false;
while (not found and not staff.at_end())
{  if (staff.current().get_name() == name)
      found = true;
   else
      staff.next();
}
```

If the loop exits because **found** is true, then the list cursor points to the element.

Now let us suppose that we had a nefarious reason to locate Harry's record—namely, to remove it from the staff list. Removing an element is not difficult. We must set the **next** pointer of the predecessor to the successor of the element that is about to be removed (see Figure 7).

In our situation there is just one small problem: We do not know the location of the predecessor. The cursor points to the current link, not the predecessor. Of course, we could find the predecessor by starting again at the beginning of the list and moving towards the cursor until we find a link whose **next** field equals the cursor. Traversing a long list can be time-consuming, though, and it is best to reduce the need for traversals whenever possible.

Figure 7

Removing a Record from a Linked List on the Heap

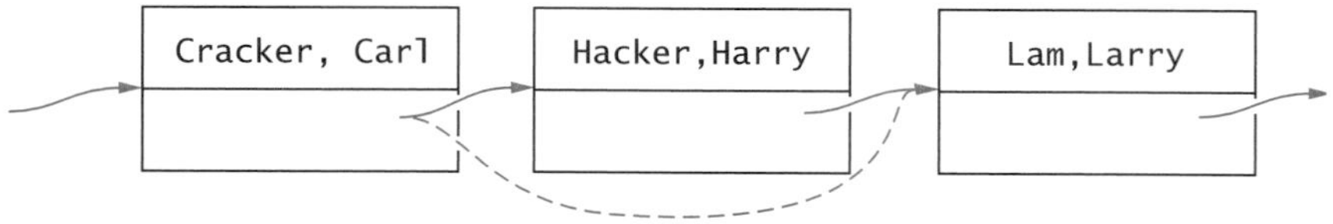

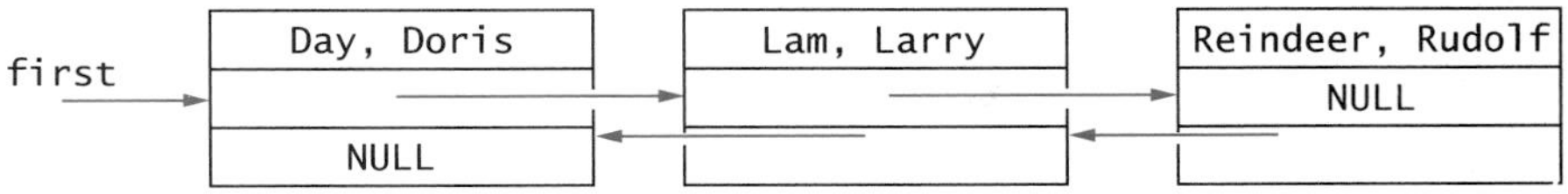

Figure 8

Doubly Linked List

One option is to give each link another pointer that points back to the predecessor. This is called a doubly linked list (Figure 8). Doubly linked lists are certainly useful, but they have twice as many links that need to be stored and that need to be updated correctly. We will not take that approach here.

Instead, we will be more clever about implementing the cursor. Rather than having it point to the current element, we will have it point to its predecessor. If the current element is the first element in the list, then the predecessor is `NULL`.

```
class EmployeeList
{
private:
   EmployeeLink* first;
   EmployeeLink* pre_cursor;
};
```

Here is the procedure to erase the cursor element. The erased link is then returned to the heap.

```
void EmployeeList::erase()
{  EmployeeLink* old_record;
   if (pre_cursor == NULL) /* first element in the list */
   {  old_record = first;
      if (first != NULL)
         first = (*first).next;
   }
   else
   {  old_record = (*pre_cursor).next;
      if (old_record != NULL)
         (*pre_cursor).next = (*old_record).next;
   }

   delete old_record;
}
```

Here is a program that inserts five records into a list, then finds and removes Harry. Note that the `insert` procedure has been changed. Rather than inserting the new employee record in sorted order, it inserts it before the cursor position. We rely on an external function, `insert_sorted`, to sort the elements. That is a useful change, because it makes the list class applicable in situations where the elements should not be sorted.

Program elist3.cpp

```
#include "ccc.h"

class EmployeeLink
{
private:
   Employee data;
   EmployeeLink* next;
friend class EmployeeList;
};

class EmployeeList
{
public:
   EmployeeList();
   void insert(Employee e);
   void erase();
   void reset();
   void next();

   bool at_end() const;
   Employee current() const;
private:
   EmployeeLink* first;
   EmployeeLink* pre_cursor;
};

EmployeeList::EmployeeList()
{  first = NULL;
   pre_cursor = NULL;
}

void EmployeeList::insert(Employee e)
{  EmployeeLink* new_record = new EmployeeLink;
   (*new_record).data = e;
   if (pre_cursor == NULL)
   {  /* make  e the first record */
      (*new_record).next = first;
      first = new_record;
   }
   else
   {  (*new_record).next = (*pre_cursor).next;
      (*pre_cursor).next = new_record;
   }
}

void EmployeeList::erase()
{  EmployeeLink* old_record;
   if (pre_cursor == NULL) /* first element in the list */
```

```
   {  old_record = first;
      if (first != NULL)
         first = (*first).next;
   }
   else
   {  old_record = (*pre_cursor).next;
      if (old_record != NULL)
         (*pre_cursor).next = (*old_record).next;
   }
   delete old_record;
}

void EmployeeList::reset()
/* PURPOSE: reset cursor to first element
*/
{  pre_cursor = NULL;
}

Employee EmployeeList::current() const
/* PURPOSE: the value stored at the cursor position
*/
{  EmployeeLink* cursor;
   if (pre_cursor == NULL) cursor = first;
   else cursor = (*pre_cursor).next;
   assert(cursor != NULL);
   return (*cursor).data;
}

void EmployeeList::next()
/* PURPOSE: moves the cursor to the next position
*/
{  if (pre_cursor == NULL)
      pre_cursor = first;
   else
      pre_cursor = (*pre_cursor).next;
}
bool EmployeeList::at_end() const
/* PURPOSE: tests if the cursor is at the end of the list
*/
{  if (pre_cursor == NULL)
      return first == NULL;
   else
      return (*pre_cursor).next == NULL;
}

void insert_sorted(EmployeeList& a, Employee e)
{  a.reset();
   while (not a.at_end()
      and a.current().get_name() <= e.get_name())
         a.next();
```

```
   a.insert(e);
}

void find(EmployeeList& a, string name)
{  for (a.reset(); not a.at_end(); a.next())
   {  if (a.current().get_name() == name)
         return;
   }
}

void print(EmployeeList& a)
{  for (a.reset(); not a.at_end(); a.next())
      cout << a.current().get_name() << "\n";
}

int main()
{  EmployeeList staff;
   insert_sorted(staff,
      Employee("Hacker, Harry", 35000.0));
   insert_sorted(staff,
      Employee("Reindeer, Rudolf", 63000.0));
   insert_sorted(staff,
      Employee("Cracker, Carl", 48000.0));
   insert_sorted(staff,
      Employee("Lam, Larry", 78000.0));
   insert_sorted(staff,
      Employee("Sandman, Susan", 51500.0));

   find(staff, "Hacker, Harry"); /* moves cursor to Harry */
   staff.erase();
   print(staff);
   return EXIT_SUCCESS;
}
```

Note how all the pointers to the links are handled by the basic list-processing procedures in the `EmployeeList` class. The functions for inserting in sorted order, for finding an employee, and for printing the list are no longer member functions. They use the list on a higher level: as a sequence of elements together with a cursor position for inspection and editing.

Advanced Topic 13.2

Templates

We have now programmed a linked list of employee records. What if we need a linked list of circles instead? Of course, we can easily program it; just replace `EmployeeList` and `EmployeeLink` with `CircleList` and `CircleLink`. That sounds boring, and it is.

C++ provides a *template* mechanism to automate this. You define the general pattern "list of T" by giving a template.

```
template<class T>
class Link
{
private:
   T data;
   Link<T>* next;
friend class List<T>;
}

template<class T>
class List
{
public:
   List();
   void insert(T t);
   void erase();
   void reset();
   void next();
   T current() const;
   bool at_end() const;
private:
   Link<T>* first;
   Link<T>* cursor;
   Link<T>* pre_cursor;
}
```

Now you can define a list of any type, by providing the type name inside <...>.

```
List<Employee> staff;
List<Circle> bubbles;
List<int> pages;
```

This is the same syntax as for vectors. `vector` is a template provided by the standard C++ library.

You also need to define templates for each member function of the `List` class.

```
template<class T>
void List<T>::insert(T t)
{  Link<T>* new_record = new Link<T>;
   (*new_record).data = t;
   if (pre_cursor == NULL)
   {  /* make e the first record */
      (*new_record).next = first;
      first = new_record;
   }
```

```
      else
      {  (*new_record).next = (*pre_cursor).next;
         (*pre_cursor).next = new_record;
      }
   }
```

You can now use `insert` on lists of any type:

```
staff.insert(harry);
bubbles.insert(Circle(Point(1, 2), 3));
pages.insert(pages, 153);
```

Advanced Topic 13.3

The Standard `list` Template

ANSI C++ defines a convenient `list` template that is easy to use. Unlike our linked lists, the linked-list template that is a part of the C++ standard does not use a cursor. It uses a more sophisticated concept: an *iterator*. Like a cursor, an iterator marks a position in the list. Our lists contain a single cursor position, but you can attach as many iterators as you like to a list.

Here is an example of how you can use those iterators:

```
list<Employee> staff;
Employee harry;
Employee angela;
Employee vivian;
staff.push_back(angela);
staff.push_back(harry);

list<Employee>::iterator first = staff.begin();
list<Employee>::iterator second = staff.begin();

second++; /* like our next */
```

Figure 9 shows the positions of these two iterators.

Here is how you insert and remove elements in a standard C++ list:

```
staff.insert(second, vivian);
Employee e = *first; /* like our current */
staff.erase(first);
```

Figure 9

Iterators

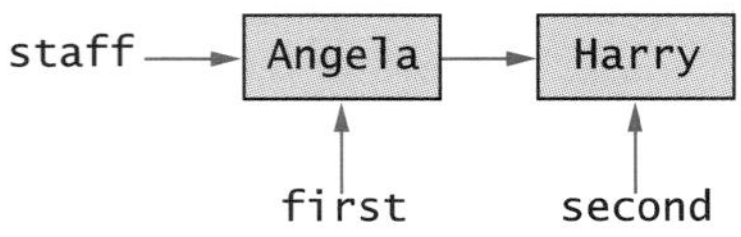

The following code traverses a list and applies a function to each of the elements:

```
list<Employee>::iterator p;
for (p = staff.begin(); p != staff.end(); p++)
   cout << (*p).get_name() << "\n";
```

The `list` template is available with every ANSI standard C++ compiler—just include the list.h header file. In your programs you will probably use the standard list class. The class introduced in this chapter is just intended to show you how a list class is implemented.

Advanced Topic 13.4

Copying Objects That Contain Pointers

The `EmployeeList` class has an unfortunate problem: It is dangerous to make copies of list variables. Consider this situation:

```
EmployeeList staff;
Employee harry;
Employee vivian;
staff.insert(harry);
staff.insert(vivian);
EmployeeList sales_department = staff;
```

The lists now appear as in Figure 10. Now we erase the first element from `sales_department`, because Harry is a programmer.

```
sales_department.reset();
sales_department.erase();
```

The lists now appear as in Figure 11. The `sales_department` list is in good shape, but the original `staff` list is completely wrecked: Its `first` pointer points to recycled memory.

This is a serious problem. There is a solution in C++, but it is complex. You must teach the list structure what it really means to make a copy. It shouldn't mean just to copy the pointers. Instead, the links containing all the list data should be copied too.

Figure 10

Before Erasing the Head of the List

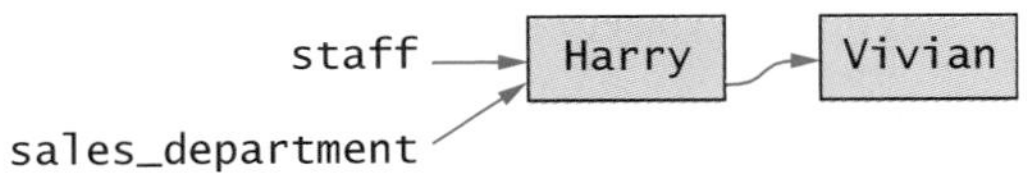

Figure 11

After Erasing the Head of the List

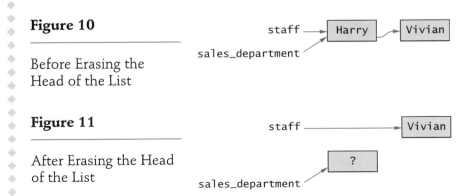

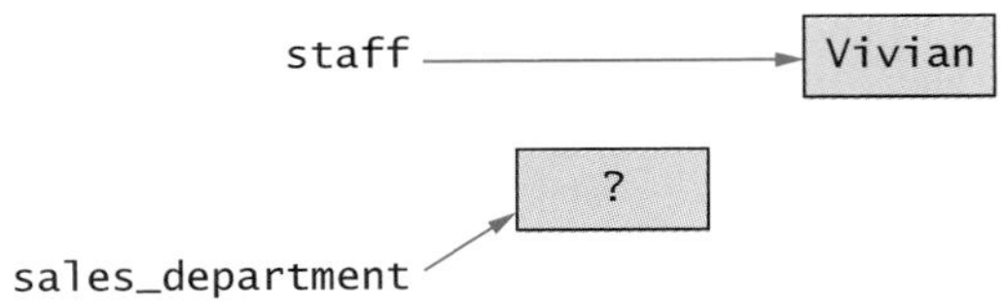

Here is what you must do to write a safe list class. First, write a member function `copy` that actually copies all the links and the cursor position:

```
void EmployeeList::copy(EmployeeList const& b)
{  first = NULL;
   pre_cursor = NULL;
   cursor = NULL;
   EmployeeLink* p = b.first;
   EmployeeLink* pre_record = NULL;
   while (p != NULL)
   {  EmployeeLink* new_record = new EmployeeLink;
      (*new_record).data = (*p).data;
      (*new_record).next = NULL;
      if (pre_record != NULL)
         (*pre_record).next = new_record;
      pre_record = new_record;
      if (p == b.first) first = new_record;
      if (p == b.pre_cursor) pre_cursor = new_record;
      p = (*p).next;
   }
}
```

Next, write a member function `free` that deletes all links in a list. When making an assignment like `sales_department = staff`, the `free` function will be called first to recycle the links of `sales_department` before copying over the links of `staff`.

```
void EmployeeList::free()
{  EmployeeLink* p = first;
   while (p != NULL)
   {  EmployeeLink* q = p;
      p = (*p).next;
      delete q;
   }
}
```

Declare these two functions in the *private* part of the list class. List users should not be able to call them.

Now you need to place the following magic commands into the list class definition:

```
class EmployeeList
{  EmployeeList()
   void insert(Employee e);
   void erase();
   . . .
   /* The "Big Three" magic commands */
   EmployeeList& operator=(EmployeeList const& b)
   {  if (this != &b) { free(); copy(b); } return *this;  }
   EmployeeList(EmployeeList const& b) { copy(b); }
   ~EmployeeList() { free(); }
```

Figure 12

Copying a List

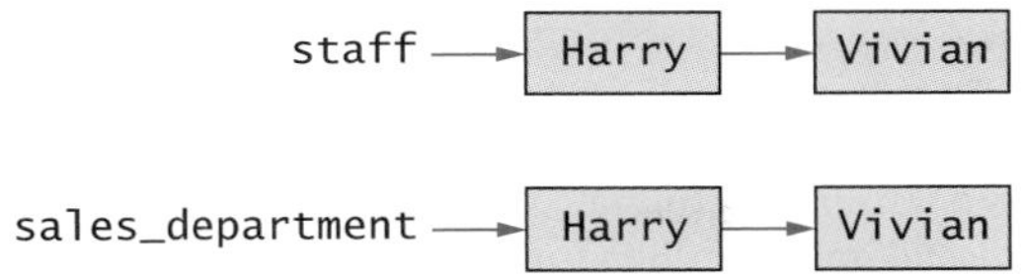

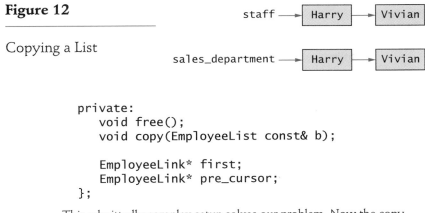

```
private:
   void free();
   void copy(EmployeeList const& b);

   EmployeeLink* first;
   EmployeeLink* pre_cursor;
};
```

This admittedly complex setup solves our problem. Now the copy

```
sales_department = staff;
```

works correctly (see Figure 12).

The magic commands redefine the assignment operator and two other essential memory management functions: the *copy constructor* and the *destructor*. These three functions are often called "the big three". They must be implemented for any structure that contains pointers. As Marshall Cline [1] says, "It's not just a good idea, it's the law".

While this law may be about as comprehensible as the tax laws to you at this point, it is not actually that hard to comply with. If your structure has no pointer fields, there is nothing to worry about. Most classes are like that—they just contain numbers, strings, vectors or objects, all of which are safe. If your class does have pointers, it is an indication that it stores its data on the heap. In that case, write two functions: `copy` and `free`. The `copy` function makes a complete copy of all the data belonging to the object. The `free` function does just the opposite, deleting all that data. Then implement "the big three" by making them call your `copy` and `free` functions.

To fully understand the issue of "big three" memory management, you need to know quite a bit more C++ that you can learn in a beginning programming course. If you are interested, look into [2] for more information.

If you need to program with linked lists or other data structures that allocate the memory for the data on the heap, you can avoid this entire issue by using someone else's classes. For example, the standard C++ library defines a `list` template that works similar to our lists. They implement all list operations, including "the big three". You can just make `list<Employee>` or `list<int>` without worrying about the memory management details.

Random Fact 13.2

Visual Programming

Programming as we know it involves typing code into a text editor and then running it. A programmer must be familiar with the programming language to write even the simplest of programs. When programming in graphics, one must compute every screen position.

A new *visual* style of programming makes this much easier. When you use a visual programming environment, such as Visual Basic or Delphi, you use your mouse to specify where text, buttons, and other fields should appear on the screen (see Figure 13). You still need to do some programming. You need to write code for every *event*. For example, you need to specify what should happen when the user clicks on a button or when text is entered in an input field.

Visual programming offers two benefits. It is much easier to lay out a screen by dragging buttons and images with the mouse than it is to compute the coordinates in a program. The visual programming environment also makes it easy to place objects with sophisticated behavior onto the screen. For example, a calendar object can show the current month 's calendar, with buttons to move to the next or previous month; all of that has been preprogrammed by someone (usually the hard way, using a traditional programming language), but you can add a fully working calendar to your program simply by dragging it off a toolbar and dropping it into your program.

Visual programming systems also make it easy to link screen fields to databases just by connecting fields and tables with the mouse.

All of this could be coded in C++. It would probably run faster that way, but user interfaces only have to be as fast as the user. Programming in a visual environment is *much* easier than the equivalent code in C++. In days a programmer can design an attractive user interface that would take weeks to complete in C++. These systems are highly recommended for user interface programming.

At this point, the Achilles heel of visual programming environments is the transfer of data between the user interface and the core application. The application code must usually run fast and interact with the operating system; it is best implemented in a language like C++.

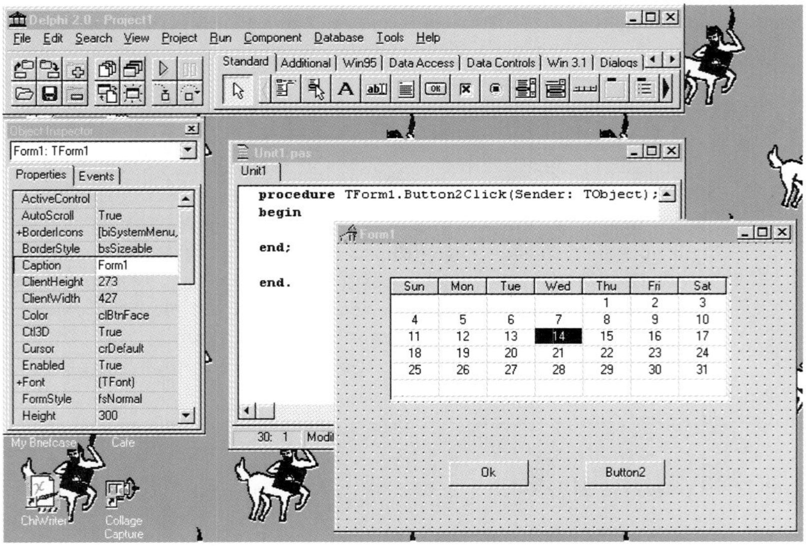

Figure 13

Visual Programming Environment

Operating systems are just now beginning to provide standards for transferring data from one programming language to another. Once these standards are in place, it will become common to write each part of an application program in the most suitable programming language for that particular task.

13.5 Binary Search Trees

When we moved from a vector of employees to a linked list and gained the advantage of fast insertion and removal in the middle of the collection, we lost one important algorithm: fast searching. Recall that binary search in an array of 1000 elements was able to locate an element in about 10 steps by cutting the size of the search interval in half in each step. That does not work for lists, which are not *random-access* data structures. To go to the middle of the list, we must start at the beginning and then go a link at a time. That makes the binary search algorithm meaningless. If we already have to traverse half the list to find its middle, that takes 500 steps for a list of 1000 elements. So we can't hope for an $O(\log n)$ algorithm.

In this section we will introduce the simplest of many *treelike* data structures that computer scientists have invented to overcome that problem. Binary search trees allow fast insertion and removal of elements, *and* they are specially designed for fast searching.

A linked list is a one-dimensional data structure. Every link has a pointer to the next link. You can imagine that all links are arranged in line. In contrast, a binary search tree is made of nodes with *two* pointers, called the *left* and *right* children. You should visualize it as a tree, except that it is traditional to draw the tree upside down, like a family tree or hierarchy chart (see Figure 14). In a binary search tree, every node has at most two children, hence the name *binary.* Finally, binary search trees are carefully constructed to have the following important property:

> The data values of *all* descendants to the left of *any* node are less than the data value stored in that node, and *all* descendants to the right have greater data values.

Figure 15 shows a binary tree that is not a binary search tree.

Let us implement these tree classes. Just as we needed classes for lists and their links, we need a class for the tree that contains a pointer to the *root node* and a separate class for the nodes. Each node contains two pointers (to the left and right child node) and a data field. At the fringes of the tree, one or two of the child pointers are `NULL`.

```
class EmployeeNode
{
public:
   void insert_node(EmployeeNode* new_record);
   void print_nodes() const;
```

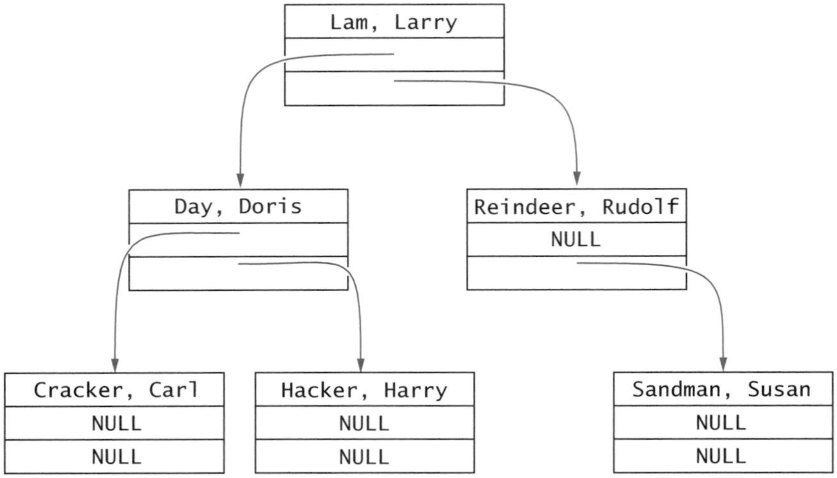

Figure 14

Binary Search Tree

Figure 15

A Binary Tree
That Is Not
a Search Tree

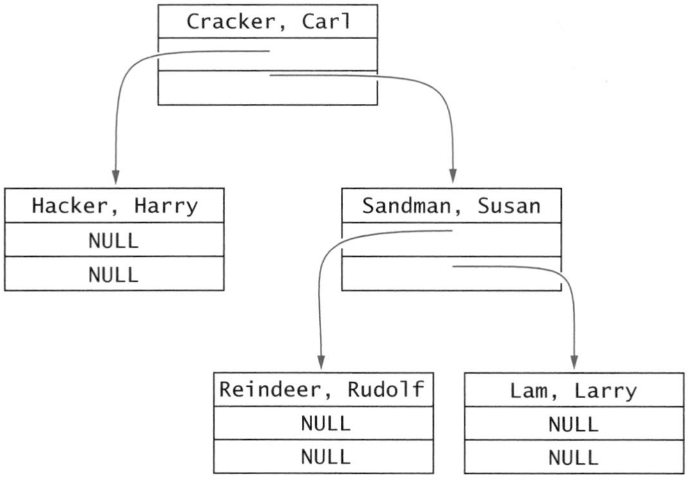

```
private:
   Employee data;
   EmployeeNode* left;
   EmployeeNode* right;
friend class EmployeeTree;
};

class EmployeeTree
{
public:
   EmployeeTree();
   void insert(Employee e);
   void print() const;
private:
   EmployeeNode* root;
};
```

To insert data into the tree, we use the following algorithm:

1. If we encounter a NULL node pointer, replace it with the new node.
2. If we encounter a non-NULL node pointer, look at its data value. If the data value of that node is larger than the one we want to insert, continue the process with the left subtree. If the existing data value is smaller, continue the process with the right subtree.

Figure 16 shows how a tree is traversed to find the location at which the new node must be inserted. Here is the code:

```
void EmployeeTree::insert(Employee e)
{  EmployeeNode* new_record = new EmployeeNode;
   (*new_record).data = e;
   (*new_record).left = NULL;
   (*new_record).right = NULL;
   if (root == NULL) root = new_record;
   else (*root).insert_node(new_record);
}
```

If the tree is empty, we simply set its root to the new record. Otherwise, we know that the new record must be inserted somewhere within the nodes, and we ask the root node to perform the insertion. That node object calls the insert_node member function of the EmployeeNode class, which checks whether the name of the new record is less than the name of the employee record stored in the node. If so, the record is inserted in the left subtree; if not, it is inserted in the right subtree:

```
void EmployeeNode::insert_node(EmployeeNode* new_record)
{  if ((*new_record).data.get_name() < data.name())
   {  if (left == NULL) left = new_record;
      else (*left).insert(new_record);
   }
```

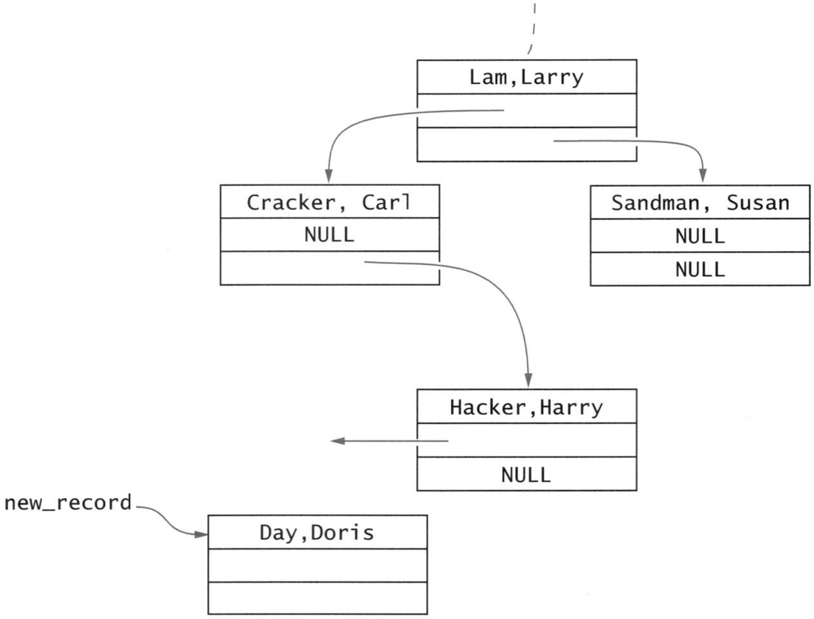

Figure 16

Finding an Insertion Location in a Binary Tree

Figure 17

Binary Search Tree after Four Insertions

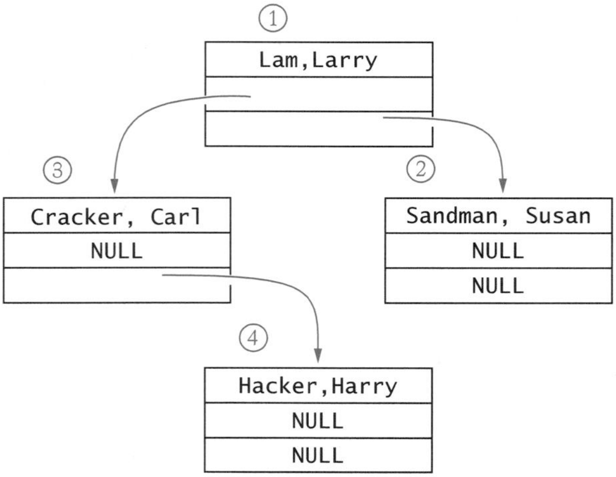

```
      else
      {  if (right == NULL) right = new_record;
         else (*right).insert(new_record);
      }
   }
```

Figure 17 shows the tree that results from inserting the records for

```
Lam, Larry
Sandman, Susan
Cracker, Carl
Hacker, Harry
```

in that order.

Let us trace the calls to **insert_node** when inserting **Reindeer, Rudolf** into the tree in Figure 11. Of course, we don't know the actual values of the pointers. They are pretty arbitrary and depend on where the memory allocator finds empty space. For this discussion, we just number the existing nodes (1), (2), (3), (4). The first call to **insert_node** is

```
root.insert_node(new_record)
```

Since **root** points to node (1), we compare the data in node (1)(**Lam, Larry**) with **Reindeer, Rudolf** and find that we must call

```
(1).right.insert_node(new_record)
```

(1).**right** is node (2). We compare the data values again and find that we must now move to the left:

```
(2).left.insert_node(new_record)
```

Since (2).**left** is **NULL**, we set (2).**left** to **new_record**, and the insertion is complete.

Note that the shape of the tree depends on the order in which we insert the elements. If we insert them in opposite order, starting with **Reindeer, Rudolf** and ending with **Lam, Larry**, then we obtain the tree in Figure 18.

Figure 18

Tree with Nodes Inserted in Reverse Order

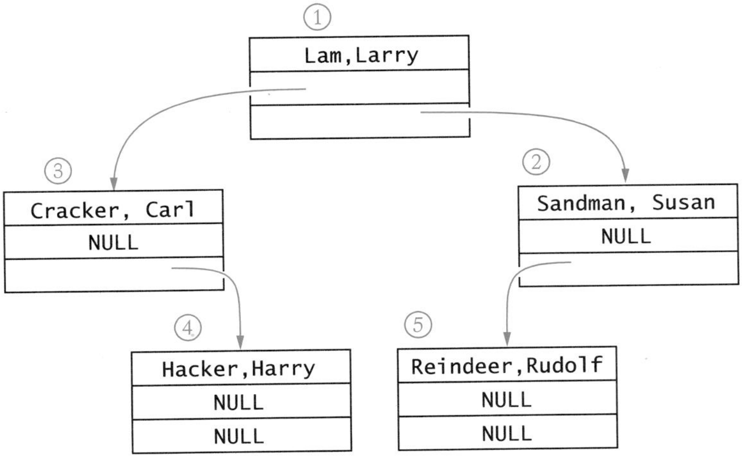

Figure 19

Binary Tree—One Order

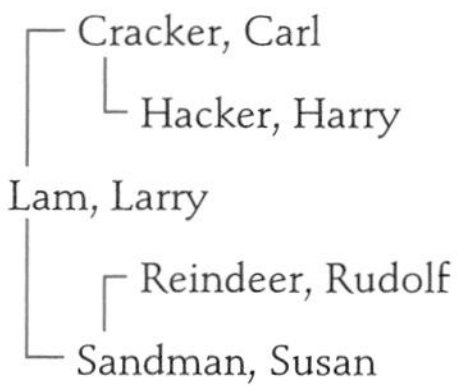

Figure 20

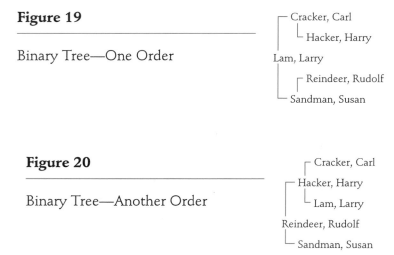

Binary Tree—Another Order

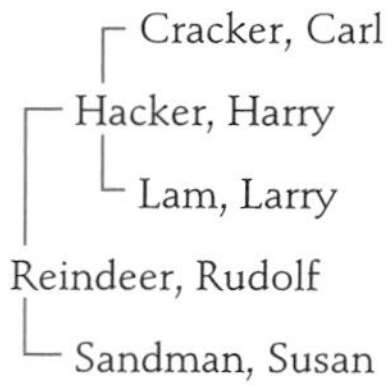

Now that we have the data inserted in the tree, what can we do with them? It turns out to be surprisingly simple to print all records in sorted order. We *know* that all data in the left subtree of any node must come before the node and before all data in the right subtree. This is expressed in the following procedure:

```
void EmployeeNode::print_nodes() const
{  if (left != NULL)
   (*left).print_node();
   cout << data.get_name() << "\n";
   if (right != NULL)
      (*right).print_node();
}
```

To print the entire tree, we start this recursive printing process at the root:

```
void EmployeeTree::print() const
{  if (root != NULL)
   (*root).print_nodes();
}
```

You should convince yourself that the records are printed in the same order no matter in which order they were inserted. Consider the two trees in Figures 19 and 20, which contain the same data, inserted in different order. To visualize the order of printing, the trees are turned sideways so that the left subtree is on top, the root is in the middle, and the right subtree is on the bottom. Even though the layout of the trees is different, the `print_node` procedure traverses them in the same order!

Here is a complete program to insert data into a tree and to print them out in sorted order:

Program etree.cpp

```
#include "ccc.h"

class EmployeeNode
{
public:
   void insert_node(EmployeeNode* new_record);
   void print_nodes() const;
private:
   Employee data;
   EmployeeNode* left;
   EmployeeNode* right;
friend class EmployeeTree;
};

class EmployeeTree
{
public:
   EmployeeTree();
   void insert(Employee e);
   void print() const;
private:
   EmployeeNode* root;
};

EmployeeTree::EmployeeTree()
{  root = NULL;
}
void EmployeeTree::print() const
{  if (root != NULL)
   (*root).print_nodes();
}

void EmployeeTree::insert(Employee e)
{  EmployeeNode* new_record = new EmployeeNode;
   (*new_record).data = e;
   (*new_record).left = NULL;
   (*new_record).right = NULL;
   if (root == NULL) root = new_record;
   else (*root).insert_node(new_record);
}
```

```
void EmployeeNode::insert_node(EmployeeNode* new_record)
{  if ((*new_record).data.get_name() < data.get_name())
   {  if (left == NULL) left = new_record;
      else (*left).insert_node(new_record);
   }
   else
   {  if (right == NULL) right = new_record;
      else (*right).insert_node(new_record);
   }

}

void EmployeeNode::print_nodes() const
{  if (left != NULL)
   (*left).print_nodes();
   cout << data.get_name() << "\n";
   if (right != NULL)
      (*right).print_nodes();
}

int main()
{  EmployeeTree staff;
   staff.insert(Employee("Reindeer, Rudolf", 39000));
   staff.insert(Employee("Lam, Larry", 48000));
   staff.insert(Employee("Sandman, Susan", 34500));
   staff.insert(Employee("Cracker, Carl", 47800));
   staff.insert(Employee("Hacker, Harry", 44520));
   staff.print();
   return EXIT_SUCCESS;
}
```

Unlike a linked list or a vector, a binary tree has no *insert positions.* We can add a new element to a vector at any position:

```
v[2] = harry;
```

We can move the cursor of a linked list to any position:

```
a.reset(); a.next(); a.next();
a.insert(harry);
```

However, we cannot select the position where we would like to insert a record into a binary search tree. The data structure is *self-organizing;* that is, each element finds its own place.

Deleting an element from a binary search tree is a little more complicated, because the children of the deleted node must be rearranged. We will leave that topic to a course on data structures.

Now that we have implemented this complex data structure, we may well wonder if it is any good. Like links in a list, nodes are allocated one at a time on the heap. No

Figure 21

Unbalanced Binary Tree

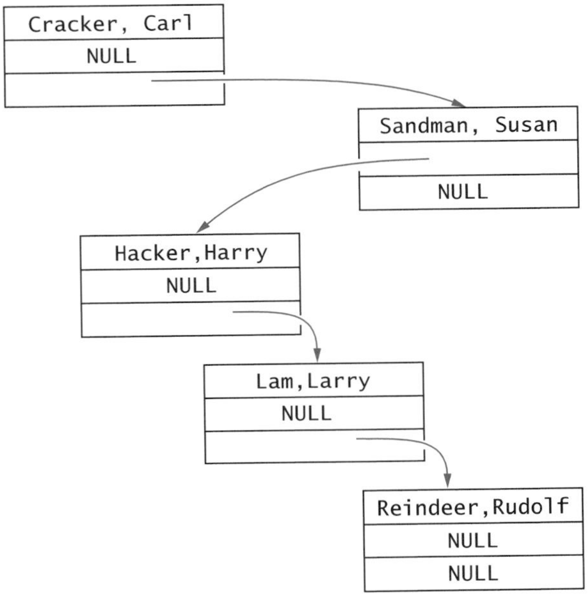

existing records need to be moved when a new record is inserted in the tree; that is an advantage. How fast insertion is, however, depends on the shape of the tree. If the tree is *balanced*—that is, if each node has approximately as many children on the left as on the right—then insertion is very fast, because about half of the nodes are eliminated in each step. On the other hand, if the tree happens to be *unbalanced,* then insertion can be slow—no faster than insertion into a linked list. (See Figure 21.)

If new records are fairly random, then the resulting tree is likely to be well balanced. However, if the incoming records happen to be already in sorted order, then the resulting tree is completely unbalanced. Each new element is inserted at the end, and the entire tree must be traversed every time to find that end!

Binary search trees work well for random data, but if you suspect that the data in your application might be sorted or have long runs of sorted data, you should not use a binary search tree. Several data structures known to computer scientists can overcome this drawback by keeping trees balanced at all times. You will encounter those advanced data structures in a later course.

Advanced Topic 13.5

Uses of Pointers

We have managed to live without pointers for twelve chapters, which was a good thing. Because the accidental mishandling of pointers is such a common error, and it can have such grave consequences, it is best to use pointers only when there is no other alternative.

C programmers are not so lucky. They must use pointers in essentially every program, for reference parameters and array parameters of functions. Because C strings are arrays of characters, string-handling functions often return pointers into C arrays. Beginning C programmers make lots of pointer errors, and quite a few of them develop the attitude that it is somehow okay to write programs that occasionally act flaky.

In C++ you must use pointers for distributed data structures like lists and trees, where the actual data are spread over a collection of links or nodes.

Another use of pointers is to express a *zero/one relationship*. For example, a department may or may not have a receptionist. You can express that with a pointer.

```
class Department
{  . . .
private:
   Employee* receptionist;
   . . .
};
```

The pointer `receptionist` either points to an employee record or is `NULL`. In fact, you can think of the `next` field in a linked list as a zero/one relationship. Either there is a next link, or there isn't.

A common use of pointers is *sharing*. Some departments may have a receptionist and a secretary; in others one person does double duty. Then one may want to have pointers to a common address:

```
class Department
{  . . .
private:
   Employee* receptionist;
   Employee* secretary;
   . . .
};
```

However, one must be very careful that the pointers are used only as long as the shared variable actually exists.

A very important use of pointers in *object-oriented programming* is *polymorphism,* a topic that we discuss in the next chapter. It is possible to have different kinds of employees, such as programmers, managers and secretaries, and have an `Employee*` pointer denote an object that may be any one of those types.

Pointers are often used for *efficiency*. It is faster to copy a pointer (usually a 4-byte memory address) than the actual object. If you use pointers for this purpose, consider references instead. References are safer to use, because you cannot make a reference that points to nowhere.

Some programming languages, such as Eiffel and Java, do not use pointers at all but provide more advanced mechanisms that allow the programmer to express all programming concepts without pointers.

Chapter Summary

1. Linked lists permit faster insertion and removal in the middle of a data set than vectors do.

2. The links of a linked list are obtained from the *heap*. Objects of any type can be obtained from the heap with the **new** operator. They must be recycled with the **delete** operator.

3. The links of a linked list are connected by *pointers*. Each link contains a pointer that either is `NULL` or specifies the location of the successor link.

4. The * operator locates the object to which a pointer points. It is a serious programming error to apply * to a `NULL` pointer or an invalid pointer.

5. Positions inside a linked list are specified with a cursor position.

6. Tree structures can significantly speed up the storage and retrieval of sorted data. We discussed the simplest of such tree structures: the binary search tree.

Further Reading

[1] Marshall Cline and Greg A. Lomow, *C++ Frequently Asked Questions,* Addison-Wesley, 1995.

[2] Cay Horstmann, *Mastering C++,* 2nd ed., John Wiley & Sons, 1995.

Review Exercises

Exercise R13.1. Draw the following linked list as a sequence of connected links, as in Figure 1.

Index	Data	Next
0	`Juliet`	4
1	`Tom`	−1
2	`Dick`	3
3	`Harry`	0
4	`Romeo`	1

Exercise R13.2. Consider a vector implementation of a linked list with the following contents:

Index	Data	Next
0	`Juliet`	1
1	`Tom`	−1
2	`Dick`	3
3	`Harry`	0

What is the contents of the vector after inserting the element **Romeo**?

Exercise R13.3. Draw the list diagram before and after the insertion of `Romeo` in the preceding example. Which links were visited during insertion? Which of them were changed?

Exercise R13.4. Consider a vector implementation of a linked list with the following contents:

Index	Data	Next
0	`Juliet`	1
1	`Tom`	−1
2	`Dick`	3
3	`Harry`	0

What is the contents of the vector after inserting the element `Albert`?

Exercise R13.5. What is the difference between the following four values?

```
Time()
Time(1996, 4, 15, 12, 0, 0)
new Time()
new Time(1996, 4, 15, 12, 0, 0)
```

Exercise R13.6. Insert the necessary code to reclaim memory in the following code:

```
int main()
{  Time a;
   Time* b = new Time();
   Time c(1996, 4, 15, 12, 0, 0)
   Time* d = new Time(1996, 4, 15, 12, 0, 0)
   . . .
   your code goes here
}
```

Exercise R13.7. Find the mistakes in the following code. Not all lines contain mistakes. Each line depends on the lines preceding it. Watch out for uninitialized pointers, null pointers, pointers to deleted objects, and confusing pointers with objects.

```
int* p = new int;
p = 5;
*p = *p + 5;
Employee e1 = new Employee("Hacker, Harry", 34000);
Employee e2; e2->set_salary(38000);
delete e2;
Time* pnow = new Time();
Time* t1 = new Time(2006, 4, 15, 2, 0, 0);
cout << (*t1).seconds_from(pnow);
delete *t1;
cout << (*t1).get_seconds();
Circle* c = new Circle(new Point(1, 2), 3);
```

```
cout << c.get_radius();
Point* q = new Point(1, 2);
cout << *q.get_x();
delete q;
Line* a;
cwin << *a;
Message* greeting = NULL;
if ((*greeting).get_text() == "") (*c).move(1, 1);
```

Exercise R13.8. A pointer variable can contain a pointer to a valid object, a pointer to a deleted object, NULL, or a random value. Write code that creates and sets four pointer variables a, b, c, and d to show each of these possibilities.

Exercise R13.9. What happens if you forget to delete an object that you obtained from the heap? What happens if you delete it twice?

Exercise R13.10. What does the following code print?

```
Employee* harry = Employee("Hacker, Harry", 35000);
Employee* boss = harry;
Employee* pharry = new Employee("Hacker, Harry", 35000);
Employee* pboss = harry;
boss.set_salary(45000);
(*pboss).set_salary(45000);
cout << harry.get_salary() << "\n";
cout << boss.get_salary() << "\n";
cout << (*pharry).get_salary() << "\n";
cout << (*pboss).get_salary() << "\n";
```

Exercise R13.11. The following code edits a linked list consisting of three links.

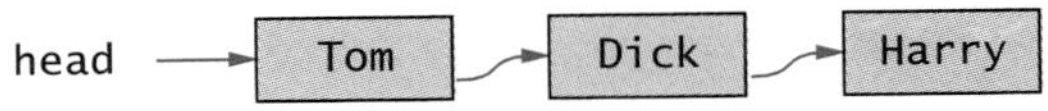

Draw a diagram how they are linked together after the code is executed.

```
EmployeeLink* p1 = (*head.next);
EmployeeLink* p2 = head;
while ((*p2).next != NULL) p2 = (*p2).next;
(*p2).next = head;
head = p1;
```

Exercise R13.12. Consider the linked list with a cursor. Explain what the following code prints.

```
EmployeeList staff;
Employee h("Hacker, Harry", 35000);
Employee l("Lam, Larry", 46000);
Employee c("Cracker, Carl", 59000);
```

```
staff.insert(h);
staff.reset();
staff.insert(l);
staff.next();
staff.insert(c);
for (staff.reset(); not staff.at_end(); staff.next())
   cout << staff.get_current().get_name();
```

Exercise R13.13. Using just the public interface of the linked list class with a cursor, write a function

```
void downsize(EmployeeList& staff)
```

that removes every second employee from a linked list.

Exercise R13.14. The `insert` procedure of Section 13.3 inserts a new element before the cursor position. To understand the updating of the links, draw before/after link diagrams for the following four scenarios.

1. The list is completely empty.
2. The list is not empty, and the cursor is at the beginning of the list.
3. The list is not empty, and the cursor is at the end of the list.
4. The list is not empty, and the cursor is in the middle of the list.

Exercise R13.15. What advantages do lists have over vectors? What disadvantages do they have?

Exercise R13.16. Suppose you needed to organize a collection of telephone numbers for a company division. There are currently about 6,000 employees, and you know that the phone switch can handle at most 10,000 phone numbers. You expect several hundred lookups against the collection every day. Would you use a vector or a linked list to store the information?

Exercise R13.17. Suppose you needed to keep a collection of appointments. Would you use a linked list or a vector of `Appointment` objects?

Exercise R13.18. What is the difference between a binary tree and a binary search tree?

Exercise R13.19. The following records are inserted into a binary search tree. Draw the resulting tree after each insertion.

```
Adam
Eve
Romeo
Juliet
```

```
Tom
Dick
Harry
```

Exercise R13.20. Consider the following tree. In which order are the nodes printed?

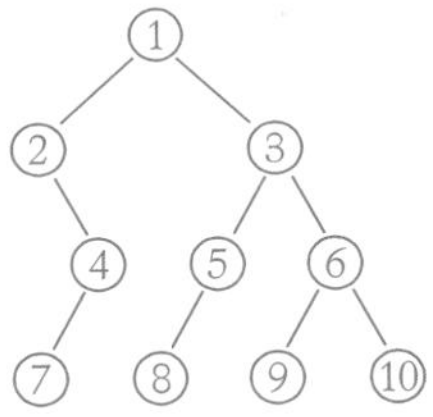

Exercise R13.21. Write a function

```
Employee EmployeeTree::smallest() const
```

that returns the smallest element of a tree. You will also need to add a member function to the `EmployeeNode` class.

Programming Exercises

Exercise P13.1. Write a vector implementation of a linked list of integers. That is, write an `IntLink` and `IntList` class.

Exercise P13.2. Write a member function `EmployeeList::reverse()` that reverses the links in a list. Use the pointer implementation.

Exercise P13.3. Change the member function `print` to display the linked list on the graphics screen. Draw each element of the list as a box, and indicate the links with arrows.

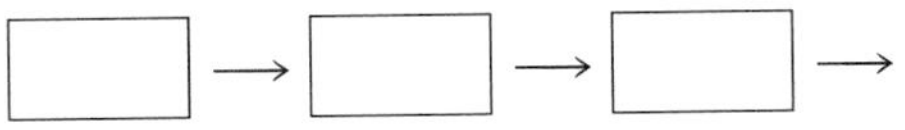

Exercise P13.4. Write a member function `EmployeeList::get_size()` that computes the number of elements in the list, by counting the elements until the end of the list is reached.

Exercise P13.5. Add a `size` field to the `List` class. Modify the `insert` and `erase` functions to update the `size` field so that it always contains the correct size. Change the `get_size()` function of the preceding exercise to take advantage of this data field.

Exercise P13.6. Write a class `Polynomial` that stores a polynomial such as

$$p(x) = 5x^{10} + 9x^7 - x - 10$$

Store it as a linked list of terms. A term contains the coefficient and the power of x. For example, you would store $p(x)$ as

$$(5, 10), (9, 7), (-1, 1), (-10, 0)$$

Supply member functions to add, multiply, and print polynomials. Supply a constructor that makes a polynomial from a single term. For example, the polynomial p can be constructed as

```
Polynomial p(Term(-10, 0));
p.add(Polynomial(Term(-1, 1)));
p.add(Polynomial(Term(9, 7)));
p.add(Polynomial(Term(5, 10)));
```

Then compute $p(x) \times p(x)$.

```
Polynomial q = p.multiply(p);
q.print();
```

Exercise P13.7. Design a structure `Set` that can hold a set of integers. Hide the private implementation: a linked list of integers. Provide the following member functions:

A constructor making an empty set

`insert(int x)` insert `x` if it is not present

`erase(int x)` erase `x` if it is present

`reset()/current()/next()/at_end()` to traverse the contents of the set

Exercise P13.8. Enhance the set class from the previous example. Write functions

```
Set set_union(Set a, Set b)
Set intersection(Set a, Set b)
```

that compute the set union and intersection of the sets `a` and `b`. (Don't call the first function `union`—that is a reserved word in C++.) Of course, you should use only the public interface of the set structure.

Exercise P13.9. Implement the *sieve of Eratosthenes:* a method for computing prime numbers known to the ancient Greeks. Choose an n. This method will compute all prime numbers up to n. First insert all numbers from 1 to n into a set. Then erase all multiples of 2 (except 2); that is, 4, 6, 8, 10, 12, ... Erase all multiples of 3, that is, 6,

9, 12, 15, ... Go up to $\sqrt{n}$. The remaining numbers are all primes. Of course, you should use only the public interface of the set structure.

Exercise P13.10. Design a `StringTree` class that stores just strings, not employee records.

Exercise P13.11. Change the member function `print` to print the tree as a tree shape. Print it sideways, as in the examples in Section 13.4. Extra credit if you instead display the tree on the graphics screen, with the root node centered on the top.

Exercise P13.12. Use the `StringTree` class from the preceding exercise to build a *parse tree* of an arithmetic expression. For example, the parse tree of the expression `a + b * (c + d)` is

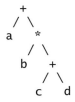

```
     +
    / \
   a   *
      / \
     b   +
        / \
       c   d
```

The parse tree of the expression `a - b - c` is

```
        -
       / \
      -   c
     / \
    a   b
```

Write a program that reads in an expression and produces a parse tree. Then print the tree.

Exercise P13.13. The `print` function of the tree class prints a tree according to the following algorithm:

Print the left subtree
Print the current node
Print the right subtree

This is called *inorder traversal.* There are two other traversal schemes, namely *pre-order traversal,*

Print the current node
Print the left subtree
Print the right subtree

and *postorder traversal,*

Print the left subtree
Print the right subtree
Print the current node

Write a program that builds a tree of strings from user input and then prints the user's choice of preorder, inorder, or postorder traversal.

Exercise P13.14. Write a member function `free()` of the tree class that deletes all nodes of a tree. *Hint:* You will also need to write a member function for the node class.

CHAPTER 14

Inheritance and Polymorphism

Objectives

- To understand the concepts of inheritance and polymorphism
- To learn how inheritance is a tool for code reuse
- To learn how to call base-class constructors and member functions
- To understand the difference between static and dynamic binding
- To be able to implement dynamic binding with virtual functions
- To understand when to use inheritance and aggregation in object-oriented design

14.1 Inheritance

Inheritance is a mechanism for enhancing existing, working classes. If a new class needs to be implemented and a class representing a more general concept is already available, then the new class can *inherit* from the existing class. For example, suppose we need to define a class `Manager`. We already have a class `Employee`, and a manager is a special case of an employee. In this case, it makes sense to use the language construct of inheritance. Here is the syntax for the class definition:

```
class Manager : public Employee
{
public:
    new member functions
private:
    new data members
};
```

The `:` symbol denotes inheritance. The keyword `public` is required for a technical reason (see Common Error 14.1).

In the `Manager` class definition you specify only new member functions and data members . All member functions and data members of the `Employee` class are automatically inherited by the `Manager` class. For example, the `set_salary` function automatically applies to managers:

```
Manager m;
m.set_salary(68000);
```

Some more terminology must be introduced here. The existing, more general class is called the *base class.* The more specialized class that inherits from the base class is called the *derived* class. In our example, `Employee` is the base class and `Manager` is the derived class.

Figure 1 is a *class diagram* showing the relationship between these classes. It is customary to show classes as rectangles, objects as hexagons. In the preceding chapters, our diagrams focused on individual objects, which were drawn as hexagons. Since inheritance is a relationship between classes, not objects, we show two *rectangles* joined by an arrow, which indicates inheritance.

To understand the mechanics of programming with inheritance, we will consider a more interesting programming problem. Our task is to display a set of clocks, as you might find on a travel agent's wall. Each clock has the name of a city, and it shows the current time of that city (see Figure 2).

Figure 1

An Inheritance Diagram

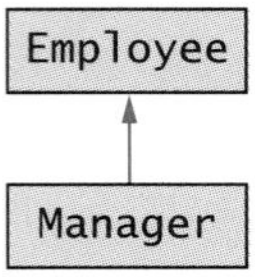

Figure 2

Clocks for Different Cities

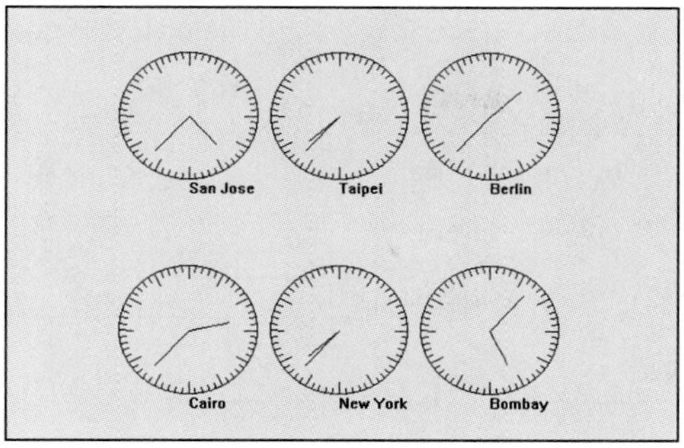

We already have a class that can show the time: namely, the `Clock` class of Chapter 9. Rather than reinventing the wheel, let us reuse that class. In particular, we want to rely on the `draw` function of the `Clock` class without touching it.

Let us see how our clocks are different from `Clock` objects. Our clocks have city names, and they show the current time, offset by the time difference between our location and a foreign city. Let us call such a clock a `WorldClock`. A `WorldClock` object differs from a `Clock` object in three ways:

- A `WorldClock` object must store the city name.
- The constructor for a `WorldClock` object receives the city name and the time difference.
- The `draw` function draws both the clock face and the city name.

When the `WorldClock` class inherits from the `Clock` class, it needs only to spell out these three differences:

```
class WorldClock : public Clock
{
public:
   WorldClock(string city_name, float hour_diff,
      Point center, float radius);
   void draw() const;
private:
   Message city;
};
```

Figure 3 shows the layout of a `WorldClock` object. It inherits all data fields from the `Clock` base object, and it gains one additional data field: `city`.

It is important to note that the data members of the base class (namely `current_time`, `center`, and `radius`) are present in each `WorldClock` object, but they are not *accessible* by the member functions of `WorldClock`. Since these fields are private data of the `Clock` class, only the `Clock` class has access to them. The derived class has no more access rights than any other class.

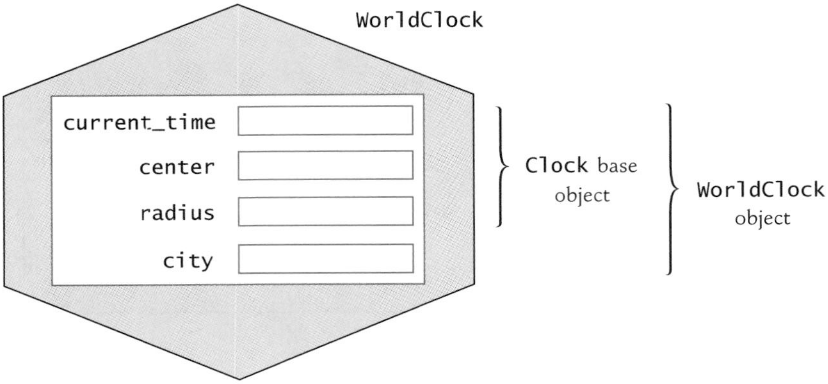

Figure 3

Data Layout of Derived Object

Common Error 14.1

Private Inheritance

It is a common error to forget the keyword `public` that must follow the colon after the derived-class name.

```
class Manager : Employee /* Error */
{ ...
};
```

The class definition will compile. The `Manager` still inherits from `Employee`, but it inherits *privately*. That is, only the member functions of `Manager` get to call member functions of `Employee`. Whenever you invoke an `Employee` member function on a `Manager` object elsewhere, the compiler will flag this as an error:

```
int main()
{  Manager m;
   ...
   m.set_salary(65000); /* Error */
   ...
}
```

This private inheritance is rarely useful. In fact, it violates the spirit of using inheritance in the first place—namely, to create objects that are usable just like the base-class objects. You should always use public inheritance and remember to supply the `public` keyword in the definition of the derived class.

14.2 Calling the Base-Class Constructor

Let us next turn to the constructor. The constructor of a derived class has two tasks:

- Initialize all data members
- Initialize the base object

The first task is straightforward:

```
WorldClock::WorldClock(string city_name, float hour_diff,
   Point center, float radius)
/* not complete */
{  Point p = center;
   p.move(0, -radius);
   city = Message(p, city_name);
}
```

The second task is not as simple. We need to construct the base object with the given center and radius. We also need to set the current time, adjusted by the time difference. The latter task is achieved through the **set_time** function of the clock class:

```
WorldClock::WorldClock(string city_name, float hour_diff,
   Point center, float radius)
/* not complete */
{  Point p = center;
   p.move(0, 2 * radius);
   city = Message(p, city_name);
   Time now;
   const float SECONDS_PER_HOUR = 60 * 60;
   now.add_seconds(hour_diff * SECONDS_PER_HOUR);
   set_time(now);
}
```

However, there are no member functions to set the center and the radius. The only way to set these values is through the `Clock` constructor. That is, we must somehow set the base object to

```
Clock(center, radius);
```

We have a problem. Unlike data fields, the base object has *no name.* There is no object that we can set to `Clock(center, radius)`. Instead, a derived-class constructor must invoke the base-class constructor before initializing the derived-class data. There is a special syntactical construct to denote the base construction:

```
WorldClock::WorldClock(string city_name, float hour_diff,
   Point center, float radius)
: Clock(center, radius)
```

```
{  Point p = center;
   p.move(0, 2 * radius);
   city = Message(p, city_name);
   Time now;
   const float SECONDS_PER_HOUR = 60 * 60;
   now.add_seconds(hour_diff * SECONDS_PER_HOUR);
   set_time(now);
}
```

The line

```
: Clock(center, radius)
```

means: Call the `Clock` constructor with parameters `center` and `radius` before executing the code inside the `{}`.

In general, the syntax for a derived-class constructor is

Derived`::`*Derived* `(`*derived construction parameters*`)`
`:` *Base* `(`*base construction parameters*`)`
`{` *derived data field initializations*
`}`

The colon is supposed to remind you of inheritance. (Actually, as explained in Advanced Topic 8.1, the same syntax can be used to invoke data field constructors as well, but then you place the name of the data field, not the name of the base class, after the colon. In this book, we choose not to use that syntax to initialize data fields.)

If you omit the base-class constructor, then the base object is constructed with the default constructor of the base class.

14.3 Calling Base-Class Member Functions

Let us now implement the `draw` function of the `WorldClock` class. To draw a world clock, we need to

- Draw the clock face
- Draw the city message

The second part is easy:

```
void WorldClock::draw() const
{  /* not complete */
   cwin << city;
}
```

But how do we draw the clock face? The `draw` method of the base class draws a clock face. Thus, we have to invoke `draw()` on some object. On which object?

The clock that we currently want to draw—that is, the implicit parameter of the `WorldClock::draw()` function. As we saw in Chapter 8, if you invoke another member function on the implicit parameter, you don't specify the parameter but just write the member function name:

```
void WorldClock::draw() const
{  draw(); /* not complete */
   cwin << city;
}
```

But this won't quite work. The compiler interprets

```
draw();
```

as

implicit parameter.`draw();`

Because the implicit parameter of `WorldClock::draw` is of type `WorldClock`, and there is a function called `draw` in the `WorldClock` class, that function will be called—but that is just the function we are currently writing! The function would call itself over and over, and the program would die in an infinite recursion.

Instead, we must be more specific *which* function called `draw` we want to call. We want `Clock::draw`:

```
void WorldClock::draw() const
{  Clock::draw();
   cwin << city;
}
```

This version of the `draw` member function is correct. To draw a world clock, first draw it as a clock, then draw the city name.

Here is the complete program that displays six world clocks. The `Clock` class has simply been copied from the code in Chapter 8, with no change. As you can see, the `WorldClock` code is quite short. This example shows how you can use inheritance to adapt existing code to a new purpose.

File clocks.cpp

```
#define CCC_WIN
#include "ccc.h"

/* This code is unchanged from Chapter 8 */

class Clock
{
public:
   Clock();
   Clock(Point c, float r);
```

```
   void set_time(Time t);

   void draw() const;
private:
   void draw_tick(float angle, float length) const;
   void draw_hand(float angle, float length) const;

   Time current_time;
   Point center;
   float radius;
};

Clock::Clock()
{
}

Clock::Clock(Point c, float r)
{  center = c;
   radius = r;
}

void Clock::set_time(Time t)
{  current_time = t;
}

void Clock::draw_tick(float angle, float length) const
{  float alpha = M_PI / 2 - 6 * angle * M_PI / 180;
   Point from(center.get_x() +
      cos(alpha) * radius * (1 - length),
      center.get_y() + sin(alpha) * radius * (1 - length));
   Point to(center.get_x() + cos(alpha) * radius,
      center.get_y() + sin(alpha) * radius);
   cwin << Line(from, to);
}

void Clock::draw_hand(float angle, float length) const
{  float alpha = M_PI / 2 - 6 * angle * M_PI / 180;
   Point from = center;
   Point to(center.get_x() + cos(alpha) * radius * length,
      center.get_y() + sin(alpha) * radius * length);
   cwin << Line(from, to);
}

void Clock::draw() const
{  cwin << Circle(center, radius);
   int i;
   const float HOUR_TICK_LENGTH = 0.2;
   const float MINUTE_TICK_LENGTH = 0.1;
   const float HOUR_HAND_LENGTH = 0.6;
   const float MINUTE_HAND_LENGTH = 0.75;
   for (i = 0; i < 12; i++)
```

```
   {  draw_tick(i * 5, HOUR_TICK_LENGTH);
      int j;
      for (j = 1; j <= 4; j++)
         draw_tick(i * 5 + j, MINUTE_TICK_LENGTH);
   }
   draw_hand(current_time.get_minutes(), MINUTE_HAND_LENGTH);
   draw_hand((current_time.get_hours() +
      current_time.get_minutes() / 60.0) * 5, HOUR_HAND_LENGTH);
}

/* This code extends the Clock code */

class WorldClock : public Clock
{
public:
   WorldClock();
   WorldClock(string city_name, float hour_diff,
      Point center, float radius);
   void draw() const;
private:
   Message city;
};

WorldClock::WorldClock() {}

WorldClock::WorldClock(string city_name, float hour_diff,
   Point center, float radius)
: Clock(center, radius)
{  Point p = center;
   p.move(0, -radius);
   city = Message(p, city_name);
   Time now;
   const float SECONDS_PER_HOUR = 60 * 60;
   now.add_seconds(hour_diff * SECONDS_PER_HOUR);
   set_time(now);
}

void WorldClock::draw() const
{  Clock::draw();
   cwin << city;
}

int main()
{  vector<WorldClock> clocks(6);

   /* populate clocks */
   clocks[0] = WorldClock("San Jose", 16, Point(-6.5, 5), 3);
   clocks[1] = WorldClock("Taipei", 7, Point(0, 5), 3);
   clocks[2] = WorldClock("Berlin", 1, Point(6.5, 5), 3);
```

```
   clocks[3] = WorldClock("Cairo", 2, Point(-6.5, -5), 3);
   clocks[4] = WorldClock("New York", 19, Point(0, -5), 3);
   clocks[5] = WorldClock("Bombay", 4.5, Point(6.5, -5), 3);

   int i;
   for (i = 0; i < clocks.size(); i++)
      clocks[i].draw();

   return EXIT_SUCCESS;
}
```

Common Error 14.2

Forgetting the Base-Class Name

A common error in extending the functionality of a base-class function is to forget the base-class name. For example, to draw a world clock we draw the hands and then show the city:

```
void WorldClock::draw() const
{  draw(); /* Error—should be Clock::draw() */
   cwin << city;
}
```

Here `draw()` refers to the `draw` function applied to the implicit parameter of the member function. The implicit parameter is of type `WorldClock`, and there is a `WorldClock::draw` function, so that function is called. Of course, that is a recursive call to the function that we are writing. Instead, we must be precise which `draw` function we want to call. In this case, we need to call `Clock::draw` explicitly.

Whenever you call a base-class function from a derived-class function with the same name, be sure to give the full name of the function, including the base-class name.

14.4 Polymorphism

In the preceding sections we saw one important use of inheritance: to reuse existing code in a new problem. In this section we will see an even more powerful application of inheritance: to model variation in object behavior.

Suppose some of the clocks on our travel agent's wall are analog clocks and others are digital (see Figure 4). Clearly, we need two classes—`AnalogClock` and `DigitalClock`—to model this situation. Each class has a `draw` function that draws the clock in the particular style.

However, if we use two separate classes, we lose something important. Consider the program of the preceding section. We were able to draw all of the clocks in a single loop:

Figure 4

Analog and Digital Clocks

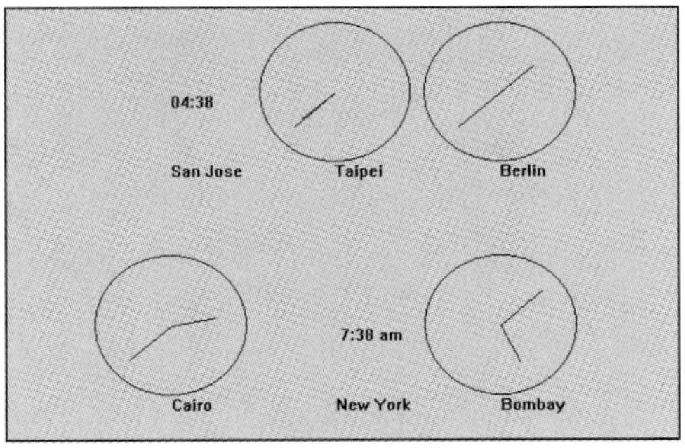


```
vector<WorldClock> clocks(6);
/* populate clocks */
for (i = 0; i < clocks.size(); i++)
   clocks[i].draw();
```

If we have two kinds of clocks, we can't collect them in a single vector. A vector holds elements *of the same type.*

However, there is some commonality between the two kinds of clocks. An analog clock is a kind of clock, and a digital clock is a kind of clock. We should be able to use inheritance to express this concept. Figure 5 shows the inheritance diagram.

The base class `Clock` of Chapter 8 is no longer suitable for us. Instead, we will create a new base class `WallClock` that expresses the commonalities between the analog and the digital clocks.

All clocks store a time and a city name. Furthermore, all clocks have a center position and a height. All clocks know how to draw themselves. Thus, we have the following definition for the base class:

```
class WallClock
{
public:
   WallClock(string city_name, float hour_diff,
      Point c, float r);
   void draw() const;
private:
   string city;
   Time current_time;
   Point center;
   float radius;
};

WallClock::WallClock(string city_name, float hour_diff,
   Point c, float r)
{  city = city_name;
   center = c;
   radius = r;
   const float SECONDS_PER_HOUR = 60 * 60;
```

Figure 5

Inheritance Diagram for Clocks

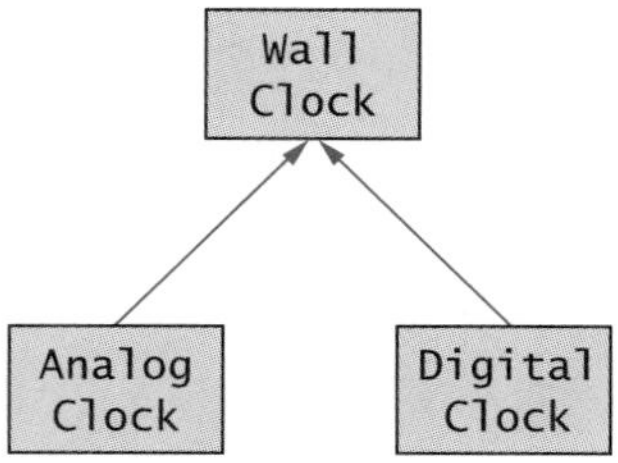


```
      current_time.add_seconds(hour_diff * SECONDS_PER_HOUR);
   }
```

We cannot do much to draw the time, because the `WallClock` does not know which style should be used—analog or digital. However, there is one service that the `WallClock` can provide: namely to draw the city name in the correct position. Because the task is common to all styles of clocks, it is a good idea to carry it out in the base class. The derived-class versions of `draw` will simply call `WallClock::draw`.

```
void WallClock::draw() const
{  Point p = center;
   p.move(0, -radius);
   cwin << Message(p, city);
}
```

Next, let us derive the analog and digital clocks.

```
class AnalogClock : public WallClock
{
public:
   AnalogClock(string city_name, float hour_diff,
      Point c, float r);
   void draw() const
};

class DigitalClock : public WallClock
{
public:
   DigitalClock(string city_name, float hour_diff,
      Point c, float r, bool am_pm);
   void draw() const;
private:
   bool use_am_pm;
};
```

Each of these classes has its own `draw` function. The analog clock draws the analog clock face (for simplicity, without ticks). The digital clock draws a message with the current time. A digital clock can display the time either in 12-hour A.M./P.M. format (2:00 P.M.) or in 24-hour "military" format (14:00).

Let us implement the **draw** function of the digital clock first:

```
void DigitalClock::draw() const /* has errors */
{  WallClock::draw();
   string time;
   int hours = current_time.get_hours();
   int minutes = current_time.get_minutes();
   if (use_am_pm)
   {  string suffix;
      if (hours < 12)
      {  if (hours == 0) hours = 12;
         suffix = " am";
      }
      else
      {  hours = hours - 12;
         suffix = " pm";
      }
      time = format("%2d", hours) + ":"
         + format("%02d", minutes) + suffix;
   }
   else
      time = format("%02d", hours) + ":"
         + format("%02d", minutes);
   cwin << Message(center, time);
}
```

Unfortunately, there is a problem with the code. While it is true that each object of type `DigitalClock` inherits the data fields **current_time** and **start** from the `WallClock` base class, accessing these data fields is not allowed. They are private data of `WallClock`.

We must design the **WallClock** class more carefully. The **WallClock** class is intended to collect the common properties of all clocks and to allow each derived clock type to carry out its own **draw** operation. Therefore the **WallClock** class must give out the necessary information for the drawing: namely the current time and clock position. We therefore supply the appropriate accessor functions in the base class:

```
class WallClock
{
public:
   WallClock(string city_name, float hour_diff,
      Point top_left, float h);
   void draw() const;
   Time get_time() const;
   Point get_center() const;
   float get_radius() const;
private:
   string city;
   Time current_time;
```

```
      Point center;
      float radius;
   };
```

The `DigitalClock::draw` function must call these accessor functions:

```
void DigitalClock::draw() const
{  WallClock::draw();
   string time;
   int hours =  get_time().get_hours();
   int minutes = get_time().get_minutes();
   if (use_am_pm)
   {  string suffix;
      if (hours < 12)
      {  if (hours == 0) hours = 12;
         suffix = " am";
      }
      else
      {  hours = hours - 12;
         suffix = " pm";
      }
      time = format("%2d", hours) + ":"
         + format("%02d", minutes) + suffix;
   }
   else
      time = format("%02d", hours) + ":"
         + format("%02d", minutes);
   cwin << Message(:get_center(), time);
}
```

You can find the code for the `AnalogClock::draw` function in the next section. It too needs to use the accessor functions to access the base class data.

Advanced Topic 14.1

Protected Access

We ran into some degree of grief when trying to implement the `draw` member function of the `DigitalClock` class. That member function needed access to the data fields of the base class. Our remedy was to have the base class provide the appropriate accessor functions.

C++ offers another solution to this problem. The base class can declare the data fields as *protected*:

```
class WallClock
{
public:
   WallClock(string city_name, float hour_diff,
      Point top_left, float h);
```

```
   void draw() const;
protected:
   string city;
   Time current_time;
   Point center;
   float radius;
};
```

Protected data can be accessed by the member functions of a class and all its derived classes. For example, `DigitalClock` inherits from `WallClock`, so its member functions can access the protected data members of the `WallClock` class.

Some programmers like the `protected` access feature because it seems to strike a balance between absolute protection (making all data members private) and no protection at all (making all data members public). However, experience has shown that protected data members are subject to the same kind of problems as public data members. The designer of the base class has no control over the authors of derived classes. Any of the derived-class member functions can corrupt the base-class data. Furthermore, classes with protected data members are hard to modify. Even if the author of the base class would like to change the data implementation, the protected data members cannot be changed, because someone might have written a derived class whose code depends on them.

It is best to leave all data private. If you want to grant access to the data only to derived-class member functions, consider making the *accessor* function protected.

14.5 Virtual Functions

Now let us write the code that generates a collection of clocks (some analog, some digital) and draws them:

```
vector<WallClock> clocks(6);

/* populate clocks */
clocks[0] = DigitalClock("San Jose", 16,
   Point(-6.5, 5), 3, false);
clocks[1] = AnalogClock("Taipei", 7,
   Point(0, 5), 3);
clocks[2] = AnalogClock("Berlin",1,
   Point(6.5, 5), 3);
clocks[3] = AnalogClock("Cairo", 2,
   Point(-6.5, -5),3);
clocks[4] = DigitalClock("New York", 19,
   Point(0, -5), 3,true);
clocks[5] = AnalogClock("Bombay", 4.5,
   Point(6.5, -5), 3);

for (i= 0; i < clocks.size(); i++)
   clocks[i].draw();
```

Unfortunately, that does not work. The vector `clocks` holds objects of type `WallClock`. The compiler realizes that a `DigitalClock` is a special case of a `WallClock`. Thus it permits the assignment from a digital clock to a wall clock:

```
clocks[0] = DigitalClock("San Jose", 16, Point(0, 0),
   0.9, false);
```

However, a `WallClock` object has four data items, whereas a `DigitalClock` object has an additional data item: namely, the `use_am_pm` flag. There is no room to store the derived-class data. That data simply gets *sliced away* when you assign a derived-class object to a base-class variable (see Figure 6).

This problem is very typical of code that needs to manipulate objects from a mixture of data types. Derived-class objects are usually bigger than base-class objects, and objects of different derived classes have different sizes. A vector of objects cannot deal with this variation in sizes.

Instead, we need to store the actual objects elsewhere and just collect their locations in a vector by storing pointers. (If you have skipped Chapter 13, you will now need to turn to Section 13.2 to learn about pointers. You can read that section independently of the remainder of Chapter 13.)

Figure 7 shows the array of pointers. The reason for using pointers is simple: Pointers to the various clock objects all have the same size—namely, the size of a memory address—even though the objects themselves may have different sizes.

Here is the code to set up the array of pointers:

```
vector<WallClock*> clocks(6);

/* populate clocks */
clocks[0] = new DigitalClock("San Jose", 16,
   Point(-6.5, 5), 3, false);
clocks[1] = new AnalogClock("Taipei", 7,
   Point(0, 5), 3);
clocks[2] = new AnalogClock("Berlin", 1,
   Point(6.5, 5), 3);
clocks[3] = new AnalogClock("Cairo", 2,
   Point(-6.5, -5), 3);
clocks[4] = new DigitalClock("New York", 19,
   Point(0, -5), 3, true);
clocks[5] = new AnalogClock("Bombay", 4.5,
   Point(6.5, -5), 3);
```

Note that each of these assignments assigns a derived-class pointer (`DigitalClock*` or `AnalogClock*`) to a base-class pointer. This is perfectly legal. A pointer is the starting address of an object. Since every `AnalogClock` is a special case of a `WallClock`, the starting address of an `AnalogClock` object is, in particular, the starting address of a `WallClock` object. The reverse assignment—from a base-class pointer to a derived-class pointer—is an error.

Of course, `clocks[i]` is a pointer to the `i`th object, not the `i`th object itself. Thus, the code to draw all clocks is

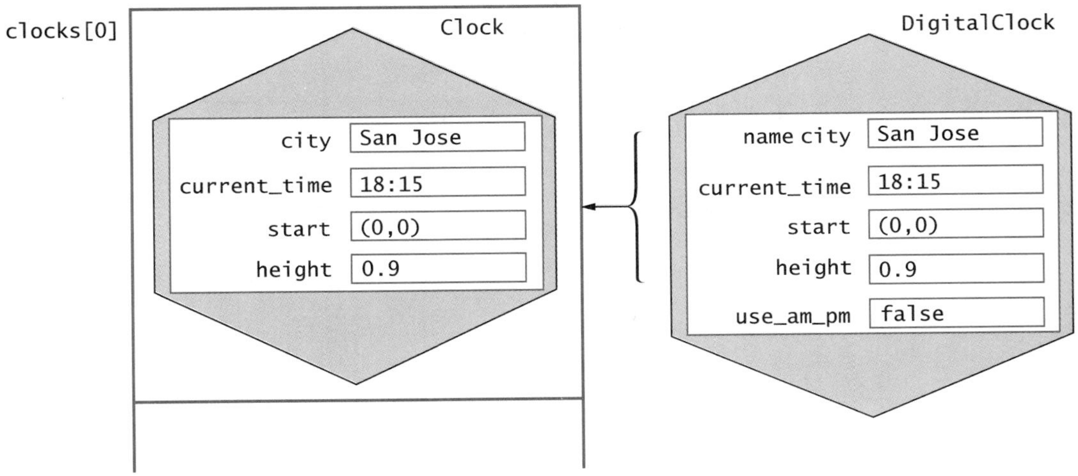

Figure 6

Slicing Away Derived-Class Data

Figure 7

A Polymorphic Array

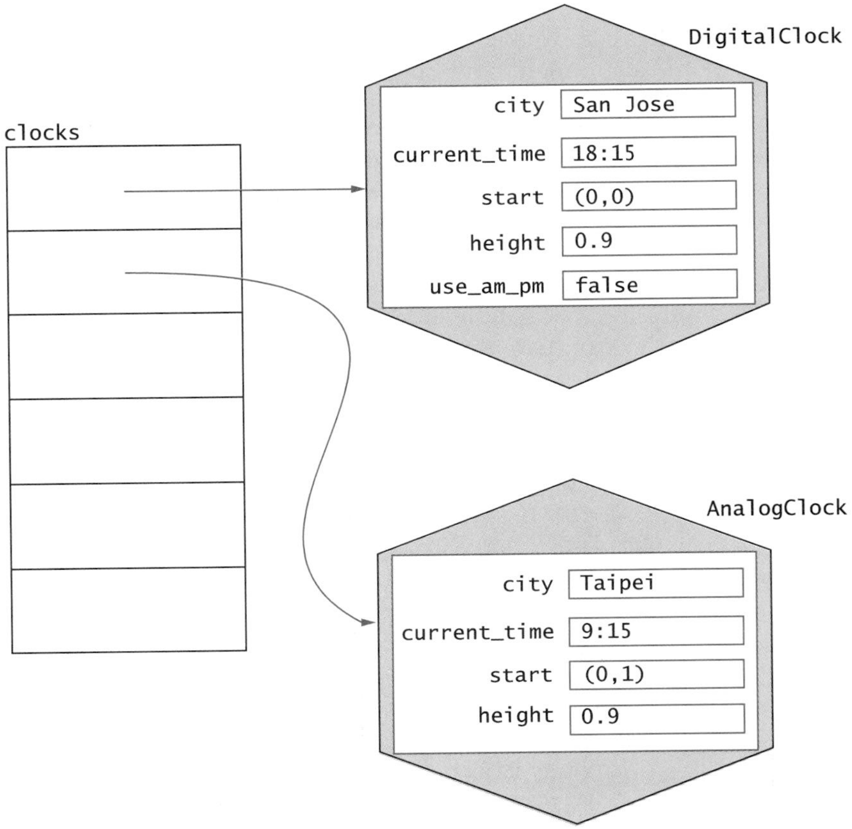

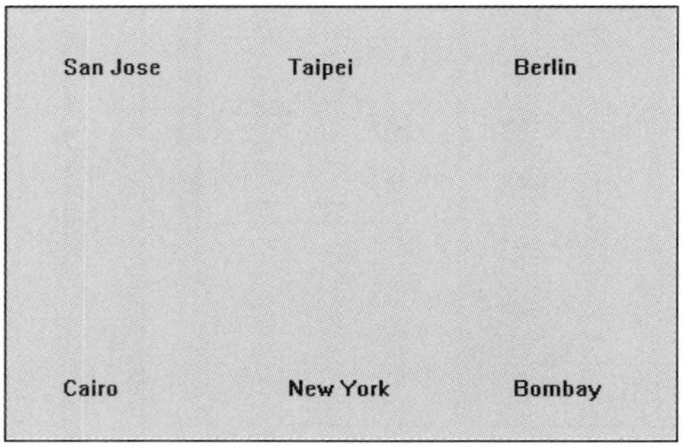

Figure 8

Result of Statically Bound `draw`

```
for (i = 0; i < clocks.size(); i++)
   (*clocks[i]).draw();
```

Unfortunately, there remains a problem. Figure 8 shows the resulting display. As you can see, none of the clocks were plotted. Only the names were displayed. The compiler generated code only to call `WallClock::draw`, not the `draw` function that was appropriate for each object.

In the compiler's defense, it actually took the correct action. A member function call is compiled into a call to one particular function. It is the compiler's job to find the appropriate function that should be called. In this case, the pointer `clocks[i]` points to the implicit parameter; it is a pointer of type `WallClock*`. The name of the function is `draw`; hence, the compiler calls `WallClock::draw`.

However, in this case we really do not want a simple function call. We want first to determine the actual type of the object to which `clocks[i]` points, which can be either an `AnalogClock` or a `DigitalClock` object, and then call *its* `draw` function. This too can be arranged in C++. We must alert the compiler that the function call needs to be preceded by the selection of the appropriate version of the `draw` function, which can be a different one for every iteration in the loop.

Such a selection/call combination is called *dynamic binding*. In contrast, the traditional call, which always invokes the same function, is called *static binding*. To tell the C++ compiler that a particular function needs to be bound dynamically, the function must be tagged as `virtual`:

```
class WallClock
{
public:
   WallClock(string city_name, float hour_diff,
      Point top_left, float h);
   virtual void draw() const;
   Time get_time() const;
   Point get_start() const;
   float get_height() const;
private:
   string city;
   Time current_time;
   Point start;
```

```
   float height;
};
```

The `virtual` keyword must be used in the *base class*. All functions with the same name and parameter types in derived classes are then automatically virtual. However, it is considered good taste to supply the `virtual` keyword for the derived-class functions as well. You do not supply the keyword virtual in the function definition:

```
void WallClock::draw() const /* no virtual keyword */
{  Point p = center;
   p.move(0, -radius);
   cwin << Message(p, city);
}
```

Whenever a virtual function is called, the compiler determines the type of the implicit parameter in the particular call at run time. The appropriate function for that object is then called. For example, when the `draw` function is declared virtual, the call

```
(*clocks[i]).draw();
```

always calls the draw function belonging to the actual type of the object to which `clocks[i]` points—either `AnalogClock::draw` or `DigitalClock::draw`.

Only member functions can be virtual. A member function that is not tagged as `virtual` is statically bound. That is, the type of the implicit parameter, as it is known at compile time, is used to select one function, and that function is always called. Because static binding is less complex, it is the default in C++. You should use virtual functions only when you need the flexibility of dynamic binding at run time.

Here is the complete clock program, using virtual functions:

File clocks2.cpp

```
#define CCC_WIN
#include "ccc.h"

class WallClock
{
public:
   WallClock();
   WallClock(string city_name, float hour_diff,
      Point c, float r);
   virtual void draw() const;
   Time get_time() const;
   Point get_center() const;
   float get_radius() const;
private:
   string city;
   Time current_time;
   Point center;
```

```
   float radius;
};

class AnalogClock : public WallClock
{
public:
   AnalogClock();
   AnalogClock(string city_name, float hour_diff,
      Point c, float r);
   virtual void draw() const;
private:
   void draw_hand(float angle, float length) const;
};

class DigitalClock : public WallClock
{
public:
   DigitalClock();
   DigitalClock(string city_name, float hour_diff,
      Point c, float r, bool am_pm);
   virtual void draw() const;
private:
   bool use_am_pm;
};

WallClock::WallClock()
{
}

WallClock::WallClock(string city_name, float hour_diff,
   Point c, float r)
{  city = city_name;
   center = c;
   radius = r;
   const float SECONDS_PER_HOUR = 60 * 60;
   current_time.add_seconds(hour_diff * SECONDS_PER_HOUR);
}

Time WallClock::get_time() const
{  return current_time;
}

Point WallClock::get_center() const
{  return center;
}

float WallClock::get_radius() const
{  return radius;
}
```

```
void WallClock::draw() const
{  Point p = center;
   p.move(0, -radius);
   cwin << Message(p, city);
}

AnalogClock::AnalogClock()
{
}

AnalogClock::AnalogClock(string city_name, float hour_diff,
   Point c, float r)
: WallClock(city_name, hour_diff, c, r)
{
}

void AnalogClock::draw_hand(float angle, float length) const
{  float alpha = M_PI / 2 - 6 * angle * M_PI / 180;
   Point from = get_center();
   Point to = from;
   to.move(cos(alpha) * get_radius() * length,
      sin(alpha) * get_radius() * length);
   cwin << Line(from, to);
}

void AnalogClock::draw() const
{  WallClock::draw();
   cwin << Circle(get_center(), get_radius());
   const float HOUR_HAND_LENGTH = 0.6;
   const float MINUTE_HAND_LENGTH = 0.75;
   draw_hand(get_time().get_minutes(), MINUTE_HAND_LENGTH);
   draw_hand((get_time().get_hours() +
      get_time().get_minutes() / 60.0) * 5, HOUR_HAND_LENGTH);
}

DigitalClock::DigitalClock()
{
}

DigitalClock::DigitalClock(string city_name, float hour_diff,
   Point c, float r, bool am_pm)
: WallClock(city_name, hour_diff, c, r)
{  use_am_pm = am_pm;
}

void DigitalClock::draw() const
{  WallClock::draw();
   string time;
   int hours = get_time().get_hours();
```

```
      int minutes = get_time().get_minutes();
      if (use_am_pm)
      {  string suffix;
         if (hours < 12)
         {  if (hours == 0) hours = 12;
            suffix = " am";
         }
         else
         {  hours = hours - 12;
            suffix = " pm";
         }
         time = format("%2d", hours) + ":"
            + format("%02d", minutes) + suffix;
      }
      else
         time = format("%02d", hours) + ":"
            + format("%02d", minutes);
      cwin << Message(get_center(), time);
   }

   int main()
   {  vector<WallClock*> clocks(6);

      /* populate clocks */
      clocks[0] = new DigitalClock("San Jose", 16,
                                   Point(-6.5, 5), 3, false);
      clocks[1] = new AnalogClock("Taipei", 7, Point(0, 5), 3);
      clocks[2] = new AnalogClock("Berlin", 1, Point(6.5, 5), 3);
      clocks[3] = new AnalogClock("Cairo", 2, Point(-6.5, -5), 3);
      clocks[4] = new DigitalClock("New York", 19,
                                   Point(0, -5), 3, true);
      clocks[5] = new AnalogClock("Bombay", 4.5,
                                  Point(6.5, -5), 3);

      int i;
      for (i = 0; i < clocks.size(); i++)
         (*clocks[i]).draw();

      return EXIT_SUCCESS;
   }
```

Virtual functions give programs a great deal of flexibility. The drawing loop needs to describe only the general mechanism: "Draw each clock". Each object knows on its own how to carry out the specific task: "Draw yourself".

Using virtual functions makes programs *easily extensible.* Suppose we want to draw two kinds of analog clocks: one with a round border and one with a square border. All we need to do is to define new classes `RoundAnalogClock` and `SquareAnalogClock`, each with its own `draw` function. Then we can populate the `clocks` array with a mixture of round and square analog clocks as well as digital clocks. The code that draws all clocks,

```
for (i = 0; i < clocks.size(); i++)
   (*clocks[i]).draw();
```

need not be changed at all! The dynamically bound **draw** function automatically selects the correct member functions of the newly defined classes.

Common Error 14.3

Slicing an Object

In C++ it is legal to copy a derived-class object into a base-class variable. However, any derived-class information is lost in the process. For example, when a `Manager` object is assigned to a variable of type `Employee`, the result is only the employee portion of the manager data:

```
Manager m;
. . .
Employee e = m; /* holds only the Employee base data of m */
```

Any information that is particular to managers is *sliced off,* because it would not fit into a variable of type `Employee`. This slicing may indeed be what you want. The code using the variable `e` may not care about the `Manager` part of the object and just need to consider it as an employee.

Note that the reverse assignment is not legal. That is, you cannot copy a base-class object into a derived-class variable.

```
Employee e;
. . .
Manager m = e; /* Error */
```

14.6 Class Relationships

Inheritance is a very important relationship between classes. It is a relationship between a more general class (the base class) and a more specialized class (the derived class). This relationship is often described as the *is-a* relationship. Every manager *is an* employee. Every digital clock *is a* wall clock.

Whenever you find two classes that are related by the is-a relationship, then it makes sense to use inheritance in the C++ program. However, like every tool, inheritance can be abused and overused.

For example, should the class `Clock` of Chapter 8 derive from `Circle`? It sounds convenient. The `Circle` base class would store the center and radius, which would reduce clutter. While perhaps practical for the programmer, this arrangement makes no sense conceptually. It isn't true that every clock is a circle. Clocks show the time, whereas circles are geometric objects. We would never envision a scenario where we have a polymorphic mixture of objects, some of which are plain circles while others are clocks.

There is a relationship between clocks and circles, though. A clock *has a* circle on the boundary. C++ lets us model that relationship, by using a data member:

```
class Clock
{...
private:
   Time current_time;
   Circle boundary;
};
```

The technical term for this relationship is *aggregation.* In C++, aggregation is implemented by using data fields.

Here is another example. Every car *is a* vehicle. Every car *has a* tire (in fact, it has four or, if you count the spare, five). Thus, you would use inheritance from `Vehicle` and use aggregation of `Tire` objects:

```
class Car : public Vehicle
{...
private:
   vector<Tire> tires;
   ...
};
```

In class diagrams that follow the so-called "unified notation" (see [1]), this has-a relationship is denoted by a line with a diamond. The diamond is placed toward the aggregating class. Figure 9 shows a class diagram with an is-a and a has-a relationship.

A central principle of object-oriented design is to capture all class relationships in a programming problem before starting to write code. Class diagrams are a useful tool for visualizing these relationships, especially for complex situations. See [2] for more information on object-oriented design methods.

Figure 9

Class Diagram with Inheritance and Aggregation

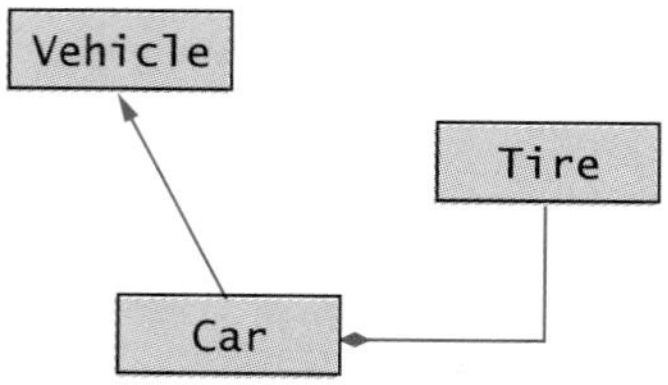

Random Fact 14.1

Operating Systems

Without an operating system, a computer would not be useful. Minimally, you need an operating system to locate files and to start programs. The programs that you run need services from the operating system to access devices and to interact with other programs. Operating systems on large computers need to provide more services than those on personal computers. Here are some typical services:

- *Program loading.* Every operating system provides some way of launching application programs. The user indicates what program should be run, usually by typing the name of the program in or by clicking on an icon. The operating system locates the program code, loads it in memory, and starts it.
- *Managing files.* A storage device such as a hard disk is, electronically, simply a device capable of storing a huge sequence of zeroes and ones. It is up to the operating system to bring some structure to the storage layout and organize it into files, folders, and so on. The operating system also needs to impose some amount of security and redundancy into the file system so that a power outage does not jeopardize the contents of an entire hard disk. Some operating systems do a better job in this regard than others.
- *Virtual memory.* RAM memory is expensive, and few computers have enough RAM to hold all programs and their data that a user would like to run simultaneously. Most operating systems extend the available memory by storing some data on the hard disk. The application programs do not realize what is happening. When a program accesses a data item that is currently not in RAM memory, the processor senses this and notifies the operating system. The operating system swaps the needed data from the hard disk into RAM, simultaneously swapping out a memory block of equal size that had not been accessed for some time.
- *Handling multiple users.* The operating systems of large and powerful computers allow simultaneous access by multiple users. Each user is connected to the computer through a separate terminal. The operating system authenticates users by checking that they have a valid account and password. It gives each user a small *slice* of processor time, then serves the next user.
- *Multitasking.* Even if you are the sole user of a computer, you may want to run multiple applications—for example, to read your email in one window and run the C++compiler in another. The operating system is responsible to divide processor time between the applications you are running, so that each can make progress.
- *Printing.* The operating system queues up the print requests that are sent by multiple applications. This is necessary to make sure that the printed pages do not contain a mixture of words send simultaneously from separate programs.
- *Windows.* Many operating systems present their users with a desktop made up of multiple windows. The operating system manages the location and appearance of the window frames; the applications are responsible for the interior.
- *Fonts.* To render text on the screen and the printer, the shapes of characters must be defined. This is especially important for programs that can display multiple type styles and sizes. Modern operating systems contain a central font repository.
- *Communicating between programs.* The operating system can facilitate the transfer of information between programs. That transfer can happen through *cut and paste* or *interprocess communication.* Cut and paste is a user-initiated data transfer in which the user copies data from one application into a transfer buffer (often called a "clipboard") managed by the operating system and inserts the buffer's contents into another application.

Interprocess communication is initiated by applications that transfer data without direct user involvement.

- *Networking.* The operating system provides protocols and services for enabling applications to reach information on other computers attached to the network.

Today, the most popular operating systems are Unix and its variants (such as Linux), the Macintosh System, and Windows.

Further Reading

[1] Grady Booch and James Rumbaugh, *Unified Method for Object-Oriented Development,* Rational Software Corporation, Santa Clara, CA, 1995.

[2] Grady Booch, *Object-Oriented Analysis and Design,* Benjamin-Cummings, 1994.

Review Exercises

Exercise R14.1. In an object-oriented traffic simulation system, we have the following classes:

```
Vehicle
Car
Truck
Sedan
Coupe
PickupTruck
SportUtilityVehicle
Minivan
Bicycle
Motorcycle
```

Draw an inheritance diagram that shows the relationships between these classes.

Exercise R14.2. What inheritance relationships would you establish among the following classes?

```
Student
Professor
TeachingAssistant
Employee
Secretary
DepartmentChair
Janitor
SeminarSpeaker
Person
Course
Seminar
Lecture
ComputerLab
```

Exercise R14.3. Derive a class `Programmer` from `Employee`. Supply a constructor `Programmer(string name, float salary)` that calls the base-class constructor.

Exercise R14.4. Consider the following classes `B` and `D`:

```
class B
{
public:
   B();
   B(int n);
};

B::B() { cout << "B::B()\n"; }
B::B(int n) { cout << "B::B(" << n << ")\n"; }

class D : public B
{
public:
   D();
   D(int n);
private:
   B b;
};

D::D() { cout << "D::D()\n"; }
D::D(int n) : B(n) { b = B(-n); cout << "D::D("<< n
   <<")\n"; }
```

What does the following program print?

```
int main()
{  D d(3);
   return EXIT_SUCCESS;
}
```

Determine the answer by hand, not by compiling and running the program.

Exercise R14.5. What does the following program print?

```
class B
{
public:
   void print(int n) const;
};

void B::print(int n) const
{  cout <<n<<"\n";
}
```

```
class D : public B
{
public:
   void print(int n) const;
};
void D::print(int n) const
{  if (n <= 1) B::print(n);
   else if (n % 2 == 0) print(n / 2);
   else print(3 * n + 1);
}

int main()
{  D d;
   d.print(3);
   return EXIT_SUCCESS;
}
```

Determine the answer by hand, not by compiling and running the program.

Exercise R14.6. What is wrong with the following code?

```
class B
{
public:
   B();
   B(int n);
   void print() const;
private:
   int b;
};

B::B() { b = 0; }
B::B(int n) { b = n; }
void B::print() const { cout << "B: " << b << "\n"; }

class D : public B
{
public:
   D();
   D(int n);
   void print(int n) const;
private:
   B b;
};

D::D() {}
D::D(int n) { b = n; }
void D::print() const { cout << "D: " << b << "\n"; }
```

How can you fix the errors?

Exercise R14.7. Suppose the class D inherits from B. Which of the following assignments are legal?

```
B b;
D d;
B* pb;
D* pd;
b = d;
d = b;
pd = pb;
pb = pd;
d = pd;
b = *pd;
*pd = *pb;
```

Exercise R14.8. Which of the following calls are statically bound, and which are dynamically bound? What does the program print?

```
class B
{
public:
   B();
   virtual void p() const;
   void q() const;
};

B::B() {}
void B::p() const { cout << "B::p\n"; }
void B::q() const { cout << "B::q\n"; }

class D : public B
{
public:
   D();
   virtual void p() const;
   void q() const;
};

D::D() {}
void D::p() const { cout << "D::p\n"; }
void D::q() const { cout << "D::q\n"; }

int main()
{  B b;
   D d;
   B* pb = new B;
   B* pd = new D;
   D* pd2 = new D;
```

```
      b.p(); b.q();
      d.p(); d.q();
      (*pb).p();  (*pb).q();
      (*pd).p();  (*pd).q();
      (*pd2).p(); (*pd2).q();
   }
```

Determine the answer by hand, not by compiling and running the program.

Exercise R14.9. True or false?

- When a member function is invoked through a pointer, it is always statically bound.
- When a member function is invoked through an object, it is always statically bound.
- Only member functions can be dynamically bound.
- Only nonmember functions can be statically bound.
- When a function is virtual in the base class, it cannot be made nonvirtual in a derived class.
- Calling a virtual function is slower than calling a nonvirtual function.
- Constructors can be virtual.
- It is good programming practice to make all member functions virtual.

Exercise R14.10. Could the `Clock` class of Chapter 8 inherit from `Time` instead of having a data field of type `Time`? Explain the advantages and disadvantages of this approach.

Exercise R14.11. Draw a class diagram of all classes in the clock game of Chapter 9. Indicate all aggregation relationships between classes.

Exercise R14.12. What relationship is appropriate between the following classes: aggregation, inheritance, or neither?

```
University—Student
Student—TeachingAssistant
Student—Freshman
Student—Professor
Car—Door
Truck—Vehicle
Traffic—TrafficSign
TrafficSign—Color
```

Exercise R14.13. Every Volvo is a car. Should a class `Volvo` inherit from the class `Car`? Volvo is a car manufacturer. Does that mean that the class `Volvo` should inherit from the class `CarManufacturer`?

Exercise R14.14. Some C++ books recommend deriving the class `Circle` from the class `Point`. Then the `Circle` class inherits the `move` function from the `Point` base class. Explain why the `move` member function need not be redefined in the derived class. Why is it nevertheless not a good idea to have `Circle` inherit from `Point`? Conversely, would deriving `Point` from `Circle` fulfill the "is-a" rule? Would it be a good idea?

Programming Exercises

Exercise P14.1. A triangle is a special case of a polygon. Implement a class `Triangle` that inherits from the `Polygon` class of Chapter 9. Supply a constructor `Triangle (Point a, Point b, Point c)`. Do you need to implement a `Triangle::plot` function, or can you inherit the `Polygon::plot` function?

Exercise P14.2. Implement a base class `Person`. Derive classes `Student` and `Instructor` from `Person`. A person has a name and a birthday. A student has a major, and an instructor has a salary. Write the class definitions, the constructors, and the member functions `print()` for all classes.

Exercise P14.3. Derive a class `Manager` from `Employee`. Add a data field, named `department`, of type `string`. Supply a function `print` that prints the manager's name, department, and salary. Derive a class `Executive` from `Manager`. Supply a function `print` that prints the string `Executive`, followed by the information stored in the `Manager` base object.

Exercise P14.4. Implement a base class `Account` and derived classes `Savings` and `Checking`. In the base class, supply member functions `deposit` and `withdraw`. Provide a function `daily_interest` that computes and adds the daily interest. For calculations, assume that every month has 30 days. Checking accounts yield interest of 3% monthly on balances over $1,000. Savings accounts yield interest of 6% on the entire balance. Write a driver program that makes a month's worth of deposits and withdrawals and calculates the interest every day.

Exercise P14.5. In the travel agent clock program, define two new classes, named `RoundAnalogClock` and `SquareAnalogClock`, each with its own `draw` function. Populate the `clocks` array with a mixture of round and square analog clocks as well as digital clocks. Draw all clocks.

Exercise P14.6. Measure the speed difference between a statically bound call and a dynamically bound call. Use the `Time` class to measure the time spent in one loop of virtual function calls and another loop of regular function calls.

Exercise P14.7. Write a base class `Worker` and derived classes `HourlyWorker` and `SalariedWorker`. Every worker has a name and a salary rate. Write a virtual function compute_pay(int hours) that computes the weekly pay for every worker. An hourly worker gets paid the hourly wage for the actual number of hours worked, if hours is at most 40. If the hourly worker worked more than 40 hours, the excess is paid at time and a half. The salaried worker gets paid the hourly wage for 40 hours, no matter what the actual number of hours is.

Exercise P14.8. Implement a base class Vehicle and derived classes Car and Truck. A vehicle has a position on the screen. Write virtual functions draw that draw cars and trucks as follows:

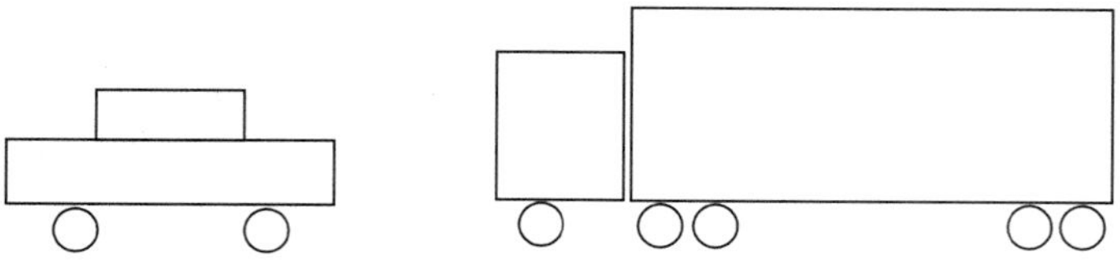

Then populate a vector of Vehicle* pointers with a mixture of cars and trucks, and draw all of them.

Exercise P14.9. Implement a base class Appointment and derived classes Onetime, Daily, Weekly, and Monthly. An appointment has a description (for example, "see the dentist") and a date and time. Write a virtual function occurs_on(Date d) that checks whether the appointment occurs on date d. For example, for a monthly appointment, you must check whether the day of the month matches. Then fill a vector of Appointment* with a mixture of appointments. Have the user enter a date and print out all appointments that happen on that date.

Exercise P14.10. Improve the appointment book program of the preceding exercise. Give the user the option to add new appointments. The user must specify the type of the appointment, the description, and the date and time.

Exercise P14.11. Improve the appointment book program of the preceding exercises by letting the user save the appointment data to a file and reload the data from a file. The saving part is straightforward: Make a virtual function save. Save out the type, description, date, and time. The loading part is not so easy. You must first determine the type of the appointment to be loaded, create an object of that type with its default constructor, and then call a virtual load function to load the remainder.

Exercise P14.12. Implement a base class Shape and derived classes Rectangle, Triangle, and Square. Derive Square from Rectangle. Supply virtual functions float area() and void plot(). Fill a vector of Shape* pointers with a mixture of the shapes, plot them all, and compute the total area.

Exercise P14.13. Use the preceding exercise as the basis for a drawing program. Users can place various shapes onto the screen by first clicking on a shape icon and then clicking on the desired screen location:

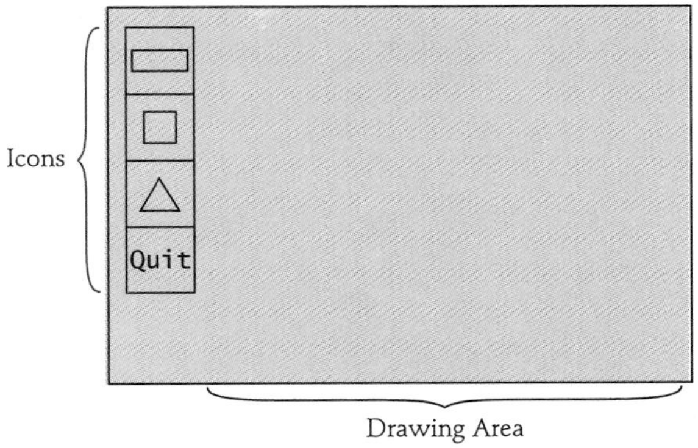

Users can save drawings to disk files and reload drawings from files. Follow the hints of Exercise P14.11.

Exercise P14.14. Extend the program of the preceding exercise by adding another shape type: `CircleShape`. (You cannot call it `Circle`, because there already is a `Circle` class in the graphics library.) Explain what changes you needed to make in the program to implement this extension. How do virtual functions help in making the program easily extensible?

Exercise P14.15. Reimplement the drawing program of Exercise P14.13 by using the `Polygon` type from Chapter 9. That is, do not use the `Shape` class, and do not use inheritance. When you are done, add the ability to draw circles, using the `Circle` type from the graphics library. Explain what changes you needed to make in the program to implement this extension. How would virtual functions have made it easier to extend the program?

Exercise P14.16. Write a base class `Chart` that stores a vector of floating-point values. Implement derived classes, `PieChart` and `BarChart`, with a virtual `plot` function that can plot the data as a pie chart and as a bar chart.

Appendix A1

C++ Language Coding Guidelines

A1.1 Introduction

This coding style guide is a simplified version of one that has been used with good success both in industrial practice and for college courses. It lays down rules that you must follow for your programming assignments.

A style guide is a set of mandatory requirements for layout and formatting. Uniform style makes it easier for you to read code from your instructor and classmates. You will really appreciate that if you do a team project. It is also easier for your instructor and your grader to grasp the essence of your programs quickly.

A style guide makes you a more productive programmer because it *reduces gratuitous choice*. If you don't have to make choices about trivial matters, you can spend your energy on the solution of real problems.

In these guidelines a number of constructs are plainly outlawed. That doesn't mean that programmers using them are evil or incompetent. It does mean that the constructs are of marginal utility and can be expressed just as well or even better with other language constructs.

If you have already programmed in C or C++, you may be initially uncomfortable at giving up some fond habits. However, it is a sign of professionalism to set aside personal preferences in minor matters and to compromise for the benefit of your group.

These guidelines are necessarily somewhat long and dull. They also mention features that you may not yet have seen in the class. Here are the most important highlights:

1. Tabs are set every three spaces (8.2).
2. Variable and function names are lowercase (8.1).
3. Constant names are uppercase (8.1).

4. There are spaces after keywords and between binary operators (8.2).
5. Braces must line up (8.3).
6. No magic numbers may be used (5.2).
7. Every function must have a comment (3.1).
8. At most 30 lines of code may be used per function (3.3).
9. No `goto`, `continue`, or `break` is allowed (7.3).
10. At most 3 global variables may be used per file (2.6).

A note to the instructor: Of course, many programmers and organizations have strong feelings about coding style. If this style guide is incompatible with your own preferences or with local custom, please feel free to modify it. For that purpose, this coding style guide is available in electronic form from the author.

A1.2 Modules

A1.2.1 Source File Layout

Each C++program is a collection of one or more files or modules. The executable program is obtained by compiling and linking these files. Organize the material in each file as follows:

- Header comment block
- `#include` statements
- Constants
- Classes
- Global variables
- Functions

A1.2.2 Header Comment

Each module starts with a header comment block in the format below.

```
/*******************************************************
COPYRIGHT (C):      1997, All Rights Reserved.
PROJECT:            CS 46A Homework #4
FILE:               wm.cpp
PURPOSE:            widget manipulation
COMPILER:           Borland C++ 3.1
TARGET:             IBM PC/DOS
PROGRAMMER:         Jenny Koo (JK)
START DATE:         6/11/97
*******************************************************/
```

Below the header comments is an optional notes block.

```
/* NOTES **************************************************

General comments go here, for example:
  - Command line options
  - File formats
  - Rules and conventions
  - Pictures of the main data structures
    ...
**********************************************************/
```

A1.2.3 Included Header Files

This section lists all included header files.

```
/* INCLUDE *********************************************/

#include "iostream.h"
#include "ccc.h"
```

Do not embed absolute path names, such as

```
#include "c:\borlandc\include\stdlib.h"  /* Don't !!! */
```

A1.2.4 The Constants Section

This section contains constants that are needed throughout the program file.

```
/* CONSTANTS *******************************************/

const int GRID_SIZE = 20;
const float CLOCK_RADIUS = 5;
```

A1.2.5 The Class Section

This section contains the definitions of classes.

```
/* CLASSES *********************************************/

class Product
{  . . .
};
```

A1.2.6 The Globals Section

This section contains the definitions of global variables.

```
/* GLOBALS *********************************************/

float annual_raise; /* this year's raise for all employees */
```

Every global variable must have a comment explaining its purpose.

Avoid global variables whenever possible. You may use at most three global variables in any one module.

A1.2.7 The Functions Section

This section lists all functions of the module. Sort the functions so that all functions are defined before they are called. Use a prototype only in the rare case of a cyclic calling pattern. Put `main` last.

```
/* FUNCTIONS *******************************************/

long dat2jul(int d, int m, int y)
/* PURPOSE:    Convert calendar date into Julian day
   RECEIVES:   d, m, y—the day, month, and year
   RETURNS:    The Julian day number that begins at noon of the given
               calendar date
   REMARKS:    This algorithm is from Press et al., Numerical Recipes in C,
               2nd ed., Cambridge University Press, 1992.
*/
{ . . .
}

/*-----------------------------------------------------*/

int main()
{  . . .
}
```

A1.3 Functions

A1.3.1 Header Comment

Supply a comment of the following form for every function.

```
/* PURPOSE:    Explanation
   RECEIVES:   argument 1—explanation
               argument 2—explanation
               . . .
   RETURNS:    explanation of return value
   REMARKS:    Preconditions, notes, and other such information.
*/
```

The `PURPOSE` comment is required for all functions. Omit the `RECEIVES` comment if the function takes no parameters. Omit the `RETURNS` comment for procedures (`void` functions).

```
long dat2jul(int d, int m, int y)
/* PURPOSE:     Convert calendar date into Julian day
   RECEIVES:    d, m, y—the day, month, and year
   RETURNS:     The Julian day number that begins at noon of the given
                calendar date
   REMARKS:     This algorithm is from Press et al., Numerical Recipes in C,
                2nd ed., Cambridge University Press, 1992.
*/
{ . . .
}
```

No function comment is required for the `main` procedure.

A1.3.2 Parameters

Parameter names must be explicit, especially if they are integers or Boolean.

```
Employee remove(int d, float s); /* Huh? */
Employee remove(int department, float severance_pay); /* OK */
```

Of course, for very generic functions, short names may be very appropriate.

Do not write procedures (`void` functions) that return exactly one answer through a reference. Instead, make the result into a return value.

```
void find(vector<Employee> c, bool& found); /* Don't! */
bool find(vector<Employee> c); /* OK */
```

Of course, if the function computes more than one value, some or all results can be returned through reference arguments.

A1.3.3 Function Length

Functions must have at most 30 lines of code (the function header, comments, blank lines, and lines containing only braces are not included in this count). Functions that consist of one long `if/else` may be longer, provided each branch is 10 lines or less.

This rule forces you to break up complex computations into separate functions.

A1.4 Variables

Do not define all variables at the beginning of a block. Define each variable just before it is used for the first time.

Every variable must be either explicitly initialized when defined or set in the immediately following statement (for example, through a >> instruction).

```
int pennies = 0;
```

or

```
int pennies;
cin >> pennies;
```

Move variables to the innermost block in which they are needed.

```
while( /* ... */ )
{  float xnew = (xold + a / xold) / 2;
   . . .
}
```

Do not define two variables on the same line:

```
int dimes = 0, nickels = 0; /* Don't */
```

When defining a pointer variable, place the * with the type, not the variable:

```
Link* p; /* OK */
```

not

```
Link *p; /* Don't */
```

A1.5 Constants

A1.5.1 Constant Definitions

In C++ , do not use `#define` to define constants:

```
#define CLOCK_RADIUS 5 /* Don't */
```

Use `const` instead:

```
const float CLOCK_RADIUS = 5; /* the radius of the clock face */
```

A1.5.2 Magic Numbers

A magic number is an integer constant embedded in code without a constant definition. You may not use magic numbers in your code. Any number except 0, 1, or 2 is considered magic:

```
if (p.get_x() < 10) /* Don't  */
```

Use a `const` variable instead:

```
const float WINDOX_XMAX = 10;

if (p.get_x() < WINDOW_XMAX) /* OK */
```

Even the most reasonable cosmic constant is going to change one day. You think there are 365 days per year? Your customers on Mars are going to be pretty unhappy about your silly prejudice. Make a constant

```
const int DAYS_PER_YEAR = 365;
```

so that you can easily cut a Martian version without trying to find all the 365's, 364's, 366's, 367's, and so on in your code.

A1.6 Classes

Lay out the items of a class as follows:

```
class Class_name
{
public:
    constructors
    mutators
    accessors
private:
    data
};
```

All data fields of classes must be private. Do not use `friend`, except for classes that have no public member functions.

Supply a default constructor for every class.

A1.7 Control Flow

A1.7.1 The if Statement

Avoid the "`if...if...else`" trap. The code

```
if( ... )
    if( ... ) ...;
else
{   ...;
    ...;
}
```

will not do what the indentation level suggests, and it can take hours to find such a bug. Always use an extra pair of `{...}` when dealing with "`if...if...else`":

```
if( ... )
{   if( ... ) ...;
    else( ... ) ...;
}   /* {...} not necessary, but they keep you out of trouble */
```

```
if( ... )
{  if( ... ) ...;
}  /* {...} are necessary */
else ...;
```

A1.7.2 The for Statement

Use `for` loops only when a variable runs from somewhere to somewhere with some constant increment/decrement.

```
for (i = 0; i < a.size(); i++)
   print(a[i]);
```

Do not use the `for` loop for weird constructs such as

```
for (xnew = a / 2; count < ITERATIONS; cout << xnew)
/* Don't */
{  xold = xnew;
   xnew = xold + a / xold;
   count++;
}
```

Make such a loop into a `while` loop. That way the sequence of instructions is much clearer.

```
xnew = a / 2;
while (count < ITERATIONS) /* OK  */
{  xold = xnew;
   xnew = xold + a / xold;
   count++;
   cout << xnew;
}
```

A `for` loop traversing a linked list can be neat and intuitive:

```
for (a.reset(); not a.at_end(); a.next())
   cout << a.current().get_name() << "\n";
```

A1.7.3 Nonlinear Control Flow

Don't use the `switch` statement. Use `if/else` instead.

Do not use the `break`, `continue`, or `goto` statement. Use another `bool` variable to control the execution flow.

A1.8 Lexical Issues

A1.8.1 Naming Convention

The following rules specify when to use upper- and lowercase letters in identifier names.

1. All variable and function names and all data fields of classes are in lowercase (maybe with an occasional under_score in the middle). For example, `first_player`.
2. All constants are in uppercase (maybe with an occasional UNDER_SCORE). For example, `CLOCK_RADIUS`.
3. All `class` names start with uppercase and are followed by lowercase letters (maybe with an occasional UpperCase letter). For example, `BankTeller`.

Names must be reasonably long and descriptive. Use `first_player` instead of `fp`. No drppng f vwls. Local variables that are fairly routine can be short (`ch`, `i`) as long as they are really just boring holders for an input character, a loop counter, and so on. Also, do not use `ctr`, `c`, `cntr`, `cnt`, `c2` for five counter variables in your function. Surely these variables all have a specific purpose and can be named to remind the reader of it (for example, `ccurrent`, `cnext`, `cprevious`, `cnew`, `cresult`).

A1.8.2 Indentation and White Space

Use tab stops every three columns. That means you will need to change the tab stop setting in your editor!

Use blank lines freely to separate logically distinct parts of a function.

Separate functions by comment lines such as `/*---------*/`.

Use a blank space around every binary operator:

```
x1 = (-b - sqrt(b * b - 4 * a * c)) / (2 * a); /* Good */
x1=(-b-sqrt(b*b-4*a*c))/(2*a); /*Bad */
```

Leave a blank space after (and not before) each comma, semicolon, and keyword, but not after a function name.

```
if (x == 0)
f(a, b[i]);
```

Every line must fit on 80 columns. If you must break a statement, add an indentation level for the continuation:

```
a[n] = ...........................................
   + .................;
```

Start the indented line with an operator (if possible).

If a line break happens in an `if` or `while` condition, be sure to brace in the next statement, *even if there is only one:*

```
if( ..............................................
   and ..................
   or .......... )
{  ...
}
```

If it wasn't for the braces, it would be hard to visually distinguish the continuation of the condition from the statement to be executed.

A1.8.3 Braces

Opening and closing braces must line up, either horizontally or vertically.

```
while (i < n) { print(a[i]); i++; }
while (i < n)
{  print(a[i]);
   i++;
}
```

Some programmers don't line up vertical braces but place the `{` behind the `while`:

```
while (i < n) {                    /* Don't */
   print(a[i]);
   i++;
}
```

Doing so makes it hard to check that the braces match. Other programmers place the `{` in a line all by itself. That isn't a good idea, because it wastes a line of precious screen space.

```
while (i < n)
{                                  /* Don't */
   print(a[i]);
   i++;
}
```

The trick is not to leave a blank line after the opening brace but to type a tab followed by the first line of the loop body.

A1.8.4 Unstable Layout

Some programmers take great pride in lining up the names of structure fields:

```
class Employee
{
private:
  string  name;
     int  age;
   float  hourly_wage;
    Time  hiredate;
};
```

This is undeniably neat, and we recommend it if your editor does it for you, but *don't* do it manually. The layout is not *stable* under change. A data type that is longer than the preallotted number of columns requires that you move *all* entries around.

Some programmers like to format multiline comments so that every line starts with `**`:

```
/* This is a comment
** that extends over
** three source lines
*/
```

Again, this is neat if your editor has a command to add and remove the asterisks. Otherwise, it is a silly thing to do, because it is a powerful method of *discouraging* programmers from editing the comment. If you have to choose between pretty comments and comments that reflect the current facts of the program, facts win over beauty.

A1.8.5 The Preprocessor

It has been said that all usage of the preprocessor points to deficiencies in the programming language. C++ fixes some deficiencies; in particular, do not use `#define` for constants or macros—use `const`, `enum`, and `inline` instead.

Do not use the `#define` facility to make your code look like Pascal, as in

```
#define begin         {
#define end           }
#define repeat     do {
#define until( x )    }  while( !( x )  );
```

Neat as they may be, these constructs are strictly outlawed. Your fellow programmers have better things to do than play preprocessor with your code.

A legitimate use for the preprocessor is conditional compilation (for example, `#ifndef NDEBUG...#endif`).

To comment out a block of code that may itself contain comments, use `#if 0...#endif`. (Recall that C++ comments do not nest.)

Appendix A2

C++ Language Summary

In this syntax summary we use "computer screen" letters for actual C++ keywords and tokens such as `while`. Italic letters denote language constructs such as *condition* or *variable_name*. Items enclosed in [...] are *optional*. Do not type the brackets!

A2.1 Types

A type can be

- A numeric type (`int`, `long`, `short`, `unsigned`, `unsigned long`, `unsigned short`, `char`, `signed char`, `unsigned char`, `float`, `double`, `long double`)
- `bool`
- A class type such as `string` or `Employee` (see Section A2.4)
- A class template such as `vector`<*type_name*> or `matrix`<*type_name*>
- A pointer (*type_name**)

A2.2 Variables

Variable definitions have the form

type_name   *variable_name*   [*initializer*] ;

Examples:

```
int n;
float x = 0;
string harry = "Harry Hacker";
Circle c;
Point p =
   cwin.get_mouse("Please click on the first point");
vector<float> data;
Time birthday(1989, 8, 1, 3, 15, 0);
Link* n = new Link;
```

The *variable_name* consists only of letters, numbers, and underscores (`A...Z`, `a...z`, `0...9`, or `_`). It must begin with a letter or underscore. Names are *case-sensitive:* `totalscore`, `TOTALSCORE`, and `totalScore` denote different variables.

The optional *initializer* has either the form

= *expression*

or

($expression_1$, $expression_2$, ...)

The first type of initialization can be used for any variable. The second type can be used only for object variables with constructors.

Variables can be defined both inside and outside of functions. When the variable is defined inside a function, it is a *local* variable; otherwise, it is a *global* variable. The *scope* of a variable is the region of the program code in which the variable is accessible. Local variables have *block* scope: They are accessible from the point of definition to the closing brace } of the block in which the definition occurs. Global variables have *file* scope: They are accessible from the point of definition to the end of the file in which the definition occurs.

A2.3 Expressions

An *expression* is a variable, a function call, or a combination of subexpressions by operators. Examples are

```
x
sin(x)
x + sin(x)
x * (1 + sin(x))
x++
```

```
cout << x << "\n"
y = x + sin(x)
x == y
x == y and (z > 0 or w > 0)
p.x
v[i]
*next
```

Operators can be *unary, binary,* or *ternary.* A unary operator acts on a single expression, as in `x++`. A binary operator combines two subexpressions, as in `x + y`. A ternary operator combines three expressions. C++ has one ternary operator, `? :` (see Advanced Topic 4.1).

Unary operators can be *prefix* or *postfix*. A prefix operator is written before the expression on which it operates, as in `-x`. A postfix operator is written after the expression on which it operates, as in `x++`.

Operators are ranked by *precedence* levels. Operators with a higher precedence level bind more strongly than those of a lower level. For example, `*` has a higher precedence than `+`, so `x + y * z` is the same as `x + (y * z)`, even though the `+` comes first.

Most operators are *left-associative*. That is, operators of the same precedence level are evaluated from the left to the right. For example, `x - y + z` is interpreted as `(x - y) + z`, not `x - (y + z)`. The exceptions are the unary prefix operators and the assignment operator. For example, `z = y = sin(x)` means the same as `z = (y = sin(x))`.

Here is a list of all C++ operators that we covered in the book. The operators are listed in groups of decreasing precedence levels. Operators in the same group have the same precedence.

`.`	Access member
`->`	Dereference and access member
`[]`	Vector subscript
`()`	Function call
`++`	Increment
`--`	Decrement
`not` or `!`	Boolean NOT
`-`(unary)	Negative
`*`(unary)	Pointer dereferencing
`new`	Heap allocation
`delete`	Heap recycling
`*`	Multiplication
`/`	Division or integer division
`%`	Integer remainder

+	Addition
-	Subtraction
<<	Output
>>	Input
<	Less than
<=	Less than or equal
>	Greater than
>=	Greater than or equal
==	Equal
!=	Not equal
`and` or `&&`	Boolean AND
`or` or `||`	Boolean OR
? :	Selection
=	Assignment

This is not a complete list of operators. There are six operators on bit patterns (~ & ^ | and << >> when applied to integers) that are of interest only when you need to manipulate the individual bits of integers.

There are assignment shortcuts (+= -= *= /= %= &= |= ^= <<= >>=). For example, `x += y` is a shortcut for `x = x + y`. The shortcuts have the same precedence and associativity as the assignment operator.

There is a curious use for a comma as an operator: *expression*$_1$, *expression*$_2$ means to evaluate the first expression and ignore its value, then to evaluate the second expression. It is more confusing than useful, and we do not cover it in this book.

The `sizeof` operator returns the size of an object in bytes. It is not very useful in C++, but it is commonly used in C to query array sizes and to allocate memory on the heap. Do not confuse it with the `size` function, which returns the size of a vector!

Finally, there are operations to convert expressions to a different type:

```
static_cast<type>()
dynamic_cast<type>()
const_cast<type>()
reinterpret_cast<type>()
```

For example, if `x` is a floating-point number, then

```
static_cast<int>(x)
```

converts `x` into an integer. In this book we always use assignment to an integer variable to force the type conversion from floating-point to integer,

```
int n = x;
```

and we use no other type conversions. In rare situations, type conversions can be necessary, but they should always be considered a matter of last resort.

You will see an old style of the static cast notation in some programs:

```
(int)x
```

This notation is now obsolete.

A2.4 Classes

Structures introduce new types. The syntax for a structure is

```
class Class_name
{
public:
    constructors
    member functions
private:
    data fields
};
```

It is also possible to have private constructors and member functions as well as public data fields, but in this book, functions are always public and data fields are always private. A data field definition has the form

```
data_type field_name;
```

A constructor has the form

$Class\_name\ (parameter_1,\ parameter_2, \ldots)$

A member function declaration has the form

$return\_type\ function\_name(parameter_1,\ parameter_2, \ldots)$ `[const];`

Here is an example:

```
class Point
{
public:
   Point();
   Point(float xpos, float ypos);

   void move(float dx, float dy);

   float get_x() const;
   float get_y() const;
private:
   float x;
   float y;
};
```

A2.5 Functions

A function definition has the form

return_type function_name(*parameter*$_1$, *parameter*$_2$, ...)
{ *body*
}

The return type is any C++ type, or the special keyword `void` if the function returns no result (such a function is often called a *procedure*).

Each function parameter has the form

parameter_type[[`const`] &] *parameter_name*

If the parameter type is followed by an &, then the parameter is passed by *reference*. In a call by reference the caller must supply a *variable*, and the reference parameter is an *alias* for that variable; any modification to the reference parameter in the body of the function actually changes that variable.

Otherwise, the parameter is a *value* parameter. The caller of the function can supply any *expression* for a value parameter, and the value parameter is a local variable of the function that is initialized with the call expression. It is not common to modify a value parameter inside a function, but if a modification does occur, it has no influence on any variables outside the function. When the function exits, all of its local variables, including the value parameters, are abandoned.

As an optimization, value parameters can be passed as `const&`. This selects a more efficient mechanism for transferring the parameter value into the function. Such parameters cannot be modified in the function.

The body of the function is a sequence of variable definitions and statements. A special `return` statement returns the function result to the caller of the function. The following is an example:

```
float future_value(float initial_balance, float p,
   int nyear)
{  float b = initial_balance
      * pow(1 + p / 12 / 100, 12 * nyear);
   return b;
}

void swap(int& x, int& y)
{  int temp = x;
   x = y;
   y = temp;
}
```

A function is called with the syntax

function_name(*argument*$_1$, *argument*$_2$, ...)

The *argument*$_i$ is either an expression, if *parameter*$_i$ is a value parameter, or a variable name or vector element, if the parameter is a reference parameter. The type of *argument*$_i$ must match the type of *parameter*$_i$.

A function can call itself. Such a function is called *recursive:*

```
int factorial(int n)
{  if (n <= 1) return 1;
   return n * factorial(n - 1);
}
```

A member function of a class has the form

return_type Class_name::*function_name*(*parameter*$_1$,
   parameter$_2$, ...) [const]
{ *body*
}

The following are examples of member functions:

```
void Point::move(float dx, float dy)
{  x = x + dx; /* that is, implicit_parameter.x */
   y = y + dy;

float Point::get_x()  const
{  return x; /* that is, implicit_parameter.x */
}
```

Every member function has a special parameter called the *implicit parameter*. The member function is called as

implicit_parameter.*function_name*(*argument*$_1$, *argument*$_2$, ...)

for example,

```
position.move(1, -1);
```

The type of the implicit parameter must match the class to which the member function belongs. The implicit parameter is a value parameter if the member function is declared as `const`, and a reference parameter otherwise.

When a data field name is used in a member function, then it denotes that field of the implicit argument. For example, the name `x` in the `Point::move` function stands for `position.x` when the function is called as `position.move(1, -1)`.

Occasionally, it is necessary to refer to the implicit parameter in its entirety, not just to its data fields. Every member function receives a pointer to the implicit parameter called `this`. For example, you can inspect `*this` in the debugger to see all data fields of the class.

A2.6 Statements

A statement is one of the following:

- An expression followed by a semicolon
- A branch or loop statement (discussed subsequently)

- A `return` statement
- A *block;* that is, a group of variable definitions and statements enclosed in braces `{...}`

C++ has two branch statements (`if` and `switch`), three loop statements (`while`, `for` and `do/while`), and three mechanisms for nonlinear control flow (`break`, `continue`, and `goto`).

The `if` statement has the form

```
if (condition) statement1  [else statement2]
```

The `switch` statement has the form

```
switch(expression)
{  case constant1a:
   case constant1b:
      ...

      statement1a
      statement1b
      ...
      break;
   case constant2a:
   case constant2b:
      ...
      statement2a
      statement2b
      ...
         break;

      ...

      default:
         ...
         statementa
         statementb
         ...
         break;
}
```

It has the same meaning as

```
if (expression  == constant1a
   or expression  == constant1b  or ...  )
{  statement1a
   statement1b
   ...
}
else if (expression  == constant2a
   or expression  == constant2b  or ...  )
```

```
{   statement_2a
    statement_2b
     . . .
}

 . . .

else
{   statement_a
    statement_b
     . . .
}
```

In this book we prefer the `if` statement over the `switch`.

The `while` loop has the form

```
while (condition)
    statement
```

The condition is evaluated. If it is true, the statement is executed. The condition is evaluated again. The process repeats until the condition is not true, and then the next statement after the `while` is executed.

The `for` loop has the form

```
for (expression_1;  expression_2;  expression_3)
    statement
```

It has the same meaning as

```
expression_1;
while (expression_2)
{   statement
    expression_3;
}
```

The `for` loop is most commonly used when a variable is incremented until it reaches an upper bound:

```
for (i = 0; i < size(a); i++)
    sum = sum + a[i];
```

The `do/while` loop has the form

```
do
    statement
while (condition);
```

It has the same meaning as

```
statement
while (condition)
    statement
```

The conditions in `if` and loop statements can be expressions of type `bool`, where the value `true` denotes success, `false` failure. They can also be numbers or pointers. A number zero or a `NULL` pointer indicate failure; any other value (not necessarily 1) indicates success.

The `break` statement exits the current loop or `switch` statement, moving to the next statement after the loop or the switch. The `continue` statement skips to the end of the current loop, so that the loop condition is tested next. Some programmers use these constructs to avoid the "loop and a half" problem in which the loop exit condition is known only in the middle of the loop body. In this book, we prefer to introduce an additional `bool` variable instead.

The `goto` *name* statement jumps to a label of the form *name*`:`. Most C++ programmers never use `goto`.

A2.7 Pointers

A *pointer variable* stores the memory location of another object. The syntax for defining a pointer variable is

type_name variable_name*`;`

For example,

```
Employee* pe;
```

There are three methods of initializing a pointer variable with a valid memory location. The `new` operator allocates a new object on the heap and returns its memory address; the `&` operator takes the memory address of an existing object; and the name of a C-style array is automatically converted to the memory address of its starting element.

```
pe = new Employee;

Employee joe;
pe = &joe;

Employee staff[100];
pe = staff;
```

In C++, the last two methods of obtaining pointers are not common, but they are essential to C programming. As a rule of thumb, all C++ pointers should point to objects on the heap.

If a pointer variable `p` has been initialized with the address of an object, then `*p` denotes that object. This operation is called *dereferencing*. For example,

```
raise_salary(*pe, 5);
cout << (*pe).get_name();
```

Because the combination `(*p).`*member_name* is so common, there is a shortcut notation, `p->`*member_name*:

```
cout << pe->get_name();
```

When an object has been allocated from the heap with `new`, it must eventually be recycled to the heap with `delete`:

```
delete p;
```

If objects are never deleted, the heap will eventually be completely filled up. If objects are deleted too early and still used afterwards, random program errors will result.

A pointer variable can be initialized as `NULL` to indicate that it does not currently point anywhere. It is an error to dereference a null pointer.

A2.8 Mathematical Functions

The following functions are defined in math.h:

`sqrt(`x`)`	$\sqrt{x}$
`pow(`x`,`y`)`	x^y. If $x > 0$, y can be any value. If x is 0, y must be > 0. If $x < 0$, y must be an integer.
`sin(`x`)`	Sine of x (x in radians)
`cos(`x`)`	Cosine of x
`tan(`x`)`	Tangent of x
`asin(`x`)`	Arc sine, $\sin^{-1} x \in [-\pi/2, \pi/2]$, $x \in [-1, 1]$
`acos(`x`)`	Arc cosine, $\cos^{-1} x \in [0, \pi]$, $x \in [-1, 1]$
`atan(`x`)`	Arc tangent, $\tan^{-1} x \in (-\pi/2, \pi/2)$
`atan2(`y`,`x`)`	Arc tangent, $\tan^{-1}(y/x) \in [-\pi/2, \pi/2]$, x may be 0
`exp(`x`)`	e^x
`log(`x`)`	Natural log, $\ln(x)$, $x > 0$
`log10(`x`)`	Decimal log, $\lg(x)$, $x > 0$
`sinh(`x`)`	Hyperbolic sine of x
`cosh(`x`)`	Hyperbolic cosine of x
`tanh(`x`)`	Hyperbolic tangent of x
`ceil(`x`)`	Smallest integer $\geq x$
`floor(`x`)`	Largest integer $\leq x$
`fabs(`x`)`	Absolute value $\lvert x \rvert$

The following function is defined in stdlib.h:

`abs(x)`	Absolute value $\lvert x \rvert$, x an integer

The following functions and constants are defined in ccc.h:

`round(x)`	Round x to the nearest integer
`float_equal(x, y)`	`True` iff x and y are approximately equal
`float_less(x, y)`	`true` iff x is less than y and not approximately equal
`float_greater(x, y)`	`true` iff x is greater than y and not approximately equal
`rand_int(a, b)`	Return a random integer $\geq a$ and $\leq b$
`rand_float(a, b)`	Return a random floating-point number $\geq a$ and $\leq b$
`M_PI`	The value of π
`M_E`	The value of e

A2.9 Strings

String constants are enclosed in double quotes `" . . . "`. Quoted strings contain characters and certain two-character combinations:

`\n`	Newline
`\t`	Tab
`\\`	Backslash
`\"`	Double quote

String variables are of type `string`:

```
string message = "Hello, \"World\ "\n";
```

Strings can be concatenated with the + operator. The `== != < <= > >=` operators compare strings in dictionary order. The following operations are defined on strings:

`s.length()`	The length of `s`
`s.substr(i, n)`	The substring of length `n` of `s` starting at index `i`
`uppercase(s)`	`s` with all lowercase characters changed to uppercase
`lowercase(s)`	`s` with all uppercase characters changed to lowercase
`stringvalue(x)`	The string equivalent of the number `x`
`intvalue(s)`	The integer value represented by `s`
`floatvalue(s)`	The floating-point value represented by `s`
`format(s, x)`	The string representation of `x`, formatted as described in `s` (see Advanced Topic 2.6)

The first two operations are ANSI standard C++; the remainder are supplied in the ccc.h library provided with this book.

A2.10 Vectors and Matrices

Vectors are sequences of values of the same type, accessed by an integer index or subscript. A vector is defined as

`vector<`*type_name*`>` *variable_name*`[(`*initial_size*`)];`

If no initial size is specified, the vector has size 0. Before any elements can be retrieved from it, it must be grown through `push_back`. For example,

```
vector<float> data;
vector<Employee> staff(100);
```

Vector elements are accessed through the subscript operator.

```
data[i]++;
raise_salary(staff[1], 5);
```

The first element in the vector `v` has subscript 0; the last has subscript `v.size()` − 1. It is an error to use a subscript outside that range.

Matrices are tabular arrangements of values of the same type. A matrix is defined as

`matrix<`*type_name*`>` *variable_name*`(`*rows*`,`*columns*`);`

For example,

```
matrix<float> a(20, 20);
```

Matrix elements are accessed through two subscripts: one for the row and one for the column index:

```
a[3][4] = 0;
```

It is an error to supply row or column subscripts outside the array bounds.

The following functions are defined for vectors and matrices:

v`.size()`	The number of elements in the vector *v*
v`.push_back(`*x*`)`	Append *x* to the end of *v*, increasing its size
v`.pop_back(`*x*`)`	Remove (but do not return) the last element of *v*
m`.rows()`	The number of rows in the matrix *m*
m`.columns()`	The number of columns in the matrix *m*

Vectors are defined in ANSI C++. Matrices are a part of the library supplied with this book.

A2.11 Input and Output

Every program running in console or text mode has a predefined output stream `cout` and a predefined input stream `cin`.

The << operator is used to print integers, floating-point numbers, and strings. Multiple outputs can be combined together.

```
cout << 3.14 << "\n";
```

The >> operator is used to read integers, floating-point numbers, and strings. Multiple inputs can be combined together:

```
int n;
float x;
string w;
cin >> n >> x >> w;
```

When a stream reads an item, all leading white space (spaces, tabs, newlines) is discarded. In particular, when a stream reads a string, a single word is read. Use `get_line` if it is important to read the input a line at a time. If a number is read but the input does not represent a number, the item is not read and the state of the stream is set to "fail"; no further input will succeed. If this is not acceptable, don't read numbers directly but first read them as strings and then convert them to numbers. The stream also fails if the end of file is encountered in an attempt to read input.

The following functions are defined for streams.

`s.fail()`	True if input has failed
`s.open(n, m)`	Open a file stream with name `n` and mode `m`; `m` is `ios::in`, `ios::out`, or `ios::in + ios::out`
`s.close()`	Close the file stream
`s.seekg(p)`	Move the get position to offset `p`
`s.tellg()`	Return the get position
`s.seekp(p)`	Move the put position to offset `p`
`s.tellp()`	Return the put position
`get_char(s)`	Get the next character as a string of length 1
`putback_char(s, c)`	Put `c` (a string of length 1) back onto `s`, to be read again in the next input operation; only one character can be put back at a time
`get_line(s)`	Get the next input line

At the time of this writing, most compilers don't support a `string` parameter for the `open` function. Use `s.open(n.c_str(), m)` instead.

Streams and the member functions listed in this table are features of ANSI C++. The `get_char`, `putback_char`, and `get_line` functions are part of the library supplied with this book.

A2.12 Graphics

Every program running in graphics mode under the graphics library supplied with this book has a predefined graphics window `cwin`. Graphical shapes can be sent to the window with the << operator.

The following operations are defined for a graphics window:

`w.coord(x1, y1, x2, y2)`	Sets the coordinate system for subsequent drawing; (x1,y1) is the top left corner, (x2,y2) the bottom right corner
`w << x`	Displays the object x (a point, circle, line, or message)
`w.clear()`	Clear the window (that is, erase its contents)
`w.get_string(p)`	Displays prompt p and returns the entered string
`w.get_int(p)`	Displays prompt p and returns the entered integer
`w.get_float(p)`	Displays prompt p and returns the entered value
`w.get_mouse(p)`	Displays prompt p and returns the mouse click point

The following shapes are defined:

`Point`

`Point(x, y)`	Constructs a point at location (x, y)
`p.get_x()`	Returns the x-coordinate of the point
`p.get_y()`	Returns the y-coordinate of the point
`p.move(dx, dy)`	Moves the point by (dx, dy)

`Circle`

`Circle(p, r)`	Constructs a circle with center p and radius r
`c.get_center()`	Returns the center point of the circle
`c.get_radius()`	Returns the radius of the circle
`c.move(dx, dy)`	Moves the circle by (dx, dy)

`Line`

`Line(p, q)`	Constructs a line joining the points p and q
`l.get_start()`	Returns the starting point of the line
`l.get_end()`	Returns the ending point of the line
`l.move(dx, dy)`	Moves the point by (dx, dy)

`Message`

`Message(p, s)`	Constructs a message with starting point p and text string s
`m.get_start()`	Returns the starting point of the message
`m.get_text()`	Gets the text string of the message
`m.move(dx, dy)`	Moves the point by (dx, dy)

All graphics classes are features of the library supplied with this book.

A2.13 Time

The time class is useful for determining the current time and for measuring the speed of an algorithm.

`Time()`	Constructs the current time
`Time(y, m, d, h, n, s)`	Constructs the time with year `y` ≥ 1970, month `m`, day `d`, hours `h`, minutes `n`, seconds `s`
`t.get_seconds()`	Returns the seconds value of `t`
`t.get_minutes()`	Returns the minutes value of `t`
`t.get_hours()`	Returns the hours value of `t`
`t.get_day()`	Returns the day value of `t`
`t.get_month()`	Returns the month value of `t`
`t.get_year()`	Returns the year value of `t`
`t.add_seconds(n)`	Changes `t` to move by `n` seconds
`t.seconds_from(t2)`	Computes the number of seconds between `t` and `t2`

This class is a feature of the library supplied with this book.

A2.14 Employee Records

The employee class is used frequently in this book for illustrative purposes:

`Employee(n, s)`	Constructs an employee with name `n` and salary `s`
`e.get_name()`	Returns the name of `e`
`e.get_salary()`	Returns the salary of `e`
`e.set_salary(s)`	Sets salary of `e` to `s`

This class is a feature of the library supplied with this book.

A2.15 Life without ccc.h

You have a license to use the library accompanying for as long as you own this book. If you don't sell the book and if instructors and graders in your other classes don't object, you can certainly use this library in the future.

If you cannot use this library but you do have access to an ANSI C++ compiler that supports the `string` class and the `vector` template, then you only have to make a few adjustments. This section tells you what to do. If you need to use a compiler that doesn't support the `string` class and the `vector` template, then you also need to read Appendix 3 to learn how to program C-style strings and arrays.

You need to include the appropriate header files for strings and vectors. According to the ANSI standard, you should `#include <string>` and `#include <vector>` (without a .h extension). However, not all compilers support this yet.

The following table shows how to express calls of the utility functions in ccc.h in standard C++.

ccc.h	ANSI C++
round(x)	(int)(x + 0.5)
float_equal(x, y)	fabs(x - y)/(1 + max(fabx(x), fabs(y)) <= EPSILON
float_greater(x, y)	(x - y)/(1 + max(fabx(x), fabs(y)) > EPSILON
float_less(x, y)	(y - x)/(1 + max(fabx(x), fabs(y)) > EPSILON
rand_int(a, b)	a + rand() % (b - a + 1)
rand_float(a, b)	a + (b - a) * rand() * (1.0 / RAND_MAX)
uppercase(s)	string t; for (i = 0; i < s.length(); i++) t += toupper(s[i]);
lowercase(s)	string t; for (i = 0; i < s.length(); i++) t += tolower(s[i]);

stringvalue(x)	char b[100];
	   sprintf(b, "%f", (double)x);
	   string s = b;

intvalue(s)	atoi(s.c_str())
floatvalue(s)	atof(s.c_str())
format("%8d", n)	cout << setw(8) << n
format("%8.2f", x)	cout << setw(8) << setprecision(2) << x

format("%-20s", str)	cout << setw(20)
	   << setiosflags(ios::left,
	      ios::alignfield)
	   << str << setiosflags(ios::right,
	      ios::alignfield)

get_char(cin)	char ch = cin.get(); string s = ch == EOF ? "" : ch;
putback_char(cin, c)	cin.putback(c[0]);

get_line(cin)	char b[512];
	   cin.get_line(b, sizeof(b));
	   string s = b;

M_PI	3.14159265358979323846
M_E	2.71828182845904523536

All of these are just tedious enough that you will probably agree that the functions supplied with this book have value, especially to the beginner.

The `vector` template of ANSI C++ does not perform bounds checking. Remedy: Don't make bounds errors. There is no matrix template in ANSI C++. Use two-dimensional C arrays instead.

Of course, the `Employee` class is not standard C++, but you probably won't miss it.

Instead of the `Time` class, use the functions in time.h. (*Ugh.*) There is no standard for graphics programming. You will need to learn how to write graphics on your platform.

Appendix A3

Moving from C++ to C

This appendix explains how to map the C++ style used in this book to C programming skills. This is necessary for students who take their first programming course in C++ and the second course in C. Naturally, it would be best if the second course were also offered in C++, but for some time that may not be the case at many institutions. Even in this setting, it is much better to learn C++ as the first language and then spend a week or two adapting to the rough-and-tumble world of C. When learning C++, you learn *concepts:* reference parameters, arrays, strings. When learning C, you learn *pointers.* It is easier to understand concepts first and then map them to the pointer implementation than to learn pointers first and then abstract from them the underlying concepts.

A3.1 Data Types and Variables

A3.1.1 Variable Definitions

In C all variables must be defined at the beginning of a block, before any statements. Simply move the variables up. That does mean that you can't usually initialize the variables at the same time you define them.

A3.1.2 Constants

In C you cannot use `const` to define constants.

```
const int LINE_LENGTH = 80; /* C++  */
```

Instead, use the **`#define`** directive:

```
#define LINE_LENGTH 80
```

Note that there is no = between the name and value and that there is no semicolon at the end of the line! The directive must be on a line all by itself.

A3.1.3 Boolean Type

There is no `bool` type. Instead, you use `int` for `bool`, 1 for `true`, and `0` for `false`. The `and`, `or` and `not` operators are not part of C. Instead, use &&, `||`, and `!`.

A3.2 Input and Output

A3.2.1 Displaying Values

C does not use `cin` and `cout`. To display values, you use the `printf` function. Unlike C++, you *must* specify the output format for every entity you want to print. For example,

```
float sum;
int count;
. . .
cout << "Count: " << count << " Average: "
   << sum / count << "\n";  /* C++  */
```

becomes

```
printf("Count: %d Average: %f\n", count, sum / count);
```

This has advantages and disadvantages. The *format string,*

```
"Count: %d Average: %f\n"
```

gives a nice picture of the output—`Count`, an integer, `Average`, a floating-point number; and a newline—whereas in C++ the output line is broken up into bits and pieces. It is also easy to specify formatting.

```
printf("Count: %5d Average: %10.2f\n", count,
   sum / count);
```

All format codes start with a %. The actual codes are the same as the ones used in `format`. The drawback of the C method is that the format codes and the data types of the output values must match exactly. If you make a mistake, such as printing an integer with an `f` code or a floating-point number with a `d` code, then the output will be wrong, and the program can even crash.

Program horror1.c

```
#include "stdio.h"
#include "stdlib.h"
```

```
int main(void)
{  int count = 10;
   float sum = 89;

   printf("Count: %f Average: %d\n", count, sum / count);
   /* NO! */
   return EXIT_SUCCESS;
}
```

A3.2.2 Reading Input

Input uses a function called `scanf`. You give it a string describing the variables(s) you want to read, and a list of the *addresses* of the inputs:

```
scanf("%d %f", &score, &price);
```

If you forget the & before the name of the variable that you want to read, the program will crash or, at the very least, not read your input.

Program horror2.c

```
#include "stdio.h"
#include "stdlib.h"

int main(void)
{  int age;
   printf("How old are you? ");
   scanf("%d", age); /* forgot & */
   printf("You are %d years older than I.\n", age);
   return EXIT_SUCCESS;
}
```

Somewhat confusingly, the format string to *print* a `float` or `double` is `%f`, and the same string is used to scan a `float`. To *scan* a `double`, however, you must use `%lf`.

A3.2.3 Finding the End of Input

There is no direct equivalent to `cin.fail()` in C. Instead, you must capture the return value of every call to `scanf`.

The `scanf` function returns a count of the successfully scanned items. Always use that return value to test whether you reached the end of input.

Program average.c

```
#include "stdio.h"
#include "stdlib.h"

int main(void)
{  int count = 0;
```

```
    float sum = 0;
    int done = 0;
    while (!done)
    {  float x;
       if (scanf("%f", &x) == 1)
       {  count++;
          sum = sum + x;
       }
       else done = 1;
    }
    printf("Count: %d Average: %f\n", count, sum / count);
    return EXIT_SUCCESS;
}
```

See Section A3.5 for instructions on reading strings.

A3.3 Functions

A3.3.1 Functions without Parameters

In C a function with no parameters has a special parameter list: `void`.

```
int get_response(void)
{  . . .
}
```

The `void` is not supplied in the call to the function—only in the definition.

```
int main(void)
{  . . .
   n = get_response();
   . . .
}
```

A3.3.2 Reference Parameters

Unlike C++, C has no reference parameters. You must explicitly take the address of any variable that a function might want to modify and write the function to take a pointer parameter.

Here is a `swap` function in C++.

```
void swap(int& x, int& y) /* C++  */
{  int temp = x;
   x = y;
   y = temp;
}
```

To swap two values, you call

```
swap(a, b); /* C++ */
```

Because **x** and **y** are references, they refer to **a** and **b**, and swapping them actually swaps the contents of **a** and **b**. In C, you must instead *take the addresses* of the reference parameters when calling the function, to tell **swap** explicitly where **a** and **b** are. Then **swap** must be written to take pointers:

Program swap.c

```
#include "stdio.h"
#include "stdlib.h"

void swap(int *x, int *y)
{  int temp = (*x);
   /* set temp to the value to which x points */
   (*x) = (*y);
   (*y) = temp;
}

int main(void)
{  int a = 3;
   int b = 4;

   swap(&a, &b);

   printf("Now a = %d and b = %d\n", a, b);

   return EXIT_SUCCESS;
}
```

Naturally, that is a pain. Here is a set of rules that should help you.

1. Replace the parameter *type*& **x** with *type* ***x**.
2. Inside the function, replace every **x** with **(*x)**. In most cases, you can drop the parentheses and just use ***x**, but there are tricky situations in which that doesn't work. In particular, ***x++** does the wrong thing—you want **(*x)++**. It is safe to use parentheses in every instance.
3. Whenever the function is called, add a **&** to every parameter that is passed by reference.

Here is another example. Let's rewrite the **raise_salary** function:

```
void raise_salary(Employee& e, float by) /* C++ */
{  e.salary = e.salary * (1 + by / 100);
}
```

In C, the function must receive a *pointer* to the employee.

```
void raise_salary(Employee *e, float by)
{  (*e).salary = (*e).salary * (1 + by / 100);
}
```

Here `e` points to the employee to be given a raise, `*e` is the employee object. The `*e` must be placed in parentheses because the dot (`.`) binds stronger than the `*`, and a dot cannot be applied to a pointer. You can use the -> operator (Advanced Topic 13.1) in this situation:

```
void raise_salary(Employee *e, float by)
{  e->salary = e->salary * (1 + by / 100);
}
```

`e->salary` has the same meaning as `(*e).salary`.

To call this function, use &:

```
raise_salary(&harry, 5);
```

A3.4 Arrays

A3.4.1 Defining Arrays

C does not have vectors. Instead, you use C arrays. Here is an example: an array of 10 floating-point numbers in C++.

```
vector<float> a(10); /* C++ */
```

In C, you use

```
float a[10];
```

This defines `a` to be an array of 10 floating-point numbers.

You have to be careful how many elements you allocate for any array. Once defined, you *cannot* resize the array. C arrays have no `push_back` function. You must know how big the array will be when you compile the program. In practice, that is usually a ridiculous assumption. When you read a set of inputs, how do you know how many inputs the user will provide? You don't. You must come with a good guess on the maximum number of inputs and be prepared to ignore any more than that maximum.

Since you must provide some amount of slack space in an array, how do you know how much of the array is actually used? C arrays have no `size` function. (There is a `sizeof` function, which gives the size of the array in bytes, but it will not tell you how much *useful* data an array contains.)

You must keep a *companion variable* that counts how many inputs you actually used. It is a very good idea, as a matter of convention, *always* to call the maximum size of an array *ARRAYNAME*`_MAXSIZE` and *always* to keep the actual size of the array in a variable *arrayname*`_size`. For example, here is an input loop for gathering data:

Program array.c

```
#include "stdio.h"
#include "stdlib.h"

#define DATA_MAXSIZE 100

int main(void)
{  int i;

   float data[DATA_MAXSIZE];
   int data_size = 0;

   int done = 0;

   while (!done && data_size < DATA_MAXSIZE)
   {  float x;
      if (scanf("%f", &x) != 1) done = 1;
      else
      {  data[data_size] = x;
         data_size++;
      }
   }

   for (i = 0; i < data_size; i++)
      printf("%f\n", data[i]);

   return EXIT_SUCCESS;
}
```

Note that we need to stop data input after the first 100 data values have been entered. There is no more room in the array.

C arrays have *no bounds checking.* If you access `data[100]` or `data[-1]`, you will simply overwrite some memory that belongs to another variable. That will corrupt the program in an unpredictable way that is often difficult to diagnose.

A3.4.2 Array Parameters

C arrays can be function parameters. In the function definition, you indicate an array parameter by placing an empty `[]` behind the parameter name:

```
float average(float a[])
```

You will occasionally see other programmers define array parameters as pointers.

```
float average(float *a, int a_size)
```

That is technically correct, but not as intuitive. You should use the `[]` notation for your own code.

Unfortunately, *array parameters* have no idea how big the array is to which they refer. (The `sizeof` operator does not work for array parameters—it works only for array variables.) Instead, you must *always pass the size of the array as a second parameter.*

Program average2.c

```
#include "stdio.h"
#include "stdlib.h"

#define DATA_MAXSIZE 100

float average(float a[], int a_size)
{  int i;
   float sum = 0;
   if (a_size == 0) return 0;

   for (i = 0; i < a_size; i++)
      sum = sum + a[i];
   return sum / a_size;
}

int main(void)
{  int i;

   float data[DATA_MAXSIZE];
   int data_size = 0;

   int done = 0;

   while (!done && data_size < DATA_MAXSIZE)
   {  float x;
      if (scanf("%f", &x) != 1) done = 1;
      else
      {  data[data_size] = x;
         data_size++;
      }
   }

   printf("%f\n", average(data, data_size));

   return EXIT_SUCCESS;
}
```

Unlike all other parameters, array parameters are always passed by reference. You can modify the array `a`, and that modification affects the array that is passed into the function. The following program contains a function `reverse` that reverses the sequence of elements in `a`. Note that you do not use the `&` and `*` to turn `a` into a reference parameter:

Program reverse.c

```
#include "stdio.h"
#include "stdlib.h"

#define DATA_MAXSIZE 100

void swap(float *x, float *y)
{  float temp = (*x);
   /* set  temp to the value to which x points */
   (*x) = (*y);
   (*y) = temp;
}

void reverse(float a[], int a_size)
{  int i = 0;
   int j = a_size - 1;
   while (i < j)
   {  swap(&a[i], &a[j]);
      i++;
      j--;
   }
}

int main(void)
{  int i;

   float data[DATA_MAXSIZE];
   int data_size = 0;

   int done = 0;

   while (!done && data_size < DATA_MAXSIZE)
   {  float x;
      if (scanf("%f", &x) != 1) done = 1;
      else
      {  data[data_size] = x;
         data_size++;
      }
   }

   reverse(data, data_size);

   for (i = 0; i < data_size; i++)
      printf("%f\n", data[i]);

   return EXIT_SUCCESS;
}
```

The situation is more complex if you write a function that adds or removes elements from an array. In that case, you need to pass the array, the maximum size (if the function grows the array), *and the size as a reference parameter*:

Program readdata.c

```
#include "stdio.h"
#include "stdlib.h"

#define DATA_MAXSIZE 100

void read_data(float a[], int a_maxsize, int *a_size)
{  int i;
   int done = 0;

   (*a_size) = 0; /* abandon old data */

   while (!done && (*a_size) < a_maxsize)
   {  float x;
      if (scanf("%f", &x) != 1) done = 1;
      else
      {  a[(*a_size)] = x;
         (*a_size)++;
      }
    }
}

void print_data(float a[], int a_size)
{  int i;
   for (i = 0; i < a_size; i++)
      printf("%f\n", data[i]);
}

int main(void)
{  float data[DATA_MAXSIZE];
   int data_size = 0;
   read_data(data, DATA_MAXSIZE, &data_size);
   print_data(data, data_size);

   return EXIT_SUCCESS;
}
```

In C a function cannot compute and return an array.

A3.4.3 Copying C Arrays

In C++ you can copy vectors and matrices:

```
vector<float> a;       /* C++  */
vector<float> b;
```

```
   ...
   a = b;
```

This discards the old contents of a and copies all elements from b into the corresponding slots in a. It doesn't even matter if a and b had different sizes before the copy. In C that is not possible; you must code an explicit for loop:

```
#define A_MAXSIZE 100
#define B_MAXSIZE 100

float a[A_MAXSIZE];
int a_size = 0;

float b[B_MAXSIZE];
int b_size = 0;

...

int i;
for (i = 0; i < b_size && i < A_MAXSIZE; i++)
   a[i] = b[i];
if (b_size < A_MAXSIZE) a_size = b_size;
else a_size = A_MAXSIZE;
```

A3.4.4 Matrices

Matrices are arrays with two dimensions:

```
#define M_ROWS 3
#define M_COLUMNS 3

float m[M_ROWS][M_COLUMNS];
m[0][0] = 1;
```

When passing a matrix to a function, you must supply the dimensions:

```
float determinant(float m[M_ROWS][M_COLUMNS])
```

It is not possible, without special tricks, to write a single function that operates on matrices with varying dimensions.

A3.5 Strings

A3.5.1 Character Arrays

C does not have a string type. Strings are arrays of characters. The type char denotes a single character. Character codes are enclosed in single quotes. For example, 'H' is of type char and denotes the single character H. That is different from the string "H", a string of length 1 containing the character 'H' and a '\0' terminator.

After the last character of every string, a zero byte is stored to indicate the end of the string. That works because no actual character has a code of zero. (The same strategy would not work to denote the end of an array of numbers, because zero could be an actual data value. There simply is no way to choose a "sentinel" value for a sequence of numbers, but a zero code can be chosen as a sentinel value to denote the end of a sequence of characters.) The zero byte code is denoted by `'\0'`. This is *not the same* as `'0'`, the code for the digit 0.

For example, the string `"Hello"` actually contains six characters: `'H'`, `'e'`, `'l'`, `'l'`, `'o'` and `'\0'`.

A string is an array of `char` values of a specified maximum length. *You* must specify that maximum length.

```
#define MESSAGE_MAXLENGTH 80
char message[MESSAGE_MAXLENGTH + 1];
```

For character arrays you should define the maximum length of the string, not the maximum size of the array. Strings are terminated with a "zero byte" code that must be stored in the array. That terminator occupies one byte. It is a common error to forget the space for this character. You can avoid that problem if you *always make character arrays* `MAXLENGTH + 1` *characters long.*

Such an array can be initialized with a string.

```
char message[MESSAGE_MAXLENGTH + 1] = "Hello";
```

In fact, you can then omit the size:

```
char message[] = "Hello";
```

Now `message` has six bytes—just large enough to hold the string `"Hello"`. That is fine as long as you never try to store a longer string into `message`. (This usage of an empty `[]` has no connection whatsoever with the empty `[]` used for array parameters of functions.)

The `strlen` function computes the length of a string. For example, the value of `strlen(message)` is 5. The `strlen` function traverses the string until it finds the zero terminator. The terminator is not counted.

A3.5.2 Reading and Writing Strings

To read a word—that is, a string of characters, separated from adjacent words by white space—use `scanf`. It is important to supply the string size to make sure the target string does not overflow through an improperly long user input:

```
#define NAME_MAXLENGTH 20
char name[NAME_MAXLENGTH + 1];
scanf("%20s", name);
```

Unfortunately, there is no easy way to supply the symbolic name `NAME_MAXLENGTH` to `scanf`. Also be very careful with the value that you supply to `scanf`. It must be the maximum *length* of the string, or one less than the size of the array. The `scanf` function assumes that there is one extra byte to fill in the zero terminator.

To print a string, use `printf` with a `%f` format.

Program sread.c

```
#include "stdio.h"
#include "stdlib.h"
#include "string.h"

#define NAME_MAXLENGTH 20

int main(void)
{  char name[NAME_MAXLENGTH + 1];

   printf("Please enter your name: ");
   scanf("%20s", name);

   printf("Hello, %s, your name is %d characters long \n",
      name, strlen(name));
   return EXIT_SUCCESS;
}
```

Run this program to see what happens if you *don't* supply a maximum length to `scanf`:

Program horror3.c

```
#include "stdio.h"
#include "stdlib.h"

#define NAME_MAXLENGTH 15

int main(void)
{  int lucky1 = -13;
   char name[NAME_MAXLENGTH + 1];
   int lucky2 = -19;

   printf("Please enter your name: ");
   scanf("%s", name);

   printf("Hello, %s, your lucky numbers are %d and %d\n",
      name, lucky1, lucky2);
   return EXIT_SUCCESS;
}
```

As you can easily test, one of the lucky numbers gets overwritten when you enter a name that is longer than 20 characters. *Moral:* Lucky people have short names.

To read a line of input, use the `fgets` function.

```
fgets(name, NAME_MAXLENGTH + 1, stdin);
```

Unfortunately, fgets wants to know the size of the character array, whereas scanf wants the maximum length of the string. You just have to remember which function needs which value.

There is also a function called gets that does not require you to specify any buffer size at all. That sounds convenient, but it actually isn't. If the input exceeds the buffer size, the function simply overwrites other memory locations. That happened to about 6,000 not-so-lucky computers in November 1988. They were running a version of the so-called finger program that used gets to read a line of input into a buffer, generously sized at 512 bytes. As a result, they were infected by the Internet Worm (see Random Fact 9.1) when it purposefully sent 536 characters to that program. *Moral:* Don't use gets in your programs.

At the end of the input file, fgets returns a NULL pointer. Test the return value to check whether any input was found:

```
if (fgets(name, NAME_MAXLENGTH + 1, stdin) == NULL)
   done = 1;
```

fgets puts a newline character at the end of the input line. That is actually useful, because it tells you whether it stopped reading input because it found the end of the line or because the buffer filled up. Here is how you can remove the newline if you don't want it:

```
fgets(name, NAME_MAXLENGTH + 1, stdin);
int len = strlen(name);
if (name[len] == '\n') name[len] = '\0';
```

To read a single character, use getchar. Unfortunately, getchar doesn't actually read a character. It reads an integer that is either a character code or the special value EOF, guaranteed not to be a legal character. Here is how you use it:

```
int c = getchar( );
char ch;
if (c == EOF) done = 1;
else ch = (char)c;
```

To print a character, use either putchar or printf with the %c format.

The functions for reading characters, words, and lines are not very consistent. Table 1 summarizes the differences.

Table 1 C Data-Reading Functions

To Read	Function	Failure Indication	Size Parameter
Word	scanf	Returns 0	Maximum length
Line	fgets	Returns NULL	Maximum length + 1
Character	getchar	Returns EOF	Not applicable

A3.5.3 Copying Strings

If you want to set the variable **message** to another string, you need to either copy it a character at a time or use the strcpy/strncpy function.

If you are absolutely certain that the target string is at least as large as the source string, use strcpy:

```
strcpy(message, "Hello");
```

This is OK as long as message can hold at least 6 characters. Unfortunately, it is often the case that the source string may be larger than the target string. Then the strncpy function must be used:

```
#define MESSAGE_MAXLENGTH 80
#define BUFFER_MAXLENGTH 100

char message[MESSAGE_MAXLENGTH + 1];
char buffer[BUFFER_MAXLENGTH + 1];

strncpy(message, buffer, MESSAGE_MAXLENGTH);
message[MESSAGE_MAXLENGTH ] = '\0';
```

The third parameter for strncpy is the maximum number of characters that can be copied into the target string message. If buffer contains a string that is shorter than MESSAGE_MAXLENGTH, then that string is simply copied into message, including the zero terminator. If, however, buffer contains a string that has MESSAGE_MAXLENGTH or more characters, then the first MESSAGE_MAXLENGTH characters are copied into message; no zero terminator is supplied. That is very dangerous; the next call to strlen(message) would fail to find the end of the string. For that reason, we must supply the '\0' terminator in the last position of message. That terminator is necessary only if the length of buffer is at least MESSAGE_MAXLENGTH, but it is faster simply to supply the terminator in all cases. Why doesn't strncpy have the grace to supply the zero terminator in both cases? It is the C way.

Because the correct copying of strings is so tedious, many C programmers use strcpy anyway and hope for the best. That is a very dangerous strategy.

Maybe you think we are making too much fuss over the zero terminator. Run the following program and explain what happens!

Program horror4.c

```
#include "stdio.h"
#include "stdlib.h"
#include "string.h"

int main(void)
{  string greeting = "Hello, World";
   int lucky1 = -13;
   string message[10];
```

```
    int lucky2 = -19;
    strncpy(message, greeting, 10);
    printf("message = %s, length = %d\n", message,
       strlen(message));
    return EXIT_SUCCESS;
}
```

The most dangerous C string error is to copy a string into random memory. Your friends will tell you that `char *` means "string" in C, but that is simply not true. For example, the following code is a recipe for disaster:

Program horror5.c

```
#include "stdio.h"
#include "stdlib.h"
#include "string.h"

int main(void)
{  char *message;
   strcpy(message, "Hello"); /* Disaster */
   printf("%s\n", message);
   return EXIT_SUCCESS;
}
```

The code will compile. When the program runs, the pointer `message` points *somewhere.* That memory location, and the five bytes following it, will be overwritten with the string `"Hello"`. Maybe you are lucky and the program dies right away. On the other hand, maybe the program will limp along for some time and act mysteriously.

```
char *message
```

is definitely *not* the same as

```
string message
```

or even

```
char message[MESSAGE_MAXLENGTH + 1];
```

As a rule of thumb, you should avoid using `char *` pointers. If you allocate strings on the heap with `malloc` or if you use certain string functions like `strchr`, then you really need `char *` pointers. But if you don't, just stick to character arrays.

A3.5.4 Concatenating Strings

In C++, it is easy to concatenate two strings:

```
fname + " " + lname   /* C++ */
```

is a new string consisting of `fname` followed `" "` followed by `lname`. Here is what you must do in C. First, you must make a character array to hold the result. Then copy the first string into the target array. Finally, append the second string after the first:

```
char lname[LNAME_MAXLENGTH + 1];
char fname[FNAME_MAXLENGTH + 1];
char name[FNAME_MAXLENGTH + 1 + LNAME_SIZE + 1];

strcpy(message, fname);
strcat(message, " ");
strcat(message, lname);
```

The `strcat` function concatenates the second string past the end of the first string. You must be absolutely certain that there is enough free space after the end of the first string.

Of course, you don't often have the luxury of having enough room in the target string:

```
#define NAME_MAXLENGTH 30
char lname[NAME_MAXLENGTH + 1];
char fname[NAME_MAXLENGTH + 1];
char name[NAME_MAXLENGTH + 1];
```

It isn't very likely that the first and last name together are longer than 30 characters, but it could happen. To make sure the target string does not overflow, you need to supply the number of characters that still fit.

```
strcpy(name, fname);
strncat(name, " ", NAME_MAXLENGTH - strlen(name));
strncat(name, lname, NAME_MAXLENGTH - strlen(name));
name[NAME_MAXLENGTH] = 0;
```

As with `strcpy`, if the source string has more characters, no terminating zero is supplied, so we must do it manually.

A3.5.5 Extracting Substrings

To extract a substring from a string, you also use `strncpy`. You must manually supply the terminating zero:

```
#define NAME_MAXLENGTH 30
char lname[NAME_MAXLENGTH + 1];
char name[NAME_MAXLENGTH + 1];
strncpy(lname, name + start, length);
lname[length] = '\0';
```

That is the equivalent of

```
command = input.substr(start, length); /* C++  */
```

A3.5.6 Comparing Strings

In C++ it is easy to compare strings. `s == t` is true if `s` and `t` are identical, `s < t` is true if `s` comes before `t` in dictionary order.

In C there is a major pitfall. The expressions `s == t` and `s < t` also have a legal meaning for C strings, but it is the wrong one. These comparisons simply test whether the starting addresses of `s` and `t` are the same, or whether `s` has a lower memory address than `t`. That isn't very useful. We don't care where `s` and `t` are located in memory; we want to compare the contents of the strings.

Program horror6.c

```
#include "stdio.h"
#include "stdlib.h"
#include "string.h"

int main(void)
{  char greeting1[] = "Hello";
   char greeting2[] = "Howdy";
   char greeting3[] = "Hello";
   char greeting4[] = "Howdy";

   if (greeting1 != greeting3)
      printf("%s != %s\n", greeting1, greeting3);
   if (greeting2 < greeting3)
      printf("%s < %s\n", greeting2, greeting3);
   if (greeting4 < greeting3)
      printf("%s < %s\n", greeting4, greeting3);

   return EXIT_SUCCESS;
}
```

In C you must use the `strcmp` function to compare strings. `strcmp(s, t)` returns a negative number if `s` is lexicographically before `t`, zero if `s` and `t` are identical, and a positive number if `s` comes after `t` in the lexicographic ordering. For example,

```
if (strcmp(command, "QUIT") == 0)
   return EXIT_SUCCESS; /* return if the command is QUIT */
```

A3.5.7 String Parameters

Here is a function with string parameters.

Program greeting.c

```
#include "stdio.h"
#include "stdlib.h"
#include "string.h"

void print_greeting(char message[], char name[])
{  printf("%s, %s\n", message, name);
}
```

```
int main(void)
{  char greeting1[] = "Hello";
   char greeting2[] = "Howdy";
   char name1[] = "Earthling";
   char name2[] = "Partner";

   print_greeting(greeting1, name1);
   print_greeting(greeting2, name2);

   return EXIT_SUCCESS;
}
```

Because the function can tell the end of the string from the terminating zero, you need not supply the length of the character array as a separate value.

C functions cannot return strings. If a function is to compute a string, the function must supply a parameter to hold the result string and a parameter to specify its maximum length. Do not try to overcome that by writing a function returning a `char *`:

Program horror7.c

```
#include "stdio.h"
#include "stdlib.h"
#include "string.h"

#define RESULT_LENGTH 100

char *make_message(char greeting[], char name[])
{  char result[RESULT_LENGTH + 1];
   strncpy(result, greeting, RESULT_LENGTH);
   strncat(result, ", ", RESULT_LENGTH - strlen(result));
   strncat(result, name, RESULT_LENGTH - strlen(result));
   strncat(result, "!", RESULT_LENGTH - strlen(result));
   return result; /* No!  */
}

int main(void)
{  char greeting1[] = "Hello";
   char greeting2[] = "Howdy";
   char name1[] = "Earthling";
   char name2[] = "Partner";

   printf("%s\n",
      make_message(greeting1, name1))

   printf("%s\n",
      make_message(greeting2, name2));

   printf("%s\n%s\n",
      make_message(greeting1, name1),
      make_message(greeting2, name2));
```

```
    return EXIT_SUCCESS;
}
```

To write this function correctly, you need to make the result string into a parameter. You also need to pass the maximum length of the result string:

Program mkgreet.c

```
#include "stdio.h"
#include "stdlib.h"
#include "string.h"

#define MESSAGE_LENGTH 100

void make_message(char greeting[], char name[],
   char result[], int result_maxlength)
{  strncpy(result, greeting, result_maxlength);
   strncat(result, ", ",
      result_maxlength - strlen(result));
   strncat(result, name,
      result_maxlength - strlen(result));
   strncat(result, "!",
      result_maxlength - strlen(result));
}

int main(void)
{  char greeting1[] = "Hello";
   char greeting2[] = "Howdy";
   char name1[] = "Earthling";
   char name2[] = "Partner";

   char message1[MESSAGE_LENGTH];
   char message2[MESSAGE_LENGTH];

   make_message(greeting1, name1, message1,
      MESSAGE_LENGTH);
   make_message(greeting2, name2, message2,
      MESSAGE_LENGTH);

   printf("%s\n%s\n", message1, message2);

   return EXIT_SUCCESS;
}
```

You will occasionally see other programmers using `char *` instead of `char []` to define string parameters.

```
void make_message(char *greeting, char *name,
   char *result, int result_maxlength)
```

That is technically correct, but not as intuitive. You should use the `[]` notation for your own code.

A3.5.8 Upper- and Lowercase

There is no standard way to convert a string to uppercase or lowercase. It is best to write a set of functions for this purpose:

```
#include "ctype.h"

void strupper(char s[])
{  int i;
   for (i = 0; s[i] != 0; i++)
      s[i] = toupper(s[i]);
}

void strlower(char s[])
{  int i;
   for (i = 0; s[i] != 0; i++)
      s[i] = tolower(s[i]);
}
```

A3.5.9 Converting between Strings and Numbers

The C equivalents of `intvalue` and `floatvalue` are `atoi` ("ASCII to integer") and `atof` ("ASCII to floating point"). The equivalent to `stringvalue` is `sprintf`. The `sprintf` function sends its output to a string instead of the standard output:

```
char text[TEXT_MAXLENGTH];
sprintf(text, "%d", count);
```

The character array `text` must be large enough to hold the output.

A3.6 Structures

Structures are the equivalent to classes in C++. However, there are no member functions, no constructors, and no private and public sections. Here is how you define a structure:

```
#define EMPLOYEE_NAME_MAXLENGTH 40

typedef struct Point Point;
struct Point
{  float x;
   float y;
};
```

```
typedef struct Employee Employee;
struct Employee
{  char name[EMPLOYEE_NAME_MAXLENGTH + 1];
   float salary;
};

typedef struct Link Link;
struct Link
{  int data;
   Link* next;
};
```

The `typedef` line sounds silly, and it is, but it is necessary in C to make the name of the structure into a type name.

Since there are no member functions, you must write ordinary functions. Make the parameter that would be the implicit parameter in C++ into the first parameter of the function.

```
void move_point(Point* p, float x, float y)
{  p->x = p->x + x;
   p->y = p->y + y;
}

Point center;
. . .
move_point(&center, 1, -1);
```

Since there is no data hiding, you can access all data fields directly.

```
Point p;
p.x = 3;
p.y = -4;
```

Therefore you don't need constructors, but you may still find them convenient. Of course, you have to invoke them explicitly:

```
void construct_employee(Employee* e,
   string employee_name, float starting_salary)
{  strncpy(e->name, employee_name, EMPLOYEE_NAME_LENGTH);
   e->name[EMPLOYEE_NAME_LENGTH] = '\0';
   e->salary = starting_salary;
}

. . .

Employee harry;
construct_employee(&harry, "Hacker, Harry", 35000);
```

A3.7 Files

The C equivalent of the type `fstream` is the type `FILE*`. Technically, a `FILE*` object is a pointer that points to a data structure, but you don't think about that when using it. To open a file, you call **`fopen`**.

```
FILE* fi = fopen("input.dat", "r");
```

The second parameter is

`"r"`	for reading (like `ios::in`)
`"w"`	for writing (like `ios::out`)
`"r+"`	for reading and writing (like `ios::in + ios::out`)

To close the file, call

```
fclose(fp);
```

Once you open a file, you can read data in with **`fgets`**, **`fgetc`**, and **`fscanf`**. You can print data with **`fprintf`**.

In C there are no separate **`get`** and **`put`** positions. There is a single file position, which is used both for reading and for writing. You set it with

```
fseek(fp, offset, from)
```

where `from` is one of

SEEK_SET	from beginning of the file (like **`eos::beg`**)
SEEK_CUR	from the current position (like **`eos::cur`**)
SEEK_END	from the end of the file (like **`eos::end`**)

You get the current file position with `ftell`. To put all these concepts together, here is the database program from Chapter 10, recoded in C.

Program database.c

```
#include "stdio.h"
#include "string.h"
#include "stdlib.h"

#define EMPLOYEE_NAME_MAXLENGTH 40
#define BUFFER_MAXLENGTH 30
#define LINE_MAXLENGTH 512
#define NUM_MAXLENGTH 10
#define FILENAME_MAXLENGTH 80

#define NEWLINE_LENGTH 2 /* or 1 on Unix */
#define RECORD_SIZE (30 + 10 + NEWLINE_LENGTH)
```

```
typedef struct Employee Employee;
struct Employee
{  char name[EMPLOYEE_NAME_MAXLENGTH + 1];
         float salary;
};

void read_employee(Employee* e, FILE* fs);
{  char line[LINE_MAXLENGTH + 1];
   char num[NUM_MAXLENGTH + 1];
   if (fgets(line, LINE_MAXLENGTH + 1, fs) == NULL) return;
   strncpy(e->name, line, EMPLOYEE_NAME_MAXLENGTH);
   strncpy(num, line + 30, NUM_MAXLENGTH);
   e->salary = atof(num);
}

void raise_salary(Employee* e, float percent)
{  e->salary = e->salary * (1 + percent / 100);
}

void write_employee(Employee* e, FILE* fs)
{  char buffer[BUFFER_MAXLENGTH + 1];
   strncpy(buffer, e->name, BUFFER_MAXLENGTH);
   buffer[BUFFER_MAXLENGTH] = '\0';
   fprintf(fs, "%-30s%10.2f%5d", buffer, e->salary);
}

int main()
{  int nrecord;
   FILE* fs;
   int pos;
   float price_change;
   char filename[FILENAME_MAXLENGTH + 1];
   Employee e;

   printf("Please enter the data file name: ");
   scanf("%80s", filename);

   fs = fopen(filename, "r+");
   if (fs == NULL) exit(EXIT_FAILURE);
   fseek(fs, 0, SEEK_END);
   nrecord = ftell(fs) / RECORD_SIZE;

   printf("Please enter the record to update: (0 - %d): ",
           nrecord - 1);
   scanf("%d", &pos);
   printf("Please enter the salary change in percent: ");
   scanf("%f", &price_change);
```

```
    fseek(fs, pos * RECORD_SIZE, SEEK_SET);
    read_employee(&e, fs);
    raise_salary(&e, price_change);
    fseek(fs, pos * RECORD_SIZE, SEEK_SET);
    write_employee(&e, fs);

    fclose(fs);
    return EXIT_SUCCESS;
}
```

A3.8 Dynamic Memory Allocation

C has no **new** and **delete** operators. Use the library functions **malloc** and **free** instead.

```
Employee* p = new Employee;
. . .
delete p;
```

becomes

```
Employee* p = (Employee*)malloc(sizeof(Employee));
. . .
free(p);
```

Glossary

Accessor function A function that accesses an object but does not change it.

Address A value that specifies the location of a variable in memory.

Aggregation relationship The "has-a" relationship between classes.

Algorithm An unambiguous, executable, and terminating specification to solve a problem.

ANSI/ISO C++ Standard The standard for the C++ language that is being developed by the American National Standards Institute and the International Standards Organization.

Argument A parameter value in a function call, or one of the values combined by an operator.

Array A collection of values of the same type, each of which can be accessed by an integer index.

Arrow operator The -> operator. `p->m` is the same as `(*p).m`.

ASCII code The American Standard Code for Information Interchange, which associates code values between 0 and 127 to letters, digits, punctuation marks, and control characters.

Assertion A claim that a certain condition holds in a particular program location; often tested with the `assert` macro.

Assignment Placing a new value into a variable.

Balanced tree A tree in which *each* subtree has the property that the number of descendants to the left is approximately the same as the number of descendants on the right.

Base class A class from which another class is derived.

Big-Oh notation The notation $g(n) = O(f(n))$ denotes that the function g grows at the same rate with respect to n as the function f. For example, $10n^2 + 100n - 1000 = O(n^2)$.

"Big three" management functions The three management functions that are essential for classes that manage heap memory or other resources: copy constructor, destructor, and assignment operator.

Binary file A file in which values are stored in their binary representation and cannot be read as text.

Binary operator An operator that takes two arguments, for example $+$ in $x + y$.

Binary search A fast algorithm to find a value in a sorted array. It narrows the search down to half of the array in every step.

Binary search tree A binary tree in which *each* subtree has the property that all left descendants are smaller than the value stored in the root, and all right descendants are larger.

Binary tree A tree in which each node has at most two child nodes.

Bit Binary digit; the smallest unit of information, having two possible values, 0 and 1. A data element consisting of n bits has 2^n possible values.

Black box testing Testing functions without knowing their implementation.

Block A group of statements bracketed by `{}`.

Boolean operator → Logical operator

Boolean type A type with two values, `true` and `false`.

Boundary test case A test case involving values that are at the outer boundary of the set of legal values. For example, if a function is expected to work for all nonnegative integers, then 0 is a boundary test case.

Bounds error Trying to access an array element that is outside the legal range.

`break` **statement** A statement that terminates a loop or `switch` statement.

Breakpoint A point in a program, specified in a debugger, at which it stops executing the program and lets the user inspect the program state.

Buffered input Input that is gathered in batches, for example, a line at a time.

Byte A number between 0 and 255 (eight bits). Essentially all currently manufactured computers use a byte as the smallest unit of storage in memory.

Call stack The set of all functions that currently have been called but not terminated, starting with the current function and ending with `main`.

Case-sensitive Distinguishing upper- and lowercase characters.

Cast Converting a value from one type to a different type. For example, the cast from a floating-point number `x` to an integer is expressed in C++ by the cast notation, `(int)x`.

Class A programmer-defined data type.

Command line The line you type when you start a program in a command window in DOS/Windows or Unix. It consists of the program name and the command line arguments.

Comment An explanation to make the human reader understand a section of a program; ignored by the compiler.

Compiler A program that translates code in a high-level language such as C++ to machine instructions.

Compile-time error → Syntax error

Compound statement A statement such as `if` or `for` that is made up of several parts (condition, body).

Concatenation Placing one string after another.

Constant A value that cannot be changed by the program.

Construction Setting a newly allocated object to an initial value.

Constructor A function that initializes a newly allocated object.

Copy constructor A function that initializes an object as a copy of another.

CPU (Central Processing Unit) The part of a computer that executes the machine instructions.

Dangling pointer A pointer that does not point to a valid location.

Data field A variable that is present in every object of a class.

Debugger A program that lets a user run another program one or a few steps at a time, stop execution, and inspect the variables in order to analyze it for bugs.

Declaration A statement that announces the existence of a variable, function, or class but does not define it.

Default constructor A constructor that can be invoked with no parameters.

`#define` **directive** A directive that defines constant values and macros for the preprocessor. Values can be queried during the preprocessing phase with the `#if` and `#ifdef` directives. Macros are replaced by the preprocessor when they are encountered in the program file.

Definition A statement or series of statements that fully describes a variable; a function and its implementation; a type; or a class and its properties.

`delete` **operator** The operator that recycles memory to the heap.

Dereferencing Locating an object when a pointer to the object is given.

Derived class A class that modifies a base class by adding data fields or member functions or by redefining member functions.

Destructor A function that is executed whenever an object goes out of scope.

Dictionary ordering → Lexicographic ordering

Directory A structure on a disk that can hold files or other directories; also called a folder.

Dot notation The notation *object*.*function*(*parameters*) used to invoke a member function on an object.

Doubly linked list A linked list in which each list has a pointer to both its predecessor and successor links.

Dynamic binding Selecting a particular function to be called, depending on the exact type of the object invoking the function when the program executes.

Dynamic memory allocation Allocating memory as a program runs as required by the program's needs.

Encapsulation The hiding of implementation details.

End of file Condition that is true when all characters of a file have been read. Note that there is no special "end of file character". When composing a file on the keyboard, you may need to type a special character to tell the operating system to end the file, but that character is not part of the file.

Enumerated type A type with a finite number of values, each of which has its own symbolic name.

Escape character A character in text that is not taken literally but has a special meaning when combined with the character or characters that follow it. The \ character is an escape character in C++ strings.

Executable file The file that contains a program's machine instructions.

Explicit parameter A parameter of a member function other than the object invoking the function.

Expression A syntactical construct that is made up of constants, variables, function calls, and operators combining them.

Extension The last part of a file name, which specifies the file type. For example, the extension .cpp denotes a C++ file.

Failed stream state The state of a stream after an invalid operation has been attempted, such as reading a number when the next stream position yielded a nondigit, or reading after the end of file was reached.

Fibonacci numbers The sequence of numbers 1, 1, 2, 3, 5, 8, 13, . . . , in which every term is the sum of its two predecessors.

Field accessor A member function that returns the value of a data field.

Field mutator A member function that sets a data field to a new value.

File A sequence of bytes that is stored on disk.

File pointer The position within a file of the next byte to be read or written. It can be moved so as to access any byte in the file.

Floating-point number A number with a fractional part.

Folder → **Directory**

Function A sequence of statements that can be invoked multiple times, with different values for its parameters.

Garbage collection Automatic reclamation of heap memory that is no longer needed. C++ does not have garbage collection.

Global variable A variable whose scope is not restricted to a single function.

`goto` **statement** A statement that transfers control to a different statement that is tagged with a label.

grep The "generalized regular expression pattern" search program, useful for finding all strings matching a pattern in a set of files.

Header file A file that informs the compiler of features that are available in another module or library.

Heap A reservoir of storage from which memory can be allocated when a program runs.

`#if` **directive** A directive to the preprocessor to include the code contained between the `#if` and the matching `#endif` if a condition is true.

Implicit parameter The object that calls a member function. For example, in the call `x.f(y)`, the object `x` is the implicit parameter of `f`.

`#include` directive An instruction to the preprocessor to include a header file.

Inheritance The "is-a" relationship between a general base class and a specialized derived class.

Initialization Setting a variable to a well-defined value when it is created.

Integer A number without a fractional part.

Integer division Taking the quotient of two integers, discarding the remainder. In C++, the / symbol denotes integer division if both arguments are integers. For example, `11 / 4` is 2, not 2.75.

Interface The set of functions that can be applied to objects of a given type.

Iterator An object that can inspect all elements in a container such as a linked list.

Lexicographic ordering Ordering strings in the same order as in a dictionary, by skipping all matching characters and comparing the first nonmatching characters of both strings. For example, "orbit" comes before "orchid" in the lexicographic ordering. Note that in C++, unlike a dictionary, the ordering is case-sensitive: `Z` comes before `a`.

Library A set of precompiled functions that can be included into programs.

Linear search Searching a container (such as an array, list, or vector) for an object by inspecting each element in turn.

Linked list A data structure that can hold an arbitrary number of objects, each of which is stored in a link object, which contains a pointer to the next link.

Linker The program that combines object and library files into an executable file.

Local variable A variable whose scope is a single block.

Logic error An error in a syntactically correct program that causes it to act differently from its specification.

Logical operator An operator that can be applied to Boolean values. C++ has three logical operators: `and`, `or`, and `not`.

Loop A sequence of instructions that is executed repeatedly.

Loop and a half A loop whose termination decision is neither at the beginning nor at the end.

Loop invariant A statement about the program state that is preserved when the statements in the loop are executed once.

Machine code Instructions that can be executed directly by the CPU.

Macro A mechanism to replace a command with a predefined sequence of other commands.

Magic number A number that appears in a program without explanation.

`main` function The function that is first called when a C++ program executes.

Make file A file that contains directives for how to build a program by compiling and linking the constituent files. When the make program is run, only those source files that are newer than their corresponding object files are rebuilt.

Member function A function that is defined by a class and operates on objects of that class.

Merge sort A sorting algorithm that first sorts two halves of an array and then merges the sorted subarrays together.

Module A program unit that contains related classes and functions. C++ has no explicit support for modules. By convention, each module is stored in a separate source file.

Mutator function A member function that changes the state of an object.

Name clash Accidentally using the same name to denote two program features in a way that cannot be resolved by the compiler.

Negative test case A test case that is expected to fail. For example, when testing a root-finding program, an attempt to compute the fourth root of −1 is a negative test case.

Nested block A block that is contained inside another block.

`new` **operator** The operator that allocates new memory from the heap.

Newline The `'\n'` character, which indicates the end of a line.

Null pointer The value that indicates that a pointer does not point to any object.

Object A value of a user-defined type.

Object file A file that contains machine instructions from a module. Object files must be combined with library files by the linker to form an executable file.

Object-oriented design Designing a program by discovering objects, their properties, and their relationships.

Off-by-one error A common programming error in which a value is one larger or smaller than it should be.

Opening a file Preparing a file for reading or writing.

Operating system The software that launches application programs and provides services (such as a file system) for those programs.

Operator A symbol denoting a mathematical or logical operation, such as `+` or `and`.

Operator associativity The rule that governs in which order operators of the same precedence are executed. For example, in C++ the `-` operator is left-associative, since `a - b - c` is interpreted as `(a - b) - c`, and `=` is right-associative, since `a = b = c` is interpreted as `a = (b = c)`.

Operator precedence The rule that governs which operator is evaluated first. For example, in C++ the `and` operator has a higher precedence than the `or` operator. Hence `a or b and c` is interpreted as `a or (b and c)`.

Oracle A program that predicts how another program should behave.

Overloading Giving more than one meaning to a function name or operator.

Parallel vectors Vectors of the same length, in which corresponding elements are logically related.

Parameter The values in the execution of a function that can be set when the function is called. For example, in the function `float root(int n, float x)`, `n` and `x` are parameters.

Parameter passing Using expressions to initialize the parameter variables of a function when it is called.

Parameter value The expression supplied for a parameter by the caller of a function.

Parameter variable A variable in a function that is initialized with the parameter value when the function is called.

Pointer A value that denotes the memory location of an object.

Polymorphism Selecting a function among several functions with the same name, by comparing the actual types of the parameters.

Popping a value Removing a value from the top of a stack.

Positive test case A test case that a function is expected to handle correctly.

Postfix operator A unary operator that is written behind its argument.

Precondition A condition that must be true when a function is called.

Predicate function A function that returns a Boolean value.

Prefix operator A unary operator that is written before its argument.

Preprocessor A program that processes a source file before the compiler. The C++ preprocessor includes files, conditionally includes code sections, and performs macro replacement.

Private inheritance Inheritance in which only the member functions can use the base-class functions.

Procedure A function that does not return a value.

Project A collection of source files and their dependencies.

Prompt A string that prompts the program user to provide input.

Prototype → **Declaration**

Pseudocode A mixture of English and C++ that is used when developing the code for a program.

Pushing a value Adding a value to the top of a stack.

RAM (random-access memory) The computer memory that stores code and data of running programs.

Random access The ability to access any value directly without having to read the values preceding it.

Recursive function A function that can call itself with simpler values. It must handle the simplest values without calling itself.

Redirection Linking input or output of a program to a file instead of the keyboard or display.

Reference parameter A parameter that is bound to a variable supplied in the call. Changes made to the parameter within the function affect the variable outside the function.

Regression testing Keeping old test cases and testing every revision of a program against them.

Regular expression An expression denoting a set of strings. A regular expression can consist of individual characters, sets of characters such as `[abc]`; ranges such as `[a-z]`; sets of all characters outside a range, such as `[^0-9]`; repetitions of other expressions, such as `[0-9]*`; alternative choices such as `+|-`; and concatenations of other expressions.

Reserved word A word that has a special meaning in a programming language and therefore cannot be used as a name by the programmer.

Return value The value returned by a function through a `return` statement.

Roundoff error An error introduced by the fact that the computer can store only a finite number of digits of a floating-point number.

Run-time error → Logic error

Run-time stack The data structure that stores the local variables and return addresses of functions when a program runs.

Scope The part of a program in which a variable is defined.

Selection sort A sorting algorithm in which the smallest element is repeatedly found and removed until no elements remain.

Sentinel A value in input that is not to be used as an actual input value but to signal the end of input.

Separate compilation Compiling each source file separately and combining the object files later into an executable program.

Sequential access Accessing values one after another without skipping over any of them.

Shadowing Hiding a variable by defining another one with the same name in a nested block.

Shell A part of an operating system in which the user types commands to execute programs and manipulate files.

Shell script A file that contains commands for running programs and manipulating files. Typing the name of the shell script file on the command line causes those commands to be executed.

Side effect An effect of a function other than returning a value.

Simple statement A statement consisting only of an expression.

Single-stepping Executing a program in the debugger one statement at a time.

Slicing objects Copying an object of a derived class into a variable of the base class, thereby losing the derived-class data.

Source file A file containing instructions in a programming language.

Stack A data structure in which elements can only be added and removed at one location, called the top of the stack.

Statement A syntactical unit in a program. In C++ a statement is either a simple statement, a compound statement, or a block.

Static binding Selecting a particular function to be called, depending on the type of the object invoking the function, which is known when the program is compiled.

`static` **keyword** A C++ keyword with several unrelated meanings: It denotes local variables that are not allocated on the stack; global variables or functions that are private to a module; class variables that are shared among all objects of a class; or member functions that do not have an implicit parameter.

Stepwise refinement Solving a problem by breaking it into smaller problems and then further decomposing those smaller problems.

Stream An abstraction for a sequence of bytes from which data can be read or to which data can be written.

String A sequence of characters.

Stub A function with no or minimal functionality.

Syntax Rules that define how to form instructions in a particular programming language.

Syntax error An instruction that does not follow the programming language rules and is rejected by the compiler.

Tab character The `'\t'` character, which advances the next character on the line to the next one of a set of fixed screen positions known as tab stops.

Template A definition for a set of classes. For example, the `vector` template defines a class `vector<T>` (a vector of `T` objects) for any type `T`.

Ternary operator An operator with three arguments. C++ has one ternary operator, `a ? b : c`.

Test coverage The instructions of a program that are executed in a set of test cases.

Test stub A program that calls a function that needs to be tested, supplying parameters and analyzing the function's return value.

Test suite A set of test cases for a program.

Text file A file in which values are stored in their text representation.

Trace message A message that is printed during a program run for debugging purposes.

Unary operator An operator with one argument.

Uninitialized variable A variable that has not been set to a particular value. It is filled with whatever "random" bytes happen to be present in the memory location that the variable occupies.

Unit test A test of a function by itself, isolated from the remainder of the program.

Value parameter A function parameter whose value is copied into a parameter variable of a function. If a variable is passed as a value parameter, changes made to the parameter inside the function do not affect the original variable outside the program.

Variable A storage location that can hold different values.

Vector The ANSI C++ template for a dynamically growing array.

Virtual function A function that can be redefined in a derived class. The actual function being called depends on the type of the object invoking it at run time.

Visual programming Programming by arranging graphical elements on a form, setting program behavior by selecting properties for these elements, and writing only a small amount of "glue" code linking them.

`void` **keyword** A keyword indicating no type or an unknown type. A procedure is a function returning `void`.

Walkthrough Simulating a program or a part of a program by hand to test for correct behavior.

Watch window A window in a debugger that shows the current values of selected variables.

White-box testing Testing functions taking their implementation into account; for example, by selecting boundary test cases and ensuring that all branches of the code are covered by some test case.

White space A sequence of space, tab, and newline characters.

Photo Credits

Chapter 1

Figures 1 and 2: Courtesy of Intel. *Figure 3:* Courtesy of Matthew R. Elman. *Figure 4:* Courtesy of Seagate. *Figure 5:* Courtesy of Lisa Passmore. *Figure 6:* Courtesy of Toshiba/The Benjamin Group. *Figure 7:* Courtesy of Maynard Electronics. *Figure 8:* Courtesy of International Business Machines Corporation. *Figure 9:* Courtesy of Intel. *Figure 11:* Courtesy of Sperry Univac, Division of Sperry Corporation.

Chapter 3

Figure 6: Courtesy of International Business Machines Corporation. *Figure 12:* Courtesy of SAS Institute, Inc. *Figure 13:* Courtesy of Autodesk Inc. *Figure 14:* From *dinopix,* by Teruhisa Tajima, Chronicle Books, Copyright ©1994 by Teruhisa Tajima. Used with permission.

Chapter 4

Figure 5: Courtesy of Digital Equipment Corporation, Corporate Photo Library. *Figure 6:* ©Sun Microsystems. *Page 161:* ©1997 by Sidney Harris.

Chapter 7

Figure 1: Naval Surface Weapons Center.

Chapter 12

Figure 3: Robert Godfrey/Courtesy of International Business Machines Corporation.

Index